TEACHING INSTRUMENTAL MUSIC

Contemporary Perspectives and Pedagogies

Edited by Bryan Powell, Kristen Pellegrino, and Quincy C. Hilliard

OXFORD UNIVERSITY PRESS

OXFORD
UNIVERSITY PRESS

Oxford University Press is a department of the University of Oxford. It furthers the University's objective of excellence in research, scholarship, and education by publishing worldwide. Oxford is a registered trademark of Oxford University Press in the UK and in certain other countries.

Published in the United States of America by Oxford University Press
198 Madison Avenue, New York, NY 10016, United States of America.

Library of Congress Cataloging-in-Publication Data

Names: Powell, Bryan, editor. | Pellegrino, Kristen, editor. | Hilliard, Quincy C., 1954-editor.
Title: Teaching instrumental music : contemporary perspectives and pedagogies / edited by Bryan Powell, Kristen Pellegrino, and Quincy C. Hilliard.
Description: [1.] | New York, NY : Oxford University Press, 2024. | Includes bibliographical references and index. | Summary: "This book focuses on the process of learning to teach music to children using instruments. It brings the field of instrumental music into the contemporary world of school music by keeping all the important aspects of previous texts (i.e., a focus on pedagogical techniques of each instrument) while broadening beyond the instruments themselves to consider the foundational musicianship and types of learner-centered classroom interactions needed for all students to enjoy playing an instrument. The project's authors represent a variety of perspectives, embodying different racial, gender, and sexual identities usually underrepresented in the field of instrumental music education" — Provided by publisher.
Identifiers: LCCN 2023007354 (print) | LCCN 2023007355 (ebook) | ISBN 9780190099725 (paperback) | ISBN 9780190099732 (epub) | ISBN 9780190099749 (ebook)
Subjects: LCSH: Instrumental music—Instruction and study.
Classification: LCC MT170 .T43 2023 (print) | LCC MT170 (ebook) | DDC 784.071—dc23/eng/20230215
LC record available at https://lccn.loc.gov/2023007354
LC ebook record available at https://lccn.loc.gov/2023007355

Printed by Integrated Books International, United States of America

TABLE OF CONTENTS

ABOUT THE EDITORS

Bryan Powell is an assistant professor of music education and music technology at Montclair State University, where he teaches classes in music technology and popular music. He also serves as the director of higher education for the nonprofit organization Music Will.

Kristen Pellegrino is a professor of music education (strings) at the University of Texas at San Antonio. From 2020 to 2022 she served as the president of the American String Teachers Association. She teaches graduate courses in research and the psychological foundations of teaching and learning, as well as undergraduate string education courses, and she supervises UTSA's String Project teachers.

Quincy C. Hilliard is a professor of music, composer in residence, and the Heymann Endowed Professor at the University of Louisiana–Lafayette. He teaches courses in composition and music education, has published numerous works for wind band, and is the author of several technique books for wind band.

ACKNOWLEDGMENTS

Bryan
Thank you to music teachers everywhere, especially modern band teachers and popular music educators, whose efforts have made it acceptable to include an entire section on popular music instruments in a book about teaching instrumental music in schools. Thank you to my students, both past and present, for the inspiration. Thank you to Liz, Ellison, and Beckett for putting up with my work-life imbalance. And thank you to my collegial coeditors, Kristen and Quincy, for the laughs and camaraderie. I'll see you both in the BBC.

Kristen
Thank you to my past and current college students for (a) helping me learn what you need on your journeys to becoming inspiring music teachers and string teachers who understand that all genres of music and forms of music literacy, as well as informal and formal ways of learning music, are valued; and (b) reading drafts of my chapters and offering constructive criticism. Thank you to all the incredible music educators and music teacher education authors who have contributed to this book, including many friends and mentors. Lastly, thank you to Chad for encouraging me to work on this project and for introducing me to my amazing coeditors, Bryan and Quincy! I'm looking forward to celebrating with you in the BBC!

Quincy
I would like to thank my wife, Rubye, and my two sons, Cameron and Alex, for their support of all my creative endeavors throughout my career. I would also like to recognize my copyist, Scott Landry, who has been by my side throughout my musical journey, working tirelessly day and night. He is the best *in the business. I would also like to acknowledge the many directors who have inspired and encouraged me along my journey. Last but not least, I would like to thank my students and graduate assistants, who have given me their insight and support. Most of all, thanks to Bryan and Kristen for their endless hard work on this project. I'll see you both in the BBC.*

Bryan, Kristen, and Quincy would collectively like to thank Hayden, Olivia, Justin, and the rest of the team at Oxford University Press for their support and assistance throughout the process. We would also like to express our gratitude to Chad West, without whom this book would not have happened. Chad did all of the early work to make this book a reality, and we are appreciative of his efforts and thankful for his vision for this book. And lastly, we would like to thank *you*, the reader, for engaging with this text (even if you didn't have a choice because it was assigned as part of a course you are taking).

CONTRIBUTORS

Sergio Alonso is a high school and community music educator in San Fernando, California, where he teaches mariachi music.

Stephen J. Benham is a professor of music education and the chair of music performance at Duquesne University in Pittsburgh, Pennsylvania, where he teaches courses in string methods and pedagogy.

John L. Benham is a professor of ethnomusicology and music education (retired/adjunct) in the School of Music at Liberty University in Lynchburg, Virginia, and has served as a music advocacy consultant working with school districts throughout North America to save, restore, and build music programs.

Aixa Burgos is a music teacher at Passaic Preparatory Academy in Passaic, New Jersey, where she teaches courses in music technology.

Scott Burstein (he/him) is the director of teaching and learning for the nonprofit organization Music Will in Montclair, New Jersey, where he manages training, musical content, and professional development.

Christopher Cayari (he/they) is an associate professor of music at Purdue University in West Lafayette, Indiana, where he teaches courses in music education, musical media, and music theater.

Mary Claxton (she/her) is the associate director of teaching and learning for the US music nonprofit organization Music Will in Montclair, New Jersey. She also teaches a course in contemporary and culturally relevant music pedagogy at the University of Northern Colorado in Greeley, Colorado.

Colleen Conway is a professor of music education at the University of Michigan, where she teaches courses in instrumental music as well as curriculum, assessment, psychology, and research.

Steven Cunningham is the director of bands at Dinwiddie High School in Dinwiddie, Virginia, where he directs the marching band, concert band, and jazz band. He also serves on the faculties at Grambling State University in Grambling, Louisiana, and John Tyler Community College in Chester, Virginia, as an adjunct music instructor teaching applied trumpet and music theory.

Virginia Davis (she/her) is a professor of music education at the University of Texas Rio Grande Valley in Edinburg, Texas, where she teaches courses in general music and popular music education.

Lonnie Easter II (he/him) is a lecturer in jazz studies and music education at the University of Oklahoma in Norman, Oklahoma. His research aims to enhance students' ability, self-efficacy, and practice room efficiency in jazz improvisation (primarily at the beginner level).

Cassandra Eisenreich (she/her) is an assistant professor of flute and music education at Slippery Rock University in Slippery Rock, Pennsylvania.

Warren Gramm (he/him) is the senior manager of program outreach for the nonprofit organization Music Will in Montclair, New Jersey, and an adjunct at Montclair State University and Thomas Edison State University in Trenton, New Jersey where he teaches music technology and music history.

Spencer Hale (they/them) is a former public school teacher and is currently the senior manager of teaching and learning at the nonprofit organization Music Will in Montclair, New Jersey, where they create educational resources for educators.

Erin M. Hansen (she/her) is an assistant professor of (string) music education at the University of Houston. Prior to teaching at the collegiate level, Erin taught fourth- through twelfth-grade orchestra and guitar for over ten years and private violin and cello lessons for over twenty years.

Karin S. Hendricks (she/her/they) is an associate professor of music and the chair of music education at Boston University, where she teaches instrumental methods and research and serves as co-chair of the Boston University Inclusive Pedagogy Initiative.

Christina Herman is a doctoral student in music education at the Indiana University Jacobs School of Music in Bloomington, where she serves as the program coordinator for Young Winds and as an associate instructor for undergraduate music education courses.

Robin Hochkeppel is the music teacher at Acadiana Renaissance Charter Academy in Youngville, Louisiana, and is the retired double reed instructor at the University of Louisiana at Lafayette. She has taught band, classroom music, and private lessons at all levels from kindergarten through college. Additionally, she is a gigging musician, clinician, and adjudicator.

Nate Holder is the international chair in music education at Royal Northern College of Music in Manchester, England.

Michael Hopkins is a professor and chair of music education at the University of Michigan in Ann Arbor, where he teaches courses in string techniques, orchestra methods, research methods, and the psychology of music teaching and learning.

Jennifer Jester (she/her) is an assistant professor of music industry at Millersville University of Pennsylvania in

Millersville, where she teaches courses in applied euphonium and tuba, live audio, modern band, commercial ensembles, and introduction to West African dance and drumming.

Erik Johnson is an associate professor of music education and director of the Trying-on-Teaching program at Colorado State University in Fort Collins, where he teaches undergraduate and graduate courses in music education.

Kelvin Jones (he/him) is the assistant director of bands at Louisiana State University in Baton Rouge, where he teaches undergraduate and graduate courses in the School of Music and leads the 325-member Golden Band from Tigerland marching band.

Brian W. Kellum is a lecturer in music education at Boston University. He has had extensive experience as a string teacher and administrator in public, community, and private settings.

David H. Knapp is an assistant professor of music education at Syracuse University in Syracuse, New York, where he teaches music education courses and directs the university's Syracuse All-Steel Percussion Orchestra (SASPO).

William L. Lake, Jr. (he/him) is an assistant professor of music education, the associate director of bands, and th assistant to the dean for Diversity, Equity, Inclusion, and Belonging for the Crane School of Music (SUNY-Potsdam), where he conducts the Crane Concert Band, facilitates the Campus-Community Band, and teaches conducting, secondary wind practices, and wind literature.

Rebecca MacLeod (she/her) is a professor of music string education at the University of North Carolina–Greensboro, where she directs the string education program and conducts the UNCG Sinfonia.

Herbert Marshall (he/him) is an assistant professor of music education at Kent State University in Kent, Ohio. There he is the early childhood and general music specialist, teaching coursework in bachelor of music, master of arts in teaching, master of music in music education, and doctoral degree programs.

Kimberly A. McCord is a professor emerita of music education at Illinois State University in Normal, Illinois, and an adjunct professor of music education at New York University. She is the founder and director of Just Accessible Music (JAM,) an equity-based music school in Connecticut.

Si Millican is a professor of music education at the University of Texas at San Antonio and the author of *Starting Out Right: Beginning Band Pedagogy*. For thirteen years prior to his university work, he was a public school teacher in Texas in the Arlington, Lewisville, and Belton school districts.

Dunwoody Mirvil is an assistant professor and director of trombone at Florida Memorial University in Miami Gardens, where he teaches applied trombone in a homogenous choir and one-on-one settings.

Asia Muhaimin is the director of bands at Warren Easton Charter High School in New Orleans, Louisiana.

James Ray (he/him) is an assistant professor of instrumental music education at Western Washington University in Bellingham, Washington. He prepares preservice teachers in string and instrumental methods, teaches music theory, and conducts the WWU String Sinfonia.

Kat Reinhert (she/her) is a professional singer-songwriter, contemporary voice specialist, educator, and entrepreneur in New York City.

Alison Robuck (she/her) teaches oboe for Missouri State University in Springfield and performs with the Odyssey Chamber Music Series and the Missouri Symphony Orchestra.

Tony Sauza (he/him) is the associate director of teaching and learning for the nonprofit organization Music Will in Montclair, New Jersey. He is also an adjunct lecturer in music education at California State University, Long Beach, where he teaches courses in popular music and music technology.

Joel Schut (he/him) is the director of orchestral studies and assistant professor of music education at Grand Valley State University where he teaches courses in orchestral performance, and music education. He previously taught at the University of Colorado–Boulder, the Crane School of Music SUNY Potsdam, and in the Michigan public schools.

Tawnya Smith is an assistant professor of music and music education at Boston University, where she teaches courses on creating healthy learning environments, arts integration, and research.

Daniel Smithiger is the director of the Percussion Area and director of the eBand at Southern Illinois University Edwardsville.

Meryl Sole is an adjunct assistant professor of music and music education at Teachers College, Columbia University, and New York University, where she teaches courses in music education.

Letitia Stancu is an adjunct professor at Montclair State University in New Jersey, where she teaches keyboard musicianship courses.

Darrin Thornton (he/him) is a teaching professor of music and music education at Pennsylvania State University in University Park, where he currently serves as associate dean for the College of Arts and Architecture.

Cynthia L. Wagoner is an associate professor at East Carolina University in Greenville, North Carolina, where she serves as department chair for music education and music therapy. She teaches undergraduate and graduate courses in pedagogy specializing in instrumental music and woodwind instruction.

Benjamin Yates is an associate professor of trombone at the University of Louisiana at Lafayette. He teaches applied lessons, coaches brass chamber music, conducts the trombone ensembles, and performs with the Louisiana Brass Quintet.

INTRODUCTION

Colleen M. Conway

This introduction provides an overview of the key concepts of the book and presents ways in which the chapters might be used in instrumental music.

Texts for the teaching of instrumental music have been present in music education for decades. The first edition of Richard Colwell's *The Teaching of Instrumental Music* appeared in 1969, and 2017 marked the text's fifth edition. *Teaching Instrumental Music: Contemporary Perspectives and Pedagogies*, however, is the first text to reimagine the teaching of instrumental music such that regardless of whether the performance at the end of a cycle of teaching occurs in a school auditorium set to imitate a concert hall or a rock stage, the process of teaching and learning is the same. This book focuses on the process of learning to teach music to children using instruments. It brings the field of instrumental music into the contemporary world of school music by keeping all the important aspects of previous texts (e.g., a focus on pedagogical techniques of each instrument) while broadening instruction beyond the instruments themselves to consider the foundational musicianship and types of learner-centered classroom interactions needed for all students to enjoy playing an instrument. The authors represent a variety of perspectives embodying different racial, gender, and sexual identities that are usually underrepresented in the field of instrumental music education. Furthermore, the authors represent a multitude of ages and experience levels, including K–12 music teachers, higher-education professors of practice, tenure-track and full professors, and music educators working in educational non-profits.

I began my own instrumental-music journey as a seven-year-old taking piano lessons with the neighborhood mom in 1973 and continued by beginning French horn in the fourth grade, in 1975, in my elementary school band in Pennsylvania. After my middle school and high school years taking private lessons and playing in orchestras, bands, jazz bands, marching bands, and chamber ensembles, as well as performing solo recitals, I found myself at the Eastman School of Music as a freshman in 1984. It was there that the idea of foundational musicianship, which included moving away from notation-only learning to include movement, singing, chanting, composing, and improvising, was first introduced to me in instrumental music. After working with elementary, middle school, and high school students along with student teachers for eight years in public school, I completed my doctoral work at Teachers College, Columbia University, in the mid-1990s and learned more about learner-centered approaches to teacher education, which I have since explored and written about in my own work. I have joined with many others over the last thirty-plus years, engaging with P–12 instrumental students as well as preservice teachers in the journey to encourage the profession to move away from the festival scores and performance-only music classrooms to embrace the excitement of learning to play an instrument (any instrument) through playing by ear, improvising, composing, and just plain having fun. It is with great pleasure that I take on this task of introducing the first-ever instrumental music textbook to bring these ideas together into one volume.

Unique Features of This Text

This text puts instruments, ways of making music, and types of music on an equal plane and does not suggest that instruments that typically perform Western art music are held in higher esteem. Instruments are considered equal, and all ways of making music with instruments, including using notation, playing by ear, improvising, and composing, are considered equal. All types of music, including classical, jazz, and popular music, are considered equal. Unlike many previous texts that focus primarily on instrument techniques or what Grunow, Gordon, and Azzara (2001) would call "executive techniques" (p. 32) of the instruments (i.e., instrument assembly, hand position, posture, embouchure, breathing, articulation), this text also focuses on balancing those executive techniques with the musicianship needed for success. Instructional sequences and methods for teaching and learning to teach are provided, with a focus on contemporary learning theories and instructional materials. In addition to providing materials and suggestions for creating solid instrumental musicians, this text focuses on the process of how to do this in a way that considers learner-centered and constructivist approaches as well as a focus on concepts of diversity, equity, inclusion, accessibility, and cultural relevance in the instrumental music classroom. This text provides all that would be needed for an instrumental music teacher education curriculum across the undergraduate degree.

FOUNDATIONAL MUSICIANSHIP

Kristen Pellegrino's opening chapter ("Transferable Pedagogical Concepts"), Pellegrino and Wagoner's "How Students Learn" (Chapter 3), Stephen Benham's "Teaching Executive Skills, Musical Skills, and Artistic Skills" (Chapter 5), and Bryan Powell's "Teaching Notation in Instrumental Music" (Chapter 6) draw the reader into the overall focus of this text as one that supports foundational musicianship. Pellegrino discusses the core music-teaching practices of modeling, sequencing, and relational capacities as needed in any type of music classroom. A sound-before-sight pedagogy, including movement, singing, chanting, call and response, improvisation, and composition before the use of notation, is consistently supported in the text. This is addressed directly in multiple chapters regarding beginners but is also pervasive in all discussions of curricular sequence.

CONSTRUCTIVIST AND LEARNER-CENTERED PEDAGOGIES

Interactions between students and the teacher that follow constructivist ideas of learner-centeredness is another constant throughout this text. Based on discussion of Vygotsky's Zone of Proximal Development (1978), Bruner's Spiral Curriculum (Bruner 1960), and general principles of the constructivist notions of Dewey (2013), Chapters 1–4, by Pellegrino and colleagues, present easy-to-understand ways that these concepts are present in music classrooms. These notions are supported by subsequent authors in Part I of the book in relation to lesson and program planning (Millican in Chapter 7 and Jones in Chapter 8), motivation (Hilliard in Chapter 9), communication (Henricks and Smith in Chapter 11), and peer mentoring (Johnson and Herman in Chapter 12).

Preservice students are encouraged to read Chapter 2 ("Learning to Teach: Preservice Teacher Experiences") whether or not it is assigned for their course, as it will assist in navigating the degree and help one consider the various teacher and musician identities that are important for growth. A key criterion for creating a learner-centered classroom is to acquire the relationship-building skills needed to interact with students, parents, and colleagues. Understanding oneself in relation to the early chapters of this text is important for developing this relational capacity.

DIVERSITY, EQUITY, INCLUSION, ACCESSIBILITY, AND CULTURAL RELEVANCE

As mentioned, authors in this text represent a variety of perspectives. At least forty-two of the chapters are written or cowritten by authors who have traditionally been underrepresented on the basis of color, gender, and sexual orientation. In addition, authors represent a variety of ages and experience levels, including those teaching in K–12, those working in educational nonprofit organizations, and college professors, from part-time professors of practice to full-time professors at every rank—assistant, associate, and full. Several chapters are specifically devoted to topics associated with diversity, equity, inclusion, accessibility, and cultural relevance including: Karin Hendricks and Tawyna Smith's "Compassion, Care, Communication, and Connection in Instrumental Learning Spaces" (Chapter 11); Kimberly McCord's "Teaching Instruments to Students with Disabilities" (Chapter 13); William Lake's "Teaching for Social Impact through Fluidity in the Twenty-First-Century Instrumental Ensemble" (Chapter 14); Antonio Sauza's "Culturally Relevant Pedagogy in Modern Band" (Chapter 25); James Ray, Karin Hendricks, and Brian Kellum's "Culturally Responsive Teaching in School Orchestras" (Chapter 31); and Darrin Thornton's "Culturally Relevant Pedagogy in Band" (Chapter 43). In addition, many other authors treat these important elements of instrumental music pedagogy in their chapters. I mention some of these later in this introduction.

INNOVATIVE ENSEMBLE APPROACHES

Authors in this text recognize the power of both large- and small-ensemble experiences, including bands (concert, jazz, marching, and rock), orchestras (string and full), chamber music, combos, and just small and large groups of students playing something. Part VII (Chapters 49–54) is devoted to these innovative approaches. Other chapters that connect to the notion of innovation in ensembles include Bryan Powell's "Integrating Technology in Instrumental Music Instruction" (Chapter 10); John Benham and Steve Benham's "Advocating for the Arts: What Every Future Music Educator Should Know" (Chapter 17); Michael Hopkins's "Building and Maintaining a Successful Orchestra Program" (Chapter 30); Aixa Burogs's "Pedagogies for Teaching Latin Percussion" (Chapter 46); David Knapp's "Pedagogies for Teaching Steel Pan and Steel Bands" (Chapter 47); Scott Burstein's "Modern Band Rehearsal Techniques" (Chapter 48); Sergio Alonso's "Mariachi Ensemble Rehearsal Techniques" (Chapter 53); and Butch Marshall's "Musical Theater Pit Orchestra Preparation and Performance" (Chapter 54).

Uses of the Text

The aim of this section is to assist students and instructors who are using this text understand how to do so in relation to coursework. No teacher education program provides a course that covers everything needed to succeed as a teacher. Undergraduate music-teacher education curricular requirements vary in relation to size of school and type of degree (BA, BS, BM, or BME). This text will be useful for those of you studying to be music teachers who take only one or two specific music education courses as well as those who take ten or more. For readers attending schools with only a few music education courses, the chapters in this book will provide important music-focused content to support what you might be learning in more generic education courses.

If you are a freshman or sophomore student in an Introduction to Music Education course (or in a program where this course is not a part of your degree and where you want to create this foundation for yourself), you will find that the chapters in Part I (Chapters 1–17) provide an excellent basis for understanding how to teach instrumental music. These opening chapters might also be used in instrumental methods courses that include work with children in private lessons or school settings. In addition to the first four chapters discussed previously, other chapters in Part I provide ideas for balancing the musicianship-focused and learner-centered practices with necessary content such as instrument fundamentals. The authors keep a constant focus on innovative and culturally relevant ideas and practices. No one way of teaching, conducting, or making music is presented as "best."

Part II (Chapters 18–25) focuses on techniques and methods for teaching popular music. Courses in secondary general music methods and courses dedicated specifically to modern band, popular music, teaching ukulele, and teaching guitar will find this section helpful. Those in teacher education programs without courses in this area will likely be struck by the similarities in sequences and learner-centered processes presented in this section and will benefit from supplementing their education with guidelines on how to teach these instruments and ensembles.

The chapters in Part III are important for those learning to teach string instruments. The first chapter (Chapter 26) in this part, by one of the editors of this textbook, Kristen Pellegrino, consolidates many of the important features of this text in one place dedicated to string teaching. It includes how to start a beginner with a focus on foundational musicianship and strategies for engaging individual learners in the process of starting strings, and it includes specific resources for choosing repertoire for strings with an eye toward diversity. The supplemental materials provided by sample lesson plans and checklists for the teacher are very helpful. Sequences for the right hand (Chapter 27) and for the left hand and tuning (Chapter 28) and shifting (Chapter 29) are combined across all the string instruments. This approach to understanding strings is helpful for P–12 teachers working in a group process setting. Chapter 30, by Michael Hopkins, on leading an orchestra program sketches out how to recruit and retain students, as well as how to plan and organize the program within contemporary motivation theories such that a learner-centered environment can be created in the orchestra class. Finally, the culturally relevant teaching chapter that concludes Part III adds to the focus on diversity, equity, and inclusion as well as new and innovative thinking for how interactions between students and teachers take place in the orchestra class. It would be useful in a string technique class as well as in instrumental methods.

Courses in the teaching of woodwinds will use Chapters 32–37 in Part IV. In Cynthia Wagoner's introduction to this section, she addresses logistical considerations for teaching woodwinds in a group setting, including the room set-up, equipment, and cost of instruments and reeds. In remarks that are particularly helpful to those who are studying to work with groups of mixed woodwinds in a woodwind class or a band or orchestra setting, she provides suggestions for instrument assembly, posture, hand position, breathing, embouchure, and articulation that would be helpful for all learners in the space. She also includes a focus on starting beginners and suggestions early in the sequence for improvising on one or two notes. The remaining chapters, on flute, oboe, clarinet, saxophone, and bassoon, return to the concepts of instrument assembly, posture, hand position, breathing, embouchure, and articulation, with additional attention to tone on each instrument. The authors of these chapters provide helpful pictures and sample exercises for learning.

Chapter 43, by Darrin Thornton, examines culturally relevant practices for band and could be studied in a woodwind, brass, or percussion techniques class in addition to instrumental methods. He begins the chapter by placing band within a historical context, drawing attention to its military roots as well as the historical focus on competition. Thornton encourages readers to consider whom they are teaching and the purposes of band in multiple settings. Strategies for providing an accessible band program that includes transferable and musicianship-focused skills while honoring learner-centered and constructivist learning practices are provided throughout the chapter.

Courses in the teaching of brass would look to Chapters 38–43 in Part V. The opening chapter in this section, by Ben Yates, presents concepts that are common to all brass instruments, including breath, embouchure, and buzzing. He also provides helpful suggestions for starting beginners on brass as well as working with the brass section in an ensemble. Chapter authors for each instrument address equipment, instrument assembly, tone, and articulation for each instrument as well as instrument-specific executive techniques in the areas of breath, embouchure, and buzzing. As mentioned, in Chapter 43 Darrin Thornton examines culturally relevant pedagogy in band that may be used in instrumental methods but might also be useful in woodwind, brass, and percussion techniques classes.

The teaching of percussion is addressed in Part VI (Chapters 44–47). Virginia Davis and Daniel Smithiger begin with a focus on snare drum and keyboard instruments, which would be typical for beginning students. They address equipment, playing positions, grips, and stroke technique as well as ear-based approaches to working with beginners. A helpful section on common mistakes made by beginners is provided. Pictures are provided, and links to notation to practice are available. The chapter on pitched and non-pitched instruments has a section on how to make percussion instruments accessible to persons with disabilities and provides a detailed description of each of the percussion instruments. Diversity of repertoire and type of music is again a focus in the remaining two chapters, on Latin percussion and steel pan/steel band respectively. Again, the work by Thornton in Chapter 43, which examines culturally relevant pedagogy, might also be useful in percussion techniques classes.

A Look to the Future

The final section of this text pushes the profession forward in considering how ensembles of any type can become places where foundational musicianship, learner-centered teaching practices, and a focus on individual identities merge to create a musical, meaningful, collaborative, and interactive ensemble environment. It is challenging in 2023 to try to predict the instrumental music of the future. However, I have no doubt that children, adolescents, and adults alike will continue to be interested in learning to play various types of instruments, and that the perspectives and pedagogies outlined in this book will assist teachers in providing musicianship-focused curricula to accomplish this task. The text is a perfect blend of past and future, with a focus on all the foundational information needed to teach traditional band and orchestral instruments as well as instruments for popular music, garage and rock bands, and songwriting. It will be fun to watch (and listen to) what the preservice teachers who have engaged with this text will be able to create in P–12 schools and community music venues.

PART I.

Teaching and Learning

1. *Transferable Pedagogical Concepts* by Kristen Pellegrino
2. *Learning to Teach: Preservice Teacher Experiences* by Kristen Pellegrino and Cynthia L. Wagoner
3. *How Students Learn* by Kristen Pellegrino and Cynthia L. Wagoner
4. *Proactive and Reactive Classroom Management Strategies* by Kristen Pellegrino
5. *Teaching Executive Skills, Musicianship Skills, and Artistic Skills* by Stephen J. Benham
6. *Teaching Notation in Instrumental Music* by Bryan Powell
7. *Planning (Lesson Planning and Curriculum) and Assessment* by J. Si Millican
8. *Strategies for Planning, Building, and Managing Music Programs* by Kelvin D. Jones
9. *Student Motivation* by Quincy C. Hilliard
10. *Integrating Technology in Instrumental Music Instruction* by Bryan Powell
11. *Compassion, Care, Communication, and Connection in Instrumental Learning Spaces* by Karin S. Hendricks and Tawnya D. Smith
12. *Peer-Assisted Learning in the Instrumental Music Ensemble* by Erik Johnson and Christina Herman
13. *Teaching Instruments to Students with (Dis)abilities* by Kimberly A. McCord
14. *Teaching for Social Impact through Fluidity in the Twenty-First-Century Instrumental Ensemble* by William L. Lake, Jr.
15. *Applications of Arranging and Transcribing for Ensembles* by Herbert Marshall
16. *Instrumental Substitutions: Rescoring for Small Bands and Limited Instrumentation* by Quincy C. Hilliard
17. *Advocating for the Arts: What Every Future Music Educator Should Know* by John L. Benham and Stephen J. Benham

CHAPTER 1

TRANSFERABLE PEDAGOGICAL CONCEPTS

Kristen Pellegrino

This chapter introduces six transferable pedagogical concepts: (a) core teaching practices; (b) sound before sight; experience, then label; (c) deconstructing and sequencing concepts; (d) teaching cycle; (e) energy profile; and (f) flow and differentiated learning.

1.1 Introduction

In this chapter, I introduce some transferable pedagogical concepts that can be applied to different musical contexts. There are six sections in this chapter: (a) "Core Teaching Practices"; (b) "Sound before Sight; Experience, Then Label"; (c) "Deconstructing and Sequencing Concepts"; (d) "Teaching Cycle"; (e) "Energy Profile"; and (f) "Flow and Differentiated Learning." These ideas will be mentioned or expanded on in other chapters, including in Chapter 4, which describes proactive and reactive classroom management strategies.

1.2 Core Teaching Practices

Take a few minutes to think about what you would consider *core teaching practices* that all music teachers could use regardless of content, context, or level of students. For example, conducting is a valuable and essential skill in large ensemble classes, but one can teach general music classes, chamber music, songwriting, piano, technology, or modern band classes without conducting. Could you identify seven *core teaching practices* for music teachers?

Millican and Forrester (2018) asked sixteen music teachers of different subjects and grade levels (K–12 and college teachers) to rate some possible core teaching practices and suggest additional ones. These teachers also chose the top three core teaching practices for preservice (college students) and in-service music teachers. (See Table 1.1) As seen in Table 1.1, both lists included "modeling" and "sequencing instruction," but "deconstructing music concepts" appeared as a top-three teaching practice for preservice music teachers, and "developing knowledge of and appropriate relationships with students" was the most important teaching practice for in-service music teachers. All four of these core teaching practices will be discussed in more detail later in this chapter, as well as in Chapters 3–5 and 7.

Also included in Table 1.1 are the results of Millican and Forrester's (2019) survey of 898 K–12 music teachers (band, choir, orchestra, and general music teachers). Millican and Forrester identified seven core teaching practices and defined each practice. The survey participants ranked these teaching practices in order of importance. Similar to their previous study, in-service teachers ranked "developing appropriate relationships with students" first, followed by both "models musical concepts" and "sequences musical instruction."

TABLE 1.1 CORE TEACHING PRACTICES (MILLICAN & FORRESTER, 2018)

Preservice music Teachers	In-service music teachers
1. Modeling musical concepts	1. Developing knowledge of and relationships with students
2. Sequencing instruction	2. Modeling musical concepts
3. Deconstructing musical concepts	3. Sequencing instruction

MILLICAN AND FORRESTER'S 2019 SURVEY

1. *Develops appropriate relationships with students*: The teacher develops and maintains appropriate personal relationships with students.
2. *Models musical concepts*: The teacher demonstrates musical concepts with his or her instrument or voice.
3. *Sequences musical instruction*: The teacher sequences student tasks to achieve musical understanding or to develop specific musical skills.
4. *Understands common student problems*: The teacher understands common mistakes, misunderstandings, conceptions, and misconceptions that students have.
5. *Deconstructs musical concepts*: The teacher deconstructs complex musical performance problems and isolates individual components separately. The teacher identifies a musical problem (live or anticipated), considers causes of the problem, and then proposes a solution or approach to solve the musical problem.
6. *Uses questioning as a teaching tool*: The teacher uses questions to lead to musical discovery, awareness, and/or understanding or to assess musical understanding.
7. *Uses representation and metaphor to explain musical concepts and skills*: The teacher uses visualizations, stories, metaphors, or other graphic representations to explain musical ideas, skills, or concepts. (pp. 89–90)

However, it makes sense that "developing knowledge of and appropriate relationships with students" was not in the top three for preservice music teachers because (a) many preservice music teachers do not teach their own students while in college, and (b) it is important to understand and develop skills in how to deconstruct and sequence instruction while in college. "Developing knowledge of and appropriate relationships with students" is absolutely a core teaching practice that needs to be in the forefront of teachers' minds, and preservice teachers need to know that this will be essential whenever they work with their own students. We will further explore the importance of this in the next few chapters, especially in Chapter 3.

1.3 Sound before Sight; Experience, then Label

When many preservice teachers begin teaching, a common issue is to over-explain a concept before students actually try anything. However, students learn better by "doing" before seeing, labeling, defining, and/or dissecting. This relates to the core teaching practice "models musical concepts" but goes a step further.

Think about how you would first teach staccato. Perhaps you explain that it means "silence before and after the pitch." Although this is correct, the next logical question is, "How much silence?" How would you answer this? Explaining it is a bit inefficient.

Instead, model four connected quarter notes and have students echo it back to you. Then, model four quarter notes with the amount of silence between notes that you want them to emulate and have them echo you back. Perhaps you ask students to describe the difference, which is core teaching practice #6, and then agree with or clarify students' answers. Next, you might show students what this looks like in the music before you show them how this applies to the music they are learning. Finally, you explain that these differences are called *articulations* and that each has a name; the connected one is legato, and the one with silence between the notes is called staccato. Now they understand through experience.

At this point, should you teach other articulations? I believe the answer is no, unless it is relevant to the music you are learning. There are always exceptions to every rule, and we will discuss one such exception in Chapter 29.

This idea of "sound before sight; experience, then label" is rooted in the work of some learning psychologists, including Bruner (1960), Dewey (2013), and Pestalozzi (2012), and these ideas have been in American music teaching for centuries. Woodbridge, a school teacher in the early to mid-1800s, traveled from Boston to Germany and Switzerland and studied Pestalozzi's teaching methods. Woodbridge shared a list of principles of music teaching with Lowell Mason, the superintendent of Boston's school system. In the first five principles, Woodbridge included "sound before signs before theory" ideas (1, 2, 5), as well as deconstructing and sequencing instruction (3, 4).

1. *To teach sounds before signs* . . . sing . . . before learn[ing] the written notes or their names.
2. *To lead [students] to observe*, by hearing and imitating sounds, their resemblances and differences, their agreeable and disagreeable effect, *instead of explaining* these things to him . . . to make [students] *active* instead of *passive* in learning.
3. *In teaching but one thing at a time.* Rhythm, melody, expression are taught and practised before the child is called to the difficult task of attending to all at once.
4. *In making them practice each step* of these divisions, *until they are master of it, before passing to the next.*
5. The giving the principles and theory after practice, and as an induction from it. (Ritter, 1884, p. 247; italics in original)

These ideas also relate to most "music methods," including Orff, Kodály, Dalcroze, Gordon, and Suzuki. For example, Suzuki's "mother-tongue approach" (1983) and Gordon (1971) compare learning music to learning a language. First, we listen to the sounds in our environment before exploring by babbling and then imitating; then, we speak words to communicate meaning (sound/experience). After that, we learn to read and write (sight/label).

Put another way, *music is located within the child* (e.g., Conway, 2019; Gordon, 1971), so we develop the internal musicianship and then label it. This is a fundamentally different approach from thinking that music is located on the page. Music is an aural art form, and in many forms of music—rock, mariachi, fiddling, jazz, folk tunes, world music, and so on—listening and imitating or modeling and echoing is the way people share music. Reading Western music notation is only one form of music literacy and should not be elevated above other types, nor should it be the primary goal in learning or teaching music. For more on different types of notation, see Chapter 6, "Teaching Notation in Instrumental Music." Although the authors of this book read Western music notation and value that skill, we caution the reader to realize that other forms of making, learning, and teaching music are even more important.

Gordon labeled the ability to make meaning of the sounds and notation and to hear it in your mind as "audiation" (1999, p. 42). Developing audiation and connecting it to what you can play on your instrument (ear-to-hand skills) is more important than decoding music notation on a page. In other words, teach people to understand music and use it to communicate ideas and express emotions, which, in turn, activates the listener's imagination and/or provokes emotional responses.

1.4 Deconstructing and Sequencing Concepts

This section begins to explore two more core teaching practices: *deconstructing concepts* and *sequencing concepts.*

DECONSTRUCTING CONCEPTS

Quincy Hilliard has a great figure that more fully explains how to deconstruct concepts. First, the director should be enthusiastic about the music. This becomes the spark that will motivate students to learn the music. Next, divide the piece of music into smaller parts to give students time to focus on a smaller portion and truly understand the music (deconstructing concepts). You may slow down the tempo to give the students the chance to read the music notation and apply the proper fingerings. *Repetition is the key to learning.* Repeat the music many times until the students feel comfortable at the slower tempo, then gradually increase the speed to the correct tempo.

During repetitions of the section, the teacher can model the correct method (M+) and an incorrect method (M-) of playing it. During the learning process, students often struggle, but when they have learned the section they will play it without struggling. Once they have learned the section, students should be able to conceptualize the piece in their minds and engage their heads, hearts, and guts (see Figure 1.1).

Also, find ways to *disguise repetitions.* You might have students say and clap the rhythm, say note names, sing note names, sing and finger along, and then play it. Additional examples would be playing a run of sixteenth notes in different rhythms or playing the same passage three times, each time focusing on a different objective.

Another approach to deconstructing concepts is creating short, succinct *repertoire-based warm-ups* (Gillespie, 2003). First, analyze the music to identify objectives that need to be taught and challenging measures that will need more attention. Then, figure out how to teach it simply following the concept of sound before sight; experience, then label. Deconstruct the concept, perhaps beginning with something students can do well and showing the difference between what they know and the new concept. Then teach it by:

1. Modeling it
2. Having students play it
3. Labeling it and showing what it looks like in the music, then playing it
4. Playing it in the musical context while looking at the music

FIGURE 1.1 How to teach

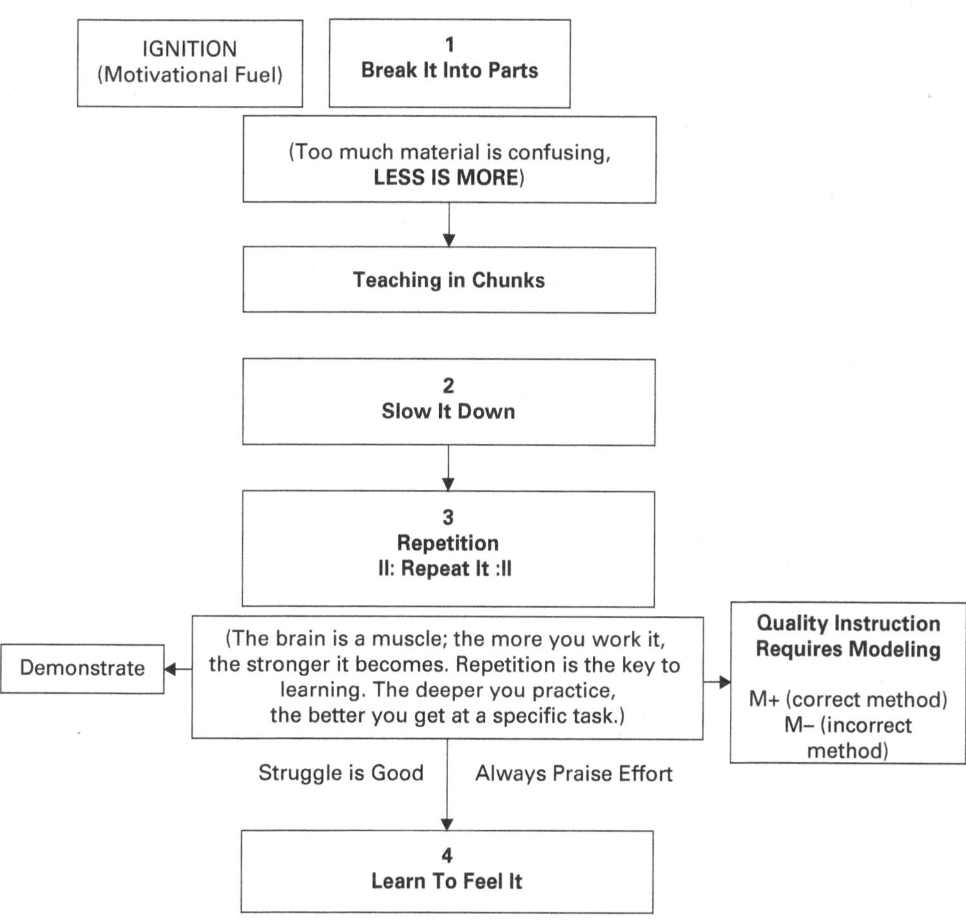

SEQUENCING CONCEPTS

Sequencing instruction relates to curriculum and will be discussed further in Chapters 3, 5, and 7. You can think about sequencing concepts in multiple ways. Two examples are thinking about which concepts should be taught first and which concepts should be taught next, or thinking about creating a spiral curriculum (Bruner, 1960). According to Johnston (2012), the features and benefits of the spiral curriculum are:

1. The student revisits a topic, theme or subject often, reinforcing and solidifying the information each time.

2. The complexity of the topic or theme increases with each revisit, logically progressing from simplistic ideas to complicated ideas.
3. Students are encouraged to apply the earlier knowledge to present learning.

This concept also influences how we have written this book, as concepts will be revisited in subsequent chapters with deepening layers of complexity.

1.5 Teaching Cycle

Imagine this scenario: A teacher says, "Let's begin at measure 9. Ready, play." Then, the teacher stops the students and says, "Let's try that again." This happens often, but do students know why they are playing it again and/or what they are supposed to focus on improving? Was there an incorrect pitch? Was a note out of tune? Were there differences in articulations, incorrect rhythms, pulse difference, poor tone production, or balance issues? There are so many options!

Instead, what if the teacher modeled and students played back similarly? Then, the teacher says, "Let's use that same tone and articulation at measure 9." The students play. When the students stop, the teacher says, "That was fantastic! Your tone was clear and focused and you sounded like one because you all played with the same articulations." Then, you move on to another section. Or, what if the feedback can come from the students themselves? The teacher asks the students, "How was that time different from the previous time? Specifically, how were the tone and articulations changed the second time?" If all agree it was excellent, then you move on to another section.

Raiber and Teachout (2014) define the teacher cycle as set, follow-through, and response. Applying this to our previous scenarios, when the teacher says, "Let's use that same tone and articulation at measure 9," this is set. Share the objective with the students so that everyone understands the focus at that moment. Follow-through is when the students play. While the students play, both the teacher and students can engage in informal assessments to inform the next steps.

There are three types of *responses*: *affirm*, *reset*, and *modified set*. After the students stop playing, the teacher says, "That was fantastic! Your tone was clear and focused and you sounded like one because you all played with the same articulations." This is one type of response—affirm. If you are pleased with the objective and everything else, this type of feedback closes the teaching cycle and you can begin the next teaching cycle. Moving on is called release.

However, students often need more feedback to continue to improve. Therefore, there are other response options. Perhaps the teacher responds, "That sounded much better than yesterday. Your tone was clear and focused but the articulations can still be clearer. Think about beginning the note with /t/ instead of /l/." Then, students play again and the teacher says, "Excellent articulations!" and goes on to the next section. When the teacher said what was good about the tone and then went on to suggest how to improve the articulation, this is reset, because the cycle began again. Then, the students played (follow-through), and the teacher gave positive feedback and closed the cycle (release).

Another option might be that the teacher gives this feedback: "The tone and articulation were excellent, but now let's work on balance. Keep that great tone and articulation, but this time, everyone listen to the tuba and trombones [or cello and bass], and if you cannot hear them, then play softer." The teacher can then ask students who are not playing to listen and give feedback about the balance afterward. "The balance was excellent!" The teacher could say, "I agree! Everyone pickup your pencil and write in your music, 'listen to the tubist and trombonists' [or 'cellists and bassists']." Then, move on to another section. In this example, the tone and articulation were great but a new objective was introduced: balance. This is an example of a modified set. Students should continue to meet the first objective, but you are adding to it. Then, students play (follow-through), and some students and the teacher gave feedback again. Since all was good, they released.

In one last scenario, the teacher says, "The tone and articulation are better but not excellent, yet. Practice that tonight and we will revisit it again tomorrow." Then the teacher offers a few practice tips. This brings the cycle to a release even though there is more work to do.

There are many other ways of referring to teaching cycles. For example, Culver (1989) wrote about the five-step teacher/student loop: initiation, response, monitor, remediation, and closure (p. 35). Whichever cycle you use, I recommend that preservice teachers limit themselves to three times around the same teaching cycle in order to keep up the pace and avoid student frustration. Of course, there are exceptions, but the rule should be broken only for good reason, and only occasionally. Remember, you might have to bring momentary closure to something. Asking students to practice it, showing them how to practice it, and revisiting it in the next class is a good option.

1.6 Energy Profile and Flow

ENERGY PROFILE

Culver (1989) observed master teachers and discovered a few commonalities, including the flow of excellent lessons (see Figure 1.2). He suggested that you first "meet the students' energy levels to begin class." Notice how students enter your room and figure out if they seem to have their usual amounts of energy. If it is different, you may want to ask if something happened so you can better relate to them and what is happening in their lives. For example, if the students are disappointed because a field trip is canceled, it would be inappropriate to start class with high energy and enthusiasm.

The structure of a lesson plan is review, extension, and motivation (p. 17). First, have a good amount of energy (medium) at the beginning of the lesson while you review and refine something students already know. Playing scales, articulations, and music with

FIGURE 1.2 Energy profile (Culver, 1989)

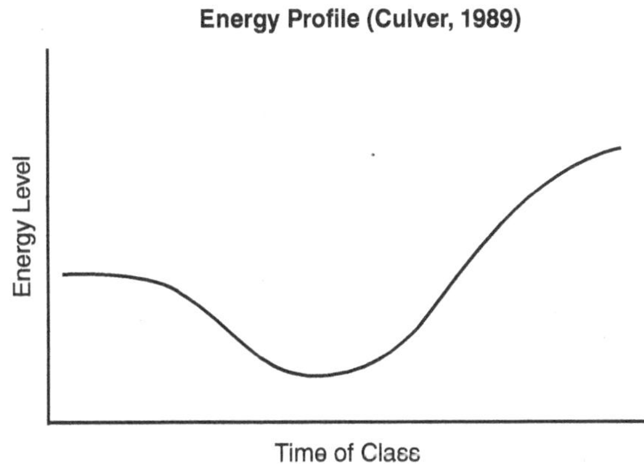

1. **Medium energy** (*Review*: meet students where they are in terms of energy and then Review and Refine)
2. **Lower energy** (*Extend*: focus and extend students' technique)
3. **High energy** (*Motivation!*: end class with success and/or fun learning games. This leaves students \with good feelings about class, encourages them to practice, and helps them be excited for next class).

This should be considered while constructing your lesson plans.

which students are familiar lets them focus on playing with excellent posture, position, tone, intonation, rhythm, style, balance, musicality, and expression at the beginning of class. Depending on the length of the class (thirty minutes, fifty minutes, an hour, or a three-hour rehearsal), the duration of the pieces, and the level of the students, you may need a few activities for them to review and refine. Have students start with success while improving what is familiar.

Second, extend students' knowledge and abilities. Teach something new—new techniques, new notes, new harmonies, new literature, and so on. The energy will be lowered because students will need to concentrate. The lower energy allows space for repetition, monitoring and remediating, guided awareness, and more individualized instruction.

Finally, leave students with feelings of success and enjoyment. This could be playing through a piece you have just worked on in sections, playing through their favorite piece, improvising, or playing a musical game. Culver called this "motivation." When students leave with high energy, this positively impacts their learning and musician identity, as explored in Chapter 3, and students are also more apt to practice and come into the next class with enthusiasm!

1.7 Flow and Differentiated Learning

FLOW

Helping everyone experience flow (Csikszentmihalyi, 2008) contributes to focus, feelings of well-being, and feeling a sense of community in the classroom. Csikszentmihalyi (2008) [pronounced "Chicks-a-me-hi"] developed a theory of flow based on his previous research studies. Csikszentmihalyi examined hundreds of "'experts'—artists, athletes, musicians, chess masters, and surgeons . . . people who seemed to spend their time in precisely those activities they preferred" (Csikszentmihalyi, 2008, p. 4). Csikszentmihalyi described "optimal experience," a psychological state when someone becomes fully absorbed in something that interests them in which they have enough skill to meet the challenge (see Figure 1.3). While engaged in the activity, they lose their sense of time and self, which results in feelings of satisfaction and a sense of well-being. "Concentration is so intense

FIGURE 1.3 Csikszentmihalyi's flow (2008)

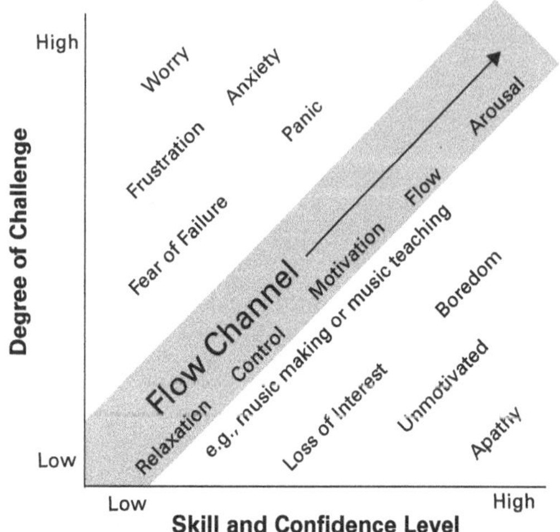

that there is no attention left over to think about anything irrelevant, or to worry about problems. Self-consciousness disappears, and the sense of time becomes distorted" (p. 71).

This was one of my favorite parts of teaching music; my students and I would often enter into a state of flow with each other. Lori Custodero (2002) suggested that flow occurs when goals are clear, feedback is immediate, action and awareness merge, concentration is deep, control is possible, and self-consciousness disappears (pp. 4–5). Additionally, flow can be contagious (Bakker, 2005; Custodero, 2012). When the teacher is in flow, students are more likely to enter into this state, and vice versa.

Do you remember being so engrossed in music making that you were surprised by a school bell indicating the class was over? If so, you might have entered a state of flow. Although entering flow is a goal, as a teacher it is also best to bring closure to the class (summarize what students have learned, what they should practice and how, and wish them a good day before they pack up).

DIFFERENTIATED LEARNING

Differentiated learning is related to flow because students should be challenged without feeling overwhelmed. To enter into a state of flow, students need to be interested in the subject and have enough skill to tackle the challenge. Therefore, you must constantly assess your students and make appropriate accommodations for them. This brings up another issue. Is "equity" giving everyone the same thing, or is it giving students what they need to be successful? I believe in giving students what they need to feel successful and motivated. Therefore, differentiated learning and flow can be a proactive classroom management strategy, which will be explored in Chapter 4.

Examples of differentiated learning vary. You might consider writing different parts for students, having students play other instruments' parts at a given time, or using advanced techniques or alternative fingerings. Another option is to give students choices during instruction. For example, you could have more advanced students model for the others while they finger along, or pair more advanced and less advanced students to help each other.

1.8 Summary

In this chapter I have presented six pedagogical concepts: core teaching practices; sound before sight and experience, then label; deconstructing and sequencing concepts; teaching cycle; energy profile; and flow and differentiated learning. All of these concepts can be applied to all music learning contexts, including peer-directed learning. Also, all concepts will be revisited in other chapters, similar to Bruner's spiral curriculum.

1.9 Discussion Questions

1. Do you agree with the list of core teaching practices in Table 1.1? Might you add something to these seven ideas? Please justify your suggestions and consider if they are equally important in all musical learning contexts.
2. Were you taught sound before sight; experience, then label? Can you see benefits to this approach? What would keep you from teaching this way?
3. Observe your conductor's rehearsals and see if you can identify teaching cycles. If not, what do you notice in the conductor's instruction and in the ensemble players' reactions?
4. Can you recall a time when a teacher had much more energy than the students at the beginning of class? How did students respond? Also, observe your rehearsals

and try to notice the energy profile of the rehearsal and the ensemble players' reactions.

5. Can you recall a time when you were in a state of flow? Did this happen when you were alone or with others? Has it happened in class, rehearsal, or a concert? Describe the experience, how you felt in the moment and afterward, and whether you can intentionally reach a state of flow often or not.
6. Can you identify five ways to differentiate instruction?

OXFORD learning link

Visit the online resources for additional documentation and exercises to help expand learning and test your knowledge further: www.oup.com/he/powell_musicle.

CHAPTER 2

LEARNING TO TEACH: PRESERVICE TEACHER EXPERIENCES

Kristen Pellegrino and Cynthia L. Wagoner

In this chapter we discuss music teacher identity development, suggest ways for you to develop a music teaching philosophy and understand its implications for your curriculum, and explore some benefits of peer and clinical teaching experiences.

2.1 Music Teacher Identity Development

Knowing myself is as crucial to good teaching as knowing my students and my subject. (Palmer, 2017)

Understanding how we bring our personal values, beliefs, goals, and individuality to the occupation of music teaching is important. We teach through who we are, bringing our inner lived experiences into our approach as teachers (Palmer, 2017). Therefore, many researchers have concluded that teacher identity is connected to teacher well-being, commitment to teaching, and belief in one's abilities, as well as to teaching effectiveness and student success (e.g., Day & Gu, 2010; Day et al., 2006; Sammons et al., 2007).

Becoming a music teacher means you will need to integrate who you are with the roles and responsibilities of a career in music education. To do this, consider what you value and your musical, teaching, and personal goals. To begin this discussion, we share a bit about core reflection and teacher presence.

CORE REFLECTION AND TEACHER PRESENCE

> *The core is the essence of the feeling that you are who you are. More specifically, it is the integrated experience of being, which is activated when you are completely present to who you are . . . and utilize your full potential for your own well-being and that of others. (Evelein & Korthagen, 2014, p. 14)*

Teacher presence is dependent on understanding yourself and teaching in a way that is true to your identity and mission and combines four components of connections: to oneself, students, subject matter, and pedagogical knowledge. Rodgers and Raider-Roth (2006) describe teaching as "engaging in an authentic relationship with students where teachers know and respond with intelligence and compassion to students and their learning" (pp. 265–266). They define presence as

> *a state of alert awareness, receptivity and connectedness to the mental, emotional and physical workings of both the individual and the group in context of their learning environments and the ability to respond with a considered and compassionate best next step. . . . Reflective teaching cannot be reduced to a series of behaviors or skills, but is a practice that demands presence. As such, it involves self-knowledge, trust, relationship and compassion. (p. 266)*

FIGURE 2.1 Korthagen and Nuijten's onion model (2022)

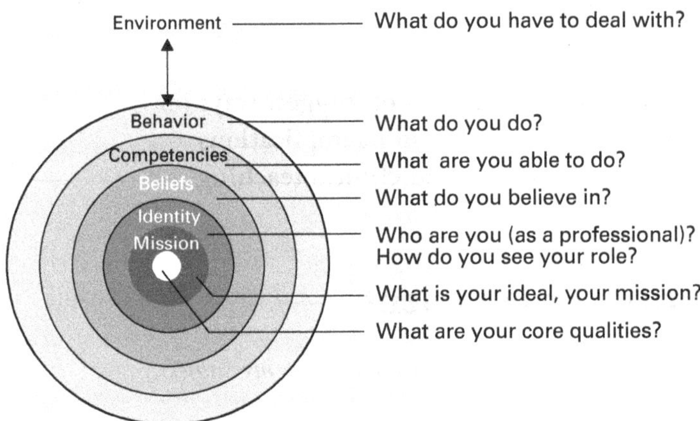

Core reflection is partially based on Korthagen's (2004) onion model, which has been updated to include some questions (Korthagen & Nuijten, 2022), as seen in Figure 2.1. Meijer, Korthagen, and Vasalos (2009) wrote that teacher presence is connected to understanding and teaching to your own strengths, as well as connecting teaching with your own beliefs, identity, and mission. Meijer et al. concluded that teachers are better able to notice and react to students' needs in meaningful and effective ways when teachers bring their personal beliefs into their professional lives, which is the purpose of core reflection. See online resources, Table 2.1, for questions Pellegrino (2019b) developed for preservice music teachers to consider based on the onion model. For more on teacher presence, including connecting teachers' personal lives and professional lives for music teachers, you can read additional works (e.g., Hibbard, 2017; Pellegrino, 2011, 2015, 2019a, 2019b).

SOCIAL-CULTURAL APPROACHES TO LEARNING MUSIC AND DEVELOPING A MUSIC TEACHER IDENTITY

Both social factors and culture impact how we learn, what musics we identify with, and how we think of ourselves. Researchers such as Etienne Wenger and Brad Olsen have investigated how humans learn, work, and think about themselves as professionals.

Wenger (1998) dissected the learning process and developed a theory called Communities of Practice (CoP). CoP refers to people participating in groups where there are implicit and explicit understandings, and people negotiate meanings in individual and social ways. CoP is the interaction of four elements:

- *Meaning*: What learning the activities means to each person.
- *Participation in practice*: Learning activities that are valued in a community.
- *Community*: The feeling of belonging that comes from being with others who value and share a dedication to the activities.
- *Identity*: How learning the activities changes who you are "and creates personal histories of becoming in the context of our communities." (p. 5)

What do these theories have to do with you and your development? If we consider Wenger's (1998) CoP theory, the activities of shared value in our community are making music in some way. Maybe you became inspired to make music after hearing someone else make music first and then thought you would like to do that too (perhaps because you had a positive reaction to the music or you looked up to the person who was making the music). At some point you began making music yourself. Maybe you were considered competent by others, had moments when you felt successful, or were inspired to continue learning. All of this represents *participation in practice*. Then you started making music with other people, and the relationships you formed with others through making music and/or the reactions from others who heard you making music seemed to provide validation and a sense of belonging (*community*). You might value music making as a form of expression, as something that connects you to others, or as something that helps you understand different cultures and/or time periods (*meaning*). Finally, you began practicing, rehearsing, and/or performing more and began to think of yourself as a musician or a specific type of music maker (*identity*). You may have experienced flow (for more on flow, see Chapter 1) or mountaintop experiences and thought about wanting to have a career in music in which you help others have similar experiences.

What we previously described might be the CoP of a music maker's cycle. However, the cycle might repeat itself with music teaching as the activity of shared value for music teachers. As a music teacher, you will then help your students participate in a music community of practice.

Wenger also viewed identity formation as a trajectory, continuously influenced by external (social) and internal (individual) forces, that incorporates what we understand about our past experiences and imagine about our future experiences in the present. He also identified five identity trajectories, three of which are (a) *peripheral trajectories*, participating in the activities of a CoP without the intention of being a full participant in its practice, (b) *inbound trajectories*, "newcomers joining the community with the prospect of becoming full participants in its practice" (p. 155), and (c) *boundary trajectories*, when participants are deciding between two or more communities of practice, such as performing and teaching. See discussion question 1 at the end of this chapter to explore this further.

Olsen (2008) believed that teacher identity is made up of the interactions among multiple parts: prior personal experience, prior professional experience, reasons for entry, teacher education experience, current teaching context and practice, and career plans/teacher retention. See Table 2.2 on the online resources site for questions to consider as you examine your journey as a music teacher. To address some people's prior personal experiences and/or teacher education experiences, we suggest some of you may want to explore literature about music experiences for music teachers (Millican & Pellegrino, 2017; Pellegrino, et al., 2021; Pellegrino, 2014; Pellegrino & Russell, 2015), cultural identity and music teacher identity development (e.g., Abu-Khader, 2019; Castañeda Lechuga &

Schmidt, 2017), and/or gender and sexual identities and music (e.g., Garrett & Palkki, 2021; Palkki, 2015a, 2015b; Talbot, 2017; Taylor et al., 2020).

Olsen (2008) suggested that preservice teachers create learning-and-teaching autobiographies where they can explore elements of their teaching identity, as described above. He also suggested they return to it later, revisiting and revising them with peers and professors. Additional suggestions include having "conversations about contradictions in the contemporary landscape of teaching, choosing the right schools for individual teachers, the many roles in early career teaching, and paying formal attention to personal and emotional effects of identity transitions" (pp. 37–38).

INTERSECTIONS OF MUSIC MAKING AND TEACHING

Pellegrino (2015) followed four student teachers with dual placements in elementary music and secondary band and found that "music making intersected with participants' personal and professional identities, wellbeing, and their teaching" (p. 189). First, "music making helped participants remember who they were as they layered on their teaching identities and they considered music making to be central to" their own *personal identity,* as well as "being a musician and music teacher" (p. 189). Also, music making intersected with *teaching* in multiple ways: "as an efficient pedagogical tool (to enhance student learning) and classroom management tool (to promote student engagement)" (p. 175).

> *Participants used music making inside the classroom to excite and inspire their students and themselves, to bring students' attention to the teacher and the music, to gain credibility and establish expertise, and to model technique and musicality in the instrumental classrooms and musical concepts and improvisation in the general music classrooms. Through music making inside the classroom, participants developed their* professional identity, *realizing what kind of music teachers they wanted to become: excited about music and music teaching, and music teachers who use music making to inspire students to be excited and engaged in music learning. (p. 175; emphasis ours)*

Finally, "intersections of music making and *wellbeing* included feeling connected to self, to others, and to their spirituality while music making, as well as music making being an expressive tool, stress management tool, and mood enhancer" (p. 175).

Past music making experiences are important in how four inservice string teachers described their beliefs about why their students enjoyed making music, and it informed their own content knowledge (Pellegrino, 2010, 2014). If a participant spoke about engaging in music making as a way to express themselves or enjoying the challenge of playing, they assumed their students had the same goals or feelings. Taken together, participants described what music making meant to them as "(a) a catalyst to discover who they were and wanted to become; (b) a challenging, fun activity; (c) a vehicle to experience success and recognition; (d) an outlet for expression; and/or (e) a sense of well-being" (p. 132). Furthermore, these string teachers used their own technical and musical experiences to inform their pedagogy, and they included many different genres in their programs and celebrated diversity in repertoire, continuing to learn different genres in professional development opportunities. However, they did not introduce genres that were new to them, underscoring the need for continual learning.

Present music making experiences (outside and inside the classroom) intersected with teaching in different ways. First, "participants used their music making *inside the classroom* to create a culture based on the love of music making; to teach technique, improvisation, music literacy; and to model musicality" (p. 137). Participants described the intersections of music making *outside the classroom* and teaching as:

a. Nurturing themselves and keeping their art alive, which "inspired," "excited," and "revitalized" them as music teachers
b. Reminding themselves what it was like to be a music learner, which led to them to being more compassionate toward student learners
c. Grappling with and solving pedagogical issues while music making
d. Inspiring students by sharing music-making stories
e. Keeping string skills accessible so they could model for their students (p. 137)

METAPHORS

Finding ways to think about who we will be as teachers can be difficult. One way we can do so is to create a teaching metaphor. Metaphors are a figure of speech in which we explain abstract concepts and link them to something more familiar to develop a deeper understanding of the abstract concept (Lakoff & Johnson, 1980). Metaphors are a common way to express ourselves, such as "apple of my eye" to describe someone who is precious to us or "heart of stone" to imply someone is stern or cruel in nature.

Metaphors can also structure our thoughts and help us understand our own assumptions and perceptions. Finding a metaphor that represents who we are as teachers may be especially helpful as we start to examine the experiences, values, and beliefs we bring to the profession with us. Researchers have found that metaphors serve as an important tool for engaging preservice teachers in thinking about how they interpret teaching and recognize their tacit understandings and personal beliefs about the profession (Thompson & Campbell, 2003; Raiber & Teachout, 2014; Wagoner, 2021).

Sample student metaphors from Wagoner's (2021) research study included:

> *Lighthouse*: The teacher is a guiding light for students, there in times of darkness or need, and silently standing by when it is light outside and the need for guidance is lessened.
> *Tour guide*: The teacher provides opportunities for students and shares information needed for a student to explore further on their own.
> *Architect* or *engineer*: The teacher has to have deep knowledge of the subject to scaffold the curriculum and classroom for optimal learning.
> *Compass*: The teacher points the way to success, leading the way when needed and allowing students to choose a direction at other times.

See discussion question 3 for an assignment about creating teacher metaphors.

2.2 Developing a Teaching Philosophy and Implications for Curriculum

We suggest that reflecting on who you are and why you want to be a music teacher, including what music means to you, should be the starting points for developing a music teacher philosophy statement. We offer a sample music teaching philosophy statement in Table 2.3 on the online resources site. We also offer assignments in discussion questions 4 and 5.

Metaphors and philosophy statements are a great starting point, but to have an impact you must take it a step further. Elements of your philosophy statement should be seen in your teaching practice and curriculum. They should also show up in your grading policies, including what you choose to assess.

2.3 Preservice Teaching Experiences

BUILDING ON PEER TEACHINGS

During peer teachings or when teaching actual students, take the time you need to prepare so that you can feel more successful and competent while you are teaching. Parkes (2015) spoke about ways to set up preservice music teachers for success based on Bandura's (1977) sources of efficacy:

- Mastery: being successful
- Physiological and emotional states: feeling well-balanced from feedback
- Social persuasion: feedback from peers (strengths and room for improvement)
- Vicarious learning: seeing excellent models

For the first peer teaching experience, we suggest that you carefully follow a lesson plan and maybe even a script and then review it or actually teach it in front of one or two trusted peers before you teach for a grade or work with students. Basically, do whatever you can to give yourself the best chance of being successful in order to promote feelings of mastery early in your development.

Preservice music teachers need positive reinforcement, so, if you are giving feedback to your peers, be sure to say specifically what went well before you offer one or two suggestions for improvement. You should think this way about your own teaching, too. We find that college students have trouble identifying what they have done well. It could be the sequencing was well executed, the teacher made excellent eye contact with students, voice projection was great, or the feedback and suggestions for improving were specific and varied. The suggestions you give for improvement should be framed in diagnosing an issue, such as talking too much, and then giving a specific suggestion for how to improve, such as modeling and letting students play it back before labeling it. Watching excellent teaching models, including fantastic peers, will help elevate everyone's teaching. You are part of the community in your school, and the more prepared you are, the more likely you are to inspire others to do well. This will also help you in your own development (mastery) as well as others' (vicarious learning).

CLINICAL TEACHING EXPERIENCES

The educational researchers Darling-Hammond and Bransford (2007) suggested that extended clinical experiences that give preservice teachers time to incorporate ideas presented in coursework are important to their overall development. Clinical experiences can include fieldwork, university partnerships, string projects, marching band camps, sectionals, and the like. These are experiences in which you are able to work with actual students. The advantage of fieldwork is that you can put into practice the concepts you are learning in class.

The advantages of long-term projects such as university partnerships and string projects are that you develop relationships with students over time you learn to lesson plan and think about long-term sequencing, and you often see master teachers working with students. Ideally, you will receive feedback in both short- and long-term experiences. Participating in clinical experiences can positively impact your inbound trajectories (Wenger, 1998), an idea introduced earlier in this chapter.

Researchers have found that preservice music teachers who engaged in a variety of clinical teaching experiences improved their teaching skills (Haston & Russell, 2012; Paul et al., 2001; Schmidt, 2005, 2010), integrated new ideas into their thinking about teaching (Ferguson, 2003; Schmidt, 2010), and developed a music teacher identity (e.g., Haston & Russell, 2012; Pellegrino, 2015, 2019). It makes sense that you develop more of a teacher identity when you have your own students and are engaging in many aspects of teaching. These may include (a) choosing literature; (b) lesson planning (including concepts described in Chapter 1 such as deconstructing concepts, sequencing, modeling, energy profile, etc.); (c) developing relationships with students; (d) working on completing teacher loops and giving informal and formal feedback/assessments (see Chapter 6); and/or (e) teaching students to practice (see Chapter 3), and more. Are there clinical teaching experiences offered through your institution? If not, is there something you could arrange? What would those look like?

In general, the more success you feel as a teacher, the more likely you are to continue in the teaching profession. Also, spend time reflecting on who you are and who you want to be. Understanding the meaning you attach to your past experiences as well as thinking about how to relate your beliefs, values, identity, and mission to your teaching will help you develop teacher presence, which impacts teacher satisfaction and student learning.

2.4 Discussion Questions

1. Thinking about Wenger's identity trajectories as described in section 2.1 (peripheral, inbound, or boundary), which one best describes your experiences so far? If you have not already done so, how could you develop an inbound trajectory?
2. Do you plan to continue making music while teaching? Why or why not? What are ways you think you might use your music making as a pedagogical tool?
3. Metaphor assignment
   a. Start with finding a visual picture or drawing a picture that represents what you think about teaching and learning.
   b. What is your selected metaphor? Include some specifics about how this metaphor supports your values and beliefs about teaching and learning.
   c. Compare your metaphor with those of your peers. What commonalities do your metaphors have? How are they different? What have you not considered? Deepen your writing after discussing the metaphor with your peers.
   d. Relate your metaphor to your philosophy of teaching. Find connections between them and deepen your writing to transfer your philosophical thoughts to your metaphor.
4. Develop a two-paragraph personal music teacher philosophy and examine your own beliefs and experiences. This essay should address your values, including your judgment of what is important. Be sure to have *only two* clearly written and concise paragraphs:
   Paragraph 1. Explain in 3–5 points what music making means to you
   Paragraph 2. Describe your philosophy of music teaching (your goals for yourself and students)

See Table 2.3 on the online resources site for an example.

5. How might your music teacher philosophy relate to your pedagogical practices, including your future grading policies? In what activities do you engage students that show the value of music as an expressive art, creative outlet, or a community-building activity, if that is your value of music? Also, how might you assess and grade those aspects of music making? If you value improvement, how would you authentically assess each student's progress and attach a grade to it? If you value helping students feel as if they belong, will that impact your music literature choices and activities (genres, diverse composers, playing by ear and reading notation, composing, songwriting, improvising, etc.)?

6. Are there clinical teacher experiences offered at your institution through your program or student musical organizations? If not, how could you arrange clinical experiences?

OXFORD learning link

Visit the online resources for additional documentation and exercises to help expand learning and test your knowledge further: www.oup.com/he/powell music1e.

HOW STUDENTS LEARN

Kristen Pellegrino and Cynthia L. Wagoner

In this chapter we explore music learning in three sections: music as a social endeavor; curriculum related to learning music (with reference to Bruner's spiral curriculum, Dewey, and culturally relevant pedagogy); and how developing a musician identity impacts learning (including teaching students through music and teaching students how to practice).

3.1 Introduction

In *The Book of Learning and Forgetting*, Smith (1998) approached learning as being a social activity in which people learn most from those with whom they identify and whom they wish to emulate, including peers and mentors. Smith also found that people learn what they can understand and what interests them. Smith's theory became the foundation for this chapter. We relate learning as a social endeavor through Vygotsky's Zone of Proximal Development and learning what students can understand to Bruner's spiral curriculum. We also relate learning what interests each student to Dewey's (2013) theory that school learning should relate to life outside of school, which includes culturally relevant teaching. Next, we discuss the impact of musician identity on learning. Finally, we explore the concept of teaching students through music and helping students learn how to practice.

3.2 Music Learning as a Social Endeavor

Learning is a social activity in which people learn most from those with whom they identify and whom they wish to emulate. Similarly, as described in Chapter 1, one of the core teaching practices in music was "developing knowledge of and appropriate relationships with students" (Millican & Forrester, 2018). Expanding on the relational aspect of learning, we explore learning through Vygotsky's (1978) Zone of Proximal Development (ZPD). ZPD is a theory that learners can achieve more with the help of a more knowledgeable other (teacher, parent, peer, and others) than they can alone. Offering a model, guidance, suggestions, and/or encouragement can help learners achieve more with you or their peers than by themselves.

Why do our students sometimes say they struggled to play something well at home but play fine in front of us? Tharp and Gallimore (1991) identified a four-step ZPD process:

- Assistance by more capable others
- Assistance provided by self
- Performance is developed
- Recursion (p. 35)

In the second step, students ("self") hear our advice in their minds without our even saying anything at that moment. In the next, "performance is developed," learners achieve "internalization, automatization, fossilization . . . [and] internal dialogue is undetectable" (p. 35). Think about something you share with friends and your shorthand way of referencing it, sometimes called inside jokes. This is an example of fossilization.

Similarly, you can create pedagogical code words. For example, for string players' left-hand position, Kristen tells a story and then uses a code word "rotten egg" to signal to her students to focus on the correct shape of the hand. This is "assistance by [a] more capable other."

Kristen also has students use a checklist so we can reduce concepts to a series of one or two words per action: rotten egg, click, land, stamp feet, snap fingers, and so on. Everyone knows the shorthand, and you can see students react accordingly. Kristen tells students, "Think about your checklist," and watches the self-corrections, which is "assistance provided by self." Eventually, students do not need reminders; they simply run through the steps automatically, representing the third step, "performance is developed."

More knowledgeable others also include peers. Therefore, giving peers time to interact and teach each other is important. When two peers teach each other, it helps solidify concepts for both of them. For more on peer-assisted learning, see Chapter 12. One additional benefit is that peer-assisted learning builds community and keeps everyone engaged in the learning process while giving the teacher time to help some students in a semiprivate way.

Thompson (2013) expanded on Vygotsky's ZPD work further, writing about eight elements that contribute to "engagement" and the "collaborative nature of the task/activity." Three of these were:

- The social context of the classroom
- The emotional context of learners: safety/risk
- Student/teacher feedback, direction, or instruction. (p. 259)

(See the online resources for more about the elements and how to implement them.) Developing appropriate relationships with and among students is sometimes referred to as attending to the social-emotional needs of students (e.g., Edgar, 2013, 2017), or elements of care (see Chapter 11).

3.3 Curriculum Related to Learning Music

Smith (1998) wrote that we learn what we can understand. This also relates to the core teaching practices in music (Millican & Forrester, 2018) as explored in Chapter 1: modeling music concepts, deconstructing concepts, and sequencing concepts, which are all addressed in Jerome Bruner's Spiral Curriculum. Bruner wrote *The Process of Education* in 1960 to emphasize that a school's educational goals should be focused on intellectual development.

BRUNER'S SPIRAL CURRICULUM

Bruner (1960) summarized his research on the cognitive development of children by presenting three modes of representation: action based (enactive), image based (iconic), and language based (symbolic). These are integrated ways that human beings construct knowledge. *Enactive* representation, which is action based, happens when we learn through using motor skills, like learning fingerings or creating an embouchure to play an instrument. These become encoded in our memory, and we do not have to think carefully about executing these skills after a period of time; they become automatic to us when we pick up the instrument to play.

Iconic representation is sensory and image based. For musicians, "sound before sight" aligns with Bruner's understanding of the ways in which we learn through motor skills and sensory information before we are able to attach symbols to what we are doing. *Symbolic* representation is language or symbol based and includes the ability to transfer the fingerings we have learned and the musical pitch or rhythms we hear to symbolic representations of notation, as well as learning the names for the notation (e.g., quarter notes, pitch names, dynamics, articulations, etc.).

Using these three steps (enactive, iconic, and symbolic) can also be a great approach to teaching music literacy. Singing the solfège syllables *mi*, *re*, and *do* while moving your hands from your head to your shoulders to your lap helps associate high, medium, and low with pitch. Then, you can draw some representation of notes that are higher, lower, and lower still. Then, you can relate these to some kind of notation. See Chapter 6, Conway (2003), West (2015, 2016), and/or the online resources for more about incorporating this idea with a composition project.

Bruner then described the spiral curriculum: "We begin with the hypothesis that any subject can be taught in some intellectually honest form to any child at any stage of development" (1960, p. 33). Basically, Bruner proposed that students learn when you deconstruct concepts and then sequence them so that they are layered and become more complex over time, including transferring those skills into new contexts. He theorized there were three stages of learning: (1) acquisition, (2) transformation, and (3) evaluation (Bruner, 1960).

The spiral curriculum requires us teachers to break a concept or task down to a simplified level or fundamental skill and then build upon those skills or concepts gradually until the student is able to perform the skill or concept at a more complex level and transfer the skill or concept to new situations: "Grasping the structure of a subject is to understand it in a way that permits many other things to be related to it meaningfully. To learn structure, in short, is to learn how things are related" (Bruner, 1960, p. 7). Therefore, you will have to think about structuring lessons that build on the last lesson and that adds more specific details or processes as the student gains more proficiency and knowledge (Stapleton & Stefaniac, 2019). An example might be learning the fundamentals of playing an instrument and then being able to use technique in a way that helps students express themselves musically.

Discovery learning is an important part of designing a spiral curriculum, where teachers serve as facilitators in the learning process to help students discover relationships in what they are learning. This relates to Vygotsky's ZPD and also incorporates Bruner's belief that children are already equipped with intelligence and are active problem solvers from the time they are born (McLeod, 2019). How does this relate to learning music?

Think about your own musical journey. Each of us had to begin learning to create sounds on our instruments, or learn to use our voices to match pitch before moving onto creating musical sounds and ideas. Over time, we were able to make more and more complex musical sounds, phrases, and nuanced musical interpretations. You certainly had encouraging teachers who helped you find your errors and learn more advanced concepts with motivating musical examples or models to hear along the way. Bruner's theory of representations and spiral curriculum can help us think more deeply about how to effectively design lessons to help students be successful early on and begin to discover the relationships between the musical sounds they hear with the concepts and motor skills they are learning. For more on curriculum, see Chapter 7 and Millican and Pellegrino (2015).

DEWEY AND CULTURALLY RELEVANT PEDAGOGY

John Dewey (1849–1952) was an educational psychologist who believed that learning in school should be related to life outside of school, and that learning should be relevant to students' lives, not separate from it (Dewey, 2013). Therefore, the goal of education is

> *to have the child come to school with all the experience he* [sic] *has got outside the school, and to leave it with something to be immediately used in his everyday life. . . . What we want is to have the child come to school with a whole mind and a whole body, and leave school with a fuller mind and an even healthier body. (p. 50)*

Recently, more authors have been writing about culturally relevant/responsive pedagogy. For example, Lind and McKoy (2016) wrote about culturally responsive teaching in music education, acknowledging that "students are unique in the ways they learn" and that we live in an "increasingly pluralistic and interconnected world which underscores the influence of factors related to race, ethnicity, and culture on student learning" (p. 1). For more on this, we have three chapters related to culturally relevant/responsive teaching in modern band (Chapter 25), orchestral settings (Chapter 31), and band (Chapter 43). We also have Chapter 14, "Teaching Instrumental Music in the Twenty-First Century," to help put students in the context of current life and events.

3.4 Developing a Musician Identity Impacts Learning

Developing a musician identity has a social component to it, adding to the foundation of this chapter, namely Smith's (1998) social learning theory. Hargreaves et al. (2018) wrote a chapter titled "Musical Identities Mediate Musical Development" in which they wrote:

> *Vygotsky's (1986) basic idea that "we become ourselves through others"—that our social relationships with others form the basis of our own individual development—has led indirectly to our own emphasis on the importance of individual* identity *in musical development. (p. 138)*

They suggest that students who identify as musicians learn more. Why? "Developing a positive musical identity can increase the extent to which individuals will engage in musical practice, which can in turn enable the development of specific musical skills" (p. 132). This also relates to Culver's motivation step of the energy profile discussed in Chapter 1 and Chapter 4. To summarize, identifying as a musician impacts interest, focus, and dedication to spending time engaged in learning music. To further encourage this, we suggest a few additional ideas to positively impact developing students' musician identity.

TEACHING STUDENTS THROUGH MUSIC

Some people say they teach music *to* students, but we believe that we actually teach students *through* music. What is the difference? We need to remember that we teach each individual in our classroom. In this way, we should resist thinking about our classes in terms of ensembles, but take each student's interests and development into consideration. This impacts our music-literature choices, our assessment decisions, pacing, motivation versus competition, and discovery of each students' meanings and values of playing an instrument. To help them develop a musician's identity, we must help each student feel successful and empowered, which may involve making accommodations and thinking about differentiated learning.

For example, if we think about the group, the concert might be the most important goal, and we may not value individual assessments as much. However, if the student is the priority, their engagement, individual progress, and happiness are important. Practically, working with a specific instrumental section on a specific passage until it is correct will benefit the whole. However, as other students wait until that one section is good enough to move on, the majority of students in the class may be bored and will be disengaged or disruptive, and motivation will wane. Placing students first might include:

- *Literature choices* (teaching popular tunes, learning songs they choose by ear, ensemble literature choices)
- *Encouraging and empowering students on their own musical journeys*, including allowing them to move at their own pace and being sure we teach for mastery (to challenge all students without overwhelming any, meaning they do not all learn the same amount of music but they have to play what they learned well)
- *Creating a community in the classroom* that encourages each person to grow musically, personally, and socially
- *Finding out students' goals and motivations*—why they want to play their instrument, what they love most about it, and what their playing goals are, and incorporating that into your teaching and assessments
- *Assessments, such as playing tests*, can be opportunities for success, individual feedback, and encouragement as opposed to moments for competition or chair challenges
- *Having rotating seating within a concert program and/or between concerts.* All parts are important, so allow students to experience different parts within their sections and sitting in different places in a string section; this also allows more students to experience musical leadership roles in your ensemble
- *Teaching students to play expressively*, which gives meaning to notes and rhythms and helps students express their emotions

In addition, there are multiple ways of learning (learning by ear, reading different types of music, composing, arranging, improvising, etc.), and all of these should be included in your teaching. We approach teaching in multiple ways in order to reach all our students as well. First, we offer many different opportunities and ways to learn and engage with music and then we encourage students to pursue and nurture their interests more fully. Teachers, we must also help identify the core issue(s) that prevent students from developing and break down barriers so that each student can move forward free of obstacles. For example, sometimes students experience technical issues, while other times they have musical, personal, or social issues. To help each student on their own musical journey, we have to know our students and be able to quickly diagnose issues. For more, please see Chapter 11 and Chapter 9.

TEACHING STUDENTS TO PRACTICE

Dweck (2008) wrote about the importance of a growth mindset—about how our ability to grow and learn is not a fixed trait but one that is malleable and influenced by context and individual persistence. Arts education has been identified as a place where socioemotional development is promoted as a growth mindset (Goldstein et al., 2017; Holochwost et al., 2021; Tan et al., 2021). Every semester Kristen has students in her string techniques classes read Suzuki's *Nurtured by Love*, and it seems to be transformational in many of her students' lives. Suzuki explained that people are not simply born with talent but rather that their own efforts in practicing regularly actually nurture talent. Relating Suzuki's concepts to Dweck's, talent is an example of "fixed mindset," whereas regularly practicing and developing talent is a "growth mindset." Austin and Berg (2006) wrote about the value of practicing:

> *The act of* practicing*—learning through systematic experience or exercise—has long been viewed as essential to knowledge/skill acquisition and development in a range of disciplines, including music. Individual practice allows musicians to reinforce learning received from instructors, engage in self-discovery, and develop habits of mind. (p. 535)*

Learning to practice entails decision making and intrapersonal skill development so students can improve with effort over time, develop strategies to improve, and view mistakes and setbacks as opportunities to learn (Burnette et al., 2018). For example, musicians learn easier keys before moving on to more difficult ones (in terms of fingering patterns and range). For example, winds learn B♭ major before E♭ or F major, whereas strings learn D, G, and A major before C or F major. There are major scales and natural, harmonic, and melodic minor scales, as well as modes. We naturally move through learning scales in a way that improves our skills over time, and students can develop specific strategies to learn new scales rather than giving up when they get harder.

We propose that the importance of practice is a combination of:

- Setting goals for each session
- Being fully attentive
- Hearing music in your mind (audiation)
- Deconstructing concepts and sequentially building them back up
- Developing muscle memory
- Associating expressive meaning to the music and using technique to create a mood or tell a story to hopefully create an emotional response in or activate the imagination of your listener.
- Learning to enjoy the process of practing as well as music making in general

Researchers found that focused, deliberate, and effective practice happens when goals are defined and appropriate strategies are used to achieve those goals (e.g., Hallam et al., 2012; Miksza, 2007; Oare, 2012; Rohwer & Polk, 2006).

For example, some people practice with metronomes as a default practice strategy. However, using a metronome is not always the most appropriate approach. When you are working on intonation, tone, and expression, metronomes are not helpful. When you are working on faster passages, you may use a metronome to slow down tempi and build it back to the appropriate tempo gradually. Another strategy for practicing fast passages might also be the use of dotted rhythms. (See online resources for a more thorough explanation within the Practicing Tips). Differentiating a multitude of strategies for various musical issues is a worthwhile endeavor.

As for setting goals, if we think about what we need to practice, we may think about different categories. How many categories do you think about when practicing? See Discussion Question #5.

Another suggestion is to teach students to structure their practice sessions according to the concept of Culver's (1998) energy profile (review and refine, extend knowledge, and end with a high/motivation). (See Chapter 1 and Chapter 4.) This may help them to enter into a state of flow (see Chapter 1 for more on flow) and be more motivated to return to practicing. It also involves being intentional about structuring practice sessions and setting goals.

For mental and physical attention, we suggest building in regular breaks and including stretching and hydrating into your practice routine. Of course, age and ability level will influence how much practice time is appropriate, but if you are going to practice more than ninety minutes, we suggest practicing fifty to fifty-five minutes during each hour. For example, you could practice for twenty-five minutes, take a break (which should include drinking some water and walking around), practice for another twenty-five minutes, stretch for five minutes, and then practice the last thirty minutes. This way one is more likely to practice with intention and maintain focus. For more suggestions for effective practice, see the online resources for (a) references, (b) specific practice strategies, and (c) effective practice charts (hint: asking for the amount of time practiced is not effective and actually invites dishonesty).

3.5 Conclusion

Again, according to Smith (1998), people learn from those they wish to emulate, including peers and mentors, and they learn what interests them and what they can understand. As the teacher, you can actively help students feel that their own interests matter, that they can be successful, and that they belong, in part because you take the time to break down learning into interesting, manageable chunks. This might lead to developing a musician identity, which leads to further learning. Lastly, be sure to teach your students that their efforts impact their learning (growth mindset) and teach them how to practice.

3.6 Discussion Questions and Activities

1. Create an example for how you can teach something based on Tharp and Gallimore's (1991) four-step process.
2. Develop a lesson plan that incorporates enactive, iconic, and symbolic ways of learning.
3. What parts of "Music Learning as a Social Endeavor" and "Curriculum Related to Learning Music" resonated with you? How might you incorporate both into your future teaching?
4. Share examples from your past and present experiences in music classrooms that relate to these theoretical concepts.
5. How would you deconstruct playing goals into different categories? Perhaps some combination of posture, position, tone, intonation, rhythm/pulse/meter, technique and speed, style, musicality, and expression. Would you add or remove categories? Why?
6. Use the energy profile to structure your practice sessions, use some new practice strategies, and use the practice chart example in the online resources for one full week. What did you like about using these tools and what would you change? How would you describe how it impacted your practice sessions?

OXFORD learning link

Visit the online resources for additional documentation and exercises to help expand learning and test your knowledge further: www.oup.com/he/powell_music1e.

CHAPTER 4

PROACTIVE AND REACTIVE CLASSROOM MANAGEMENT STRATEGIES

Kristen Pellegrino

You create the climate in your classroom

I've come to the frightening conclusion that I am the decisive element in the classroom. It's my daily mood that makes the weather. As a teacher, I possess a tremendous power to make a child's life miserable or joyous. I can be a tool of torture or an instrument of inspiration.

I can humiliate or humor, hurt or heal. In all situations, it is my response that decides whether a crisis will be escalated or de-escalated and a child humanized or de-humanized. (Ginott, 1965)

I had this quote taped to my desk and gradebook when I taught high school orchestra in Virginia and then Rhode Island. It guided me and my reactions when I was at my best. Researchers found that preservice and early-career in-service music teachers are particularly concerned about developing effective classroom management techniques (e.g., Berg and Miksza, 2010; Regier, 2021). In this chapter, I present proactive classroom strategies, such as using your musicianship, developing great habits, engaging students, setting them up for success, and building community, and briefly discuss some reactive classroom strategies.

4.1 Proactive Classroom Management Strategies

Ideas explored in the first chapter are reiterated here because I believe that good teaching principles will help to keep students engaged and motivated. I discuss developing proactive classroom management strategies in four subsections: (a) use your musicianship, (b) develop great habits, (c) engage students and set them up for success, and (d) build community.

USE YOUR MUSICIANSHIP

How will you bring yourself as a musician into your music teaching? I suggest using your own music making (on primary and secondary instruments, including singing) in the classroom, making musical teaching decisions, and limiting teacher talk.

Use Your Music Making in the Classroom

Sharing yourself as a musician is an important element of teaching music. As an orchestra teacher in the public schools and then as a researcher, I first noticed and then examined the intersections of music making and teaching (Pellegrino, 2010, 2014, 2015a, 2015b, 2015c, 2019) and found many benefits. When music teachers used their primary instruments in the classroom, they found (a) student engagement and classroom management improved; (b) student learning improved, (c) students and teachers seemed more excited and felt more present, and (d) the musical interactions aided personal rapport between teacher and students.

Teachers used their primary and secondary instruments to model posture, position, tone, intonation, rhythm, technique, musicality and phrasing, playing together, cueing, and moving to the music. Teachers also modeled the tone and timbre they wanted students to emulate instead of asking them generally to play louder or softer, which I highly recommend. Improvisation was taught through modeling and audiation skills were connected to music literacy. Lastly, some teachers even used music-making during transitions between pieces or activities.

After watching videos of their students' reactions, the teachers felt that playing their primary instrument in the classroom inspired students and motivated them to want to play like the teacher. The teachers felt they could share their "musical voice" when modeling on their primary instruments. Also, the teachers thought that their students saw them as artist-teachers (expert music makers and teachers) and believed that helped them build relationships with their students and create a culture based on the love of music making.

All teachers could model on all instruments and sing. Teachers were more likely to use secondary instruments when they played larger instruments (e.g., cello, bass, tuba). They explained that the smaller instruments were less cumbersome and more mobile (they could walk around while playing), and that most of the students in the room played a higher-pitched instrument.

Make Musical Teaching Decisions

Wait to stop students until the end of a phrase! It is a good musical instinct to cadence and play until the end of a phrase. However, teachers often try to stop students in the middle of the phrase and then become frustrated when students continue to play.

Also, let students play until you know what you want to say and have them do to improve (what and how). Having students wait while you think about how to respond is an invitation for students to begin talking, as it is human nature to talk to fill the silences. It is also important to let students play more than you talk.

Breathe to cue students to begin and have them breathe with you as opposed to counting, clapping, or stamping. This is true whether cueing with your instrument in hand or when conducting. Students will have to watch you and make eye contact with you, which also helps with building relationships with students and keeping their attention. While students are watching you for a cue to begin, communicate the mood of the music in your musical gestures and face. You stop less often to ask for different articulations, dynamics, tone, phrasing, and expression when you work to show musical cues *while* they are making music instead of just waiting until afterward.

Finally, spend significant time working on developing the meaning of the piece and being expressive. I believe music should activate one's emotions and/or imagination. Have students work with you to help create a story or identify a mood or feeling so that the technical elements of playing are serving an emotive, musical purpose. This is the reason many of us love music, and sharing this is an integral part of being a music teacher.

Limit Teacher Talk

Give clear and concise instructions, have students play more, and, again, use modeling! In the first chapter I gave an example of teaching staccato for the first time in two ways: first through explanation and second through modeling and having students echo back what they hear. Teaching "sound before sight; experience, then label" will help teachers limit talking and allow students to play more. When you do talk, give clear, concise instructions. Get to the point and then have students *do* something musical immediately afterward. This way, when you share the background of a piece, share stories, or give directions, students will pay attention.

In a study (Pellegrino, 2019) with two undergraduate students who taught their own students in two hour-long group lessons (about thirty-five students in each group) twice a week, "Ashley" and "Xander" discovered a link between talking too much, not having students play enough, and classroom management issues. Xander said:

> *How much the students play really affects their learning experience in the classroom. After we did the assigned exercise where we kept track of how much time the students were playing versus how much they weren't playing, there was much less playing and more of me talking than I expected! When students weren't playing for longer periods of time, it would be kind of difficult to get the control back sometimes; the students would lose focus. Things would start happening either in their playing or behaviorally that wouldn't happen when they would be playing or constantly engaged. (pp. 19–20)*

Again, being proactive means that you work to keep students' attention.

DEVELOP GREAT HABITS

I recommend (a) developing consistent and clear expectations, (b) establishing classroom routines, and (c) preparing for smooth transitions.

Consistent and Clear Expectations (Musically and Behaviorally)

Once you are aware of what you consider most important, you can set clear expectations. I suggest that instead of having a long list of classroom rules that outlines exactly what students can and cannot do, instead, try to sum up the rules in five to seven ideas. They may spell a word, like MUSIC, with each letter standing for a rule. Your school may have a schoolwide policy. I borrowed the rules below from a music teacher in San Antonio, Mrs. Johnson, and then I added the sixth rule. These rules are not punitive but instead offer clear guidance about the positive behaviors expected from students in your classroom. Be:

- Prompt
- Prepared
- Productive
- Polite
- Positive
- A problem solver

I posted musical expectations in my room, too, which formed the basis of my playing tests (20 percent each). I began with *posture and position*, because they are foundational in producing a good *tone*. Playing with excellent *intonation* involves playing with relaxed, balanced, supported *posture and position*, a clear, ringing *tone*, audiating, and playing the correct pitches.

- Posture and position
- Tone
- Pitch accuracy and intonation
- Rhythm, pulse, meter, and tempo
- Style, musicality, and expression

Pulse, meter, and rhythm and *style* (articulations) are imperative to ensemble playing and can help clear up intonation issues before you work on playing at an *appropriate tempo*. Playing with the same sense of *style* (articulations) also contributes to clearly expressing ourselves musically, but we must also have the same *musical and expressive intentions* so that we can activate the audience members' imaginations and/or emotions.

Classroom Routines (Musical and Behavioral)

Establish procedures and expectations for how students enter the room, where students put their instrument cases and backpacks, what should be on the stand, and how to prepare to play before instruction begins. What is the tuning procedure? What is the playing test procedure? Where should students submit forms? When are announcements made? What are attention-getting signals? I have seen many routines for beginning class or rehearsal that work, such as communicating that students should be quiet when anyone steps on the podium or puts their bow on their head. Practice your chosen procedures until they become automatic, and be consistent with your expectations.

You should also establish playing routines as well. I had a default canonic scale warm-up for my high school string students that I could cue students to begin without my conducting. For my elementary beginning violinists and violists, they play standing up so they move their whole bodies until the scroll faces me. After the first couple of times, I stamp my feet to remind them to move their bodies until the scroll faces me instead of telling them. A position checklist works for beginners through high school students. I remind students to think about the checklist and I observe their behaviors as they adjust their posture and position accordingly. Similarly, Hilliard (2005) has three steps for seated playing positions:

1. Sit on the *edge* of the chair
2. Keep feet flat on the floor (sit tall and *no* "wrinkled" stomach)
3. *Hold still* and *listen* for instructions.

Prepare for Smooth Transitions

Students often lose focus during transitions. Be sure to tell students what you expect from them. For example, "Place your instrument silently and carefully in its case. Without talking, stand up and spread out for stretches." The music begins, and you or a student lead the students in stretches. Students will respond accordingly, but you must intentionally lead them with clear routines. Therefore, when you plan your lesson, be sure to write clear, concise, one- or two-sentence transitions and/or plan another way to signal the activity, such as playing the first few phrases of the next piece.

ENGAGE STUDENTS AND SET STUDENTS UP FOR SUCCESS

Engaging students has many elements, and will be discussed in two main sections (a) keeping everyone involved in the learning process (with three subsections: flow, differentiated learning—challenge everyone without overwhelming anyone, and nonverbal cues) and (b) energy profile, positive feedback, and the teaching cycle. See the online resources for more on setting students up for success: deconstruct concepts and sequence instruction, and setting realistic long- and short-term goals.

Keep Everyone Involved in the Learning Process

In Pellegrino (2019) Ashley wrote, "I have learned that pacing is usually the key to efficient classroom management in a music classroom; if I keep my pace up, I keep the students on their toes and they don't have time to be distracted" (p. 19). If students are constantly learning and playing music, then there will be very little down time.

Notice what each individual student is doing during your class, not just your pace of instruction. For example, if you are working with trumpets, what is everyone else doing? Just listening is not enough engagement. Instead, ask students who are not playing to watch one student who is playing and analyze one specific thing (articulation, bow speed, etc.). Give a thumbs-up if their person was successful and a neutral thumb (to the side) if we need to keep working. When the students are specifically being watched by their peers, they seem to focus better and achieve success more quickly, and the students who are not playing are more engaged.

Another option is to teach everyone a technique first. Then, when that one section applies it to the piece, the others evaluate and can give specific recommendations based on their experience. Even better, if students use the same technique elsewhere in the music, find all of the places people use it and have them play together, even if they play in fifths.

"FLOW"

Here is another example of a good teaching habit discussed in Chapter 1 contributing to good classroom management. Csikszentmihalyi (2008) described the state of flow as becoming fully absorbed in an activity of interest and having enough skill to tackle an appropriately challenging activity. The result is losing a sense of time and self, which results in feelings of satisfaction and a sense of well-being: "Concentration is so intense that there is no attention left over to think about anything irrelevant, or to worry about problems. Self-consciousness disappears, and the sense of time becomes distorted" (p. 71).

Therefore, you must take students' playing levels as well as their personal and musical interests into consideration. Building relationships with students, engaging them musically and socially in what they consider to be meaningful ways, and motivating students all relate to proactive classroom management strategies. One example is to offer a few literature choices and have students vote on which to play. The trick is to be sure that the options you offer are thoughtfully considered in relation to curricular considerations. (For more, see Chapter 3.)

What prohibits people from entering into a state of flow? In Figure 4.1 I show the connection between skills and the challenge of a task. If something is too easy, students usually feel bored and lose focus. On the other hand, if something is too challenging, then they can feel frustrated and become discouraged. Both ends of the spectrum have behavioral implications, as students often tune out or start joking or misbehaving, either to entertain themselves or to deflect attention. When something is too difficult, sometimes students will say, "This is dumb," or "I don't care about playing."

FIGURE 4.1 Csikszentmihalyi's flow (2008)

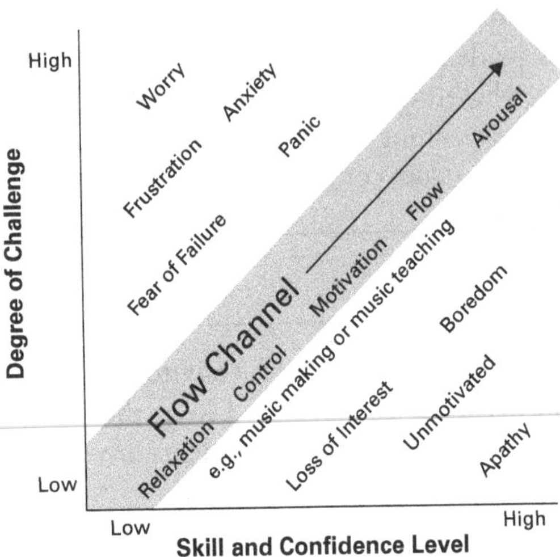

Therefore, it is important to first choose music that is at an appropriate level for the students in your class. However, what is a great choice in general is not always a great choice for each individual in your class. This leads us to the next section.

DIFFERENTIATED LEARNING—CHALLENGE EVERYONE WITHOUT OVERWHELMING ANYONE

Musically, I had a rule with both elementary and high school students (the two levels I taught before teaching in college) that *whatever* they played, they had to play well. What are the repercussions of that statement? Not every student played everything during the concert, or sometimes they played a simplified part. However, I reminded them often that the amount of time and effort they put into practicing directly impacted how much they learned, harking back to the growth mindset discussed in Chapter 3.

This rule allowed me to accept people of differing levels and let them play in parts of the concert. I had students who played piano or wind instruments ask if they could join the high string orchestra even though they had not played a string instrument before and we did not offer a beginning orchestra. I would teach them alone, pair them with an orchestra buddy, have them join the group while we rehearsed "their" piece, and then let them practice.

Based on observing your students, ask yourself, "What do students need from me right now in order to be successful?" Do they need reminders, repetition, more time to develop these techniques, more practice strategies, more deconstruction of concepts, more encouragement, more examples, or something else? Treating everyone the same is not the same as giving all students what they need, when they need it. Helping every individual excel should be our goal. (See Chapter 3.)

If needed, I suggest simplifying parts for some students and challenging others (differentiated instruction). Maybe students could play up or down an octave. For string players, they could be challenged to play in a different position (often third or fifth position) or add vibrato. Also, maybe the students who can play it can take more responsibility, such as putting in fingerings and bowing or teaching others.

Another approach to simplifying music is to play eighth notes (the first and third sixteenth notes) instead of a full passage of sixteenth notes. This is an example of deconstructing and perhaps sequencing instruction. You could have a section that is resting or playing an easier part double the part of another section to offer a challenge. Basses or tubas, for example, might play a cello or trombone part for a challenge or vice versa to simplify parts. Whether that is for practice only or they play it in the concert is up to you. Additionally, some people with learning disabilities may need simplified parts or other forms of assistance, such as color-coding their music, making the print larger, or printing it on colored background. For more ideas, see Chapter 13.

Therefore, setting students up for success includes (a) differentiating instruction—challenging all without overwhelming anyone, (b) deconstructing concepts and sequencing instruction, and (c) setting realistic long and short-term goals. See the online resources for more on this.

NONVERBAL CUES

Being intentional with your nonverbal cues helps keep students engaged. Nonverbal cues include eye contact, facial expressions, vocal inflections, and proximity. Have you ever heard a student say, "Mr. X doesn't care about me. He never even looks at me"? Nonverbal and verbal connections are often misconstrued as indicating whether a teacher cares about the student or not. Intentionally connecting with each student in your class with eye contact, encouraging smiles, and proximity will help students stay connected with you and engaged.

Energy Profile, Positive Feedback, and the Teaching Cycle

I defined and described Culver's (1989) energy profile in Chapter 1, describing an optimal flow of a classroom or rehearsal. Culver suggested you meet students' energy level at the beginning of class, which is usually medium to medium-high. Then, review and refine so students feel successful and play with good posture, position, tone, intonation, rhythm, speed and style, expression, and so on. Next, introduce new concepts and extend their knowledge (lower energy). Finally, end with success! This is high energy, and it should help students feel excited and more motivated to both practice and come back to class next time (see Figure 4.2). Again, good teaching helps students feel engaged, motivated, and focused.

FIGURE 4.2 **Energy profile (Culver, 1989)**

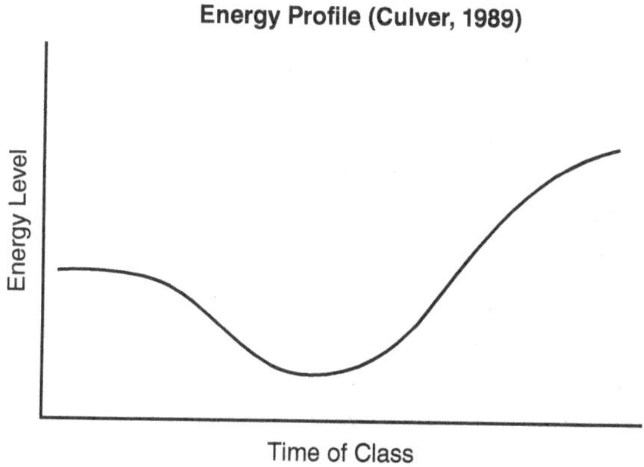

1. **Medium energy** (*Review*: meet students where they are in terms of energy and then Review and Refine)
2. **Lower energy** (*Extend*: focus and extend students' technique)
3. **High energy** (*Motivation!*: end class with success and/or fun learning games. This leaves students \with good feelings about class, encourages them to practice, and helps them be excited for next class).

This should be considered while constructing your lesson plans.

Giving positive, encouraging, and specific feedback can help keep students engaged. Think about the teaching cycle described in Chapter 1. First, be explicit about what students should focus on so that everyone is working toward the same goal. After students play, there is a response. If the response is only telling students what they should fix or what they did wrong, some might find that demoralizing (though others might be motivated by such criticism). If posture was excellent but intonation was not, share what you want students to continue doing well while they address improving another aspect. This contributes to building community, addressed in the next section.

BUILD COMMUNITY

My colleague Dr. Eugene Dowdy recommended that our preservice teachers work to "catch their students doing something well" and praise them. We want to help students be aware of what they are doing well and help them continue to do so. After students played a passage particularly well, maybe say, "That was beautiful!!! What were you thinking about just then?" When the students answer, we could say, "Let's write that in the music and let's all think about that every time." In Pellegrino (2019), Ashley spoke of experiencing connections between deconstructing sections, feedback, and classroom management:

> *There was a tricky transition and after spending a few minutes building up to being able to play the entire transition well, the students completely nailed what we were working on. I got so excited in that moment that I exclaimed LOUDLY in joy (Pellegrino-style ☺) and told them everything that I loved about what they just did. When we went to repeat the phrase again after that, I think the class in general felt more confident about what they had just done and, once again, they played it awesomely. I learned that my feedback controls the climate of the classroom quite a bit. (p. 19)*

We can also work intentionally to promote an environment that is conducive to learning and encourages everyone to be their best selves. If we foster a spirit of "we are all in this together," then students will be more willing to offer constructive comments and be more open to suggestions. They will also be less embarrassed when they make mistakes because they will realize that mistakes are part of the learning process and can be seen as opportunities for learning and improving.

I believe that pairing students together to help each other is important. I suggest you begin by assigning students to watch for something specific. For example, beginners might watch for position issues (curved right thumb and pinky, straight left wrist, or elbow hanging toward the ground) but more often they need feedback about keeping the bow halfway between the bridge and fingerboard, tone issues (a good balance between bow speed, placement, and weight or, for wind players, playing with consistent air speed), or playing the correct pitches in tune. In Pellegrino (2019), Xander said:

> *A great teaching moment was when I had the students partner to assess each other's playing. The students played the same excerpt and gave specific feedback on what they did well and what they could improve on. It was exciting to see the students helping each other improve, which helped me value partner activities in the classroom. This is definitely something that I plan to include in my future teaching. (Questionnaire, p. 22)*

There are many benefits to peer teaching. First, it lets students see what something might look like when another student tries it. Second, to teach something is to help solidify it in the teacher's mind. Third, students like to be helpful, and other students might want to hear something worded a bit differently. Fourth, it lets the teacher have time to go right to the student or students who were struggling and give them a little extra attention while everyone else is engaged. Fifth, it builds a community of support in the classroom. For more on this, see Chapter 12.

Using humor, taking students' musical and personal interests into consideration, having social activities inside and outside the classroom, helping students feel present and connected to each other, and offering additional performance opportunities are all ways to build community. For more ideas, see the online online resources and Chapters 3, 11, and 12.

4.2 Reactive Classroom Management Strategies

Table 4.1 is a list of classroom do's and don'ts. Although it is not comprehensive, you can start to imagine yourself in different scenarios. For example, instead of engaging in a "discussion or disagreement" with students in front of the class, ask them to stay after class. This gives both of you time to cool down, respects privacy, and is more likely to promote true conversation and understanding. If it is something that needs immediate attention, assign your class a section to play and lead the student outside. If the student is not ready to join the class, ask them to stay outside the classroom for five minutes and then report to you.

If someone is misbehaving, focus on communicating with your nonverbal cues, such as eye contact, proximity, and/or facial or vocal inflections. When I began teaching, I realized that I was sending mixed signals because I often had a smile on my face. I had to work on my neutral and disappointed or disapproving look so I could access a wider range of facial expressions. Sending clear messages can help students stay engaged.

Changing the energy in the classroom can be a positive reactive classroom management strategy. Redirect students' attention to the music and give them a learning task: (a) have everyone play, (b) have half the room evaluate something specific you are teaching the other students, or (c) teach everyone the technique and then only apply it to one section. Also, you can quickly change pieces or activities. For example, if students seem tired, have them put their instruments down and begin stretching, or begin improvisation, composition, or listening activities.

Understanding what your school management strategies are is also important. After you are hired, you should inquire about school-wide procedures regarding principal referrals as well as emailing, calling, and setting up in-person parent conferences. Be prepared, though, and document your interactions with your students, including how often this happened, descriptions of what the student was doing, and descriptions of how you reacted.

There are also ways to use music-making as a reactive classroom management strategy. Reese (2007) wrote, "Music is the reason we become music teachers, and it's the reason the students come to our classroom. The content of music class can be a powerful motivator and manager" (p. 28). Reese suggested using the four C's of classroom management: commendation, communication, consistency, and content-represent: "Using the four Cs helps establish an efficient, supportive, and safe environment to nurture positive experiences in music learning" (p. 24). As an example of Reese's content-represent approach, if you know that the student wants to play and be part of the group, music-making could be a consequence as you gradually escalate reactive steps.

My colleague Dr. Si Millican suggested having a behavior plan. You can create your own or use something like the following list.

1. Redirect people's attention
2. Use nonverbal cues
3. Remind students about the rules
4. Have students stop music making momentarily
5. Talk to students:
   Describe problem–"I noticed . . ."
   Ask questions—get at the root of the problem
   Document interaction/agreement
6. Parent conference
   Document interaction/agreement
7. Principal referral—schedule change

TABLE 4.1 REACTIVE CLASSROOM MANAGEMENT TECHNIQUES—SOME DO'S AND DON'TS

DON'T	DO	DO
Engage in an argument about a student's behavior during class.	Ask the student to stay after class so that you can speak privately with them.	Have a can of 10 pencils and an empty can and move a pencil into the empty to indicate that they have "lost points" for the day/establish what having points or losing points means to the class.
Yell at your students.	Use physical proximity, eye contact, and/or facial and vocal inflections to indicate that behavior is inappropriate.	Redirect students' attention and/or change activities. For example, if students seem tired, have them put their instruments down and begin stretching. Or begin improvisation, composition, or listening activities. Or simplify their part or offer a more challenging part.
Reprimand students for talking when you are working with another section or expect students to wait patiently for long periods of time.	Redirect students' attention to the music and give them a learning task: (a) have everyone play, (b) have half the room evaluate something specific you are teaching the other students, or (c) teach everyone the technique and then only apply it to one section.	*Have a plan* 1. Remind them of the rule 2. Temporarily do not play For example, "Percussionists, put your sticks down on the ground and come back in when you're ready to be a part of the class." 3. Pack up, send to office, and follow up with call to parents
Embarrass students, especially in front of others.	Find students in the act of doing something well and compliment them.	Create a signal to show me when they are ready. "Show me that you are ready to play by . . ."
Always wait for everyone to be ready.	Begin class on time and begin by tuning and playing as soon as possible.	Limit teacher talk and pick up the pace.
Complain about missing students at beginning of class.	Thank your students who were there on time and ready to play and encourage them to bring others with them next time.	Begin with a long-term, fun activity or play students' favorite piece at the beginning of class.
Show frustration when students are having trouble with certain passages.	Break passages down and practice with them. Have people audition for a solo or reduced section solo, etc.	Simplify the parts as a preliminary step or for the concert. If you want them to practice more, schedule a playing test for 3 days later.
Assume students who are talking are always off task.	Ask if you can clarify something. If not, you now have their attention, so move on.	"Is everything okay?" or "Music is organized sound and talking is getting in the way of the music."
Be sporadic in your reactions.	Be consistent and enforce the established classroom rules.	Be a truth seeker instead of assuming students' intentions. Open lines of communication.

This list is not comprehensive. What can you add to the table?

4.3 Summary

Although it is important to have reactive classroom management strategies ready to implement, I reiterate that I highly recommend working to proactively engage students in order to help nurture their intrinsic desire to learn and be the best versions of themselves. This includes challenging students without overwhelming them, taking students' interests into consideration, working to achieve flow, and being the most musical music teacher possible. Good teaching strategies help create musical environments based on the love of music making, which might help you avoid many typical classroom management issues.

4.4 Discussion Questions

1. Did your music teachers play instruments or sing in the classroom? Do you remember why they used their instruments, how you felt when they played or sang, or your or your fellow students' reactions? What kind of lasting impression did it leave on you, if any?
2. Activity: Record yourself teaching and reflect in three ways.
   a. Write why you chose to use your instrument at that moment, what you hoped the students would learn from it, and what you noticed about their students' reactions on the video.
   b. Time how many minutes students are playing their instruments, singing, and/or moving. Adding this together, is each student actively engaged in some kind of music making at least 60 percent of the time? If not, how will you readjust your lesson plan for the next lesson?
   c. Were there classroom management issues related to playing short segments, being cut off before the end of the phrase, too much time talking, or not playing enough during the lesson?
3. Consider this statement: Musically, everything that has a sound can be taught with sound first. Is that true? Give five examples for when it is true and when it is not, and explain.
4. What classroom routines and tuning procedures will you create?
5. I mentioned engaging students in literature choices. In what other ways can you imagine engaging students in choices?
6. Can you recall a time you experienced flow in a classroom? Describe the circumstance and how you felt during and afterward.
7. What other ways might you simplify parts, make them more challenging, or make appropriate accommodations to best address each student's needs?
8. Discuss some reactive strategies you have found to be effective (in your teaching, observing, or remembering when you were a student). Then share some reactive strategies that have not gone well. Can you think of an alternative approach for that situation?

OXFORD
learning link

Visit the online resources for additional documentation and exercises to help expand learning and test your knowledge further: www.oup.com/he/powell_music1e.

CHAPTER 5

TEACHING EXECUTIVE SKILLS, MUSICIANSHIP SKILLS, AND ARTISTIC SKILLS

Stephen J. Benham

This chapter provides an overview of curricular structure for instrumental music classes, focusing on three strands of instruction: executive skills and knowledge, musicianship skills and knowledge, and artistic skills and knowledge.

5.1 Introduction

It can be overwhelming to think about how many instruments you need to learn to become a qualified and certified music educator. Most teacher-training programs include methods and techniques courses in brass, woodwinds, percussion, strings, classroom instruments, voice, and keyboard, but this is just a starting point for the skills you will need.

You may be one of those who came into college with multiple musical experiences—you sing, play the piano, were in band, choir, and orchestra, and took upper-level music theory courses—but most did not. If your background is voice, a keyboard instrument, or guitar, then an instrumental methods course may be your first interaction with brass, woodwind, percussion, and string instruments. Regardless of your prior experience, this chapter will help you develop a framework for how to approach learning and teaching *any* instrument. If you have already taken technique classes, this chapter will help you apply that knowledge to instructional design and delivery.

You might be thinking, "I'm never going to teach strings, I'm going to be a high school choir director!" But then you find out that your only job offer for next year includes teaching violin to middle school students, beginning brass, one period of guitar, and two periods of choir. (In my first five years of teaching, I taught K–12 strings, elementary general music, band 4–8 in public and private schools; I also served as section coach for French horn and saxophone at marching band camp and conducted adult church choirs. Each was a valuable experience and made me a better teacher, and I continue to use the skills I learned from these jobs to this day.) Let me encourage you to be that student who takes full advantage of every opportunity to study every instrument in depth. You can be the teacher who is comfortable conducting a choir accompanied by strings, working with a full orchestra, playing by ear, or leading a mariachi ensemble.

In Chapter 1 you learned about seven core teaching practices (CTP) that guide excellent music teachers. Discussion in this chapter relates directly to four of those practices:

- CTP 2b: Sequences musical instruction
- CTP 4: Understands common student problems
- CTP 5: Deconstructs musical concepts
- CTP 6: Uses questioning as a teaching tool

The topics I cover in this chapter will also help inform your lesson planning and your understanding of curriculum development and assessment (see Chapter 7).

5.2 A Common Framework for Teaching Instrumental Music

The best educators approach teaching in a strategic, intentional, and methodical manner. A helpful way to orient yourself toward teaching music is by using a framework to analyze and approach each instrument in a common, systematic, and structured way. The framework in this chapter is based on more than three decades of observations of hundreds of music educators and the expert advice they give, experiences working with music education majors in multiple institutions, teaching in multiple teaching settings from preschool through adult classrooms, and interacting with thousands of music educators in professional development workshops in multiple international educational programs. It is informed by the expert advice of artist-level teachers from universities, conservatories, and professional musical ensembles and the research and writings of experts from all instrument disciplines. Finally, this framework draws heavily on the fields of the psychology of music teaching and learning, educational psychology, developmental psychology, neuropsychology, and biomechanics.

The framework covers three content areas of skills and knowledge common to every instrument: executive skills and knowledge, musicianship skills and knowledge, and artistic skills and knowledge. These areas are interconnected. The ability to play artistically, for example, requires the performer to be able to produce a beautiful sound and play with a good sense of rhythm, pitch, and articulation. These content areas are also useful in that they:

- Provide a structure for planning instruction in a thoughtful, intentional, and detailed manner that is useful for both daily and long-term planning.
- Help guide instructional delivery and classroom activities that are comprehensive, student focused, and musically sound.
- Provide a framework for evaluating students in both informal and formal settings, using summative and formative assessment procedures and guiding student self-reflection and self-directed learning.
- Are applicable for use with a wide range of repertoire and musical practices.
- Are sequential (i.e., one idea builds on a previous idea) and comprehensive.
- Help administrators and educator colleagues understand that teaching and learning music is not a matter of chance, pure talent, or luck. It requires skill, dedication, and careful planning.
- Help parents understand what is involved in learning an instrument and how their child will be assessed in the ensemble.
- Provide a basis for administrators in evaluating the quality of instruction.
- Inform the process for hiring of well-trained, qualified music educators.

COMMON UNDERSTANDINGS FOR ALL INSTRUMENTS

Seven common pedagogical understandings apply to all instrumental music teaching situations:

1. All students have music aptitude.
2. The laws of acoustics govern tone production regardless of how sound is produced.
3. All instruments produce sound by creating vibration.
4. The ability to learn and perform musical skills and concepts is a brain-based activity.
5. Each instrument family has a specific sequence of executive skills and knowledge.
6. The ways in which musicianship skills and knowledge are developed are universal and apply to all instrument families.
7. The ways in which artistic skills and knowledge are developed are universal and apply to all instrument families.

All Students Have Musical Aptitude

All children have the potential to learn music and benefit from music education in the same way that all children have the capacity to learn a language. Unfortunately, far too many people still believe that formal music instruction should be reserved only for the most talented students. They are wrong! Our music programs should be places where all children, regardless of prior experience and music aptitude, are welcome. (See Section 5.1, "Music Aptitude," in this book's online resources.)

The Laws of Acoustics Govern Tone Production Regardless of How Sound Is Produced

The laws of acoustics apply to everything from tone quality to dynamics and articulation. If you have an opportunity to take a class in acoustics during your program, do so. It really will help your understanding of how sound works. Understanding basic concepts of acoustics such as frequency, amplitude, and intensity is essential for the music educator. (See Section 5.2, "Basic Concepts of Acoustics," in the book's online resources.)

All Instruments Produce Sound by Creating Vibration

The families of musical instruments (brass, woodwinds, percussion, and strings) look and sound quite different from one another but are tied together by a common thread: all produce sound by creating vibrations. Sounds simple, right? It's not. These vibrations cause air molecules to vibrate, which in turn causes our eardrum to vibrate. The eardrum transmits those vibrations through tiny bones and fibers in the ear directly to the nerves that communicate with the brain. The brain then processes and interprets the sounds. Furthermore, a child's capacity to process and interpret sound is influenced heavily by the quality of their music education. A child's ability to perceive, understand, produce, and control tone, pitch, intonation, rhythm patterns, a steady pulse, melody, harmony, musical form, and musical expression is tied directly to the experiences they have in early childhood, well before they start playing an instrument. This is one of many reasons it is so important for instrumental music educators to support their general music colleagues and advocate for strong general music programs in early-childhood and elementary education.

Brass musicians form an embouchure (the term used for how the lips, tongue, and teeth are used and positioned) and use the buzzing of their lips, supported by the movement of air, against a mouthpiece to produce sound. Woodwind players also form an embouchure and, except for flutes, create and control the vibration of a reed against a mouthpiece or of two reeds against each other. Flutes have a unique embouchure compared to the other woodwinds and produce sound by blowing a focused airstream across a small hole in the head joint of the flute. Vibrations are created in a more complex way on flutes than they are on reed instruments, but the fundamental idea of sound production is the same.

String musicians create sound by moving a bow across a string (the hair of the bow causes the string to vibrate). They also will pluck the strings of their instruments (a technique called *pizzicato*) to create tone. String bass players tend to use pizzicato more than the other instruments, especially when performing in jazz, folk, or other types of ensembles.

Percussionists create sound by striking an instrument, which sets up a vibration on a membrane (e.g., a drum), a piece of metal (e.g., bells), or a piece of wood (e.g., xylophones). Pianos are also considered part of the percussion family because sound is created when a felt-covered hammer strikes a string.

The Ability to Learn and Perform Musical Skills and Concepts Is a Brain-Based Activity

Did you know that our brains have specialized areas dedicated to specific musical functions? Musical functions, skills, and understandings are processed in multiple parts of the brain—for all instruments. (See Chapter 17 and also Section 5.3, "The Musical Brain," in the book's online resources.)

Each Instrument Family Has a Specific Sequence of Executive Skills and Knowledge

Executive skills and knowledge are those abilities that relate to producing tone on any instrument. Some music teachers may use the term *technique* to describe executive skills, but that term can be confused with a teaching technique (i.e., a strategy, such as repetition or asking questions) that teachers might use to help students learn something.

The Ways in Which Musicianship Skills and Knowledge Are Developed Are Universal and Apply to All Instrument Families

Musicianship skills and knowledge are common among all instruments and are broken down into several subcategories: tonal aural skills and ear training, rhythmic skills and ear training, and creative musicianship. These skills are based on the ways children learn music, an understanding of musical aptitude, and the importance of developing foundational musicianship skills prior to beginning formal study on an instrument. Because these skills are universal and sequential, they apply to any instrumental setting.

That might sound overwhelming, but the good news is that each student with whom you will work has an instrument in common—the human body. The development of musicianship skills and knowledge starts with learning how to use our ears to listen, our voices to sing, and our bodies to move. This foundation influences other essential musical skills, including how well we perform and comprehend pitch, tonality, melody, harmony, form, intonation, rhythm patterns, and pulse.

Musicianship skills are essential prerequisites for reading music with comprehension and being able to compose, arrange, and improvise. They also serve as the foundation for creative musicianship, which is far too often left out of the student experience. Instead, teachers may introduce notation too quickly, before a student has the aural and musical framework in place to comprehend what is written. Imagine if we taught children to read English *before* they had substantial experience listening to and speaking the language: our ability to improvise (be creative) in language would be severely limited. Unfortunately, this is what happens for most students in music education. They rarely develop the basic skills required to compose, arrange, and improvise.

The Ways in Which Artistic Skills and Knowledge Are Developed Are Universal and Apply to All Instrument Families

The category of artistic skills and knowledge encompasses music literacy, ensemble skills, musical expression, historical and cultural elements, and the evaluation of music and musical performance. This is an area where teachers can explore a wide range of repertoire and musical styles and genres, including popular music and music from different cultures and eras. The skills and knowledge in this area can be applied to multiple types of ensembles, from a large symphony orchestra to a small jazz combo, rock ensemble, or fiddle group.

With these common ideas in mind, you now have a basic structural framework to use for teaching any instrument. As you progress through your program and especially during your instrumental methods and techniques classes, think about the commonalities of each instrument. What is universal? What is unique? What can you transfer from one instrument to another?

5.3 Three Content Areas of Skills and Knowledge

As you learned already, three content areas of skills and knowledge form the core of instruction. In this section, I discuss each of those areas in more detail and provide sample sequences of instruction. At the end of this chapter, you will find key questions that you should be ready to answer by the time you enter student teaching.

TEACHING EXECUTIVE SKILLS AND KNOWLEDGE

Executive skills and knowledge are an essential part of any lesson or rehearsal and should be included in every lesson plan. The fields of biomechanics, kinesiology, anatomy, and physiology all inform the order in which we teach executive skills. An understanding of how our body works, moves, and functions is essential to promoting good health, preventing injury, and maximizing the development of executive skills. We also need to understand that our body, mind, emotions, and spiritual selves all interact with and affect each other. A basic understanding of anatomy and physiology as related to our specific instruments helps us understand why and how certain muscles, nerves, and our limbic system function and work together.

The term *sequential pedagogy* is often used to describe how we talk about the acquisition of musical skills and the order in which they should be taught. The specific skills for each instrument vary, but the general sequence in which skills are taught is universal:

1. *Body posture and format*: Focus on the body before the instrument is introduced.
2. *Instrument position, hand placement, and for winds only, forming the embouchure*; This often includes preliminary steps such as just using a mouthpiece before moving to the instrument (for woodwinds and brass), playing in guitar position (for strings), or using a practice pad (for percussion).

3. *Tone production*: The goal for all students is to produce a characteristic sound on their instruments. For strings, this means learning the fundamentals of controlling bow weight, speed, angle, and placement. For winds, this includes breathing, embouchure, and articulation. For percussion, this includes how and where to strike the instrument (drumhead, mallet instruments, etc.).
4. *Performing different pitches and rhythms*: Pitch and rhythm are taught as separate skills, then combined (see the section on teaching musicianship skills and knowledge).
5. *Articulation*: Students start with playing simple connected and separated rhythm and tonal patterns. As students gain competence, they incorporate a variety of bowing techniques or tonguing techniques.
6. *Dynamics and musical expression*: Musical artistry and the ability to express emotion are an important goal, but far too many teachers sacrifice long-term executive and musicianship skill development for short-term gains in the rush to prepare for a concert or by choosing music that is too difficult.
7. *Speed and style*: A student's ability to perform with technical fluency and an appropriate sense of musical style is also connected with a strong foundation in executive and musicianship skills.

TEACHING MUSICIANSHIP SKILLS AND KNOWLEDGE

In the past fifty years our understanding of how children learn and develop musical skills and knowledge has advanced greatly. When I was a beginning teacher, I did not know about Carl Orff, Zoltán Kodály, or Edwin Gordon. Partly that is because they were not discussed during my undergraduate education (which focused almost exclusively on instrumental music), but I admit that I was also ignorant and thought that the ideas of these great teachers applied only to general music classes. I could not have been more wrong. I also did not know much about music aptitude or the ways children learn music. I did my best with the knowledge I had, but my early failures and successes as a teacher showed me areas where I needed to learn and grow.

The framework in the next section provides a structure for how teachers might approach teaching musicianship skills and knowledge in a sequential and systematic way. The examples are excerpted from the baseline levels of the *ASTA String Curriculum* (Benham et al., 2021).

A SAMPLE FRAMEWORK FOR DEVELOPING TONAL MUSICIANSHIP SKILLS AND KNOWLEDGE

1.1. Students perform, by ear, melodic tonal patterns in major and minor tonalities (vocally, first on a neutral syllable, then with solfège; then on the instrument).
1.2. Students identify whether two performed melodic tonal patterns are the same or different.
1.3. Students correctly associate the words *high* and *low* with relative pitch differences (e.g., with the use of Curwen hand symbols and vocal solfège).
1.4. Students correctly identify the direction of melodic motion (within a tetrachord).
1.5. Students perform, by ear, primary (i.e., tonic and dominant) harmonic tonal patterns (vocally, first on a neutral syllable, then with solfège; then on the instrument).
1.6. Students improvise melodic tonal patterns (vocally, first on a neutral syllable, then with solfège; then on the instrument).

A SAMPLE FRAMEWORK FOR DEVELOPING RHYTHMIC MUSICIANSHIP SKILLS AND KNOWLEDGE

1.1. Students maintain a steady pulse while singing or chanting rhythm patterns.
1.2. Students demonstrate a sense of meter while singing or chanting rhythm patterns.
1.3. Students maintain a steady pulse while playing rhythm patterns.
1.4. Students demonstrate a sense of meter while playing rhythm patterns.
1.5. Students perform rhythm patterns containing rests.
1.6. Students perform rhythm patterns containing ties.
1.7. Students perform rhythm patterns containing upbeats.
1.8. Students improvise rhythm patterns corresponding to items 1.1–1.7.

A SAMPLE FRAMEWORK FOR DEVELOPING CREATIVE MUSICIANSHIP SKILLS AND KNOWLEDGE

1.1. *Rhythmic creativity*: Students derive rhythm patterns from speech and environmental sounds and link them with the motion of the bow hand or connect with performance on a single pitch.
1.2. *Tonal* (melodic and harmonic): Students create one-note solos against a class-generated accompaniment.
1.3. *Textural*: Students reproduce sound effects from their environment on their instruments (exploratory focus).
1.4. *Compositional*: Students invent scoring techniques based on common objectives.

DEVELOPING MUSIC LITERACY

Being musically literate means much more than simply knowing the names and durations of notes, identifying key signatures, and understanding vocabulary. The teacher should emphasize tonal, rhythmic, and creative musicianship skills before introducing music reading skills. According to Benham et al (2021, p. 3):

> *Students demonstrate sequential music literacy skills (decoding and comprehension), defined as an association of sound-tosymbol, in a given musical context, which includes predictive components (understanding of reading based on audiation of written material) and knowledge of symbols and notation related to pitch, rhythm, dynamics, tonality, clef, articulation, etc., based on the principle that sound comes before sight.*

This concept was first introduced in Chapter 1 of this textbook and is a core principle of high-quality music teaching.

A SAMPLE FRAMEWORK FOR DEVELOPING MUSIC LITERACY

1.1. Students correctly identify and perform basic music notation and symbols associated with the following skills and understandings to each corresponding curricular level.
1.2. Students sight-read basic music notation and symbols.
1.3. Students understand chord symbols in root position.
1.4. Students correctly identify the following key signatures: C, G, D, and F major (with their relative minors) for strings; C, F, B♭, and E♭ (with their relative minors) for wind instruments; or other keys as appropriate.
1.5. Students correctly identify accidentals (sharp, natural, flat).

TEACHING ARTISTIC SKILLS AND KNOWLEDGE

By now, you have probably figured out that executive and musicianship skills and knowledge are the building blocks for the final category: artistic skills and knowledge. Artistic skills and knowledge do not quite follow the same orderly sequence as the prior categories, but this is the area where teachers can provide unbelievable musical experiences for their students. This is also an area where larger, abstract thinking can be emphasized and where writing might be incorporated into the ensemble. The four areas listed below form the framework for artistic skills and knowledge.

1.1. *Ensemble skills*: Students learn to play simple melodies with accompaniments as part of a group; many teachers will teach students the melody *and* the bass line to a folk song even in the first lessons. Students alternate playing these parts and progress to canons, rounds, and other simple two- and three-part songs. First year experiences include improvising melodies or rhythm patterns as part of an ensemble.

2. *Expressive elements*: Students acquire the skills to play with expression from the earliest lessons but by the second year of instruction should be able to employ the expressive elements of music to communicate abstract thoughts, ideas, and meaning and for self-expression and understanding.

1.3. *Historical and cultural elements*: Students should listen to, respond to, and perform music from a wide range of genres in a culturally authentic manner, reflecting the diverse nature of people groups and cultures. Student performances demonstrate an understanding of historical and cultural contexts and reflect stylistic traditions and practice.

1.4. *Evaluation of music and musical performance*: Students are directed to critically assess their own performances from the first lessons. This includes the ability to discriminate between a given example and their own playing. Far too many teachers simply give students the answer instead of guiding the students to analyze their own performance in the comparison to what is correct. Providing specific criteria for students to evaluate is essential (e.g., tone quality, articulation, intonation, etc.).

5.4 Conclusion

As you begin your career, plot out a map of where you are the most experienced and where you need the most growth in each of the areas listed in this chapter. Your college experience is an excellent point of departure, but there's no way to prepare you for the expertise you need on each instrument to be a master teacher in four years. Professional music education associations provide excellent ongoing professional development. When you consider graduate study, look for schools that will help you increase your breadth and depth of knowledge beyond what you received in your undergraduate training. A final word of encouragement: the best teachers I know continue learning for their entire lives. Having a systematic plan in place can help you achieve your goals.

5.5 Discussion Questions

1. *Applications for instructional design and delivery*
   a. How will you plan to incorporate executive skills and knowledge in each class? Can you break down the sequence of executive skill development to a more detailed level for your personal instrument? Can you do the same for all the woodwind, brass, percussion, and string instruments?

   b. How will you plan to incorporate musicianship skills and knowledge in each class? How will you know which rhythm patterns or tonal patterns you should teach, and in what order? (See Chapter 7.)
   c. How will you incorporate the systematic and sequential development of the four areas of artistic skills and knowledge into each class?
   d. How can you teach these skills through nonverbal and experiential learning?
2. *Applications for assessment of student performance*
   a. How will you assess student performance in each of the three content areas? (See Chapter 7.)
   b. What questions might you use to guide students to a deeper understanding of their own performance as part of an ensemble or in comparison to other ensembles and musicians?
3. *Applications for teacher self-reflection*
   a. Is your personal level of performance on secondary instruments strong enough that you can produce a characteristic tone on each instrument and play with correct posture, body format, and instrument position? What instruments do you need to spend more time studying to feel competent teaching?
   b. Is your personal level of musicianship strong enough that you are comfortable using tonal solfège or rhythmic syllable systems in the classroom? List areas on which you need to spend more time. (See Chapter 2.)

OXFORD learning link

Visit the online resources for additional documentation and exercises to help expand learning and test your knowledge further: www.oup.com/he/powell_music1e.

CHAPTER 6

TEACHING NOTATION IN INSTRUMENTAL MUSIC

Bryan Powell

This chapter examines various examples of music notation and explores some ways in which music teachers can incorporate these types of notation into their teaching.

6.1 Introduction

Think about your approach to music making. Can you hear a melody and play it by ear? Are you able to easily improvise on your instrument? Are you a songwriter or composer who creates your own music? Chances are that if you are a music education major, the answer to at least one of these questions is "no." While there may be a few reasons for this, one of them almost certainly has to do with your relationship to traditional music staff notation. When I was a young trombone player in high school, in order to play my instrument, I needed to have my sheet music with me. In jazz band, in order to feel comfortable improvising, I needed to have my chart in front of me. I was a competent trombonist, but as soon as you took the music notation away, I was lost. My musicianship on the trombone was dependent on having other people's compositions in front of me. I was good at reading compositions written by other people, but I was never encouraged to create my own musical ideas and play my trombone without having the music notation on a stand.

I was a musical story *reader,* not a musical story *teller.*

Notation is an important part of many instrumental ensembles, but in most bands and orchestras, it has historically been taught with traditional music staff notation (TMSN). In many music education spaces, we actually refer to the music notation *as* music. "Get out your music" means "Get out your music notation." When someone asks, "Do you read music?" they actually mean, "Do you read music staff notation?" While it is certainly true that a knowledge of TMSN is an important part of comprehensive musicianship for many musicians, music teachers can engage students with a deeper and more creative understanding of the elements of music by teaching them musical practices that do not start with reading TMSN on a music stand (Clauhs, 2018). Elements of creative music making can include vocalizing, practicing rhythms, and incorporating audiation, which is the process of hearing and understanding in our minds music that we have just heard or that we are about to play (Gordon, 1999).

When thinking about teaching instrumental music with non-band and non-orchestra instruments (think of ukuleles, bucket drums, and iPads), TMSN is not necessarily useful in those contexts and could possibly be detrimental to a student's progress if we start to teach those instruments using TMSN. Sometimes music teachers approach instrumental pedagogy with the belief that because the skill of decoding TMSN is useful in learning certain kinds of music, it is useful in learning music from *all* musical traditions. This is not the case, and even some of our traditional ensembles can benefit from the inclusion of various types of notation during the learning process.

This chapter examines various examples of music notation and explores some ways in which music teachers can incorporate these types of notation into their teaching. The goal of this chapter is not to pit one style of notation against another to see which is "better" or "worse," but to demonstrate how different approaches to teaching music notation can help students expand their sense of creativity and overall musicianship.

6.2 Definitions of Notation and Literacy

Words are important. What music educators say in the classroom shapes the ways in which students view themselves as music makers. Perhaps you have heard music teachers say, "I emphasize reading music because music literacy is important." A couple of phrases in that sentence need to be examined: "reading music" and "music literacy." Let's start with "reading music." As you might be aware, nobody *reads* music—we *listen* to music and we *make* music. What musicians read is *notation*, and there are many different types of notation. The National Coalition for the Core Arts Standards (NCCAS, the organization that created the most recent national standards for music that are used by NAfME and most state music education associations) defines musical notation as a "visual representation of musical sounds." This means that *any* visual representation of musical sound can be considered music notation, including TMSN, shapes, squiggly lines, numbers, colors, body gestures, and any number of other symbols.

If notation can be defined in any of these ways, then what exactly is "standard notation"? You might be surprised to learn that the NAfME lists many types of standard music notation and defines it as a "system for visually representing musical sound that is in widespread use; such systems include traditional music staff notation, tablature notation (primarily for fretted stringed instruments), and lead-sheet notation" (NAfME, 2014). So when reading one of the NCCAS performance standards, MU:Pr4.2.5b—"read and perform using standard notation," you should keep in mind that there various types of "standard notations" can be used. In fact, the New York State framework modified this standard for clarity and changed the standard so that it now reads: "When analyzing selected music, read and perform using standard notation, *as appropriate to the musical tradition*" (New York State Education Department, 2021; emphasis added). The added language "as appropriate to the musical tradition" is important because it recognizes that different types of standard notation are appropriate to various musical traditions. For example, using TMSN to teach the trumpet is the appropriate standard notation, whereas teaching the ukulele might rely more on other types of standard notation such as chord diagrams and tablature.

6.3 What Is Music Literacy?

The phrase “musically literate” is often used to refer one’s ability to read music staff notation. However, according to NAfME, the definition of “music literacy” is not synonymous with the ability to read traditional music staff notation. NAfME defines “music literacy” as the “knowledge and understanding required to participate authentically in the discipline of music by independently carrying out the artistic processes of creating, performing, and responding” (NAfME, 2014). While music literacy can certainly include knowledge of reading TMSN and an understanding of how signs and symbols represent sound, also included is the ability to create music and transfer skills and capacities to other contexts for lifelong engagement in the arts. Imagine a guitar player who plays in a band, writes their own songs, uses different types of music notation, can easily improvise, and can hear a song on the radio and figure it out by ear. That person is musically literate, whether they read TMSN or not. I would argue there are also many different musical traditions in which someone can be literate. A beatmaker who performs using Ableton Live and samplers such as an Akai MPC is literate in one musical tradition, but not necessarily in the traditions required to play Western art music.

6.4 Iconic Notation

The National Association for Music Education defines iconic notation as the “representation of sound and its treatment using lines, drawings, [and] pictures” (NAfME, 2014) and includes iconic notation in several of the performance standards. For example, music standard MU:Cr2.1.2 states: “Use iconic or standard notation and/or recording technology to combine, sequence, and document personal musical ideas” (NCCAS, 2014, p. 2). The use of iconic notation can help students learn notation organically in a way that is developmentally appropriate (West, 2016). The following section is a review of some examples of iconic notation used in music.

ICONIC NOTATION FOR BAND, CHOIR, AND ORCHESTRA INSTRUMENTS

Iconic notation is often used in elementary-school music to teach rhythms, such as using pictures and the names of fruit to teach different rhythms (e.g., “watermelon” = ♬♬). Iconic notation can also be combined with traditional music staff notation to allow students to understand the duration of notes. In the notation example in Figure 6.1, the duration of the played note is indicated by the length of the physical note, and colors are used to represent certain pitches.

FIGURE 6.1 **Music notation created by United Sound (unitedsound.org)**

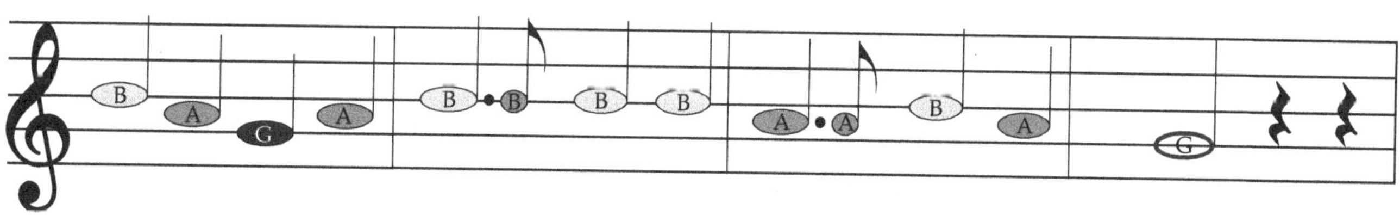

In Figure 6.2, the notation is a depiction of the rhythmic word (i.e., the quarter note “cake” looks like a cake, the half note soup looks like a bowl of soup, etc.).

FIGURE 6.2 Iconic music notation created by United Sound (unitedsound.org)

These types of iconic notation are designed to help all students (including beginning students and/or students with disabilities) understand the duration of notes.

In another example, the Figurenotes system in Figure 6.3 presents color-coded notes with different shapes to match the shapes and colors on the keyboard. These color-coded notes can also be used as notation to play songs. This type of notation "lowers the threshold for learning and teaching music, and is especially applicable in educational situations where the student's cognitive load needs to be lessened" (Kivijärvi, 2019, p. 654).

FIGURE 6.3 Figurenotes (figurenotes.org)

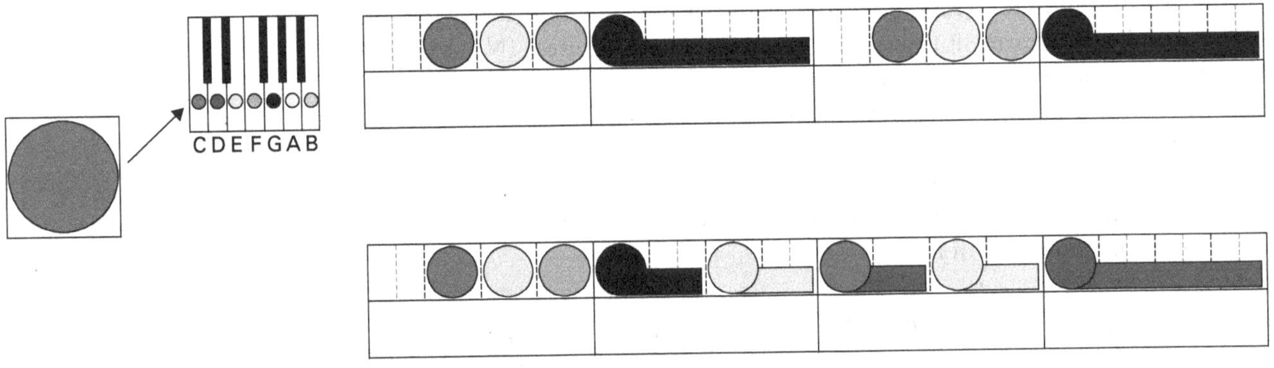

There are also examples of iconic notation used to indicate individual notes on various instruments. In Figure 6.4, the notes of the C blues scale are represented on a fretted violin fingerboard.

FIGURE 6.4 Iconic notation violin scale. Developed by Music Will (musicwill.org)

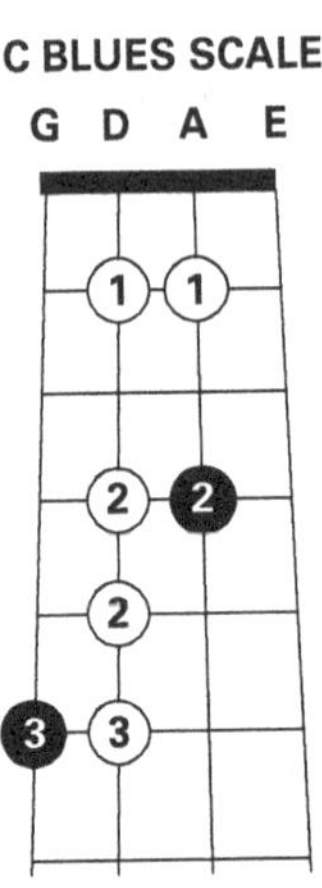

In Figure 6.5, the familiar representation of the notes of the trombone slide positions and partials (left) can be altered to create an iconic notation representation of individual notes, similar to guitar tablature. The tablature image on the right indicates the low (first) partial, middle (second) partial, high (third) partial, and super-high (fourth partial). The trombone tablature on the right indicates that you would play the notes A (second position on the high/third partial) and G (fourth position on the high/third partial).

FIGURE 6.5 ***Left*: trombone slide positions and partials; *right*: trombone tablature**

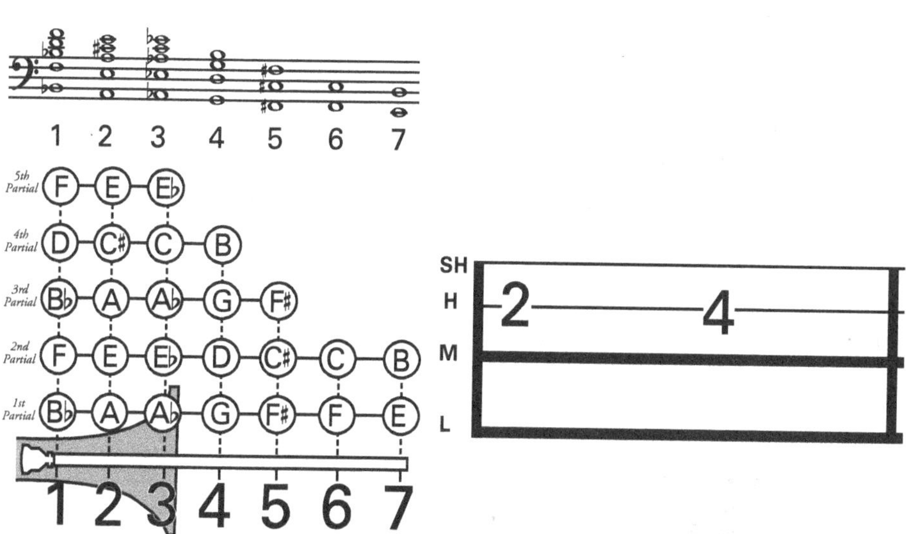

NOTATION IN POPULAR MUSIC INSTRUMENTS

There are many different types of notation used in popular music. Examples include chord diagrams, piano-roll notation, grid-based beat sequences, and depictions of fretboards and the keyboard with notes indicated through dots or the shading in of keys. While this chapter does not present an exhaustive list of different types of notation used in popular music, a few examples are listed in the next section. For more on popular music notation, check out Clauhs, Powell, and Clements (2020).

Chord Diagrams

Chord diagrams for fretted instruments show a representation of the fretboard and indicate which string and fret should be held down to play the chord. In some cases there are numbers inside of the black dots which indicate which finger to use. In Figure 6.6 the chord diagram for the C chord on the guitar indicates that you play the chord by using the first, second, and third fingers to hold down different strings at different frets. The "X" above the string on the left indicates that you do not play that string when strumming a C chord. The "O" symbol that appears above some of the other strings indicates that you play those strings "open," without pressing down on the string anywhere. Chord diagrams provide a visual map of how to play a chord on a guitar. Students do not need to know what notes they are playing or even the pitches of the six guitar strings to play the chord. They simply make the shape that they see in the diagram, press down, and play the chord.

FIGURE 6.6 Guitar chord diagram

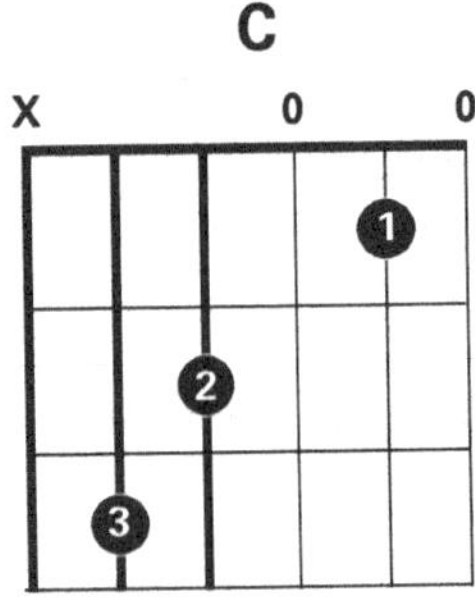

Fretted instruments such as the guitar and ukulele are not the only ones that use chord diagrams. Chord diagrams are also useful when teaching the keyboard. Figure 6.7 is a representation of a piano keyboard in which the notes of a C major chord are shaded. Although the piano is usually an instrument that relies on traditional music staff notation, the shaded-in chord diagram provides a fast way for students to understand what they are supposed to play without having to decode notation on a staff.

FIGURE 6.7 Piano chord diagram

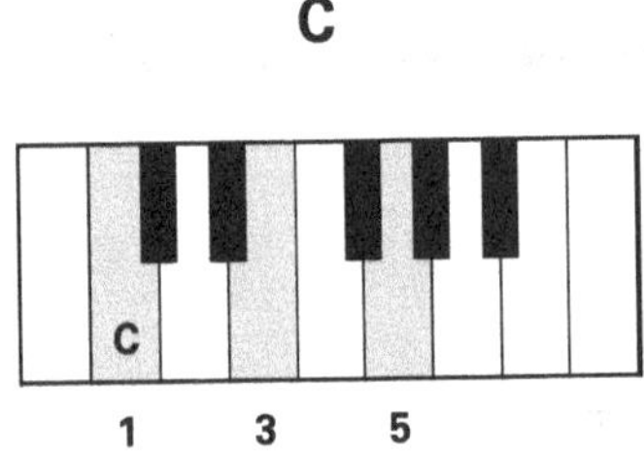

When using a keyboard in a digital audio workstation (DAW), you will likely encounter piano-roll notation. This type of iconic notation uses a representation of the keyboard, and the pitch and duration of the notes are indicated by the shading in of the rectangle that aligns with each note. This type of music notation is used in software such as Synthesia and can be more effective than traditional music staff notation in enabling beginning students to quickly master beginning-level songs (Cremata & Powell, 2016). Figure 6.8 shows two parts represented on piano-roll notation.

Grid-Based Notation

Common rhythms can also be represented through grid-based iconic notation. In the depiction of the drumbeat in Figure 6.9, there are pictorial representations of the drums and cymbals which are placed in a grid with subdivisions of the beats underneath the pattern. When compared to the traditional percussion clef notation below it, you can see how this use of iconic notation might provide easier access for beginning students to know which parts of the drum kit to play.

Similar grid-based notation can also be used to depict notes on the scale. In Figure 6.10, the light gray squares represent different notes on the scale. Students could create their own pattern to notate melodies before transitioning to traditional music staff notation.

FIGURE 6.8 Piano-roll notation

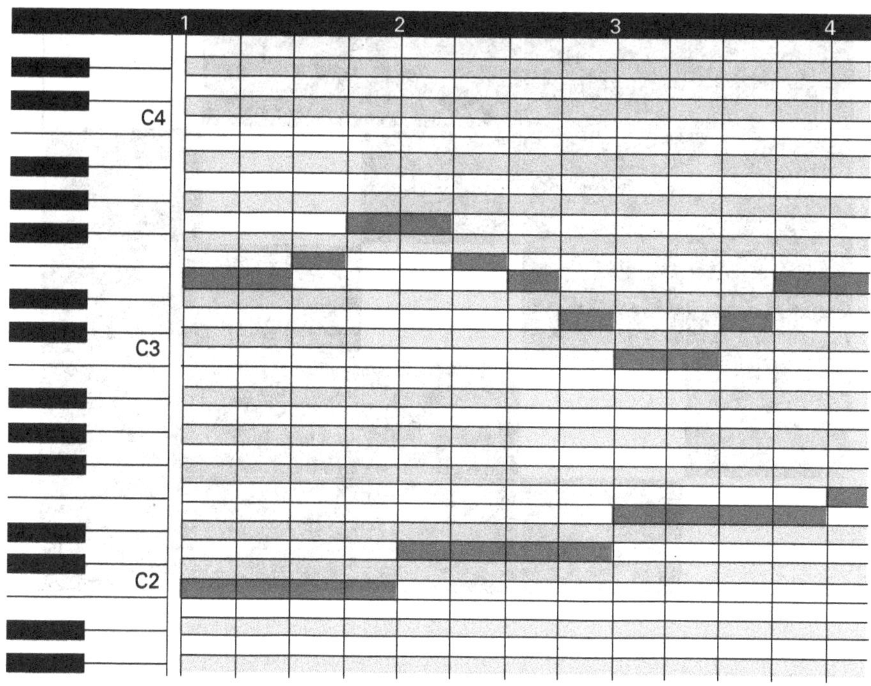

FIGURE 6.9 Grid-based drum kit notation and percussion clef notation

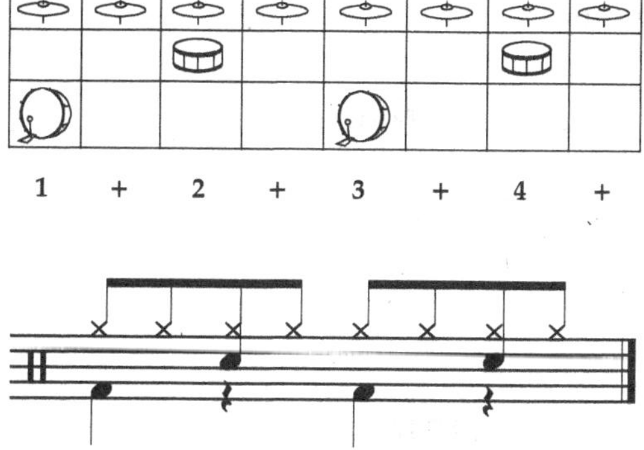

Rhythmic Notation

Numbers are often used as a substitution for traditional rhythmic notation. For example, the representation of the rhythmic pattern in Figure 6.11 is shown by using quarter notes and eighth notes; the same rhythm is then notated using numbers and plus signs.

Pictorial iconic notation can also be a useful way to depict rhythm. In Figure 6.12, the size of the engine indicates the length of the note. Note how the iconic notation imitates traditional rhythmic notation as well. Young students can visually grasp the relationship between the pairs of eighth notes for the first three beats and the quarter note on the fourth beat. Imagine an activity where your instrumental-music students had to create iconic notation to represent both the pitch and rhythm of a melodic line. What might that look like?

FIGURE 6.10 Grid-based notation for individual notes

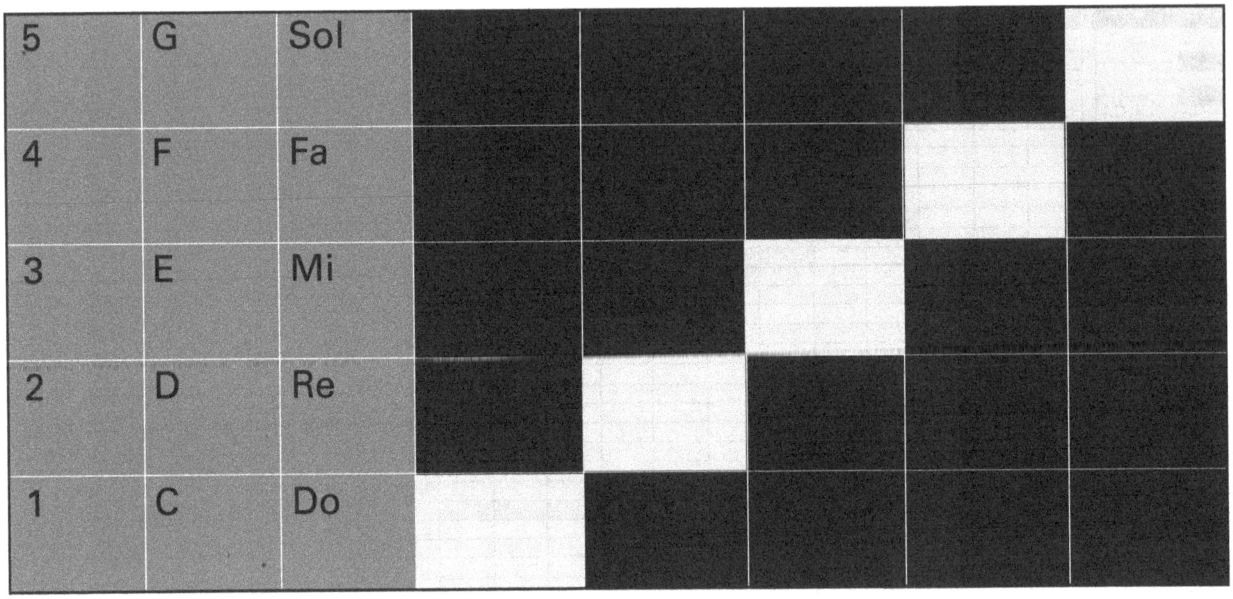

5	G	Sol					
4	F	Fa					
3	E	Mi					
2	D	Re					
1	C	Do					

FIGURE 6.11 Numbers-based rhythmic notation

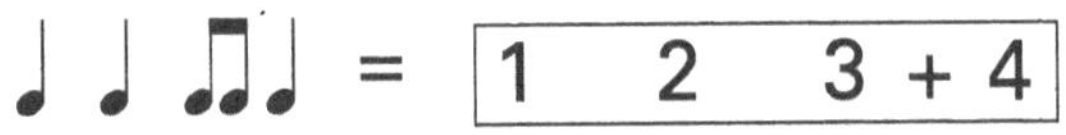

♩ ♩ ♫♩ = 1 2 3 + 4

FIGURE 6.12 Pictorial representations of rhythms

TEACHING TRADITIONAL MUSIC STAFF NOTATION

Music educators generally have a good deal of experience with TMSN, both as a performer and as a teacher. While there are several approaches to teaching TMSN, many educators have advocated against simply starting with reading the notational symbol (e.g., "the first space on the treble clef is F, and here is how you play it on your instrument"). Before teaching the actual notes, there are a few things that music teachers can do to prepare students to read TMSN.

Sound before Symbol

Many approaches and music methodologies promote the concept of "sound before symbol," which can be described as the process of engaging with the sound of music through listening, singing, understanding the difference between pitches, and audiation before connecting this knowledge to the written symbol. Music education scholars such as

Pestalozzi, Kodály, Suzuki, Gordon, and many others have all promoted a "sound before symbol" approach to music learning. Music teachers can engage students with opportunities to explore different pitches on their instruments, improvise, and play by ear before turning to TMSN to match these pre-notational activities with the written note. As explored in Chapters 1, 3, 38, and 39 of this book, exploring pitch matching, audiation, and learning by ear *before* introducing the written note can increase students' overall musicality and help them to play in tune.

INCORPORATING VARIOUS TYPES OF NOTATION

There are various types of notation that instrumental music educators can utilize in their instruction. Even though most music ensembles prioritize the use of TMSN, incorporating a variety of types of music notation in the early stages can stimulate a student's curiosity about music notation in general: "Many children, on seeing staffs of many different shapes, colors, and sizes in their surroundings, become inspired to draw their own and notation begins to take place naturally" (Jacobi, 2012, p. 14). Through the creation of their own versions of iconic notation, students can develop a more holistic understanding of the connection between musical sounds and notational symbols.

6.5 Conclusion

As mentioned previously, this chapter does not present an exhaustive list of the various types of notation that music teachers can use in the classroom, and certain types of notation may make more sense with certain musical traditions than with others. Consider that even if your goal is for students to be able to read traditional music staff notation, it should not be the only type of notation used when teaching an instrument. Try bringing in different types of notation to enhance the learning process and even allow students to create their own notation systems to deepen their musical experiences. Alternative notations can be applied to many different learning styles and help even the youngest or most novice student to build their musical creativity and take ownership of the musical process.

6.6 Discussion Questions

1. How were you taught notation in school? How did this approach have an impact on your musicianship?
2. How might the incorporation of different approaches to teaching various types of notation free students from being "notation-dependent" musicians?
3. What types of notation might you be able to use in your future teaching context?
4. What are some of the limitations of teaching iconic notation to instrumentalists?

OXFORD learning link

Visit the online resources for additional documentation and exercises to help expand learning and test your knowledge further: www.oup.com/he/powell_music1e.

CHAPTER 7

PLANNING (LESSON PLANNING AND CURRICULUM) AND ASSESSMENT

J. Si Millican

In this chapter I will look at ways music teachers can plan for and assess their students' learning and development.

7.1 Introduction

When teachers plan, they outline the knowledge, skills, and dispositions pupils will develop as a result of their work in and outside the classroom. Assessment is an essential part of planning and refers to the ways in which teachers evaluate students' retention and use of the knowledge, skills, and dispositions presented in a unit of instruction. Planning can be long- or short-term and includes everything from the day-to-day task outline within a single class session to program-wide plans for what students should know or be able to do over a broader time frame. Assessment can be as formal as an evaluation of progress at the end of an instructional period or as informal as simply part of a teacher's daily work, though they are equally important.

7.2 Planning: Charting the Course

Careful planning helps to ensure efficient and purposeful student learning. Without a plan, teachers might miss important aspects of their students' education or be less efficient with their rehearsal or class time. Rather than focusing on what activities the students will complete, this type of planning is centered on what students should know, feel, or be able to do at the end of their time in the classroom. As an example, imagine a high school orchestra teacher who is working on Elgar's *Enigma Variations*. A teacher who is *task oriented*—one who is focused on what the students will do—might say to herself, "Today, we are going to work on Variation V of the *Enigma Variations*." On the other hand, a teacher who is *goal oriented*—focused on what the students will learn, feel, or be able to do—might say, "Our goal today is to balance the volume of the different moving lines in Variation V." A task-oriented teacher might say, "I want to play these three pieces for my next concert," while a goal-oriented one might say, "These three pieces give us an opportunity to learn these skills or this list of terms effectively."

TYPES OF PLANS

Various types of plans exist to help teachers plan within a variety of time frames. The time frame and focus for these plans can range from the micro level, such as a daily lesson plan, all the way up to a lengthier overview, such as a yearly outline of intended student knowledge, skills, and attitudes. In the next section I will look at each of these types of plans beginning at the micro level with the activity plan.

Activity Plans

When teachers set out to map out exactly what will happen within a single class session, they work with *activity plans* to structure effective instruction on a specific concept or skill within a particular exercise, activity, or piece of music (see Figure 7.1 of the online resources). Teachers usually combine several activity plans that are then sequenced within a single class session. For example, a teacher might plan to spend class time on different activities: (a) have a brief warm-up, (b) do technical exercises, (c) rehearse a section of a concert tune, (d) work on the chorale section of another piece, and finally (e) finish with a run-through of an upbeat piece of music. Each of these five activities, in order to be efficient and effective, requires an activity plan.

Each activity plan contains at least three parts: *objective*, *assessment*, and *activities*. While the tendency for some novice teachers is to begin with designing the activities of a particular lesson first, the efficient, goal-oriented teacher begins with an objective. The objective is a clear statement of learning goals, such as, "The students will play the legato section of the last movement of Holst's *First Suite in E-flat* with accurate dotted eighth and sixteenth note rhythms at performance tempo." With this information, the teacher may now design an assessment for the lesson. Continuing with this example, the assessment might be as simple as, "The students will align note changes precisely in measures x through y at a tempo of half note = 110."

After the objective and assessment have been considered, the teacher can develop activities to help their students achieve those goals. This part of the activity plan lists exactly what the students will do in step-by-step detail to achieve the objectives of the lesson. There are several characteristics that are common in effective and efficient activities:

- Include only *activities that are directly related to the objective.* For example, if your objective includes working on intonation, you will not want to include steps in your plan that address key signatures or rhythmic precision. While both of those musical elements are important concepts, they do not relate directly to the knowledge and skills associated with intonation.
- Begin at an appropriate starting point in which *every student can be successful.* For example, if not all of the students would be successful playing the correct rhythms of a passage up to tempo, playing the rhythms of the section slowly on one note is a more appropriate starting place.
- As students move through each new step in the activity, effective teachers *change one thing at a time.* Continuing with the previous example, skipping from playing the passage on one note at a slow tempo to playing the notes and rhythms together at performance tempo skips a lot of important steps.
- If students are unsuccessful after multiple attempts on any step, *consider "leaping back" several steps in your lesson to a point in which everyone was successful* (Duke, 2009). By the time teachers notice that a significant number of students are

struggling on a particular step, it is likely that some of them began struggling several steps earlier.

- Effective teachers plan in great detail every step of their lesson. Novice teachers should plan in such detail that *someone else could teach the lesson* using the plan. This allows teachers to think through each step carefully and prepare themselves effectively.

Teachers often include a list of *materials* that are needed for the planned activity. This list can serve as a reminder for the needed equipment in advance. Preparation that includes considering the materials needed promotes efficient teaching and improved classroom management, since teachers will not need to scurry about hunting for items they may need for their lessons.

Daily Lesson Plans

A *daily lesson plan* lists all of the activities within a single class session or rehearsal (see Figure 7.2 of the online resources). Just as careful planning of the objectives, assessments, and activities that are a part of activity plans helps to promote efficient rehearsals and lessons, a well-thought-out daily plan organizes how those pieces fit together. Effective teachers often list the timing for each activity in their lesson plans to the exact minute. This helps them to estimate how many activities they can include in a class session and to keep track of time as they are teaching. If a teacher planned to spend ten minutes working on a particular activity plan yet find that they've actually spent twenty minutes, they can adjust timings and move on to the next activity.

Weekly Lesson Plans

Weekly lesson plans include the highlights of each daily lesson plan for an entire week (see Figure 7.3 of the online resources). These weekly plans do not go into as much detail as the daily lesson plans or activity plans, but they serve an important planning function. In many cases, weekly plans are submitted to campus administrators for evaluation purposes. Teachers are often required to list how the plan aligns with state or national performance standards. Teachers can also take into account the weekly calendar of school and local activities. For example, a grade-level assembly that requires a significant number of students to be out of class one day may affect the weekly plan.

Unit Plans

Effective teachers, in their weekly and daily plans, string together activities designed to accomplish longer-range goals into a *unit plan*. Unit plans allow teachers to structure instruction into longer-range, logical sequences within a given theme or to accomplish a particular set of knowledge and skills. For instance, a teacher might plan a week's lessons to include (a) a short warm-up activity that improves performance fundamentals, (b) technical exercises to develop executive skills, (c) rehearsal of problematic areas in repertoire for an upcoming performance, and (d) sightreading of some short pieces. Each individual part of these ((a)–(d)) may be planned across a longer period of time to create a unit of study with its own logical pedagogical intent.

Units can be inserted into daily plans in a variety of ways depending on their purpose. Some units are designed to be cycled through, as in a sequence of scales. Others outline ways to rehearse a piece for an upcoming concert; when that concert is over, the next repertoire unit can begin as the ensemble prepares for the next concert. Some units are seasonal, such as preparing a marching band show for a halftime performance or working on holiday tunes. These different types of units may end simultaneously with a particular event such as a concert or grading period, but the units often do not align nor overlap with each other.

7.3 Curriculum: Setting the Framework

When we look at the performance and learning goals that drive unit plans, we turn our attention to more long-term planning through *curriculum development*. Curriculum influences instruction across longer spans of time and may include (a) yearly plans, benchmarks, and goals inspired by state and national standards for learning, (b) district curriculum guides, (c) teacher-developed goals and objectives for various grade levels, and (d) particular philosophies or systems of teaching such as the Comprehensive Musicianship through Performance model (Garofalo, 1983; Pagliaro, 2014; Wisconsin Music Educators Association, 2021).

One method for long-range planning includes the organization of benchmarks for student knowledge and performance. Benchmarks are standards of progress that the typical student should achieve by a particular time and may be organized by grade level, campus, program, or across the entire span of a student's PK–12 musical development.

Program goals outline student development across the entirety of their experience in the instrumental music program at a particular campus or group of campuses. The development of these goals and benchmarks often requires cooperation between middle school and high school music teachers. When program benchmarks and goals are shared across campuses—between elementary and middle school teachers, for instance—teachers understand better what is expected when students move from campus to campus as they advance in grade levels. These long-term benchmarks give teachers the opportunity to align instruction across grade levels to help ensure that important knowledge and skills are developed throughout the student's experiences in a school district.

Another source for broader curriculum goals includes state or national learning standards such as the ones developed through the National Coalition for Core Arts Standards in conjunction with the NAfME (National Coalition for Core Arts Standards, 2015). Most state and national standards are divided by grade level to help provide teachers with benchmarks for what their students should know or be able to do at various times in their musical development. Some also provide differentiated levels of achievement such as *proficient*, *accomplished*, and *advanced* (National Coalition for Core Arts Standards, 2014).

Some school districts have developed curriculum guides outlining achievement goals and benchmarks. These district curriculum guides can refine instruction within individual schools and programs as well as help to align instruction between schools within the district. As mentioned earlier, the alignment of instruction among and between schools can help students as they transition from campus to campus and move through programs within a district, particularly in larger school districts.

Whether the benchmarks used by teachers are developed by their school districts, the state, or a national arts coalition, it is beneficial to have a broader curricular plan of instruction for students. Having a curriculum that informs planning helps to ensure that students are developing the knowledge, skills, and dispositions that they will need to be musically literate performers, listeners, and creators.

7.4 Assessment

Assessment can refer to two different but equally important processes: *formal assessment* and *informal assessment*. When teachers engage in formal assessment activities, they evaluate how students have retained or used the knowledge, skills, or dispositions that they intended them to learn. This kind of assessment often results in a grade in a gradebook, a rating at a festival, or formal written feedback on a project, performance, or activity. Informal assessment, on the other hand, occurs more frequently and is a part of the teaching process. With informal assessment, rather than assign a grade or rating, teachers use collected data to determine how well students respond during a lesson.

Consider an example to help illustrate the differences between the two major types of assessment by imagining a learning goal of playing a particular rhythm accurately. Students would complete various activities designed to accomplish that goal such as echoing a model of the rhythm or playing the rhythm on each note of a major scale. As teachers monitor students' responses during these activities, they continually engage in a process in which they compare a detailed *mental model* of the accurate version of that rhythm in the correct style with what the students actually play. That process of comparing the mental model to what the students play is one type of informal assessment. If later the teacher assigned the students to play the rhythm for a grade based on their performance, that would be an example of a formal assessment of that learning goal.

INFORMAL ASSESSMENT

Informal assessment is any type of evaluation in which a teacher makes a judgment based on student performance without assigning a formal grade. Teachers use informal assessment to inform the decisions they make in determining the next instructional steps during a lesson. Informal assessment is an integral part of the process of teaching and learning; without monitoring how well students are doing during the lesson, teachers cannot be sure that the students have developed the knowledge and skills set forth in the objective.

Raiber and Teachout (2014) presented a model showing the role of informal assessment in the *teaching cycle* (see Figure 7.4 of the online resources). This cycle is made up of three basic parts: the *set*, the *follow-through*, and the *response*. The teaching cycle begins with a set, which refers to the pedagogical instructions that the teacher provides the students. The follow-through occurs when the students attempt what the teacher asks of them in the set. It is at this stage that the teacher compares what the students do in the follow-through with a mental image of the ideal performance.

The response part of the teaching cycle follows this informal evaluation and is determined by whether the students' performance matches the teacher's mental image. If the performance matches the teacher's mental image, the teacher can *confirm* that accomplishment. If the response does not match the mental image, then the teacher can decide to either *reset* the cycle by going back to the original set, *modify* the set by changing the instructions, or *release* the students from the cycle. Research has shown that teachers are more effective when they have clear mental images of student performance and these mental images are vital components of the informal assessment process (Millican, 2013).

FORMAL ASSESSMENT

While informal assessment is an integral part of the everyday teaching and learning process, formal assessment is a more official and often more structured evaluation. Formal assessments often establish a record of how a student has achieved on one or more established longer-term benchmarks (see the previous section, "Curriculum: Setting the Framework"). These tangible records of student achievement can be documented in ways such as grades in the gradebook, ratings at a festival, or standardized scores on an aptitude test.

Educators generally acknowledge two broad types of formal assessment: *formative* and *summative assessment*. A summative assessment is recorded to help teachers document what has been learned at the end of a particular unit of instruction. An exam on the

Italian expression and tempo terms used in a selection of concert music is an example of a summative assessment. A contest rating of "superior" or "excellent" is another example of summary feedback, helping students understand how they performed on a piece of music prepared for a festival. Summative assessments, because they give an evaluation at the end of a unit of instruction, tend to carry more weight than formative assessments.

Formative assessment occurs earlier during the learning process and gives students a snapshot of their progress toward a final goal. This type of assessment can provide records of students' initial knowledge or skills at the beginning of a unit of instruction or their progress towards established learning goals. Giving students a pre-test on the Italian terms for the hypothetical concert mentioned earlier might be an example of a formative assessment. Having students play portions of that same festival music for a grade as they prepare for the concert is another example of a formative assessment. In each of these examples, the assessment is intended to help students understand where they are in relation to the final learning goals. Formative assessments, because they are more forward-looking and occur at an earlier point during a unit of instruction, tend to carry less academic weight than summative assessments.

ASSESSMENT TOOLS

Educators can use several tools to help them evaluate students formally. Some of these assessment tools include *holistic grading*, *checklists*, *rating scales*, and *rubrics* (Millican, 2012). Other assessment methods might include *student portfolios* or *journals*. Each of these tools has its advantages and disadvantages.

Holistic grading is the process of assigning a grade based on the teacher's overall opinion of how the performance did or did not match the teacher's mental model for performance. For example, the students play a line from a beginning method book, and the teacher then records a grade based on their very quick mental evaluation. The problem with this approach is that it is subjective, and it can be difficult for students to know why they earned a particular grade. Even if teachers have clear criteria for the holistic grades they assign, they run the risk of forgetting important student performance details.

To remove some of the inherent subjectivity in holistic grading, teachers can specify the most important criteria they will evaluate in a grading *checklist*. A checklist outlines essential performance elements so students know how they are being evaluated (see Figure 7.5 of the online resources). One of the disadvantages of the checklist is the all-or-nothing nature of each of the items: either a student meets the standard and receives a check, or the student does not. This can create the dilemma of having to decide whether a student should receive a check on an item such as "All notes played correctly" if they miss one note in one scale.

One solution to the yes-or-no checklist is to use a *rating scale* to give more subtle shading to the evaluation of the criteria being assessed. A rating scale allows teachers to document how well a student achieved a particular performance requirement along a range of scores (see Figure 7.6 of the online resources). This format allows more flexibility and specificity in the assessment. Leaving room for constructive comments from the instructor in the margins or bottom of the rating scale is often useful, or one can further refine the rating scale by modifying it into a rubric.

A rubric is a specific type of rating scale that adds descriptive text defining the criteria for each score within the range of the rubric scale (see Figure 7.7 of the online resources) Using the scale performance example again, a score of 5 might indicate that the student "plays *all* of the pitches accurately in *each* of the scales," whereas a 4 might mean the student "plays *most* of the pitches accurately in *most* of the scales." At the lower end, we might have a 1, signifying that the student "plays *none* of the pitches accurately in *any* of the scales." While this level of detailed feedback can be helpful to students, a rubric can be time-consuming to complete and can quickly become overwhelming to both the teacher and the student.

Two other methods of assessing student achievement include student *portfolios* and *journals*. A portfolio is a collection of student work that can include sound recordings, written tests, copies of teacher feedback, adjudicators' comment sheets, and so forth. Most advocates of portfolios suggest that it is best to allow the students to select the work in the collection that they feel best represents their growth and progress. Students can complete *journals* by writing free-form reflections about anything related to their participation in the music learning process, or they can respond to prompts given by the teacher. For example, perhaps the teacher asks students to reflect upon strengths and areas for improvement following a performance. Allowing students to share their voice through journaling can give them a feeling of autonomy and ownership.

7.5 Summary

Careful planning from the program level through activity planning within a daily lesson plan helps music instructors be thorough and effective in their teaching. Different types of plans require different levels of detail, and educators should know the purpose, scope, and characteristics of each kind. Assessment is not only a formal process, it is also an informal way to help guide everyday teaching and feedback. Informal assessment is an important component of the teaching cycle and incorporates comparison between a teacher's clear mental image of the ideal student performance with how their students actually perform. Formal assessments represent a structured measurement and documentation of student performance that is often recorded in gradebooks or festival results. Teachers use formative assessment to give students feedback regarding their progress toward a long-term goal, while summative assessment documents student achievement after the work toward that goal is complete. Assessment tools can include checklists, rating scales, rubrics, portfolios, and journals; each has its own unique advantages and disadvantages. Effective planning and assessment will help teachers document and organize student learning while strengthening the instructional effectiveness of their teaching.

7.6 Discussion Questions

1. List the types of plans discussed in this chapter, including how they help you organize your time.
2. Identify and discuss aspects of long-term planning through curriculum development.
3. Describe formal and informal assessments, including examples from the chapter as well as examples from your own experiences.
4. List the types of assessment tools discussed in this chapter, including bulleted points of the advantages and disadvantages of each type.
5. Create three checklists to use for playing tests: one for beginners, one for middle school intermediates, and one for advanced students in high school.

OXFORD learning link

Visit the online resources for additional documentation and exercises to help expand learning and test your knowledge further: www.oup.com/he/powell_music1e.

CHAPTER 8

STRATEGIES FOR PLANNING, BUILDING, AND MANAGING MUSIC PROGRAMS

Kelvin D. Jones

This chapter provides strategies for developing and sustaining a diverse music program regardless of demographic.

8.1 Introduction

The goal of this chapter is to provide music programs in any setting (rural, suburban, urban, inner city, etc.) with techniques and strategies to help build diverse and multifaceted programs consisting of a variety of ensembles, such as marching and concert bands; chamber, jazz, and percussion ensembles; string and full orchestra; choirs; and popular music ensembles. Throughout this section you will uncover strategies for planning, building, and maintaining your music program, from developing your program's philosophy, advocating for your program, and gaining community support, to incorporating tangible strategies to develop musicianship.

8.2 What Is Your Program Philosophy?

Before thinking about the accolades you desire for your program, you should have an idea of how your program should function. What do you value? What is the crux of your program philosophy? Will it be heavily focused on competitions, focus solely on ensembles, or offer a diverse range of experiences? Will your program travel? Visit other college campuses? Participate in all-county, district, or state-level festivals? These are all things to consider when determining the backbone of your program philosophy.

Once you have an idea about your philosophical beliefs, create a three-, five-, and ten-year plan of what you will want to see with the program; this will help reinforce your vision for the program. The author Stephen Covey (2020) calls this strategy "beginning with the end in mind." This is no different from traveling. You put the address of your destination into your GPS system and then follow the directions. You must know where you want to go first and then chart a path to get there, just like the directions you get in your traveling app after putting in the final destination. From here, you can create

SMART goals (things that are Specific, Measurable, Attainable, Relevant or Realistic, and Timely) to chart a path for your three-, five-, and ten-year plans (Yemm, 2013).

A specific goal has a much greater chance of being accomplished than a general goal. A general goal would be "improve tone quality in the ensemble" or "to sound better," but a specific goal would be "improve tone quality in the ensemble by incorporating seven minutes of dedicated long tone exercises in the marching band daily." Goals that are *specific* involve answering the five "W" questions:

1. Who is involved?
2. What do I want to accomplish?
3. When should this be accomplished (days, months, years)?
4. Which requirements and/or constraints are involved?
5. Why is this important?

Measurable goals establish concrete criteria for measuring progress toward attaining your desired outcome. Goals that are measurable involve answering questions such as How much? How many? and How will I know when it is accomplished? *Attainable* goals occur when you identify goals that are most important to you and you begin to figure out ways you can achieve them. By planning your steps wisely and establishing a time frame for carrying out the steps, you can make goals that seem far-fetched more attainable. For example, you want your students to memorize all halftime music. Instead, split the focus into smaller goals, such as, "Students will memorize ten measures of music each day of camp until all music is learned by the end of camp."

Similar to attainable goals, *relevant* or *realistic* goals help determine whether you believe the goal can be accomplished. Have you accomplished anything similar in the past, and/or can you identify the conditions that would have to exist to accomplish this goal? To be realistic, a goal must represent an objective toward which you are both willing and able to work. *Timely* goals are goals that should be grounded within a time frame. With no time frame tied to it, there is no sense of urgency. When do you want to accomplish your goal? For example, students will effectively march an 8-to-5 by the second day of band camp. Putting time stamps on your goals emphasizes the time frame in which to accomplish them.

These SMART goal processes can help you home in on your big philosophical goals and convert them into targeted and tangible action items. The same pedagogical approach can be applied to your vision of music instruction in regard to the sound concept you desire for your program. Again, this all happens before the students arrive.

The more clearly you can define your vision, the more students and staff will have clarity in implementing your philosophy effectively. Create a master calendar of all events, performances, competitions, and trips. Begin to work backward on how you plan to achieve goals for each one. This could involve musical goals, visual goals, and maybe even fundraising, community, engagement, outreach, or recruiting goals. The key word here is goals. We must have them and then create standards to achieve them.

After you have spent time solidifying your program's philosophy, done a SWOT analysis, and charted a vision for the program, you can focus on the other strategies that can help make this vision a reality and set it up for success.

8.3 SWOT Analysis

Before starting rehearsal, planning your big trip, or meeting with students and parents, you will need to have an idea of your vision and expectations for your program. You can't come into the program expecting things to be the way they were when you were in school or facing the challenges you experienced in your college days. You need to have perspective on the strengths and challenges of your current position. In order to assess this, I suggest you perform a technique used in the business sector called a SWOT analysis. This is a strategic planning technique used with companies to identify various aspects within the business.

Keep in mind that your music program is similar to a business. You are the CEO of the program and likely need to answer to a board of supervisors (i.e., your administration), and you will be responsible for setting your employees (i.e., your students) up for success. A SWOT analysis will enable you to assess the needs and identify key areas of the program. Let's break down each meaning:

The S in SWOT stands for *strengths*. What are the strengths of your music program? Are there inherent advantages? Examples of advantages include programs that have a private lesson system already in place, have a strong feeder system, have funding for support staff such as a drumline/percussion instructor, travel, sectional coaches, chamber music coaches, mariachi instructors, and so on. These are all resources that can be used to supplement and aid the program in a positive way.

The W in SWOT stands for *weaknesses*. What are the weaknesses of the program? Are there inherent disadvantages? Examples include little or no funding for the program, lack of instrumental inventory, poor retention, or a weak feeder system. Any of these factors can make it challenging to be successful. Having little to no funding in your budget will make it hard to secure instruments, music, equipment, travel, and even cleanings. Make sure you understand the budget decision-making process in your district. Inheriting a program with a weak feeder system will make it harder to recruit and retain students for your program.

The O in SWOT stands for *opportunities*. Are there areas within the program that present opportunities of which you can take advantage? Examples include strong parental involvement, committed administrators, a school located close to a university where you can use college students for private lessons or supplemental instruction, a nice performance hall or auditorium, and the like. You can leverage any of these depending on the opportunity. You can use parental involvement for fundraisers or engaging the community. Being located near a university can allow college students to come and provide lessons or masterclasses at discounted rates. Having a nice performance hall can allow you to host music festivals or guest artists on campus.

The T in SWOT stands for *threats*. Are there areas within the program that can be threats you need to be concerned about in your position? Examples can be lack of support from administration, negative involvement from the parents' booster club, systemic issues from prior directors, and so on. These issues are things you not only need to be aware of, but also have a plan on how to navigate through. Such threats can make or break the success and efficiency of your program.

Doing a SWOT analysis can take a few days, but once completed it will provide you with important insights not only into the steps needed to have a successful program but also into implementing a strategic method for doing so.

8.4 Building Advocacy and Community Support

The ability to develop relationships and community support is vital to any plans for your program. Students have to know that you value them in order to build trust. Former United States president Theodore Roosevelt has been credited as saying, "People don't care how much you know until they know how much you care." The same applies not only to your students but also to your community, as it is important to have buy-in and develop a family dynamic from all stakeholders. Everyone must steer the boat in unison in order to maximize the speed at which we head toward our destination. The following are people you need on your side in order to effectively implement your vision for the program.

ADMINISTRATION

These are the decision makers for the school. They have the power to approve nearly everything you request, including whether you will be allowed to travel to events, order equipment, budget for sheet music and instruments, and so forth. It is imperative to keep a positive relationship and open line of communication with your administration at the school and school board level.

COUNSELORS

These are the masters of the scheduling and can make your job easier or very complicated. Be sure to stay in their good graces and work with your counselors to help find solutions for your band program. It is always better to think through issues and provide them with potential solutions to your concerns rather than expecting them to handle all of your concerns on their own. Remember, they have to focus on the entire school, so if you can provide a solution for them, this takes one more thing off their plate, and they will appreciate your contribution to that. The easier you can make their jobs, the more they will want to go above and beyond for you.

CUSTODIANS

Custodians not only work hard to help keep the school clean but are also the people who know the ins and outs of the entire school and can get you into your classroom when you forget your keys at home for the fourth time. It is great to have them as allies and an ear-to-the-streets perspective to keep you abreast of the latest news on campus. Often they can forewarn you of issues before they arise, such as student conduct in other classes, policies that may come down the pipeline, community developments, and other things that can impact your program.

SECRETARIES

In most cases, these are the people who run the campus and provide insights that can make your job easier or much more difficult. Be sure to keep an open line of communication with your secretary, as they can control your access to travel requests, purchase expenditures, requisitions, fundraisers, and more. Secretaries are invaluable resources for your success.

PARENTS

Parents are the biggest potential advocates of your program. They can make or break any situation. Helping parents understand and agree with your vision helps ensure your ability to implement your vision without issues arising from within. This is incredibly vital if you operate a parent booster organization of any type as well.

COMMUNITY FIGURES

School board members, political figures, and community and business leaders can be important figures to have on your side as well, especially for fundraising or important items that involve school board advisories. Be sure to promote any positive press to all your stakeholders. People love good news, especially if they feel they are partially responsible for it.

COACHES

Coaches do not have to be your enemies. The old saying is true: you really do catch more flies with honey than with vinegar. It is always better to foster a positive relationship with your coaches and other teachers. You never know when you will need their support.

STUDENTS

Last but most important, the students are the "why" of what you do. Taking steps to develop trust, compassion, and understanding is vital to their individual success and the overall success of your program. Students are more inclined to help when they know that you genuinely care about them and their development, so be sure to make your social deposits now for withdrawals later.

You will need positive relationships with each of these entities in order to effectively implement your vision. Strategies to help develop relationships with each group include inviting administrators or coaches to guest-conduct a piece on your concert and sending biweekly or monthly newsletters to parents and community leaders. You can create a standard template through a software program like Adobe Spark or Canva and just update content to send electronically to your stakeholders.

For students, have every positive student or ensemble accomplishment announced on the morning and/or afternoon school announcements. Post achievements on the school website and social media platforms. Send letters to school board members highlighting the program's achievements. Advertise your program through multiple avenues—the local newspaper, morning announcements, social media, and creating a website—as this adds legitimacy to your program. There are plenty of user-friendly platforms: Wix, Weebly, Squarespace, WordPress, and GoDaddy, to name a few. Be sure to check with your administration to make sure you adhere to any district online guidelines.

Let students have buy-in and involve them in the music selection process. In your program, make it a point to learn each student's name and specific things about them. What are their hobbies, interests, musical preferences, and so on? Find social activities to do with the students on campus to help build rapport such as a day of basketball, flag football, or dodgeball after a practice. Another idea can be a day of card games or a water balloon fight during a hot day of summer camp. Finding moments allowing you to bond as a unit is vital in building rapport with your students.

Utilize your SWOT analysis to develop ways to make your program special and unique. Students want to be a part of something "cool" and lasting, so how can we create an educational and musical experience that is unique and the "it" thing on campus? Be consistent in your expectations, standards, and approach. If resources are one of the weaknesses of your program, fundraising will be the name of your game. Find what works in your area so that you are not repeating an endeavor another group on campus is doing. This can be a SWOT analysis by itself. Where are there opportunities to do something no one else is doing that can add value to your program? Incorporating different fundraising strategies such as writing grants, writing letters to businesses for donations, food sales, 50/50 raffle sales at sporting events, and running concessions at sporting events can all help you reach your fundraising goal.

Another idea can be a rehearsal-thon where students get pledges for the number of hours they rehearse. For example, a person commits to giving someone $5 for every hour they rehearse. After securing pledges, you as the director set up a five-hour rehearsal on an available Friday evening, say from five to ten in the evening. and use this time to bring in people to provide master classes for the students and a clinician to work with the ensembles. The money raised from the pledges can help offset the costs of bringing in the clinicians or the student's fees, among other things. This approach can be a win-win for all involved.

8.5 Building Ensembles

Again, hopefully one of the pillars in your philosophy is to create a multifaceted, well-rounded music program, whether it features a chamber orchestra, marching band, full orchestra, concert ensemble, jazz band, percussion ensemble, or even just small chamber ensembles. To achieve this, you'll need to get creative with your scheduling. This goes back to having a great relationship with the counselors and administration, who can help you with scheduling endeavors.

Also of importance is building numbers (recruitment) and keeping them (retention). If you do not have a strong feeder system, you may need to start beginners at your school to bridge the gap while you work with your feeder pipeline. To help with retention, taking small trips to colleges, going to in-state festivals, and/or forming honor bands can provide a lot of exposure for students that can lead to bigger trips out of state and also expose students to deeper levels of musicianship than they are accustomed to locally.

8.6 Building Musicianship: Self and Program

Your program will only go as far as you will take it. We must continue to learn and grow in order to provide the best musical experience possible for our students. We cannot ask students to do things we are not committed to doing ourselves. Bringing in clinicians to rehearse your ensemble or provide master classes to the students are great ways of bringing skill into the classroom. Also, attending district meetings, local honor ensembles, conferences, and other rehearsals are great ways to continue to learn and develop by taking ideas from other skilled professionals.

Another idea for your program's development is to seek out opportunities for your own professional development (PD). Ask your administration if you may be excused from school to watch another master teacher. Again, this goes back to having great relationships with your administration. Instead of spending time at a school-wide professional event that will have little direct impact on your instruction (e.g., learning about science test-taking skills for state exams), ask your administration if you can go to another director's classroom in the district to observe, learn, and take notes. Make a point of developing positive relationships with the local master teachers in your area. These are the people who can visit your classroom rehearsal and provide insights and strategies to help you and your students improve. In the same vein, get involved in the local ensemble director functions. For example, volunteer to serve as the chair for local honor band events. This will put you in direct contact with experienced clinicians, and you can watch their rehearsals and take notes. A connection from this experience could lead to someone serving as a mentor to you. Most successful people want to help others. After all, we are in the education profession.

For student development, you should consider setting up a private lesson structure for your program. If resources are limited, look into partnering with a local university to have undergraduate students provide lessons for a discounted rate, let's say $10 per student. The undergraduate student would look for the teaching experience and as directors we can certainly use the expertise to help our students. The students can pay half ($5) and the booster club or a grant can pay for the other half ($5) for a thirty-minute lesson. Let's say you have ten students in one section: this would be equal to $100 for the private instructor undergraduate student on a weekly basis. A definite win-win scenario for both parties.

8.7 Conclusion

One of the best skills any educator can possess is being organized. As you plan for how your program will operate, be sure to begin with the end in mind. How will your program function when it's up to speed? What experiences will the students have after four years under your leadership? Once you envision how this will look, begin to work backward with your SMART goals to chart a path forward to achieve them. The more organized you become in your vision, the better you will be able to implement your goals for your program.

8.8 Discussion Questions

1. What are things you value in your program? What are key traits you want from your students as they matriculate?
2. You set a goal for your students to learn twelve major scales by the end of the school year in May. Working backward, discuss ways to achieve this goal and tangible outcomes.
3. How can doing a SWOT analysis on your program be advantageous to you as an incoming teacher?
4. What are some fundraising ideas that have worked for you in high school?
5. What are the pros and cons to having stakeholders involved in your program?

OXFORD learning link

Visit the online resources for additional documentation and exercises to help expand learning and test your knowledge further: www.oup.com/he/powell_music1e.

CHAPTER 9

STUDENT MOTIVATION

Quincy C. Hilliard

This chapter examines several different ways to motivate students.

Motivation is the ability to inspire in another a need to want to accomplish, work together, achieve, and so on.

As music teachers, we can no longer just teach our subject matter and content. The teacher's role today includes being a motivator that facilitates what is possible for every child. You can read Hopkins' Chapter 30 on the online resources site for some of the theoretical concepts of motivation. In many cases, we have students from diverse cultural and economic backgrounds where some are ready to learn and others must be convinced that learning is in their best interest. The key factor in motivation is the teacher. I have seen many successful teachers over the years with many different techniques; each has their own techniques that work for their situation. What I would like to discuss in this chapter are some of the characteristics I have used and observed over the years that can lead to motivating students.

9.1 A-P.I.E. (Attitude of Positivity, Inspiration, and Enthusiasm)

As music educators we must know that our classes and ensembles mirror our beliefs systems and most importantly our attitude. It is the difference between being a thermostat that sets the environment or simply a thermometer that reports, reflects, and responds to the environment. Having a positive attitude can be extremely uplifting to students. It can be a teacher's most important trait, as it helps set the climate and culture for the classroom. I have found this can-do attitude to be an essential element to both student and teacher success. Having a positive attitude, unfortunately, can be the most difficult attribute to maintain on a consistent basis owing to situations that will arise that the teacher did not foresee or have control over. With students coming from so many different home environments, it is absolutely essential that a teacher maintain a positive attitude: our students feed off of our energy more than we often realize. For some students, the only positive influence that they receive might be from their teacher.

It is important that teachers try to be as upbeat as they can and present their lesson plans or run rehearsal with as much enthusiasm as possible. If the teacher is excited about what they are doing, this energy will become contagious and energize the students. A simple self-help reminder for teachers to say to themselves is, "If you act enthusiastic, you'll be enthusiastic!" Another positivity-power-up tool is this: in difficult times simply smile and say to yourself, "Thank you," for the situation you find yourself struggling with, because gratitude is the fuel that will let you win the day. Gratitude helps you see your situation as what it truly is: a lesson, not a loss. Using positive energy and enthusiasm can be an incredibly powerful motivating force. Enthusiasm is contagious! When teachers use energy and excitement to motivate others, the teachers themselves can affect more people than they will ever know (Clark, 2004).

It is important to remember that you are "attractive," but not in the way you might think. Whatever emotional energy you put out will attract that same energy. In my years of teaching and observing teachers, I have observed many teachers with negative or unenthusiastic qualities. These traits often can lead to small or almost nonexistent programs. The students will have a lackluster attitude toward the program, and every day will seem like a chore for the teacher, students, and the administration. I once observed this attitude lead the principal to cancel the music program. In other instances, I have witnessed a positive and energetic teacher, following a negative teacher, excite and build a program that flourished. The teacher makes the difference, and if students are excited about the state of the program, they will continue to enroll in the class. It is the teacher's job to lead, develop, and inspire the program.

In motivating students, teachers should try to exhibit traits that will inspire all students. However, in some cases, there are going to be some students who will need more motivation than others. Clark (2004) suggested some traits that teachers can use with less motivated students to give them more attention.

- Praise them more
- Call on them more
- Give them some classroom responsibility
- Provide them with positive feedback and sincere criticism (Clark, 2004, p. 6)

The teacher's expectations are also important. A motivating teacher will have high expectations of all students; anything less would be destructive to the student and the program. In getting students motivated to learn, you will build their self-esteem. This will cause the students to become self-motivated, because they will feel good about themselves. Giving kids an opportunity to experience a win helps to make everyday a "WINS-day" for them and ultimately for you as well. Teachers should expect good work, praise effort, honor success, and give honest and sincere criticism. This will allow the students' pride in themselves and their work to grow. Note that it will be hard to maintain a high level of enthusiasm every day. However, the more enthusiasm you can muster, the more it will become a part of your teaching style. Keep in mind that the school year is not a sprint, but it is a 180-day marathon that is as easy "A-P.I.E." By that I mean your actions and commitment to A-P.I.E. principles cannot be limited to a week, a month, or a grading period; rather, it should be committed to for the year if it is to come to fruition. A teacher must arouse a need in students to want to be around them and a desire to be a part of the program. Kids learn better from people they like and situations they enjoy. See Pellegrino and Wagoner's Chapter 3, "How Students Learn," for more on this.

9.2 Get to Know Each Student

More than anything, children need a sound, trusted adult in their lives. It has been said that students do not care what you know until they know that you care. When students feel that a teacher is truly and sincerely invested in them, they feel confidence in working with that teacher. It is important to note that getting to know the student must be kept in the proper perspective. A close friend of mine, the high school band director Terry Kenny (retired from his former job in Georgia), made a statement that I think encapsulates this idea: "In working with the students: BE FRIENDLY, but not FRIENDS."

I have observed many teachers who have tried to become their students' friends. In becoming friends, they lose the students' respect, and they have problems maintaining control of the class. Directors like Kenny have been extremely successful in building a strong program by observing this rule.

One way of getting to know the students is to develop a questionnaire that will give you insight into their thoughts and feelings. Below is a sample list of questions that can be used. The teacher can add or delete questions to fit the situation.

1. I am very proud that I ______________.
2. Something that worries me is ______________.
3. Two of my favorite things I like to do:______________.
4. Name one thing that you do well: ______________.
5. My favorite movie is ______________.
6. My favorite TV show is ______________.
7. I would like to travel to ______________.
8. I get depressed when ______________.
9. I think that I am very good at ______________.
10. To help me do better in school, I wish that my teacher would ______________.
11. Two things that make me happy: ______________.
12. Two things that make me sad: ______________.
13. I wish I could ______________.
14. Two things I want my teacher to know about me: ______________.
15. My best friend is ______________.
16. Two things that worry me: ______________.
17. If I had the chance, I would like to ______________.
18. I feel I know a lot about ______________.
19. Two traits I would like to see in my teacher: ______________.
20. One of my best accomplishments is ______________.

Many successful teachers have also taken time to attend an after-school activity that one of their students was participating in. Here are some examples of activities that a director can attend:

- Sporting events
- Outside solo performances at churches, malls, etc.
- Exhibits or class projects that are school-related
- Choral or orchestra concerts
- Plays

When I was teaching, I had a student who was very shy and withdrawn. As I passed by his music stand one day, I observed that he had some beautiful artwork on his folder. I asked him who did the drawings, and to my surprise, he said he did. So I immediately came up with the idea that he would design the cover art for all of our future programs. He took it one step further and designed every program based upon events and stories about the music and the band. He also designed all the flyers we would put up around the school and local businesses to advertise each concert. Next, he designed the band T-shirt. This brought him out of his withdrawn state, and he later was elected band president.

Jessica Fain, director of bands at Bluff Middle School in Prairieville, LA, uses a portion of her Monday morning class period to do something called Monday Musings. She states, "I ask students to share something cool about their weekend. As the year progresses, students begin to share more or join in for the first time. If I forget Monday Musings, students are quick to remind me" (Fain, 2018). This idea gives the director some insight into the student's lives and some information on how to communicate with them and what about.

Getting to know the students on an individual basis is best. Some students will come motivated. Those who do not come motivated will need you to individualize your effort to reach them. The more you know about your students, the more you can help them, and they will respond because they know you care.

9.3 Set Goals

If you do not know where you are going,

you will never reach your destination.

We talked about making every day a "WINS-day" and that is also connected to setting SMART goals.

- Specific
- Measurable
- Achievable
- Reasonable
- Timely

Setting goals from day to day, week to week, and month to month allows the students to see their progress. These goals should involve each student's progress on a weekly, monthly, and yearly basis, as well as including goals for the class or group. As students begin to track and see their accomplishments, they become excited and motivated to go further. Many small accomplishments by each student will in turn bring about a change in the accomplishments of the group as a whole. Luke Wilcox, a member of the National Board for Professional Teaching Standards, says that daily learning goals (learning targets or "I can" statements) should be posted, visible, and referenced on a daily basis. Establishing the "goal of the day" at the start of the lesson gives purpose to the students' learning. Students can also formatively assess themselves at the end of each lesson by checking to be sure they have met the learning goal (Wilcox, 2018).

It is important to note that the daily and weekly goals should be small enough for each student to attain. For example, a teacher could teach a rhythm each day. The teacher can write the rhythm on the board and, most important, have the students write it down in their notebooks with the proper counting notation. The teacher can have the students count, clap, and sing the rhythm. Afterward, the students can perform the rhythm on a scale pattern or in a particular chord structure.

A good weekly goal can be to learn a different scale each week. The teacher can begin by discussing the scale, writing it on the board, and showing the key signature and how it relates to the scale. It would also be a good idea to have the students write this scale in their notebooks for future assessments. A helpful approach might be to play or sing the scale slowly for a few classes before increasing the tempo. If it is a very young class, teach the scale four notes at a time before combining them.

A good monthly goal could be to learn a portion of a composition that you will be performing in the future. The half-year goal could be your Christmas/winter concert.

Other goals would be preparing for ensemble and solo assessment, school performances, the spring concert, and so on. The total music goal would be to increase the level of music that your students will perform throughout the year.

One of the most important aspects of achieving goals is for the students to observe their progress. A large chart of the year's events should be posted in a planned site and checked off after each one is accomplished, alongside a smaller chart for personal accomplishments. This one is for scales, music tests, and the like. This is one of the best ways for the students to evaluate themselves and the whole group. Seeing is believing!

It is the director's job to decide the direction of the program, and in small ensembles such as rock bands the direction of the group will be decided by the student leader in charge of that group. Therefore, setting goals is vitally important in order to maintain and grow the program. One of my students took over a school that did not have a band program. His first fifth-grade beginning band class had an enrollment of eight students. The second year, he had twelve students, and the third year, he had forty beginners. He told me that he had a third of the total fifth-grade class in his band and that his goal for the next year was to get half of the fifth-grade class enrolled. His future goal was to increase that to at least 60 to 70 percent of the fifth-grade class. The principal was so impressed that she gave him a larger room for band class.

Goal setting is a bit like learning to walk. You set small goals; for example, learning to sit up, roll over, then crawl, all the while keeping your eye on the bigger goal of learning to walk. If you attain your goals too fast, set new ones. It is important to note that some years you will be able to attain your goals more easily than others. This is due to many different factors, such as scheduling, student desire, class climate, and so on. A teacher should always try to set goals that are attainable. Expectations and goal setting are very similar. If the teacher has low expectations, then the goals that are attained will be few or nonexistent. However, if the expectations are high, then the goals will be higher, making for a very successful program. The teacher should make a personal goal chart every year and evaluate it at the end of the year.

9.4 Give Honest and Sincere Praise and Objective Criticism

There is a saying that you can con a con and fool a fool, but you can't kid a kid. Children know when you are being authentic and keeping it real with them. Keeping students motivated with authentic, positive praise and feedback is very important. This gives them a sense of self-worth and accomplishment. *Whenever possible, always praise before you criticize.* When students work hard, they need to know that their time and effort was appreciated. I witnessed a rehearsal in Hawaii once where, at the end of the rehearsal, the director had the students stand, whereupon he thanked them for their time and effort. I was so surprised by this that I asked the director why he did that. He stated to me that no matter how the rehearsal goes (well or poorly), he wanted the students to know that their time and effort was appreciated, and he said he did this after every after-school or special rehearsal. I know of another director who told me that he never passes by a student practicing on their own without praising them. These two directors have outstanding programs. The students in their programs are highly motivated, feel appreciated, and have a sense of pride in their work. Students are able to sense empty phrases and know that they are not real. It should be noted that the praise must be sincere and honest. It can be detailed or brief, depending on the student and the circumstance. Here are a few quick words that a director can use to praise students for a specific accomplishment:

- Perfect!
- Great effort!
- Awesome!

- Nice job!
- Excellent!
- Way to go!
- Nice work!
- Super job!

A teacher should also avoid backhanded praise:

Backhanded praise: "Well, you didn't mess things up like you did before."

Positive praise: "Things are sounding a lot better today! Keep up the good work."

Backhanded praise: "This is not the worst rehearsal I have had."

Positive praise: "You can do better. I expect better. You are not giving me what you are capable of. Let's try it again."

Backhanded praise: "How did you ever get that done?"

Positive praise: "You did it! Your hard work paid off! I am so proud of you."

Praise is one of the key factors in motivating a student and helping them to build a good self-concept. When criticizing or making helpful suggestions, I have found that giving praise first often lessens the sting of criticism. Criticism can be very damaging to students, especially to those who are just beginning. A teacher must learn that a healthy amount of praise with small amounts of constructive criticism keeps students motivated. Also, students are not all alike. It is the teacher's job to learn what motivates each individual student. A good teacher can motivate by challenging the student, praising them, and criticizing them. The word "criticism" might have a negative connotation when it comes to motivating students. In some cases, it might become necessary to replace the word "criticism" with *helpful suggestions*, *comments for improvement*, or *critiques*. When giving individual criticism, it may be necessary to do it in private. Praising, however, can be done in public and private. A teacher must remember that constructive criticism is designed to point out mistakes and show how to make improvements. Any person can criticize, but showing how to correct the problem gives the student a path to solving it.

As a young teacher, your problem solving toolkit for correcting problems will be limited. Your toolkit will grow as you mature as a teacher. You must gather more tools by talking to more experienced directors; attending workshops, clinics, and seminars; and reading and studying about your craft. In addition, observing successful directors' rehearsals at their school, having them come and rehearse your group, and watching guest conductors of honor groups are also great tools. It is important that young directors *take notes* and keep a notebook of ideas that they have gathered.

This will become your toolkit, and you can refer to it when you need to review or solve a problem. A strong, healthy toolkit will help the young director when giving comments or criticisms. The toolkit will be infinite! Some ideas or tools will grow old and need to be replaced or updated with new ones. Remember: A teacher is a student who never stops learning and improving. You must strive to be up-to-date on all the latest student behavior and teaching techniques.

9.5 Patience

The only way to help children persevere from their potential to their promise is with patience. Teaching students music is similar to teaching them a new language with a device that creates sound. I feel it is imperative that the teacher and student remain patient in this new endeavor. We live in a world where instant gratification seems to be expected.

The problem with this is that it creates, in both the student and sometimes the teachers, the idea that if things cannot be done quickly, let's give up and move to something else. The teacher must learn and instill in the student that they must "give up on giving up." Not everything happens quickly. Some students and teachers will experience success before others. Those who have to work harder than others need to know it's important to praise the effort that is given and to continue moving forward toward their goals. I often tell my teachers it will take about five to seven years before they are able to start feeling successful. During this time they must experiment, redefine, and shape their teaching strategies into a framework that fits them. In working with students, the teacher should impress upon them that hard work, discipline, and persistence are some of the keys to learning to play an instrument.

The teacher must also learn to be patient in working with administrators. My wife was a middle school principal. I was astonished at how busy every one of her days was, even on weekends. She was always dealing with an extreme issue, whether it concerned a student, a parent, the school board, or state mandates. I went to visit her on one occasion, waited about an hour and a half with her telling me "just one more minute" every ten minutes, and then left and *never* visited her at her office again. As a teacher, when dealing with the administration (principals and counselors), it is important to take a slow and patient path to getting your program to the level you have planned. As you start to prove yourself, the administration will begin to accept your ideas and wishes.

Nowhere is it more apparent that the proverb "patience is a virtue" holds true than in teaching. I constantly have to remind my young teachers that teaching has up days and down days. In the beginning there will be many down days. This is where perseverance and patience are needed. As the years go by, the down days will become fewer or less important, and you will begin to focus on having more up days. In addition, as you become comfortable and settled into your job, the down days will not be as frustrating. It can take five or more years to develop a successful program. I have seen outstanding programs built over many years torn down in one semester or one year by bad administration and/or scheduling.

Great teachers have to be willing to be patient and build a successful program *brick by brick.* When faced with a challenge, it's best to outline a course of action. This course of action can be on weekly, monthly, and yearly bases. This outline can be modified and updated until the challenges are overcome. This is the challenge that you will face entering the profession.

9.6 Sense of Humor

"The most wasted of all days is one without laughter."

E. E. Cummings (1894–1962)

Laughter is contagious, and it can be a powerful force in helping us relate to others. When present in the learning environment, the joy and delight that come from humor can be powerful tools when getting students to put forth effort and achieve at the highest level. (Clark, 2004, p. 166) When teaching students, it's a good idea to help them learn to deal with stress and frustration through humor. I have noticed that some students tend to take every little problem more seriously than it merits. The teacher's role is to help the students learn to face their problems or frustrations, and sometimes laughter is the best solution. In this day and age, some students are afraid of failure or mistakes and see them as overwhelming. Students must learn that it's okay to make a mistake as long as they keep trying. In my teaching, I have heard students say, "I am just dumb and I will not get it." I am quick to say, "No you are not! You just have not yet grasped the principles that will help you to overcome the problem."

I can remember a rehearsal I was doing with a middle school honor band. We had been working hard on a section that was not coming together. In repeating that section one of many times, a trumpet player played the wrong note, and I started to laugh. I stopped the rehearsal and we all laughed. I told them that was the funniest thing I had heard all day. Afterward, we repeated the section and they played it perfectly. I am sure that the laughter removed the tension and stress of learning to play the section. Several directors told me afterward how they appreciated me not getting angry and belittling the student.

Teaching is an arduous job, and that in itself can be overwhelming. It helps sometimes to stop and laugh with your students to let them know that you are human. The award-winning humorist Linda Edgcombe has said: "Learn, love, laugh. If you are not laughing, you are not learning. All successful people in the world have a great sense of humor." During my master's degree, my composition teacher, Jared Spears, taught a composition class that I never missed because of his humor, whether it was directed at me or another student. Spears was the same way in my private lessons. When I was frustrated with my writing, he encouraged me, made me laugh, and sent me on my way to fix the problems. I learned so much from him as a composer and as a teacher. I now use a lot of humor when working with my students. Laughter is powerful: it can take away the blues, mend a heart, dry an eye, and doctor the soul. It can pull us together, lift us up, and put a smile on any face. In every classroom there should be some form of laughter (Clark, 2004).

As teachers we possess great power in making a difference in students' lives. We must build their self-confidence and self-esteem. Using humor is a nice contrast in relieving stress and frustration.

9.7 Flexibility

Flexibility is the ability to change and adapt to situations as they occur. This adaptability may have to be done with scheduling, rehearsals, extra practices, administration, parents, and so on. Teachers who are very rigid in their approach to teaching have found themselves disappointed, frustrated, and stressed, to say the least.

Because we live in an ever-changing environment, situations are going to occur where the teacher will have to make adjustments. Example 1: Some students are involved in several school activities or organizations, and this can sometimes conflict with your rehearsals or performances. I have found that if the teacher speaks with the other adult involved, they can usually resolve the problem. *The two teachers should try to resolve the problem before approaching the administration.* It is very important that you not get the student caught in the middle. If that happens, it can lead to the student's becoming frustrated and leaving one or both of the organizations. I know of a director who had several of his band members on the soccer team. After talking with the coach, they agreed to share the students except on days of band performances or soccer games. It made the students happy that they were able to enjoy both activities. On some occasions, the band students would even go and perform at the soccer games.

Occasionally teachers try to do what is "fair and equal" and apply it to all students. The teacher must learn what is fair is not always equal, and what is equal is not always fair. Before teachers make a steadfast rule, they should take into account all contingencies. I once had a director who only had one tuba player in his band. The tuba player was also a starter on the football team. In the fall, the student learned his music during his off period and before school. The director wrote the halftime marching show in a way that the tuba player had limited involvement in the drill. The coach agreed to let the student miss football practice on Monday and Tuesday to practice with the band. On Friday night during halftime, when the team went to the locker room, the student got his tuba and performed in the halftime show in his football uniform. When I saw this, I was astonished. The student did not get a football scholarship to go to college, but he did get a music scholarship and majored in music education. Now he is a successful band director.

Example 2: One of my former students had taken a job at a school where the band was all but nonexistent. He had very few instruments and little sheet music or equipment. The superintendent wanted to have a strong band program, so after he was hired he was able to get a few instruments and some equipment. The superintendent asked him to submit a five-year budget plan for instruments and equipment, which the board approved. Shortly afterward came the financial crisis of 2008. The school system had layoffs and cutbacks. Over the next two years the director got instruments and equipment through donations, fundraising, pawn shops, government supply warehouses, and other nontraditional sources. In the summer of 2011 the superintendent called the director to this office and told him that he was going to get him everything on his five-year plan at once and more during the upcoming year! The school board even approved remodeling the band room. The director was so excited. He told me it was like Christmas! The superintendent praised him for being patient and flexible and told the director how much he appreciated his looking for other funding sources. It took the director almost eight years to get what he needed, but being flexible paid off. The teacher often asked me during the dark times if he should leave this school, and I always told him no. Occasionally, when he had few instruments and limited instrumentation, I would write some pieces that he would play with his small group.

Example 3: During the COVID-19 pandemic of 2020, teachers had to adjust their teaching approaches and become very flexible and creative. Band, orchestra, and choir directors had to discover how to teach without having complete ensemble rehearsals. Many had to teach their students online individually and/or in small groups. Here are just a few of the ideas and teaching strategies that they developed:

1. Teaching private lessons online via Zoom.
2. Teaching ensembles groups online via Zoom.
3. Since marching band was not an option in some states, the director had smaller classes where they taught theory and musicianship concepts.
4. Inviting composers, musicians, and/or clinicians to serve as guest lecturers online.
5. Teaching on a hybrid schedule with half of your ensemble every other day.
6. Focusing their teaching strategies more on music fundamentals (rhythms, music theory, music history, etc.) than on performing music.
7. Teaching outside under tents with six-foot spacing.
8. Some other examples: six feet of spacing, wearing masks at all times, thirty-minute rehearsals only, nylon coverings for all instrument bells (from oboe to tuba), proper ventilation system, proper disinfectants for cleaning the band room, and other mitigation measures.
9. Students had choices. If they were at home, daily lessons and testing were all via Zoom.

Teachers should also be flexible in their teaching styles. As a teacher you are trying to reach as many students as possible. Sometimes a new approach to teaching an existing concept might help the student comprehend it quickly. Talking with experienced teachers can also be helpful in learning to be flexible in your teaching style. Teaching will forever be a changing profession. Being flexible is one of the characteristics you must have to last in this profession.

9.8 Discussion Questions

1. List some ideas for what a director can do to foster a positive attitude in the classroom. In working with less motivated students, list some ideas you have observed that might work with them. List some ideas for building confidence in the students.
2. List some ways of getting to know your students that can be done in an appropriate manner. How did your directors let you know that they cared about you?
3. List some personal goals you have set for yourself that you accomplished? What feelings did you get when you accomplished your goals? Can you help students set and accomplish their goals?
4. List some examples of positive praise that made you feel uplifted. List some examples of backhanded praise that you have observed. Discuss objective criticism and how and when to use it in an uplifting way.
5. What are some of the challenges you have had to face that took time and patience for you to overcome? List some challenges in your musical studies which you have had to overcome with patience. When faced with a large challenge, what are some of the characteristics that you must have to overcome it?
6. Discuss some instances where you have observed humor being used to aid in learning. Discuss the role of humor in your life and how it has helped you get through a difficult situation.
7. What characteristics must a teacher have to be flexible? List some ways that you could teach students music without their instruments. What musical concepts would you teach if the students were not allowed to have instruments?

OXFORD learning link

Visit the online resources for additional documentation and exercises to help expand learning and test your knowledge further: www.oup.com/he/powell_music1e.

CHAPTER 10

INTEGRATING TECHNOLOGY IN INSTRUMENTAL MUSIC INSTRUCTION

Bryan Powell

This chapter provides an overview of some of the ways that music technology can be incorporated into the music classroom.

10.1 Introduction

The use of technology in instrumental music teaching and learning provides opportunities to engage students in ways that would not otherwise be possible. This has been especially true in recent years, as the COVID-19 pandemic required teachers to pivot to online teaching and utilize various technological platforms to connect with students and allow them to collaborate musically. This chapter outlines different ways in which music educators can use technology in their teaching, both in individual lessons and in ensemble rehearsals. I will not provide a comprehensive list of apps and software platforms in this chapter because those are constantly evolving. Instead, the purpose of this chapter is to showcase the different ways that technologies can be incorporated in the classroom. To help organize this chapter, the discussion of technology in music instruction is divided into three categories: technology for recording, technology as a teaching tool, and technology as an instrument.

10.2 Technology for Recording

Even with the proliferation of affordable music technologies over the past two decades, video and audio recordings are the most common ways that instrumental music teachers incorporate music technology into the classroom. Teachers often record their students to allow them to listen back to themselves or watch their performances as part of self-evaluation and assessment. Engaging students in self-assessment is an important part of any music class, and with the proliferation of smartphones, it has become increasingly easy for students to record rehearsals or performances themselves to view outside the classroom as they practice or simply reflect on their performance.

The use of video and audio recording in music rehearsals can allow students to take an active role in providing feedback on their performances. Instead of relying only on the director's feedback, students can listen to the ensemble play and provide feedback based on what they hear. This is especially important because what a musician hears when they are performing with an ensemble and what they hear when they listen back to the performance are often different. Researchers have found that student perceptions of their performance can change after they listen to a recording of their performance (Silveira & Gavin, 2016).

DIGITAL AUDIO WORKSTATIONS

The use of digital audio workstations (DAWs) has become increasingly common in recent years. The term applies to both hardware configurations (e.g., computers with audio interfaces and recording software, standalone devices) and software applications (e.g., GarageBand, Audacity, FruityLoops/FL Studio, Soundtrap, Pro Tools, Logic). DAWs allow the user to record, edit, manipulate, and produce audio files. Some DAWs also include loops that users can drag and drop to create musical compositions.

During the COVID-19 pandemic, many teachers incorporated the use of DAWs to create virtual ensembles where each student would record their individual part and send it to their music teacher, who would then mix all of the parts together into a single audio file. In order to achieve a consistent tempo from all players, students often listened to a recording of the piece or a metronome click-track in their headphones, or watched a video of the music teacher conducting the piece while they played or sang their part.

As many teachers who created virtual ensemble performances realized, all this is a lot of work. The mixing together of several separate performances (and a hundred or more parts for large ensembles) is a laborious process for even the most accomplished audio engineer. The creation of virtual ensembles also introduced new considerations for music teachers, such as what to do with out-of-tune parts. Many DAWs allow some pitch correction, but doing so may create a version of the students' performance that is not a realistic representation of the sound of the ensemble. These digitally altered performances might then create an "ethic of expectation" (Talbot and Bernard, in press) that is unfair to the students and music teachers. And what about muting certain parts of a student's performance that are out of tune or out of time? Is this the same thing as telling a vocalist to "mouth the words" to a song without singing because they sing out of tune? As is hopefully clear, the introduction of DAWs to create virtual music performances for school-based ensembles introduces a variety of considerations for the music teacher.

DAWs can also be used in small group or individual lessons. Cloud-based DAWs such as Soundtrap and BandLab make it easy for students to record themselves playing at home and then share that recording with their music teachers. These students could be practicing long tones or playing scales over a drumbeat, improvising over a loop, or creating melodies to accompany a preexisting backing track. Teachers can also select loops from DAWs (or find backing tracks online) to use as accompaniment for students practicing scales or long tones on their instrument. Most DAWs allow the user to change the tempo and key of the loop, enabling teachers to select appropriate keys to match the music exercise. There are many possibilities.

MUSICAL COLLABORATION

Some apps and software allow students to collaborate with others or record multiple parts themselves to create music. As detailed in the DAW section above, DAWs can allow students to record parts to different tracks. With a cloud-based DAW such as Soundtrap or BandLab, students can collaborate with other students to create music together, or they can record multiple parts themselves. Most instrumental method books include duets or trios, which allow a student to use a DAW to record each of those parts to play a duet or trio with themselves. Apps such as Acapella also allow students to collaborate with others or create all of the parts themselves.

10.3 Technology as a Teaching Tool

Technology can also be used as a teaching tool in the classroom. There are many websites, apps, hardware, and software platforms that allow teachers to demonstrate music concepts and allow students to practice their instruments and create music. As mentioned previously, this chapter is not meant to be an exhaustive list of websites, apps, and brands of technology available to music teachers. It is instead designed to be an overview of the specific *types* of technology that teachers can utilize. Most music technologies for teaching have accompanying websites with tutorials and resources for educators. However, if you cannot find the answer on the company's website, YouTube is usually a great resource to find answers to issues or frequently asked questions.

ONLINE MUSIC LEARNING SOFTWARE

Some software platforms offer students the opportunity to play and get feedback when they are not at school. Software such as SmartMusic, Noteflight Learn, and PracticeFirst allows students to play along to music staff notation and receive instant feedback on the correctness of their pitch and rhythm. For popular music instruments including guitar, bass, ukulele, keyboards, and vocals, the platform Yousician offers similar instant feedback on note and pitch correction for instrumentalists. Software platforms like these can be a valuable addition to a music teacher's music program but should not be seen as a replacement for actual in-class instruction. Obstacles to using these platforms include financial barriers due to a subscription fee for each student, and inconsistent experiences as a result of unreliable internet access or using older computers, Chromebooks, iPads, or phones to access the websites or apps.

NOTATION SOFTWARE

Most music teachers are familiar with music notation software such as Finale and Sibelius. There are a growing number of options for music notation software that teachers can use, including free options such as MuseScore and cloud-based options such as Flat.io and Noteflight. One nice option with cloud-based notation software is that students can collaborate with one another to create new pieces of music or notate their own melodies. Cloud-based notation software such Flat.io and Noteflight also integrate with common learning management systems such as Google Classroom, Schoology, and Canvas, making it easy for teachers to create assignments that students can complete on Chromebooks. Because the software is cloud-based, there is no need for students to download any notation software to complete the assignments. Music notation software can also be used for more than just traditional music staff notation. Most music notation software offers options to create chord charts and tablature as well for fretted instruments such as the ukulele and guitar. For more on different types of music notation, see Chapter 6, "Teaching Notation in Instrumental Music."

MUSIC STREAMING

The proliferation of music streaming services gives music teachers and students the opportunity to share music easily. Gone are the days of providing students with CDs of the concert music, or needing students to bring in CDs (or tapes!) of their favorite music to share with the class. Utilizing streaming services such as Spotify, Apple Music, or Amazon Music or sharing YouTube links can allow teachers to share music with students that they are learning in class, as well as allow students to share music with the teacher that is personally meaningful to them. Music streaming services can also allow students to listen to several versions of the same piece or song, analyzing and comparing the musical features of each version.

In all of my classes, I create a public Spotify playlist that I share with my students. I ask all of my students to add at least one song to the playlist that is personally meaningful to them, and I always add a few songs myself. Students do not need to have a paid Spotify subscription to do this, and if they would prefer not to register for a free Spotify account, they can tell me the name of the song and I can add the song to the playlist for them. As a result of this activity, each semester I have an entire list of music that is relevant to my students. I listen to all of the songs in the playlist and then pull examples from the playlist when I want to talk about musical concepts. Co-creating this playlist with my students serves a variety of goals: I learn new music, the students learn that their music is important to me, and it provides a common group of songs that I can use for future lessons. As with any music sharing activity, it is important to have a class discussion about what types of music the students think should be included on the list. Ask the students if they think songs with explicit lyrics are appropriate for the playlist. This conversation can lead to a common understanding of the role of music in and outside the classroom, including what types of music might be fine for at-home listening but problematic inside the classroom. Each school is different, with different parental and administrative expectations, so having these discussions with the students and administrators before asking students to share their music to a playlist is a good idea.

ALTERING THE TEMPO OR PITCH OF A SONG

Play-along videos are becoming increasingly popular in the music classroom, especially in modern band classes where students are playing popular music on instruments such as the guitar, ukulele, bass, keyboard, and drums. There are many technologies that allow teachers to slow down the tempo of videos or audio files so that students can play along to the track at a slower tempo as they are learning the song. The web browser Google Chrome offers an extension called "Transpose" (to find it, simply search Google for "Chrome extension transpose"). This extension allows the user to slow a video down or speed it up, change the key or pitch of the song in the video, or loop a section of the song for students to practice the same section over and over. Software such as Amazing Slow Downer, available for both Mac and PC, allows you to loop, transpose, speed up, and slow down songs and save the song to a new file with the changes. Changing the key for a song can allow teachers to put it in a more comfortable vocal range for students to sing and/or put the song in an easier key for students to play on their instruments.

SILENT REHEARSAL OPTIONS FOR ELECTRONIC INSTRUMENTS

There are a few options for modern band teachers who want to allow students to rehearse silently or want to rehearse multiple ensembles in the same room. Most electronic instruments in K–12 classrooms, including keyboards and amplifiers for electric guitar or bass, have headphone jacks that can allow students to practice their parts in relative silence. You are probably familiar with keyboard labs where everyone practices quietly using headphones. For mixed-instrumentation bands made up of four or five students, hardware such as the Roland HS-5 Session Mixer or a different mixing board can be used to allow students to plug in their instruments to the mixer and listen to the group through headphones. The use of these devices for popular music ensembles works best with an electronic drum kit that can also plug into the mixer. These options can range in price, and some are expensive (the Roland HS-5 is around $670 as of 2023). However, for schools that have a budget for this type of technology, it can facilitate the rehearsal of multiple ensembles in the same room.

10.4 Technology as an Instrument

More and more, music educators are viewing technology such as the iPad as an instrument to be used in the classroom. While it might be strange for some students to think about the iPad as an instrument, the music educator David Williams points out that there are many commonalities between the iPad and a traditional concert band instrument: both can be played either well or poorly; both take practice to get better at playing it and build technique; both are inanimate objects that require someone to touch them in order to make sound; both have limitations on the types of music that can be performed; and both are more appropriate in certain musical circumstances than others (Williams, 2014).

On the iPad, the GarageBand app includes a wide variety of virtual instruments that can provide familiar, or unusual timbres, to any music ensemble. There are options with the virtual instruments in the iPad that allows the user to play chords with a touch of a button, or create drum beats by simply moving icons around a grid. Other apps such as ThumbJam allow the user to pick the instrument, scale, and range for instant access. For example, a student can choose a grid with only the notes of the appropriate pentatonic scale and instantly improvise in the desired key with a move of the finger.

Other pieces of music technology hardware, such as the Skoog, Soundbeam, and Makey Makey, can allow students to create music through touch or gesture, opening up a world of possibilities for all students who might not be able to play, or might not want to play, traditional band instruments. These technological instruments can be incorporated into the band or orchestra ensemble or can be part of an expanded ensemble that welcomes any and all musical instruments (including those that are technologically mediated).

10.5 Drum Machines and Beatmaking

There are several free online websites and apps that allow students to engage in music creation through beatmaking and samplers. Online drum machines provide great ways to engage students in creating rhythmic compositions by clicking on boxes or tapping their device's screen to trigger sounds. Drum machines can replicate a variety of sounds, including sounds from a traditional drum kit as well as synth-based sounds. Many online drum machines can also mimic the sounds of other well-known drum machines, such as the popular Roland TR-808. Some software drum machines allow the user to tap out simple rhythms directly from the device or use a sequencer to program more complex beats.

In Figure 10.1, the website Drumbit (drumbit.app) allows users to create drumbeats using a variety of sounds, effects, and filters. The rhythm represented in the beat sequencer on the left is represented on the right through iconic notation (top right) and percussion clef notation (bottom right).

Creating rhythms on a drum sampler can be a fun activity for all students (not just drummers!) because it allows students to expand their knowledge of creative music technologies while allowing the teacher to teach such musical elements as subdividing a beat, rhythm, timbre, tempo, and so on. In a popular music ensemble, drummers can start by using a drum sequencer to recreate a drum beat to a familiar song before learning to play the rhythm on the drum kit.

FIGURE 10.1 **Drumbit notation**

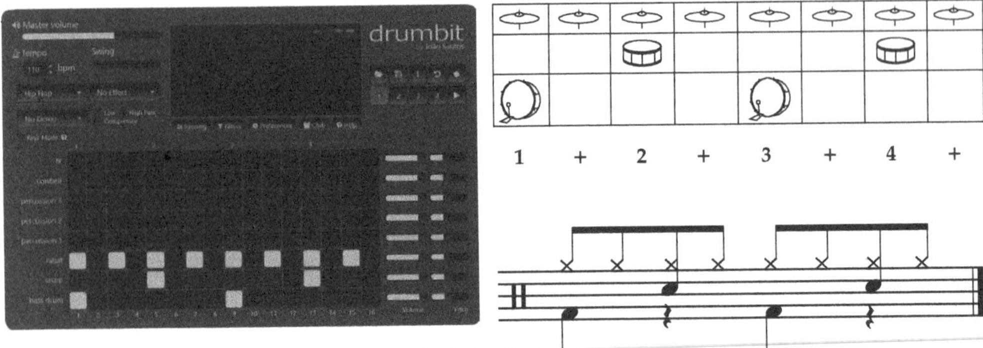

10.6 Conclusion

There are a number of ways that technology can be incorporated into instrumental music instruction. The use of technology might also allow teachers to engage students who would not otherwise be able to participate, or might not want to participate, in instrumental music instruction. It is useful to think through the use of technology through the categories discussed in this chapter—recording with technology, technology as a teaching tool, and technology as an instrument—so that music teachers can better understand the types of technology that they are integrating into their music classrooms. It is also important to interrogate the reasons for using music technology in instrumental music instruction. If teachers are using music technology just to check a box, then they are likely missing out on the myriad ways that technology can provide access and relevance to music instruction.

It is also important to remember that music teachers do not need to be technology experts; technology is constantly changing, and keeping on top of the latest app, piece of hardware, or software platform can be daunting. However, many technologies for music instruction are pretty accessible to even novice music technologists, and there are many valuable resources available, including YouTube tutorials and social media groups, dedicated to music technology instruction. It is okay to sit alongside your students as a co-learner of the technology. You can explain to your students that some of the music technologies are new to you and you will be learning together. It is also okay to start small when it comes to integrating technology into instrumental music instruction. Pick one technology that you would like to integrate and use that as a jumping-off point to explore other types of music technology. As mentioned, the use of technology in instrumental music instruction can provide increased access and relevance for students participating in your music classroom, which is an exciting opportunity for all music educators.

10.7 Discussion Questions

1. Think back to your music programs in elementary, middle, and high school. What types of technology (if any) were used?
2. How might the integration of music technology in instrumental music instruction be able to engage more students?

3. What are some of the challenges that you might anticipate from the integration of music technology into instrumental music instruction?
4. What types of technology are you most likely to integrate into your future music classroom?

OXFORD learning link

Visit the online resources for additional documentation and exercises to help expand learning and test your knowledge further: www.oup.com/he/powell_music1e.

CHAPTER 11

COMPASSION, CARE, COMMUNICATION, AND CONNECTION IN INSTRUMENTAL LEARNING SPACES

Karin S. Hendricks and Tawnya D. Smith

This chapter offers research-based strategies for creating positive, productive, and sustainable instrumental learning environments.

11.1 Introduction

One unfortunate myth believed by some music educators is that teachers must be tough, or even mean, to encourage the highest levels of musicianship from their students. Ensemble programs in the United States have a long history of association with the military, where recruits were broken down physically and emotionally so that they would follow authority without question. For much too long, and far too often, many ensemble directors have attempted to motivate students to practice or to work harder by running such a tight ship that students have had little voice or choice in the learning process (Allsup and Benedict, 2008). In some very unfortunate cases, music teachers have relied upon external, negative reinforcements (such as public embarrassment, physical and/or emotional abuse, or pitting students against one another in divisive ways) to instill a fear of mistakes rather than emphasizing internal positive reinforcements that might foster a love of exploration and learning (Lewis, Weight, and Hendricks, 2022).

Is it possible to get the same kind of high-level musical results without negative reinforcements? We answer emphatically: yes—and more so! In this chapter we argue that teachers do not need to make a choice between high standards and kindness—that they can be both demanding and benevolent, both inspirational and compassionate. Furthermore, we draw upon research to explain how the highest levels of musical expression and expertise may be fostered in nurturing and supportive environments—where students have teachers who care *for*, *about*, and *with* them in ways that forge meaningful musical connections. Finally, we draw upon nonviolent communication (NVC) principles to provide examples of effective and nurturing communication practices in instrumental ensemble settings.

Why is it important to emphasize care and compassion in music education? First, neuroscience suggests that learning is stifled if students do not feel safe (Leahy, 2021). Experiences of stress or fear inhibit the connections in learners' brains between the limbic system (where emotions are processed) and the frontal cortex (the area responsible for reasoning and problem solving), and the amygdala responds to perceived threats by sending the body into survival/protection mode (Goswami, 2008). It makes sense that if students feel any sort of danger—whether physically, emotionally, or of any other kind—their attention will be diverted to hypervigilance and protection, away from learning or trying new things.

In contrast, the more trusting an educational environment is, the higher the levels of achievement (Bryk and Schneider, 2002). Even among professional musicians, creating a safe and empathetic space with other musicians is critical in terms of facilitating musical communication and expression (Davis, 2020). Safe spaces are necessary to foster musical risk taking such as trying out different interpretations of a phrase, improvising, and playing out fully (Hendricks, Smith, and Stanuch, 2014). It is imperative that ensemble directors facilitate a space of safety and trust, given that (a) music students may spend more time with their ensemble director than any other teacher, (b) musical expression requires a relatively large amount of personal vulnerability, and (c) music ensembles often require more cooperation and teamwork than other academic subjects.

The field of education has shifted away from the older practice of blaming students who demonstrate acting-out behavior, now acknowledging that a great number of such students are survivors of trauma. Childhood trauma can include witnessing or experiencing domestic and/or sexual violence, homelessness, hunger, accidents, extreme weather events, ongoing abuse and neglect; and growing up in a household with adults who are substance abusers, have poor mental health, or are away for long periods due to incarceration or forced separation related to immigration policies. The Centers for Disease Control reports that 61 percent of adults have experienced at least one adverse childhood experience (ACE) with one in six, or around 16 percent, reporting at least four (Centers for Disease Control, 2021). This statistic is concerning not only in relation to maintaining a healthy and safe classroom environment, but also because some students who have been traumatized may be triggered by some music class activities such as being singled out (even to be praised) or having a teacher yell over the ensemble (even if just to invite students to play louder). Other students who have been traumatized might be more prone to developing symptoms of music performance anxiety (McGrath, Hendricks, and Smith, 2016).

Similarly, teachers may have personal trauma histories, can be traumatized at work, or can develop secondary traumatic stress as a result of working with traumatized students (Smith, 2021). Impacted trauma survivors (both students and teachers) may have brain and neurological damage, which causes their nervous systems to respond to stressors differently than those who have not been traumatized (van der Kolk, 2014). Given the prevalence of trauma survivors and the way the trauma interferes with teaching and learning (Jennings, 2019), there is a clear need for educators to exercise trauma-informed care for themselves and their students.

Declining mental health within the school-age population is also a concern. There is a sharp upward trend in the number of children and young adults getting treatment for anxiety, depression, and suicidal ideation (Mental Health America, 2021). Before 2006, fifty years of mental health tracking showed no significant changes in adolescent mental health trajectories (Costello et al., 2006). However, between 2009 and 2017 major depressive episodes increased by 52 percent (Twenge et al., 2019). Additionally, between 2007 and 2015 emergency room treatments of suicide attempts and suicidal ideation doubled for adolescents (Burstein et al., 2019). In a study of undergraduate music education majors, over 50 percent reported moderate to severe depression, and over 70 percent reported moderate to severe anxiety (Payne et al., 2020).

Music teachers often serve as the "first line of communication" for adolescents with anxiety and depression (Dirks, 2020, p. 98). Given the prevalence and increase in both self-reported and documented treatment for mental illness, there is a clear need to design and implement trauma-sensitive curricula and provide differentiated approaches to support all students' emotional and mental well-being. Music can be instrumental in healing, or it can lead to further harm. It is important that we all understand how to create healthful and supportive musical experiences—what we call "compassionate music teaching."

11.2 Understanding Compassion

The word "compassion" has many different interpretations, some of which are more appropriate to music education than others (Hendricks, 2018). As shown in Figure 11.1, definitions of compassion that lean toward the "pity" end of the spectrum would imply that music students have something wrong with them and somehow need help being "lifted up" or "saved" by teachers. This understanding places the teacher in a position superior to students and implies that students need to be rescued by a teacher-hero. Such assumptions place all the responsibility for learning on the teacher and negate the many potential strengths that individual students bring. Students are potentially disempowered by compassion-as-pity relationships, while teachers may be left unnecessarily burdened or overwhelmed. Other harmful notions of compassion-as-pity might suggest that teachers do not challenge students to their full potential because they do not want to make them uncomfortable.

On the other hand, interpretations of compassion that lean toward the "shared enthusiasm" end of the spectrum assume that students have inherent strengths and passions for learning, which are enriched through symbiotic relationships with teachers and peers. Compassion-as-shared-enthusiasm honors the various strengths that every person brings to the learning space. On this end of the spectrum, music students and teachers not only share a love of music but also work together to reach shared goals. There is no need for external, fear-based motivation strategies in these kinds of relationships because students are more likely to experience intrinsic motivation, owing to their sense of autonomy, competence, and relatedness (Deci and Ryan, 1985; Hendricks and McPherson, 2023; Ryan and Deci, 2000).

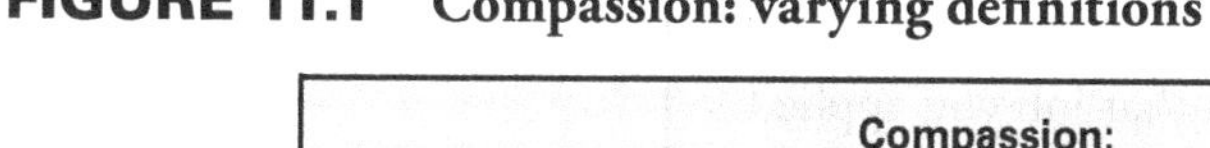

FIGURE 11.1 **Compassion: varying definitions**

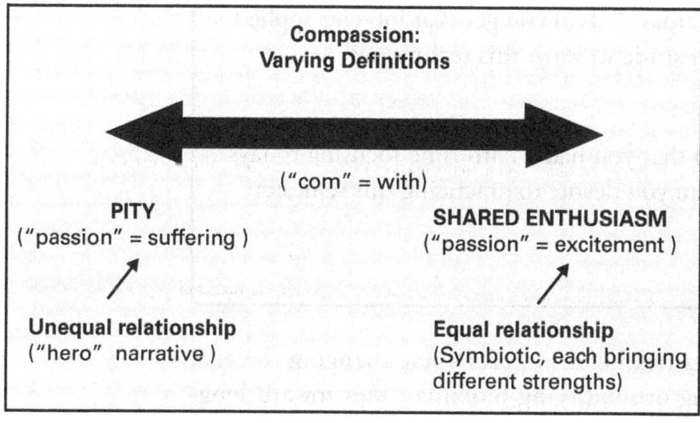

According to Hendricks (2018), compassionate music teaching is not about giving in to students. It is not weakness, nor is it letting students walk all over you. Instead, it involves believing in the highest and best in students, being attuned to students' desires and goals, and communicating in honest and specific ways to help them reach their goals. Compassionate music teaching also involves maintaining healthy and professional boundaries, with music teachers modeling self-care and self-compassion (Hendricks, 2018, pp. 6–8).

Compassionate music teaching is flexible and creative, and involves six capacities:

- *Trust*, which is both relational (person-to-person) and collective (group confidence);
- *Empathy*, or the ability to understand the feelings, needs, and interests of others;
- *Patience*, which involves long-range goal setting, short-term adjustments, and a practice of continued curiosity;
- *Inclusion*, or a radical welcome of a broad range of student identities, experiences, and voices;
- *Community*, or a focus on peer support, a sense of belonging, and collective achievement; and
- *Authentic connection*, or an experience of socio-emotional bonding through music. (Hendricks, 2018, 2021)

Compassionate music teaching involves an interactive, engaging, and democratic process where teachers act as co-learners and exercise curiosity. Activity Box 11.1 contains different types of questions that might be asked in a compassionate music classroom (see discussion question 1).

ACTIVITY BOX 11.1

Try out some compassionate questions

GUIDING

Ex.: "What did you like about that?" "What would you do differently?" "What do you want to improve?"

INSPIRING

Ex.: "What does this song remind you of?" "How would you like to phrase this passage?" "Which instrument do you think would sound good with this?" "What piece would you like to pick from this list?"

CONNECTION

Ex.: "How did your soccer game go yesterday?" "Did you get that job you applied for?" "Would you like to help [a younger student] learn this technique?"

GOAL-CLARIFICATION

Ex.: "Do you like this piece?" "I noticed that you had a hard time focusing today. Is everything okay?" "How much time can you devote to practicing this semester?"

(Adapted from Hendricks, 2018, p. 9)

Compassionate music teaching also involves flexibility in goals—not changing the goal or lowering standards, but instead adjusting or modifying proximal steps toward long-range goals as teachers and students engage together in continual self-assessment and self-reflection (Hendricks, 2018; see discussion question 2).

11.3 Care and Communication

Compassionate music teaching requires acts of care—caring *about*, caring *for*, and caring *with* students (Hendricks, 2023). One can care *about* people by feeling and/or expressing concern for them but not necessarily take action or respond to others' needs. Some ensemble directors might care about the members of their ensemble and work with them toward certain goals but not necessarily consider the individual needs or nuanced personalities that each student brings to the ensemble. Caring *for*, on the other hand, involves "direct attention and response" (Noddings, 2013, p. 11) and signifies a relationship where one individual strives to meet the needs of another.

In a compassionate music teaching relationship, ensemble directors extend beyond caring about and caring for to care *with* students—to engage with them in working toward shared goals that are mutually determined, and to connect with them as collaborators in the music-making and learning process. Looking again at Figure 11.1, caring with students would fall toward the shared-enthusiasm side, where ensemble leaders might engage with students less as directors and more as facilitators of learning. In a space of co-learning and collaboration, ensemble facilitators can guide and support student learning while also promoting brave spaces where students are encouraged to take musical risks, assume various leadership roles, and challenge one another toward positive musical and social transformation (Berg, 2009). To be effective, this kind of caring-with ensemble facilitation requires particular attention to healthy and robust communication practices.

If we are honest with ourselves, most of us find that effective communication can be challenging in certain relationships or situations. Sometimes certain people trigger us or remind us of past situations that were harmful or even abusive in nature—which can make it harder to be open to considering others' perspectives. When this happens, we often react rather than respond, or have emotions that interfere with our ability to stay focused and communicate in a healthy way. Many of us have learned ineffective communication patterns from our caregivers or families. Some of us work with people who are manipulative or just more assertive than we are accustomed to being, and that may cause us to feel disrespected or unheard. This can lead to the breakdown of effective communication and interrupt the possibility of "caring with." In such situations, it might be helpful to learn and implement the nonviolent communication (NVC) practice developed by Rosenberg (2003a) in order to address the structural issues in schools that prevent teachers and students from communicating effectively. NVC consists of a four-step process:

- I state what I observe that does not contribute to my well-being (observing without evaluation or judgment)
- I state how I feel in relation to what I observe
- I state what I need or value that causes these feelings
- I clearly request that which would enrich my life without making a demand (Rosenberg, 2003b, pp. 6–7)

STATE AN OBSERVATION WITHOUT EVALUATION OR JUDGMENT

When we make a judgment or evaluation about a situation or blame someone for doing something in a way we do not agree with, we automatically send the message that the other person is wrong and not entitled to their feelings or values. However, by stating what we observe to be a problem without blaming, judging, or evaluating, we can clarify what we think is problematic without immediately putting the other person on the defensive. Blaming, judging, or evaluating is likely to cause the other person to have a strong emotional response, which could interfere with their ability to receive the communication.

For instance, I could say, "You ruined the performance!" or I could say, "When you missed the entrance at letter C, and it confused those who entered after you and we were not together for about eight bars." The first statement is a judgment and does not effectively communicate the problem. The second is an observation; it is specific, instructive, and does not assign blame. It also sets the stage for the next step: expressing your feelings. See two additional examples of observation versus evaluation in Figure 11.2.

FIGURE 11.2 **Observation vs. evaluation**

Observation vs. Evaluation	
Did anyone notice intonation issues at letter B? Why might this be happening?	Trumpets, you were very sharp at letter B again. How many times do I need to tell you to stop overblowing?
Would you agree that we weren't quite together?	Violins, you have to listen to the basses!

STATE HOW YOU FEEL

When you can communicate your observations to others without judgment, they might be more receptive to listening to how you feel because they are not struggling with their own feelings of defensiveness or rejection. Communicating feelings without blame can also help the other person to empathize with your situation more easily. For example, you could say, "I feel disappointed that you missed your entrance, because it caused other students to get lost when they didn't hear you come in." In this case, you are making it clear that the miscue caused others to make an error—something for which you and the other person will share disappointment. Figure 11.3 offers additional examples for how feelings might be expressed and received, first in judgmental ways, and then as observations.

FIGURE 11.3 **Feelings: judgments and observations**

Clearly expressing how **I am** without blaming or criticizing	Empathically receiving how **you are** without hearing blame or criticism
We didn't get a superior rating at contest because the percussion section screwed up and one of the clarinets squeaked.	You always put the blame on others, maybe we should listen to the recording and see how many times your section messed up!
OR	OR
I am disappointed that we did not get a superior rating at contest.	I understand that you are disappointed in our ensemble's performance.

STATE WHAT YOU NEED OR VALUE

Once you have expressed how you feel, it is very important to express *why* you feel that way. Others may have different value systems or priorities and may therefore not immediately understand why the stated situation is a problem. To help the other person empathize with you more fully, it is important to share your value system or a rationale for your perspective.

For instance, a student could say something like, "I feel upset because that is my favorite section of the piece, and I missed the opportunity to play the beautiful solo line." By communicating their love for the music and love for playing the solo line, they make clear to the other person how their missed entrance impacted them. Perhaps the person who missed the entrance is feeling similarly, in which case they might be able to share feelings of disappointment. In cases where the other person does not feel similarly or has different values or aims, at least you have shared where you are coming from, so they can sense what is important to you.

OFFER A REQUEST

Offering a clear request after communicating observations, feelings, and needs/values can be the beginning of a negotiation process. When you state what it is that you want the other person to do, you don't leave the other guessing as to what you want, and you refrain from using passive-aggressive communication tactics, which are ambiguous and often confusing. For example, rather than saying sarcastically, "Well, that shows how much we've all been paying attention," you might say, "It would help the rest of the ensemble hear how their parts fit if you spent some time at home listening to recordings so you know exactly when to enter." When a direct request is made, the other person can choose to honor your request, ask for further clarification, or refuse your request. In any case, you have been straightforward and respectful throughout the process. You have honored your feelings and asserted what you need.

KEEP EXPECTATIONS REALISTIC

It is not realistic to expect everyone to respond to communication structured in this way, nor is it realistic to expect that everyone will honor your request. Often the other person might return the four steps to you and hope that you will listen to what they observe, feel, value, and request. It is important to listen with the same focus that you would want the other person to give to you. Perhaps when you have heard each other out and have two requests on the table, you may find that each of you can agree to honor the other's request. Sometimes you will find that you cannot and need to continue to work out a solution either that day or sometime in the future.

Nonviolent communication has been found to be an effective tool for de-escalating tensions and helping those on both sides of a difficult situation to understand something about the other's perspective. When practiced regularly, NVC can help to establish a climate of trust, because communication is delivered in a nonjudgmental manner, feelings are owned and expressed without blame, values or perspectives are made transparent so that each person can have the opportunity to understand why the issue is important to the other, and a potential solution is put on the table to begin the process of negotiating. Activity Box 11.2 includes some scenarios in which you might practice the four NVC steps (see discussion question 4).

ACTIVITY BOX 11.2

Practice the four nonviolent communication steps in each of the following scenarios:

You notice that your student has not practiced for a lesson or playing exam.
You notice that a significant number of students leave their personal belongings or trash in the music room.
You learn that one of your students is being bullied by a small group of students in the same ensemble.
A student says, "You suck! I hate your stupid class!"
A student proclaims, "I hate this piece!"

11.4 Connection: It's Why We Do This!

Can you recall when you decided you wanted to be a music teacher? Likely it had to do with some sort of connection you made—to the music, to a music teacher, to friends or family through music, or to something within yourself. When making music with others, there is always an element of unpredictability and surprise, not only because music learning is variable at times, but because human relationships are as well.

When rehearsals become challenging and tensions begin to rise, it may be helpful to keep in mind why and how students fall in love with music and strive to maintain that love by exercising compassion and curiosity, practicing nonviolent communication, and creating spaces where students feel brave enough to take musical risks. Connection will also involve culturally responsive teaching where multiplicity is honored (Ray, Kellum, & Hendricks, chapter 31, this volume), and will thrive in spaces where students develop capabilities for lifelong music making.

Finally, it is imperative for us to create healthier work environments in our communities and to create a culture of wellness within the field of music education (McGrath, Hendricks, & Smith, 2016; Smith, 2021). As ensemble directors, we can practice compassion and care by also practicing *self*-compassion and *self*-care—by being gentle with ourselves, advocating for our needs, and prioritizing our mental and physical health. By modeling self-care in addition to engaging in caring and compassionate practices, we can encourage students to recognize music study not only as a means of connecting to others, but also as a way to connect to their own health and well-being.

11.5 Discussion Questions

1. Reflect upon the compassionate questions in Activity Box 11.1. What other questions could you ask within each category?
2. Think about a difficult musical passage you might rehearse.
   a. What is the long-range goal?
   b. What are some proximal steps to reach that goal?
   c. What are some different scenarios or student needs that require modifications or adaptations to your plan?
   d. How might you modify or adapt certain steps?
3. Describe some ways of caring *for*, *about*, and *with* in an instrumental ensemble setting.
4. Recall an ensemble rehearsal where things got frustrating and/or stressful. Using Activity Box 11.2 as a guide, how might you have practiced nonviolent communication in that situation?
5. What are some ways that enacting compassion might better support student and teacher well-being?

OXFORD learning link

Visit the online resources for additional documentation and exercises to help expand learning and test your knowledge further: www.oup.com/he/powell_music1e.

PEER-ASSISTED LEARNING IN THE INSTRUMENTAL MUSIC ENSEMBLE

Erik Johnson and Christina Herman

This chapter provides an overview of focused approaches to peer-assisted learning, including ways to transform traditional teacher-led ensembles into collaborative spaces for peer-to-peer learning.

12.1 A Tale of Two Classrooms

The music classroom can be a place where students take control of their own learning; however, this is only possible when teachers and students work together to create space for this type of experience. The following vignettes illustrate two types of classroom environments: the first makes limited use of peer interaction, and the second incorporates peer interaction in a responsive, student-centered way.

1. Jayda is sitting in the back row of the music room as her teacher, Mr. Burgess, writes a rhythm on the board. She sinks into her chair, silently willing Mr. Burgess to call on anyone but her as he turns to face his students. "It's not that I can't count rhythms," Jayda mentally reassures herself, "but everyone else seems to get it faster than me." She lets out a sigh of relief as Mr. Burgess says, "Sam, what are the counts for this rhythm?," and the student sitting directly next to her answers correctly. However, Jayda finds herself confused as Mr. Burgess writes in the counts. Not wanting to embarrass herself by asking in front of the class, Jayda leans over to Sam and says, "Why is it counted that way?" Jayda has always been grateful to be seated next to Sam because he likes helping her and never makes fun of her for asking questions. However, before Sam can respond, Mr. Burgess says "Jayda, you are distracting Sam; let's move you to a different row." Reluctantly, Jayda moves to her new seat, silently hoping that another student will help her as Sam did.
2. There is a noticeable air of excitement as students enter Ms. Williams's music classroom. Payton and Jessie are particularly eager to begin class, moving hurriedly toward their seats and encouraging other students to do the same,

remarking, "Hurry! The sooner you sit down, the sooner we can start!" Ms. Williams's instructions are brief, and soon Payton and Jessie launch themselves out of their chairs and toward the other members of their group because they cannot wait to work on their group composition project. This is their third group meeting, and today their task is to add four measures to their group melody. "What if we have it go higher here, since we started lower in the beginning?" says Payton to the rest of the group, and they immediately begin discussing this new idea. Elsewhere the classroom is buzzing with similar conversations as Ms. Williams circulates the room, answering questions, making little suggestions, and listening to students eagerly test out different ideas for their own groups. Before they know it, the students are called back to their seats to complete a reflection activity, and Ms. Williams is pleased to answer a chorus of "When do we get to do this again?"

12.2 Understanding Peer-Assisted Learning

WHAT IS PEER-ASSISTED LEARNING?

Peer-assisted learning (PAL) is an instructional arrangement whereby peers help each other to gain knowledge and skill through active help and support (Topping & Ehly, 2001). Beneficial to collaborative instrumental ensembles, PAL entails individuals sharing knowledge until it becomes a common possession. Different from "show and tell," PAL requires that individuals experience working together in two specific ways. First, individuals must be connected interdependently to feel like they are going to sink or swim together. Collaborative music making is rife with examples of this. For example, playing music together requires performers to trust and depend on the rhythmic and pitch accuracy of one another's performance. Second, individuals foster meaning together in order to collaboratively influence each other. For example, if two students work through solving a musical challenge (e.g., memorizing a piece together, mirroring each other's phrasing, mimicking and influencing each other's articulation style) there are shared meanings created between individuals that are responsive and contextualized to specific challenges and moments.

Learning Explained

Two learning theories help us to understand how PAL aids learning. First, the Zone of Proximal Development (ZPD; Vygotsky, 1978), highlights how two individuals—one a novice and one who is more advanced—collaborate to accomplish a shared task as the more novice individual advances their understanding. Second, a concept known as cognitive conflict—a process wherein students wrestle with concepts that are confusing in an effort to ultimately achieve understanding (Piaget, 1952)—highlights how both novice and more advanced individuals develop through assimilating or accommodating new information into previous understandings.

Let us discuss a few examples. Imagine a situation where a student says, "I like learning and working with people who are better than I am at a specific musical skill. It helps me to see and understand how the music should go." Another student might say, "I like working with my friends who have the same confusion about concepts that I do. It makes me feel less awkward and alone and helps me to know that we are all in this together." These two sentiments and many more are common when teachers give students the chance to learn together. Understanding the ZPD and cognitive conflict helps teachers to understand the learning process of individuals with similar or divergent abilities while working together.

Embracing the Challenge

However, it is not all a walk in the park. Many students after experiencing PAL still feel frustrated in a way that some teachers call a "pooling of ignorance." Sometimes that is exactly what we want as teachers. Allowing students to make confusions known with a peer helps the teacher orient their support. In simple terms, the struggle is real, and it is okay and important for the teacher to cultivate a space where the struggle to learn (Payne, 1998) is part of a healthy educational process. Responsive instruction requires that teachers create spaces where students can reveal and construct their own understandings (Allsup, 2012; Green, 2008). Allowing students the space to become the architects of their own education helps to support a more democratic approach to learning, as opposed to environments that are purely teacher directed (Dewey, 1916). Responsive approaches to teaching can also create space for students to bring their thoughts, feelings, values, and misconceptions to the table in a supported environment.

Mentoring Chains

Mentoring chains help to conceptualize how the PAL process can benefit students as knowledge is shared between more expert and novice students in your classroom and program. As part of a lineage of knowledge and skill, students in instrumental ensembles participate in mentoring chains until knowledge is a common possession. Directing the more experienced students is critical to making mentoring chains work.

Direct approaches to mentoring chains include structuring experiences where roles and outcomes are clear. An adopt-a-student program, where older students spend thirty minutes a week working on specific music-related tasks (e.g., a tenth-grader adopts an eighth-grader), or a collaborative project where students are paired together to compose a short duet, are examples of direct approaches. Indirect approaches may be less obvious but are just as powerful in aiding mentoring chains to take flight. Examples of indirect approaches include seating students who are more advanced closer to less experienced students and jigsawing lesson plans, where learning tasks are broken into three parts and students rotate in short succession between problem-solving groups (e.g., counting rhythms, audiating challenging melodies, learning new fingerings).

Utilizing student aides where advanced students are assigned to work in specific classes can help to also create fuel for mentoring chains and develop the skills of advanced students. For example, if an eighth-grade student who has been playing an instrument for three years is assigned to help the beginning sixth-grade class, the benefit for the more advanced student is revisiting previously learned concepts in a new light. A potential benefit for the younger student is having a near-peer example to encourage them to overcome challenges.

Cultivating mentoring chains requires all members of the learning community to be highlighted (e.g., students in a single class or students across an entire program). Through mentoring chains, everyone has the opportunity to be responsible actively for cultivating a positive, productive learning climate. However, building positive mentoring chains takes time and requires specific attention to reinforce the following socio-emotional learning practices (CASEL, 2003): self-awareness, social awareness, responsible decision making, self-management, and relationship skills.

The general traits of an engaged student working in a mentoring chain remain the same as in any other learning context. The difference is that in the context of learning through mentoring chains, knowledge and skill have a focused vehicle to become visible and take flight the more that they are shared and become a common possession.

IMPLEMENTING PAL IN SECONDARY MUSIC CONTEXTS

Practical considerations for implementing PAL in your instrumental music classroom include student pairing and the scope of projects you will have students complete. In addition to the information discussed under the next heading, please see Section 12.1, "Additional Reading and Resources for Peer-Assisted Learning in the Secondary Music Classroom," on this book's online resources site.

Student Pairing

In general, pairing students who are more similar in ability can help to expose potential misunderstandings, while pairing students who are more divergent in ability can help to inspire and raise the ability of the more novice student (see Table 12.1). However, consider first pairing students who have similar personalities and who are close in age and then gradually introducing pairings that involve students who are further apart in age and ability. Successful beginnings include keeping experiences short (five minutes) and rotating student pairings after two or three experiences.

TABLE 12.1 GROUPING CONSIDERATIONS FOR PAL EXPERIENCES

PAL grouping	Advantages	Special considerations
Student chosen	Social appeal; added fun for students	Potentially low focus on achievement; students feeling left out if not chosen
Ability level	Sense of safety between peers of similar ability; more likely to admit confusion or ask real questions	Some students miss out on teaching or learning from peers of different ability levels; apprehension about assigned partner
Random grouping	Builds group dynamic and camaraderie (especially in short, frequent rotations); good for introducing students to one another	Low focus on achievement and student personalities

SCOPE OF CONCEPTS

When beginning PAL with your students, keep the scope small (focused) when deciding what information you are asking them to learn or rehearse. Consider breaking down the task into three or four specific parts. The more detailed steps they need to follow, the better. Avoid expectations of mastery at the start; the beginnings of PAL can simply be a primer to get the students ready for what you have to offer them when you take back over instruction.

IDEA BOX 12.1

Cooperative to Collaborative: Why Group Work Fails

Many educators and students lament the fact that group work often fails in many ways, both in meeting project goals and with participants not holding up their end of the bargain. Understanding the difference between *cooperative* and *collaborative* learning structures is a great tool for improving the quality of group work. Cooperative learning is typically characterized by a division-of-labor approach whereby individuals take a job and piece it together to form a product at the end of the experience. Collaborative learning scenarios can be elusive, because they require a level of cohesion and buy-in amongst students. Collaborative learning becomes possible when peers work together to directly impact on the outcome in real time. Ideally, student motivation comes from shared interdependence relying upon each other's engagement in the present moment.

12.3 The Process of PAL: How it Works

TEACHER PLANNING: PREPARING FOR TAKEOFF

Quality preparation is key for ensuring a smooth transition from teacher-led instruction to successful PAL sessions. Attempting PAL without a plan will likely result in frustration for all participants involved. Instead, give yourself enough runway (i.e., planning and prep time) to achieve a smooth takeoff. Just as a pilot does not take off without knowing the plane's destination, teachers should plan each PAL session with the end in mind. One of the great benefits of PAL is its flexibility: it can be used on both a small and a large scale. Therefore, teachers can consider guiding questions related to:

- *Format:* How will we balance teacher-led instruction and PAL?
- *Scope:* What is the length and frequency of each PAL session?
- *Materials:* What tools will my students need?
- *Logistics:* How will students be grouped together?
- *Goals:* What should students to gain from this experience?

PAL Possibilities

Given the incredible amount of technology available to students, it is possible for PAL to take place in online and hybrid settings as well as traditional face-to-face classrooms. In fact, PAL is a great way to bolster social interactions and stave off feelings of loneliness that often arise in online classes. Regardless of setting, PAL experiences should focus on achievable tasks that encourage student interaction. *Think, pair, share* is a great strategy for scaffolding student responsibility while also encouraging groups to work collaboratively to complete a task.

IDEA BOX 12.2

Think, pair, share (TPS) is a low-maintenance way to implement PAL (Jellison et al., 2017). In TPS, students think on their own, meet with a partner, and share thoughts and information regarding the task at hand. This strategy can be utilized amongst stand partners, or students can be allowed to move around the room to a partner of their choice, which allows for observation of student interaction prior to beginning a larger PAL unit.

Students Working Together

Peer-to-peer interactions are at the heart of every PAL experience; therefore, teachers should give considerable thought to potential student groupings during the planning process. It is beneficial to experiment with various group sizes depending upon student personalities as well as the task at hand. Additionally, rotating between teacher-selected and student-selected groups is a great way to get a feel for what works with your students. When in doubt, start with pairs of students, rotating the members frequently, and work up to small groups of four to six students during a larger unit. PAL is not a one-size-fits-all approach; in fact, PAL works best when teachers and students have the flexibility and freedom to experiment with different formats and strategies.

STUDENT PREPARATION: TAKEOFF

An important part of getting a PAL unit off of the ground is guiding students through the process of creating procedures, rules, and goals. Teacher-led training sessions vary in scope and sequence; however, they are key to helping students understand the PAL process. Preparation sessions should address such social and logistical aspects of PAL as: respectful dialogue, goal setting, and staying on task. The power for students to customize their own rule system through joint decision making sets PAL apart from group work that students may have experienced in the past.

IDEA BOX 12.3

PAL 101: Sample Student Prep *(3 class sessions, 20-minutes each)*

- Step 1: Teacher selects a mini-goal related to project
- Step 2: Teacher guides student pairs/groups through example PAL session:
    - Students determine goals and rules for interaction with help from prompts:
        - *What are our shared goals?*
        - *How will we ensure that everyone is contributing?*
        - *What will we do if we disagree?*
        - *How will we stay on task?*
    - Students practice interaction with teacher assistance
    - Peers give feedback and reflect on the process
- Step 3: Students repeat Step 2 again without teacher assistance
- Step 4: Final questions and clarifications from student groups before beginning PAL session

KEEP GOING: IN-FLIGHT CONSIDERATIONS

Assessment is a crucial component of PAL that helps all participants gather information and course-correct when necessary. Because PAL is a responsive, student-centered approach to learning, it is to be expected that needs will shift over time as students adjust to learning together. Assessment that takes place "in-flight" during a PAL experience should be low-stakes and involve students giving frequent written and verbal feedback, both about themselves and about their group. Additionally, consider what tools are available to students to help them work through problems that might arise, such as class notes, technology, other peers, and the like. With access to the proper learning tools, students can become more autonomous, critically thinking learners and ultimately build confidence in their own abilities.

WRAP UP: LANDING THE PLANE

Reflection activities are an effective way to make the most of the transition back to teacher-led instruction. This is a pivotal point in the PAL process, similar to trying to catch a connecting flight once your plane has landed. It is crucial to find productive ways for students to frame their struggles (i.e., cognitive conflict) as questions within the teacher-led instructional format—or, in other words, to connect what took place "in flight" during the PAL process to the next leg of their journey. The following exercise is one way of helping students make this connection:

IDEA BOX 12.4

WHAT I FEEL	WHAT I WANT
(struggles/misconceptions)	*(questions for teacher)*
I feel . . .	I want to feel . . .
I am . . .	I want to be . . .
I don't know . . .	I want to know . . .

12.4 How to Structure PAL

INSTRUCTIONAL PROPORTION: TEACHER LED SUPPORTED BY PAL

When students have short PAL episodes, the pace and feel of instruction feels less hurried and gives students the opportunity to build connections with their peers in ways unique to their understanding at specific points in the learning process. With anywhere from 5 to 25 percent of instruction being allotted to PAL, a variety of arrangements can be made to support student learning. Some of the pertinent details that a teacher needs to consider in this arrangement are listed in Table 12.2. Note that peer interactions can be either in the reciprocal or fixed role format and that the role of the teacher is more observational, with leading endpoint group summarization at the end of the PAL experience in this format.

TABLE 12.2 SAMPLE STRUCTURES FOR PAL EXPERIENCES

	Format	Length (In one 50-minute class)	Suggested teacher tools	Peer interactions	Teacher-student interactions	Student goals	Student prep	Student groups
Teacher led	Majority of time spent in *teacher-led instruction* interspersed with **short segments of PAL** work time	1 or 2 PAL sessions lasting **5–10 minutes**	**Worksheets** and **processes** *with clearly defined steps*, common **question prompts** to get conversations started	**Reciprocal** (students trade taking on the teacher role), **fixed role** (one student stays in the teacher role the entire time) *Note*: Fixed role may be more efficient owing to time constraints	**Teacher listens, observes, and summarizes** at the end of PAL cycle	*Short*, **skill-based objectives** set by the teacher	Teacher-led class discussion where *simple guidelines* for **taking turns**, **asking questions**, ways to **identify challenging tasks** are identified by full group.	**Pairs**, *matched* or *divergent* in ability
Half and half	**Even split** between time spent in *teacher-led instruction* and *PAL*	Frequent sessions varying from **5 to 15 minutes** dependent upon teacher and student needs	Short **problems** or **prompts** that support teacher instruction and build over time	Rotate between **reciprocal** or **fixed role** depending on project goals	**Students report out** to teacher after each session; **teacher instruction is highly responsive** to student needs	*Short*, **skill-based objectives** set by students and teacher that build toward **deeper understanding** of a concept	With guidance from teacher-led instruction, students meet in groups to discuss **guidelines for PAL interactions**	**Pairs** or **small groups**, using a *variety of grouping strategies* (chosen by teacher, students, or at random)
Student led	Majority of time spent in *PAL groups* supported by **teacher assistance, as needed**	Students help determine length and frequency of sessions—typically lasting **25–35 minutes**	**Checkpoints** with *clearly defined expectations* to help students stay on track and reflect	**Reciprocal** interactions: students rotate through roles with specific *job descriptions*	**Students guide interactions**, ask for support and additional tools from teacher throughout the PAL cycle	**Clear, measurable, student-determined** short- and long-term goals *set/reviewed at the beginning of each PAL session*	**Previously engaged** in teacher-led PAL sessions; **group meeting** to determine goals and *student roles*	**Pairs**, *matched* or *divergent* in ability, or **small groups** determined with input from *teacher and students*

INSTRUCTIONAL PROPORTION: HALF AND HALF

After students have experience with shorter PAL sessions, balancing instruction with alternating formats where students slowly become responsible for more PAL learning can buoy momentum toward success. Imagine this scenario: students start with five-minute PAL sessions interspersed with five-minute teacher-led instructional interruptions. Interruptions should take the students out of PAL just as they become thirsty and engaged, with the teacher providing feedback at or just above the observed level of performance. If the task stays the same throughout these alternating sessions, students then have the chance to become introduced, revisit concepts after further explanation, and ultimately gain confidence in their ability through repeated practice. Additionally, a half-and-half PAL format is a great way to take students from declarative understandings toward more procedural understandings, especially if the steps needed to accomplish the task remain the same. For example, if students are working to apply a counting system to a challenging excerpt or worksheet, they can start small with limited excerpts and grow to assume more and more responsibility as they become familiar with applying the specific procedural steps to subdividing the rhythm, writing out the counts, and ultimately embodying the knowledge of how to count the rhythms being studied by performing the excerpt(s) with a deeper fundamental understanding of their underlying construction. Again, this approach becomes powerful the more that the teacher is able to focus their instructional efforts in between PAL sessions where students have the chance to learn through trial and error within a supported and scaffolded structure.

INSTRUCTIONAL PROPORTION: PAL SUPPORTED BY TEACHER-LED

Longer student-led PAL sessions should build upon the shorter, teacher-led PAL sessions described above. In this format, anywhere from 50 to 75 percent of instruction is allotted to PAL, with the remainder of class time focused primarily on group discussion and reflection of PAL experiences. Typically this format takes place one or more times during the week and is used for longer-term projects (e.g., group composition, listening projects, etc.). From the teacher standpoint, this format provides a valuable opportunity to see how students may struggle to learn (i.e., cognitive conflict) and to scaffold their growth. Oftentimes the problems and questions that arise in the student-led PAL format are what help clarify and guide future teacher-led instruction. Note that in this format students are part of the decision-making process from start to finish, which includes determining length and frequency of PAL sessions, goals, and increased responsibility to ask for teacher assistance where needed.

12.5 Summary

When approached thoughtfully and with the student experience in mind, PAL can be a fun, effective, and motivating way to engage your students with making meaningful connections with their peers and to develop deeper understanding of content, all at the same time. Music requires collaboration. Music making thrives when students move from a mindset of *individual accuracy* toward one of *collaborative interdependence*. Teaching students to make meaning with their peers around the music that is being studied takes time, willingness, and patience—especially for those who are uncomfortable with relinquishing control of the ensemble-based endeavor. Still, a balance between a teacher sharing what they can to deepen student learning coupled with students being allowed to step into the space where they can take ownership can bring much magic to the whole music-making process. While a balanced approach to secondary music instruction includes both teacher- and student-centered models, allowing students the space to collaborate can also be the necessary ingredient for students to embody a deep love and understanding of music itself.

12.6 Discussion Questions

1. How might PAL be useful to teachers who want to diversify the way that students experience music?
2. Identify some pairing and/or grouping considerations that teachers should be aware of when utilizing PAL?
3. What are some of the challenges that teachers and students might encounter when learning in PAL formats? What can teachers do to reframe challenges into potential positives for students?

OXFORD learning link

Visit the online resources for additional documentation and exercises to help expand learning and test your knowledge further: www.oup.com/he/powell_music1e.

CHAPTER 13

TEACHING INSTRUMENTS TO STUDENTS WITH (DIS)ABILITIES

Kimberly A. McCord

This chapter focuses on strategies for teaching instrumental music in differentiated classes and ensembles.

13.1 Introduction

Special education terms are always evolving to ensure that descriptions used to address certain groups are as positive and accurate as they can be. For example, the now outdated and offensive term "handicapped" dates to the nineteenth century, when people with (dis) abilities stood or sat with cap in hand, begging for money. Of course, it makes sense that no one wants to be thought of as so helpless that they must spend their days begging.

That brings me to inclusion. In the early 1990s teachers were guided to change their word choice from "mainstreaming" to "inclusion." Mainstreaming meant that students who were primarily educated in self-contained special education classrooms were included most often for art, physical education, and music. During this time there was a plethora of research (Downing, 2008; Fox & Ysseldyke, 1997; Kennedy & Horn, 2004; Peterson & Hittie, 2010) that supported the idea of all children receiving the same curriculum in the same classroom. Socially, this was a vital step in children's understanding and having compassion for peers with (dis)abilities. Students with (dis)abilities received the same curriculum, though with accommodations and adaptations, as directed by their most recent Individual Education Plan (IEP).

However, does inclusion mean an accessible curriculum? When we include Rachel in one of the high school choirs, does that ensure that she can fully access the choral curriculum? If Rachel has dyslexia, she may have difficulty reading a choral octavo because of its many parts and words. She perhaps elects to memorize her part and holds the music but does not read it. The choral curriculum is, therefore, not accessible.

Creating an accessible instrumental program has additional challenges. This chapter will address barriers and solutions to accessing instruments, music notation, learning by ear, and performing. I will also suggest you consult professionals in your school building, school district, and community who can help you. The goal is to help students enrolled in instrumental music to meaningfully access curriculum, classes, and ensembles.

13.2 Accessible Instruments

We teach ensembles of musical instruments not only because we love the music our groups create, but because we love musical instruments. We might especially love certain types of instruments, semi-hollow-body electric guitars, vintage vibraphones, or Steinway pianos. Some of us hang instruments on our walls, wear jewelry made from cymbals, or decorate our houses with unplayable instruments that now serve as lamps. I am sure I am describing many of you.

Robert is a twelve-year-old student with a physical (dis)ability that leaves him very weak. He participates in the same courses as his peers with support from special educators, paraprofessionals, and therapists. He uses a wheelchair. He currently sings in one of the high school choirs, but he dreams of playing an instrument. He wants to play drums. One day he stops by the music room after school and asks me if I can help him play a cymbal. He wants his mother to see him playing a cymbal with a drumstick. I tell him of course I can teach him how to play a cymbal, although I'm not sure I know how.

Occupational therapists (OT) are assigned to almost all students in a given school district who have a physical (dis)ability. They are masters at making things that help students access the curriculum. I find the OT assigned to Robert, and she begins by building an arm support that attaches to his wheelchair armrest and is flexible enough to be adjusted to match the height and angle of the cymbal. With this support Robert does not have to lift his arm and keep it up to play the cymbal. We try out the support with Robert and discover that there is another problem or barrier: Robert is too weak to hold a drumstick. The OT tries to create a strap of sorts that supports the stick without his needing to hold the stick. The strap goes around his hand with a pocket that keeps the stick firmly in place. It is still too heavy, though.

That night I go to the local music store in search of the lightest drumstick made. I buy a pair; Robert cannot lift the new stick either and immediately drops his hand with the stick in it. I know he wants to play with a real drumstick, but the OT and I are beginning to think that drumsticks will not work. Later on I run across a recorder cleaning rod. The cleaning rod is a plastic stick that is smaller in diameter than a pencil or chopstick. It works; he can play the cymbal for about ten seconds before he tires. He rests a bit and jumps right back in on the cymbal part until he tires, but at the end of the song I look at him and he is smiling—what the teacher and researcher Markku Kaikkonen calls "The Big Smile" (Kaikkonen, 2016, pp. 10–11). Robert is telling me with his big smile that he is happy; even though he is not playing with a drumstick, and he only plays his part intermittently, he is doing it! Robert has accessed the instrument he wants to play. Six weeks later, Robert's mother attends the concert and sits in the audience where she can see Robert in the percussion section playing the cymbal.

I needed the occupational therapist to help me figure out how to approach Robert's request. She helped, but I also had to puzzle out the problem of an accessible drumstick. It turned out drumsticks were not accessible at all. I had to let go of the idea of drummers playing with sticks, the kind we buy at music stores. Years later I discovered wooden dowel rods at a craft store. They looked more like a drumstick and sounded better too. Dowel rods are also bundled and wrapped and played like drumsticks. With the help of the student's occupational therapist, teachers can create bundled dowel rod sticks that can be customized to weight and length.

Ultimately it was Robert's decision to use whatever stick he wanted to use. I had to let go of the custom of the teacher or the conductor making those decisions, realizing that the teacher should make these decisions in partnership with the student. It is important to honor the way students prefer to play the instrument, even if it is not the accepted way the teacher was taught to play and teach the instrument. Many students with (dis)abilities are unable to articulate why they prefer to play a guitar flat on a table as opposed to the traditional way.

FIGURE 13.1 Walk-up guitar stand

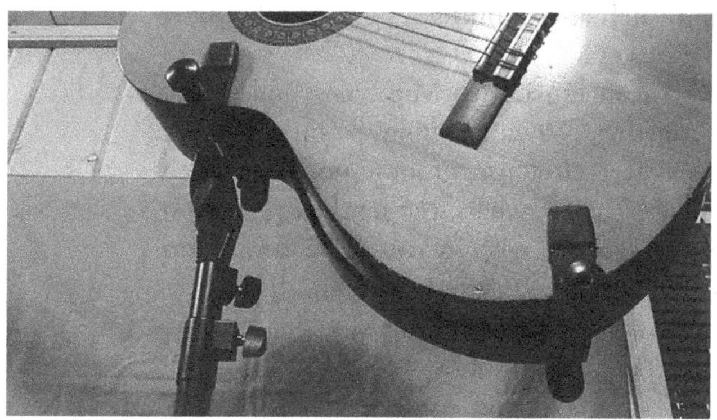

Orienting the guitar to lie flat instead of the traditional way (see Figure 13.1) benefits all sorts of musicians, whether or not they have (dis)abilities. Other students may be embarrassed that their autism makes them sensitive to loud, high frequencies to the point of outbursts and other behaviors. And some students may have chronic illnesses that cause them to be hospitalized or feel sick at school. Missing rehearsals is essential for them but does not negate their passion for performing with their ensemble. The point is, know who the students are with IEPs and 504 plans and trust them to let us know when they need us to develop accommodations and adaptations.

13.3 Accessible Classrooms

As music teachers, we have one of the best jobs. Children want to be musical, they want to play instruments, and they want to sound good. They are motivated when they walk through our doors. We have the opportunity to be facilitators who develop an individual student's musicianship while also developing the ensembles to which they contribute.

Now imagine a child with a (dis)ability. Maybe they have mild cerebral palsy and a slightly unsteady gait. They might try to sit toward the back of the room to avoid your attention because they want to play the trumpet, even if they are not sure they are capable of doing so. They have dreamed of someday playing trumpet and today the dream finally comes true. How do we support and care for this new trumpet player? See the online resources for more on making instruments accessible for students with specific learning (dis)abilities, emotional or behavioral disorders, vision loss, and/or physical or orthopedic (dis)abilities, along with ways to adapt instruments and your teaching.

CREATING A WELCOMING CLASSROOM

A welcoming classroom starts with the teacher. Stand outside your classroom; make eye contact with each student and say hello to them. Get to know each one and remember to ask them about their soccer team, or their trip to Chicago over the Thanksgiving break. If you notice a student who seems upset or down, ask them to come stand next to you for a minute and when no one is within hearing range ask, "Is everything ok?" They do not have to reveal all the details, but if they do admit to being upset, ask them if they need to sit out and cool down before playing today.

Have a spot in your room where a student can sit somewhat away from the others. A beanbag chair doubles as a sensory space for students with autism. Some teachers provide a clipboard with a worksheet asking some general questions the students can answer if they feel comfortable such as, "I feel ________________ because ________________."
This gives you the opportunity to be empathetic and recognize that students experience

very upsetting incidents at school, even if they seem minor to us. You might be missing your only cellist for the rehearsal, but attending to the student as a person first helps their well-being and might prevent them acting out, such as beginning a fight or sobbing in front of their peers.

Practice compassion and kindness with all your musicians. Music ensembles are a community, and a strong community works together. When teaching, be mindful that, in some instances, students with (dis)abilities may feel self-conscious or respond negatively if they feel singled out or patronized—not only by their teachers, but by their peers, too. Research has found that having a (dis)ability is associated with increased "victimization, assisting, and defending behavior" (Malecki et al., 2020), and students with (dis)abilities have been found to experience nearly double the rate of bullying of non-disabled students (Bear et al., 2015: Eisenberg et al., 2015; Janssen et al., 2004; Robinson & Espelage, 2012). In addition, eliminate problematic and outdated phrases and words such as "insane," "handicapped," "special," and "wheelchair-bound" from communication within your community of musicians. Instead, say "person with a (mental health/physical) disability."

Assume that students with invisible (dis)abilities might not be out to their peers. Some people hide their (dis)abilities if they can, and we should be careful not to reveal them unless they give permission. Students with visible (dis)abilities need respect and appropriate support too. Their peers probably know they have a (dis)ability but might not understand it. For example, physical (dis)abilities can sometimes be particularly difficult because of the many physical barriers at school and the obvious difference in appearance or ability.

Talk to your students with (dis)abilities. Ask them when peers are out of earshot whether it is okay if you help with adaptations and accommodations. Let them know it is a joint decision and that they have veto power. Ask the student what they want to play and whether they anticipate any barriers to playing that instrument. Ask them if they have ideas for ways to remove the barrier. Often they have researched and thought about this and can offer good ideas that might work better than others.

13.3 Keeping Everyone in Our Classes and Ensembles

In a 1997 study of middle school band students and the use of computer-assisted theory instruction to increase the ability of poor music notation readers to read music at the same level, students with specified learning (dis)abilities were the only students who did not show any improvement in music reading. In addition, most students with disabilities did not continue band the following year (McCord, 1997). This was a red flag to me and my colleagues who participated in this study. We discussed whether we could do anything to keep these students in our programs.

The biggest change we made was reassessing the way we taught and becoming more student centered and flexible. Our students began to describe us as "nice." Nice meant one or more of many different things: accessible, available, flexible, caring, playful, and welcoming, as well as listening to the thoughts and requests of our students and doing what we could to make their efforts to play an instrument successful—for example, learning American Sign Language well enough for us to converse about music and other interests of our students with hearing loss who use ASL. Many of us also became more aware of students with ADHD and the need to do something different with our long rehearsals, which became frustrating for those who required more breaks. We offered alternate seats to move between, seat cushions that swivel, one-legged stools, and seat cushions with small bumps on them that provide just enough stimulation to help with focus.

Mostly, we worked on the "nice" descriptor. We kept extra pencils in cups all around the room for those who needed them, we created recordings of individual parts for practice purposes, and we learned everyone's names and used them. When you know your students' names, it indicates that you care about them. We find reasons to call home whenever we can to let parents know about what their child is doing that is *right* instead of wrong. It could even be something as small as remembering to play the last note softly on one of the pieces. It may seem insignificant, but it can change the climate of the entire family.

I look for art and photographs of musicians with (dis)abilities playing instruments to display in my classroom. It's a powerful thing to see oneself in an image that has been chosen as a representation of great musicianship. My best images are those of my former students. Ask for permission and get them printed in poster size. I like to also ask for quotes from the musician on the poster, along with their name and dates.

Most of these things are easy and inexpensive. Feature your musicians with (dis)abilities and celebrate their contributions. Imagine this scenario: Scott is a football commentator at the high school games and has become quite good at describing the action. Scott does not have friends, though, and often sits by himself at lunch. He used to play in band but switched out of the class at the beginning of the semester. How about asking Scott to emcee your next concert? This could honor his strengths and give him a community to which he might feel he belongs.

Many music teachers who take their groups to competitions worry that having students with (dis)abilities in their groups could ultimately lower the ensemble's scores. Competitions can be stressful for all musicians; however, if you feel it is a beneficial event for your students to experience, then it is a beneficial event for *all* your students. Work with your special educators to find ways to prepare individuals for what to expect and make a consistent effort to describe the upcoming contest as an opportunity to perform in a new environment and share music with others.

TEACHING AND USING TRADITIONAL MUSIC NOTATION

Reading music notation is a major barrier to musicians with certain types of learning (dis)abilities, intellectual (dis)abilities, and vision loss. All these groups of musicians appreciate flexibility in finding the least frustrating way to learn music. Sometimes colored overlays reduce glare and help notation be more readable. Dorico notation software offers some excellent ways to adapt notation for struggling musicians. There are many ways to customize music within the software to make reading much easier for the musician. Braille music notation is a good tool for notating music; however, it is difficult to play most instruments and read the music with one hand.

FIGURENOTES

An excellent research-based music notation system is Figurenotes©, invented at the Resonarri Special Music Centre in Helsinki, Finland. The music is notated using colors for pitch and shapes for octaves and is very intuitive and readable. It relies on stickers on the instrument that match what the musician sees in the music. Drake Music Scotland sells Figurenotes software and stickers and provides simple online training. Dorico can also print in Figurenotes colors.

PLAYING BY EAR

Many musicians prefer to learn by ear and use their own ways of remembering music. Provide recordings of the music you are rehearsing to help with learning by ear. Make sure the recordings are in the same key and use the same arrangement. If either of these elements are different, be sure to let the student know where the recording is different and what to expect instead.

BRAILLE MUSIC NOTATION

Dancing Dots is an excellent resource for AT and training to learn and use Braille music. The Library of Congress also holds a large collection of music in Braille, including scores of major symphonies. Most of the devices at Dancing Dots require training for the teacher and student. Fortunately, the same law that pays for the equipment also pays for training if it is written on the IEP.

CUSTOMIZING MUSIC NOTATION

It is always best to ask the student about their own preferred way to learn music. For example, if they learn by writing the names under the notes in their music, guide them to write the names alongside the note head so they see the name and associate it with how it looks in the music. Dorico and Figurenotes can be customized to print the name of the note inside the note head. Wonderful musicians with flourishing careers are on record sharing their personal struggles with learning to read music, including the singer-songwriter Paul McCartney, the jazz drummer Tony Williams, and the composers Irving Berlin and Danny Elfman.

FINGERING CHARTS

Some students also have trouble with visual perception or spatial skills. Traditional fingering charts are difficult to decode because they don't look like the instrument does in the students' hands. You might notice them turning the instrument around to make it look like the orientation of the fingering chart. Taking pictures of chords from the perspective of the instrument in the hands of the player helps make guitar chords make sense for the first time.

13.4 Summary

The responsibility for all students to be able to access the curriculum rests on the teacher. This does not mean that the teacher must know everything about adapting for the student. Ask for help from professionals in your school and outside of school. Use available devices and instruments that can be classified as assistive technology. If these devices are written into a student's IEP, the school receives federal funding to purchase the device and provide training if needed. Always remember, your best resource is the student. The student should be the first person you consult.

Federal law mandates that all children have the right to a free and appropriate education in the least restrictive environment (which means removing barriers and making learning individualized). Music teachers cannot, for example, use auditions as a barrier to keep students with (dis)abilities out of ensembles and classes. The audition should be accessible and fair to students who do not sight-read music well due to their (dis)ability. Students have the right to experience instrumental music in meaningful and accessible ensembles, classes, and lessons. All students should be welcomed and allowed to participate in trips and contests. Understanding how to adapt and prepare students for such events is important and can be assisted by the special educator and his or her team. Awards are not always the goal: rewards such as the "big smile" or the joy of playing music with others are a different type of success. Being part of a community that values all musicians and their contributions is an award that all can celebrate.

13.5 Discussion Questions

1. Do you remember having students in your music classes who required accommodations? Describe your memories of those students. Then imagine how you would have accommodated them if you had been their teacher.
2. How could you turn your classroom into a Welcoming Classroom? Consider all possibilities of students who might enter your classroom and any barriers that exist, such as furniture, student musicians who might bully, instruments, ability to see or attend to a conductor or leader, and inability to read traditional music and learn in traditional ways.
3. As you prepare to teach students with (dis)abilities, create a checklist to help guide you through the process of working with students. Include who you will reach out to, what laws you need to consider, and a list of possible accommodations and considerations, always checking with the students themselves.
4. Describe ways to make music notation more accessible for students with different (dis)abilities.

OXFORD learning link

Visit the online resources for additional documentation and exercises to help expand learning and test your knowledge further: www.oup.com/he/powell_music1e.

CHAPTER 14

TEACHING FOR SOCIAL IMPACT THROUGH FLUIDITY IN THE TWENTY-FIRST-CENTURY INSTRUMENTAL ENSEMBLE

William L. Lake, Jr.

This chapter presents a framework for teaching in the twenty-first-century instrumental ensemble centered around fluid musicianship and social relevance.

Fixation is the way to death. Fluidity is the way to live.
(—Miyamoto Musashi, Japanese philosopher)

14.1 Introduction

At the time of writing this chapter, it is the twenty-first year of the twenty-first century. The world is in the middle of one of the deadliest pandemics in recorded history. According to Johns Hopkins University's *Coronavirus Report* (2021), the United States of America alone accounts for more than 1 out of every 6.5 deaths globally. In the spring of 2020 public and private schools at all levels hastily transitioned to virtual teaching, fears of an airborne disease on everyone's mind. In the world of music education, band, orchestra, choir, and general music rooms went silent as virtual music making became the standard for large-ensemble music experiences through the aid of digital audio workstations (DAWs) and prerecorded, socially distanced performances.

While there are few, if any, substitutes for live performance, remote learning forced curricula to stumble, trip, and nosedive finally into twenty-first-century modalities with some measure of success. Across the country, the educational experience was sustained with lectures by guest composers, performers, and other specialists through videoconferencing. Instrumental ensembles presented live or premiere recordings using various multisensory mixed media presentations creating new ideas for performance practice (Dale, 2021). It will be realized, in hindsight, that it took an entire pandemic to add these elements to the student experience, although these resources were accessible years if not decades prior.

Concurrently, 2020 was wrought with social unrest as racial inequity continued to plague American society. The murders of George Floyd and Breonna Taylor, among many others, sparked the most significant civil rights protest movement in the country's history, fueled by isolation mandates and viral consumption of the sights and sounds of a nation at odds with each other on social media and television (Buchanan et al., 2020). The nine-minute-and-thirty-second video of George Floyd's murder prompted a mass wave of allyship by America's cultural and industrial leaders, including the education sector. Institutions posted black squares and drafted solidarity statements in corporate and educational spaces announcing their commitment to action against systemic inequities. The collision of these two social phenomena will mark American society in ways unparalleled since the terrorist attacks of September 11, 2001.

These major societal influences are occurring during a period when the United States is experiencing the slowest population growth since the Great Depression (Mackun et al., 2021). This demographic change will herald low school enrollment in the coming decades at all levels. Students entering the education system will be more diverse than ever before, with the US Census reporting an 8.6 percent decrease in the white, non-Hispanic population, the largest since 2010 (Census Bureau, 2021). In summation, the field of education is experiencing difficult times—a pandemic, cultural unrest that reverberates through schoolhouse walls, and declining enrollment, all of which will require reimagining the future of the education system.

14.2 After the Caesura

As instrumental music education and performance emerge from this period of caesura, the field must confront five crucial questions that will affect sustainability in this unfamiliar and rapidly changing social landscape. These questions position music education to truly consider a student-centered curriculum that meets the demands of the twenty-first-century musician: What are we teaching? What aren't we teaching? Who are we teaching? Who aren't we reaching? Why are we teaching?

In Pamela Pike's 2015 article, "The Ninth Semester: Preparing Undergraduates to Function as Professional Musicians in the 21st Century," she writes:

> *In addition to the requisite synthesis of musical skills, [the twenty-first-century musician] must understand their strengths and weaknesses, know about types of jobs in the music industry, think creatively about acquiring musical work, and set realistic short and long-term career goals. (p. 2)*

She further adds ten categories to these areas of focus as provided by Michael Hannan in "Expanding the Skill Set" (2012), including: performance skills, stagecraft skills, aural recognition skills, notational skills, theoretical knowledge, compositional skills, technology skills (music specific), other technology skills (multimedia, web design, etc.), business skills, and generic skills (communication, creativity, etc.). Although Hannan's list of skills might appear exhaustive, it is negligent not to include intracultural skills, social awareness, and cultural (musical) fluidity as necessary competencies in today's market. Twenty-first-century musicians are required (if they desire a steady stream of income) to be familiar with, perform, and embrace various musical styles authentically while engaging with a wide variety of audiences and consumers.

American music education curricula center on Western European musical traditions at the expense of the many diverse styles of US-born musical traditions (Whitehead, 2021). Until recently, and by no means in equal representation, music genres of other cultures found room in artistic programming in professional and educational spheres.

It is possible for students and audiences never to encounter non-white composers and non-European derivative cultural expressions in entire matriculation cycles and concert seasons. Widening the musical lens through the performance of a diverse array of music and ensemble configurations within the larger instrumental groups (band and orchestra) will provide opportunities for education and build on often forsaken musical skills (see Chapters 15–16 and 48–54).

Students who identify as Black, Indigenous, or a person of color are the largest demographic of public-school-aged students in the United States (National Center for Education Statistics, 2020). Thus, instrumental music education and performance in the twenty-first century must reflect the myriad of global cultures that students will encounter musically and socially. Gay (2010) underlines culturally responsive teaching as validating, comprehensive, multidimensional, empowering, transformative, and emancipatory (see Figure 14.1).

FIGURE 14.1 Culturally responsive teaching graphic, adapted from Gay, *Theory, Research, and Practice* (2010, Teachers College Press)

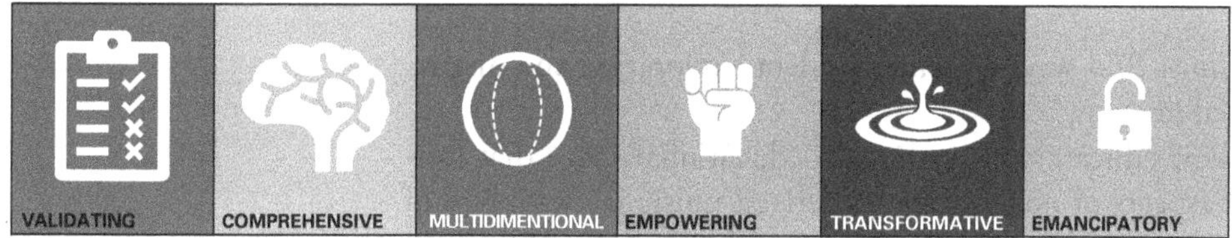

When programming reflects diverse cultural identities, students, professionals, and audiences will find a sense of belonging and ownership as their varied cultural identities are presented and promulgated through championed performance. Expanding the intracultural and intersectional character of music education experiences benefits all students as they navigate an ever more interconnected world and empowers them to seek new knowledge and understanding individually.

In settings where one engages with cultures outside of their identity, the musical experience provides a window artistically, and human interaction with authentic stories and narratives (Garoutte and McCarthy-Gilmore, 2014). The cultural capital acquired from immersive and broad musical experiences yields mobility and fluidity in students' career pursuits. Twenty-first-century musicians can navigate various cultural idiosyncrasies with fluency, understanding, compassion, and appreciation.

14.3 Fluidity: The Path Forward

The education profession has embraced two terms that are becoming standard pedagogical vocabulary and practice: *cultural responsiveness* and *cultural relevance.* These terms, though often used interchangeably, are very different. Furthermore, the ability to respond is often predicated on the level of sensitivity the responding entity has to that stimulus.

On the other hand, relevance can only be measured by social impact over time (see Chapter 39). Thus, the two terms are a sequential process. First, instrumental music educators must respond to the cultural musical identities of their students through interest, inquiry, and appreciation. When this occurs over an extended time, with frequent space and presence within the instructional experience, the student's cultural identity becomes relevant in the classroom environment.

The educational television show *Sesame Street* asks an important question: "Who are the people in your neighborhood?" Do we know who our students are? Do we know the unique cultural traditions, rituals, and ceremonies that define our community? It is easy to assume a biased position that our school performance organizations are the sole providers of music expression in a community. This is not true. Music exists outside of the walls of our educational institutions without any need for engagement from educational institutions (Gay, 2010). Creating relationships between the community and academic spaces is forged in trust, appreciation, and dialogue. Lind and McKoy, in *Culturally Responsive Teaching in Music Education* (2016), write:

> *Culturally responsive teaching acknowledges the value of the cultural heritages of differing groups both in terms of curriculum content and in terms of these respective cultural legacies influence students' attitudes, dispositions, and ways of learning. Because culturally responsive teaching incorporates information from a wide variety of cultural resources and materials for instructional use in all subject and skill areas in school, learners recognize that their culturally specific ways of knowing are appreciated, valued, and worthy of attention and exploration in the formal curriculum. (p.18)*

Twenty-first-century educators must find ways to center student exploration and discovery in the classroom to gain social impact.

Expanding curricula will allow educators to provide an educational space that mirrors society. One of the unique aspects of non-European-derived music is ownership of the performer through improvisation, composition, and aural acquisition of performance practice. Though there is evidence of this in European-influenced curricula, engaging with the musical practices of other American genres and music traditions worldwide opens many unique possibilities. The presentation of music solely as a notated art form centers written conventions over aurally promulgated genres. Presenting written music as the only means of musical knowledge acquisition creates a need for a knowledge bearer (teacher) to guide the learning process, removing the individual agency of the musician, in part, until some level of literacy is achieved. Many musical traditions outside of these genres position leadership within the performer musician or the ensemble. Individual or group exploration independent of a musical leader or in proxy (a written score) creates space for ear-based learning. This experience not only strengthens audiation in aural traditions but enhances individualized musicianship overall (Mills & McPherson, 2006). Unfortunately, owing to scheduling restraints, lack of resources, and training, these modalities are rarely experienced either in the classroom or in in pre-professional experiences (McNeil, 2021).

Teaching with the evolving responsibility to nourish the twenty-first-century music student isn't easy. The primary difficulty is that college curricula are outdated and very slow to change. After the challenges of the last year and a half, the sustainability of arts programs is more critical than ever as institutions work to reintegrate themselves into their communities. Music is a cultural expression; thus, the relevance of musical institutions will depend on their ability to make a lasting impression on patrons and stakeholders in the residential area. The "continuum of impact" framework authored by the Animating

Democracy program of the organization Americans for the Arts provides a measurable framework within which to formulate, implement, and assess the relevance of classrooms and institutions. The organization writes:

> *[Twenty-first-century artists and art] reflect society. Attuned to the social, political, and cultural currents of their time, [diverse arts experience reveals] untold stories and embodies and heralds the issues of the time. Artists' work enters the public consciousness and public discourse. Artists and cultural organizations are increasingly playing a more deliberate role in making social change. Beyond reflection:* The Arts Engage. The Arts Animate. The Arts Influence.

Adopting a social impact mission in curricular reform immediately expands the scope and outcomes of music education experiences available to students. Depending on geographic location and other intersectional identifiers, music education should look uniquely different from state to state and even from region to region.

The continuum of impact framework comprises six measurable outcomes: knowledge, discourse, attitudes, capacity, action, and conditions (see Figure 14.2).

FIGURE 14.2 **Continuum of impact graphic**

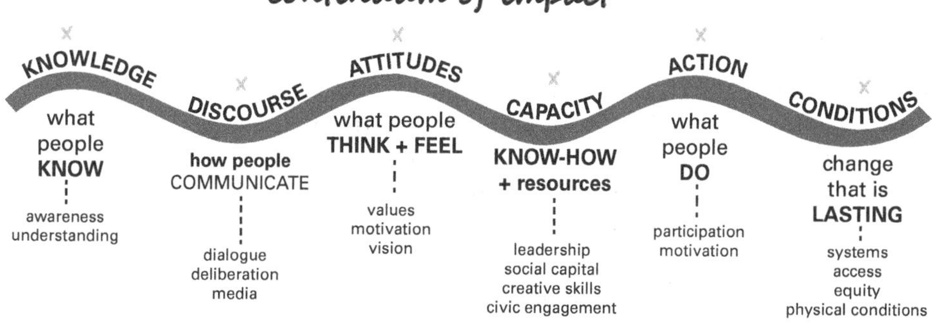

Source: Continuum of Impact Guide | Animating Democracy. (2017). Retrieved December 3, 2021, from https://animatingdemocracy.org/continuum-impact-guide.

Twenty-first-century instrumental music pedagogy that embraces these ideals will find growth in relationships with students (they will invest their committed energy into the program), the entire school community (they will advocate for the program), and a broad array of stakeholders (they will fund the program) who are interested in investing and supporting the program (see Figure 14.3).

The first outcome, knowledge, relates to a communal advancement in a specific issue or opportunity (e.g., global warming, gender equity, civil rights, hunger, homelessness, etc.). As an instrumental music educator, providing opportunities for repertoire and performances to extend to social issues and points of interest extends the stage to the audience—and thereby outside the concert hall. Pre- or post-concert talks, intentional social media engagement, and space for partnerships with activist organizations and special interest groups extend the audience experience beyond the mere existence of an active listener. For musical knowledge, opportunities to expand the audience's musical understanding can be achieved through instrument petting zoos,

FIGURE 14.3 **Continuum of impact outcomes for instrumental music education indicators**

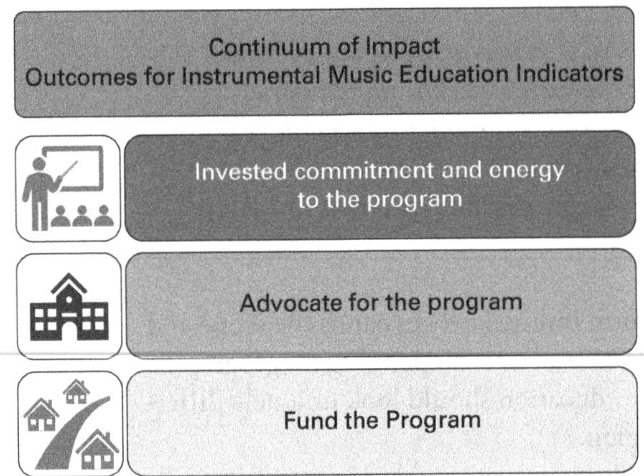

virtual program notes, and real-time motivic form presentations for solo, chamber, and large-ensemble settings. Involving students both in the research of material presented and the actual dissemination of those findings is a beautiful way to share this responsibility.

Providing a space for discourse is the second tenet of the continuum of impact. Now more than ever, society needs opportunities to wrestle with topics of debate. Art—specifically, music—allows such exploration as audiences and musicians dialogue face to face (safely) and share multiple views. More important than the subject presented, audiences and performers learn the art of listening, conversation, and discovering new truths unimagined. Storytelling has a lot of power; it provides space for unheard voices to be championed and allows audiences to experience various phenomena through different people. An example of a concert that would create such a space for discourse is included in Figure 14.4.

This concert, Peace & Love, was the first concert of the Crane Concert Band after two years of not performing in person together due to the COVID-19 pandemic. The concert was curated to allow students and the Crane School of Music Community to reflect on the last two years' events in celebration, lament, and hope.

This powerful concert could be augmented with the audience submitting videos of their thoughts of American patriotism, memorials for those who lost their lives in the COVID-19 pandemic, or testimonials of hope for our society as we move forward through social unrest and a health crisis. These submissions could be curated as a series of montages throughout the concert from diverse perspectives. A panel discussion could serve as a post-concert event involving civic organizations to respond to the many different representations of nationalism presented in the music. Visual artists could be solicited to create a pre-concert queue to personify the various works featured on the concert as the audience enters the concert hall.

One of the ever-present goals for engagement in music as a student, performer, or audience member is the hope that the experience will have a lasting effect on everyone involved. Changes in attitudes are signs of social impact on a personal level. When making the case for music and music education, the transformative power of music mentally, socially, and emotionally underlines many requests for funding, support, and inclusion in curriculum. If one were to inquire of those engaging with the musical experience as performer and audience, "How has the musical experience impacted their behaviors, attitudes, and dispositions?" what would be their response? For the audience, one might

FIGURE 14.4 Crane Concert Band Peace & Love Concert poster

consider inviting real-time and post-concert commentary while watching the performance to provide a way to engage with the often silent participant in the concert experience.

One of the most prominent criticisms of the American music education program is its elitist and often exclusionary history (Elpus & Abril, 2011). The fourth tenet of the continuum of impact framework—capacity—addresses how multiple people interact with the artistic mission of the curriculum or institution. Who is and who isn't drawn into the curriculum is an essential question that will reveal the capacity of the organization to expand both to those within its walls and beyond. As pedagogical and curricular reform advances toward equity (correcting the imbalance of Eurocentric ideals) and, ultimately, equality (a curriculum that centers all cultural expressions and competence), music education will move beyond being a space of exclusion to a haven of belonging for all students. The intentional efforts to advance knowledge (from diverse purveyors) create space for discourse and debate and, in doing so, will draw the surrounding musical ecosystem to seek the instrumental program as a source of interest. Capacity also refers to the amount of agency that participants find within the curriculum and performance experiences to create, perform, and make decisions within the artistic experience. The fifth tenet of the framework inspires action: "Does one's audience decline, sustain, or grow in attendance?" "Is the level of engagement increasing?" These questions evaluate whether or not the impact of the musical center (school program or professional) is expanding beyond the institution's walls.

Lastly, if all of the previous benchmarks are achieved with measurable success and growth, the actions taken within the organization will lead to lasting change outside of the organization. It is possible that an artistic position could lead to lasting change. This should be the goal of all art. At some level, continued experiences lead to changes in political and social norms, advancement of sensibilities, and the inspiration for entrepreneurial and independent expressions.

The road ahead for instrumental music in the twenty-first century will look very different from the road behind. Students have changed, teachers have changed, and communities are looking for stimulating sources of change. There is no more pressing means for sustainability than a renewed focus on how the arts bring people together to feel, listen, emote, and communicate. Curricula that have room for each of these integral human experiences will thrive even through the unknowns of the future. It is the job of the twenty-first-century music educator to be an inspiring facilitator of this growth and a champion for the entire community. The future of music and music education is being rewritten as we charge ahead. Our ability to adapt and to be relative, relevant, and fluid will be the secret to music education's survival.

14.4 Discussion Questions

1. How have the COVID-19 pandemic and the social justice movement impacted your teaching philosophy?
2. Using the continuum of impact as a guide, create a concert experience that has elements before, during, and after to fulfill all of the tenets of the continuum.
3. Research a musical genre that is unfamiliar to you. Consider how you will introduce this music to your current or future students. Identify critical areas that you will need to become familiar with and plan how to teach this music to your students. Remember to involve your students in building the context for the music you study and eventually perform.
   Then . . . *do it*!

OXFORD
learning link

Visit the online resources for additional documentation and exercises to help expand learning and test your knowledge further: www.oup.com/he/powell_music1e.

CHAPTER 15

APPLICATIONS OF ARRANGING AND TRANSCRIBING FOR ENSEMBLES

Herbert Marshall

This chapter explores arranging and transcription, skills many music educators use to create learning experiences tailor-made for their students in terms of developmental ability, interest, and cultural relevance. In addition, the process of transcribing and arranging reinforces essential skills and knowledge such as audiation, notation, range, intonation tendencies, blend, balance, transposition, and learner-centered instruction.

15.1 Introduction

As you near the end of your studies in instrumental music education, one of the best ways to aggregate the many skills and understandings you have developed is to transcribe and arrange music for instrumental ensembles. In your pedagogy classes (woodwinds, brass, strings, and percussion), you have learned much about these instruments, but you may not have had opportunities to focus on them as unique choirs with specific tone qualities, technical challenges, and intonation tendencies. Further, the technical challenges of each instrument in different ranges become apparent when you write, rehearse, and perform chamber ensemble music for these choirs. Finally, culturally responsive teaching means sharing content with your students that is relevant to their lives, including content that might be culturally significant to them as well as content that helps to open a window on a culture of interest. Because no school library, state repertoire list, or publisher can know your students as you do, the way to best diversify their musical curricula is for you to arrange pieces uniquely suited to their needs. In this chapter I will take you through some of those processes.

15.2 Terminology

Because the way we conceive of these terms varies with the context, the way that I will be using creativity terminology is as follows:

- Arranging: using familiar (audiated or written) musical ideas in a new way
- Composition: any new musical ideas, written down or recorded
- Improvisation: creating and performing music in the moment with some parameters as to meter, tonality, harmonic or rhythmic function, style, length, and so forth
- Orchestration: arranging that takes specific instrumental qualities into consideration, such as range, tone quality, harmonics and overtones, technical demands, and so forth
- Secondary instrument: several of the activities call for secondary instruments, which includes all band and string instruments that are not your primary instrument as well as the vast array of vernacular instruments (keyboard, guitar, digital), classroom instruments (hand drum, glockenspiel, boomwhacker, recorder) and non-Western instruments
- Transcribing: capturing sounds aurally that are audiated, in the environment, or shared live or via electronic means

15.3 Making Time for Creativity

When we engage in original thinking and music making or facilitate this process with our students, we are working toward one of the central reasons the performing arts are in schools: to create. Music pedagogues have described the parallels between language learning and music learning (Gordon, 2012; Suzuki, 2018). The analogy follows that speaking extemporaneously is like solo improvisation and carrying on a conversation is two- (or more) part improvisation. Reading someone else's speech may involve performance skills and interpretation, but it does not engage the upper levels of learning in the New Bloom's Taxonomy the way that creativity does, in which the highest process includes "Create, Generate, Plan, and Produce" (Hannah, 2007, p. 10). For teachers and students alike, creativity matters.

In their article introducing a seven-step instructional model, Robinson, Bell, & Pogonowski report that "personal encounters with musical processes—improvisation, composition, and performance—cultivate students' deeper conceptual understandings and musical independence" (2011, p. 50). The authors list dispositions that help us be creative teachers:

1. To teach creatively, one must be creative.
2. Teachers must ask open-ended questions that stimulate thinking.
3. Music educators must function within the culture of their classroom as the "guide on the side" rather than the "sage on the stage."
4. Much care must be taken to establish a safe and nurturing environment (p. 51).

These prerequisites apply to the instrumental methods class, modeled by the college instructor, as well as to the P–12 classroom, embodied by the educator.

In a study with undergraduate and graduate students taking instrumentation and orchestration and choral arranging, McConville (2015) applied Resnick's description of kindergarten students' creativity as a model for inspiring creativity in collegiate arrangers. Resnick's "creative thinking spiral" describes this process as "imagine, create, play, share, reflect, imagine" (p. 3). College students used Noteflight technology for their creating and sharing and blogging for their reflecting. This proved to be, for them an effective model to facilitate creativity.

15.4 Improvising, Arranging, and Orchestrating at the College Level

Given the importance of creativity and the necessity of nurturing beginning steps in this direction, I will provide a layered approach. First, we will follow the wisdom of Duke Ellington: "If it sounds good, it's good music" (Ellington, 1973, p. 455). Thus, any music that piques your interest, that inspires you, and that you can share thoughtfully and respectfully is appropriate for arranging and transcribing projects. If you are borrowing from a culture that is not your own, then you and your students should research the piece to provide historical and cultural context. When possible, consult with a culture bearer for authenticity. I will be providing folk and vernacular examples, but you should use what inspires you and lends itself well to instrumental writing. Likewise, I will be basing my examples around melodic and harmonic tunes, but complex rhythmic structures and spoken-word rhythms are excellent ideas to explore.

Gordon's research (2012) suggests that musicians vary in their aptitude for tonal and rhythmic audiation. As you begin to transcribe, audiate, and create, you may notice that some ideas come easier than others. For instance, some musicians hear harmonies and chord progressions more readily, while others gravitate first to complementary rhythms and subdivisions. That is fine. Knowing yourself as a musician and a composer is an essential part of being an effective music educator. Collaborating with a peer who has complementary strengths may be a great way to approach these activities.

ONE-PART IMPROVISING AND ARRANGING

Create a variation on a melody, perhaps adding rhythmic variations and melodic ornamentations or altering the fundamental musical structure by changing to a different meter or mode. Choose a familiar tune for which you can audiate the harmonic changes or the accompanying rhythms. Improvise on that tune with a secondary instrument and record your favorite ideas. By using a secondary instrument, you reinforce your skills on more instruments and experience the activity like a less technically proficient player. The fewer pitches you know, the more like a beginner you become and the more purposeful you are about repertoire, key, and tempo. Transcribe your improvisation.

TWO-PART IMPROVISING, ARRANGING, AND ORCHESTRATING

Create a two-part texture using a familiar melody. This could be a tune with a chord roots (just the roots of the harmonic structure), a melody with a rhythmic or melodic ostinato, or a melodic duet. Improvise on any of the parts to create an embellished line, like a bass line with passing tones or added rhythmic figures. Share this with a peer and play your arrangement on secondary instruments. As you create, there are many decisions to make. Do not trust any published harmonizations you find; rather, use your own musical taste and revise if needed. Given known parameters of range, balance, blend, and technique, orchestrate your piece using instruments that can achieve the effect you desire. Consider the instruments and performers and what you know about developmentally appropriate practice for these players. Consult a comprehensive guide for transpositions, ranges, and pitch tendencies, such as *The Technique of Orchestration* (Kennan & Grantham, 2002) or *Contemporary Orchestration: A Practical Guide to Instruments, Ensembles, and Musicians* (Miller, 2015).

In Figure 15.1, the tune "New Britain," by an anonymous composer from 1829, is used. The tune became more famous when it was used to set the hymn "Amazing Grace," written by John Newton.

FIGURE 15.1 Extract from "New Britain"

THREE-PART IMPROVISING, ARRANGING, AND ORCHESTRATING

A round, such as "Shalom Chavarim," provides opportunities to learn the melody and tonality: play it as a round and then add accompaniment or harmony parts as an arrangement. The round can be played with the suggested starting points designated with the + sign (see Figure 15.2).

FIGURE 15.2 Extract from "Shalom Chavarim"

Next, you might try a simple, elemental approach with a drone or bordun that reinforces the modal quality of this piece (see Figure 15.3). If your elementary colleagues use an Orff approach to general music, then your students are already familiar with the sound of drones and borduns to provide simple accompaniment. The work of Goodkin (2002) and Cribari and Layton (2019) may provide insights into elemental style and help you meet your students where they are.

FIGURE 15.3 Extract from "Shalom Chavarim" demonstrating elemental approach

A piece like this, with its simple harmonic structure and repetitive rhythmic patterns, lends itself well to melodic variations. I happen to hear this piece in Aeolian mode, but if you hear it in harmonic minor, you would make those adjustments to fit your audiation. Creative musicians naturally noodle with the melody to make it their own. The second (bordun) line can feel like a harmony part or like an alternative melody that provides additional harmonic and rhythmic interest. You could also improvise a second melody that sounds like a counter-melody or a descant. Take turns being the person on the main melody, the alternative melody, and the chord roots. It can be a test of a young player's independence and fortitude to maintain the pulse and style of the main melody while an alternative melody weaves in and out. For a deeper dive into the improvisational aspects of this process, consider the research and materials of Christopher Azzara. His article "An Aural Approach to Improvisation" (1999) may be a good starting point.

When you make orchestration decisions, consider the balance and range of the first two parts. Consider also the plight of bass-clef instruments, always relegated to slow-moving bass lines parked on tonic and dominant. What would it sound like to pass the melody throughout the three parts so that the low voices play melodic material (see Figure 15.4)? What might the treble instruments learn by listening "down" to a melody in the bass voices and having to blend and balance with it?

FOUR-PART IMPROVISING, ARRANGING, AND ORCHESTRATING

A familiar four-part texture might be an active melody, a simple bass line, and a harmonized inner part, such as that often played on rhythm guitar. To add complexity, we might put this melody in triple meter with a secondary dominant. If the melody is familiar, however, and you can audiate the chord progression, the other parts should fall into place. In Figure 15.5 I included chords to show how I audiate this tune. This is somewhat subjective. The way we audiate familiar tunes depends on many factors, particularly a tune such as this, which I sang hundreds of times before I ever saw notation. If you prefer a different harmonic progression, then make this tune your own.

Because the melody is so active, the bass line can be less so, primarily reinforcing the root and the fifth and adding some passing tones (see Figure 15.6).

FIGURE 15.4 Extract from "Shalom Chavarim" demonstrating the melody being passed around all parts

Andante

5

FIGURE 15.5 Extract from "Over the River and Through the Wood"

For the inner parts, choose a rhythm pattern that provides additional rhythmic interest and fills in the remaining pitches of the harmonies (see Figure 15.7). Use your knowledge of common-practice part writing to guide you in doublings and voice leading. Use your instrumental pedagogy to consider range, technique, and intonation considerations for the orchestration. Perhaps a pattern like this complements the melody well.

FIGURE 15.6 Extract from "Over the River and Through the Wood" demonstrating bass line

FIGURE 15.7 Extract from "Over the River and Through the Wood" with different rhythmic pattern

In using this process, I am trying to connect with literature and concepts you may know as well as honoring the culture, genre, and style of this tune. You may break these rules whenever there are good musical, pedagogical, and artistic reasons to do so, particularly when you are exploring music of other time periods and cultures. For this Western folk song, when you combine those different elements you arrive at something like the example in Figure 15.8.

15.5 Transcribing at the College Level

When transcribing, your prodigious aural skills are brought to bear, as well as your knowledge of theory and musical styles to predict what is likely to be the structure and intent of the piece you are transcribing. Choose your environment and tools wisely. It takes many hearings of a piece to capture it accurately. I need a melodic instrument and a chordal instrument by my side so that I can try to replicate what I have just heard. A good sound system, comfortable furniture, and a quiet space are all beneficial.

One of the exciting things about transcribing is that you can capture pieces that no one has seen in notation yet. In terms of relevance, these may be works that are current and thus will be immediate touchstones to contemporary culture. However, you might also capture sounds from an international radio station, a YouTube video that inspires you, or a video game theme. Choose something that is worth your time and effort. The more you work at transcription, the better you will become—it's sort of addictive. For our purposes, I am going to follow through with notating the transcription, but of course, you could just make a lead sheet with brief notations and try performing tunes for your friends.

One decision to make is whether to pursue a literal transcription or an "inspired by" type of transcription. In terms of vernacular music, you might choose a literal transcription, or cover, of a popular piece, notating it as faithfully as possible. When transcribing for students at school, they typically want the piece to be as close to the original as possible, so a literal transcription is often a good choice. However, you may choose to create

FIGURE 15.8 "Over the River and Through the Wood" full example

your own take on a piece, in the style of "Postmodern Jukebox," "Pomplamoose," or "The Roots" on *The Tonight Show Starring Jimmy Fallon*. Their musical interpretations of pop hits—often featuring the original artists—are a great example of this kind of transcription and arrangement. Once a hit becomes popular and familiar, it may be a good candidate for an interpretation or parody, as the audience members can hear the original inspiration behind your arrangement and are comparing your version to the original. This is an audiation game that we play with P–12 students all the time, and it is fascinating to see it gain such a following in the wider culture.

Consider the aforementioned process for arranging, in which we considered texture and kept adding complexity and depth by adding more voices. We will follow a similar process for transcription. You may transcribe as many or as few of the voices as you can discern and notate. There may be instruments that use unique or nontraditional notation, like harp or theremin. Some non-Western instruments use an alternative notation system, such as gamelan ensembles. This is an opportunity for you to learn both a new notation system and how to communicate with those players. Texture is vertical, as notated. Think about limiting your transcription by restricting it horizontally as well, as in time. Perhaps plan to transcribe one complete thought, such as a verse or chorus, a complete statement of a melody, or the most impactful part of the piece. In this way you can transcribe an excerpt that stands on its own while at the same time being able always to return to the project and complete another section.

ORDER OF TRANSCRIPTION WITH CHECKPOINTS

With my students, I ask them to choose literal or inspirational transcriptions so that I can make informed feedback. I suggest that they go through the process in this order and send me periodic drafts so that I can help guide the process. Before we start, I ask them to consider transcribing directly in the same key as the original, then transpose later if needed. Also, I suggest that our guitar colleagues are always the first people to share lead sheets for popular music; you can find these on various websites. Because this is available to us, it is a timesaver to use this harmonic analysis as a starting point, but with a critical ear, changing anything that may be inaccurate or unmusical.

1. Capture the melody and add harmonic analysis in the form of chord symbols (letter name chords are best, but I–V7–I will work); if the melody has words, add a lyrics line and capture the words gradually as you can, because they may help guide the transcription.
2. Add the bass line, or whatever functions as the lowest voice, comparing this to the harmonic analysis.
3. Add other melodic lines, such as harmony lines that are somewhat homorhythmic with the melody, variations on the melody, descants, and countermelodies.
4. Add any other pitched rhythmic parts, such as a rhythm guitar, comping keyboard, or other lines that reinforce the harmony and add rhythmic interest; continue to compare these to the harmonic analysis to make sure there is consonance when intended and dissonance when intended.
5. Add the non-pitched rhythmic part(s), such as all the membrane and idiophone instruments, body percussion, and so forth, noticing how these complement the melody and pitched rhythmic parts to create a complex rhythmic texture.
6. Add anything else not included thus far and continue to edit until you are satisfied.

Figure 15.9 shows a typical pop tune accompaniment, inspired by Bruno Mars's "Count On Me."

FIGURE 15.9 Extract inspired by Bruno Mars's "Count On Me"

P–12 STUDENT APPLICATIONS

Virtually everything you have been exploring up to this point can be passed on to your P–12 students. As stated earlier, if you enjoy this process of playing by ear, capturing sounds from your environment, replicating current music that resonates with you, and recalling familiar pieces and making them your own, then this may be a gift you want to pass along to your younger students. The more excited about this you can be and the better you can model the process, the more likely it is that you will be successful in guiding learners through these activities.

You might consider a backward design model to guide you (Wiggins & McTighe, 2005). If you want a chamber program in your high school in which quartets or quintets transcribe a piece to play on a chamber concert, then that is the curricular goal. Those pieces will have advanced meters, rhythms, harmonies, and techniques and may be five to seven minutes in length. This chamber project will involve transcribing, improvising, arranging, orchestrating, rehearsing, editing, and performing. It can be a culminating project for your experienced students in grades 11 and 12.

If that is the goal for grades 11 and 12, then what sorts of understandings and skills will they need to be developing in grades 9 and 10? Perhaps similar musical goals, but within sections, so that there is only one timbre? With that in mind, what sorts of understandings and skills are required of your middle school students so that they have the necessary readiness? Thus, it follows that your beginners are probably learning to play by ear, capturing songs they hear from social media and video games, and arranging simple duets with a stand partner. Think of the potential for actual creativity, artistry, and individualized achievement when your beginners improvise their own variations on relevant, engaging tunes. Consider what you can learn about their skills and what they can teach themselves in the process. One of my favorite years with beginners was the year I had a fourth-grade trombone group who all had tickets to a minor-league hockey team with a live pep band. Every Monday they came to school with a new pop or funk tune that they had heard at the hockey game and had started learning by ear. Although half of them couldn't reach seventh position, they were developing valuable skills that would serve them well in the future.

COPYRIGHT CONSIDERATIONS

Newly composed music is the gold standard for creative activity. It showcases your students' creativity and musicianship and demonstrates that living composers walk among us. Many states now have statewide showcases for young composers in recognition of the importance of this process. While public domain music is a constantly moving target, this too is a safe category for arranging, improvising, orchestrating, and transcribing. Determining what is in the public domain, and therefore free to use, is complicated. The copyright protections expire every year for a new group of pieces, making them available to use. This chart from Cornell University may help: https://copyright.cornell.edu/publicdomain

For current vernacular music and many works composed in the past hundred years, most music educators will strive to meet the conditions of fair use. Fair use in education includes research and analysis of works in the classroom. If you are purchasing recordings but then rote learning pieces with the recording or even transcribing sections of a piece to analyze in class, that would appear to be a fair academic use of copyrighted material. If, on the other hand, you are transcribing entire pieces and publishing an arrangement or performing the work in a commercial way (including a pep band being broadcast on local television during an athletic event), then you may be infringing on the copyright owner's ability to profit from their creative work. NAfME has a wealth of resources on this topic and may be the best place for you to start to research this topic. https://nafme.org/my-classroom/copyright/#MainResources

15.6 Create!

1. Turn to the second half of any beginning string or band book you know and pick a tune you like. Write variations on the tune that include changing the meter, mode, or rhythms, and add ornaments, bass lines, or a descant.
2. Choose a current pop song, video game theme, or snippet of a film score that appeals to you. Transcribe a few phrases of the melody and any other lines you can decipher. Try out your transcription with a peer to see how accurate you are.
3. Pick your most challenging secondary instrument. Arrange a classical or Broadway theme for a duet or trio setting that you could perform with a little practice.

4. Select a folk or patriotic piece that you foresee programming in a school setting for chamber or full ensemble—one that upper elementary students could sing or play on recorder. As a recruiting activity, arrange the piece for a standard high school chamber ensemble to accompany the elementary students playing or singing the melody. Consider reinforcing the melody somewhat, but make sure that the younger students have the spotlight in your arrangement.

OXFORD learning link

Visit the online resources for additional documentation and exercises to help expand learning and test your knowledge further: www.oup.com/he/powell_music1e.

CHAPTER 16

INSTRUMENTAL SUBSTITUTIONS: RESCORING FOR SMALL BANDS AND LIMITED INSTRUMENTATION

Quincy C. Hilliard

This chapter explores alternative ways to rescore for those band programs that are struggling with unusual or small instrumentation. The author's aim is to show which instruments are most suitable when rescoring parts for your ensemble.

16.1 Introduction

Declining enrollment, lack of funding, class load requirements, extracurricular activities, and after-school jobs have all had a tremendous effect on the size of large band programs. Small programs are fast becoming the rule rather than the exception. Additionally, a program that depends largely upon its feeder schools might not have much control over its size or instrumentation from year to year. These problems, along with others, have hurt the school band program, making ideal instrumentation difficult to achieve.

As a director, you must work with the instrumentation you have and try to provide the students with a successful learning experience. If you have a problem with limited or unbalanced instrumentation, it can cause enormous balance problems when trying to perform many of the selections for today's concert band.

There are several solutions to this problem. They will require both a small amount of time devoted to rewriting parts and some creative imagination on the part of the director. For example, let's examine the following brass section: ten trumpets, one French horn, one baritone, two trombones, and one tuba.

A major problem with this instrumentation is that there are not enough low brass to balance the large upper brass section; and of course, like all high school bands, it is made up of amateur musicians. Also, the trumpets will overbalance the section when playing *f* or *ff.* Here is the solution: move one trumpet to horn, one trumpet to treble-clef baritone, one trumpet to trombone, and one trumpet to tuba. Thus, the instrumentation will look like this:

6 trumpets
2 horns
2 baritones
3 trombones
2 tubas

First move—Trumpet to horn: rewrite the horn part for B♭ trumpet. If you have an extra baritone, move the trumpet player to baritone and have the student sit next to the horn player and play the second horn part on the baritone. If you do not have an extra baritone, transpose the part to B♭ trumpet and have the trumpet read the part with a bucket mute at all times. The use of the mute will take the edge off the trumpet's tone quality and give the instrument a dark tone close to that of the horn.

Second move—Trumpet to treble-clef baritone: simple!

Third move—Trumpet to third trombone: for the first solution, provide the student with a valve trombone; transpose the part as if it were for treble-clef baritone (a ninth—octave and a step—up). The student will be able to read the music on the valve trombone with the same fingering as the trumpet. As part of the second solution, transpose the third trombone part to treble-clef baritone and provide the student with a baritone. The student will then be able to read the third trombone (now treble-clef third trombone) as though it were a treble-clef baritone part.

Fourth move—Trumpet to tuba: to avoid making the student read a new clef, transpose the tuba part to B♭ by moving up two octaves and a step. Now the part will be in treble clef like the trumpet part, and all of the fingerings will be the same as on the trumpet. The student only has to make an adjustment to the sound of each pitch, which can occur within two to four hours of scale practice.

As a director with a small band or unbalanced instrumentation, it will be to your advantage to have a couple of valve trombones and three or four baritones in storage. Many of the low brass parts for horn, baritone, trombone, and tuba can be covered by switching trumpet players. A director should be aware of the following ideas when selecting music for an unbalanced or limited instrumentation:

1. Music selection is critical. Finding the right music for your group requires that you examine a vast amount of literature each year. Make a list of possible pieces each year, and over a period of three to four years you will have a large collection of music from which to choose. Make notes on the instrumental challenges presented by each piece on the list; for example, maybe a piece is low brass–heavy or has an exposed horn part or a solo oboe. This way you can have a running cheat sheet on instrumentation of the piece.
2. The director must know the transposition of each instrument as well as the characteristic tone quality in each of its different registers. Also, an effort should be made to make each substitution match the original color scored by the composer.
3. Be realistic; you have to work with what you have and do the best you can with it.

The purpose of this chapter is to examine what instruments can be substituted or used for doubling weak sections with regard to range and tone color (Note: in all cases, only one or two instruments can be substituted in doubling a weak section; in addition, the instrumental substitutions are listed in order of preference.)

16.2 Flute

The ideal tone quality of this instrument is one that is bright and crisp in the upper register, dark and mysterious in the low register. In the upper register, for a fast staccato passage, the flute can be doubled with the xylophone as written or an octave lower (see Figure 16.1). In the upper register, a slow or fast lyrical passage should be doubled with the bells. If the passage in the flute is similar in range to the one as shown in Figure 16.1, it can be scored for one or two clarinets to play when it occurs in the music (see Figure 16.2). The instrumental substitutions for the flute are listed in Figure 16.3.

FIGURE 16.1 **Fast staccato passage with xylophone doubling flute**

FIGURE 16.2 **Clarinet doubling flute in same register**

FIGURE 16.3 **Instrumental substitutions for the flute**

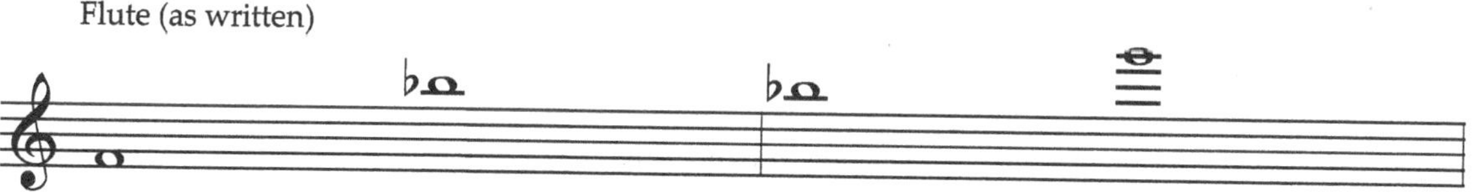

1. B♭ Clarinet
2. Bells (legato passages)
3. Xylophone (marcato passages)

1. Xylophone (marcato passages)
2. Bells (legato passages, use soft mallets)

16.3 Oboe

The oboe usually doubles the flute or clarinet; thus, no significant material is missed when the part is omitted. If there is an important part, it can be played by the clarinet, trumpet (with straight mute), or alto sax (see Figure 16.4). The trumpet (with mute) is more suitable for the light, playful passages, whereas the slower, more lyrical passages are suitable for the clarinet and alto saxophone.

FIGURE 16.4 **Instrumental substitutions for the oboe**

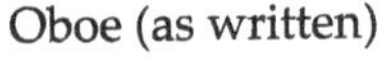

1. B♭ Clarinet (lyrical passages)
2. B♭ Trumpet (playful passages)
3. B♭ Soprano Saxophone

1. E♭ Alto Saxophone (lyrical passages)

16.4 B♭ Clarinet

This instrument has three distinct registers. The upper register is bright, the middle register is warm, and the lower register is dark and full. Instrumental substitutions are listed in Figure 16.5.

FIGURE 16.5 **Instrumental substitutions for B♭ clarinet**

16.5 E♭ Alto Clarinet

In recent years this instrument has become obsolete in the concert band. The part is often omitted and carries no significant weight. In some of the older selections, where the part is important, it is usually doubled with the baritone and tenor sax (see Figure 16.6).

FIGURE 16.6 **E♭ Alto Clarinet part doubled with the baritone and tenor sax**

1. Baritone (1 player only)

1. B♭ Tenor Saxophone (muted or covering over bell)

16.6 B♭ Bass Clarinet

This instrument is very important in creating a balanced woodwind section. Often a band will have thirteen clarinets and one bass clarinet. As a rule, there should be one bass clarinet for every three or four Bb soprano clarinets in the band. The instrumental substitution for the ranges is shown in Figure 16.7.

FIGURE 16.7 **Instrumental substitution ranges for B♭ bass clarinet'**

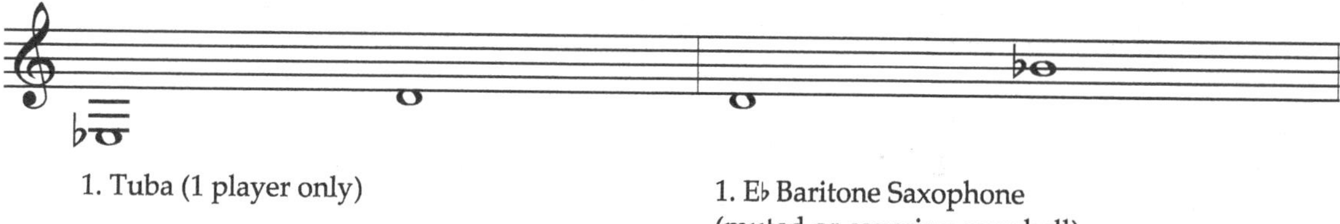

16.7 E♭ Contralto Clarinet and B♭ Contrabass Clarinets

These instruments serve as the tuba of the woodwind section. Many directors neglect their importance in creating a solid foundation for the woodwind section and for the band as a whole.

As a rule, there should be at least one contralto or contrabass clarinet for every two to four bass clarinets in the band. The instrumental substitutions for the range are shown in Figure 16.8 and Figure 16.9.

FIGURE 16.8 **Instrumental substitutions for E♭ Contralto Clarinet**

FIGURE 16.9 **Instrumental substitutions for B♭ Contralto Clarinet**

16.8 Bassoon

The bassoon has a unique sound in the woodwind section. Many of the orchestral transcriptions and most of the grade four and five literature will have roles or important parts written for the bassoon. The instrumental substitution for the range is shown in Figure 16.10.

FIGURE 16.10 **Instrumental substitutions for bassoon**

1. B♭ Bass Clarinet
2. E♭ Alto Clarinet
3. E♭ Contralto Clarinet

1. Baritone (1 player only)
2. B♭ Tenor Saxophone (muted or covering over bell)
3. E♭ Baritone Saxophone (muted or covering over bell)

16.9 E♭ Alto Saxophone

In recent years this instrument has become the most popular one in the band. The alto saxophone can cause many intonation and balance problems for the band when played or used incorrectly. Recently, it has been used to double the horn line. Most solos for the alto saxophone are cued for the trumpet as a suitable substitute. The instrument substitution for the range is shown in Figure 16.11.

FIGURE 16.11 **Instrumental substitutions for E♭ Alto Saxophone**

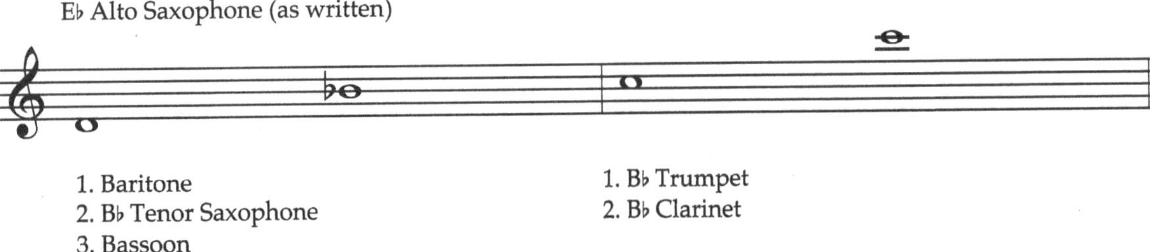

1. Baritone
2. B♭ Tenor Saxophone
3. Bassoon

1. B♭ Trumpet
2. B♭ Clarinet

16.10 B♭ Tenor Saxophone

The tenor saxophone is usually doubled with the baritone or trombone line. In some instances it can be used to reinforce the clarinets in their low register. A good example of this type of doubling can be observed in most march trios, where the clarinets play the melody in the low register. The instrumental substitution for the range is shown in Figure 16.12.

FIGURE 16.12 Instrumental substitutions for B♭ Tenor Saxophone

B♭ Tenor Saxophone (as written)

1. B♭ Bass Clarinet
2. E♭ Alto Clarinet

1. E♭ Baritone Saxophone
2. Baritone
3. Trombone

1. B♭ Trumpet
2. F Horn

16.11 E♭ Baritone Saxophone

The baritone saxophone is another bass voice in the woodwind section. Often it is played too loudly by young students, creating problems of balance and intonation.

The color is dark in the lower register and nasally harsh in the upper register. The instrumental substitution for the ranges is shown in Figure 16.13.

FIGURE 16.13 Instrumental substitutions for E♭ Baritone Saxophone

E♭ Baritone Saxophone (as written)

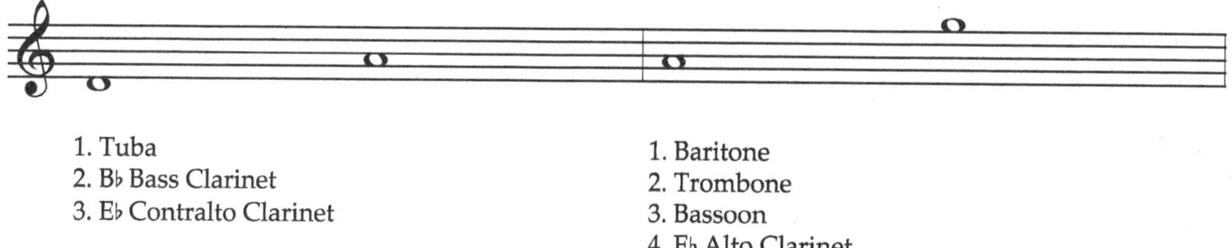

1. Tuba
2. B♭ Bass Clarinet
3. E♭ Contralto Clarinet

1. Baritone
2. Trombone
3. Bassoon
4. E♭ Alto Clarinet

16.12 B♭ Trumpet

The trumpet is one of the strongest instruments in the band, with a clear, penetrating tone quality. This instrument can be used to switch students to other brass instruments or to treble-clef baritone so as to cover trombone and horn parts. The instrumental substitution for the range is shown in Figure 16.14.

FIGURE 16.14 Instrumental substitution for B♭ trumpet

B♭ Trumpet (as written)

1. E♭ Alto Saxophone (muted or covering over bell)

16.13 F Horn

The horn is one of the most important instruments for the band. It is the *only* instrument that blends with both the woodwind and brass sections. The tone of this instrument is full and warm in all registers. Often the alto saxophone is doubled with horn. When this is done, the saxophones must play one dynamic level softer in a supporting role, being careful to never overbalance the horns.

In substitution or doubling, it will aid the blend if the saxophone uses a mute or some type of covering over the bell to produce a dark sound without any edge. The instrumental substitutions are shown in Figure 16.15.

FIGURE 16.15 **Instrumental substitutions for F horn**

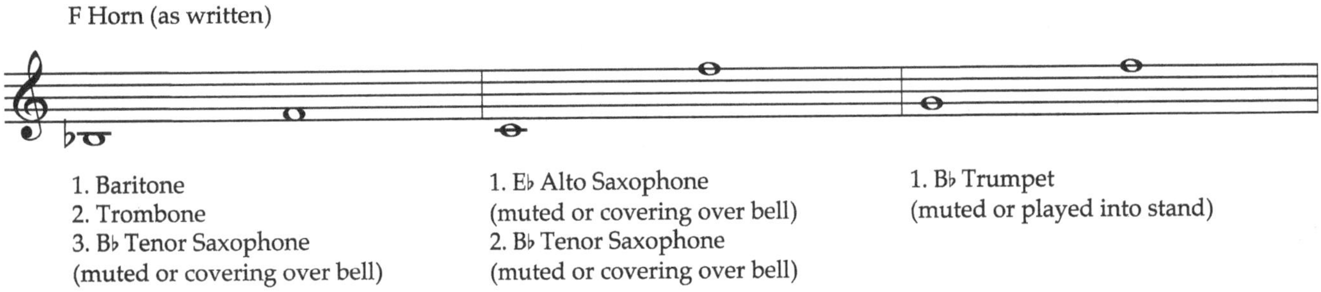

16.14 Trombone

The trombone is the heart of any brass section. It is used mostly for harmonic scoring to produce a solid chord structure in which the melody will be played by the upper instruments of the band. The tone quality is dark in the deepest register and triumphant in the upper register. If you have a small trombone section (one or two players), the parts can often be doubled with a baritone in bass clef or in treble clef (the latter transposed up an octave and a step). The importance of this instrument cannot be overemphasized in cases where the scoring calls for it to produce a solid chordal background. The instrumental substitutions are shown in Figure 16.16.

FIGURE 16.16 **Instrumental substitutions for trombone**

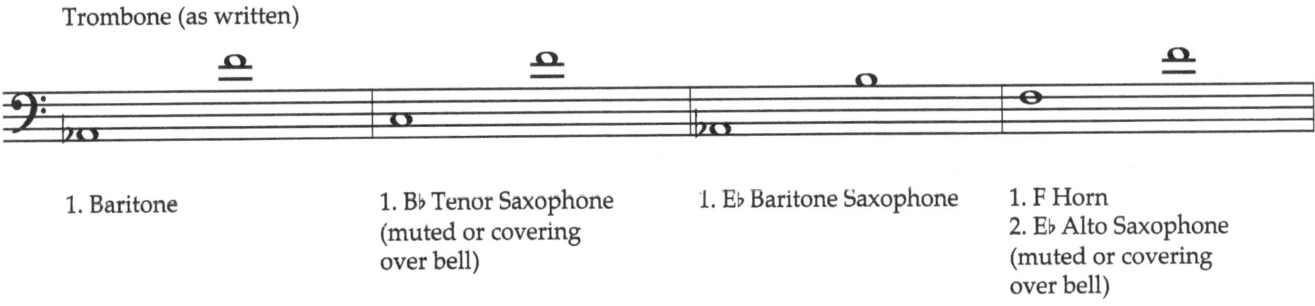

16.15 Baritone

The baritone is another important member of the low brass section and is known primarily for its solo and melodic capabilities. The instrument can be used in both bass and treble clef, thus making it possible to cover trombone parts in bass clef.

Parts for the trombone can be transposed to treble-clef baritone, and trumpet players can be used to cover the part on baritone. The instrumental substitutions are shown in Figure 16.17.

FIGURE 16.17 Instrumental substitutions for baritone

Baritone (as written)

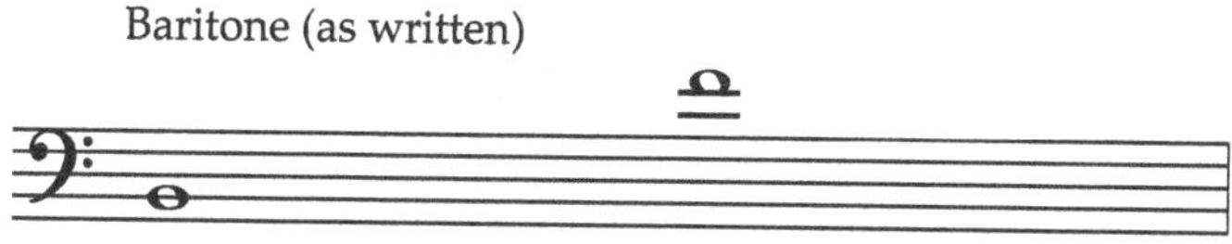

1. Trombone
2. B♭ Tenor Saxophone (muted or covering over bell)
3. B♭ Bass Clarinet (in chord structures only)

16.16 Tuba

The tuba is the foundation of the band. It is valued for its strength and beauty in playing low notes. The tuba is eminently useful for doubling (an octave lower) the baritones and trombones, the group to which it belongs. These qualities also make it a fairly flexible instrument. In extreme cases, an electric bass may be substituted to play the bass line. Another idea is to use an electric keyboard but as a low synth to emulate the bass line. Care should be taken to control the volume of this instrument. The instrumental substitutions are shown in Figure 16.18.

FIGURE 16.18 Instrumental substitutions for tuba

Tuba (as written)

1. E♭ Contralto or B♭ Contrabass Clarinet
2. Electric Bass or Keyboard
3. String Bass

1. E♭ Baritone Saxophone
2. B♭ Bass Clarinet
3. String Bass

Many of the substitutions mentioned here will capture the color that the composer intended. As a composer, I have no objection to a director's rescoring parts of my music to adapt it to a particular situation. In fact, I admire a director who uses their skills to adapt his or her instrumentation to the compositional requirements of a piece. As stated earlier, many directors do not have control over their feeder system; I am sure that if they did, many of their instrumentation problems would not exist. Listed below are some quick and easy solutions to doubling in weak situations.

- *Weak clarinets in the middle to low register or weak third clarinets*: Use one or two alto saxophones on the part or one tenor saxophone in the lower register, *always* muted or with a covering over the bell.
- *No contralto or contrabass clarinets*: Score important lines for one baritone saxophone or one tuba, depending on the range.
- *No bassoon*: Rescore important lines for the baritone horn or tenor saxophone (muted or with a covering over the bell).
- *Weak third trumpets*: Rescore part for one or two alto saxophones (mute or with a covering over the bell).
- *Weak horns*: Rescore important parts for one or two alto saxophones (muted or with a covering over the bell) one dynamic level lower. A trumpet (with a bucket mute) or a baritone can also be substituted.
- *Weak trombones or baritone*: Transpose the part to treble clef and have it played by a trumpet player switched to baritone. The part can also be doubled by the tenor saxophone or baritone saxophone.
- *No tuba*: In extreme cases use an electric bass keyboard, but be careful of the volume!

When the alto, tenor, or baritone saxophone is rescored to be doubled with other instruments, the saxophone should be muted or have some type of covering placed over the bell to muffle or darken the instrument's bright tone. In addition to using a covering, a different mouthpiece (one with an open lay) can also be used to darken the saxophone's tone quality.

The ideas in this chapter should give the director new direction in coping with the problem of unbalanced instrumentation. Always keep in mind that selecting music and trying to match the original color are the most important elements.

16.17 Discussion Questions

1. What are some of the benefits of rescoring instrument parts to achieve a better balance?
2. What are some of the considerations to keep in mind when engaging with instrumental substitutions?
3. What are some factors that are important when selecting music for unbalanced or limited instrumentation?

OXFORD learning link

Visit the online resources for additional documentation and exercises to help expand learning and test your knowledge further: www.oup.com/he/powell_music1e.

CHAPTER 17

ADVOCATING FOR THE ARTS: WHAT EVERY FUTURE MUSIC EDUCATOR SHOULD KNOW

John L. Benham and Stephen J. Benham

This chapter provides strategies and approaches to music advocacy, emphasizing the role of the music coalition (politics), the music profession (unity), and budget analysis (reverse economics) in saving, restoring, and building music programs.

17.1 Introduction

Formal music education in public schools in the United States was established in the early nineteenth century. Lowell Mason was one of the first advocates of formal music education in public schools. His efforts led to the adoption in 1838 of music education as a curricular subject in Boston. The first national professional association for music education––the Music Supervisors National Conference––was established in 1907. It is now known as NAfME, the National Association for Music Education.

Historically, music advocates have emphasized the cultural value of music and the expectation that a well-educated individual should have knowledge of the arts. In the late twentieth century several factors arose threatening the existence of music education in the public schools. Among these were educational reforms such as block scheduling, magnet or charter schools, tax voucher systems, the school-to-work movement, school choice (open enrollment), and STEM. Often these reforms were implemented by new administrative teams intending to demonstrate innovative leadership as agents of change. Such efforts were adopted with promises for success but were not accompanied by a clear set of goals or a system of assessment.

Financial crises have continuously threatened music education programs since the 1970s. Taken together, modern educational reform movements and financial challenges make music education a frequent target for cuts and expose an underlying philosophy in the educational system that music is not an essential curricular subject. Music education, in this view, is not only expendable or irrelevant, but extremely expensive.

The earlier philosophical approach was no longer effective as the sole means of defense. In the 1980s the theory of reverse economics was developed, followed by the mobilization of a political power base led by the National Association of Music Merchants, a primary driving force behind the advocacy movement in the early 1990s.

This chapter is divided into three sections. In the first, we explore essential music advocacy concepts, define advocacy, and discuss various approaches to advocacy. In the second, we help you understand the process of becoming a music education advocate. And in the third, we present practical tools for building, restoring, and saving music programs.

17.2 Essential Music Advocacy Concepts

DEFINING ADVOCACY

Advocates are people who support specific causes, events, or ideas. You've probably already been an advocate in your life for a cause that's important to you. Most of you reading this book are now eligible to vote in local, state, and national elections, but that's just one way to advocate for your beliefs.

Advocacy is *organizing, equipping, empowering, and mobilizing all constituents in the local school district for the advancement of music education for all students.* We believe that the goal of music education is equipping the general population to be lifelong participants and patrons of the art of making and enjoying music.

APPROACHES TO MUSIC ADVOCACY

Music advocacy is most effective when there is a *proactive*, long-term, coordinated effort by all constituents (teachers, community members, school board, and district administration) in the educational system. Unfortunately, most advocacy efforts are *reactive*—that is, they only begin in response to a crisis. Successful advocacy includes strategic use of *philosophical, psychological and developmental*, and *economic* approaches.

Philosophical Approaches to Music Advocacy

During your studies, you may be asked to write a rationale or personal philosophy of music education. (We strongly recommend that you have a well-constructed philosophy in hand before you start your job interviews.) Typically, a philosophical approach toward music advocacy focuses on *why* music is important for the individual and for society, but it also answers questions about intellectual, practical, and moral issues (Elliott & Silverman, 2019).

Psychological and Developmental Approaches to Music Advocacy

Psychological and developmental approaches to music advocacy gained popularity in the late twentieth century, with the *Music Makes You Smarter* campaigns. The underlying argument was based on research from SAT scores that showed a correlation between the length of time students studied music and their achievement on standardized test scores. (There is also a similar link between high grade point average and length of time students have participated in music programs.) The problem is that these studies do not show a causal effect—that is, we can't say with any certainty that participation in music, by itself, makes the difference. There are likely other contributing factors over which we have no control, such as socioeconomic status, involvement of the parents, quality of the music program, whether students take private lessons, and so on.

Another argument in this category was the "Mozart effect," which showed that student achievement on spatial reasoning tests increased after listening to classical music. Music advocates quickly latched onto this idea as one more way to argue for the importance of music. Unfortunately, similar research studies showed either different results or that the same positive results could be achieved using other stimuli.

A more promising field for music advocates is the area of brain research in relation to music education. Research in this field reveals several important claims about the value of music education (Helding, 2020).

- Participation in music during childhood is linked to improved cognitive function in senior adults.
- Participation in music is linked to improved mental health and general well-being.
- Music making activates nearly all of the brain, including the cerebrum (cognitive functions), the cerebellum (motor functions), and the limbic system (part of the emotional system).
- Participation in music results in more complex brain structures, which serve as the background structure for all other types of learning. Music making also strengthens the connections between the neurons and helps preserve the neural pathways used for thinking, emotion, and physical function.

Economic Approaches to Music Advocacy

The economic approach to music advocacy, often called reverse economics, was developed in the mid-1980s. Reverse economics was used to counter the assumption that music programs are more expensive than other programs, which resulted in some school boards choosing to cut music in the midst of economic crises. This approach is discussed in detail later.

Political Approaches to Music Advocacy

Political approaches to music advocacy occur at the local, state, and national levels. At the national level, organizations such as the NAfME, have helped unify efforts in music advocacy. The Music Education Policy Roundtable is a coalition of national educational, professional, and commercial organizations and associations that work together to influence policy, laws, and financial support for the arts and arts education. However, federal mandates for music education may not affect the local level, because funding for arts education does not come primarily from the federal budget: most funding decisions about schools take place at the state and local levels.

The majority of states have a board of education that oversees funding for the arts, but budgets are politically influenced. Thus, statewide coalition efforts for the support of music education are essential. Individual state music education associations, state chapters of national organizations, and regional and local arts funding agencies often work together to provide support for music advocacy. Efforts focus on enacting laws to provide access to arts education for all and securing funding for education and performers. State-level advocates attempt to influence policy related to music requirements for K–12 schools and improve the overall level of teacher training in the state.

At the local level, schools are usually governed by a district- or county-level school board. The local level is where immediate decisions are made and where most crises occur. It's also where the music advocate has the greatest influence.

17.3 Becoming a Music Education Advocate

Unfortunately, many music educators start their careers with little knowledge of what they can do to prepare their programs from facing cuts. As a result, they often display a sense of denial, helplessness, or apathy and don't know how to advocate for their program. What does this look like?

Denial: Through naivete, neglect, or complacency, teachers deny the vulnerability of the program. It's so easy to think that *our* program will never face cuts. Worse, we may think we have greater power than we actually have to prevent any cuts to our program. As you will see in this chapter, teachers are at the bottom of the decision-making chain of command. Unfortunately, teachers may not realize this until their own program has been threatened.

Helplessness: Teachers experience a sense of helplessness once they learn about potential cuts. Some teachers retreat and accept the loss, not realizing that there are real solutions available through the power of a music coalition.

Apathy: The most apathetic and selfish teachers are often those with tenure. Because their own job is secure, they won't act on behalf of the students. A common strategy used by unethical administrators is to promise some teachers in a district that their own program will not be cut if they agree to not fight the cuts in other areas of the music curriculum, and it often works. These administrators use a divide-and-conquer strategy to create conflict and division among the music staff. Teachers who participate in this practice are also unethical; their attitude is completely self-centered, with no consideration of the impact potential cuts will have on the students.

Advocacy: Advocates fight for the students and know that the battle is ongoing. Advocates educate the public about what can be done to support music. Advocates put students first. They know that students in the program now may become future administrators, board members, businesspeople, doctors, politicians, and/or supporters of the arts. They know that their own behavior and professionalism will have a major impact on the way future decisions are made.

The greatest obstacle to the advancement of music education may be the disunity of our own profession.

What's the solution? Music educators must view themselves as a team, putting the students first. It isn't *my* band, *my* orchestra, or *my* choir. The program belongs to the community, and to the students. Excellent music educator advocates don't compete, they collaborate.

POWER STRUCTURE

Understanding the power structure of your school system will help you gain a better perspective on how decisions are made. Do you know who has actual authority over schools? Is it the federal, the state, or the local government? In most places, the local community has authority through its elected or appointed board. The board then hires an administrative team to manage the district and serves as the liaison between the community and the district. Unfortunately, many officials elected to the board lack experience with and understanding of the inner workings of the system, including things such as budgets, policies, and curriculum. As a result, the board must rely on the information that the administration gives them—information that may be biased, incomplete, politically motivated, or inaccurate.

Typically, the central administration submits recommendations to the school board after consulting with local school administrators, and the school board accepts and approves those recommendations. Sometimes this leads people to accuse school boards of being rubber stamps for the administration. In their defense, if no one provides any alternative information, how are they supposed to know?

Ultimately, the primary constituents in the school district are the community, the parents, and their children. Too often music educators view the school board, administration, and classroom teachers as hostile to the music program. Instead, music educators should establish relationships of trust with these individuals, become informed about the political process in the schools, and participate as full members of the local school community. This can only be accomplished by the investment of time and actions that demonstrate your position as one of collaboration.

You inherit the reputation of all of those who precede you. You help establish the reputation of those who follow you.

THE MUSIC COALITION

So, knowing now that you have limited authority to influence policy and budget decisions, what can you do? Empower, equip, and educate parents, community members, and local business leaders to exert the legal authority they have to influence the board. These individuals form a *music coalition*––a unified group of individuals committed to advancing music education. As a young educator, you should work with the veteran teachers in your program to find out if a coalition exists and promote unity within your department. You should also quickly get to know parents and other individuals who have a vested interest in the music program.

There is no group of people more capable of raising rapid political furor than a well-organized music coalition.

The coalition is the primary advocate for music education, working with the district and music educators to ensure that all children have equal access to a high-quality music education. The coalition monitors administrative proposals under consideration by the board and local schools, informing decision makers about potential impacts on the music program. The coalition also serves as the primary defender of the program in the face of threats such as budget cuts. This process protects teachers and allows them to focus on their primary job: educating students.

The coalition is a single unified entity representing all areas and levels of the music program. Subcommittees within the coalition may focus on:

- Marketing strategies, social media campaigns, newsletters, membership recruitment, and so on;
- Communication with both central and site administration, such as monitoring the status of the district, having as least one identifiable member at every school board meeting, awareness of proposals, financial status;
- Assisting the department in advancing curricular proposals, especially as related to the mission and vision of the music department; and
- Assisting in the management of statistical information related to student enrollment, helping in the development and presentation of information from and about the music curriculum, and finances related to fundraising.

ANNUAL STATUS REPORTS

One of the most effective means of advocating for music education is the annual status report (ASR). The coalition uses the ASR as a practical means of demonstrating the philosophical basis for a strong music program and music's importance as a core component of the student's intellectual and socioemotional development.

The ASR focuses on four areas of analysis: *faculty issues*, *curricular issues*, *student participation issues*, and *economic issues*. Faculty issues relate to concepts like FTE (full-time equivalent positions), staffing, and student-faculty ratios. Curricular issues include things such as the availability and diversity of performing ensembles and other music courses, the presence of a written curriculum, and the systematic assessment of student achievement and program outcomes. Student participation issues include enrollment data, rates of recruitment and retention, and program access. Economic issues (sometimes called fiscal issues) include budgeting, fiscal responsibility, the financial advantages of large enrollment, and FTE value (see the section on reverse economics). The ASR does not include a discussion of political issues, which tend to drive decisions by administrators and school boards. However, it often reveals underlying philosophical and political issues related to educational reform and budget decisions.

The ASR requires the active participation of the community in the decision-making process, specifically the involvement of the coalition representing all areas of the music curriculum. Examples and templates of ASRs are included in the online resources.

Fundraising is *not* a primary function of the coalition. The ability to raise significant funds in support of the program often becomes an excuse for the district to deny budgetary requests or reduce the program's budget. We recommend that you restrict all fundraising to extracurricular aspects of the music program.

CRISIS-MANAGEMENT AND PREVENTION

As a future music educator, you should be aware that any of the following may signal a potential threat to a program:

- Economic issues
  - Budget cuts, budget restructuring, including hidden cuts (e.g., not replacing retired teachers, restructuring teaching assignments).
- Student participation and curricular issues
  - Educational reform movements, in which political agendas are most plainly evident
  - Educational trends, for example, changing the structure of the schools within a district, school calendar changes (e.g., year-round vs. traditional, quarters vs. trimesters vs. semesters), school-day schedule changes (block-type schedules, reducing the number of periods in a day, implementing required study halls [*extra help* or *tutoring* periods], early release programs [allowing HS students to leave for work]), dual enrollment (post-secondary education programs), new curriculum movements, new state or national standards
  - Lack of a written, district-approved music curriculum, with specific student learning outcomes and related assessments for each curricular area
  - Lack of administrators trained in supervising the curriculum or providing effective feedback for music educators; the unique aspects of the group/ensemble teaching process are not often understood
  - Lack of meaningful, systematic, program-level assessment by the central administration. Educational reformers and new administrators often fail to assess what is currently in place to determine whether change needs to happen; likewise, they fail to assess new programs to determine whether implemented initiatives have had any effect.
- Political issues: Personal and political agendas of colleagues, parents, board members, and administrators; educational consultants and corporate interests focused on adult-centered issues instead of student-centered issues.

UNDERSTANDING THE BUDGETING CYCLE

School board budget discussions begin immediately in the fall for the following year; however, teachers may not learn about proposed budget cuts for several months. It is essential that a member of the coalition be present at every board meeting and work session from the beginning of the budgeting cycle. This helps the coalition provide timely information to the board about potential cuts and prevent unexpected crises. It also shows the board that the coalition is not just there for the crisis, but for the long term.

17.4 Practical Tools for Building, Restoring, and Saving Music Programs

DEVELOPING THE FINANCIAL CASE FOR MUSIC ADVOCACY

The advocacy case starts with the ASR. The key task is developing a case showing that cuts to the music program may result not in financial savings, but in a loss. The ASR provides the data showing the music program's fiscal viability in a way that can be clearly understood by those responsible for making decisions. It provides a factual picture of issues that reveal factors—such as the distribution of music-instructional FTE, curricular opportunities or needs, equal access to music education for all students, and the economic value of the music program—related to student participation in music. Many districts use an ASR as a proactive means of keeping music education off the budget-cut list. If program enrollment doesn't show a positive FTE Value, an effective ASR may provide a statistical basis for restoring, maintaining, and developing strong music programs.

Basic to establishing the financial viability of a music program is understanding the *ratio point*, *full-time equivalent* (FTE), and *FTE value*. With the collection of the data and its analysis, you can determine the financial status of your program as compared to other areas of the curriculum.

The ratio point is a calculation used to determine the allocation of funds related to the staffing of schools. Essentially, it is the amount of money available divided by the average salary of the particular category (teachers) of the budget. It is directly related to the average class size. For example, if the ratio point is set at 25:1 and the average teacher salary is $50,000, the school will receive $50,000 for every twenty-five students enrolled in that school.

Example 1. In a financial crisis, the central administration may change the ratio point to 26:1 or some other determined ratio, in which case the principal receives $50,000 for every twenty-six students. For example, if the budget deficit is $300,000 and the average salary $50,000, the ratio will be changed to reflect the cut of 6.0 FTE faculty positions.

How this looks in practice and what the administration missed:

- A 6.0 FTE reduction requires low-seniority faculty to be cut first. These positions are always at the bottom of the pay scale.
- Because the administration based their recommendation on average salary, it is impossible to save $300,000 by eliminating just 6.0 FTE.
- At the end of the fiscal year an audit will show a continuing budget deficit, so the process will begin all over again.

FTE is the equivalent of 1.0 full-time position and is based on *average* salaries, class sizes, and student loads for each position. But this is where a fundamental problem occurs: the assumption underlying an FTE cost is usually wrong, because it is based on an incorrect, theoretical assumption. For example, if the typical teacher teaches five classes in a district where thirty students is the average class size, the district will calculate that each teacher teaches 150 students a day. This assumption is applied to every curricular area, even though there may be huge differences in class sizes between subjects.

FTE value is the determination of the average FTE of the individual teacher or group of teachers within a specific area of the curriculum and gives a more accurate picture of the cost factor. In music, FTE value is the key factor in demonstrating the financial viability of secondary music performance teachers. Normally, elementary general music teachers are funded as a means of providing planning time for classroom teachers and rarely appear on the cut list.

REVERSE ECONOMICS

Reverse economics is the concept that savings anticipated from proposed program cuts will result in further immediate or long-term budget deficits. Imagine a business owner facing a financial crisis in which he or she needs to reduce the sales staff by 20 percent. Does the owner look at all of the salespeople in the company and cut the two people with the least amount of time on the job? Of course not. The sales records of all employees are examined and the two with the lowest sales are released, regardless of their length of service. The smart business owner considers costs *and* benefits in evaluating where to invest.

The coalition develops the same type of case, showing the strong economic value of the music program compared to others. They compare the average FTE value of the secondary music performance teacher with that of the average FTE value across the district. In most cases, the FTE value of music educators is much greater than that of their classroom colleagues because they see more students in each class. Typical secondary music ensemble teachers with a five-period day have average student loads of 200 students, compared with average classroom teachers with 150 students. The excess load of the music performance teacher is fifty students, the equivalent of two extra classes. This gives the music performance teachers an FTE value of 1.4 compared to the FTE value of 1 achieved by classroom teachers. This effect is potentially very large when there is a larger number of secondary music teachers. For example, 6.0 FTE secondary music teachers, with a 1.4 FTE value each, provide the district with a cumulative FTE value of 8.4. That's an excess value of 2.4 FTE. The excess value provides several advantages to the district:

- It justifies the cost factor of secondary smaller performance ensembles.
- It assists the district in maintaining smaller classes in all academic areas.
- It provides financial justification for the funding of 2.4 FTE elementary instrumental music teachers.

Some boards respond to this by proposing to eliminate the elementary instrumental pull-out programs. However, any cost-benefit will be short-lived and ultimately cost more. Why? Statistical analyses of districts who cut elementary programs demonstrate a *decline* in secondary instrumental music enrollment of 65 percent or more. Further, districts that begin instrumental music later than fifth grade can expect 65 percent less participation at the secondary level (Benham, 2016).

Here is how this looks in practice and what the administration missed:

- Teachers of secondary band, orchestra, and related performance ensembles normally have significantly larger loads that often give them the highest FTE value of all curricular areas.
- The larger FTE value at the secondary level supports the financial viability of the rest of the music program. This is of particular importance when it comes to justifying the elementary instrumental program, especially when elementary classroom teachers and administrators often view the pull-out scheduling of those classes negatively.

- The financial benefit of large secondary music performance classes is lost; the district has to hire 1.4 FTE for every music teacher cut and/or make significant increases in class size in all academic areas.
- Students are eliminated from the program and miss out on the extraordinary benefits of a music education.

As you learn the concept of reverse economics you will come to understand, as I do, that money is not saved by cutting music programs.

—*Burton M. Nygren, retired superintendent of schools*

RESOURCES FOR THE MUSIC ADVOCATE

Music educators may feel isolated, especially if they are in a smaller community or travel between buildings. However, many resources are available to support music educators in all teaching situations. Professional associations, the music industry, federal and state education departments, arts organizations, and higher education institutions can be valuable partners in advocacy efforts. Be sure to become part of your professional network!

17.5 Discussion Questions

1. Discuss the different approaches to music advocacy and their benefits, as described in this chapter.
2. Outline the steps toward becoming a music education advocate.
3. Describe signs that music programs might be threatened.
4. What steps can you take to develop a case showing that cuts to the music program may *not* result in financial savings, but a loss?

OXFORD learning link

Visit the online resources for additional documentation and exercises to help expand learning and test your knowledge further: www.oup.com/he/powell_music1e.

PART II.

Popular and Nontraditional Music

PEDAGOGICAL CONSIDERATIONS FOR TEACHING MODERN BAND INSTRUMENTS

Bryan Powell

This chapter provides an overview of the rationalizations for the inclusion of popular music ensembles in K–12 music education.

18.1 Introduction

The inclusion of popular music instruments in K–12 music education has become more common in the twenty-first century owing to many factors, including the expansion of modern band programs, the growing popularity of the ukulele, and the increasing affordability of music technology. As a result, preservice music teachers benefit from learning how to facilitate musical experiences using popular music instruments so they will be prepared to incorporate popular music instruments and popular music ensembles into their future music programs. This introductory chapter will outline some key considerations regarding the inclusion of popular music instruments in K–12 music education programs. Following this introduction, individual chapters are dedicated to several popular music instruments, including guitar, electric bass, keyboard, drum kit, ukulele, and vocals in popular music settings. It is worth noting that almost all popular music uses aspects of music technology and recording technology. You can read more about music technology in instrumental instruction in Chapter 10, "Integrating Technology in Instrumental Instruction."

Throughout the instrument chapters in this section, you will seem that many of the authors use the term "modern band." Modern band is an instrumental and vocal ensemble that incorporates popular music, student-chosen music, and songwriting on popular music instruments including guitar, bass, drums, keyboard, ukulele, technology, and voice (Powell & Burstein, 2017). Initially introduced by the nonprofit organization Little Kids Rock (now named Music Will) in 2002, there are now thousands of modern band programs in K–12 schools throughout the United States. Additionally, there are over seventy-five college and university music education programs that incorporate aspects of modern band into their preservice music teacher education programs (Powell, 2022).

18.2 Why Popular Music?

Most music education majors had a positive experience in band, choir, and/or orchestra as high school students. These ensembles work well for many of the students who participate in them, and as a result, some students decide to major in music education. However, the majority of students in high schools are not participating in school music. In fact, research has shown that, on average, over 75 percent of students in high school are not participating in school music offerings (Elpus & Abril, 2019). This is a striking statistic; in a time when the vast majority of students have access to streaming music and can create, collaborate, and share their music with others, only one in every four secondary students is participating in school music programs. There are a few reasons that students do not participate in school music. One is that school music offerings often do not reflect the musical experiences that students are passionate about. For a student who is interested in making their own music using music technology or learning to play an instrument such as the guitar, traditional school music ensembles often lack relevance for those students.

The incorporation of popular music instruments into K–12 music education can help to bridge the gap between school music and music in society. Popular music education can increase the relevance of music programs and can attract students who are currently not participating in school music programs. There is research that demonstrates that when a new music class is offered such as a modern band ensemble or a music technology class, the majority of students who are participating in those classes are not also in the band, choir, or orchestra (Dammers, 2010). Additionally, popular music ensembles and modern bands are more likely to attract students of color, and students from lower socioeconomic backgrounds, compared to traditional band and orchestra programs (Clauhs & Cremata, 2019). This research indicates that the addition of more contemporary music ensembles can increase participation in school music for more students without negatively impacting existing ensembles.

Another reason to engage students with popular music instruments is to incorporate a focus on lifelong music making. It is a goal of many music educators to provide students with the knowledge and skills to enjoy playing music throughout their life. And if we look at music outside of school, it is pretty clear that the instruments that most people are playing in society can be categorized as popular music instruments (which includes technologically mediated instruments). In 2020 the most popular instruments sold in North America were the guitar, ukulele, and keyboard (NAMM, 2020). Despite the popularity of guitars in society, it is still a gendered instrument that is more commonly played by people who identify as male. Incorporating traditionally gendered instruments into school music programs can provide access for all students to participate (Powell, 2019).

Other researchers have shown that most students who participate in band or orchestra through their senior year of high school stop playing their instruments as soon as they go to college, unless they become music majors (Mantie & Tucker, 2008). With this in mind, the music education community must come to terms with the fact that if we want to engage students in lifelong music making, we need to be incorporating the instruments that society uses to make music.

18.3 Feeling Prepared to Teach Popular Music

Most beginning music teachers feel unprepared to teach popular music instruments in school (Springer, 2016). This is in part because the average music education major comes from a band, choir, and/or orchestra background and likely does not have the same level of experience playing popular music instruments. Despite the potential lack of experience on popular music instruments, music teachers can still facilitate popular music ensembles in the classroom. As mentioned in Chapter 10, "Integrating Technology in Instrumental

Music Instruction," sitting alongside your student as a co-learner can be a powerful dynamic in the classroom. Preservice music teachers are often taught that they need to be the musical expert in the classroom, and good music teachers certainly do need to have expertise in fingerings for notes on each instrument, which instruments transpose, how to hold the bow for a string instrument, and so on. However, in popular music ensembles, teachers can learn alongside their students as the teacher embodies the role of a facilitator in the classroom. For example, when starting a ukulele program, it is okay to let the student know that you will be learning alongside them and staying one step ahead of them as you learn chords. There are a growing number of resources for how to play popular music instruments on YouTube and websites such as Music Will's Jam Zone (jamzone.musicwill.org).

There are many aspects of popular music that allow it to be introduced in the classroom by teachers who do not have a great deal of experience playing popular music instruments. Many popular music songs utilize only a few chords (I, IV, and V). This means that if you know how to play three or four chords on the ukulele or guitar, there are thousands of songs that you can play. Similarly, there are a couple of common rhythms on the drum kit that are used in thousands of popular music songs. If a student knows how to play one drum rhythm with the snare drum on beats 2 and 4, there are many songs they can play. For more information on ways to start with popular music instruments, see each of the instrumental chapters in this section.

18.4 Facilitation in Popular Music Ensembles

Teachers can leverage the prior musical experiences of the students in the classroom when it comes to teaching popular music instruments. Since instruments such as guitar and drum kit are commonly used in music making outside of the classroom, it is likely that some students will have prior experience with these instruments. Teachers can leverage the students' knowledge of the instruments and use peer mentoring in the classroom to allow them to work with other students (Gramm, 2021). Music teachers can also leverage student access to technology to look up chord diagrams for the guitar or ukulele, search for chord charts to songs that they want to play, and record their own original music. Empowering students to take ownership of the learning can be a powerful opportunity for you to see your role in the classroom as a "facilitator" more than a "director."

The role of a music teacher as facilitator involves letting go of the idea that the music teacher is in charge of all aspects of the rehearsal process. Cremata (2017) stated that the teacher-as-facilitator "employs constructivist learning approaches through student-centered experiential processes" (p. 64). In a popular music ensemble, the music facilitator engages all members of the class and responds to the needs of the students to determine when they should step in to make a correction and when they can let students work through a music problem by themselves. As a facilitator, the music teacher in a popular music ensemble also engages students in leadership roles in the classroom, allowing students to have a primary role in choosing repertoire, leading rehearsals, running the sound board, making flyers to advertise performances, and deciding what they will wear for the gigs. This democratization of the music classroom changes the power dynamic between the teacher and the students and releases ownership of the musical decision-making process to the students.

18.5 Opportunities for the Inclusion of Popular Music Instruments

The cost of instruments is often a barrier to starting any new instrumental music program; they can be expensive. Popular music instruments for beginning students, on the other hand, are often affordable. A quality student ukulele costs around $50, and a decent-quality student guitar can be purchased for roughly $100, which makes them much more affordable than the instruments used in a concert band or orchestra. And since instruments like the guitar are popular in society, it is often possible to get popular music instruments through donations. When I first started teaching music in an East Harlem public school in New York City, many of the instruments for my after-school rock band were donated by friends, parents, and community members.

There are also many ways to incorporate popular music instruments into school music programs. My journey with including popular music instruments in my teaching started with an after-school rock band and then transitioned into a guitar program with many of the classes that I saw throughout the week. These guitar classes included opportunities for students to cover their favorite songs as well as write their own. Music teachers can also incorporate popular music instruments into their concert bands and orchestras. Likewise, music teachers can incorporate traditional school instruments into popular music ensembles. I currently facilitate a popular music ensemble that includes several concert band and orchestra instruments.

As detailed in Chapter 48 of this book, there are many ways to work with a popular music ensemble or modern band in school music programs. Music teachers can start with only one instrument and then add others gradually. For example, teachers can have all students start with the ukulele and then add some students on keyboard, drums, bass, Orff instruments, and the like. Music teachers can also introduce several instruments at the same time and have different stations that students rotate through. There is no one right way to introduce popular music instruments into music programs. I recommend having conversations with your students about which instruments they might like to play and then coming up with a plan to work with your school administration to incorporate popular music instruments into the school's music program. In my experience, school administrators are usually receptive to modern band programs and popular music ensembles once they understand that these ensembles are likely to include more students, as well as a greater diversity of students who are not currently participating in school music programs.

18.6 Discussion Questions

1. What are some reasons to include popular music instruments in K–12 music education programs?
2. How might you include popular music instruments and/or popular music ensembles in your future music program?
3. What are some of the challenges you anticipate in including popular music instruments into your music program?

OXFORD learning link

Visit the online resources for additional documentation and exercises to help expand learning and test your knowledge further: www.oup.com/he/powell_music1e.

CHAPTER 19

PEDAGOGIES FOR TEACHING UKULELE IN POPULAR MUSIC EDUCATION

Christopher Cayari

This chapter provides an overview of various ways to teach the ukulele and how to integrate multiple modes of teaching that can lead to their application for many of the musical skills desired for classroom and ensemble students.

19.1 History of the Ukulele

The ukulele's history began in 1879 when the cavaquinho, a four-string fretted instrument from Portugal, was introduced to Hawaiians, who adapted the instrument and gave it a name that translates as "jumping flea." The instrument was initially used to encourage traditional Hawaiian music and dance on the islands and was brought to California in 1915, where its prevalence spread across the United States in folk and popular genres, particularly vaudeville and Tin Pan Alley. It was a prominent staple in popular music genres, being used for musical shtick: Roy Smeck played it behind his back or with a violin bow, Tessie O'Shea fingerpicked on the banjo ukulele while singing her signature song "Two Ton Tessie from Tennessee," and Herbert Butros Khaury, more widely known as Tiny Tim, accompanied his falsetto voice singing "Tiptoe Through the Tulips." The instrument seemingly went dormant in the 1960s but experienced a resurgence of popularity in popular music from the 1990s onward. The Hawaiian native Israel (Bruddah Iz) Kamakawiwo'ole was a key figure in giving the instrument a reputation for creating happy, easy-listening renditions of popular pop songs; Jake Shimabukro used classical fingerpicking techniques to adapt both classical and popular music for ukulele; and popular music artists and bands, Elvis Presley, Taylor Swift, Jason Mraz, Train, Sara Bareilles, Twenty One Pilots, and Panic! at the Disco—have incorporated the instrument into their recordings and concerts.

The ukulele has become a staple in many music education programs because of its affordability, portability, and ease of use. While ukuleles come in various shapes and sizes, the soprano, standard/concert, and tenor are the ones most commonly used in school music programs. Their strings are tuned using G–C–E–A, and tradition is that one sings "My dog has fleas" when plucking each string. Knowledge of other fretted string instruments and how to teach them can be applied to the ukulele, and the chapters on guitar and bass in this volume can inform readers on how to approach reading various notations, including staff and tablature, as well as how beneficial it may be to start with simple tasks such as playing single notes; after all, a student can play single notes on ukulele to serve as a (not-so-) bass line to accompany others.

In this chapter I share the three activities I teach on the first day of class, whether I am working with fourth-graders, college students, or older learners, as I believe the ukulele is a versatile, easy-to-learn instrument that can be used to teach many musical aspects. After that, I explain the usefulness of rote learning, staff notation, tablature, and chord reading and how they can be used individually or in tandem to provide students with a well-balanced music education. I close the chapter by discussing adaptations for the instrument whose concepts can be applied not only to ukulele, but to all instrumental learning activities.

19.2 Day 1: Let's Get Playing

My first session has three goals: help students learn how to hold the instrument, have students play single notes, and get students to play chords. Depending on the age level and how students are responding, I add a variety of exercises, tips, and tricks to expand upon each goal. Below I describe what I have found to be the simplest, most efficient to enable students to accomplish these tasks.

HOLDING THE UKULELE

I give my students an anatomy lesson of the ukulele so that students know the difference between the head and the body. We count the frets and the strings. I tell them there are three main points of contact. The left hand holds the neck, and the instrument is stabilized between the player's body and right arm. I have straps available for them to use if they would like, as they allow the instrument to be placed in the optimal position regarding angle and height. Every player's body is different, so there is no single position that should be described as the way to play. The options that teachers can give their students include resting the cutout on the knee, holding it at a 45-degree angle like a classical guitar, wearing a high neck strap like the Beatles, or embodying the *ainokea* lifestyle (a Hawaiian pidgin phrase meaning "I don't care" or "No worries, it's cool") by lying in a beanbag chair or hammock.

MAKING SINGLE SOUNDS

I teach ukulele with the philosophy that there are a lot of ways to make sound on the instrument, but some are healthier and more efficient than others. Therefore, I teach good technique and explain what the best practices are for the right and left hands while also giving my students choices that foster autonomy. (For a ukulele anatomy lesson and three ways to pick the string, search 'Introduction to the Ukulele - Parts of the Uke and right hand picking by Dr Cayari'). I choose not to introduce picks in the first lesson because they add another variable. I ask my students to give me a thumbs-up and then let their thumb fall to their index finger naturally, thus forming their makeshift pick. I explain to them that they should move their forearm in a circular counterclockwise motion from the elbow, ever so slightly, and let that circle move their thumb as it strikes the first (bottom) string in a steady beat. I move around the room, monitoring and helping students as needed. Once the class is playing in unison, we move to the second string, which is more difficult because another string is on either side of it. We work our way up the strings and then play a game where I shout out random strings. We also play aural skills games where I turn my back and start playing a different string, and students have to figure out which one. We keep going until everyone is playing in unison, and then I change strings.

We then turn our attention to the left hand. (For beginning ukulele finger exercises for the left hand, search 'Beginner Ukulele Finger Exercises - Left Hand - First Steps by Dr Cayari'.) I tell my students to show me an American Sign Language C with their hands and explain that they want to keep their hand in a relaxed C curve. The students are instructed to place their thumbs lightly on the back of the ukulele's neck and use the tips of their 1-finger (index finger) behind the first fret of the first string. The tip of the finger should create a tight seal between the string as it rests behind the fret. We then get our right arm circling and achieve unison. Students are then asked to put their 2-finger (middle finger) behind the second fret of the first string, and the process is repeated. I then decide if it is time to move on or try different exercises. They could include adaptations and combinations of the following: playing on a single string and calling out the finger/fret; playing a fixed number of times on each fret (e.g., 1-1-1-1-2-2-2-2, etc.); playing a pattern using numbers as a guide (e.g., 1-2-3-4, 1-3-2-4, etc.); and allowing students to develop their own patterns, which lays the groundwork for them to make their own melodies in the future. When developing patterns, it is helpful to start with the 1-finger because it can anchor the player's hand to the instrument; thus the finger can stay pressed against the fretboard for the whole exercise as the other fingers change the pitches of the notes.

PLAYING CHORDS

I then teach students how to play chords that only require one finger on the left hand. (For an example of using one finger on the left hand to play chords, search for 'Learn Achy Breaky Heart on ukulele by Dr Cayari'.) I explain chord charts by showing students how the strings and frets are represented by lines and the circles represent where you would place a finger. Then, we learn which chords are in our repertoire for the lesson. Teachers can choose from C, C7, F2sus, and Am (see Figure 19.1).

FIGURE 19.1 **Playing chords**

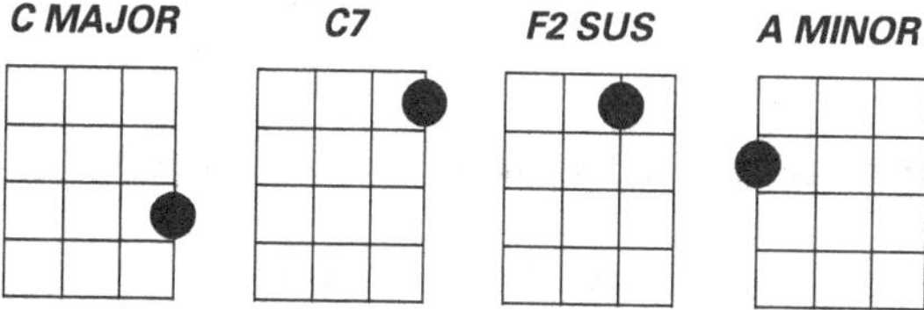

Using these chords provides options from a plethora of songs that employ I and V chords in the key of F major; I, IV, and vi in C major; or i, III, and IV in A minor. For strumming, I have my students shape their right hand like a bird's beak with an overbite with their index and thumb and explain that the fingernail of the index finger strings strikes the strings at about a 45-degree angle. A rule of thumb (pun intended) is that if it hurts, you may be playing it wrong. Either the player is pushing too hard and scraping the flesh of their finger, or they are approaching the string at a degree closer to perpendicular, which will also cause undue wrist tension.

To get the group playing together, I pick a chord and have them strum a whole note. Students then release their left hand and tap the ukulele with their right hand for four beats. Their goal is to put the chord back as we get ready to play another whole note. We then progress in difficulty by playing half notes and tapping two times, then play quarter notes with one tap in between. The same process is used to get a handle on every individual chord (see Figure 19.2). Then I have students play alternating chords in the same whole-, half-, and quarter-note progression with tapping (Example A). Alternatively, students can play the equivalent number of quarter notes (Example B). Eventually, we try playing chords in a progression with pauses (Example C), and, finally, without a pause (Example D).

FIGURE 19.2 **Strumming whole notes**

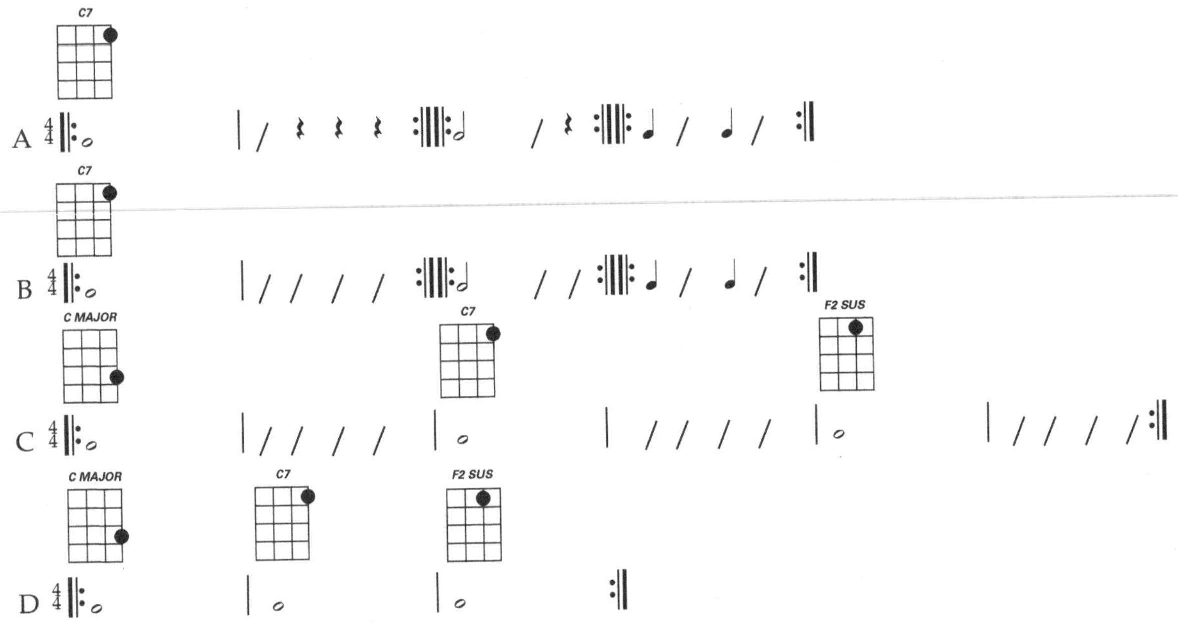

The progression I choose is always taken from a song, and I ask students if they know what song we are playing. Once someone guesses the song or I tell them, we add the lyrics and have a good ol'-fashioned sing-along. An aural skills game can also be played using chords by turning my back to students and playing a chord that we just learned and having students figure out which of the options I am playing by strumming along until we are in unison.

19.3 Developing Well-Rounded Musicians with Ukulele

The first lesson has students learn how to use their ears and also lays the groundwork for chord charts, tablature, and even Western classical notation. In the following section, I discuss various literacies educators can teach with the ukulele.

STAFF NOTATION: WESTERN CLASSICAL ART MUSIC AND CHAMBER MUSIC LEARNING

Most music educators are required to learn and be able to teach standard music staff notation for licensure. While that was not the custom for ukulele initially, the instrument can be used to teach the same note reading concepts so useful for orchestral, concert band, and choral ensembles. Like classical guitarists, some ukulele performers have used staff notation to organize their thoughts and arrange popular music favorites. Exemplars of this crossover style are Taimane Gardner, the Ukulele Orchestra of Great Britain, and Jake Shimabukuro. Whether approaching the ukulele as a solo concert instrument, an accompaniment instrument for a choir, or one of many in an ensemble, teaching students how notes on a staff align with the strings and the fretboard can be useful.

The ukulele has an optimal range of one octave starting at middle C (the open third string), which makes it a great companion to the soprano recorder and treble voices.

Method books for ukulele can be purchased for students, or teachers can use the plethora of Orff, Kodály, and recorder books stashed on their shelves as a starting point. Additionally, chamber music, whether it was originally for string quartet, trumpet trio, woodwind quintet, or any other group, can be (re)arranged for a group of ukulele players, and if a lower instrument is desired, a guitar, bass ukulele, or even piano could be added. Finally, it is possible to replace the fourth string on a ukulele—which is traditionally the G above middle C—with a thicker one that plays an octave lower, thus extending the range of the instrument down a perfect fourth.

TABLATURE AS AN ALTERNATIVE TO STAFF NOTATION

Tablature is notation that provides a visual representation for fretted string instruments, and often associated with the guitar. Modern guitar tablature dates to 1536, with Luis de Milán's *Libro de música de vihuela de mano intitulado El maestro*, and thus was not simply used for popular music as some might think. However, in contemporary society, tablature is associated with popular music genres, even though the staff is often translated to tablature. A knowledge of how tablature works—the numbers represent the frets, and the lines represent the strings—can be applied to all fretted string instruments, so teaching tablature on ukulele can make a transition to playing guitar or bass easier, and in contrast, if a musician can already read guitar tablature, it is simple to apply the same concepts to ukulele. Aspects common in staff notation can be included in tablature including note lengths, rests, articulations, and dynamics. Additionally, some publishers opt to include both staff and tablature notations in a conjoined staff to allow musicians to choose their preferred visual representation (See Chapter 20, "Pedagogies for Teaching Popular Music Guitar in Popular Music Education," for more on reading tablature).

The internet is a repository of copious resources for learning to play tablature as well as visual resources to play and practice. While the reader may no longer have access to the same sites that were available at the time this chapter was written, internet searches can provide websites with tablature sheets and video streams in which tablature scrolls across the screen while providing aural examples. In sum, tablature is another visual representation of music that can be used in place of or in tandem with other music notation.

CHORD CHARTS: UKULELE ACCOMPANIMENT

Ukulele playing can also be visually represented through chord charts, depicting what the instrument can play as accompaniment. A chord diagram is often placed above lyrics or notation to suggest what can be played on the ukulele to accompany. Fakebooks, piano reductions of popular music, and lyric sheets are common forms of music in which chord charts are found. The chord diagrams—vertical lines representing strings, horizontal lines representing frets, and circles or numbers representing fingers—guide the player in a variety of explicit and improvisatory ways. For example, in a lyric sheet, a chord chart may simply have the letters of chords above the line of lyrics to be sung, requiring the musician to listen to the lyrics to know when to change chords. To help students learn aural skills, teachers can have students listen to a song and raise their hands when the chords change. This can be done with or without a lyric sheet to serve as a guide that gives them hints as to when the changes happen. The chords that are used can then be given to students, and they can try to strum when they hear the chords change. Again, this can be used with or without the guide of visual cues, notation, and various other resources a music educator might apply from their bag of tricks.

Guided chord charts may have notation—staff or tablature—that shows strumming or picking. These markings are found above the notes or tablature numbers. Common down-strum marks are D, a down arrow, and a bracket. For up-strums one might see U, an up arrow, or an upside-down caret. These symbols can also be applied to using a pick to play individual notes. Fingerpicking symbols are marked below the notation and are denoted with the first letter of the Spanish names of each finger, which was popularized in the classical guitar tradition. The symbols for the thumb, index finger, middle finger, and ring finger are *p* (*pulgar*), *i* (*indice*), *m* (*medio*), and *a* (*angular*), respectively. The pinky is rarely utilized, but *c* (*chiquito*) may be used.

Teaching students to use fingers and picks for both strumming and individual note playing can help them build dexterity in their hands, and exercises can be created to focus on whatever goals are needed. For example, if students need more work on changing between the C major and G major chords, the whole class can work on left-hand skills, with more advanced players playing the fingerpicking pattern *pimiaimi* in eighth notes, students who are struggling with switching chords playing *pimi* and then turning their attention to the left hand, and others simply strumming whole notes.

19.4 Developing Opportunities for Learning and Music Making

When going on a trip, it is necessary to first decide on a destination. After all, if one does not have a clear destination in mind, how will they know where they are going? Therefore, instrumental teachers should decide what is important for their students to be able to do before starting to teach how to play an instrument. As can be seen in my suggestions for the first day of class, I want my students to be able to move the fingers of their left hand independently and be able to make sounds with their right hand. I think it is also important for them to be able to play a song on the first day of class. Therefore, I build up to that moment by introducing the anatomy of the instrument, how to hold it, how to use the left hand, how to use the right hand for single tones, and finally, how to use the right hand for multiple tones. As I plan my courses, I think about what the end goal might be, and I often encourage students to identify their musical goals and serve as a facilitator in order to help them along their journey as music makers. Examples may include students performing a concert; students producing an album; and students playing for a school-wide sing-along of our favorite popular music. Each event might require the teacher to focus on certain skills. Tasks could require a teacher to develop ensembles that are student or teacher led, using notation to promote chamber music in popular, folk, classical, or a combination of the genres. Some chord-based activities could be used to accompany boomwhackers, recorders, mallet instruments, wind band instruments, and/or voices. Songwriting activities could be developed to showcase at the concert, and the event could end with an audience sing-along. Informal music pedagogy could guide student-led projects in which groups create covers or original songs centered around a theme for a recording. Some educators may even want to have students guide the learning with the aid of online tutorials so prominent on video sharing websites. For example, the teacher may encourage digital and technological literacies such as how to use search engines by telling students to find a ukulele tutorial, learn a new skill, and then show their small group or the whole class what they learned. The teacher and student then help everyone else in the course learn how to acquire the new skill.

19.5 A Participatory Music Making Model for Ukulele

The ukulele is an accessible instrument that can be used to teach music to a wide range of students. It is possible, though, that varying proclivities, dedication, outside resources, body shapes, physical limitations, and disabilities may require adaptations in either the instrument or the teacher's approach to teaching, or both. Elsewhere I have discussed how participatory music making is a great way to structure ukulele activities in the classroom (Bernard & Cayari, 2020). In sum, teachers identify various ways for students to achieve a collective goal through teaching multiple skills that students can choose from to participate. For example, when playing a I–IV–I–V pattern, students could choose between the following: play whole notes; play half notes; play quarter notes; play only the I chord; improvise a strum pattern; improvise strumming that never repeats; learn a notated riff to play during beats 3 and 4 of the V chord; improvise a riff during the IV chord; sing the melody while playing; hum the root of each chord while playing; fingerpick *pimapima* on the I chords; or improvise fingerpicking during the first two beats of each measure; Each option can be practiced through group exercises and turn taking in a large group or during structured and unstructured practice in small groups or individual work time. Teachers could introduce a skill, model it, and then give students half a minute to two minutes to practice the skill before coming together as a class to try it together or have students volunteer to show their progress. Students can brainstorm these as well as the teacher providing starting points. After all, the possibilities on ukulele are limited only by the imagination.

19.6 Concluding Thoughts

I believe that the ukulele is a versatile instrument that can be easily incorporated into many classrooms because it has a low barrier of entry, it is affordable, and students see a plethora of examples for its use in popular culture. It is prevalent in many music styles and genres including (but not limited to) folk music, Top 40, rock and roll, classical, and alternative. Its size lends itself to young players while remaining a viable option for adults. Although some might consider it simply a gateway instrument that helps prepare students for other music making, it is an incredible option for music making in its own right. It truly is an instrument that is loved and accessible to the masses.

19.7 Discussion Questions

1. Who are some musical artists who are prominent in the your and your students' lives who play the ukulele? How have they adapted the instrument to their genre or style?
2. Consider the adaptations listed in this chapter and consider who the same aspect of *ainokea* can be applied to other instruments of ways of making music that allows people to experience music in various ways.
3. What are the benefits and drawbacks of using ukulele for teaching staff notation?
4. How might you sequence the ukulele in a music program where you have students for three or more years?

OXFORD learning link

Visit the online resources for additional documentation and exercises to help expand learning and test your knowledge further: www.oup.com/he/powell_music1e.

CHAPTER 20

PEDAGOGIES FOR TEACHING GUITAR IN POPULAR MUSIC EDUCATION

Warren Gramm

This chapter provides an overview of teaching guitar within the context of popular music, approaching the instrument with a sound-before-sight mindset.

20.1 Introduction

The guitar is one of the most iconic and celebrated instruments in the popular music canon. It is versatile, capable of playing melodies and harmonies as well as serving as a lead or supporting instrument. This chapter includes pedagogical implications for using the instrument, approaches for scaffolding in an ensemble, and ways to integrate composition and improvisation as key tenets for learning guitar in a popular music ensemble. In countless other places, the guitar has been described in detail regarding its various parts, holding the instrument, and proper left- and right-hand technique. Therefore, I will not repeat those explanations but instead shed light on how to approach learning and playing the guitar in a popular music ensemble. Educators should strive to implement a methodology that enables learners of all abilities to participate and be successful while embracing a sound-before-sight mentality.

20.2 Pedagogical Considerations

The most significant pedagogical consideration to be made at the onset of this chapter (having already been discussed in earlier chapters) is that learning should be approached with an execution-before-explanation mentality regardless of instrument or genre. In this chapter, I offer an approach to teaching guitar that is an alternative to the one presented in method books where students begin their learning through identification of parts of the instrument, reading whole notes, and learning how to use only one string at a time. Nor will I advocate for teaching in which the primary focus is on learning the names of notes, reading five-line staff notation, and playing songs that are often unknown to the player and meant to teach skills and techniques rather than engage the learner in relevant, exciting, and meaningful music making, even at an introductory level, utilizing visual representations and iconic notation. Learning through many guitar method books remains a static endeavor regarding songs that are played and learning objectives, and it often mirrors how many other instruments are taught at the introductory level. Many approaches for learning the guitar in a traditional context focus on honing technique in a teacher-centered, non-creative, and non-compositional approach. In fact, none of the contributors to this book recommend this approach, as noted in earlier chapters.

Learning the guitar in a popular music ensemble or classroom context should be approached with a creativity mindset in a student-centered environment. A nonformal (Mok, 2010) approach (a hybrid of informal and formal methods and approaches) to learning the instrument brings a student's learning a step closer to how popular musicians learn outside of educational contexts. Instead of defaulting to note reading through five-line staff notation, guitarists who embrace learning popular music would most likely learn through listening, watching YouTube videos, and reading tablature (discussed in detail later) and chord charts. Before standard notation as we understand it today, the guitar's predecessor, the lute, was approached using tablature. Tablature is commonplace when it comes to learning how to play melodic and harmonic passages on the guitar in a popular music context. Most students who learn the guitar this way will visit sites such as ultimateguitar.com or guitarinstructor.com, or search for tablature online to learn guitar riffs and solos and other guitar related material.

This chapter does not discuss approaches to reading five-line standard music notation. The methods discussed in this chapter are focused on student-centered learning and how popular musicians more authentically learn and interpret iconic notation (tablature, chord charts, etc.). One approach is not superior to another but should be understood as contextual and authentic to the music being learned. While studying for my master's degree in classical guitar performance I relied heavily on reading traditional music staff notation, but as a middle school teacher I focused on starting students with reading iconic notation such as chord charts and tablature to fully engage learners in various ways. A rock guitar solo would not commonly be learned using standard five-line notation, just as a classical guitarist would not typically learn pieces using guitar tablature and chord diagrams. Educators should approach the guitar within a popular music context by using student-centered repertoire, culturally responsive pedagogies, and scaffolding of ability levels within the same ensemble experience. Again, authors in this book suggest similar approaches to teaching all instrumentalists. Similar to how a popular music ensemble may be constructed, players of differing experience levels can all make music with each other and learn from their peers with an educator who approaches teaching more like a facilitator rather than a director (Gramm, 2021).

Learning through the lens of popular music pedagogy often relies heavily on aural learning and replicating what is heard with the support of chord diagrams and other forms of iconic notation. Relying on and developing skills related to learning by ear are tenets important to learning many nuances of popular music that seldom translate well to the written page. When dealing with the guitar's many sounds that are not exactly related to the notes that are played, learning by ear remains the most accurate method to properly imitate and subsequently obtain skills necessary to playing guitar in a popular music context. Check out the song examples at the end of many sections for context to put learning into practice.

DAY 1

Learning the guitar in a popular music setting should begin with playing music. While there are many important things students will need to know and work on as beginners, chords, melodies, songwriting, and improvisation are four main areas that we will focus on. To work on these skills in an authentic manner, educators should not approach learning in a vacuum but through student-centered song choices. While it may seem anxiety-triggering to jump right into playing if you are somewhat unfamiliar with the instrument, the methods that work with your students are helpful for educators as well. As a harmonic instrument, the most crucial building block of learning the guitar in a popular music setting is the understanding of chords, so let's jump in!

20.3 Chords

As a foundational tool at all levels of guitar playing in any genre (but especially in popular music), chords make up the majority of what most guitarists will play. The understanding of playing chords remains a formative and crucial tenet of learning with the instrument. For initial learning purposes, as a student begins playing the instrument, chords can be assigned to four categories: simple, open, power, and barre. Each of these groupings increases in complexity, the need for physical dexterity, and fullness of sound. They should be approached sequentially while taking prior experience into account. Be sure to approach learning these chords within a song's context. Sections may include a sample song to work through as your and your students' skills progress.

SIMPLE CHORDS

Simple chords are a way to engage even the most novice of guitarists. The guitar is set up in such a way that many chords are easy to play when approached in a simple manner. While these types of simple chords do not immediately utilize the full functionality of the instrument or the depth of its sound, they enable beginner guitarists to play almost immediately and contribute to a classroom or ensemble's sound landscape. Some of the most common chords in this category are G major, C major, A minor, and E minor. As you examine the chord diagrams demonstrated in Figures 20.1, 20.2, 20.3, and 20.4, remember that the vertical lines represent the strings (the thicker strings are represented in the graphic by thicker lines), the horizontal lines represent the frets, and numbers tell the learner which finger to use on their fretting hand (commonly the left hand). The index finger is no. 1, the middle finger is no. 2, the ring finger is no. 3, and the pinky is no. 4. Students should depress the string with the tip of their finger and strum all strings that have an "O" marked above them or have a fretted note. It is important to be aware of which strings are played and which are not (marked with an X). Encourage your students to use a guitar pick and strum the strings downward toward their feet starting with the lowest-pitched string (that is applicable to the chord), closest to the ceiling. For reference, the strings are numbered like the floors of a building. String no. 1 is closest to the ground, and string no. 6 is the farthest away. While these chords can be used in many songs, be sure to try out "What's Up?," by 4-Non Blondes.

FIGURE 20.1 Open G chord diagram

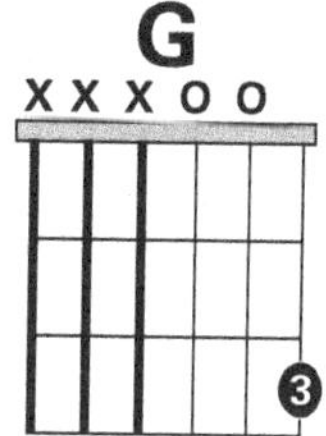

FIGURE 20.2 Open C chord diagram

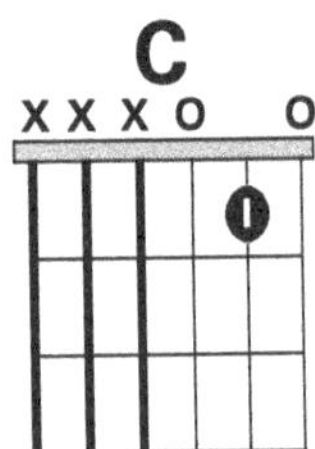

FIGURE 20.3 Open Am chord diagram

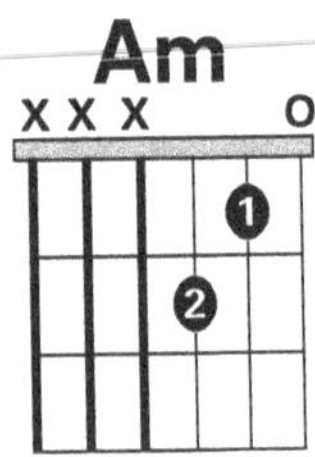

FIGURE 20.4 Open Emi chord diagram

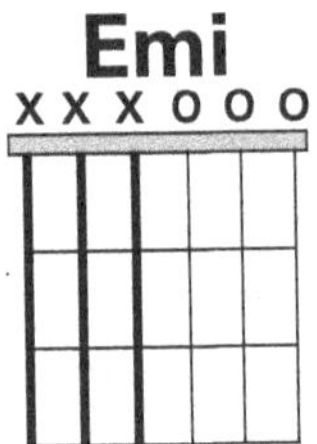

OPEN CHORDS

Open chords are named for their utilization of open strings and are often located within the first three frets of the guitar. While simple chords use open strings as well, open chords maximize the available notes within the first three frets of the instrument. The notes in simple chords are found as part of these larger, open chords. Open chords are very commonly used in popular music and represent authentic ways that guitarists can learn chords found in their full versions in many genres. First, examine the four chords referenced in the previous section and note their differences as compared to the simple chords. Some notable increases in complexity and sound are detailed below.

The G major chord now utilizes all six strings and can be played in a few different ways. Based on its functionality and hand positioning, this is the most preferred.

FIGURE 20.5 Preferred finger placement for open G chord

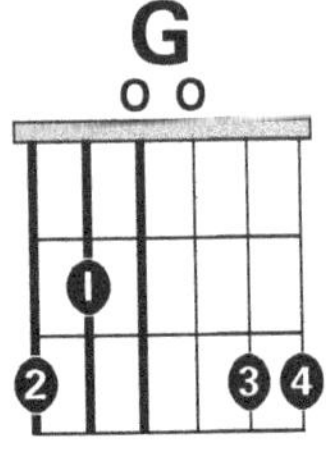

The C major and A minor chords now utilize five of the six strings. Take note of the fact that the lowest string (no. 6) is to be avoided as much as possible.

FIGURE 20.6 **Preferred finger placement for open C chord**

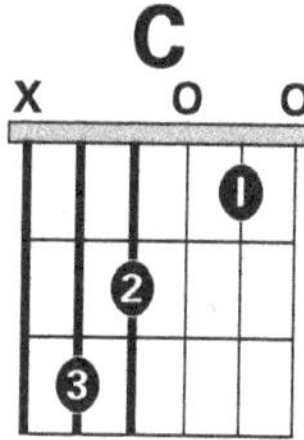

FIGURE 20.7 **Preferred finger placement for open Am chord**

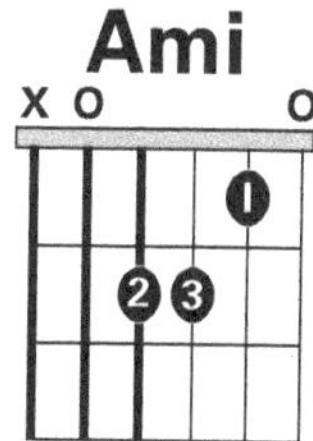

The E minor chord can be played in two different ways, as diagrammed in Figures 20.8 and 20.9. The notes are the same in both, and preference should be given to the player initially as to what they feel most comfortable with, taking into account the chord(s) that precede or follow it for maximum economy of motion.

FIGURE 20.8 **First way to play open Emi chord**

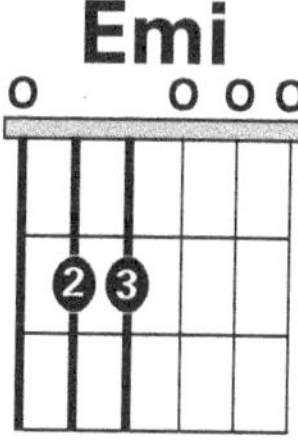

FIGURE 20.9 **Second way to play open Emi chord**

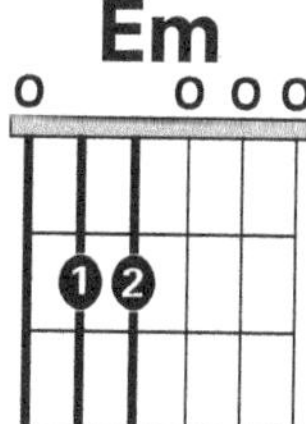

A few other commonly used chords to take note of in this category are A major, D major, D minor, E major, and a simplified F major chord for the purposes of skill building on the way to a more comprehensive F major chord found in the following sections.

FIGURE 20.10 Open A major chord diagram

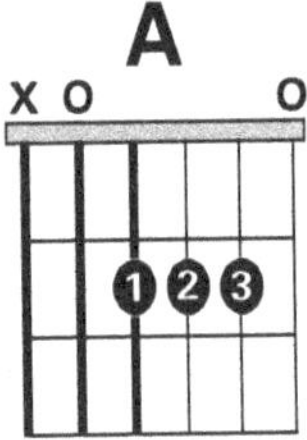

FIGURE 20.11 Open D major chord diagram

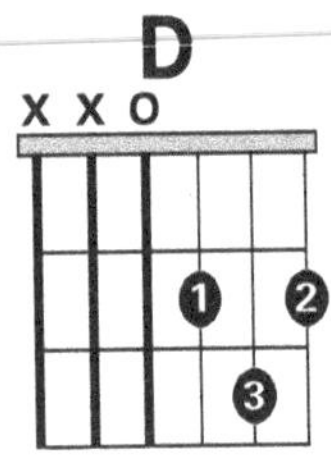

FIGURE 20.12 Open D minor chord diagram

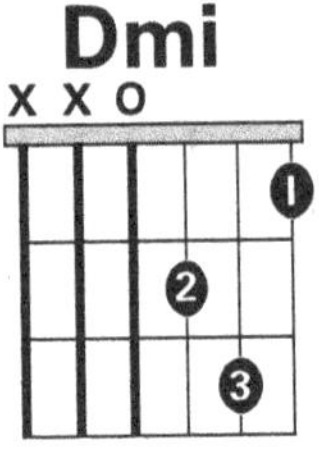

FIGURE 20.13 Open E major chord diagram

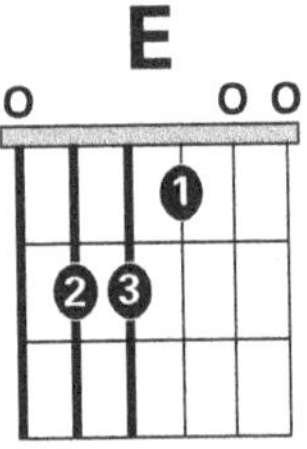

FIGURE 20.14 Open F major chord diagram

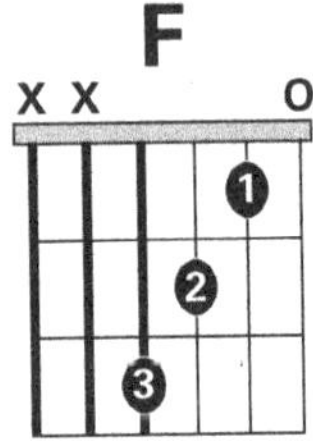

Song example: The Beatles, "Let it Be"

POWER CHORDS

One of the most versatile, authentic, and commonly used chords on the guitar in the context of popular music is the power chord. A power chord is neither a major nor minor chord: it consists of the root, a perfect fifth above the root, and the doubled root one octave higher. Because it lacks the third, the chord can substitute for more complex chords on the guitar that are not simple or open, but it also serves as a stylistic choice, especially in the genres of rock, pop, and heavy metal. As you can see in Figures 20.15 and 20.16, the power chord can be replicated on any fret and its shape does not change when the root of the chord (played by the first finger) is found on the fifth or sixth string. When students are learning power chords, a way to scaffold the dexterity needed is to forgo the octave above the root and just play the root and fifth above. It becomes a crucial step in playing the power chord that open strings are not played, as they can often cause dissonance with the fretted notes. A helpful way of avoiding this is to keep the right hand strumming very focused but also use the index finger on the fretting hand to lightly touch the strings that are not in use. This takes some practice, but it enables the player to strum without worrying about hitting errant open strings. The examples below depict F♯ and B♭ power chords. Power chords are labeled with a "5" after the root note in chord charts.

FIGURE 20.15 **Power chord starting on E string, second fret**

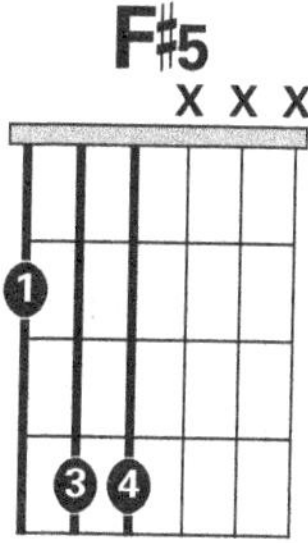

FIGURE 20.16 **Power chord starting on A string, first fret**

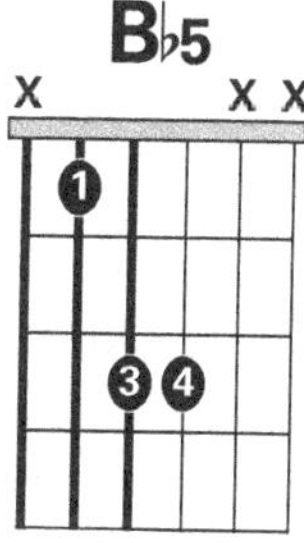

Song examples: Deep Purple, "Smoke on the Water," and Nirvana, "Smells Like Teen Spirit."

Through scaffolding of simple chords to more complex ones, students can find success on a variety of levels as they begin and progress through learning the guitar. While the aforementioned set of chords is in no way meant to be comprehensive, it serves to highlight the chords most common to learning the guitar in a popular music setting and ways to have success with your students. Whether they are starting on simple chords or working their way through familiarity with more complex barre chords (see the information found in the online resources), all students can participate and make music!

20.4 Songwriting and Soloing

A guitar can easily be used as a tool for composition. In popular music, composition and improvisation may more accurately be termed "songwriting" and "soloing," respectively. When students look to begin a journey of creativity with music making, the guitar is an instrument that can lead to success due to its user-friendly construction and pattern-based approach. Songwriting becomes an attainable endeavor once a guitarist understands even basic chords, and soloing can begin early once a student understands some of the guitar's basic scale patterns. Creativity and composition should be regarded as equally important to playing preexisting music. While it is tempting to play the music of others, the guitar has the potential to be a useful tool for students to create music of their own.

CHORD PATTERNS

Encouraging your students to compose music using their guitar is a small step forward after they learn basic chords. The guitar can be utilized as a great songwriting tool, even at the most basic level, using simple, three-note chords. Many of the chords that make up popular music are found as open chords on the guitar. While there are many chords that a student can choose from, setting parameters for which ones they should be using makes the activity much more successful. For instance, writing songs in the following keys with the notated chords will lead to success for many guitarists.

Key of C major – C major, D minor, E minor, F major, G major, and A minor
Key of G major – G major, A minor, C major, D major, and E minor
Key of A major – A major, D major, and E major

Writing songs within these three keys permits a variety of song structures and should work well for fitting a song within the vocal range of any student. To facilitate songwriting using the guitar, simply pick a key, give students the chord options, and ask them to make different combinations using the guitar. Ask them to pick randomly, try out different patterns, and find interesting progressions. While many of these combinations work well for diatonic progressions, encourage your students to explore nondiatonic progressions as well. Take any of the chords that have been discussed and create a progression. It is helpful to start composing by creating four-bar phrases and using existing popular music songs as templates for songwriting. Encourage your students to explore creatively using the chord chart templates found in the online resources.

STRUMMING PATTERNS

As part of songwriting on the guitar and playing chords in general to go along with any song, a guitarist needs to determine what strumming patterns they will use. The variety of chords used is complemented by varying the strumming patterns that are chosen. Strumming patterns, much like the scaffolded approach to chords, can begin simply and grow in complexity. In popular music contexts, chordal rhythms are often transcribed in nontraditional ways. While a traditional approach would write out rhythms using whole, half, quarter, and eighth notes, another way of transcribing rhythmic strumming patterns on the guitar within popular music contexts is to use numbers and plus signs to denote playing on the downbeat and upbeat, respectively. Examine the strumming patterns in the online resources that increase in complexity. When a numbered downbeat is colored gray, it is not to be strummed. When strumming patterns exhibit various levels of syncopation, downbeats will be "missed" during strumming to create variation.

A helpful tip in strumming is to continuously move the strumming hand up and down with the rhythm of the music to always be ready for a strum while keeping in time.

When practicing strumming patterns, it is crucial to practice along with existing songs. The chord progression of an existing song is predetermined, but the strumming pattern leaves room for creativity. Students can create their own strumming patterns by experimenting with their own combinations of downbeats and upbeats. Check out the online resources for a list of various strumming patterns.

SOLOING AND RIFFS

The guitar has been established as a chordal, harmonic, and supportive instrument, but it also plays a crucial role as a lead instrument in popular music contexts. The main way that scales, riffs (short, often repeated passages), and solos are transcribed, as noted earlier, is through tablature. A further explanation of how tablature works is necessary before one embarks on a discussion of playing melodic passages on the guitar. Tablature is broken down into horizontal lines and numbers that intersect them. The horizontal lines represent the strings. The top line in tablature represents the highest-pitched string of the guitar, the first string, commonly tuned to an E. The bottom line represents the lowest-pitched string, the 6th string, commonly tuned to E as well, unless noted otherwise. The numbers represent the frets that are to be played on whichever string they are intersected by. Figure 20.17 is an example of a passage in tablature, with the same music in standard notation above for comparison.

FIGURE 20.17 **Passage in tablature with standard notation written alongside for comparison**

Guitar tablature has become commonplace for learning existing songs, riffs, and solos as well as for communicating various scales to be used for creative music making, be it solos, riffs, or demonstrating scales and technique. While many songbooks print various transcriptions for the guitar in standard notation, the authenticity of guitar tablature makes it easier for nontraditional guitar learners to accomplish their task. Tablature provides guitarists with the notes to play but often excludes the rhythm, which further reinforces the need for guitarists in popular music to develop and utilize their aural skills.

Writing riffs, playing solos, and other melodic endeavors can be accomplished easily from the start of guitar playing. When approaching the instrument in a nontraditional way, playing should come before a deep understanding of the music theory and the notes behind each of the scales being used. Most guitarists learn the patterns of notes to play on the guitar's fretboard rather than the names of the individual notes being used. Working within these parameters of scales, patterns, and shapes allows all guitarists of any level to be successful on the instrument when it is approached in an authentic context of popular music.

The most common scales on the guitar within this context are the major and minor pentatonic. These scales are a great starting point for soloing and can be scaffolded for any player by utilizing the first string to begin with and then adding in the notes on each adjacent string as comfort and dexterity increase. The knowledge of note names on the sixth string becomes increasingly important for determining where to start each scale. These scales are great starting points for learning and should be seen as the first step toward learning more. The scale diagrammed in Figure 20.18 shows the guitarist which notes to play once the starting note has been determined. The diagram is lacking fret numbers because, as mentioned before, the patterns and shapes of the scale are most important. These two scales (Figures 20.18 and 20.19) can serve as a user-friendly and proven method of success for any guitarist. Visit the accompanying website for a more in-depth explanation of how to best use these scales.

FIGURE 20.18 The major pentatonic scale

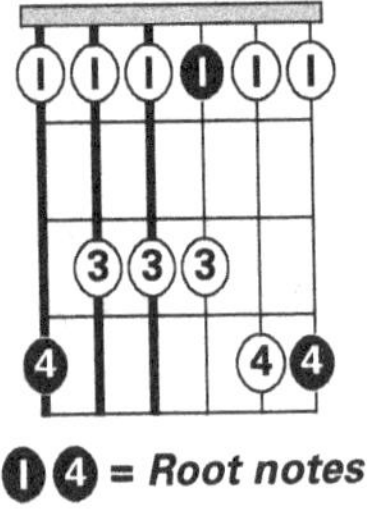

FIGURE 20.19 The minor pentatonic scale

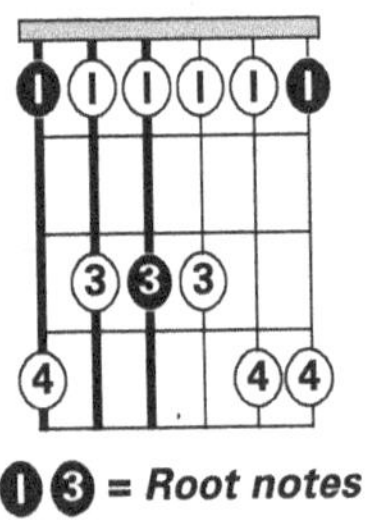

When playing guitar in a popular music context, these scales should be understood as the building blocks to soloing. Once a guitarist knows what notes to play, it is equally important to know what to do with those notes. Encourage your students to try varying the *way* they play the notes and how they move from one to another. Some common variations here are to slide from one to another (ascending or descending), to bend the string with their fretting fingers, and to explore more complicated techniques such as hammer-ons and pull-offs. Variation is the key to success when soloing. Encourage your students to also move away from thinking that they are successful if they play the greatest number of notes possible within a set time. While each student should strive to create their own style, learning from other musicians' soloing and improvisation and their songs is a helpful way to learn and encourage creativity. Simple riffs are the key to popular music guitar playing. Listen to the Rolling Stones to hear great examples of iconic and memorable guitar riffs.

20.5 Lesson Ideas to Build Creative Musicianship

The previous sections are not meant to be an exhaustive and comprehensive look at everything possible with the guitar when playing in a popular music context. Instead, they should be seen as jumping-off points to spur creativity and skill building. In the classroom, the skills acquired through learning chords, scales, and soloing possibilities will serve to enhance every student's musical experience, whether they are playing the music of others or their own original compositions. To that end, it is important to engage students with creative and exciting student-centered lessons. Try any of the following in part or whole based on the context of your teaching and your students' abilities and experiences:

1. Identify a simple three- or four-chord song (internet searches will yield plenty of examples) and encourage all students to take turns soloing over the chord progression. Use the internet to play an instrumental play-along of the song if students cannot play the chord progressions themselves.
2. Have each student write a riff consisting of only five notes that are repeated many times to go along with an existing song.
3. Using G major, C major, D major, and E minor, have students create various combinations and patterns for verses and choruses while other students determine the strumming patterns to be used.
4. Pair up more experienced students with less experienced ones to foster peer mentoring in your classroom or ensemble. For more on peer mentoring, see Chapter 12.
5. Split your classroom in half. For four measures, half of the room plays a student-composed chord progression while the other half solos. Then, without stopping, switch parts. Add in a prerecorded drum track to make it more interesting.

It is extremely important that all students be given the chance to play the guitar according to their ability level. Having students of multiple abilities play with each other is a common practice in popular music. Scaffolding is a term used to describe an ensemble experience where, for example, guitarists who are just beginning can play simple chords while more advanced players can utilize barre chords to play with each other. There are other accommodations to learning the guitar that educators should make to provide success for all. One accommodation that can be made for students with physical limitations is to tune sets of guitars so that open strings form various chords to align with particular progressions. This way, students do not have to fret any notes but can simply strum the strings as they are. Half- and three-quarter-size guitars can be detuned more easily than full-size ones because of the string tension. While this may require some creative thinking from each educator, the benefits are great when it comes to getting all the students involved.

20.6 Discussion Questions

1. How can educators use the guitar to not only recreate the music of others but to encourage students to make their own?
2. While playing and learning chords, how can educators ensure that every student, regardless of ability level, is included?
3. How can peer mentoring help guitar learners within classrooms?
4. How can educators encourage creativity and the creation of original music while learning the guitar within their classroom or ensemble?

OXFORD learning link

Visit the online resources for additional documentation and exercises to help expand learning and test your knowledge further: www.oup.com/he/powell_music1e.

CHAPTER 21

PEDAGOGIES FOR TEACHING ELECTRIC BASS IN POPULAR MUSIC EDUCATION

Spencer Hale

This chapter provides a step-by-step guide to helping students be successful bassists from day 1, and helping them continue to grow as musicians.

21.1 Introduction

The bass guitar is probably the youngest instrument in this book. As the time of this writing in 2022, the bass guitar has not yet had its hundredth birthday. It was developed to be a less burdensome double bass, and anyone who plays both electric and upright will tell you which they would rather haul to the gig. Bass players over the last century have continued to develop new techniques of playing and applying the bass guitar to music. I bring this up to say this: there is no one way to play the bass, but throughout this chapter I will cover several of the ways to get students hooked.

Physically, the bass guitar works like most other string instruments: the performer adjusts the length of a string by pressing it against a solid surface and then makes that string vibrate. Developed as a gig-friendlier version of its predecessor, it parallels the double bass in its register, standard tuning (E, A, D, G), and the one-octave transposition in its notation on the bass staff. (Figure 21.1)

FIGURE 21.1 Bass guitar pitch of open strings, written vs sounding

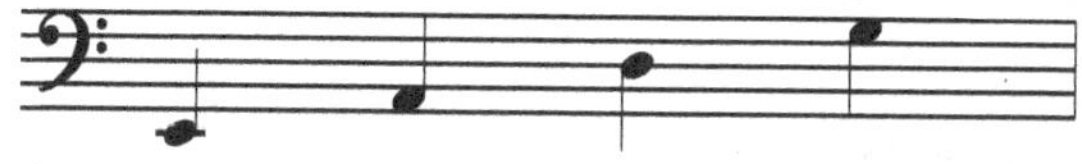

21.2 Everybody Should Play the Bass

One of the best things about the bass guitar is its low bar for entry. Playing steady quarter notes on the E string is a perfectly respectable bass line—ask Van Halen. It's a great introductory instrument for students who are struggling with others. Guitar and keyboard often require playing multiple notes and coordinating multiple fingers at the same time. Bassists usually just play one note at a time.

More important than the ease of getting started is the role the bass player takes. Bassists are often in support roles. They build bridges between the drummers and the harmonic instruments. They rarely take solos and almost never play the melody. However, if you took out the bass the music just wouldn't be the same. Like a touch of salt that kicks up all the other flavors, the bass just makes everyone sound better, often without recognition for doing so. Bassists are always listening to make *others* sound better. Bass playing is humbling, ego taming, and eye opening. To grow as a bassist is to grow as a musical empathizer.

21.3 How to Get Started Playing Bass

FINGERS VERSUS PICKS

Most bass players play with either a plastic pick, like many guitar players, or with their fingers. Picking technique is comparable to guitar picking, but bassists will often use a thicker pick to produce a stronger attack on their notes. For finger technique, players often rest their thumb on the pickup and play the strings with their index and middle fingers. A common mistake here is to pull the strings *up and away* from the instrument, but the most common technique here is to bring the finger *through* the string. This produces a less aggressive attack.

JUST PLAY ONE NOTE

Imagine this scenario: A new student comes to your class. They have no musical experience and are feeling down on themself. There are many advanced musicians in the classroom. But the teacher hands them a bass and says, "Just play this one note here and the band will do the rest." Add a backbeat, some guitar strumming, and maybe a keyboard riff, and that student will feel like an accomplished musician on day 1, ready to keep learning and growing.

There are several songs that, for some or all of the song, center on a pitch that is one of the open strings on the bass. Students can begin building walking or picking technique with just one hand.

E string: The Doors, "Roadhouse Blues," and George Thorogood, "Who Do You Love"

A string: Muddy Waters, "Mannish Boy," and The Doors, "Five to One"

D string: Yo La Tengo, "Ohm"; Creedence Clearwater Revival and "Run through the Jungle"; and Wilson Picket, "Land of 1,000 Dances"

G string: Sly and the Family Stone, "Everyday People," and Deep Purple, "Smoke on the Water"

With this method, students get to focus on rhythm, note length, and timing rather than stressing about changing or even fretting notes. More advanced students can practice the techniques I'll get to later, or they can sing while they play.

If you'd like to see this in action, search for "Homer Plays Bass" on YouTube and watch that clip from *The Simpsons* (season 26, episode 8; Groening et al., 2014). That is *prime* electric bass pedagogy. While the salesperson in this clip is likely just working on commission and trying to get Homer to buy something, his pedagogical approach is amazing. As educators, we aren't trying to get our students to give us money, but we *are* trying to help them feel amazing about playing music as quickly as possible.

In the clip, the salesperson sees that Homer lacks confidence. He can't get Homer to feel great about playing guitar quickly, so he suggests bass instead. The salesperson shows Homer how easy it is to play, then immediately lets him play with the "band" (in other words, the salesperson). Homer thinks it's *so* cool that he can play the bass with other people ("I'm amazing!").

The bassist and educator Victor Wooten says, "Never lose the groove to find a note." While learning the notes on the bass is important, playing rhythmically trumps all. It's hard to spend too much time on the one-note exercise. Gaining control over your fingers and your rhythm and learning to lock in with the drummer takes time. Spend ample time on this with your students and use it as a recurring exercise to focus on those fundamental skills.

PLAYING MORE THAN ONE NOTE

In a chord-based context, where students are learning to play chords to play the harmonic changes of a song, the bass player can just play the root notes. There are a lot of different ways to teach students where the notes are.

Color-Coded Stickers

The color-coded sticker method assigns each chord a color (e.g., C is yellow, F is blue, G is green etc. Please note, colors in diagrams have been transposed to different shades of gray. Yellow = lightest; blue = second lightest; green = darkest.). For the bass player, you can place one colored sticker on the fretboard between the frets under the appropriate string. For example, if C major is yellow, you can place a yellow sticker between the second and third fret underneath the A string. You can do the same for all the chords your students are learning on keyboard, guitar, ukulele, or whatever other instruments they're playing.

Your fretboard might look something like this for a beginner (see Figure 21.2):

FIGURE 21.2 **Beginner's fretboard**

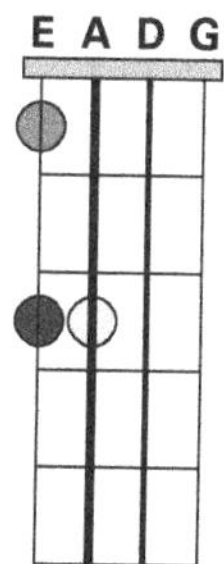

So a song with a chord progression such as (see Figure 21.3):

FIGURE 21.3 **Beginner's chord progression with chord names**

C F G C

𝄆 / / / / | / / / / | / / / / | / / / / 𝄇

could be written like (see Figure 21.4):

FIGURE 21.4 Visual representation of chords

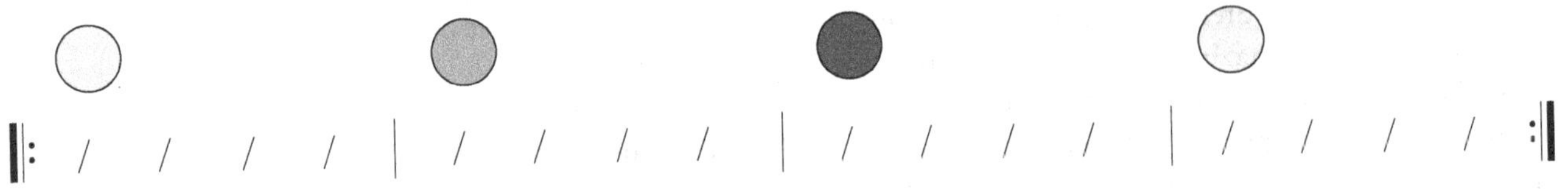

The bass player can find the correct dots and play along.

This method works great for getting students started, but think of it as training wheels. My word of caution is to practice restraint. Pick a maximum of four or five chords or notes to mark this way. You may do more harm than good if your student has to hunt for the yellow circle in the rainbow soup of frets rather than spot it from the four or five dots. As you plan your curriculum, take the chords you'll start your semester with and mark those. If your students want more stickers after that, you can encourage them to move on to a new form of notation now that they're more comfortable with the instrument.

Numbered One-String Charts

With this method, a student again plays just the root notes of the song, but plays them all on the same string. Rather than using colored dots, the student is counting which frets to play on. The student knows which string to play on because you assign all the numbers to the same string. In Figure 21.5, the student would play notes on the first, third, and eighth frets of the low E string (F, G, and C, respectively).

So a song with a chord progression such as the one in Figure 21.3 could be written in Figure 21.5 as:

FIGURE 21.5 Numerical representation of chords

Because a student can play a full chromatic scale from frets 0 to 11 (0 meaning the open string), the student can play *any* root note of *any* chord in *any* key. A chart for Rihanna's "Umbrella," originally recorded in B♭ minor (see Figure 21.6), could look like the one shown in Figure 21.7.

FIGURE 21.6 Rihanna, "Umbrella"—chord name version

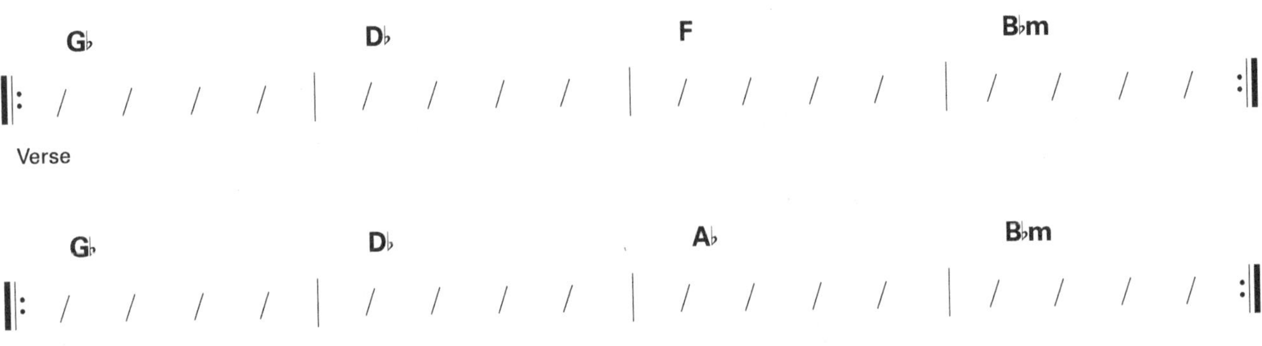

FIGURE 21.7 Rihanna, "Umbrella"—one-string fret version

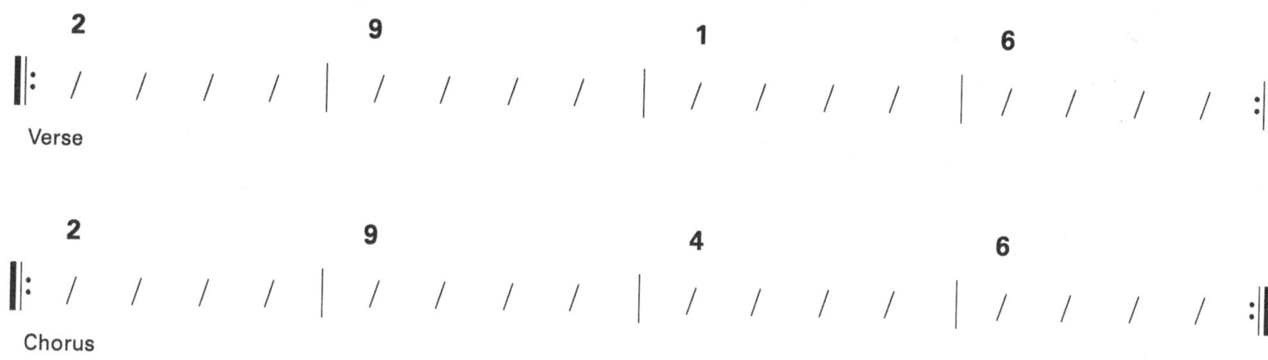

All of a sudden five flats doesn't look so daunting—it's just numbers.

With this method, students can focus on counting and finding frets, shifting position quickly and accurately, playing in time, learning song form, playing different rhythms, getting a good tone on the instrument, and listening as a band member. More advanced students could also work on any other performance skill, such as singing and dancing while playing. This method works on any string, as the student has access to the full chromatic scale from frets 0 to 11.

A tip for finding frets more easily is to use the fret markers. These are the small dots on the side and often front of the fretboard. They're there to make it easier for bass players to navigate the neck of the instrument. They're most commonly placed at the third, fifth, seventh, ninth, and twelfth fret. The twelfth fret is double-dotted to delineate the octave. Beyond that, the pattern repeats until the end of the fretboard.

This method saved me when I was teaching modern band ensembles. I had a student who excelled at keyboard and another who was quickly mastering guitar. They came to me wanting to learn "Isn't She Lovely" by Stevie Wonder. I wasn't worried about their ability to learn the six-note chords in C♯ minor—I was worried about the brand-new student my principal informed me was just joining my class. To help this complete beginner and these seasoned performers play together, I gave one group a song chart with the chords and the other student a chart with numbers. "Just stay on this string, keep counting to four, and follow the numbers!"

With this method, there was no song that had too many chords or was in too complex a key for my brand-new students, and that student felt great about being able to play with more experienced musicians.

Fretboard Diagrams

Once my students really got a handle on fret + string = note, I'd move them on to fretboard diagrams. Again, this method of getting started has the bass player playing just the root notes of the song. This method helps the student learn the names of the notes on the fretboard using a few different forms of iconic notation.

Note Diagrams

These look like chord diagrams that a guitar or ukulele player might use. The only difference is that they show just one note, rather than a whole chord, and therefore don't specify chord quality.

So a song with a chord progression such as the one in Figure 21.8:

FIGURE 21.8 Beginner's chord progression

could be written as (see Figure 21.9):

FIGURE 21.9 Beginner's chord progression written with note diagrams

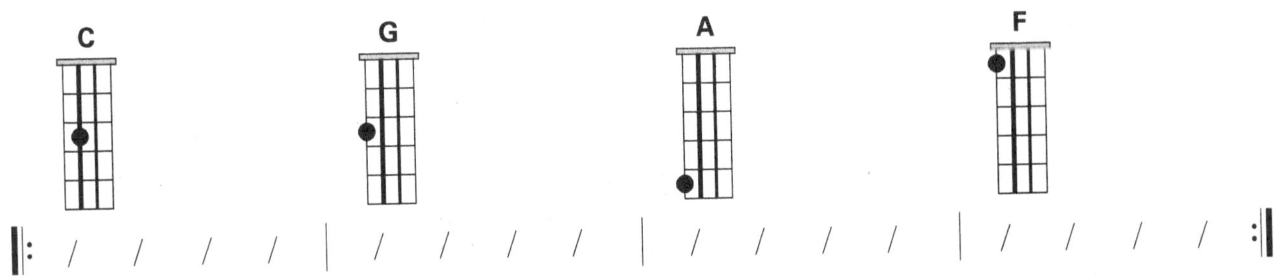

Again for Figure 21.8, more advanced students could be given a chart with chords and a reference diagram, like the one in Figure 21.10.

FIGURE 21.10 Chord chart for more advanced students

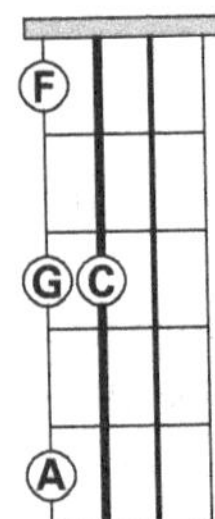

With this chart, the student is learning how to read a diagram and find notes. They could be provided with a more complete fretboard diagram, like the one in Figure 21.11:

FIGURE 21.11 Complete fretboard diagram

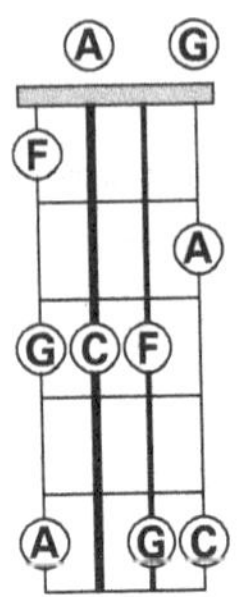

. . . and make choices about whether to play notes in higher or lower registers, developing their musical decision-making skills. The student can listen to the songs and other musicians and determine what rhythms would be best to play or how long the notes should be.

Once students understand how to read a fretboard diagram, they can play the root notes to any song they want to play. As a bassist, that is 75 percent of what I play on any given gig with a pop band, and it's 99 percent of what anybody besides the bass player wants to hear.

There's a joke about a brand new bassist who takes two lessons, learns the first five notes on the E and A strings, and then ditches their third lesson because they have a gig. I know people who played their first gig on the same day they first played the bass.

GOING BEYOND THE ROOT NOTE

If your student is bored with their root-note-only bass lines, they can start thinking about intervals. The most commonly used intervals are fifths and octaves. The nice thing about a bass is that once you learn how to play the interval with one note, you've learned it for every note.

To play an octave, take any note and find two strings and two frets higher (see Figure 21.12). That's an octave. Just remember that 2 + 2 = 8. Play this interval anywhere on the neck of the instrument and all of a sudden everything will sound *funky*.

FIGURE 21.12 Playing an octave

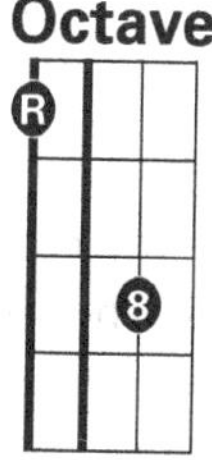

To play a fifth above a note, go one string higher in pitch and two frets higher (see Figure 21.13. Just remember 2 + 1 = 5 (your math teacher co-worker will love you). Play root-to-fifth in quarter notes and you've got a solid 1960s pop bass line.

FIGURE 21.13 Playing a fifth

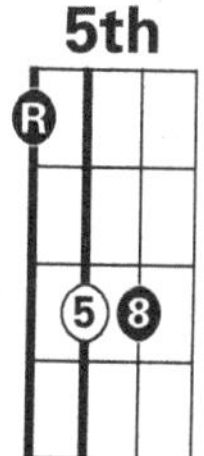

A popular song that uses this interval is "Love Me Do" by the Beatles. McCartney goes between the G and C chord playing root and fifth every two beats.

You can also go one string lower in pitch on the same fret to play a fifth below the root note. This is also your classic country interval. Also notice how the fifth above and below the note are two frets and two strings apart from each other—because those are octaves.

ADDING PASSING TONES AND NEIGHBOR NOTES

Before we get into licks and riffs and tab reading, students can start writing their own beyond-the-root-note bass lines by adding in some passing tones. A passing tone is a non-root note that a bassist adds while going from one chord to another. If I were playing this progression with steady quarter notes (see Figure 21.14), I might play A on beats 1, 2, and 3, and then add a passing G on beat 4 before arriving on F on beat 1 of measure 2. Or I might add some motion by playing two eighth notes on beat 4, playing A on the downbeat and G on the upbeat.

FIGURE 21.14 **Progression with steady quarter notes**

Passing tones take a root-notes-only bass line and quickly turn it into something memorable. The bass line in "Zombie," by the Cranberries, is mostly root notes, but a few passing tones and neighbor notes make it stand out.

Students can begin playing passing tones this same way. Beat 4 is a great place to start. For whatever chord progression they're playing, they can play root notes until the last beat before the chord changes, then add in a passing tone or neighbor note.

"Which note should I use?" a student may ask.

I would advise against prescribing notes to students, as this can hinder creativity and decision making. I would say to a student, "Try a few out and see which sounds best." If the student feels overwhelmed by that amount of choice, I would say, "Try playing the notes one and two frets higher (or lower). Which sounds better to you?" I might even play those few measures with the whole band and let all the students hear it and make a decision.

As a bassist, I know which I would play, but I don't want to hinder the exploration and creativity of the student. In the short term, it might make for a quicker rehearsal and a great sounding concert if I say, "Add this note here on beat 4." But my end goal as a teacher is not a great-sounding concert; it's to help students grow into creative and independent music makers. Exploring different sounds is part of that process. If they pick a note that I think is wrong (outside of the key, clashes with another note being played, jumps too high or too low), I let them play it. My opinion there *doesn't matter.* I will eventually teach my students about playing in a stylistically appropriate manner for certain contexts, but I want them to explore the instrument and make musical decisions on their own as well. Encouraging them is more important than teaching them standardized theory, and absolutely more important than my ego and opinions.

LYING TO YOUR STUDENTS

If you watched the clip from *The Simpsons* mentioned earlier, you might remember the guitar store employee said that Homer played a "lick." While this is a little lie, it was told for the sake of encouraging a student. I like to think of teaching music as a series of smaller and smaller lies. Common lies I told my students were:

"Every chord on the keyboard looks like this," as students play through diatonic triads in C.

"Music happens in groups of four," as we learned to count songs.

"The bass just plays the root note," as I get a new bassist started.

"Chords are either major or minor," as I explained why some chords have "mi" in their name.

"I don't care which sound you pick," as students select timbres on their electronic keyboards.

Please don't take this out of content, but I believe lying can be good pedagogy. It simplifies complex concepts such as meter, chord structure, chord quality, tonality, and form and makes them easier for students to digest. I'm fine making a blanket statement about music that I will clarify later. I know I'm not the only one. My level 1 chemistry teacher in high school regularly said, "This is a lie, but, . . ." and when I took advanced-placement chemistry, he clarified those lies.

LICKS AND RIFFS

I like to think of licks and riffs as melodic bass lines. Not every song has a bass part that just plays root notes or basic intervals; some have a melodic contour. For some bass lines, that melodic contour comes from basic intervals. The bass line to "Despacito," by Luis Fonsi, is just arpeggios.

Moving beyond the root notes is important. Many songs just wouldn't be the same without their iconic bass lines, and students want to be a part of that iconography. Imagine "Come Together," by the Beatles; "Billie Jean," by Michael Jackson; "Another One Bites the Dust," by Queen; and "Good Times," by Chic, without their bass lines.

Tablature is a great way to learn these bass lines. A Google search for "<name of song> bass tab" will work for almost any song. There are also a number of YouTube tutorials. Take all of these with a grain of salt, as most are user generated, meaning they may contain errors. As an educator, start listening for the bass in songs and make note of any time you hear a cool bass line. Bringing these songs to your students is a chance to highlight the bass player and challenge them to play beyond the root notes.

TECHNIQUE

As a bass player, most of my practice time is focused on two things: note length and stopping sympathetic vibration.

NOTE LENGTH

It's not glamorous, but mastery over note length is a sign of a seasoned bassist. You master note length by stopping the note when you want to. You stop the note by stopping the vibration of the string.

To begin getting a handle on note length, students can first try muting open strings with their fretting hand. Play the open E string and then gently place the fretting hand over the string to stop the vibration. To make this a little more fun, students can play along with a variety of drumbeats in different styles and tempos. To build technique and musicianship, they can focus on listening to determine whether longer or shorter notes feel more appropriate to match the track. Then they can practice the coordination of the left and right hand, playing the notes in time and muting them when it feels appropriate.

Next, students can do the same with fretted notes. To mute a fretted note, a player can lift their finger so it's no longer depressing the string, but without fully lifting their finger off the string. To aid this, they can also gently lay their other fingers on the string.

STOPPING SYMPATHETIC VIBRATION

Sympathetic vibration occurs when the resonance from one string causes another one to vibrate. For example, playing G on the low E string will cause the open G to ring out. This might sound like a cool way to play more notes at once, but it can quickly get muddy. A good bass player has control over this and will only play more than one note when they *intend* to. Fortunately, there are several solutions.

If you've played other fretted string instruments, such as guitar, ukulele, banjo, or mandolin, you've probably heard that you should curl your fingers when fretting chords. On those instruments, that is an important technique because you want all those strings to ring out freely. However, on bass you want to *stop* those other strings, so your fingers should *not* be curled. While chord strummers focus on playing with the fingertips, bassists will often play slightly closer to the pad of the finger.

Play with just a slight curve in your fingers, no more than when you let them rest and sit naturally. When you play a note on the E string, gently place your other fingers against the other strings on the bass, helping to mute them. Your fingers should almost always mute the strings that are physically lower than the note you're playing.

This is a basic technique that should be introduced fairly early on and will dramatically increase the tone and clarity of bass playing, but it takes years to master. I wouldn't worry about this all the time, but I would check to see if students are doing basic muting.

21.4 Where Do We Go From Here?

Honestly, you could have a bass career if you master this chapter. The bass is both extremely simple and endlessly complex. I recommend that students double in the modern band classroom—that they each play more than one instrument. Bass is a great instrument to double on because it puts students in that support position, humbling the spotlight hogs and serving as a home to the modest. For students who want to focus on bass, they'll always have somewhere to grow and improve. For students who want to play bass because their other instrument is too hard, they'll have a space where they can feel successful. For you, yourself, there is probably a band looking for a bassist in your neighborhood. So find an old Fender on Craigslist, learn a few notes, and get gigging!

21.5 Discussion Questions

1. What role does the bass guitar typically play in a musical ensemble? What are some examples counter to that?
2. What effect does the length of the note have on my musical performance? Which musical contexts does this affect more or less?
3. There are many places to play each note on the bass, and no two are exactly the same. What effect do the different notes have on the overall sound of the band? How do you determine which to play?
4. What innovations have been made to bass playing over the last century?
5. What do the knobs on the bass do?

OXFORD learning link

Visit the online resources for additional documentation and exercises to help expand learning and test your knowledge further: www.oup.com/he/powell_music1e.

CHAPTER 22

PEDAGOGIES FOR TEACHING KEYBOARD IN POPULAR MUSIC EDUCATION

Letitia Stancu

This chapter provides an overview of teaching keyboard in a popular music classroom.

22.1 Introduction

One of my favorite things to do as a kid was to listen to songs on the radio and figure out how to play the melodies on my piano. My family did not have internet access, and I had to rely mostly on memory to recreate the melodies and accompaniments I heard. I homed in on that skill in my teenage years and felt really happy when I could figure out a Van Halen or U2 song and play along with the recording! That skill came in handy when I started playing in rock bands. As a keyboardist, sometimes you need to figure out your part from a recording, because there may not be a song chart or a score available. At other times you need to hear all the different parts that could be played on a keyboard and decide which ones are prominent in the song and that you want to bring to a live setting. Beginner keyboardists can choose which sound (patch) they want to play in a song, while more advanced keyboardists can choose two or more sounds per song. There is a lot of work involved, but it is fun and rewarding.

After a couple of years of working as a keyboardist, I was hired to co-coach a music camp's rock band. Our keyboard students were of various ages and experience levels. Typical students included some with little or no piano/keyboard experience, others with some rock band experience, and others with classical piano backgrounds but no prior experience playing in a modern band. Their eclectic music backgrounds worked out great for song possibilities and student grouping. Beginner students would work on something like "Wild Thing," by the Troggs, with the keyboard player doubling the guitar part. Experienced students would cover something like "Superstition," by Stevie Wonder. Classically trained students would get a keyboard-prominent song such as "Clocks," by Coldplay, or "Don't Stop Believin'," by Journey. Time was not on our side, since the bands needed to be ready to perform in under two weeks. However, practicing and rehearsing every day did wonders for each student's musical growth. In addition, the daily contact with students forced me to grow as a teacher and become more efficient at breaking down specific skills such as chord progressions and comping patterns. The lessons I learned about teaching rock band at camp informed the following approaches I discuss in this chapter.

The chapter will primarily focus on strategies for teaching beginner keyboard students. Some of the topics discussed include:

- Types of keyboards and equipment
- Getting students familiar with the keyboard, posture, finger numbers, and root-position chords
- Iconic notation, comping patterns, and chord chart notation
- Warm-up exercises
- Bringing creativity to lessons and classes
- Strategies for keeping keyboard students engaged and challenged

22.2 Types of Keyboards and Equipment to Consider

The ideal modern band set-up will need at least one touch-sensitive keyboard with full-size keys, preferably sixty-one keys or larger, with weighted or unweighted keys. If there is the option of having multiple keyboards and there is the choice of purchasing a seventy-six-key or eighty-eight-key keyboard, go for the eighty-eight-key full-size keyboard, which is the same size as an acoustic piano. It might also be important to consider an eighty-eight-key full-size keyboard controller to connect to a laptop and your desired music software. Using a keyboard stand for each keyboard as well as a keyboard amp or amps and corresponding equipment are also important. Sustain pedals are not needed for beginner students but can be used by intermediate and advanced players. There are several great resources, such as *Popular Music Pedagogies: A Practical Guide for Music Teachers* (Clauhs et al., 2020), that discuss the difference between keyboards and synthesizers as well as touch sensitivity, weighted keys, MIDI controllers, mini-keyboards, and various keyboard and synthesizer features.

22.3 Pedagogical Considerations and Beginning Classes

The first few classes or lessons can be spent on getting students familiar with the instrument, hand position, finger numbers, getting comfortable playing chords, and jamming along. Consider using traditional piano method books as resources and supplements to your beginning lessons. *Bastien Piano Basics: Piano Level 1* (Bastien, 1997) for younger students, *Alfred's Basic Piano Chord Approach: A Piano Method for the Later Beginner* (Palmer et al., 1987), and *Adult Piano Adventures: A Comprehensive Piano Course: Level 1* (Faber & Faber, 2001) for older or fast-learning students are some possibilities to start with. *Crash Course in Chords* (Evans, 2013) is a chord and music theory supplement for older or fast-learning students. In addition, the *Modern Band Method*'s keyboard book (Burstein et al., 2020) provides music concepts, exercises, and songs to work on with your keyboardists and a full modern band. This modern band method book starts students with playing triads to play popular songs, as opposed to starting by learning individual notes and music staff notation. You might find that a chord-based approach for beginners allows them to play in a popular music ensemble more quickly than starting with reading individual notes. This method book also has online resources, including instructional videos, jam cards, and audio tracks, that you can use to keep things moving on track.

In addition to method books and series, consider using online content in lessons and homework. The organization Music Will (2023) offers free online resources for educators which are very useful for different instrument levels and skill sets. There are a variety of YouTube channels, such as Pianote (2008), offering free online piano lessons and tutorials. You may also choose to create and share your own video tutorials specific to your class curriculum.

POSTURE FOR SITTING OR STANDING AT THE KEYBOARD

Playing the keyboard while sitting or standing requires healthy hand, wrist, arm, and torso positions. As with learning to play an acoustic piano, it is important to teach students the correct positions to strive for so they can develop and maintain healthy playing habits. As a teacher, it is also important to model the correct posture for your students (see Figures 22.1 and 22.2). Remind your students to maintain their healthy posture as much as possible while they are playing and ask them to demonstrate a healthy resting position when they are not.

FIGURE 22.1 **Sitting posture**

FIGURE 22.2 Standing posture

GETTING FAMILIAR WITH KEYBOARD FINGER NUMBERS

Keyboard or piano finger numbers are the same for each hand (see Figure 22.3). A quick finger number warm-up in the beginning classes will reinforce the finger numbers for the right hand (RH), left hand (LH), and both hands.

FIGURE 22.3 Keyboard finger numbers

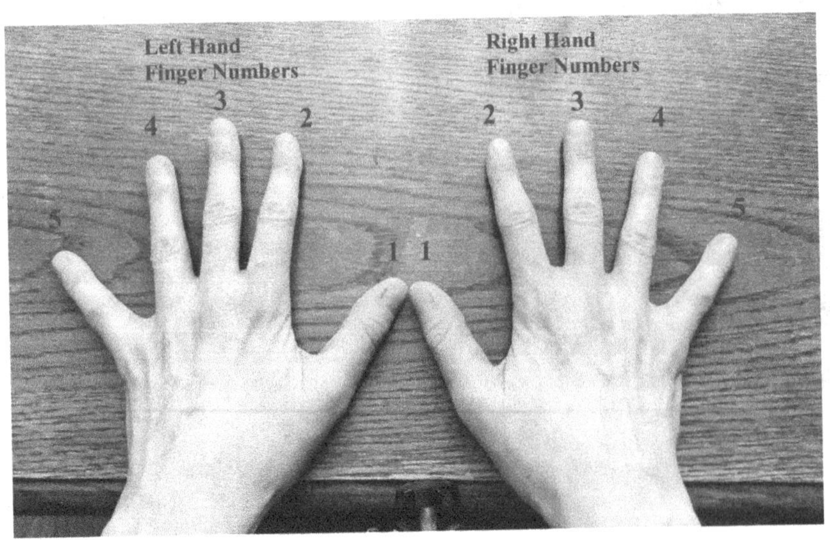

GETTING FAMILIAR WITH THE KEYBOARD

Introduce the students to the different registers of the keyboard—low, middle, and high—as well as the concept of going up (to the right) and down (to the left) on the keyboard. Then show your students the groups of black notes: twos and threes. Direct them to locate C to the left of the group of twos and F to the left of the group of threes (see Figure 22.4). Next, introduce the students to the music alphabet and have them play and say the note names going up or down on the keyboard. If working with younger and inexperienced students, it is important to ease into note name recognition on the keyboard, and also to use visual aids for the students by labeling all the white keys with letter stickers or with a permanent marker (which you can wipe off with rubbing alcohol once the students learn the notes). Once students are familiar with the individual notes, they can start creating simple melodic ideas over a backing track or over a built-in beat common on many keyboards.

FIGURE 22.4 **Black note groups: twos and threes**

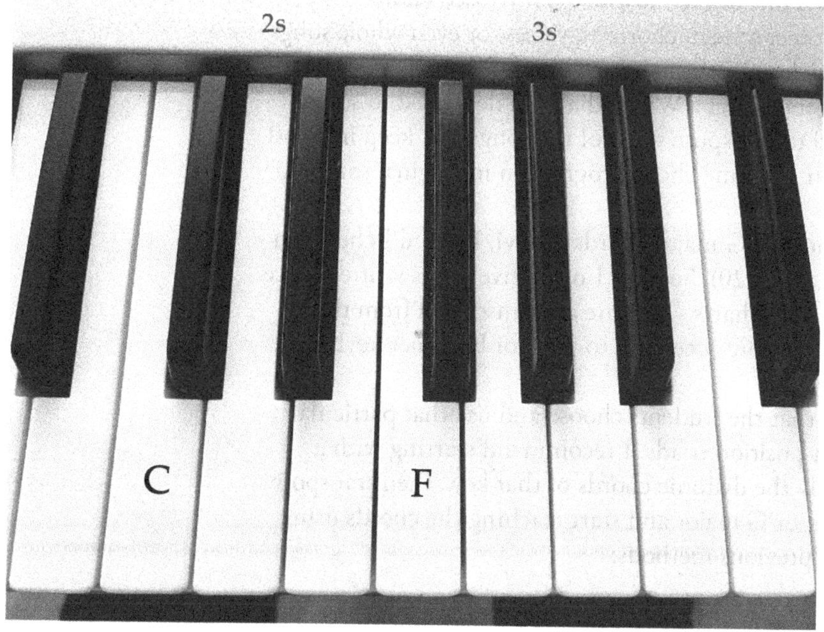

It is also important to realize that while keyboards might look similar to acoustic pianos, there are a lot of things that keyboards can do that pianos cannot do. Many popular keyboards used in schools allow the user to choose different sounds, have built-in beats, and transpose, and some can even split the keyboard into two different sounds. Allowing students to explore what the buttons do in the first class can be a fun activity to get students excited about learning the keyboard. If headphones are available for each keyboard, multiple keyboardists can explore different sounds and beats at the same time without disturbing the whole class.

ROOT-POSITION TRIADS

Once the students can find the Cs and Fs on the keyboard, they are ready to learn root-position chords, which will enable them to start playing along with the band, a backing track, and each other. By learning the diatonic C major chords, students can jam with a variety of popular songs using two, three, or four chord progressions.

Show students how to build a C major chord using fingers 1, 3, and 5 of the RH. Then ask them to explore and find other chords using the same hand shape, moving up or down on the keyboard and playing the white notes. Encourage students to share what they have found and then share with them the names of the chords. Let students explore the sounds of different chord patterns and introduce the concept of chord progressions. The following are some chord progressions you might consider using in the first classes.

1. Using the C major and F major triads (the I and IV chords in C major), you can teach the introduction and beginning verse of the Rolling Stones' classic rock song "You Can't Always Get What You Want." Direct students to play each chord on beat 1 of every measure.
2. Use the C major, G major, A minor, and F major triads (the I, V, vi, and IV chords in C major). Because this is one of the most frequently used chord progressions in popular music, you can teach choruses, verses, or even whole songs with just these four chords. A quick online search for four-chord songs on piano will lead you to many selections, including a Wikipedia page dedicated to songs using these chords. You will need to transpose some of the songs and keep in mind that in later classes, you can teach the same chord progression in original song keys.
3. Begin with the E minor, C major, and G major chords (the vi, IV, and I chords in G major), as used in Burstein et al. (2020). Section 1 offers five songs written since 2015 along with jam tracks and song charts. They are all transcribed from the original keys to G major so that they are accessible to play for beginner keyboard, bass, and guitar students.
4. Adapt a song or a part of a song that the students choose and use that particular song to teach the beginning root-position triads. I recommend starting with a song in a major key that uses only the diatonic chords of that key. Then transpose the chord progression to C major or G major and start teaching the chords using the same techniques as with the previous methods.

ADDING BASS NOTES IN THE LH: THE ROOT NOTES OF THE CHORDS

Once the students can play their first chord progression in the RH, you can introduce playing bass notes for the LH. Show students how to find the roots of the chords they already know. LH root notes should be played an octave lower than the RH chords. Students can use finger 2 for LH root notes; for an extra challenge, they can switch fingers on the different notes. Once students can play the RH chord changes with the roots in the LH, they are ready to learn comping patterns.

ADAPTIVE CHORDS FOR YOUNG STUDENTS AND STUDENTS WITH PHYSICAL DISABILITIES

Playing root-position chords with one hand is not feasible for all students. The following are a few options to make chords adaptable for various abilities.

1. Play the bottom note of the triad with an LH finger and the top two notes of the triad with two RH fingers. When changing chords, ask the students to keep the shape of their hands and move both hands to the next chord in the progression.
2. Play the bottom two notes of the triad only, with one hand or both hands, depending on ability and comfort level. Little Kids Rock (2019, now called "Music Will") refers to these chords as two-note chords or mini chords.
3. Use an iPad or tablet to access the keyboard instrument in Garage Band or a comparable app. After selecting the desired keyboard sound and key, students can play full triads with one finger.
4. Use the Makey Makey hardware and software to connect a laptop accessing a music program to everyday objects such as Play-Doh and fruit. Students can then touch the fruit or Play-Doh to trigger the desired chords. (Clauhs et al., 2020)

STRATEGIES FOR TEACHING CHORDS TO STUDENTS WITH VISUAL IMPAIRMENT

Students with visual impairment or low vision can learn chords quickly once they are familiar with the feel of the keyboard. Start with the C major and F major chords and use the familiarity of those chords to help students find the other diatonic chords of C major for the particular song you are teaching. The next step is to have your students feel the grooves in between the white keys, which will help them find other root-position triads in C major.

22.4 Introducing Iconic Notation, Comping Patterns, and Chord Chart Notation

Iconic notation for keyboard can be illustrated as a small portion of a keyboard with keys highlighted to indicate which notes should be played in a chord or a scale (see Figures 22.5 and 22.6). A quick internet search for piano chords or piano scales will get you started on the various options available for sale, including *Basic Piano Chord Chart* (Tomlins, 2004).

FIGURES 22.5 and 22.6 **Examples of iconic notation root-position triads: G major and E minor**

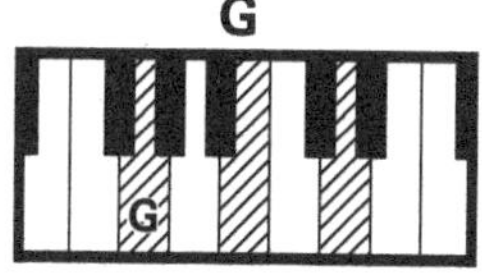

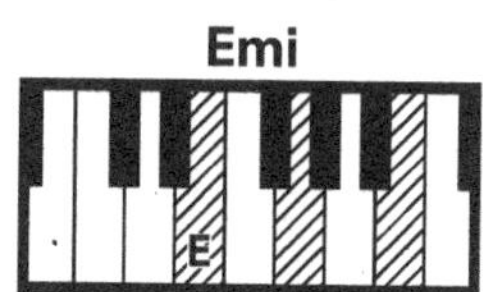

In addition, iconic notation can indicate chord changes within a song chart as well as comping patterns. Music Will (2019) developed a version of iconic notation which is also used in *Modern Band Method* (Burstein et al., 2020). Through their website, you can access free chord diagrams, scales (Figures 22.7, 22.8, and 22.9), comping patterns and a template for customizing your own song charts.

FIGURES 22.7, 22.8, and 22.9 Examples of iconic notation scales

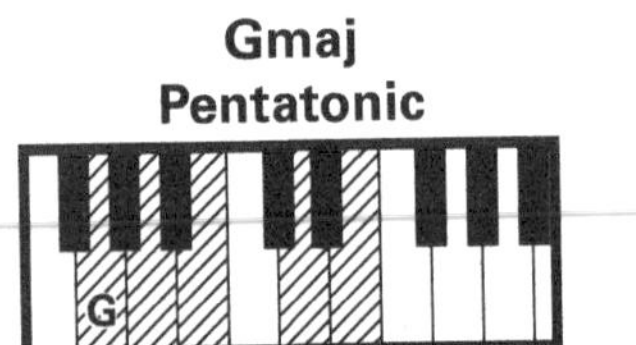

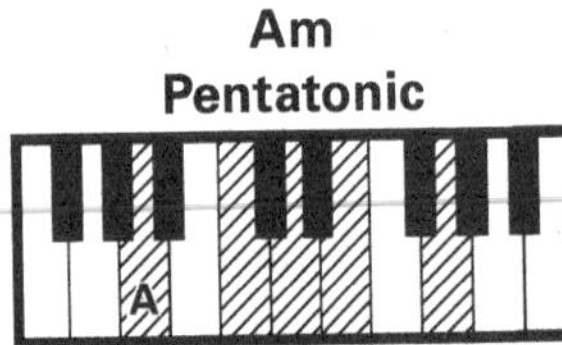

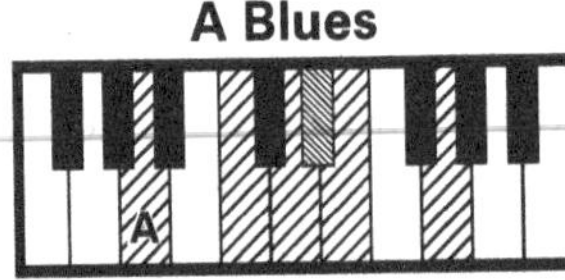

COMPING PATTERNS

Playing rhythmic patterns using chords is referred to as *comping*. Similar to guitarists strumming different patterns to match the feel of a song, keyboardists comp using different comping patterns (Clauhs et al., 2020). Comping patterns follow the groove of the song and are used to propel the melody and rhythmic feel of a song. Have students listen to a song with a strong piano part and have them clap along to the comping pattern played by the piano. Once they can clap along to the pattern, help them figure out what the chords are and then have them play along with the recording. Another way to help students work on this skill is to play a rhythm track, provide the students with a set of chords or even just a single chord, and have them figure out their own comping patterns using the rhythmic feel provided by the groove.

As an additional resource, the Music Will (2019) comping pattern diagrams use four beats subdivided into eighth notes and illustrate which beats the RH chords and LH bass notes need to play on. The three dots in the RH diagram represent the three notes of the chord. In more complex comping patterns, the RH can play one or two notes of the chord at a time (see Figures 22.10, 22.11, and 22.12).

FIGURES 22.10, 22.11, and 22.12 Examples of iconic notation comping patterns

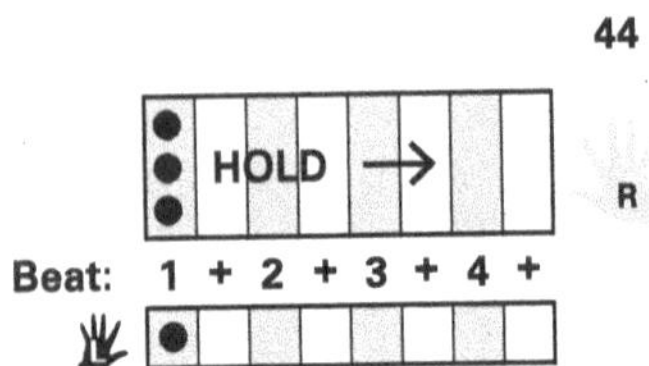

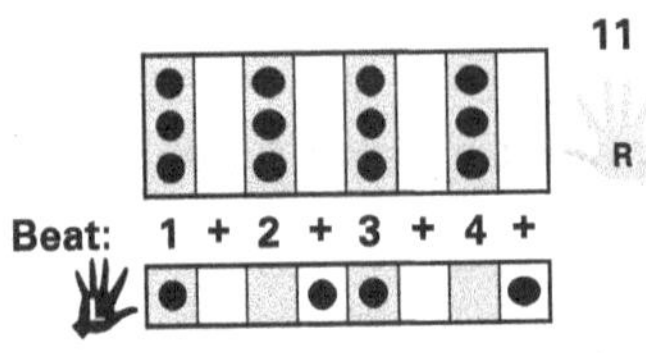

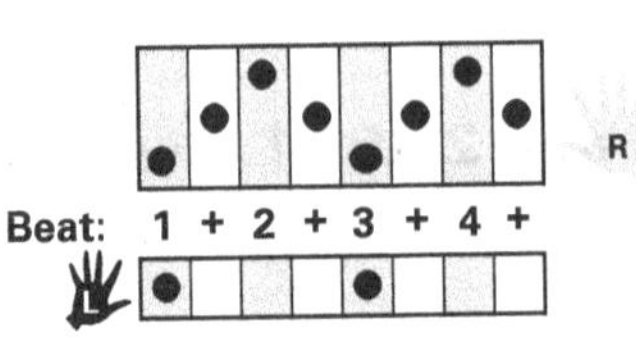

CHORD CHART NOTATION

An important aspect of popular music notation is a chord chart. You can ease into it with your students by using a verse or chorus only, rather than a full song chord chart. For example, if you are teaching songs with C–F chord progressions, you can customize a partial chord chart with the chords over the bars and the comping pattern or possible patterns underneath.

When the students are ready to play a whole song, have them create a chord chart for the song they are listening to. Alternatively, have the students create an eight- or sixteen-measure chord pattern using the chords they have learned and then create a chord chart that matches the way the chords move.

There are many free chord charts available online. There are also many free chord charts available on the Music Will (2019) website to use as is or as a reference for how you may want to consider building your own lead sheets. In Burstein et al. (2020), the song charts are provided.

Other ways to help students create chord charts are to search online for uploaded songs with lyrics and chords. Guide students to figure out the song's time signature, how many measures are in the song's sections, and the comping pattern. Students can then create chord charts using the lyrics and chords as a reference.

22.5 Lesson Ideas for Creative Musicianship

Encourage and inspire your students to explore their own creativity from the beginning classes by using improvisation and song recreation.

IMPROVISATION USING FAMILIAR NOTES

Improvising can be approached from the very beginning. Once students can play the first five notes of a C major scale, have them play around with discovering melodies using the notes in that scale. Have them share what they find with their classmates. Alternatively, have them simply play any white-key notes while a chord progression, such as I–vi–IV–V, plays in C major in the background.

After students are comfortable playing their first chord progression, guide them to improvise on single notes of those chords while you comp on the progression or use a jam track. You can also teach the pentatonic scale that is appropriate to use for the particular chord progression or song you are working on. If you have multiple keyboard players, have them take turns on improvising and comping.

RECREATING SONGS BY EAR

Figuring a song out is like a treasure hunt for all: fun and with great rewards. Once you know the specific part or parts to a song, you can guide students to hear and recreate the part. For example, if you are working on figuring out a short melodic line commonly found in many songs, these next steps break down the process.

1. Share with the students what they are listening for and play that section of the recording.
2. Sing it for them, ask them to sing it back, then play it again.
3. Ask them questions about the direction of the melody line or part. Ask them how many notes are being played. If they understand intervals or steps and skips, ask them about what they are hearing.
4. Share with them the starting pitch and remind them of what they learned in step 3. Then let them figure it out. Keep singing, remind them to sing, and continue playing the recording as needed.

Teaching your students this strategy for figuring parts out on their own will help them hone their listening skills and give them the freedom to explore whatever songs they like.

22.6 Strategies for Keeping Keyboard Students Engaged and Challenged

Going back to my summer camp days and coaching the keyboard section, I remember having to strike the right balance with my students as far as giving them a part that they can handle and that also could be expanded upon to make it more challenging, if needed. I learned that while some students need daily reinforcement and review of chords, comping patterns, finger numbers, and so forth, others are always ready for new challenges. The following topics offer some strategies for continuing to challenge your students at various musical stages.

TEACHING TRIAD INVERSIONS

Moving from one root-position chord to another is fine for the beginning keyboard player but becomes problematic when attempting more challenging comping patterns. For instance, keeping steady eighth notes in an arpeggiated pattern will feel either rushed or students will fall behind the beat when changing chords if they use only root-position chords. This is where using inversions is helpful. It is much more efficient to stay in the same area of the keyboard than to move up and down on the keyboard using root-position chords. In addition, most songs you will cover do use inverted chords, so students will play a more authentic version of the song when using the correct inversions.

TRANSITIONING TO READING TRADITIONAL MUSIC NOTATION

Students of various levels can transition to reading staff music notation while continuing to use song charts and iconic notation. Recycle songs or parts of songs that students already know to teach certain notes. A keyboard- or piano-prominent song can be the motivational tool needed to teach the notes and rhythms used in that particular song. Use music notation software to transcribe songs into accessible keys for your students' various levels.

CHALLENGES FOR PLAYING PARTS WITH BOTH HANDS

Challenge self-driven students to play two keyboard parts in addition to an RH comping pattern. For instance, a student working on "Clocks," by Coldplay, can play an RH arpeggiated comping pattern using a piano sound and LH blocked chords using a strings or synth pad sound. The keyboard would need to be edited and split so both sounds could be played on the same patch: one on the bottom, one on the top. Another challenge using the same song is for the student to play the RH comping pattern and the moving bass line in the LH, essentially doubling the bass part. This type of challenge involves more coordination between the hands than a static bass line.

SINGING AND PLAYING

Challenge your students from the very beginning to learn the lyrics of the songs they are playing. Lead the class to sing along with the recording. Then direct the students to sing the chorus on repeat while they play their respective parts. An additional possibility is to assign backing vocals and harmonies to those students that need extra challenges.

MOVING AND PLAYING

Encourage the students to feel the songs physically so they can move their bodies while playing. Leading the class into simple head-bopping to the beats, swaying from side to side or front to back while listening to recordings, can be helpful and fun. Then have the students to repeat the movements while playing a familiar song or chord progression.

22.7 Discussion Questions

1. How is learning to play the keyboard similar to, and different from, learning the piano?

Song selection:

1. What song or songs mentioned might you consider teaching in your first classes?
2. What songs do your students like? How might you incorporate your students' musical preferences into your teaching?
3. How can you engage the students in exploring and creating songs themselves and within the band using these chord progressions?

Improvising:

1. What improvising strategy do you want to use in your first or second class?
2. How can you encourage students to engage with improvisation?

Song recreation:

1. How can you engage the students in finding songs that they want to figure out?

22.8 Takeaways

- Start teaching root position chords in the first class by familiarizing students to their instrument, posture, finger positions and hand shape needed for chords.
- Use online resources to teach iconic notation and song charts as well as access video lessons and tutorials.
- Encourage students to be creative by using teaching tools for improvisation and song recreation.
- Use challenges to maintain students' interest.

OXFORD learning link

Visit the online resources for additional documentation and exercises to help expand learning and test your knowledge further: www.oup.com/he/powell_music1e.

CHAPTER 23

PEDAGOGIES FOR TEACHING DRUM SET IN POPULAR MUSIC EDUCATION

Mary Claxton

In this chapter we will explore drum-set concepts and the pedagogical considerations that go along with them. This instrument can be intimidating to some, but with the right preparation and classroom environment, it is a ton of fun.

Over the course of this chapter, you will learn about:

- Body drumming
- Beatboxing and transcription
- Set-up and posture
- Notation
- Drum grooves
- Improvisation
- Technique
- Role(s) in ensembles
- Basic maintenance and upkeep

Owing to the volume of drumming and typical equipment restrictions, body drumming can be a great place to start. Let's jump in!

23.1 Body Drumming

Body drumming is an immediate and accessible way for students to practice the coordination needed for drum-set playing. A simple beginning exercise is for them to take their cymbal hand and place it on their shoulder, while placing their snare-drum hand on their leg.

(*Note:* For most drummers [regardless of their dominant hand], their right hand is their cymbal hand and their left is their snare-drum hand. Playing the cymbal beat with the left hand is called playing "open handed" and is another option for drummers.)

Have the students start with the sequence of cymbal hand and both hands (alternating) in Figure 23.1. Let them repeat it several times or until it feels comfortable. This

FIGURE 23.1 Playing open handed

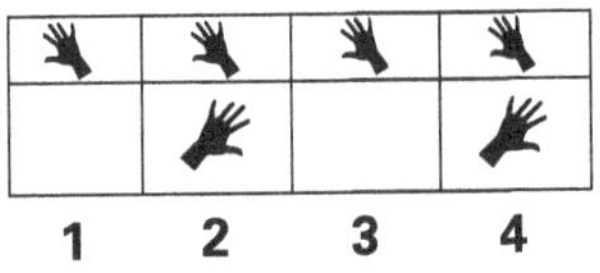

1 2 3 4

beat is the foundation of the *backbeat*, which they will play later. This basic, hands-only approximation can be put to use with many popular songs, such as:

"No One," by Alicia Keys
"Let's Dance," by David Bowie
"Seven Nation Army," by the White Stripes
"Dynamite," by Taio Cruz

On drum set, the notation will look like the kind shown in Figure 23.2.

FIGURE 23.2 Backbeat notation

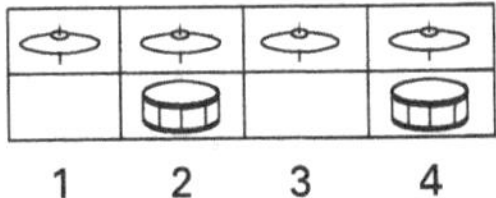

Next, students can change their cymbal rhythm to eighth notes, as shown in Figure 23.3.

FIGURE 23.3 Backbeat notation with cymbal playing 8th notes

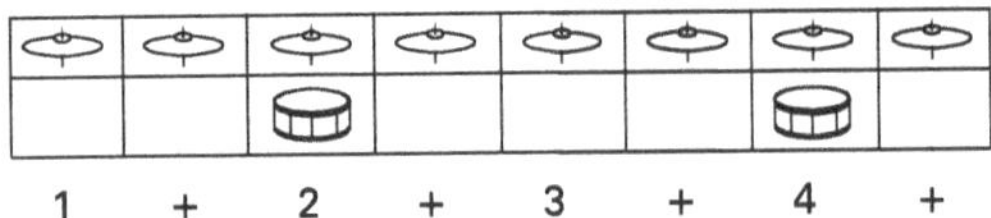

After practicing this, students can add in their right (bass-drum) foot, as shown in Figure 23.4.

FIGURE 23.4 Backbeat notation with bass drum added

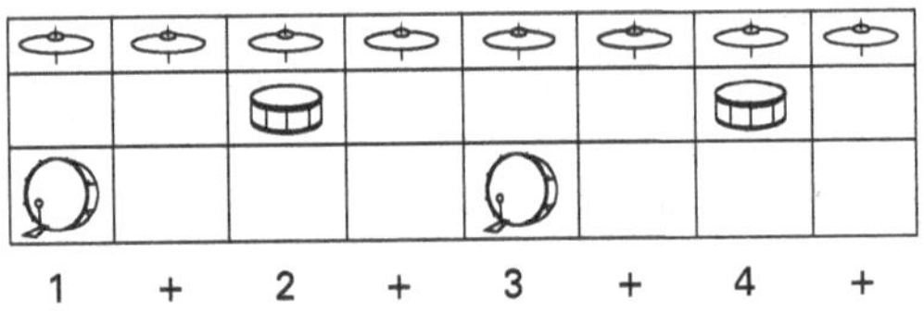

1 + 2 + 3 + 4 +

Introducing three-limb coordination is most attainable if students first practice the various two-limb combinations that make it up. For example, they started with their hands. They can then try bass drum and snare drum.

The beat students are now playing, the backbeat, is foundational to popular music spanning many genres. They can practice it with songs such as:

"Love on Top," by Beyoncé
"Comfortably Numb," by Pink Floyd
"Grandma's Hands," by Bill Withers
"Roar," by Katy Perry
"She's Everything," by Brad Paisley
"Dynamite," by BTS

As you go through the various groove examples outlined in this chapter, remember that students can always practice them with body drumming.

23.2 Beatboxing and Transcription

Let's start by having students listen to "Clint Eastwood," by Gorillaz (the clean version if you prefer). Have them try beatboxing along to the drum part. If they are new to beatboxing, have them listen to the sounds of the drum part and see if they can replicate some of those sounds vocally using a different sound for the kick, snare, and hi-hat. For example, a "tss" sound might work for a hi-hat, while a "kuh" sound might work for the snare drum.

Vocalizing drum patterns brings the students' attention to many essential elements of the music they are trying to emulate, such as tempo, groove, subdivision, tone, articulations, and dynamics. With beginning students, some of this can happen subconsciously without further dissection until they are ready to analyze and process the information. As they grow, we can ask such questions as:

- Have you heard this beat in a song before?
- Can you emulate the pattern happening between the bass drum and the snare drum? Can you write it down?
- What syllables or articulations mimic the *tone* of the drums in this recording?
- Which of the drum sounds is the loudest? Which is the softest?
- How long are the sounds? How do these translate to things like the tightness of the hi-hat, the tuning of the tom-toms, or the size of the bass drum?
- Are the sounds acoustic or electronic? How can we best translate to an acoustic setup *or* use electronics to supplement our sound?

These questions demonstrate some musical knowledge we can glean from vocal transcription. In another practical sense, it is often the case that drummers are not provided with written music. Unlike other rhythm section players, who have collections of lead sheets and tablature like Ultimate Guitar easily available, drum music for popular music is much less accessible. In addition, learning the rhythmic subtleties (related to subdivision, tone, etc.) is particularly important for the role of the drums. Therefore, it is in the best interest of any drummer to develop their ability to learn by ear from the very beginning of their practice.

23.3 Sitting at the Kit

Drumming is a very physical activity, and good posture is essential for safety as well as for musical facility and tone. Sitting at a drum set should be comfortable. While seated securely (not leaning left, right, forward, or back), the student should be able to reach all of their drums and cymbals with the tips of their sticks. Students can play in front of a mirror or use a video camera to review their posture.

In a classroom setting, it is important that students be empowered with the knowledge and permission needed to adjust the drum set to their bodies. This may mean an extra moment between songs or at the beginning of a rehearsal, but it is an essential step for a drummer's long-term health.

Figures 23.5 and 23.6 demonstrate common posture problems at the drum set—slumped posture and tense posture. In true Goldilocks fashion, drummers want to be "just right" and sit up straight without tension, as shown in Figure 23.7. Additionally, though playing drums doesn't require breath support in the direct way that, say, trumpet does, steady and relaxed breathing while playing helps drummers avoid tension.

FIGURE 23.5 (top left): Slumped

FIGURE 23.6 (top right): Shoulder tension

FIGURE 23.7 (bottom): Relaxed

23.4 Types of Notation

There are several types of notation used by drummers. We have already seen grid notation, like that shown in Figure 23.8.

FIGURE 23.8 **Standard grid notation for drummers**

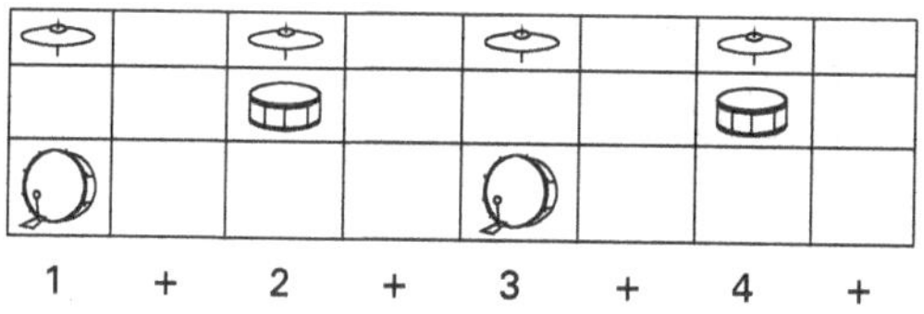

1 + 2 + 3 + 4 +

Grid notation sometimes uses dots, and other times an icon of the instrument being played. Either way, when it is ordered correctly, it transfers very nicely into percussion clef notation (see Figure 23.9).

FIGURE 23.9 **Percussion clef notation**

A grid is a very functional way to remember and communicate patterns. As previously mentioned, the drum set has a long history of aural tradition, so for certain styles this may be enough information for a player. Its limitations, however, become more apparent in a jazz big band, pit orchestra, or other more formal settings. Drummers who would like the option to perform in these types of ensembles should be encouraged to also read standard percussion-clef notation.

Here are the most commonly used instruments seen in drum notation. For a more complete list, see Audio Graffiti's *Guide to Drum and Percussion Notation.*

FIGURE 23.10 **Representation of each drum on percussion clef notation**

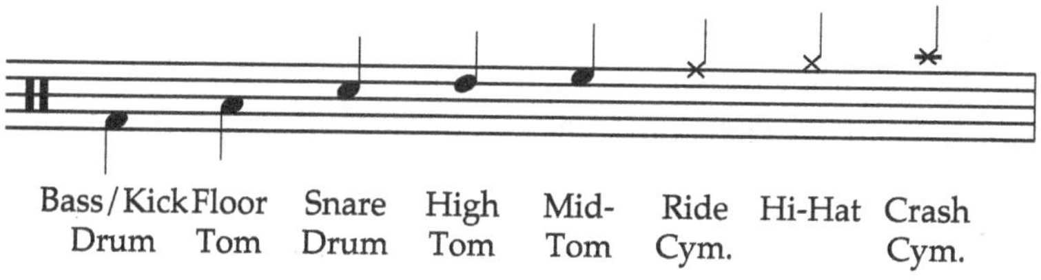

23.5 Comping

In a general sense, *comping* is making spontaneous rhythmic, harmonic, or melodic choices to support a musical performance. On the drum set, comping involves having a core groove for a given section and then making small creative choices to support the music.

For example, if the core groove is a backbeat (see Figure 23.11),

FIGURE 23.11 **Backbeat as core groove**

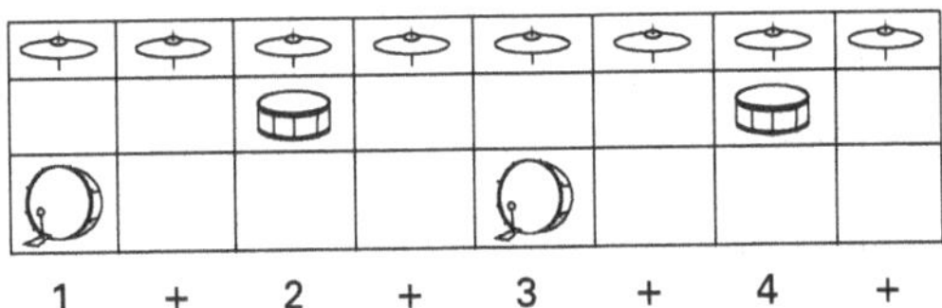

then students can use a bass-drum variation like the one seen in Figure 23.12 to emphasize something happening on the "and" of 2 in the music.

FIGURE 23.12 **Bass drum variation on backbeat groove**

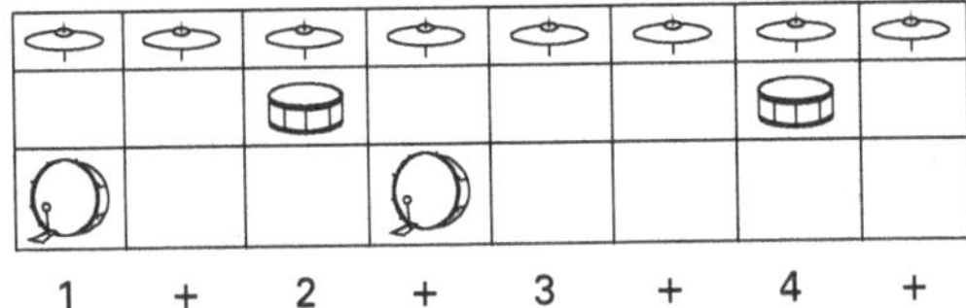

Or, they might indicate the end of the phrase by lifting their hi-hat pedal on the "and" of 4 (see Figure 23.13).

FIGURE 23.13 **Hi-hat variation on backbeat groove**

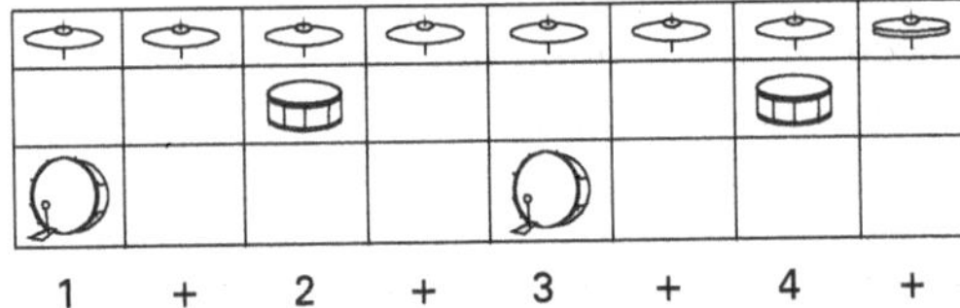

As a general rule, jazz involves the most comping, particularly in subgenres such as bebop. In other styles, such as pop, there is typically much less variation in the drum groove within sections, and the drummer is more inclined to rely on hits and fills (discussed next) to support the music.

HITS

Hits emphasize rhythmic and melodic ideas happening in music. A clear example of hits comes from the introduction of "Power of Love," by Huey Lewis and the News, where the drummer plays crash cymbals (and later open hi-hats) along with various synthesizer figures. In "Crybaby," by Lizzo, there are snare drum hits that emphasize the synthesizer figures.

Figure 23.14 presents a melodic figure that might be a good candidate for drum hits.

FIGURE 23.14 **Melodic figure on treble clef**

Students can use their own creativity to orchestrate hits along with this figure. Below are a few options you can give them to consider.

- Play the figure just on the snare drum to practice the rhythm (see Figure 23.15).

FIGURE 23.15 **Melodic figure played on snare drum**

- Experiment with various "stickings" (right or left hand).
- Consider the melodic arc. Can you approximate the line onto various instruments based on high and low pitch? (See Figure 23.16.)

FIGURE 23.16 **Melodic figure approximated onto various drums**

- Consider the note length. Is the band playing this figure legato or staccato? Can you use a longer-ringing instrument like a cymbal to play the longer notes and a shorter-ringing instrument like closed hi-hat or snare drum to play the shorter ones? (See Figure 23.17.)

FIGURE 23.17 **Melodic figure with cymbals playing the long tones**

Hits are indicated either with rhythms notated within the staff or using rhythms above the staff to show another instrument's part that should be emphasized.

FILLS

Fills are typically used to emphasize a new musical idea or section in the form of a song. Like hits, they can emphasize rhythmic or melodic ideas, but often they set, rather than reinforce, the tone.

Figure 23.18 shows the same melodic figure we saw in the "hits" section.

FIGURE 23.18 **Melodic figure on treble clef**

Now, imagine that after the final quarter rest, a chorus was about to start. The student may want to fill in that rest with a musical idea that will set the tone for volume, subdivision, and other musical elements. There are many options, both simple and complex, that would work in this space. For example, Prince famously had many fills that were a single snare drum hit on beat 4. To emulate that, they could play something like what is shown in Figure 23.19.

FIGURE 23.19 Example of a Prince-inspired drum fill

Or, they could play a busier idea to keep momentum going through the long note, as shown in Figure 23.20.

FIGURE 23.20 Idea for a busier drum fill

In general, it's common for an inexperienced drummer to see a fill as an opportunity to play many notes. While there is certainly a time and place for this, drummers' primary responsibilities are to complement the music, keep the time, and signal a new section to the band (and the listener).

In drum charts, composers and arrangers will often use text to indicate places where they expect drummers to fill. In charts for beginners, the writer may notate the fill, but it is more commonly up to the drummer's own discretion to decide what they would like to play in that space.

FIGURE 23.21 Percussion clef notation leaving space for drum fill

23.6 Groove Guide

First, a word of caution on learning drum grooves: any drummer is best served by learning drum grooves from audio musical examples. While it is helpful to see approximations of multiple styles cleanly notated in a book such as this one, genres are filled with subtleties that are difficult to capture on paper. There can even be a significant difference in the way two drummers approach the same written-down groove.

Next, a word of encouragement: the coordination used in drum-set playing is incredible, and at its best it is a fun challenge. Students of any age should be encouraged to have patience with themselves, focus on progress over perfection, and be willing to approximate.

Start by exploring some common backbeat variations. For notated examples for backbeat variations, see this book's online resources.

AFRO-CARIBBEAN DANCE BEAT

This family of grooves is extremely popular and wide-ranging. Depending on the region, variations on this beat include soca, reggaeton, dancehall, bomba, calypso, and legba. For examples of common variations of Afro-Caribbean dance beats, see this book's online resources.

CUMBIA

Cumbia music originated in Colombia and was typically played with traditional hand and stick drums, including the alegre, the guacharaca, the llamador, and the tambora. The rhythms were adapted to drum set after cumbia became an international success and entered the world of popular music. Currently, drums in cumbia music can also include sequenced patterns and electronic sounds.

HIP-HOP

Hip-hop DJs started by looping *drum breaks* from drummers on funk records. Because of this, hip-hop grooves often use sixteenth-note, syncopated ideas (see Figure 23.22). These days, these are often programmed using beat sequencers or other sampling technology.

FIGURE 23.22 **Hip-hop groove with syncopation**

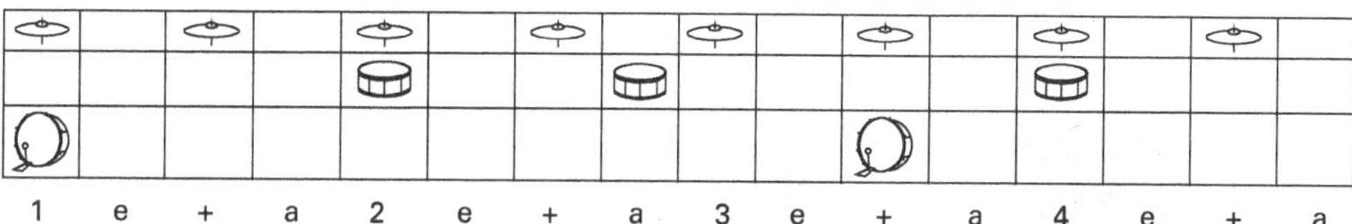

For more examples of syncopated drum grooves, including rhythms that use triple meter, see the online resources for this book.

23.7 Improvisation

Have the students start with an activity using the following steps.

1. Have the student put on any of the previously mentioned songs that use the backbeat or a variation of it.
2. Have them play quarter notes, starting on the snare drum and then moving to whatever drums or cymbals they choose.
3. Now, ask them to leave some quarter notes out completely.
4. Have them try doing this while keeping a steady quarter-note beat in one or both feet.
5. Next, have them mix in eighth notes.
6. Have them mix in some triplets.
7. Finally, try having them infuse some melodic ideas. Can they play along with the vocal melody of the song they chose? They can start on the snare drum, spread it around the kit, and give it their own spin!

At its best, improvisation is this easy. Just like language, the more *vocabulary* students can incorporate into their repertoire, the more they will be able to say. Like grooves, drummers typically learn their favorite solo material from recordings.

For drummers, improvisation either takes place

1. over *the form* of a given tune (even if chordal accompaniment is not being provided),
2. over a *vamp* section, or
3. in an *open* section (where time, feel, & harmony are fluid).

As we get into the next section, you will be able to see how the technique behind rudiments opens up another layer of rhythm and articulation possibilities in students' improvisation.

23.8 Technique

HANDS

Have the students wrap their hands around their drumsticks with their palms flat. There are multiple accepted and codified techniques for holding drumsticks, but the majority of popular music drummers play with *matched grip*. This means both hands use this grip.

FIGURE 23.23 Matched grip

FEET

Students can either play with heels slightly up or down, resting on the pedals. Many drummers do both depending on the musical context. What is most important is that they not rely on their feet to stay balanced.

RUDIMENTS

Play the snare drum with the following sequence (L = left hand, R = right hand):

L R L L/R L R R

Now congratulate your students—they just played your first rudiment, the *paradiddle.* Some folks think of rudiments as being the building blocks of drumming. Others think of them as tools in your drumming toolbox. In plain terms, they are names for just about every *sticking* combination that you can imagine. Have your students try some more. To begin, have them practice with their sticks feeling very even (the same motion and volume).

- Single strokes (see Figure 23.24)

FIGURE 23.24 **Single strokes**

- Double strokes (see Figure 23.25)

FIGURE 23.25 **Double strokes**

- Paradiddles (see Figure 23.26)

FIGURE 23.26 **Paradiddles**

A fantastic book for practicing sticking combinations is *Stick Control,* by George Lawrence Stone. Although it is conceptually simple, it has been valued by many drummers since the 1930s. Here are a few more rudiments (Figure 23.27):

FIGURE 23.27 **Rudiment example**

- Flam: A flam is played by adding a quieter grace note with one stick before the second stick plays on indicated beat. This doubling, accomplished by using two different stick heights (see Figure 23.28), creates a slightly thicker sound and is common in many styles of drumming.

FIGURE 23.28 **Drummer playing rudiment**

- Double-stroke open roll: A double-stroke open roll is played by letting each stick bounce twice before switching to the other stick. Ideally, both bounces will have the same consistency in volume and articulation.
- Multiple bounce roll: As the name suggests, multiple bounce rolls are played by letting each stick bounce multiple times (more than two). The number of bounces can vary by style, speed, and chosen technique.

There are more rudiments that are made up of various combinations of these previous elements. The Percussive Arts Society lists "International Drum Rudiments" along with audio examples on their website. Students can use creativity to combine bits and pieces of rudiments to make solos, fills, or melodies. You can also give them rudimental exercises to practice foot coordination and/or go between hands and feet. For example, paradiddles can be practiced between the right hand and bass drum. Finally, rudiments are often used to enhance the imitation of other instruments. For example, a long note on vocals could be imitated by playing a multiple bounce roll on the snare drum, while a short bend on the trombone might be well represented by a flam on a tom-tom.

EXTENDED TECHNIQUES

- Cross-stick: A cross-stick is played by holding the tip or bead of the stick on the head of the drum and striking the butt of the stick across the rim of the drum (see Figure 23.29). This creates a sound not unlike that of a clave. This sound can be used to play a snare drum rhythm with a different volume and/or texture.

FIGURE 23.29 Cross-stick technique

- Rim shot: A rim shot is played by striking the head of the drum with the tip or bead of the stick and the middle/shaft of the stick simultaneously (see Figure 23.30). This creates a rather loud and distinct sound, commonly used in emphatic passages of rock, funk, and more.

FIGURE 23.30 Rim shot technique

23.9 Roles in Ensembles

ESTABLISHING AND/OR REINFORCING SUBDIVISION

One of the primary roles of a drummer is to establish and/or reinforce the *subdivision* for the song at hand. *Straight* subdivision refers to the space between quarter notes being split evenly. *Swung* subdivision, at its simplest, refers to the space between quarter notes being split into three. The reality, however, is that swung subdivision often falls somewhere between groups of two and groups of three. For example, the subdivision of Joseph "Zigaboo" Modeliste's playing on "Hey Pocky A-Way" (the Meters) could certainly be called swung. So could Allison Miller's feel in "Goddess of the Hunt" (ARTEMIS), though it is certainly a very different spacing between notes. Terry Lyne Carrington's playing on "The Nurturer" has a straight eighth-note subdivision, but the sixteenth notes are swung. All of these musical choices are fantastic, but they only work if the drummer's feel is matched up with the subdivision used by the rest of the band or group. The indefinable nature of swing (and its subdivision) is one of the things that makes it fascinating. It is also another great reason to reference audio examples in addition to written ones, as so much of that subtlety is lost in notation.

BALANCE CONSIDERATIONS

Balance is a potentially challenging consideration for drummers. They have to consider balance between their own multiple instruments as well as their overall balance with the rest of the ensemble. Both elements of balance shift by genre and by time period. It is common in contemporary popular music for the bass drum and snare drum to be prominent, with a lighter cymbal sound.

Drums are intended to be loud, but not every classroom or performance space lends itself to drums being played at full volume. As the teacher, you can incorporate mutes to help reduce the decibel level. These can be purchased or made from materials such as cloth or rubber matting.

Note: It is highly recommended to use ear protection whenever playing drums to avoid long-term hearing loss.

23.10 Basic Maintenance and Upkeep

CLEANING

Drums and cymbals should be wiped down regularly with a clean, dry cloth. If you are working in a classroom setting, assign this as a regular practice with your students and allow them to care for the instrument(s).

Note: While cymbals *can* be cleaned and/or polished with a specific cymbal-cleaning solution, many drummers prefer the sound of aged or weathered cymbals (some go so far as to bury them in the ground for a while, which I am not personally suggesting).

CHANGING DRUM HEADS

Drum heads need to be changed periodically, though how often is highly dependent on the amount of use they receive. The top head, or the one that is struck, is called the *batter* head, and the bottom head is called the *resonant* head. In general, batter heads will need more frequent replacement. Here are some simple steps to follow during this process.

It should be noted that there are some variations in tuning systems on drums, but the process detailed below is fairly standard on contemporary drum sets.

1. Remove the old drum head (see figure 23.31). Loosen each lug around the hoop until the tension rod can be taken out. To do this, you will need a drum key (a crescent wrench works in a pinch).

FIGURE 23.31 Drum key

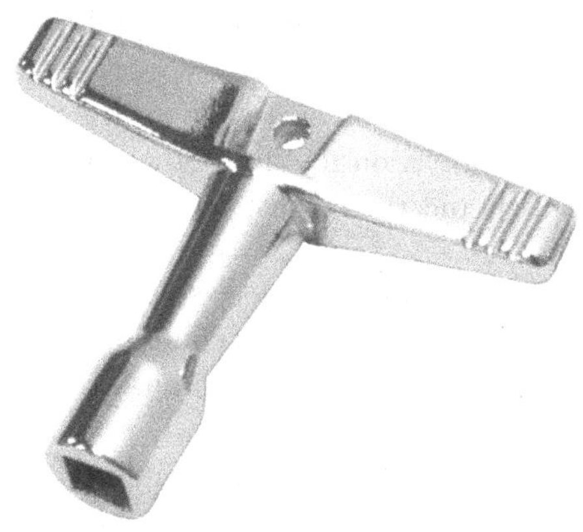

2. Clean both the hoop and the drum with a dry cloth. Ensure that no dirt or dust is inside the drum.
3. Place the new head onto the drum, making sure it sits evenly.
4. Replace the hoop onto the rim of the drum.
5. It is recommended to use a small amount of lubricant on the bottom of each tension rod. Many drum companies sell a variation of this grease, which will help facilitate smooth motion during the tuning process.
6. Using your fingers, tighten each tension rod down to the hoop.
7. At this point, you can begin to seat the head. This looks strangely like administering CPR chest compressions. Press firmly on the head to loosen it. It is normal to hear some stretching sounds. This step helps your initial tuning to hold longer.
8. Your drum head has been replaced, and you may now tune your drum. For an initial or more serious tune-up, it is recommended to use a star pattern (see the order of Figure 23.32), which helps hold tension evenly.

FIGURE 23.32 Star pattern for tuning drum head

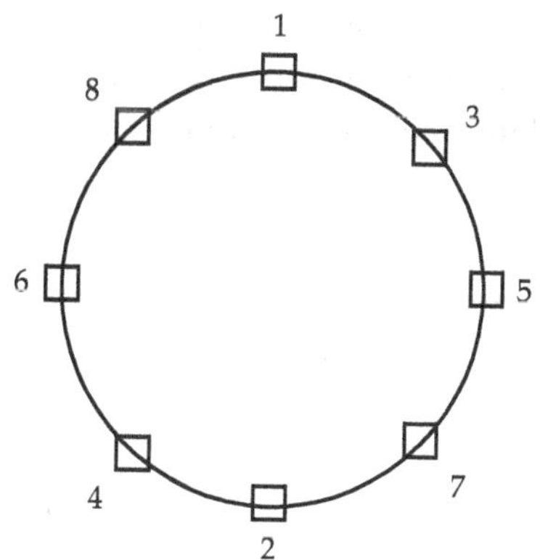

TUNING

Unsurprisingly, drum heads that get repeatedly struck with sticks will stretch out and go out of tune. Learning to tune drums takes practice, though the principle is simple: create equal tension at all of the lugs around the head using your drum key.

To tune by ear, drummers tap lightly near each of the lugs, about an inch from the rim. They then compare the pitches and tighten or loosen each lug to reach the desired tension. While some drummers aim for a given pitch, others solely aim for a tension and/or timbre that fits their musical needs.

There are also various devices, both analog and digital, that measure tympanic pressure when placed on the head. For the beginner or busy educator, this can be a very helpful tool.

Both the top (batter) and bottom (resonant) heads will need to be tuned. There are various schools of thought about how to tune drum heads in relation to one another. A good place to start is to tune both heads to the same pitch and then adjust the top or bottom in half-step increments.

Ultimately, tuning is a personal preference, though it is common to use recordings of drummers in your preferred style as a reference point. That as a starting place, combined with experimentation, will ultimately lead to a preferred sound (or sounds) and a knowledge of how to achieve them.

Note: Tuning should be done regularly, depending on level of use. However, if dimpling or wrinkling ever appears on a head, tune immediately to reduce the risk of permanent damage.

MUFFLING

After tuning, you may find that you want a shorter or dryer sound out of your drums or cymbals. Many, if not most, drummers use muffling, particularly in situations such as the recording studio. Ultimately, models, experimentation, and the ear are the best ways for students to learn to mute. Here are some suggestions to get them started.

- Several companies make gels that are designed for drums or cymbals, are removable, and do not leave residue. In a classroom setting, make sure to leverage student leadership to keep gels in good shape and in a consistent storage location.
- Gaff tape is a useful tool for drummers, as it does not leave a residue but holds up fairly well. Students can use strips of gaff tape on its own for drums or cymbals, or they can use it to attach a small mute (paper towels can even be effective here).
- You may be familiar with the idea of putting a pillow, blankets, or other muffling inside a bass drum. This is a legitimate muting technique. However, it has two potential drawbacks. First, unless you have a porthole (a circular hole for inserting a microphone into the resonant head) that your muting will fit through, you will not be able to easily adjust the amount of muting material. Second, sometimes "over-muting" is used as a replacement for having a drum properly tuned. With these two considerations, I would recommend trying gaff-tape solutions before an overreliance on muting within the drum itself.

23.11 Discussion Questions

1. What connections and differences are there between learning drums and other instruments?
2. What are the differences and similarities between comping, hits, fills, and improvisation?
3. Describe ways that you could incorporate drumming into various class settings.
4. What challenges might you face with drum materials and maintenance? What are some ways to overcome these?

23.12 Suggested Further Reading

- *Kick It: A Social History of the Drum Kit*, by Matt Brennan
- *Modern Band Method—Drums, Book 1*, by Scott Burstein, Spencer Hale, Mary Claxton, & Dave Wish
- *Rudimental Ritual*, by Alan Dawson
- *Mel Bay's Drum Cookbook*, by John Pickering
- *When the Drummers Were Women: A Spiritual History of Rhythm*, by Layne Redmond
- *Progressive Steps to Syncopation for the Modern Drummer*, by Ted Reed
- *Women Drummers: A History from Rock and Jazz to Blues and Country*, by Angela Smith
- *I Think, Therefore I Drum*, by Gareth Dylan Smith
- *Stick Control*, by George Lawrence Stone
- *The Sound of Brushes*, by Ed Thigpen
- *The Essence of Afro-Cuban Percussion and Drum Set*, by Ed Uribe

OXFORD learning link

Visit the online resources for additional documentation and exercises to help expand learning and test your knowledge further: www.oup.com/he/powell_music1e.

CHAPTER 24

PEDAGOGIES FOR TEACHING VOCALISTS IN POPULAR MUSIC ENSEMBLES

Kat Reinhert

This chapter is designed to give popular music ensemble directors a basic understanding of the voice and how it works so as to help them empower the singers in their ensembles.

Many ensemble leaders are tasked with helping young vocalists develop their voices through singing in an ensemble. Whether you're a choral teacher leading a pop a cappella group or a bass player working with the lead singer in a rock band, understanding the basics of how the voice functions is important. Just like understanding how a trumpet or saxophone works, this knowledge can assist the ensemble director in helping the singers in their ensemble achieve their best.

24.1 The Voice: Five Basic Systems Working Together

One way to think of the voice and how it makes sound is the power-source-filter model (Russo et al., 2020; see Figure 24.1). The power is the breath, the source is where sound is made, and the filter is how the sound can be altered above the level of the vocal folds. Within each section of this model are systems that work together to enable the production of sound.

FIGURE 24.1 Power-source-filter model

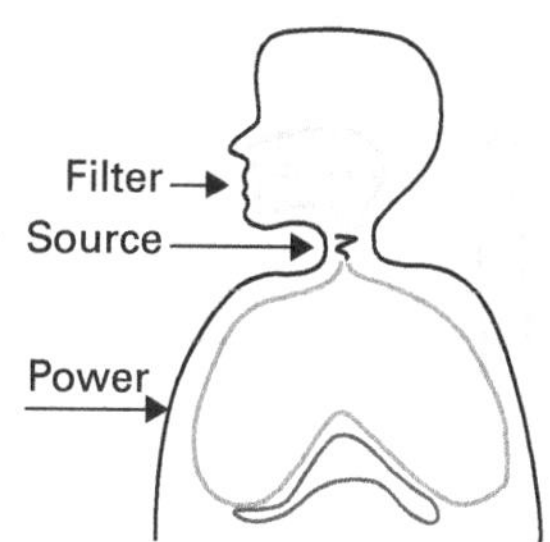

POWER

The power for singing starts with the breath, located within the respiratory system. Understanding the basics of how the system works can help students use their air more effectively so as to produce sound that is supported and efficient.

When inhaling, the air travels through the mouth, past the vocal folds, and into the lungs. The diaphragm, an umbrella-shaped muscle that separates the lungs and abdominal muscles, is connected to the rib cage. As the muscles connected to the rib cage expand, the dome of the "umbrella" flattens downward, and air rushes past the vocal folds and into the lungs. Then, as those same muscles connected to the ribs contract, the umbrella recoils back to its original position and the air rushes back out past the vocal folds. Voilà—breathing.

Breathing is where the power for singing is generated. Whether someone wants to sing soft or loud, the regulation of air past the vocal folds is necessary. Without adequate and efficient breath management, singers often struggle with singing long or loud phrases, as well as staying in tune on certain vowels at certain volumes. Volume (loud and soft, and everything in between) is determined by the amount of time the vocal folds stay closed versus open and how much air moves past them during a phase of vibration.

For additional breathing practice exercises, visit the online resources.

SOURCE

The larynx (*lehr*-inx) is the system within the voice where sound is produced (Figure 24.2). It is located in the throat beneath the epiglottis (the covering that directs food to the stomach instead of the lungs). The front part of the larynx is sometimes referred to as the Adam's apple.

FIGURE 24.2 **Larynx, from *Anatomy of the Voice* (Dimon, 2018)**

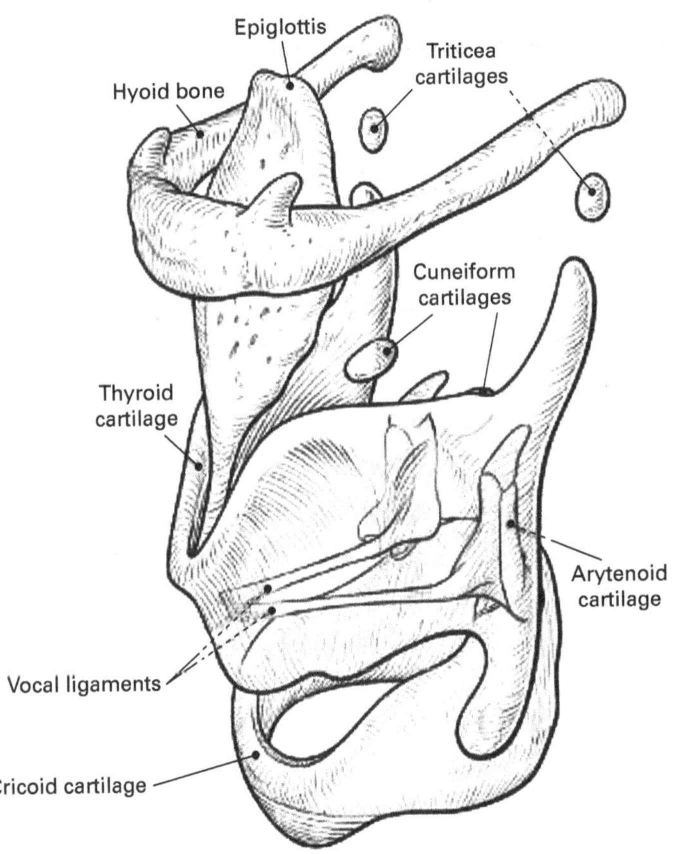

For a resource on how to find the larynx, visit the online resources.

Located at the center of the larynx are the vocal folds. The vocal folds (also known as vocal cords) are a valve that allows air in and out of the lungs. They are also the sound generator within the human body. To make sound, the vocal folds are drawn together and begin to oscillate, generating sound waves that pass into the space above the larynx, creating what we know as vocal sound (Dimon, 2018, Leborgne & Rosenberg, 2014, 2019; Malde et al., 2016). Whatever pitch someone is singing is how fast the vocal folds are oscillating per second. For example, if someone is singing A440, that means the vocal folds are coming together and apart 440 times *per second*. That's pretty amazing, right?

The words "chest," "head," and "mix" are often used to describe vocal sound. Chest-dominant sounds are most easily found in lower pitches, and the term "chest" comes from the sensation that the sound are waves resonating within the chest cavity. Head-dominant sounds are most easily found in higher pitches, and the term "head" comes from the sensation of the sound waves resonating within the head and nasal cavities (Dimon, 2018, LeBorgne & Rosenberg, 2014, 2019; Malde et al., 2016).

For further explanation of registers, visit the online resources.

Singing in tune has to do with the ability of the muscles to hold a certain pitch on a certain vowel with a certain loudness, all while coordinating with the neurological and audio feedback loops. If the muscles are weak, the ability to match pitch will also suffer.

FILTER

The pharynx and the face encompass everything above the larynx and vocal folds—the tongue, soft palate, face, and mouth (Figure 24.3). By moving parts of the pharynx to direct the air in specific ways, specific sounds are elicited from the system that then result in sensations—and perceived emotions (Dimon, 2018, Leborgne & Rosenberg, 2014, 2019; Malde et al., 2016).

FIGURE 24.3 **Pharynx, from *Anatomy of the Voice* (Dimon, 2018)**

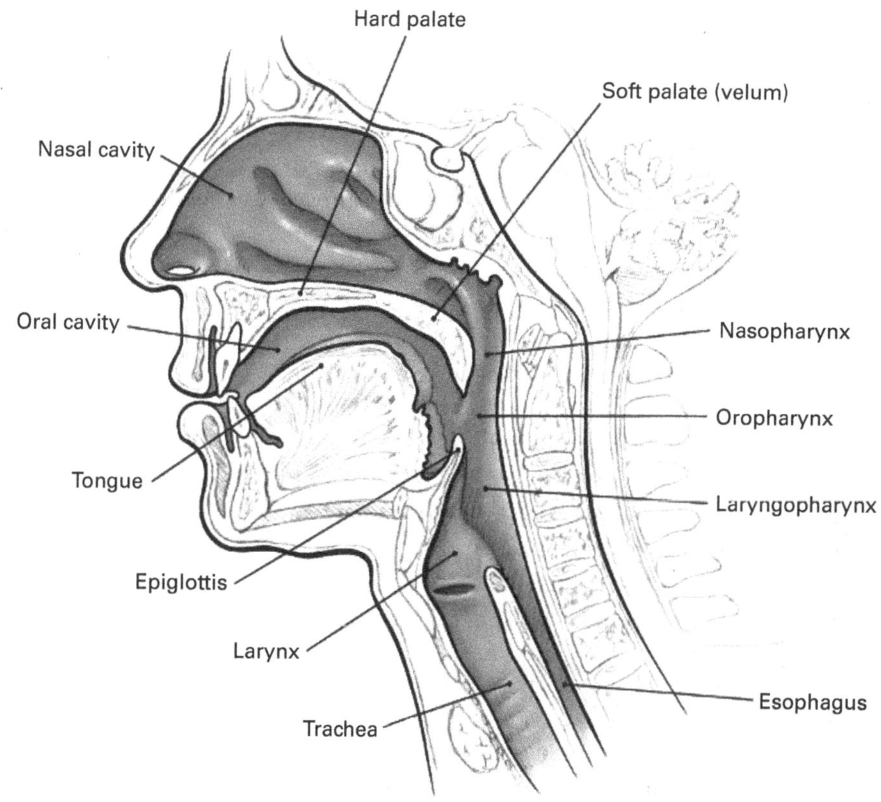

Vowels are made within the pharynx. Think of vowels on a continuum of dark to bright, not only with reference to themselves, but in relationship to other vowels, with /o/ as in *glow* and /ɑ/ as in *not* (dark) on one side, and /e/ as in *bee* and /æ/ as in *cat* (bright) on the other. Sometimes, if a singer is struggling with intonation, helping them shape the vowel in a way that helps direct the airflow may improve intonation. Shifting and changing vowels can also be an asset when moving between different genres, such as from a blues sound to a more indie-pop sound.

For further explanation of vowel shapes, visit the online resources.

Articulation has to do with the movement of the lips and the tongue and how they interact with the teeth. The common musical theater saying "To the lips, to the teeth, to the tip of the tongue" is actually a great exercise to help students understand articulation.

For further demonstration of articulation practices, visit the online resources.

In review, the voice is a complex muscle system. It is made up of three large sections (power, source, and filter) that work together to produce myriad sounds and timbres. With this working knowledge of voice function, now it's time to consider how this looks in practice. For more in depth understanding and diagrams, I recommend *Anatomy of the Voice*, by Theodore Dimon.

24.2 Pedagogical Considerations

CONTEMPORARY SINGING METHODS

There are many approaches to teaching contemporary, popular, and commercial singing (Benson, 2020; Hoch, 2018; Hughes, 2010, 2017; LeBorgne & Rosenberg, 2014, 2019). However, there is an agreed understanding that popular music is amplified music (Benson, 2020; Edwards, 2014; Hughes, 2017; Reinhert, 2019). Amplification allows vocal sounds to be heard above a band (Benson, 2020; Edwards, 2014; Hughes, 2017; LeBorgne & Rosenberg, 2014, 2019).

VOCAL HEALTH AND WELLNESS

A vocalist's instrument is located within their body. This presents a unique challenge in terms of maintenance of the instrument. Stress and anxiety can have profound effects on the ability of someone to make sound. One of the most common issues vocalists will face is vocal fatigue. Extensive voice use over the course of a day can negatively impact the vocal mechanism, potentially causing vocal strain or injury. Vocal load, which is "the amount of voice use within the parameters of intensity, pitch and duration" (LeBorgne & Rosenberg, 2019, p. 145), has a profound effect on the health of the voice. Educating singers in popular music ensembles (PMEs) about vocal load, efficient breath management, and effective speech patterns can help alleviate some vocal fatigue. Other factors that can help prevent vocal fatigue are adequate hydration, warming up before singing, effective technique while singing, and microphone and monitor use during rehearsal. Singing should not be painful, involve straining, or cause loss of voice. If any of these are happening with a singer in your ensemble, seek advice from a voice professional, an ear, nose, and throat specialist, or an otolaryngologist as soon as possible.

WARM-UPS AND EXERCISES

When singing in PMEs, it is important to warm up and exercise the system using sounds that are found in popular music. This helps to align the vocal tract and prepare the muscular system for the work it will be doing. There are some basic exercises that can help students gain more facility within their voice and can often produce results fairly quickly.

When choosing an exercise, consider what the exercise is doing in relation to the function of the voice and what the student might need or request in terms of help. Once the goal is identified, it is then possible to use combinations to create exercises that will address specific aspects of vocal production (Baldwin, 2021).

Figure 24.4 provides some basic warm-ups and exercises to work on specific aspects of the voice.

For a demonstration of the exercises within the guide, visit the online resources.

REPERTOIRE

Student choice is important in PMEs. Provide opportunities for the students to suggest repertoire and to give reasons they want to play it, and ask them to demonstrate why they think it would be good for the band.

Things to consider when helping students choose repertoire:

1. Key
2. Playability (too hard vs. too easy: find the sweet spot)
3. Adaptability
4. Style
5. Original music

KEYS AND RANGE

Helping students choose a key is about consistency of style and intention. If the original key does not work, find keys for songs that allow the desired sounds endemic to the style to be made in a comfortable manner. Consider the overall vibe and message of the song and how it fits into a singer's voice and range. When playing with a band, it is also worth considering how to navigate between what the instrumentalists can play and what the singer or singers can sing. Usually there is a way to negotiate between the two that works for both entities, but with an awareness that the vocalist will be limited by their biology.

If you notice that the student is doing any of the following, most likely the song is out of their range (too high or too low) and they are struggling to sing the song.

1. Chin goes up or is tucked in to "get" the note—as if that is the only way to reach it
2. Visible tension in the jaw
3. Unintentional rasp or artifact in the sound
4. Distorted vowels
5. Body distortion—raised shoulders, standing on tiptoes, head tilted to one side
6. Low notes sound distorted and muffled as if in a vacuum, not as an effect

If any of these sounds occur, suggest a key change and see if even a whole step in one direction can make a difference, or give suggestions for alternative songs in a similar style that have a different key. Alternatively, suggest that a voice professional work with them to help develop their voice. This is a long-term solution, taking months and/or years. It can be an opportunity to bring in an outside expert or enlist the help of a colleague.

AGE-BASED CONSIDERATIONS

In middle school, as students move through puberty, the male voice will most often exhibit the most profound change, sometimes with the ability to only sing within a three-to-five-note range. The female voice will also exhibit changes, possibly losing some upper

FIGURE 24.4 Vocal workout guide

EXERCISE TYPE	SOUND, VOWEL, LOCATION	SCALE DEGREE PATTERN	WOMEN: PITCH RANGE
WARM UP	lip trills, straw kazoo, raspberries, humming (/m/ or /n/), straw in water	1,5,1	starting on middle D and then going down, then up to a moderately high pitch that is easily accessible then back down to starting pitch
WARM UP	ah or oh	1,5,1	starting on middle D and then going down, then up to a moderately high pitch that is easily accessible then back down to starting pitch
WARM UP	ha, hee, ho	1,3,5,8,5,3,1	starting on A below middle C and then going down, then up to a moderately high pitch that is easily accessible then back down to starting pitch
WARM UP	ga-da, ba-da, nah-nah	1,1,3,3,5,5,8,8,5,5,3,3,1,1	starting on A below middle C and then going down, then up to a moderately high pitch that is easily accessible then back down to starting pitch
FLEXIBILITY	eh, ah, ae,	1,2,3,5,6,5,3,2,1	starting on A below middle C and then going up to about an A or B above middle C, then back down to starting pitch
FLEXIBILITY	any	123, 234, 345, 4321	starting on middle C and going up in half step intervals with each iteration of the exercise until about a high D
STRENGTH	Oh	1 - 2 - 1	A below middle C, down a few notes, then back up to about an E above middle C
STRENGTH	meah, ming	1,2,3,2,1	starting on A above middle C in head register and going up to about a G if accessible
BREATH EFFICIENCY	ha	1,3,5, 3,1	starting on A below middle C and then going down, then up to a moderately high pitch that is easily accessible then back down to starting pitch
BREATH EFFICIENCY	sss or zzz or fff	none	none
BREATH EFFICIENCY	any, can also use lip trill or straw blowing into water	one note hold	any
RELAXATION/TENSION RELEASE	straw bubbles into water	1,5,1	starting on A below middle C and then going down, then up to a moderately high pitch that is easily accessible then back down to starting pitch
RELAXATION/ TENSION RELEASE	straw phonation glides	1, 5, 1 or 1, 8, 1	starting on A below middle C and then going down, then up to a moderately high pitch that is easily accessible then back down to starting pitch
PHYSICAL EXERCISES	neck	looking slowly over shoulder left to right	none
PHYSICAL EXERCISES	neck	ear to shoulder	none
PHYSICAL EXERCISES	neck & shoulders	shoulders to ears	none
PHYSICAL EXERCISES	jaw	palm flat on cheek	none

MEN: PITCH RANGE	VOLUME (1=SOFT 10=LOUD)	EXECUTION
starting on D below middle C and then going down, then up to a moderately high pitch that is easily accessible then back down to starting pitch	medium-soft (3-4)	sliding between pitches
starting on D below middle C and then going down, then up to a moderately high pitch that is easily accessible then back down to starting pitch	medium (4-5)	sliding between pitches
starting on D below middle C and then going down, then up to a moderately high pitch that is easily accessible then back down to starting pitch	medium-soft (3-4)	jumping between pitches, light execution, smiley face, tongue and jaw neutral
starting on D below middle C and then going down, then up to a moderately high pitch that is easily accessible then back down to starting pitch	medium (4-5)	jumping between pitches, light execution, smiley face, tongue and jaw neutral
starting on A octave and a 3rd below middle C and then going up to a moderately high pitch that is easily accessible and back down to starting pitch	medium-soft (3-4)	glottal attack, then breathy attack, then coordinated sound
starting on D below middle C and then going down, then up to a moderately high pitch that is easily accessible then back down to starting pitch	medium-soft (3-4)	quick, light, as smooth and connected as possible at the given speed. accuracy is more important than speed, especially at beginning - as flexibility grows, speed can increase
D below middle C, down a few notes, then back up to about a G below middle C	loud (6-7)	chesty, bright, smiley. Can place tongue over straw or chopstick while singing. Maintain equal volume between two pitches.
starting on A below middle C in head register and going up to about a G if accessible	medium (4-5)	nasty, bright, forward sound. head register strengthening.
starting on A octave and a 3rd below middle C and then going up to a moderately high pitch that is easily accessible and back down to starting pitch	medium (4-5)	skipping, short staccato notes, engaging the abdominal muscles/diagraphm with intension
none	soft (1-2)	inhale as if through a straw, expanding into rib cage and lower part of the lungs so that abdomen expands, then belly button to backbone on the exhale - using one of the fricatives (s,z,f)
any	any	hold one note on either one constant vowel or a series of vowels while maintaing steady breath pressure which will result in even-ness of the sound
starting on A octave and a 3rd below middle C and then going up to a moderately high pitch that is easily accessible and back down to starting pitch	Medium-soft (2-3)	slides while blowing even bubbles into the water. concentrate on maintaining even breath flow = even bubbles
starting on A octave and a 3rd below middle C and then going up to a moderately high pitch that is easily accessible and back down to starting pitch	soft (1-2), medium-soft (2-3)	blow into straw like using a small kazoo. not too loud, focus awareness on open-ness of the throat
none	quiet	slow, deliberate, holding in each position for at least 10 seconds before swiveling neck in other direction. At least two times in each direction - looking for a point further than the last on each iteration - but without forcing
none	quiet	ear to shoulder - NOT shoulder to ear. slow, deliberate motion, holding in each position for at least 10 seconds before moving to alternate side. At least two times in each direction Ideally, head should hang heavy
none	quiet	bring shoulders up to ears in exaggerated shrug and hold for at least 10 seconds. drop shoulders and roll head around gently. At least 3 times up and down.
none	quiet	press palm gently into cheekbone on one side of face while simultaneously pressing jaw into the palm - hold for 20-30 seconds. repeat on opposite side

range. A slightly breathy tone may also be present in the voice at this time. In high school, although many in this age group have grown past the initial stages of puberty, there are still physical changes occurring in the voice and body. There is also a growing body of evidence on nonbinary students that can provide specific knowledge. Keys should be chosen to adequately support the changing voices.

These stages of vocal development can be very uncomfortable for singers. As the body adjusts to the new mechanism, sounds that were once easily made may become difficult, and vice versa.

Confidence in their new voices may take time to develop. Be kind.

24.3 Other Considerations

PLAYABILITY

Can the students in the PME play the music? Is it learnable in the desired amount of time? If it's too hard, can the original arrangement be adapted? Could the key be changed? Could some parts be altered or moved to other instruments (e.g., horn parts moved or embellished on a synth)? Be creative. I highly recommend *Coaching a Popular Music Ensemble*, by Steve Holley, as a resource for more on this aspect of PMEs.

STYLE AND GENRE

Choosing music—or helping guide students to choose music—in a diverse set of styles and genres will help the overall musicianship of the PME thrive. Additionally, this will allow the different kinds of voices one might find in a PME to shine with their own light, while other voices can shine as backup singers. Exposing students to different genres can also provide experiences for them to explore music outside their—and your—comfort zone.

ORIGINAL MUSIC

Original music is a meaningful choice to consider in regard to repertoire. If anyone in the band is interested in writing, have them connect with the singer of the band (it may or may not be the same person) and have them co-write a song. Or, if anyone in the band has written a song, ask them if they would want to front the band for that song.

CULTURAL CONSIDERATIONS

Acknowledging the rich history, culture, and traditions of popular music can highlight areas of diversity, equity, and inclusion in a PME (Smith & Shafighian, 2014). The ongoing importance of avoiding hegemony and creating inclusive spaces of all kinds, while simultaneously promoting democratic and culturally relevant teaching that ultimately leads to self-expression, is the goal (Allsup, 2008; Hess, 2019; Woodward, 2017).

TECHNOLOGY

It is vital for any PME leader to be comfortable with technology, and one of the most important pieces of music technology in regard to vocal health is the microphone.

MICROPHONES

Microphones and monitors are essential equipment for singers in popular music ensembles. It is physically impossible for a young singer to out-sing a drum set, electric guitars and bass, and keyboards. Vocal fatigue and potentially damage could occur to the singer or singers if a microphone is not employed. Microphones and monitors (see Figure 24.5) are required in PMEs to amplify voices so that the singers can hear themselves and the band can hear them.

FIGURE 24.5 Dynamic microphone

Dynamic Microphone

1) Sound strikes diaphragm (thin plastic membrane)
2) Diaphragm vibrates in response
3) Voice coil (attached to diaphragm) vibrates
4) Vibration of voice coil and magnet create magnetic field
5) As voice coil moves, magnetic field turns acoustic energy into an electric signal

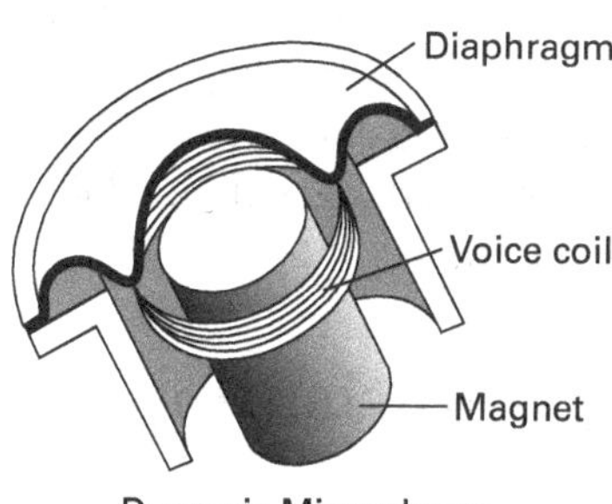

Dynamic Microphone

There are three kinds of microphones: dynamic, condenser, and ribbon. For a PME, a dynamic microphone is going to be the most effective and affordable option (see Figure 24.5). *For a demonstration of good microphone technique, visit the online resources.*

MICROPHONE STANDS

I recommend boom microphone stands. This allows the most flexibility and use—straight up, at the piano, or with an instrument.

CABLES

XLR and quarter-inch cables are used. XLR cables are three-pronged microphone cables that are used in conjunction with quarter-inch cables. XLR and quarter-inch cables are often used for connecting other parts of the set-up—the guitar into the amp, the mixing board into the monitor, the monitor into the amplifier.

For a demonstration of the different cables, visit the online resources.

Typical output devices for microphones are monitors, power amplifiers, sound mixers, public address (PA) systems, and digital audio workstations (DAW).

MONITORS AND AMPLIFIERS

Monitors provide auditory feedback for the singer. The signal chain of sound goes out of the microphone into a mixing board or other interface and then into a monitor. Two common monitors are in-ear monitors (IEMs) and wedge monitors. Wedge monitors sit on the floor and should face the band and the singer or singers, and/or be placed nearest the singer or singers. IEMs are headphones connected to a wireless system that gets signal from the board. Amplifiers for bass, guitar, and keyboards—and outfacing for the vocals—are also important. Being familiar with the different kinds and be able to troubleshoot in the event that there is an issue will help the PME rehearsals run smoothly. (See also Holley's *Coaching a Popular Music Ensemble.*)

STAGE SETUP

The way all the equipment and humans are configured is also important to assist with managing vocal load. I find two options work best. One is ideal for rehearsal (circle facing in) as it provides more visual feedback between the band and singer, thus helping to decrease confusion and potentially vocal load, the other ideal for performance preparation or sharing opportunities (outfacing).

24.5 Performance

Popular music of all genres deserve the same goal of mastery as any other music. Mastery, as Sarah Lewis states in her book *The Rise*, is "not merely a commitment to a goal, but to a curved-line, constant pursuit" (2014, p. 8)—meaning that one should strive to be the best given what one has to work with (which will be different for all groups depending on age, prior experience and goals of the ensemble, and so on) and improving all the time. This will look different at each of these levels, but it will always look like working with the skills students have and toward whatever goals are designed for the ensemble.

24.6 Lesson Ideas to Build Creative Musicianship

ARRANGING

Have the students create interesting arrangements of cover songs. For example: a metal rock version of Dolly Parton's "Jolene"? A punk version of Norah Jones's "Don't Know Why"? A country version of Beyoncé's "Single Ladies" ("Put a Ring on It")? Giving students autonomy to come up with both simple and crazy arrangements of pre-existing repertoire can give them collaborative agency over their own learning process.

EXPLORING SOUND AND HARMONY WITHOUT JUDGMENT

Learning to harmonize with others and make up harmony parts on the spot is a skill most PM singers possess. A basic understanding of major and minor scales and triads is beneficial for knowing what kind of harmony to create. However, the best way to learn is to simply have the student try. See what they come up with that "fits" into the chord and works with the melody.

MOVEMENT

Coordinated and even choreographed movement is often necessary for a dynamic PME performance experience. Engaging students in movement can help to make a performance easier, as well as more fun for both the audience and the performers (Murnak, 2021).

RECORDING

Regularly recording rehearsals can be a very effective rehearsal technique. A simple voice memo recording of a rehearsal that is shared with the ensemble for listening before the next rehearsal can help with consistency of songs as well as engage students in effective rehearsal strategies—especially when working with original music.

Multitrack recording in a digital audio workstation (DAW) is another way to provide a more real-life experience for the students. The feedback loop and recording experience can help the singer hear when they need to work on their intonation or phrasing. As most music today is created in the DAW, this experience will be closer to what is happening in the professional music industry.

SONGWRITING

Engaging students in the creation of their own material for that particular PME can instill a sense of pride and ownership, as well as provide collaborative, student-centered spaces for creativity and musicianship skill building. If songwriting is something you're new to exploring, there are some great resources available to help you learn how to help your students write songs, including *Songwriting for Music Educators* (Reinhert & Gulish, 2021)—an online course specifically designed for music educators—and the book *Music, Lyrics, and Life* (Errico, 2022), along with other listed resources.

PERSONAL NOTE

More than anything, when working with a voice, lead with kindness. When someone is told their voice isn't something—whatever that is (too loud, too soft, to brassy, ugly, too pretty . . . the list is endless), it can have potentially adverse and lifelong effects on that human's relationship with their voice. The voice is how we communicate with the world. It is often how we feel most seen. So, always, be kind. If someone can make a sound, they can sing. Singing is a human condition. Not everyone who sings will have the drive or desire to make it their career or their life's calling—but if we are physically capable of making sound, we can experience joy expressing ourselves through singing. Allow space for all voices.

24.7 Conclusion

The voice is a multifaceted, multisensory instrument located within the body. Working with voices in PMEs requires some basic knowledge of vocal anatomy that can be applied to helping singers grow. In addition, technology, repertoire, age-based parameters, vowels, movement, performance, and cultural awareness are all pedagogical considerations when working with a PME. Remember to be kind, have fun, and learn right along with everyone—that's part of the fun.

24.8 Discussion Questions

1. What is the model discussed for making sound? Describe how each part of the model works and engages in the overall ability to produce sound.
2. What are some pedagogical considerations to consider when working with a PME?
3. What challenges do you foresee for yourself when working with singers? How might you work to overcome those challenges? What do you not know, and where might you find the information?
4. When working with repertoire, what are things to consider?

OXFORD learning link

Visit the online resources for additional documentation and exercises to help expand learning and test your knowledge further: www.oup.com/he/powell_music1e.

CHAPTER 25

CULTURALLY RELEVANT PEDAGOGY IN MODERN BAND

Tony Sauza

This chapter provides an overview of culturally responsive pedagogy and its potential applications within the music classroom.

25.1 Representation Is Only the Beginning

Representation within a music classroom context can be considered across several areas, including the artists you and your students select for musical study as well as your approach to ensuring a diverse representation among lead roles in the band. Representation is often described as a key aspect for working toward an inclusive environment that celebrates all cultures and people. It serves as a clear indicator for demonstrating how students from various backgrounds are integrated into a music program. As valuable as representation may be, culturally responsive pedagogy (CRP) emphasizes the need to view representation as a prerequisite for entering this type of pedagogical practice. Digging deeper beyond representation leads us to a wealth of possibilities when it comes to CRP.

25.2 The Music Making Process Itself Should Be Culturally Responsive

There are many pathways to developing a culturally responsive music program. One of the most impactful ways of doing this is by encouraging diversity through repertoire selection. In CRP, a significant portion of every ensemble's repertoire consists of student-selected music. There are many ways to go about deciding how to facilitate the song selection process in each class.

- *Surveys*: Ask students who they're currently listening to or the top listening choices of their siblings, cousins, or parents. Oftentimes they will enjoy learning a song their parents enjoy, even if they initially did not like the song. Finding out about your students' listening habits and learning about how they experience music listening are essential pieces of information that will help inform your curriculum design.
- *Playlists*: Playlist assignments are effective ways to learn more about your students and which artists they value. YouTube is typically the best option in terms of price

(free), and it is Web-based, which allows most devices to access the playlist. If your school has a firewall preventing you and your students from accessing YouTube, there are other options, such as SoundCloud.com. Once most of the class has submitted a playlist, you can select a handful of songs that would be great for your students to learn.

- *Dialogue*: Sometimes it might be helpful to listen to songs as a class and have informal discussions around things your students enjoyed or things they didn't like. Going through this process should give you plenty of insight into the type of music your students enjoy.
- *Follow the charts*: Following various music industry charts on a consistent basis is a key pathway to staying current on the most popular songs and artists out there. The Billboard Hot 100 chart lists the songs that are generating the most streams, radio airplay, video plays, and downloads. Here you will learn about artists representing many different genres and backgrounds who have managed to make it into the world of popular music. Beyond the Hot 100 there are also other categories such as Hot Latin and Hot Country songs. Apple Music, Spotify, and other streaming services publish their own charts based on data from their own platforms.
- *Artists, composers, and musicians representing various groups*: Whether it be through race, gender, geographic region, specific time period or era, age, or any other element that helps shape and form identity, there are many ways to go about celebrating different groups of people. Historically speaking, the contributions of women musicians and songwriters have continually been underreported, omitted, or flat-out ignored. Ensuring that women and other marginalized groups are represented for their work and contributions should be nonnegotiable, especially when it comes to repertoire selection.

25.3 A Student-Centered Approach Is by Definition Culturally Responsive

The concept of decentering the music educator is a key component of establishing a music program that integrates CRP. By doing so, we allow students to become the focal point and creators of their own knowledge, which is otherwise known as *student-centered learning* or a *student-centered approach* (Crumly, 2014). In a student-centered music class, students drive learning processes through various types of activities, including:

- *Facilitating jam sessions and rehearsals*: Allowing students the opportunity to call out cues for the band or lead the group in improvisation activities are great ways to empower them and build confidence. Having section leaders and various student roles do this promotes the concept of autonomous and peer-to-peer learning.
- *Backline setup and breakdown*: Let's be real—most of us hate schlepping gear around, whether it is in your classroom or for public performances. Giving your students the opportunity to learn how to pack things away and set them up again begins to expand their understanding of the various components involved with making music in this type of ensemble setting. Certain students will even be attracted more to learning about live sound than music making. This also serves as a great opportunity to discuss careers in the music industry and how most jobs correlate to each other when preparing and producing a musical performance.
- *Instrument self-selection*: I once heard a story from a band teacher who "knew" his students would "all" want to play the trumpet. In order to balance out the

instrument assignments, during selection day he would turn one of the trumpet valves over so it would be out of position and would prevent any airflow from going through. To the disappointment of each student, they were led to believe they were not meant to play the trumpet. He would then offer up a different instrument such as the French horn. They would end up easily producing a tone, which allowed the teacher to encourage them to switch over. When it comes to instrument selection, we want to do the exact opposite of what this teacher did. Allowing students the opportunity to choose their instrument contributes to an environment where students feel safe taking risks and are encouraged to try new things. Having students switch instruments for different songs is also a great strategy. Through this approach, students experience the various roles each instrument plays in a band.
- *Improvisation*: Creating opportunities for students to improvise also nurtures an environment in which expression is encouraged and celebrated. Improvisation does not always have to be a lead solo for sixteen measures. Improvisation can take many forms, including improvising the song's arrangement, trying different combinations of collective improvisation, adding in a call-and-response section where various students take turns doing the calling, and many other possible activities. Hip-hop emceeing activities could also be fun ways to improvise individually and as a class.
- *Student collaboration*: Having students work together on creative projects is one of the best ways to nurture a student-centered learning environment. Whether it is remaking a song they all enjoy or focusing on composing a song together, any project that requires shared thinking and problem solving allows students to develop skills they can use for the rest of their lives. Quite often, especially toward the beginning of the year, students will approach me to complain about their bandmates. Usually it is either a disagreement about a creative decision that needs to be made or a student's displeasure with the group's work habits or vice versa. As long as the students are not disrespecting each other, I encourage them to work through their issues and find solutions on their own that makes sense to all parties involved. This approach gives students the ability to engage in higher-order thinking and develops their social awareness within a project-based environment.
- *Planning and preparing school concerts*: This is one of the most fun components when applying a student-centered learning approach. Involving students in the planning process and behind-the-scenes production work allows students the opportunity to experience and develop skills around other elements of a musical concert. Having students be in charge of wardrobe and outfits while other students focus on performance schedules and staging areas are excellent ways to empower your students. The various roles each student can play are broad and can vary depending on your school's rules and layout of the performance facility.

25.4 Program and Curriculum Design

It is important, when designing a program and curriculum, that they be reflective of the cultural values and communication preferences of at least some or even all your students (Claxton & Hale, 2020).

DO YOUR HOMEWORK

Whether you have been engaging in CRP for many years or this is your first attempt at designing such a program and curriculum, it is important to do your research so that you can familiarize yourself with your school's community. There are many ways to go about learning more about your students and their community. Interviewing community culture bearers can be a highly effective strategy for further understanding the people living in the area. This could include musicians, artists, actors, or any other respected figures who could give you insight into certain things you might not find through a Google search. This could also lead you toward finding out more about the musical history of your school community. Are there any musicians from the area who made significant contributions to the music world? Were there any notable concerts that took place in the area? Are there historic landmarks or venues within the city that once hosted some of the country's best artists?

MOVING BEYOND THE TEACHER-AS-CONDUCTOR FORMAT

I previously mentioned the value of handing the baton (or drumstick) over to your students during rehearsals and even performances. Having your students play the role of facilitator works best when your class is set up in a full circle or a semicircle with the student facilitator signaling everyone in the middle. Another highly effective format involves having students work together in small groups or bands. In this setting, the teacher might lay out certain parameters for ensuring student growth and focus, but the students themselves are at the center of their own learning here. In this collaborative model, students must apply real-life skills toward their group's development. This could involve having students set a tempo and count everyone in at the top of a song or ask questions that facilitate the lyric-writing or songwriting process.

REFRAMING THE MUSICAL PERFORMANCE

When establishing a culturally responsive music program, a paradigm shift could begin to occur as you reassess the role music plays in the lives of all of our students. Some of them experience music through their religion during church services, while other students might have a sibling who is in a local band. You might have a student whose father performs in a mariachi ensemble or whose sibling creates beats on their computer. There are many ways to conceptualize school and public performances. As music educators, we are often guilty of devoting the majority of class time to rehearsing for the winter concert or for the next competition. This unfortunately leans into a product-based model, where learning is demonstrated, evaluated, and critiqued at a culminating event. A lot of nerves and anxiety usually accompany the job of performing, although many seasoned performers find this uneasiness beneficial when preparing for a performance. We must be aware that these types of high-stakes environments have the potential to either elevate a student's self-esteem or create a traumatic moment that stays with them for the rest of their lives.

While there is a lot of value in providing performance-based experiences for our students, we must also acknowledge that music making is not solely a performative pursuit. Music takes on many roles and functions throughout societies across the globe. Music is used for religious rituals, rite-of-passage ceremonies, therapy and healing, soundscapes, and many other functional purposes. As a result, shifting our attention toward process-based music-making activities can serve as a great way to exemplify the value music brings to people's lives in various ways. Working on a recording project is a valuable way to facilitate process-based music making. While there is obviously an end product (a produced sound recording), the students themselves will begin to see how the songwriting and recording process will allow them the opportunity to grow and develop in ways they never imagined. Going through this process repeatedly only helps to reinforce the value of the approach while further advancing the intricacy of student compositions.

25.5 Practical Applications for CRP in the Music Classroom

CULTURAL RESPONSIVENESS THROUGH SONGWRITING AND COMPOSITION

Developing and encouraging an environment consisting of original student work is key to achieving a culturally responsive music program. If your students are composing their own songs, do your best to find ways to acknowledge their accomplishments. One way to do this is by allowing a student to share their song with the band so they can all perform it together. If you have a large class ensemble, you could work toward developing a set consisting mainly of original student songs. A similar approach can be applied to music production and beat making. Both having regular listening parties and sharing the recordings with the entire school are fun ways of celebrating students and the cultural elements they put into their music.

EXEMPLIFYING COMPOSITIONS AND ARTISTS USING DIFFERENT LANGUAGES

This strategy is a great way to introduce unfamiliar music to your students. Sharing recordings with them that are sung in a language other than English allows them the opportunity to experience music in a unique way. This is also a great way to honor the languages spoken at home by some of your students. Sharing music sung in Spanish, Arabic, Mandarin, or any other language representative of any of your students sends a clear, although sometimes subliminal, message to each student in your class that they are valued in your program and on your school's campus. Providing translations of the lyrics also helps to create opportunities for students to identify with the song.

BRINGING IN LOCAL MUSICIANS REPRESENTATIVE OF YOUR STUDENTS' BACKGROUNDS

I have already outlined the value of establishing relationships with local musicians and other artists. If you find local songwriters or music producers, inviting them to speak to your students can have a lasting impact on your class. Having them speak about their songwriting process and approach can inform and validate a lot of the experiences of your young student composers. Along with speaking about the process, having local songwriters speak to your students shows them how people who are similar to them have achieved success with their craft.

ALLOWING STUDENTS TO PLAY INSTRUMENTS THAT ARE UNCOMMON IN MODERN BANDS AND IN DIFFERENT ENSEMBLES

Having taught middle school music, I would occasionally get a student who was coming in with a background on an instrument not typically used in a modern band setting. One example is of a student who had two years' experience playing the violin. Her development on violin occurred mainly through a mariachi musical environment. Although we had a mariachi ensemble at our school, this student was insistent on joining the modern band. While it was challenging at times to find ways of incorporating her and her instrument into arrangements of pop songs, it really pushed her and me both to think creatively and in ways that encouraged originality in regard to her approach. On the flip side, I had a couple of other students who always did well in music class but never participated in any school ensembles. Initially during my first few years of teaching, I had only a modern band group and a Brazilian drum line. After some time, we were able to establish the school's first ever mariachi. To my surprise, these previously reluctant students were now joining the mariachi, and many of them were gravitating toward playing the violin. These students found a home within the mariachi ensemble and showed me that different students engage and identify with various types of music and musical groups, highlighting the importance of having a diverse set of ensemble offerings that attract different groups of students. Brass and woodwinds can also be applied to modern band and there are many examples of bands and artists that have integrated these instruments into their sound. Incorporating various types of hand percussion as well as adapting instruments that are prominent regionally are great ways of demonstrating CRP in action.

ANALYZING YOUR STUDENTS' FORMATION OF THEIR MUSICAL IDENTITY

Earlier I discussed the value of surveying your students for the purpose of understanding their musical interests. Beyond learning about their favorite artists and songs, it is helpful to consider the various ways your students are experiencing music. Family events such as birthday parties and weddings serve as sources of musical influence, even if the students are not aware of the process that is occurring. Along with these examples, there are musical sources out in the world such as at stores, in elevators, at sporting events, and at other places where your students are being exposed to different types of sounds.

Nowadays, unless your students are crate diggers, odds are they are listening to and experiencing music through some type of streaming service. Learning about which streaming platforms your students tend to use can help give you insights into what artists and types of music they are being exposed to. Also, learning about their behaviors within the platform can yield some valuable information. Do they mainly listen to playlists, or do they actually listen to entire albums? Do they know what an album is? Do *we* still know what an album is? Do they listen to Spotify- or Apple Music–curated playlists, or do they lean toward user-created playlists? There are clear differences between the ways we access music on YouTube versus Spotify versus SoundCloud, and any number of other possibilities. Understanding these nuances between each platform helps to inform your perspective on various ways your students are accessing musical recordings at any given point in time.

ASSESSMENTS

Through gradual integration of CRP within your music classroom, you and your students can begin to build a foundation that continues evolving to meet the needs of all students. Similarly, assessments can be used as a tool and a resource to better understand these student needs. Quite often, our go-to forms of assessment tend to focus on standard quizzes and juried-type performances. While these have their respective values and purposes, looking toward other forms of determining student learning should be examined and implemented. The network of modern band–focused teachers throughout the country is strong and active. Music teachers share best practices and exchange pedagogical approaches within a modern band format. While my two decades of performance experience helped to inform my own approach to assessments and modern band in my classroom, it must be mentioned that many of these practices have been used and developed among modern band teachers from across the country. The following are some examples of ways to diversify student assessments. They should be designed and presented in various ways that allow students multiple opportunities to demonstrate their growth and development.

- *Peer to peer*: Having students perform for each other in pairs or small groups takes the focus and pressure off each individual student. In this format, students assess each other and develop criteria for providing feedback.

- *Private audio recording*: Instead of having students perform, consider allowing them the option to record their performance. This is a great option for students who experience overwhelming anxiety while performing. The recording can remain private if the student prefers.
- *Public audio recording (SoundCloud)*: Allowing students to publish their recording transforms their song from a private demo to a publicly accessible song. There are privacy options available on platforms such as SoundCloud where only people with the link can access a particular recording. It is also a good idea to inform yourself about intellectual property rights as they relate to minors.
- *SoundTrap*: Having students create and develop musical ideas and/or compositions on an online (digital audio workstation (DAW) such as SoundTrap allows them the opportunity to be musically creative in ways they might not be able to be on a physical instrument. Approaching music making through a DAW encourages students to think and listen like producers.
- *Private video (Flipgrid)*: If it is allowed at your school district, Flipgrid is a great and efficient way of receiving student video submissions.
- *Public video (Flipgrid)*: Allowing students to post videos where their peers can view and comment on them are a fun way for students to share and interact with each other. This allows students to view as many videos as they would like in order to inform their own growth.
- *Community performances*: There's nothing like the real thing! One of the best ways for students to realize their growth and development is through live public performances. These do not always have to take the form of school concerts. Having your modern band perform at city events or in front of supportive businesses can give your students real experience performing in public environments.

25.6 Final Thoughts

First, I would like to encourage you to read chapters 31 and 43, where the authors discuss CRP within a school orchestra and a band setting respectively. Learning how CRP looks in these ensemble settings will help you to develop a more comprehensive understanding of the approach.

Culturally responsive pedagogy within a modern band setting will also bring various challenges that are a part of the process. As mentioned before, being grounded in current research around this topic could prove quite beneficial when you are speaking with administrators or your colleagues. Having a well-informed support system is also of the utmost importance in terms of ensuring desirable outcomes. Whenever I have the chance to visit a program that is highly culturally responsive, it quickly becomes apparent that students feel valued and respected as individuals. These students feel safe, and they trust not only their peers but also their teacher. It is a form of support that encourages students to take risks and place themselves in vulnerable situations. Culturally responsive pedagogy will continue to evolve over time; however, the core values will remain relevant for years to come.

25.7 Discussion Questions

1. How can some of the strategies discussed here be transferred to other ensembles? Are there any examples here that you find problematic for your students and program?

2. Take a moment and reflect on your program's current format and approach. Does it align with many of the topics discussed in this chapter? What differences do you see?
3. Taking your previous knowledge or lack thereof into consideration, what are some next steps that you could take to help integrate CRP into your classroom?

OXFORD learning link

Visit the online resources for additional documentation and exercises to help expand learning and test your knowledge further: www.oup.com/he/powell_music1e.

PART III.

Teaching Strings

CHAPTER 26

PEDAGOGICAL CONSIDERATIONS FOR TEACHING STRING STUDENTS

Kristen Pellegrino

In this chapter, I address preparing to teach string students content considerations, and how to teach beginners, progressing from preparing to teach strings, to teaching the first day, to offering an overview of teaching the first year.

26.1 Introduction

Unlike teaching woodwind instruments, much of teaching orchestral bowed string instruments is visible as well as similar and transferable. For example, orchestral string instruments:

- have four strings tuned in perfect intervals from lowest to highest (unlike most ukuleles)
- share finger logic (change pitches in the following ways):
  - add fingers or move to a higher string for higher pitch; remove fingers or move to a lower string for lower pitch
  - adjust pitches:
    - sharper by moving fingers toward the bridge (shortening the string)
    - flatter by moving fingers closer to the scroll (elongating the string)
  - address notes on one string as well as connections between strings
  - can play multiple notes at a time (notes on two, three, or four strings at once)

Also, examples of technical similarities include:

- the second knuckle of the left hand fingers stays over the strings
- the right thumb is bent like a spiral
- everyone lands their bows silently halfway between the bridge and fingerboard to begin
- the tone is determined by a combination of:
  - bow: *p*lacement on the string, *a*ngle to the string, *w*eight, and *s*peed (PAWS)
  - left hand: a ringing tone is achievable only when the strings and pitches are in tune with the instrument, causing sympathetic vibrations with the open strings

In this chapter I address preparing to teach orchestral string students (violin, viola, cello, and bass, referred to generally as string or strings in this chapter and section), content considerations, and suggestions for how to teach beginners, progressing from preparing to teach beginning strings, to teaching the first day, to offering an overview of teaching the first year (see online resources).

26.2 Preparing to Teach String Students

Preparing to teach string students is dependent on your teaching context, content considerations, and preparing for the first day of strings.

TEACHING CONTEXT

The instrumentation of the students in your classes, the students' ages, the number of meetings per week, and class size will all impact your instruction. First, the instrumentation of students in your class will impact your instruction. Although strings are often taught in heterogeneous classes, sometimes they are split into homogeneous classes (by instrument) or into high string and low string classes. Also, the age of the students will impact your instruction. For example, *when* beginning strings are taught varies among states and districts, often occurring in fourth to sixth grades, but sometimes students are grades P–3. You will need to plan to teach fewer concepts and repeat them more often when teaching younger students. What you can accomplish will also vary based on how often you meet students and for how long. For example, teaching students twice a week for thirty minutes (not recommended) will be very different from teaching five times a week for thirty to sixty minutes. I have heard of teaching small groups of students (fewer than ten) to large groups (twenty-five to sixty!). This will impact how many individualized instruction and assessment opportunities each student will receive. In any of these varied settings, the teaching fundamentals remain the same.

CONTENT CONSIDERATIONS

Some content considerations include choosing a method book and other literature and/or materials, making teaching decisions, and learning from string pedagogues.

Choosing a Method Book

We are lucky to have a plethora of good method books for string students at all levels. However, the way I teach strings is not dependent on any method book and does not change significantly based on my choice of method book. My philosophy is that I am the teacher and the method book is one tool I use. For intermediate and advanced students, I often create my own warm-ups and repertoire-based warm-ups (Gillespie, 2003). Whichever book I choose for beginners, I do not introduce it right away unless there are great pictures of posture, position, instrument care, and/or accompaniment tracks.

There are many things to consider when choosing a method book. I offer a sample in Figure 26.1 of the online resources, which you can use when comparing method books. I include thirteen categories, but you can add or change any of them. I suggest you think about categories that are important to you first and then look at my list.

FIGURE 26.1 **Example of notation for beginning violinists, for home practice only**

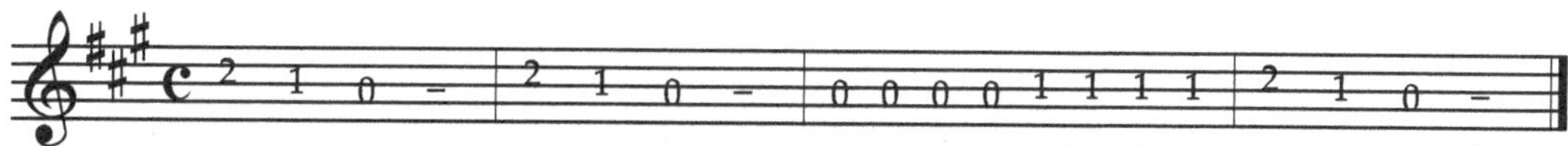

I also suggest using your own supplemental materials. I created a "string pack" for beginning and intermediate students so that they could move at their own pace. The pack included songs, technical diagrams, bow games, and beginning composition details. Although I initially teach beginners by rote in class, I send home some musical notation to help them remember what we practiced in class. You can create various kinds of musical notation and composition activities that make sense to you. See Figures 26.1 and 26.2 for an example of "Hot Cross Buns" notation and details for a beginning composition experience.

FIGURE 26.2 **Example of a beginning composition for strings**

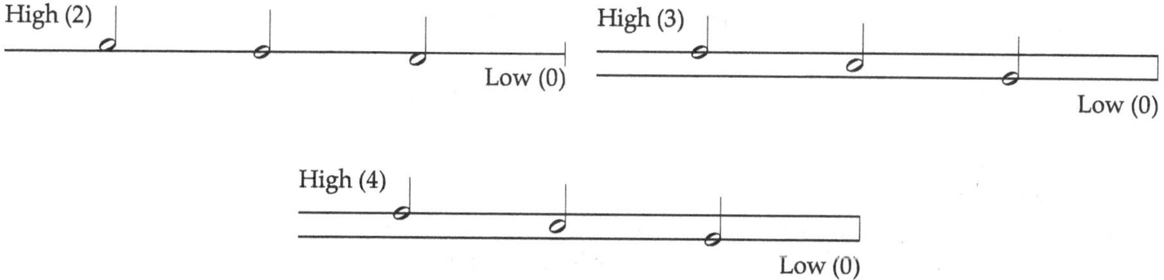

ASSIGNMENT: For today's composition, you can use:

1. Three pitches (high, medium, and low)
   (*mi*, *re*, *do*)
2. Begin on high (*mi*).
3. The last note of the second measure is a half note on medium (*re*).
4. The last note of the composition is low (*do*).

Either give all students the same rhythm, which you provide, or have the students work together to determine a rhythm just using quarter, half, and eighth notes.

Then, we learn to play the student compositions with this procedure:

1. *Say* the rhythm
2. *Sing* letter names until you can sing them in rhythm
3. With letter names and/or finger numbers, *sing and pizz.* in *rest* position
4. *Sing and pizz.* in *playing* position
5. *Play with the bow*

I also have a string pack for more advanced students so they can continue to be challenged. My rule is that students perform whatever they can play with excellent posture, position, tone, intonation, speed, and style. Therefore, not all students perform everything, but I explain that when students have more time to practice, they can often learn more songs. This relates to Carol Dweck's (2008) growth mindset.

I also teach the beginnings of improvisation within the first few weeks of learning to play strings. I begin by having students improvise rhythms on an open string and then add additional pitches, one at a time. Then I continue offering improvisation opportunities as they progress through exercises and by including pieces with improvisation opportunities in them (e.g., "Pepperoni Pizza Rock" by Brian Balmages for beginners, and Tuttle Island String Quartet's "Skylife," for advanced students).

After students can play a few songs, I always have students learn a chorus from a song they love, whether from a television show, movie, game, or anywhere else. I ask them to sing it to me and bring a link to a recording so that I can help them figure out how to play it. This often involves playing it in a different key and teaching them new rhythms, bowings, and pitches. In fact, I introduce new notes (such as F naturals on the D string, B flats on the A string, and C# on the G string for all except bassists) while teaching a pop tune to the whole class.

Choosing Literature for Students of All Levels

We should always intentionally include music from diverse genres and historically underrepresented composers, and there are many resources available. At the time of writing this, there are databases that highlight music by of underrepresented composers, such as https://www.orchestra4all.com/, which features music by women and Black, Indigenous, and people of color (BIPOC), and www.composerdiversity.com, where you can use search filters to find categories of composers, such as LGBTQIA+ composers. According to the Adore Project, they offer orchestral repertoire that is accessible and diverse (broadening it), and equitable (highlighting under-represented composers) https://theadoreproject.org Also, Rachel Barton Pine is the president and founder of the Music by Black Composers Project (MBC), which began in 2003. MBC's mission is threefold:

- to inspire Black students to begin and continue instrumental training by showing them that they are an integral part of classical music's past as well as its future
- to make the music of Black composers available to all people regardless of background or ethnicity
- to help bring greater diversity to the ranks of performers, composers, and audiences and help change the face of classical music and its canon. https://www.musicbyblackcomposers.org/

The Kronos String Quartet, in honor of their fiftieth anniversary, also offered fifty compositions "for the future" (https://50ftf.kronosquartet.org/composers). Finally, the American String Teachers Association (ASTA) is working in partnerships with Rising Tide Publishers and ACDA and with grants from the NEA and Sphinx Organization to help create places where BIPOC composers who are early in their careers can publish their compositions and even receive professional development advice on how to compose for different levels of school ensembles.

There are so many wonderful teaching resources that explore multiple genres for all levels of string students. For example, Bob Phillips has worked with experts in various genres and created pedagogical materials for students at various levels. Examples include *fiddling* (with Andrew H. Dabczynski), *fiddling and song* (with Crystal Plohman Wiegman and Renata Bratt), *jazz* (with Randy Sabien), *rock* (with Daryl Silberman), *mariachi* (with John Nieto), and *Latin* (with Victor López). You may use some ready-made materials or create your own arrangements and compositions!

Making Teaching Decisions

There are many good reasons to teach in different ways; you have to decide which ways you will choose, and you should understand what fuels your decisions. See Table 26.1 on the online resources for twelve issues related to teaching beginners before reading some of my decisions.

Thinking about teaching beginning string players, I always teach "sound before sight" and "experience, then label." I also want students to sing during every lesson, learn by ear first, and then to learn to read music notation later. An even more controversial choice is that I teach playing with the bow during the first lesson. These are my preferences. Addressing each item in the online resources' Table 26.1, I teach the following:

1. with finger markers on the fingerboard *and* harmonies to help with intonation
2. violinists and violists use some sort of shoulder rests
3. violinists, violists, and bassists play standing up, and with chairs and stools available for them to sit on when not playing with the bow
4. everyone sings every day, on letter names, finger numbers, and sometimes solfège
5. I begin students playing by rote so they can concentrate on posture, position, tone, intonation, and playing together by watching my bow (I play for and with them)
6. everyone learns to hold the bow and bring the bow to the string the first day
7. I have a simple, three-or-four-step general process for teaching bow hold

8. everyone plays "Hot Cross Buns" (melody) pizz. *and* with the bow on the first day
9. I assess students individually (regular playing tests)
   - I have them play alone in front of others, although not always in front of the whole class
10. I include many genres in class, including popular, folk, "classical," holiday, fiddling, jazz, music by historically underrepresented composers, and so on
11. I teach the beginnings of improvisation and composition soon after they begin learning to play. I use composition to help teach music literacy using three pitches, three note values, and four measures.
12. I usually cue (one-beat preparation), although I occasionally sing "rea-dy play" or "your turn."

I try to set students up for success from the first day of teaching strings, and each choice I make has a reason associated with it. For example, I use a one-beat cue for multiple reasons. First, students have to look at me (instead of just listening to me), which positively impacts ensemble issues and classroom management. For ensemble, I teach with my violin in hand so students will match the amount of bow I use as well as the changes in direction. This sets students up for success when they play with others, as they should be moving their bows at the same time and in the same way as their section leader. This also helps students play together, which is part of "ensemble skills" (Benham et al., 2011). One-beat cues also save time and transfer into conducting with one-beat preparation, as well as teaching students to watch the conductor.

Second, the one-beat cue helps with classroom management because (a) we begin in silence, (b) it helps keep a fast pace, and (c) students look me in the eyes before and while we play. I also arrange violin and viola students so they can see me, their left-hand fingers on the fingerboard and their bow on the string, being sure to keep it "on one track, halfway between the bridge and fingerboard." Again, these are my choices and reasons, which are right for how I teach and why I teach. You can explore the merits of these and other ideas in your methods and/or pedagogy classes.

Learning from String Pedagogues

I strongly encourage you to learn from some amazing string pedagogues who contributed to our understanding of group process teaching. String pedagogues include but are not limited to Suzuki, Rolland, Green, and Bornoff (See Table 26.2 on the online resources site), Samuel Applebaum, and Robert Klotman, as well as those who adopted elements of different pedagogues such as Marvin Rabin, Jacquelyn Dillon, Robert L. Culver, Phyllis Young, Mimi Zweig, Robert Gillespie, Bob Phillips, Stephen Benham, and many more. There are also what the American String Teachers Association has labeled "eclectic styles" or "multi-styles" pedagogues. These include but are not limited to Daryl Anger, Renata Bratt, Christian Howes, Julie Lyonn Lieberman, Martha Mooke, John Nieto, Mark O'Connor, Tracy Silverman, David Wallace, Mark Woods, and many more.

We will never know everything about teaching strings, so continued professional development is imperative. I attend multiple conferences every year so that I can gather ideas from many fantastic teachers. From state conferences, to American String Teachers Association conferences, to National Association for Music Educators meetings, to workshops offered during the year or in the summer, I have been a conference junkie. Now there are many virtual conferences, too, so learning from great pedagogues in our field is even more accessible. Although we can learn a lot from others, we must also remember to be "present, in the moment" so that we can problem-solve and anticipate what will help our students musically, as learners, and as people. (See Chapters 2 and 3.)

PREPARING FOR THE FIRST DAY OF STRINGS

Before you meet your students, you must prepare for the logistics of the first day of classes. For intermediate and advanced students, what is the most efficient way to begin the year? Will you prearrange locker assignments, have music already in folders, have handbooks ready, and so on? Will you have students play the first day, and if so, will you teach a rote tune, play a piece they already know, improvise, or compose? There are so many decisions to make.

For beginners, how you will tune each instrument, put on tapes, fit students with shoulder rests, and so on? At some schools I arranged to have students lay their violin and viola cases on the floor and open the lids so I could prepare the instruments before class. I opened the cello cases and was able to have basses available at the school already. If this was not possible, I modified the logistics by only putting two tapes on their fingerboards, or tuning students' open strings while teaching, making sure at least all of their D strings were in tune (see Chapter 28 for more about tuning).

Will you ask students to purchase and bring to class accessories such as shoulder rests and rock stops, or will you provide them? Will you recommend brands? Sometimes I cut an egg-crate mattress into smaller pieces to fit students and bring large elastic bands to keep them in place. Other times I ask students to purchase shoulder rests, rock stops, an extra set of strings, and a method book. Districts provide different materials and have different policies and budgets, so please check with your district after you are hired.

If you expect your students to bring shoulder rests (violin and viola) or rock stops (cello and bass), extra strings, a method book, and the like, you must be clear in your communications with parents. You may also include practicing expectations, strategies, and journals. I frame it as ways parents can help children succeed on their string instrument. As you can see, teachers make many pedagogical and logistical decisions before you even meet with students.

Here is a list of materials and accessories you may consider bringing, purchasing, or having students bring.

1. Finger tapes and scissors
2. Chin rest gadgets
3. Shoulder rests
4. Rock stops
5. Bow hold forms
6. Extra strings
7. Stands or no stands
8. Handouts (music, information, practice suggestions, etc.)
9. Method books
10. Practice journals and/or access to audio and/or video practicing technologies
11. Other

26.3 The First Days of Teaching String Students

The way I play influences how I teach. My decisions are based on my experiences with many different string teachers, all of whom I greatly respect. However, teachers have suggested different variations to my playing and I ultimately decide which techniques I adopt into my playing and/or teaching.

Although there are many ways to be a great string teacher, I offer one way of teaching beginning string students. This is *not* meant to be presented as *the* way to teach strings. Instead, this is a way that worked for me and is based on ideas I gleaned from former professors, such as Robert Culver; my former public school teacher, Carol Pellegrino; former violin private teachers, such as Eric Rosenblith, Lynn Blakeslee, Paul Kantor, Robert Culver, Camilla Wickes, Gregory Fulkerson, William Preucil, Andrew Jennings; ideas from great pedagogues such as Suzuki, Roland, Gordon, and Bornoff; ideas shared with me by students and teachers; and some of my own ideas. I also understand that reading something and implementing it are two very different experiences.

I have provided a sample lesson plan for violinists and violists and another lesson plan for one way to teach the first day of strings in heterogeneous settings (see Tables 26.3 and 26.4 of the online resources). Even though I have scripted these lesson plans to share with you as an example, I do not teach the first lesson the same way every time. Even so, my goals remain the same, to have students sing and have them learn rest position, playing position, pizzicato (pizz.), bow hold, putting bow to string, putting left-hand fingers on the strings, and to sing, pizz., and play with their bows "Hot Cross Buns" on the first day. I *show,* students *do.* Basically, I set the pace, expectations, and teaching style during the first class, and they learn posture, position, aural skills, tone, rhythm, ensemble skills, and more.

Again, I borrow ideas from many pedagogues and string teachers. For the violinists and violists, I teach rest position and playing position sequence as my professor at the University of Michigan, Robert Culver, taught me, but it was itself partially borrowed from other pedagogues. For the bow hold, I teach a sequence taught to me by Eric Rosenblith and use a poem that my first cousin once removed shared with me over two decades ago from her elementary string teacher from Pottstown, Pennsylvania. (I am so sorry I do not know the teacher's name.) Some ideas are mine, but most are compiled from various people.

There are a few general pedagogical concepts that I use to teach. First, *repetition is essential!* We help students learn what to think about before they play. By saying what they should be doing and thinking, we guide them. First, I teach students each step individually. Eventually I refer to a checklist, and we move through the steps silently. I say, "Think about the checklist," and we all land silently, halfway between the bridge and fingerboard, click your pinky (violinists and violists), bend your thumb, relax your arm, put the egg in place, hand parallel to the fingerboard, and have fingers dance on top of the strings. See the beginner checklist for strings.

BEGINNER CHECKLIST FOR STRINGS

- Land silently halfway between the bridge and fingerboard
- Click pinky (violin and viola)
- Relax shoulder and arm
- Pet frog
- Bend thumb
- Cello and bass
  - Water bottle—"C" for cello and bass and thumb behind second finger in center of fingerboard
    - Shoulders level
    - The arm to wrist should be a straight line; no droopy elbows or collapsed wrists
    - Bass face (thumb in ear, middle finger on nose, pinky on bottom lip, index finger on eyebrow)
- Violin and viola
  - Left elbow hangs toward floor
  - The arm to wrist should be a straight line; no droopy elbows or collapsed wrists
  - Neck sits on top of fleshy side of finger above biggest knuckle near the nut and thumb sits across
  - Thumb feels seam between fingerboard and neck

- Put egg in place
- Hand parallel to the fingerboard
- Fingers dance on fingerboard (second knuckles *over/above* strings)

I refer to the checklist because we all need reminders so that bad habits do not creep into students' playing. Checklists help students internalize and automatize the skills so they become second nature (see Chapter 3 for more on this process). Even with my advanced students, I continue to remind them to "land, click, bend, and relax" in order to avoid letting tension creep into their playing (see Chapter 27 for more). This helps set students up for success.

For suggestions about how to plan an overview for the year and beginning strings teaching competencies for teacher preparation programs (Hopkins & Pellegrino, 2019, pp. 768–769), see Table 26.5 on the online resources site.

I began this chapter by stating that string techniques are visible, similar, and transferable. In the upcoming chapters in this section, we will explore generally teaching the right hand (Chapter 27), teaching the left hand and tuning (Chapter 28), teaching shifting and vibrato (Chapter 29), maintaining a successful orchestral program (Chapter 30), and culturally responsive teaching in school orchestras (Chapter 31).

26.4 Discussion Questions and Assignments

1. What are your goals for the first day of class? What do you want your students to think, feel, know, and be able to do at the end of the first class? Answer questions from the online resources.
2. Assignment: reviewing method books. See the online resources.
3. What literature would you explore in terms of genres and music by underrepresented composers? How would you approach teaching these to students?
4. Assignment: communicating with parents. Prepare two written communications: (a) recruiting new students, information about what is needed for the first day, how to help your children succeed on their string instruments; and (b) inviting parents to an Orchestra Parents Association meeting. These are great opportunities to discuss tone and writing in a clear, concise manner, highlighting what is most important.
5. Looking at the beginner checklist, what kind of checklists would you create for your beginning students?
6. Looking at the playing and teaching competencies listed in the Table 26.5 of the online resources, list which are your strengths and which you need to spend time improving.

OXFORD learning link

Visit the online resources for additional documentation and exercises to help expand learning and test your knowledge further: www.oup.com/he/powell_music1e.

CHAPTER 27

PEDAGOGIES FOR TEACHING THE RIGHT HAND TO STRING PLAYERS

Kristen Pellegrino and Joel Schut

This chapter provides an overview of strategies for teaching the right hand to string players by addressing the teaching of bow hold formation, tone development, rhythmic control, bow direction, stroke differentiation, and expressive elements.

27.1 Introduction

The bow is a string player's breath and voice. Careful development of the right hand is important from beginning instruction through advanced refinement. This includes teaching bow hold formation, tone development, rhythmic control, bow direction, stroke differentiation, and expressive elements. This chapter builds upon Chapter 26 with steps for advancing right-hand skills and incorporates Joel's and Kristen's experiences as string players, public school teachers, and college professors. Additional activities and troubleshooting can be found in the supplemental materials.

27.2 Establishing the Bow Hold

Beginning with a lengthened, balanced, and fluid body posture is fundamental for all string skills. The right-hand fingers should be naturally rounded and free of tension. Bow hold is best learned independently from instrument playing position and is sometimes taught using a pencil, straw, or pipe cleaner before transferring this activity to the bow. Consider marking guide dots on the bow or fingers to help remind students of proper placement.

There are many traditions and pedagogical preferences for teaching bow hold. The next section provides information about three prominent traditions: German, Franco-Belgian, and Russian.

GERMAN, FRANCO-BELGIAN, AND RUSSIAN BOW HOLDS

Three of the most common bow hold traditions are German, Franco-Belgian, and Russian. Differences include:

- Range of pronated index finger contact points
- Engagement of the wrist
- Engagement of the fingers
- Leverage of the arm
- Angle of bow hair and stick

The German hold, developed by Louis Spohr and advocated by pedagogues such as Shinichi Suzuki, features little pronation, with fingers relatively close together. The Franco-Belgian hold, developed by Charles de Beriot and advocated by pedagogues such as Paul Rolland, has slight pronation with space between all the fingers. The Russian hold, developed by Henryk Wieniawski and advocated by pedagogues such as Kato Havas, features a highly pronated hand with limited space between all fingers except the pinky. These bow holds can be understood as being on a spectrum of pronation from most to least pronated: Russian, Franco-Belgian, and German.

For heterogeneous string classes, it is possible to teach a simplified bow hold that can be transferred and modified between the bowed string instruments. This simplified bow hold permits the natural transfer of weight in the arm and an efficient change of directions without significantly altering the angle of the hand or fingers. This is in opposition to beginning with an overly flexible wrist and fingers that "cushion" the bow changes.

The next section provides steps for teaching the simplified bow hold. It is organized in a movement-based experience with a poem that can be practiced and repeated together in class and at home. While the full poem is for violin and viola, this bow hold can be used with cello and bass French bow holds. The most fundamental change between high strings and low strings is the placement of the pinky finger: perched on the stick for violin and viola or draped over the stick for cello and bass.

TEACHING SIMPLIFIED BOW HOLD

- Pick the bow up at its balance point with your left hand, frog facing right
- Keep your left arm in front of your body
- Lightly grab your arm with your right hand (thumb underneath arm). Look down and notice the spaces between your fingers. That is your natural bow hold.
- Slide second knuckle of fingers over hand and onto stick over the frog
- Thumb is bent and underneath the frog. "It won't always live here but just for now."
- Say this poem after me:

  "Four little frogs swimming in the pool," [cellists and bassists stop here]
  [Violinists and violists:] "The little one gets out and sits on the stool" [click your pinky on top of the stick]

Depending on a student's hand size, strength, and flexibility, thumb placement can be taught in a two-step process beginning with the thumb under the frog. This provides wider space and an easier curved thumb visual. After students demonstrate fundamental shape and fluidity, they can move their thumbs inside the stick. Gradually transfer students' thumbs to the stick between the frog and padded grip. For violin and viola, create a C shape and touch the top knuckle of the thumb to the bow hairs. For cello and bass, the thumb is higher above the hair.

FIGURE 27.1 C shape for violin and viola bows

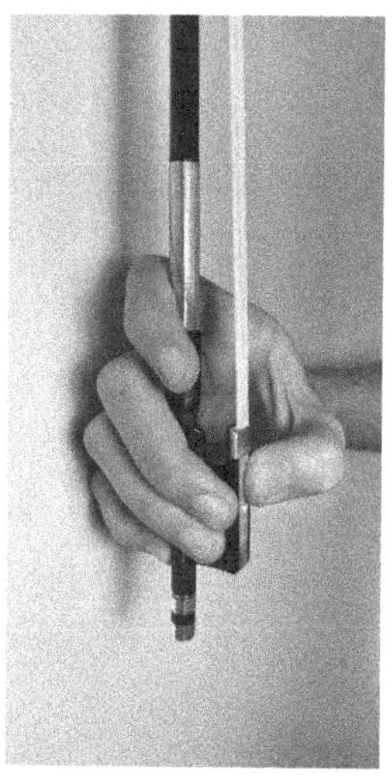
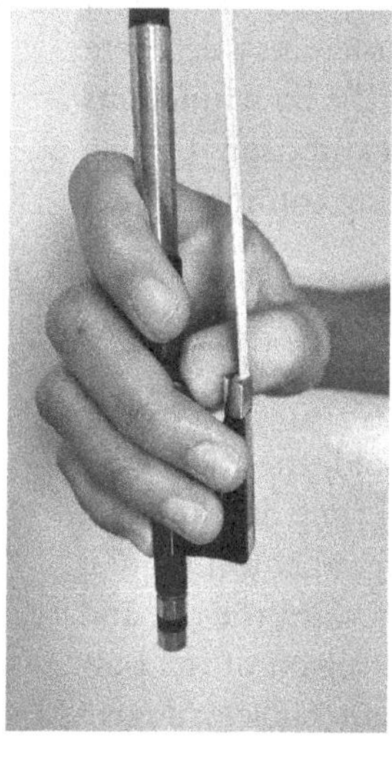
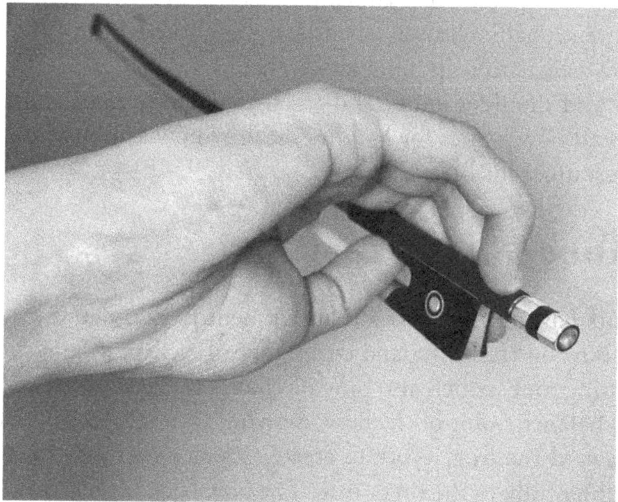

While the simplified bow hold is easily transferable between all instruments, basses have another bow hold option, the German bow. The shape of the German frog is wider and requires a unique bow hold, with the thumb and index finger on top of the stick, two fingers in the frog, and the pinky beneath the frog, as shown in the following figures. It is even possible to start students on French bow for a unified approach and later transition students to German bow.

FIGURE 27.2 Transitioning from French bow to German bow

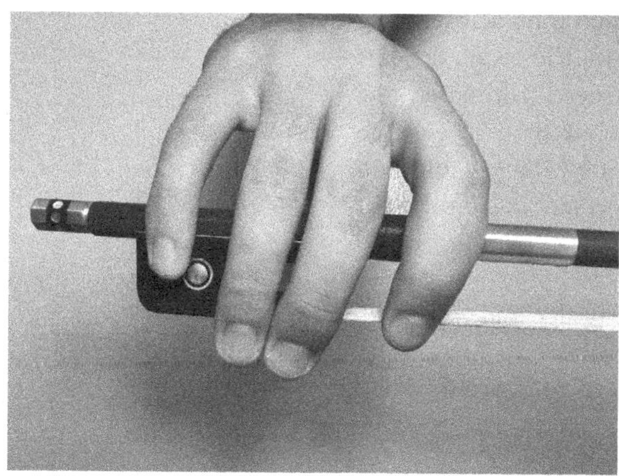
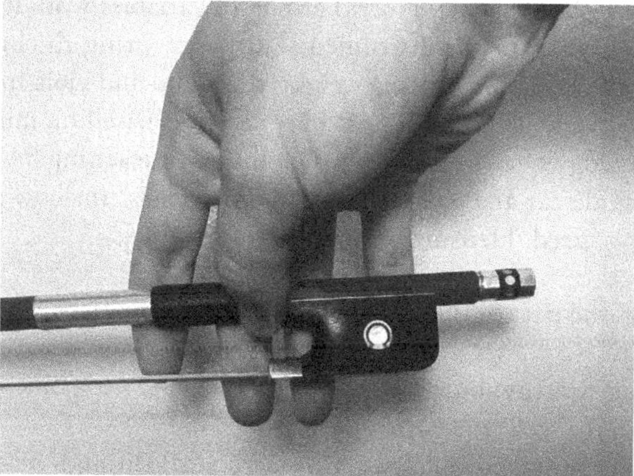
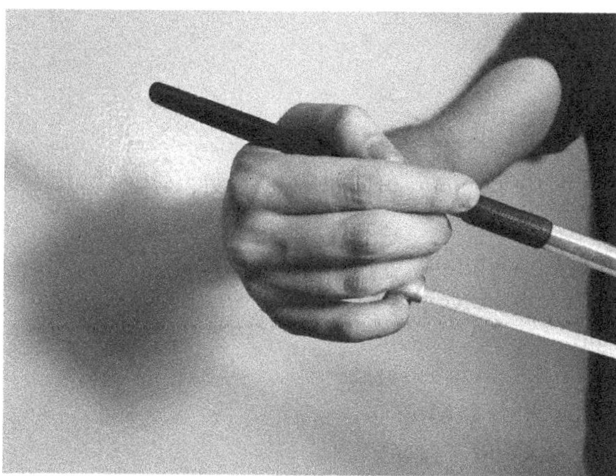
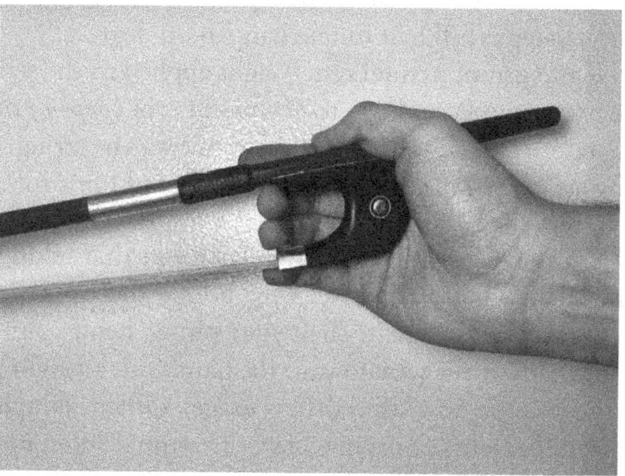

Bow hold fundamentals should be reviewed frequently. Reinforce a naturally bent thumb with space between the palm and the bow. Like all string techniques, tension will have to be intentionally released when learning and refining any right-hand skill. There are many bow games to help build an excellent bow hold, understand the bow functions of the elbow and shoulder joints, and teach control, rhythm, and bow direction. Online we share several bow games for building healthy bow arms and avoiding common issues (see online resources for Bow Games).

27.3 Tone

Once students have reliable posture, instrument position, and bow hold, they are ready to place the bow on the string and create tone. Teachers should spend time developing a reliable, pleasing tone, which also provides motivation before extending other techniques. Begin at the balance point of the bow, drawing through the middle, toward the tip, and then back toward the frog. Work to create a clear tone in the middle region of the bow before extending fully to the tip or frog. The bow stick tilt has two default choices: angled toward the scroll (violin and viola) and away from the scroll (cello and bass), or flat hair with the stick above the hairs. Playing with a great sound (tone) makes it easier to facilitate intonation (left hand [LH]) and articulation (right hand [RH]).

The four main variables affecting string tone production are placement, angle, weight, and speed (PAWS). While there are other acronyms and orderings, using PAWS helps students remember the variables in a pedagogically logical sequence that reviews and reinforces basic posture and position. Like a beginning juggler, students should first experiment with only one or two PAWS variables at a time. For example, when working with beginners, you may have them keep the placement and angle the same and guide them to vary the weight and/or speed. Explore variable combinations first in pairs, then trios, and then as a full PAWS quartet. Note that not all variables work in equal ways across string instruments. Owing to the instruments' different string thicknesses, the cello and bass generate a high yield from varying weight, the violin and viola from speed. Ultimately, the goal is to give students the skills to adjust variables based on musical needs.

Using analogies can be especially helpful when teaching PAWS bow usage. Common examples include car analogies such as "driving lanes" for bow placement and "miles per hour" for bow speed. Here are some examples:

- *Placement:* the part of the bow applied to the string between the bridge and fingerboard
  - Teaching strategy: bow placement (middle, balance point, tip, three-quarters point, etc.)
  - Teaching strategy: Bow lanes: 1 (fingerboard) through 5 (bridge)
- Angle: the amount or angle of the bow hairs to the string
  - Teaching strategy: full hair to one hair (0–90 degrees)
- Weight: the amount of natural arm weight applied to the string
  - Teaching strategy: Pounds: 0- to 10-pound arm (*ppp–fff* dynamic extremes)
- Speed: the rate at which the bow hair travels over the string
  - Teaching strategy: miles per hour: 0–100 (speed limit zones)

Common language in the orchestra classroom that addresses PAWS elements may include: "land silently halfway between the bridge and fingerboard at the balance point" (placement), "with flat bow hair, click your pinky, bend your thumb" (angle), "using a relaxed your arm, lower the stick toward the hairs with an eight pound arm" (weight), and "pull and push a 70mph bow" (speed/bow usage). Other examples may include rowing the bow for angle adjustments or having a favorite animal sit on top of the stick for weight.

Tone development involves continuous refinement at all levels of playing. To produce a beautiful tone, one must listen for *ring* and *resonance.* Ring, sometimes called spinning sound, is the idea of a note played with well-balanced PAWS variables, allowing the instrument to naturally vibrate and project. Resonance includes an added intonation step to ring, where sympathetic vibrations allow open strings to vibrate, creating a sound rich in overtones. For example, a bow played with balanced PAWS variables and a fingered G on the D string, when in tune, will resonate with the open G string. Suzuki builds this skill through exercises called "tonalization." Achieving tonal ring and resonance requires well-planned combinations of both PAWS variables and left-hand intonation (see Chapter 28). Consider the following activities for exploring PAWS variables.

PAWS VARIABLE ACTIVITIES

What do you notice when you:

1. Play in different bow lanes? Do you hear a difference in volume or dynamics based on bow placement? Explain the difference between each lane and which you prefer.
2. Move the bow nonparallel to the bridge? What sounds are associated with different bow skew, such as with moving the frog toward the scroll or keeping the bow parallel to the bridge?
3. Float the bow across the strings versus carve into the string? Use arm weight to bring stick toward bow hairs when "carving into the string."
4. Imagine having a hummingbird, bunny, cat, dog, or baby elephant sitting on top of your bow stick.
5. Move the bow slowly across the string (15 mph), and then three more times, increasing the speed each time (35 mph, 50 mph, 80 mph).
6. Keep the bow parallel to the bridge with flat hair but compare playing: (a) in lane 5, no animals on the bows, and 75 mph; (b) in lane 3, a cat on the bow, and 50 mph; and (c) in lane 2, a dog on the bow, and 100 mph; (d) how does the sound of a 35 mph bow on the G string compare to that of a 35 mph bow on the A string?

Tone issues may be resolved by addressing technique, equipment, and musical demands. See the supplemental materials for suggestions for troubleshooting tone issues. They also feature a table that shows common tone issues with possible solutions.

27.4 Rhythm

Bowing and rhythmic issues are often related for string players. With the exception of multi-note slurs, the bow arm is primarily responsible for rhythm, sustain, and articulation. Precursor bowing strategies, such as "rhythmic air bowing," are useful for building visual, aural, and kinesthetic awareness of rhythmic skills. Additionally, observing bow rhythm can help students demonstrate and teachers diagnose bow rhythm understanding.

There are two basic "rhythmic air bowing" strategies: *vertical air bowing* and *shadow bowing.* Vertical air bowing is done with the bow tip pointed upward and helps keep the bow weight from disrupting well-formed bow hands. This helps show "up and down directions," similar to the pull of gravity. Be aware that this may be counterintuitive for cello and bass players, who ultimately bow on a horizontal plane. Shadow bowing tracks the bow in the crook of the arm (violin and viola) or behind the bridge (cello and bass). This version is great for facilitating bow direction in an approximated natural playing plane as well as for incorporating the feeling of string crossings. It is possible to combine shadow playing with left-hand fingering. During any air bowing practice, remember to say the rhythm (ex. syllable or counting), bow direction (ex. up or down), or distribution (ex. whole, half, etc.) while moving the bow.

Other strategies that build rhythmic skills include using bow tracking aids such as toilet paper tubes, rosin cakes, or a pencil between bow stick and hair. Like tone, rhythmic accuracy often atrophies with increased left-hand difficulties. For added complications such as rapid string crossings, practice a passage without the left hand using only the open strings required.

27.5 Bow Strokes and Techniques

Bow arm development can be organized into three sequential levels, each comprising unique goals, strategies, and vocabulary.

BEGINNERS

For beginners, the primary goal is establishing an excellent bow hold and characteristic tone. We suggest using imaginative and descriptive vocabulary with the goals of habit formation, disguised repetition, and student-driven "look-fors." Example: students practice the "four little frogs" bow hold poem each day and describe the placement of each finger.

Beginners first learn "on-the-string bow strokes" including detaché and staccato, followed by legato, slurs, and hooked bowing, as found in the first figure in this chapter. Beginner bowing is best started at the balance point or in the middle of the bow and later extended outward to the extremes (tip and frog). For violin and viola this makes a "square," sometimes termed the Suzuki square. Begin with compact rhythms (e.g., play your name: "Kristen Pellegrino" or "Joel Schut") that keep the bow hand intact. Gradually extend toward the tip or frog using slurred staccato or portato strokes, recentering if the bow hold collapses. It is important to note that a mature bow hold requires flexibility to get to all parts of the bow. As a result, a frog bow hold will look different from a tip bow hold. Work to return to a balanced, neutral bow hold in the center of the bow when returning from either the tip or the frog. In general, open the elbow hinge to guide the bow across the string and engage the shoulder hinge to change string levels.

INTERMEDIATE

For intermediate players, the primary goal is ability and fluency using all parts of the bow. We suggest using specific, referential, and scientific language, with the goal of versatility and comfort playing with a characteristic sound in all parts of the bow. Example: students land silently at major points of the bow (frog, balance point, middle, three-quarter point, and tip) and connect through these points using a full bow.

Intermediate players develop and refine "on-the-string strokes" such as martelé, portato, and tremolo, in addition "off-the-string strokes" including spiccato, as found in Table 27.1. For intermediate players, use exercises that develop access and fluency in all parts of the bow and a balance-point home base for "off-the-string strokes." Once students are able to play in all parts of the bow, understanding the function and fulcrum of each part of the bow is essential for refinement. For example, down and up whole bow strokes can be broken into two parts each and physical functions:

- Down bow stroke
  - Frog to middle: arm releases naturally with gravity, elbow leads (drop)
  - Middle to tip: open elbow, forearm extension, wrist leads (open)

TABLE 27.1 BOW STROKES

On-the-string strokes	Definition	Visual example	Sound
Detaché	Naturally back and forth; change in bow direction provides articulation		"Dah"
Staccato	Short with bow stopping the sound		"Tot"
Legato	Smooth and connected, working to minimize bow change articulation		"La"
Slur	Multiple notes/strings in one bow	 	"LaLa LaLa" "LaLaLaLa"
Hook	Two notes in the same bow direction separated with stopped sound	 	"Ka Ka"
Martelé	Hammered; starts with a "click," ends with a "ring"		"Ka" or "Ping"
Slurred staccato	Staccato strokes in the same bow direction		"Tot Tot"
Louré or portato	Legato slurred staccato; the bow remains moving in a continuous direction with nudges in bow weight		"Wa"

Off-the-string bow strokes	Definition	Visual example	Sound
Spiccato	Bounced at balance point		"Pa"
Sautillé	Jumped at camber point		"Pah"
Ricochet or Jeté	Rebounded near three-quarter point		"Pl-l-l"

Off-the-string bow strokes	Definition	Visual example	Sound
Col legno	Played with the stick of the bow	Col legno 	"Tik"

Special-effects bow strokes	Definition	Visual example	Sound
Tremolo	Quick bow shaking usually in the upper half		"tik-l-l-l-l-l-l-l"
Sul tasto	Over the fingerboard	Sul tasto 	Whisper tone
Ponticello	Near the bridge, creating "ghost" overtones	Sul pont 	Ghost tone
Collé	Rapid finger expansion/contraction; pizzicato with the bow	*No specific marking for style	"Click"

- Up bow stroke
  - Tip to middle: close elbow forearm retraction, wrist leads (close)
  - Middle to frog: arm lifts, elbow leads (lift)

While this basic approach leads to a brilliant bow arm, each string instrument has subtle refinements of this process. For example, the violin and viola middle to tip involve a slight scoop into the string owing to the rapid loss of natural bow weight. Similarly, the cello and bass may feel a greater sinking of the shoulder in the lower half and an extension of the elbow in the upper half.

ADVANCED

For advanced players, the primary goal is pairing bow usage with communicating artistic decisions for a flexible, controlled, and stylized sound. We suggest using coloristic, communicative, and expressive language to inspire creative ownership of decisions. Example: students can play a single bow stroke (i.e., spiccato) with multiple lengths and intensities to varying musical contexts.

Advancing players refine and extend bow strokes to include a wide range of on- and off-the-string strokes, such as slurred staccato and sautillé, in addition to special effects such as ricochet, ponticello, and collé, as found in Table 27.1. It is critical to develop two centers of gravity for use in on- and off-string strokes that permit even sound. The middle of the bow is home base for repeating-on-the-string strokes such as detaché and martelé. The balance point is home base for repeating off the string strokes such as spiccato. With increased speed, off-string spiccato strokes become easier moving toward the frog. Depending on the bow and player, this eventually requires transition to a sautillé stroke best played at the camber point located roughly one to two inches toward the tip from the balance point. Special effects strokes such as sul tasto and ponticello allow a wide range of color variations. Similarly, the collé stroke allows virtuosic articulation.

Issues with posture and instrument hold are often compounded in intermediate and advancing strokes. For example, a student lacking a bent bow-hold thumb will find great difficulty refining a spiccato stroke. A student with locked fingers will find great difficulty playing repetitive downbows near the frog. For advanced players, performance goals such as projection may involve flexing some variables, such as dropping the shoulder or using a weighted elbow earlier in the bowing process. For additional activities developing beginner, intermediate, and advanced bow strokes, see the supplemental materials.

Bow strokes can be classified as: (1) on-string strokes, (2) off-string strokes, and (3) special-effects strokes. All bow strokes, regardless of classification, originate from the string, with the exception of ricochet and col legno. Table 27.1 provides a sequence of bow technique development listed in progressive order of difficulty within each category. Note that the sound examples may vary with stylistic or artistic choices.

27.6 Articulations and Refinement

String players are able to produce more than thirty articulations (Rabin & Smith, 1990) with the most common reflected in Table 27.1. Learning to achieve and control a wide palette of attacks and releases is important. After basic detaché stroke and bow direction is achieved, students can make great leaps forward by refining the martelé stroke. The martelé stroke is fundamental for advanced techniques, as it requires the ability to load and release bow friction in a single motion. Sonically, the martelé stroke starts with a "click" and ends with a "ring," as described by the word "Ping." Table 27.2 shows common problems and tips for diagnosing solutions associated with the martelé stroke.

TABLE 27.2 COMMON MARTELÉ STROKE DEVELOPMENT DIFFICULTIES

Sound	Visualization	Description
Goal: "Ping"	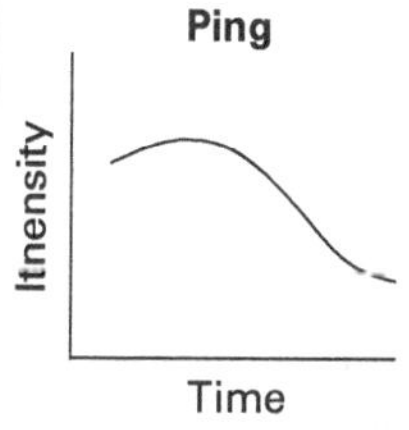 Ping Itnensity Time	Ideal martelé: Starts with a "click" and ends with a "ring." Look-fors: Ensure that the stick is brought close to the hair with loaded weight before the stroke is initiated. At the end of the stroke, look to ensure that the weight is released with the hair away from the stick.
"Phing"	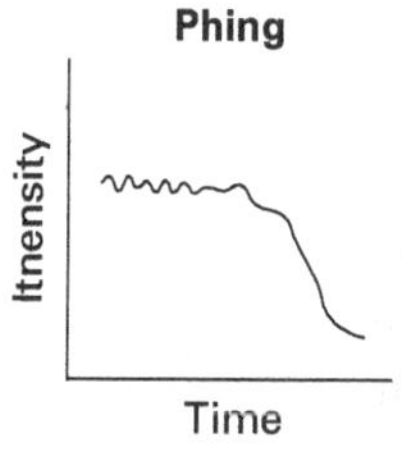 Phing Itnensity Time	Problem: Insufficient contact at beginning of stroke (an airy sound onset) How to fix: Load weight into the string, bringing the stick closer to the hair.
"Pink"	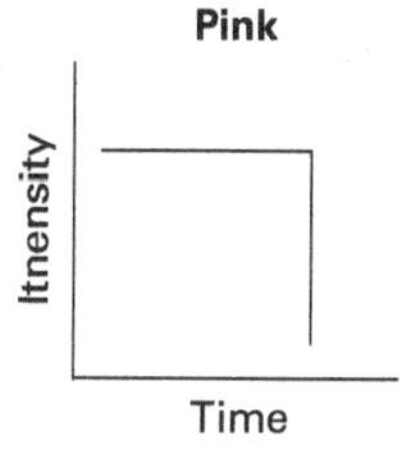 Pink Itnensity Time	Problem: No release at end of stroke (a clear beginning followed by a clipped staccato sound) How to fix: Release weight from the string at end of stroke. Look for tension to release in right hand thumb, forearm, and shoulder.

Sound	Visualization	Description
"Phiph"	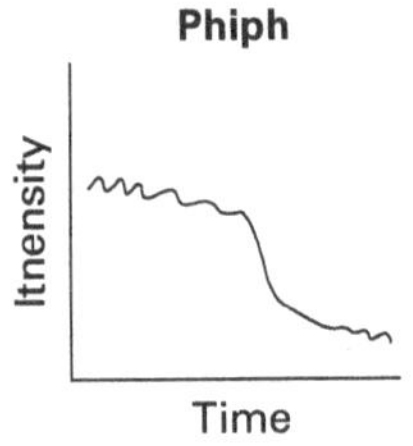 Phiph Itnensity Time	Problem: Insufficient contact at beginning and end of stroke (an airy sound at beginning and end) How to fix: Load weight into string, bringing stick closer to hair, and allow bow speed to slow down, at end of stroke, producing a natural ring
"Phink"	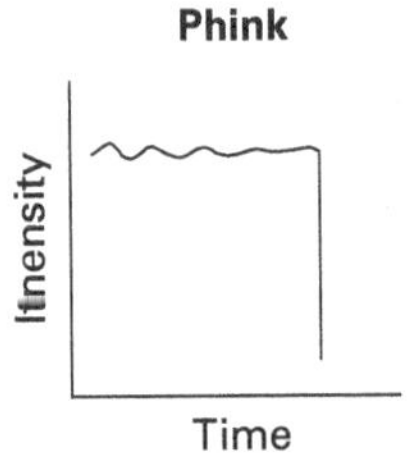 Phink Itnensity Time	Problem: Insufficient beginning contact, stopped ending (a swell and sudden clip of sound) How to fix: Load weight into string, bringing stick closer to hair, and release weight from the string at end of stroke. Think of stroke as one motion originating from initial set-up.

27.7 Musical and Expressive Elements

A large percentage of artistry occurs through a string player's right hand. While the left hand changes pitch and some tone colors with shifting and vibrato, significant artistry in articulation, tone, rhythm, timing, and communication is created through careful right-hand decisions. We draw a distinction between musicality and expressivity. The ability to control and decide aspects of bow usage helps string players develop and progress from playing musically to expressively.

MUSICALITY

A musical player will select the appropriate use of PAWS variables to create tone colors and generate phrases. For example, a common way to phrase musically is creating crescendos and decrescendos within a phrase. For beginner players, this may be done by choosing one PAWS variable, such as speed or weight, with faster or heavier bows leading the crescendo and slower or lighter bows creating the diminuendo. Intermediate and advanced players may combine multiple PAWS variables.

Musical players will also respond to harmonies by leaning into dissonances and chromatics, carving out double stops and chords, singing through larger intervals, and playing with appropriate note length for style. For example, a musical player may use more weight (dog on the stick) and a medium bow speed (40 mph) to bring out a dissonance. Resolve to a lighter weight (hummingbird) and a slower (15 mph) bow speed to end a phrase beautifully.

In general, the wider the interval, the more the bow carves into the string. For larger intervals, prioritize the bottom note like gold, using more weight and speed, and the top note like silver, letting it "float" to the top. This can be combined with left-hand elements such as vibrating the note *before* the goal note or the most beautiful note. For chords, use a heavier bow near the frog for the bottom two notes, played together, and then "break the chord" at the balance point, using a slightly lighter, faster bow for the top two notes. This works whether it is a three- or four-note chord.

EXPRESSIVITY

An expressive player will use the bow to go one step beyond musical idioms and conventions and use PAWS variables for communication. Expressive players create musical meaning and play with intent, thinking about communicating an emotion, mood, story, or scene. They make technical decisions to convey their intent while considering audience experience (listener), audiation intent (hearing the music in their minds), imagination (story line, creativity), and room geography (projection).

An expressive player starts with a sound in mind. They design a beginning, middle, and end to each sound, using articulation consonances and listening critically for specific timbres. For example, you may flavor a martelé with a pointed bee-sting "click" followed by a core tone with an elegant exhale "ring." This might be selected to project in a large space, in a thick texture, or for a dramatic telling. Use vivid, descriptive language that creates memorable personality and meaning. Creating a plan and being responsive to your environment are essential.

Audiation intent involves translating what you hear in your mind to bow distribution and usage. This entails considering the musically appropriate ways to "save" or "spend" the bow. Bow distribution will adjust based on uneven distribution, rhythmic stress, style, and phrasing. Therefore, you must plan how much bow, which part of the bow, and specific placement on the string to create the quality of timbre to match your expressive goals.

One goal of expressive string technique is activating the audience's imagination or emotions. Examples of using moods and stories to inspire expressive playing include projecting a picture and asking students what it makes them think or feel. Then translate this image into bow technique to create a timbre that invokes similar thoughts or feelings. Another example is having students create a story line so that everyone has the same projection goals or intentions at the same time. That way, the audience can imagine different characters and moods. The key is for bow technique to serve the player's expressive musicianship.

Varying expressive choices may impact bow arm technique. For instance, the geography of the room may require varying projection needs. If projection is your priority, you might play in lane 2: more weight, bow stick over the hairs, full bows with faster speed, simple bow changes, and slight skewness. If you prefer a sweet sound, you may prefer lane 3: medium weight, bow stick slightly tilted with medium speed, and smoother bow changes, focusing on finger flexibility and wrist action. These more advanced concepts may change depending on personal preference, performance setting (orchestra, chamber music, solos), and the music you are playing and interpreting.

27.8 Conclusion

Building an excellent bow arm is a journey of refinement. Through thoughtful bow hold formation and tone development at the earliest stages to rhythmic control and stroke refinement at later stages, players can progress from rudimentary playing toward expressive communication. While the simplified bow hold is helpful when teaching group process instruction, continued instrument-specific refinement for healthy and communicative playing is to be highly encouraged in players at all levels. The ultimate goal is to develop a reliable and versatile bow arm, leading toward musical expression.

27.9 Discussion Questions

1. How does the simplified bow hold poem help students memorize, practice, and retain the formation of a healthy bow hand?
2. Why is it important to establish a healthy tone before extending right-hand bow technique?

3. How might your language change when extending bowing skills working with beginner, intermediate, and advanced string players? What are some examples?
4. Why is an understanding of right-hand bow mechanics important for helping string players play expressively? What are some examples?

OXFORD learning link

Visit the online resources for additional documentation and exercises to help expand learning and test your knowledge further: www.oup.com/he/powell_music1e.

CHAPTER 28

PEDAGOGIES FOR TEACHING LEFT-HAND POSITION, INTONATION, AND INSTRUMENT TUNING TO STRING PLAYERS

Erin M. Hansen and Kristen Pellegrino

This chapter provides an overview of strategies for teaching the left-hand position and technique, ways to develop accurate aural skills, how to play with good intonation, and how to teach string players to tune their instruments.

28.1 Introduction

Teaching a group of students to play in tune on buttonless or fretless instruments can seem daunting. However, beginning string students can learn to tune and play their instruments with excellent intonation while still having fun. A key to playing with good intonation is establishing a proper left-hand and arm position, which is how we begin this chapter. Then we suggest ways to help students learn to play in tune through use of finger-spacing patterns and rote instruction as well as singing, audiating, associating intonation with tone, and improvising. Lastly, we connect teaching intonation to tuning one's instrument.

28.2 Establishing the Left-Hand Position

For all musicians, tension can lead to playing issues. Therefore, it is paramount for string musicians to play with a relaxed—yet supported—posture and instrument position. Tension-free playing includes keeping the left-hand muscles and knuckles soft and pliable. Additionally, strings are depressed from both arm weight and the fingers dropping onto the fingerboard.

PREPARING THE INSTRUMENT FOR LEFT-HAND INSTRUCTION

When inspecting string instruments, make sure the bridge is straight and placed properly on each instrument. Next, check the height of the highest and lowest strings, at both the nut and the end of the fingerboard. Strings that are too high are difficult for beginners to depress and can lead to excess tension and improper technique. There is a lot information online about proper string height for beginning string players, but Erin finds it helpful to discuss instrument set-up with the string shops and repair people with whom she works.

Once instruments are properly set up, use stickers or tapes on the fingerboard to temporarily mark approximately where students should place certain fingers. Finger markers help establish and reinforce correct finger spacing and hand frame, especially for students with developing aural skills. However, the finger markers are only temporary aids and are to be used while also developing audiation skills.

28.3 Introducing Left-Hand and Arm Positions

VIOLIN AND VIOLA

Kristen teaches a simple playing position to beginners on the first day (see the next section, "Steps to Forming the Left-Hand Position: Violin and Viola"). Based on what she learned from Robert Culver at the University of Michigan, Kristen has students raise the instrument up over the head and then relax the muscles when lowering it onto the shoulder. Next, when placing the left-hand fingers on the fingerboard, let the arm relax and the elbow hang toward the floor. To change strings, the left arm moves from the shoulder hinge as one unit (fingers to arm), the elbow freely swinging under the instrument; this keeps the hand and finger angle consistent when compared to the string.

Help students think about moving their fingers as a unit, connected by three knuckles. Students can practice collapsing the hand at the crease below the base knuckles of the fingers, but above the thumb; this is the point from which the fingers drop onto the strings. Additionally, practice "hand claps" by "clapping" the fingers against the palm of the hand.

To teach students where to place their hands on the instrument neck, have students locate the space just below the crease at the base of their left-index finger. Hopkins (2019) and other pedagogues, such as Mimi Zweig, refer to this as "X marks the spot." Some use a washable marker to draw a line on this crease and a letter X underneath the line. The neck of the violin or viola rests on the X so that the line is even with—or just visible above—the top of the fingerboard. The thumb rests softly across from the index finger, where the fingerboard meets the neck of the instrument. Erin has students imagine that the neck of the instrument is relaxing in a hammock tied between the base of the first finger and the center of the thumbprint. Make sure the hammock is properly placed so that the instrument does not fall onto the ground (i.e., the webbing between the thumb and index finger).

Many students avoid using the fourth finger because it feels weak. However, we like to introduce it on the first day to help create a strong hand frame. So that all four fingers can reach their spots on the fingerboard without adjusting the hand, we teach that the left hand should be parallel to the fingerboard. For additional finger support, we teach students to use "block fingering" and keep all fingers on the fingerboard whenever possible. For example, when playing fourth finger, the first, second, and third fingers should also be down.

STEPS TO FORMING THE LEFT-HAND POSITION: VIOLIN AND VIOLA

1. Place the fleshy part on the side of the index finger—above the bottom knuckle—against the instrument's neck, near the nut.
2. Place the thumb on the neck, across from the first finger. The thumbprint feels the seam between the fingerboard and neck.*
3. Let the elbow hang toward the floor. There should be a straight line from arm to wrist: no crooked wrists!
4. Let the fingers "dance" on the fingerboard by alternately tapping the fingertips. Make sure fingers are dropping without squeezing the thumb. Then, place all of the fingers down at once. Look for *curved*, "mountaintop" fingers.
5. Place each finger on the fingerboard, and use the right hand to pluck each note four times while singing the finger numbers. Example: open, open, open, open; 1, 1, 1, 1; 2, 2, 2, 2; 3, 3, 3, 3; 4, 4, 4, 4. You can have students play this on another string.

*Some teachers prefer variations in violin and viola thumb placements, based on hand size or philosophy: across from 2, across from 1, in between 1 and 2, or slightly behind 1.

CELLO AND BASS

Because cello and bass strings are thicker and more difficult to depress, we teach students to form the left-hand position on their arms (Figure 28.1). Ask students to follow along while reading the steps in the following section. Having students play songs on their "arm cellos" and "arm basses" is helpful in reinforcing left-hand shape, buddy fingers, arm weight, and playing without thumb pressure.

FIGURE 28.1 **Students form cello left-hand positions on their arms.** ***Alicia Verdier Photography***

STEPS TO FORMING THE LEFT-HAND POSITION: CELLO AND BASS

1. Form a fist with your right hand. Then, put your fist under your chin.
2. Extend your left arm to the side and pretend to hold a can of your favorite beverage. Notice that your arm is like a flat stretch of highway, with no "valleys" or

"peaks" in your elbow or wrist. Your fingers should be rounded, without tension (i.e., soft), with slight spaces between them.

3. Tap your thumb and middle finger together. These are your "buddy fingers," and they are always opposite each other (until fourth position, but that comes later).
4. Bend your left elbow so that your left-hand fingertips rest on the back of your right arm and your left thumb hangs below your right arm. Your fingers should look similar to how they looked in step 2. If you are a cellist, your fingers are rounded and evenly spaced. If you are a bassist, extend your first finger back on your arm, toward your face.

Bass face: Before moving on, let us pause to discover how far bass players should extend their first fingers by making a "bass face." First, put your left thumb in your left ear. Then, place your index finger on your eyebrow, your middle finger on the tip of your nose, your ring finger on your top lip, and your pinky on your bottom lip. Notice there is more distance between your first and second finger and your thumb is opposite your second finger. Now, repeat step 4 before moving to step 5.

5. Now that your fingers are in position, "hang" from your left fingertips (maintaining rounded fingers) and notice how heavy your arm is. Practice hanging with different amounts of weight in your left arm. Your elbow should "float" so that your forearm is flat, from knuckles to elbow.
6. Place your left thumb under its buddy (second finger). When you play notes with your left hand, the strings should depress from the natural weight of your arm, never from squeezing with your thumb.

After establishing the left-hand position on their arms, have students establish a good instrument position. Repeat steps 2 through 6 on their instruments, this time without the "bass face." When students perform step 4, tell them to land so that their pinky fingers land on the fourth-finger sticker. From there, students can slide their other fingers back into place. Using the fourth finger to place the hand, rather than the first finger, helps maintain the necessary curve of the weaker pinky finger.

ALL STRINGS

To help form a strong left-hand frame, we tell another Culver story:

I went to a farmers' market and bought lots of fruit, vegetables, eggs, and milk, but when I came home, I found I bought a dozen rotten eggs! At first I was disappointed, but then I thought about bringing them into class and putting them between your hand and the neck of your instrument. Then, if you squeezed too hard it would crack and ooze down your arm and you would stink all day! Also, if your hand was too far from the neck (SPLAT!), *it would slip out and fall to the floor. Then, I realized the custodians would hate me, so we will just pretend.*

We pretend to place a rotten egg in the palm of their hands. We have used our fists or plastic Easter eggs to help students feel what the shape of their hands should be. Consequently, students automatically reshape their left hands whenever they hear "remember your rotten eggs!" You can then help cellists and bassists make the connection between their "rotten eggs" and their "canned beverages," as described in the previous section (step 2). A word of caution: some teachers describe attaching thumb tacks to the back of violin and viola necks, to encourage students to play with straight wrists. We do *not* recommend this. Ouch!

FINGER-SPACING PATTERNS

String players rely on muscle memory and often think in terms of finger-spacing patterns, based on where half steps (symbolized by ^) and whole steps occur in music. Most beginning string literature will be in the key of either D major or G major. These keys allow all string players to play on their instrument's middle strings (A, D, and G) and primarily require just two finger patterns. Table 28.1. illustrates the finger-spacing patterns most common in beginning orchestra music. Violinists and violists think about which fingers are close together, often touching (half steps), and which ones are about a finger's width away (whole steps). See Figure 28.2. Cellists and bassists think about what fingers to use, instead of the spacing between fingers. As string students advance, they will encounter music in multiple keys and tonalities, at which point new finger-spacing patterns are introduced.

TABLE 28.1 INITIAL FINGER-SPACING PATTERNS (IN FIRST POSITION)

	First pattern introduced	Second pattern introduced
Violin & Viola	**2-3 Pattern** 0 - 1 - 2^3 - 4 Ex. D E F♯G A	**1-2 Pattern** 0 - 1^2 - 3 - 4 Ex. D E F G A
Cello	**1-3 Pattern** 0 - 1 - 3 - 4 Ex. D E F♯ G	**1-2-4 Pattern** 0 - 1 - 2 - 4 Ex. D E F G
Bass	**1-4 Pattern** 0 - 1 - 4 - 0 Ex. D E F♯ G	**1-2 Pattern** 0 - 1 - 2 - 0 Ex. D E F G

Note: The caret (^) denotes a half step and fingers touching or almost touching for violinists and violists. Light grey numbers represent the fingers not used for that pattern.

FIGURE 28.2 Students demonstrate the "2^3 Finger Spacing Pattern" for violin and viola. ***Alicia Verdier Photography***

String teachers call these finger patterns by different names. We label violin and viola patterns by the location of the half step(s) (e.g., 2^3 finger spacing pattern) and ask them to hold up their left hands with the correct spacing between their fingers (see Figure 28.2); we identify low-string patterns by the fingers used. Some string pedagogues, such as

Bornoff (see Chapter 26), number the finger patterns and have students play patterns one through five (Lyle, 2018). For more on finger spacing patterns, see "Finger-Spacing Patterns" on the book's online resources site.

28.4 Developing Left-Hand Technique

VIOLIN AND VIOLA

All string players play C and F naturals on the A and D strings with the second finger. However, when first teaching violinists and violists to play these "low" second fingers, as they are often called, Kristen has them slide their second fingers down over their first finger and fingernail to feel the closeness of the half-step. To reinforce this relationship, students then demonstrate and compare the 2–3 finger–spacing pattern (1–2^3–4) and the 1–2 pattern (1^2–3–4) by keeping their first, third, and fourth fingers stable while sliding their second fingers on the string between touching their third fingers to touching their finger fingers.

When beginning and intermediate violinists and violists encounter notes a half step above the third finger, we have them play a low fourth finger instead of a high third finger (see Figure 28.3). This technique helps maintain a consistent hand position (i.e., the third finger remains in place) and helps students feel the half-step distance between their third and fourth fingers. As a result, the notes before and after the target are more likely to be in tune because the basic hand shape is maintained. However, students' instinct is to use an extended third finger because it makes intellectual sense to them and their third fingers are stronger. Therefore, it is imperative to help them understand that playing the entire passage in tune is the goal. I often let them try it both ways and then they understand.

FIGURE 28.3 **Low fourth finger on a viola.** ***Alicia Verdier Photography***

For teaching low ones (e.g., B♭ on the A string), Kristen uses the bass-face exercise as a reference. After forming a bass-face hand position, students move their first fingers between their eyebrows to the top part of their noses to feel how to open the hand while keeping the other fingers in place for pitches that follow. This also works for cellists when playing backward extensions, which is addressed in the next section.

CELLO AND BASS

As stated in "Finger Spacing Positions," cellists and bassists do not change the spacing between their fingers but choose different finger patterns, depending on the music. However, because of the longer string lengths and the limited number of notes the left hand can play in one position, cellists and bassists need to use different techniques to play additional notes. Such techniques include extensions and thumb position discussed next, as well as shifting (Chapter 29). Cellists and bassists will also need to read music in tenor and treble clef when playing in higher positions.

As they advance, cellists will add extensions to their finger patterns. Extensions require cellists to create a whole step between their first and second fingers, resulting in a bass-hand shape. Additionally, depending on whether the music requires a backward (as we have seen) or a forward extension, cellists will need to slide their thumbs up and down the cello neck to keep their buddy fingers aligned and support the weaker fourth finger. Teachers can prepare students for passages containing extensions by marking in the music when to extend and close the hand (see Figure 28.4) and by introducing the extension motion through simple exercises (See "Extension Exercises" in the book's online resources).

FIGURE 28.4 **Mark when to extend and close the left hand in cello music**

Lastly, more advanced pieces require both cellists and bassists to play in thumb position, at which point the thumb acts like a movable capo on a guitar. As the left hand moves toward the bridge, the spacing between pitches becomes smaller. Owing to the closer proximity of pitches and the shape of the left hand in thumb position, cellists and bassists need to use different finger spacing patterns. More information on thumb position is included in the book's online resources.

28.5 Teaching Intonation

Many people associate beginning strings with out-of-tune sounds. However, beginning string players can and *should* play with good intonation. In this section we describe strategies for teaching intonation by singing, addressing tone, teaching by rote, and using improvisation.

SINGING TO DEVELOP AURAL SKILLS

Singing and humming help develop pitch accuracy and often are a more accurate indication of students' aural skills than playing, as equipment and playing technique can affect a student's performance (Segado et al., 2018). Aural skills can be developed through various singing activities and pitch-matching games. See "Activities to Develop Aural Skills" in the book's online resources for demonstrations of and instructions for several pitch-building activities. We also teach students to sing the melodies and root melodies of songs they will learn to play. Root melodies are made up of chord roots. Erin uses this tern instead of "basslines" so that all strings players understand that bass players also play the melody and virtuosic music. Songs can be sung in a variety of ways, including singing them with words (if they have lyrics), on a neutral syllable or with solfège, note names, or fingerings. Not only does this build tonal acuity, it also helps students when learning to play songs by rote.

Asking students to match their playing to their singing helps turn something that is inaudible and intangible (i.e., audiation) into something audible, concrete, and useful when assessing their playing. We teach students to intentionally break intonation into a four-step process:

1. Sing and then audiate the music (i.e., hear it in your mind)
2. Play music and listen to the pitches
3. Compare pitches from the instrument to audiated sounds
4. Quickly adjust fingers to match audiated sounds (move toward the scroll to lower pitches and toward the bridge to raise them)

In addition to singing, students can develop pitch accuracy by connecting aural information (i.e., what they audiate) to theoretical knowledge (e.g., key signatures, half steps, and whole steps) and to physical manipulation by way of finger-spacing patterns. Initially, these aural and oral and physical activities take time, but they teach students to independently address intonation issues, saving time in the long run.

ASSOCIATING INTONATION WITH TONE

Interestingly, excellent intonation is dependent upon a combination of left- and right-hand skills. In Chapter 27 we discussed how tone is a combination of bow placement, angle, weight, and speed (PAWS). However, a ringing and resonant tone also depends on the correct left-hand placement on the string. If students are not playing in tune, teachers will have to differentiate between equipment (e.g., false strings, out-of-tune open strings, etc.), musical (e.g., not matching instrument sounds to audiated sounds), and technical issues (e.g., playing in the wrong key, playing with an incorrect hand position, etc.) in order to help students.

ROTE INSTRUCTION AND BASIC IMPROVISATION TO STRENGTHEN INTONATION

Learning to play a string instrument requires several distinct physical and motor skills: forming instrument and bow positions, vertically moving the left-hand fingers, and horizontally moving the bow with the right arm. It is a lot to think about! That is why we feel that music reading should be introduced *after* students can successfully play their instruments with a stable position and clear tone. Teaching by rote is an efficient method of instruction that provides a model of posture, position, intonation, tone, and more (Hamann & Gillespie, 2018).

Rote instruction works best with songs with which students are already familiar, such as short songs they learned in their elementary school general music classes, folk songs, and popular tunes and melodies (e.g., themes from television shows and movies and music they listen to for fun). Rote instruction is a fabulous way to expand students' aural vocabulary by introducing them to songs in different modes and meters. When teaching new notes outside of D major on the D and A strings, Kristen often has students play popular melodies they can audiate while playing. Overall, learning by rote allows students to develop the necessary executive skills to play in tune and with beautiful tone as well as play together (ensemble skills). For more on transitioning from rote to note, see Chapter 6.

Introducing improvisation early in students' development helps foster creativity, audiation, playing with excellent posture, position, intonation, and tone, as well as self-confidence when leading and playing in front of others. We begin improvisation instruction with short, controlled experiences before asking students to improvise full passages. These activities progress sequentially so that students may experience multiple successes and develop confidence. Even if you are not comfortable improvising, you can plant the improvising seed in your students so they can develop these skills throughout their musical careers. See "Improvisation Activities" in the book's online resources.

28.6 Teaching Tuning

Tuning a string instrument is made up of two components: an aural component (i.e., being able to hear whether or not a note is in tune) and a mechanical component (e.g., turning fine tuners to raise or lower the pitch of a string). Before asking students to tune their instruments, time must be spent developing students' aural skills and introducing students to the mechanics of tuning. Most frustrations occur when students are asked to tune their instruments before they are able to discern differences in pitch.

While aural skills are developing, students can become familiar with the terminology and mechanics of tuning. Common tuning terms address whether or not a pitch is too low (flat) or high (sharp) and how to correct it (see Table 28.2). Try to include these terms in as many activities as possible so they become part of students' vernacular. For example, when playing Simon Says: "Simon says to stand and turn clockwise, three times." Similarly, ask students to glissando "higher" or "lower."

TABLE 28.2 INTONATION TENDENCIES AND MECHANICAL RESPONSES

How it sounds	What to do
Flat or low	Tighten the string; raise the pitch; turn the fine tuner clockwise; righty-tighty; slide your finger toward the bridge
Sharp or high	Loosen the string; lower the pitch; turn the fine tuner counterclockwise; lefty-loosey; slide your finger toward the nut

When students are first learning to tune their instruments, they often feel overwhelmed from having to: (a) hear and discern pitch; (b) manipulate fine tuners, tuning keys (bass), or pegs; (c) produce a clear sound; and (d) support their instrument with a good position. Therefore, prior to asking students to tune their instruments, it is important to practice the following physical skills:

- Support their instruments without hands
- Find the fine tuner/tuning key that corresponds to each string
- Play arco while touching the fine tuner/tuning key
- Turn the fine tuner/tuning key in the correct direction while in tuning position

Once students are comfortable with these skills, they can practice the mechanics of tuning by using a tuner to tune their open strings.

When students are comfortable with both the mechanical and aural aspects, they are ready to begin tuning their instruments. When introducing a tuning procedure, it is helpful to establish visual cues you will use during the somewhat cacophonous tuning process. Erin uses the following cues with her students:

1. "When I raise my hand, you are to stop playing, raise your hand, and wait for my instructions."
2. "You may begin tuning your instrument once I give this cue" (musically cue with head and scroll of violin).

To prevent tuning from taking too much class time (and frustrating students), start by having students tune just one string (e.g., the D string). Add one string to tune (e.g., the D and A strings) as they become more efficient and accurate when tuning. By the time they can tune all four strings, tuning should take only five to ten minutes.

Once students have developed aurally and can successfully tune their open strings while using fine tuners/tuning keys, they are ready to tune using their pegs. After demonstrating the tuning process for tuning with pegs, Erin distributes an instructional handout (see "Tuning with Pegs" in the online resources) and has students work in pairs to lower and then raise to pitch one of their strings while using pegs.

28.7 Conclusion

We hope you recognize the connections between playing with good technique and intonation, developing aural skills, and learning to tune a string instrument. Developing these skills sets up string students for future musical successes. In the next chapter, we discuss more advanced left-hand techniques in shifting and vibrato.

28.8 Discussion Questions

1. How did the authors define "tension-free playing"? What are ways in which tension affects your performance on your primary instrument? From the chapter, identify any pedagogical activities or techniques you think would prepare students to play without tension.
2. When watching string students play, what visible characteristics would indicate a good left-hand and arm position? See if you can identify four components for violins and violas and four for cellos and basses.
3. Identify six or more elements of teaching intonation, as discussed by the authors. Would any of these elements transfer to teaching intonation to other instrumentalists? Would you feel uncomfortable with teaching any of the audiation or intonation-building activities, as described in the chapter? Why or why not?
4. Did you sing in instrumental music classes? Did you know why you were singing? How do you feel about having students sing in class and helping them realize that singing helps them understand how to play with excellent intonation?
5. The authors recommend using finger markers when starting string players; they also recommend building students' audiation skills before asking them to tune their instruments by ear. Considering these recommendations, when do you think it would be appropriate to remove students' finger markers?
6. Why did the authors suggest that string students start learning to play their instruments without notation? What are your experiences with rote learning? What are your experiences with teaching by rote? Would rote instruction benefit other beginning instrumentalists? Why or why not?

OXFORD learning link

Visit the online resources for additional documentation and exercises to help expand learning and test your knowledge further: www.oup.com/he/powell_music1e.

CHAPTER 29

PEDAGOGIES FOR TEACHING SHIFTING AND VIBRATO TO STRING PLAYERS

Kristen Pellegrino and Erin M. Hansen

This chapter provides an overview of strategies for teaching shifting and vibrato to string players.

29.1 Introduction

This chapter furthers the discussion from Chapter 28 about teaching left-hand skills to string players in group settings, specifically shifting (sliding to move fingers and hand to a different place on the fingerboard) and vibrato (controlled, steady oscillations of pitch). We begin with ways to determine when students are ready to learn these techniques and offer fun preliminary exercises that you can teach early in a string player's development. Then we suggest activities for teaching shifting and vibrato to beginning through advanced students.

29.2 Determining Readiness

People often wonder when to teach shifting and vibrato. Although your specific context matters (e.g., how often and for how long you see your students), there are two good indicators: (a) when a student consistently plays with a relaxed, balanced, supported posture and position; and (b) when students can match pitch when singing and playing.

POSITION

A lengthened, relaxed, and balanced position is a prerequisite for learning advanced techniques. For violinists and violists, excellent position includes laying the instrument on the shoulder and using the weight of the head to keep the instrument in place while resting the side of the jaw on the chin rest. This allows the left hand and arm to move freely around the fingerboard. Also, students need a solid left-hand and arm frame, which includes:

- a consistent and balanced left-hand position
- using correct finger spacing patterns based on the tonality of the piece
- moving the arm as a unit, from the finger knuckles to the elbow.

See Chapter 28 for more on left-hand frame.

Cellists and bassists need to play with a lengthened, relaxed posture and to feel that their instrument securely rests against them. For this reason, we recommend that bassists play from a seated position when first learning how to shift and use vibrato. Make sure that low-string players use chairs and stools of the correct height, as this contributes to the ease with which the left arm moves freely around the fingerboard. Both cellists and bassists should consistently play with proper hand positions (see Chapter 28) and be able to depress the strings using primarily arm weight and without thumb pressure.

MATCHING PITCH

Students should be able to match pitch when singing and playing instruments before learning to shift or play with vibrato. Having students sing every day, beginning on the first day, establishes the basis of playing with excellent intonation. Additionally, we teach students to audiate while playing. See Chapter 28 for activities to develop students' aural skills.

29.3 Teaching Pre-Shifting Activities

Shifting is not a big deal! Simply slide your entire left hand to a different location on the fingerboard; moving closer to the bridge shortens the string length and raises the pitch. Fingerboard locations are labeled with a position number (e.g., third position), and most string players begin playing in first position. Reasons to play in different positions include (a) playing higher notes that you could not otherwise reach; (b) the timbre of a lower string being more musically appropriate; (c) avoiding open strings; and/or (d) making certain left-hand passages easier to play.

When shifting, one should release all tension and slide or glide lightly on top of the string, allowing the thumb, hand, and arm to move as a single unit. To help students feel comfortable moving around the fingerboard, teachers can introduce pre-shifting activities that promote tension-free motion and build confidence. Although there are many strategies teachers can use, the next section describes the six strategies that we most commonly use: push-aways, ski jumps, polishing the strings, sirens, engaging in musical conversations, and creating sound effects for a story. The first two strategies—push-aways and ski jumps—are specific to upper or lower string instruments, respectively. The other four strategies work for all orchestral string instruments.

PRE-SHIFTING ACTIVITIES

Push-aways are specifically for violinists and violists (vlns/vlas) and are precursors for both shifting and vibrato. The goal is to form a C-shaped hand, similar to that used by cellists and bassists, without moving the thumb. First, hold your instrument in ***seated rest position*** (like a cello), with the scroll near your chin and your left hand in playing position and fingers resting on a string. Next, leave your left thumbprint on the side of the fingerboard/neck but push the inside of your left hand away from the opposite side of the fingerboard/neck. Notice the profile of your first fingernail; now, keeping the first finger on the fingerboard, rotate your arm until you are looking at your entire fingernail. You may describe this as moving a hand on a clock; the scroll points to 12, your first finger knuckle moves the hour hand from the one o'clock position to the three o'clock position. Next, practice this in *playing position.*

Ski jumps are for cellists and bassists. The goal is for an Olympic "skier" (i.e., the left hand) to feel a release in their shoulders and upper arms as gravity pulls their left hands down the slope (i.e., the fingerboard). At the bottom of the slope, the skier "catches air" when the left hand soars off the end of the fingerboard, jumping high in the air and landing at the starting gate (i.e., the nut). In order to make use of gravity, bass players are encouraged to play in the seated position, releasing the left hand from providing any support for the bass.

All students can participate in the following activities:

Polishing the fingerboard is also a precursor of vibrato. Put a tissue underneath the strings, where the bow lands, and bring it up between the strings and fingerboard. Then, put all four fingers on the tissue in between the two middle strings. Put your thumb in the appropriate place and, after vlns/vlas do a push-away, polish the fingerboard with the tissue, moving the thumb, hand, and arm as one unit. Students can also perform this exercise without tissues.

For *sirens* or *ghost sirens,* use the same motion as *polishing the fingerboard* but use arm weight to bring the string to the fingerboard and then slide one finger from the nut to the bridge while using long, smooth bows. This will imitate the sound of an emergency vehicle siren. To make *ghost sirens,* we suggest beginning on the pitch D on the A string, which would be third finger for violinists and violists and fourth finger for cellists; use one finger that lightly touches the string (do not depress the string to the fingerboard), creating harmonics rather than "solid" pitches. We also introduce *ghost sirens* first, as it is a tension-free left hand movement.

In general, the thumb, hand, and arm should move as one unit. As cellists and bassists move toward the bridge, buddy fingers will keep the thumb and second finger moving together until fourth position (first finger and thumb align at the base of the neck). Once the left hand moves past the instrument's shoulder, players thumb positions will change. For violinists and violists, the thumb travels from the side of the fingerboard to underneath the curved part of the neck; those with small hands sometimes move their thumb to the opposite side of the fingerboard. Low-string players let their thumb move from behind the neck to hovering above the strings. All should move in a way that keeps a consistent finger to string angle.

Lastly, students can have *musical conversations* using sirens. One person asks a musical "question," and the other provides a musical "answer." You can suggest that if one person ends with the pitch going higher, that is like a question, and the answer might end with the pitch going lower. You can give other guidance, such as having the second person start around the same pitch as where the first person ended. What other directions might you give? You could *create sound effects for a story* using sirens. Do you have other ideas for games?

We suggest that teachers speak about moving fingers "toward the bridge" or "toward the scroll," as these directions work for all string instruments. To describe a pitch as "higher" and "lower," one must clarify for students that those terms refer to how the pitch sounds, not the direction of hand movement. Otherwise, using the terms "higher" or "lower" to describe motion is problematic because (a) cellists and bassists move higher in pitch when their hands move lower on the fingerboard; and (b) violinists and violists move their hands horizontally, rather than vertically. Since bass players need to begin shifting earlier than other instrumentalists owing to the limited range of pitches in first position, we suggest teaching pre-shifting activities to everyone so that all players begin the process together.

29.4 Teaching How to Play in Different Positions and Shifting into Positions

There is a difference between teaching shifting *between* positions and playing *in* a new position. Many find it easier to play a song in a new position, rather than tunes that require a change between positions. When first playing in new positions, we suggest that students revisit melodies they played in first position, such as "Hot Cross Buns" or "Mary Had a Little Lamb." Many simple melodies can be played in multiple positions and on multiple strings. See Figure 29.1 for an example of how Kristen teaches students to play "Hot Cross Buns" in third or fourth position. Note: basses may choose to play their open G strings for *do*, and cellists use 4, 2, x1 (extend the first finger backward).

FIGURE 29.1 Introducing "Hot Cross Buns" in third position

To teach students to move between positions, we use harmonics, as they do not require hand strength (helping students shift without pressure) and have a wide range in which they sound in tune (helping students feel successful in their motion). Figure 29.2 illustrates two versions of "Twinkle, Twinkle Little Star." In the first version, instead of open strings, students play the octave harmonic in the middle of the string (i.e., the first harmonic).

FIGURE 29.2 Using harmonics to shift between positions

The second version is similar, but has students play the second harmonics (i.e., a twelfth higher) at the base of the neck; violinists and violists will play these with their second fingers, and cellists and bassists will use their first fingers. This sets students up to shift between first and third position (upper strings) and first and fourth position (lower strings), which are the most common positions to first learn to shift. Once students can easily play this version of "Twinkle" with harmonics, they can make the notes solid (depress the string) and voilà—they are shifting! Can you think of more ways to experience these concepts?

Because violinists and violists can play more notes in one position, here are two additional ways to teach violinists and violists to shift. First, they need to perform a push-away. Then, playing the pre-shifting activity sirens, students release their thumbs before gliding on top of the string until their first fingers are playing the harmonic D on the A string. Students "walk up," D, E, F♯^G. See Figure 29.3 for another example that combines an exercise from Whistler (1989) with push-aways and "Hot Cross Buns."

FIGURE 29.3 Combination of Whistler (1989) exercise and "Hot Cross Buns"

*PA = pushaways

Notated music uses several different methods to indicate a left-hand shift. Regardless of which system you use, it is important to remain consistent when talking about shifting and when notating shifting and fingerings. Figure 29.4 illustrates one way to indicate shifts. For additional information on shifting, bass-specific considerations, and notated musical examples, refer to "Shifting Supplemental Materials" in the book's online resources.

FIGURE 29.4 Written symbols associated with shifting

Symbol	-	1, 2, 3, 4	e.g. "1^{st}_{p}" or "3_{p}"	I, II, III, IV
Meaning	Shift (i.e., move arm & thumb)	Finger numbers (i.e., Arabic numbers)	Position on neck (i.e., Arabic numbers + lowercase "p")	String (i.e., Roman numerals; I = highest sounding string, IV = lowest)

FIGURE 29.5 Musical example of shifting

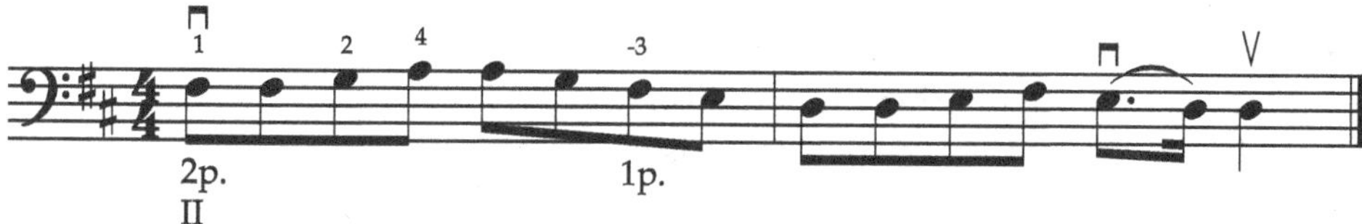

29.5 Choreographing Shifts and Advanced Shifting Concerns

When deciding on when and how to shift, it is important to look at the music around the shift and plan accordingly. Here are some general "rules" and strategies, first in a list, then with descriptions.

- Audiate the destination note, before you shift
- Shift on half steps
- Shift to a secure-feeling position
- Stay in one position for as long as possible
- Find a position where the finger spacings stay consistent from string to string
- Shift rhythmically (appropriate speed) and metrically
- Shift musically and stylistically

When given the choice, we suggest shifting on a half-step. That could happen on the same finger (e.g., 1–1, 2–2, etc.) or between two fingers (e.g., 2–1, etc.). Another option is to shift to a position where you feel most secure (often first, third, and fifth positions). However, sometimes it is more important to find a position that works best for a longer period of time rather than shifting between positions. This often involves finding a position where you can play the same finger spacing pattern on more than one string.

For more advanced students, there are strategies that help people shift smoothly and play in a variety of stylistic and expressive ways. Decide whether to shift on the old note (slide on the old finger to the new position, then put down the new finger), to shift on the new note (put the new finger down and then slide for a Romantic-style shift), or a combination of the two (begin shifting on the old note and switch to the new note mid-shift). Similar decisions must be made regarding the timing of shifts and bow changes (e.g., shift on the old bow, disguise the shift in between bow changes, or shift on the new bow). One must experiment with each possibility and decide based on sound preference and which technique results in greater accuracy.

We suggest thinking about choreographing your shifts in three different ways. First, shift in musically appropriate ways, which includes shifting rhythmically, metrically, and in appropriate places within a phrase. Next, for each shift, plan to execute it in an appropriate part of the bow for that passage and practice it the same way every time. Then think about measuring your shift with *ghost tones,* which involves imagining an intermediate note. For example, when shifting from a B to a G on the A string, violinists and violists can first practice moving their hands until their first fingers travel from B, past C and C♯, up to D before placing their fourth fingers on the G; cellists continue traveling until their first finger rests at the note E. Practice drawing the bow so you can hear the ghost tones and feel the gliding motion. Then, practice the same motion without drawing the bow but check the arrival pitch. Finally, gradually speed up the process.

Lastly, always audiate the destination pitch before your shift so that you have a goal pitch and will know when you arrive. It is okay to slightly hear the shift as it is happening. There are other techniques that help string players shift with great intonation, including by concentrating on changing finger spacing positions (Chapter 28), putting your hand in the shape it will be in in higher positions before your shift, compressing your hand during the shift, or moving the thumb into the crook of the neck in higher positions and developing hand balance and finger independence. However, addressing the previously discussed considerations will get you pretty far. To learn how to troubleshoot shifting issues, please see "Common Shifting Issues" in the book's online resources.

29.6 Vibrato

For all string players, the fundamental motion of vibrato consists of rolling the fingertip back and forth on the string, oscillating around a single pitch. For example, when playing the pitch E, the fingertip will roll above, through, and below the fingered note, causing the pitch to fluctuate several cents above and below the fundamental pitch. There are different hand and arm motions involved in this process, and we will discuss ways to teach those.

As with shifting, there are some approaches better suited for upper strings, some intended for lower strings, and subtle differences between each instrument. Let us begin by identifying pedagogical strategies that we feel are universal among string instruments.

TEACHING VIBRATO: UNIVERSAL PEDAGOGICAL STRATEGIES

- Practice vibrato motion between strings, before on the string, to reduce left hand tension.
- Begin teaching vibrato using the second finger, as this is often easiest for string players.
- Practice the vibrato motion with just the left hand. When the motion is correct and rhythmically steady, add the bow in the following sequence:
    - The student closes their eyes while maintaining vibrato; then, another student or teacher draws the bow across the string.
    - The student establishes the vibrato motion. They then add their bow to an open string that is different from the one with vibrato (e.g., vibrato F♯ on the A string and sustain open D).
    - The student establishes vibrato motion and then adds their bow to the same string.
    - The student begins to incorporate vibrato on sustained notes within their music.
- Vibrato that has correct motion, is tension free, and is rhythmically steady is preferred over fast vibrato that is tense and irregular. Keep in mind that instruments with thicker strings have a slower vibrato.

PRE-VIBRATO EXERCISES

Similar to teaching pre-shifting activities, we begin with pre-vibrato activities. These activities reduce left hand tension and introduce the vibrato motion. Some of these exercises come from the method book *Viva Vibrato!* (Fischbach & Frost, 1997) and the accompanying video *The Art of Vibrato* (Fischbach, 2002), which are wonderful resources for string teachers.

PRE-VIBRATO EXERCISES

Push-aways are specifically for violinists and violists and are precursors for both shifting and vibrato. (See *pre-shifting activities* above for the explanation.)

Swing plops: At your side, freely swing the left arm backward and forward, like the pendulum of a grandfather clock. Feel how heavy and relaxed the arm is. Then, on a forward swing, swing the arm up above your instrument and let your left-hand fingertips plop onto the fingerboard. Feel the weight of your arm dangling from your flexible and curved fingers. Notice your relaxed left arm and shoulders (Fishbach, 2002).

Heel pats: With a good left-hand position, slide your left hand and thumb toward the shoulders of the instrument until the heel of your hand touches them. The thumbs will rest at the base of the neck. Upper-string players perform a push-away. Keeping your thumb in place, let the heel of your hand rhythmically pat your instrument's shoulder. Pat a steady rhythm or different rhythmic patterns. Your thumb and the webbing between your thumb and index finger should feel secure but flexible. (Fishbach calls this exercise "palm pats.")

Rhythmic polishing: Once you can *polish the fingerboard (see pre-shifting exercises)* with one finger, perform the same motion on top of a string. Start polishing at a steady tempo. We recommend sliding to the eighth-note pulse, quarter note = 70 bpm. Keeping the same pulse, gradually polish a smaller and smaller distance until your finger gets "stuck."

If your arm becomes tense or your polishing become arrhythmic, go back to polishing the distance at which you were last steady.

VIOLIN AND VIOLA VIBRATO

Violinists and violists use two main types of vibrato: arm and wrist vibrato (although advanced players can also use finger vibrato, in fast passages). Before you try to vibrate, you should first do a push-away. Although Kristen plays with arm vibrato or a combination of arm and wrist, she initially teaches wrist vibrato, as she found it clearer to teach wrist vibrato and *then* teach some students to play with arm vibrato if it begins to happen naturally for them.

The wrist vibrato motion is essentially moving the hand back and forth at the wrist joint while the arm is still and balanced. To teach this, Kristen uses three ideas. Pretend you are a southern grandmother rocking on her rocking chair on the porch and say, "Oh, my, it's *sooo* hot!," and fan yourself with your hand. Then pretend you are making a gesture like an Italian American from the northeast, like me: make a circle with your middle finger and thumb and shake your hand while saying, "What's the mattah you?" or "What'a you doin'?" The third is to use an egg shaker so students can see, hear, and feel the motion.

Next, bring the hand to the instrument by placing two drops of imaginary glue on the heel of your left hand and pretend to glue it to the ribs of the instrument by the base of the neck. Then do a push-away and fan yourself, keeping the heel of your hand "glued" to the ribs; after a while, let your fingers lightly drag back and forth on the strings. Be sure the hand is moving at the wrist joint on top of a balanced arm. Next, place a drop of imaginary glue on the fingertip of the second finger and pretend to glue it to the A string (around fourth or fifth position). Making sure your hand is still pushed away from the side of the fingerboard, move your hand at the wrist joint while rolling the fingertip back and forth on the string.

Some students begin to naturally play with an arm vibrato. If they do, I intentionally teach them to open and close their elbow hinge, moving their hand, wrist, and forearm as one unit. Beginning with a *push-away*, I have them *polish the fingerboard*, gradually narrowing the movement. Next, they put their *fingertips on the shoulder of the instrument* and roll their fingertips until their hands move away from the shoulder of the violin and back, making sure to open and close the forearm at the elbow hinge (as opposed to the wrist hinge). Finally, as with the wrist vibrato, we move the fingertips to a string by pretending to put one drop of glue on the fingertip. Roll the fingertip on the string with the forearm, wrist, and hand moving as one unit in a single motion.

CELLO AND BASS

We have found that cellists and bassists develop vibrato fairly easily by practicing pre-vibrato exercises. However, it is important to remind low-string players not to squeeze with their thumbs and to monitor their left-arm motion for movement from the elbow. Cellists and bassists should never try to achieve vibrato by pronating and supinating the arm, as you would to turn a doorknob.

WHEN AND HOW TO INTRODUCE VIBRATO WHILE PLAYING

After students move with the correct motion, have them close their eyes while someone else draws the bow across the string. If they can keep the motion going, then have them try it on another finger; many students prefer this finger order 2, 3, and then 1 or 4. When they are comfortable with keeping a consistent motion, have them silently place the bow onto a string other than the one they are vibrating, with controlled motion. If the motion is still consistent, have them draw the bow. Caution: using the bow often interrupts the left-hand motion. If this happens, start this process again.

After the first day, only spend two to five minutes a day on vibrato. As they improve, they can add their own bow. Plan on practicing vibrato motion for at least a month before it can be used in any piece. After that, we suggest having students apply a wide, slow vibrato to their music when they can play long notes in position, such as the first three notes of Pachelbel's Canon for violins.

ADVANCED VIBRATO CONCEPTS

Vibrato can be considered as an expressive element with which to manipulate and use strategically. For vibrato mastery, string players must learn to keep vibrato consistent from finger to finger (between notes) as well as being able to blossom notes (starting slower and increasing speed and width and then decreasing width and speed again within a note) or phrase between notes (starting slower and increasing speed and width and then decreasing width and speed again from note to note). Another important concept is to vibrate the note *before* the destination note, the one you want to make sing. Finally, use vibrato as an ornament and learn to vary the speed and width of the vibrato to highlight the style and character of the piece.

For troubleshooting vibrato issues and further resources, visit the online resources.

29.7 Conclusion

Teaching shifting and vibrato to string players is an exciting time, as it marks a pivotal moment in a string player's development and presents more expressive options. Learning to shift and to play with vibrato are long-term endeavors that take time and patience and can only be the focus of a lesson for short periods of time. By introducing pre-shifting and pre-vibrato activities to students early in their development, they will be excited when they encounter these advanced string techniques and ready to execute them expressively and with good technique.

29.8 Discussion Questions

1. Which precursors for shifting and vibrato would you feel most comfortable teaching? Are there precursor exercises for shifting and vibrato that you would not feel comfortable teaching? Why or why not?
2. What were the gestures associated with teaching vibrato for the different instruments? Can you think of another fun gesture that occurs in real life that you could apply to teaching vibrato?
3. Identify the root problem and possible remedies for these common shifting issues. What precursors and strategies would you use to help students resolve these issues and why?

Common Shifting Issues

- Not making it up to the note or going past the note
- Sounding too intense on the top note
- Stuttering
- Hearing the shift or too much of the shift
- Sounding nervous

4. Identify the root problem and possible remedies for these common vibrato issues. What precursors and strategies would you use to help students resolve these issues and why?

Common Vibrato Issues

- Moving the wrist back and forth
- Moving the fingers up and down
- Moving the fingers only
- Sliding the fingers on string
- Jittery-sounding vibrato
- Pitch sounding flat

OXFORD learning link

Visit the online resources for additional documentation and exercises to help expand learning and test your knowledge further: www.oup.com/he/powell_music1e.

CHAPTER 30

BUILDING AND MAINTAINING A SUCCESSFUL ORCHESTRA PROGRAM

Michael Hopkins

In this chapter, I offer suggestions for recruiting and retaining students in your program as well as tips for effective teaching, understanding students' needs, school and community relations, and ensemble administration.

30.1 Introduction

In most schools, the orchestra is an elective class, so your success as a teacher hinges on your success in these two areas. Children choose to play instruments based on influence from parents, professional musicians, and their peers (Hamann & Gillespie, 2012). Once students have chosen an instrument, they quickly learn that playing an instrument is challenging and requires sustained involvement and self-regulated practice habits. Over time, students may become frustrated if they are unable to cope with the many challenges they will face (McPherson & Davidson, 2006). Therefore, retention is often more challenging than recruitment.

There are many factors that will contribute to retention of students in your program, including effective teaching and classroom management (for more, see Chapter 4), understanding the needs and motivations of your students (for more, see Chapters 3, 9, 11), school and community relations (for more, see Chapters 8 and 17), and ensemble administration (for more, see Chapter 8). Many of these topics are addressed in detail in Part 1: Teaching and Learning. In this chapter, I will focus on ideas specific to school orchestra programs. Much of the material in this chapter is adapted from my book *The Art of String Teaching* (Hopkins, 2019).

30.2 Recruiting Students to the Program

When you take a new job, learn what the established traditions are in all areas of the program, including the recruitment procedure. Your music teaching colleagues, especially the band director, will help you learn what has been done in the past. If you have the opportunity to meet with the outgoing orchestra director, it may be extremely beneficial.

If you find yourself in a situation where you need to develop your own recruitment procedure, start by creating a recruiting procedures document that provides answers to the following questions:

1. What time of year will you recruit—spring or fall?
2. Will you recruit at the same time as the band and/or choir?
3. How will your recruitment efforts support the other parts of the music program (band, choir, etc.)?
4. How will you coordinate the building, teacher, and student schedules for the recruitment demonstrations?
5. What are your equipment and transportation needs?
6. When will you send thank-you letters, and who will you send them to?
7. What type of recruitment demonstration will you do and who will be involved?

RECRUITMENT DEMONSTRATIONS

Musical demonstrations on the stringed instruments are the key to effective recruitment. You may need to demonstrate the instruments yourself for the recruits, but if you can coordinate a performance by students who are currently in your program, that will be the most effective way to recruit new students. Most schools begin orchestra in fourth, fifth, or sixth grade. Depending on your situation you might arrange for your current students to travel to elementary schools and perform for an individual class or grade level (e.g., all the 5th grade students) or play at an elementary school assembly. Perhaps elementary students could travel to your middle school for a performance. Once you learn the traditions, think about how you can effectively recruit given the schedule and resources you have available. Here are some tips for the recruitment performance:

- Prepare your current students well for their recruitment performance.
- Perform music from a variety of genres that the recruits will recognize and keep the pieces short! For example, you could play some of Pachelbel's Canon in D, the Star Wars Theme, game music (i.e., Legend of Zelda or Halo), and a fiddle tune.
- During the performance, take time to demonstrate each individual instrument.
- Find ways to involve the audience.
- Let the recruits ask questions.
- Let the recruits make sounds on the instruments.

Unless there is an arrangement in the district to begin strings earlier than band, the recruitment of students to new string programs should parallel the recruitment procedure currently used for band and should occur at the same date/time. Recruitment should be a cooperative, joint effort. A recruiting demonstration, ideally including students who currently play winds, percussion, and strings, should be designed to promote interest in the full instrumental department through performance, verbal information, and printed information. Also, regardless of the time of year that you do your official recruitment demonstration and follow-up communications, try to find opportunities throughout the year to be visible to the students you will be recruiting.

COMMUNICATING WITH RECRUITS AND PARENTS

After the recruitment demonstration, follow up with the recruits to learn what instrument(s) they are interested in playing, then send a letter home to their parents that includes information about the student's instrument choice, the benefits of music instruction, and the procedure for instrument selection and rental. Build relationships with your local instrument dealers and give them the opportunity to rent or sell to your students. Be clear about your expectations for instrument quality and specs, accessories, and books. You may wish to hold an "Instrument Rental Night" where local merchants will come to the school and parents can rent or purchase an instrument. Provide parents with information about all their quality options and encourage them to contact you before they purchase an instrument. Horror stories abound in our profession of parents buying "violin-shaped objects" online for less than $50 that are totally inadequate for instruction.

30.3 Retention

Many excellent resources have been published on the topic of recruitment including Selby, Rush and Moon (2016), Cooper (2004), and Hamman & Gillespie (2012).

The music education profession is characterized by dedicated teachers who approach their subject with a missionary zeal. Many music teachers go into schools and literally transform the entire community. But it is important for teachers to remember that there are certain things that are in our control, and some that are not. Your students will have varied motivations for participating in music, and your motivation for music teaching and learning that has led you to this point in your career is very different from the motivations of most of your students.

In almost all orchestra programs, even those taught by highly effective teachers, there will be some students who drop out for one reason or another. Research suggests that when students switch school levels (elementary to middle or middle to high school) is when they are most likely to discontinue instrumental music instruction (Cook, 2013). What should your retention goals be? Research on retention suggests the national average for retention between school levels is around 73% (Hamman, Gillespie & Bergonzi, 2002). As an example, if you start 100 students in fifth grade in elementary school, 73 of those students would continue in middle school. A few more students are probably going to drop during middle school years. There will be 73% retention from middle school to high school, with a few more students dropping during high school. Under this scenario, it is likely that between 30 and 40 12th graders would still be playing in orchestra. As music teachers, we are deeply passionate about our students' learning and we don't want to see our students quit. In a perfect world, we would have 100% retention, and more students would join throughout the upper grades. However, the retention rates in the aforementioned scenario are averages based on demographic research of string programs across the country.

When you interview for a teaching position, try to get a sense for the historical retention rates in that district. If they are really high, you know that you will have work to do. When you take the position, learn the reasons why students drop out, and take steps to address those issues. Perhaps there is a scheduling issue that can be addressed by working with the school administration. If the elementary students know (and like) the middle school orchestra director, they will be less likely to quit when changing school levels. The same is also true when changing from middle school to high school. A great retention technique is for the high school orchestra director to invite all the eighth graders to play in the final high school concert of the year on one piece.

Students may be losing motivation for reasons that are in your control to address. (see chapters 1, 3, 4 and 8 for more about this.) Students influence each others' opinions so they tend to drop in clusters, not as individuals. Develop relationships with the counselors in your school. Ask them to not let students drop orchestra without you having a chance to talk with them and their parents. Even if they do end up leaving your program, at least you will know why so you can take steps to better address your students' needs and motivations in the future. In the remaining sections of this chapter, I will focus on the reasons students typically drop out of music programs and steps you can take as the orchestra director to foster student retention and maintain a successful program.

30.4 Effective Teaching

Highly effective teaching that addresses the needs of all students is the best retention strategy. Effective teaching is complex and varied, and is addressed in every chapter in this volume. I will simply add my top ten list of things you can do to be effective and increase retention in your orchestra program:

- Create a classroom environment designed to meet the needs of all students.
- Be respectful, polite, and fair to students.
- Have high expectations of all students for learning and participation.
- Provide musical demonstrations on an instrument or using singing voice.
- Address important and appropriate musical concepts based on students' achievement level and where they are in the performance cycle.
- Monitor student learning and provide meaningful feedback to students that furthers learning.
- Adjust instruction in response to evidence of student understanding (or lack of it).
- Use clear, concise, accurate directions and explanations and teach with suitable pacing, neither dragged (talking too much) nor rushed (avoiding feedback).
- Ask clear questions and make use of effective questioning techniques that encourage higher-order thinking and deepen student understanding.
- Provide accurate answers to students' questions (and say that you will look it up if you are unsure).
- Use a variety of rehearsal strategies that involve different styles of learning.
- Provide time for closure at the end of class.

Be mindful of the way you rehearse an ensemble. Ensemble rehearsing can be absolutely mind-numbing, bland, and tiresome if the director is overly negative, focuses exclusively on technical details, and does not vary rehearsal strategies. People want to be inspired when they play music. Listen to your students and address their needs and interests. Give them opportunities for input on repertoire. Be flexible and creative in your lesson planning and programming. Help your students make emotional connections to the music and understand the relevance of the music program to their lives. Most importantly, communicate the joy of music making in every rehearsal.

30.5 Understanding Students' Needs

All teachers make decisions and take actions that influence student learning. Developing a comprehensive, systematic understanding of what is happening in your classroom or private studio serves as a guide for action (Abeles, Hoffer, & Klotman, 1995). As Holz and Jacobi (1966) wrote, "the teacher must realize that the important activity in the class is not teaching, but learning, and that learning depends on the desire to learn. . . . if learning depends on wanting to learn, then teaching is the art of making students want to learn" (p. 47). Modern theories of motivation focus on the relation of beliefs, values, and goals with action (Eccles & Wigfield, 2002). In the online resources for Chapter 30, I describe how you can apply theories of motivation in your classroom to address your students' psychological and emotional needs.

30.6 School and Community Relations

To retain students you need to foster healthy relationships with the other adults in their lives. Open strong lines of communication with your students' parents. Develop relationships and cultivate an understanding of your program with your teaching colleagues, school counselors, administrators, and school board members. Be active in your community to advocate for the value of your program.

String programs that are successful at retaining students establish a tradition of excellence through high-quality performances. Invite school and community leaders to your performances, recognize them, and involve them when possible (e.g., narrating for a novelty piece). Recognize your students for their achievements through awards, jerseys, letters, and medals. Provide social opportunities for your students, such as fundraisers, field trips to hear professional orchestras, overnight trips, or tours. Collaborate with professional musicians and collegiate faculty for clinics or performances. Get involved in the larger school community and create visibility for your orchestra program by providing music for school and community events. There are many opportunities for orchestra students to provide music in the community including:

- Community fairs
- Senior residences
- Street fairs and parades
- Business and civic events
- Church events
- Sporting events
- Service clubs

It is vital for you to not only develop strong professional relationships with your students, but to also develop strong positive relationships with adults in the community.

30.7 Ensemble Administration

STRING SEATING

Seat your higher achieving students on the outside of the stand, paired with lower achieving students on the inside, and distribute your highest achieving students between the front, middle, and back of the sections so your orchestra plays with the fullest and most balanced tone (Adey, 1998). Orchestras with all the strongest players in the front and center play with a thin, forced tone. Placing all your highest achieving violinists in the Violin 1 section leaves no leadership or strength on the Violin 2 part. The Violin 1 part is higher than the Violin 2 part, however, it is not more important.

Develop leadership and build confidence in all your students by rotating the stands each rehearsal (or each week). As you get closer to the concert, establish what the concert seating will be, so students get used to hearing their part from a consistent location within the ensemble. Deemphasize competitive attitudes and put the emphasis on working as a team towards a common goal. Think creatively about seating your students in a way that helps to put the focus on learning and high levels of music making.

PERFORMANCES

"Overprogramming" is a common problem in our profession, and can have serious consequences for the health of orchestra programs (Kjelland, 2001). If all the pieces you have chosen are a little too difficult (and therefore underprepared), the cumulative effect is that none of the pieces sound good at the performance. Vary the difficulty level of the music you are performing. If you have a program with four pieces, select one piece that really challenges the students, two that are well within a comfortable performance level, and a concert opener that might be a little too "easy" but gives your students an opportunity to stretch their musical expression potential.

Be careful to not select too many pieces of music for a single performance. Your students' parents really don't want a two-hour concert. Twenty to 30 minutes of great sounding music always will be a better concert than 60–90 minutes of underprepared music. In my entire career I have never had anyone complain to me that a concert was too short!

You need to spend some time preparing your students, on-stage presence. Some basics of concert stage presence you will need to teach include:

- the tuning procedure when the concertmaster enters the stage.
- standing when you enter the stage.
- facing the audience when they stand. Orchestras typically don't bow, only the conductor.
- how to sit in rest position.
- when to bring their instruments and bows into playing position.
- standing up on your cue following a piece.
- waiting to get out the next piece of sheet music until the applause ends following a piece.

Concerts involve lots of little tasks. I suggest assigning groups of students to various tasks associated with preparing for the concert, including set-up, tear-down, making announcements during the concert, and creating the concert program. It is a great way to motivate students, while also taking some of the burden off your shoulders. Get parent volunteers involved in helping with various tasks.

If you are sharing a concert with the band or choir, spend time planning the stage transition in advance. Assemble a large crew of student/parent helpers available with assigned duties. Aim for a five-minute transition between ensembles.

I recommend that when musicians take the stage, they be allowed to warm up on their instruments until the performance is ready to begin and the concertmaster/mistress enters the stage. I've witnessed concerts where the whole orchestra enters the stage and then sits in awkward silence for several minutes, waiting for the concertmaster/mistress and conductor. This is not authentic professional practice. Encourage your students to go on-stage and warm-up.

EVENT COMMUNICATION

Make sure you inform your students, parents, teachers, and administrators far in advance about the concert date, and keep the reminders coming as the date approaches. Check to make sure your concert dates don't conflict with other important events. Involving your administrators and board members in your concerts will get them to your events and educate them about the value of your program to the school and community. If they are at your concert, make sure you publicly thank them for coming.

Concert programs are often thrown together in haste. Programs have the potential to be important historical documents, but make sure to include the following information:

- School name
- Administrator's names

- Date (including year), time, location
- Names of ensembles
- Your name and other director's names
- All students' names, organized by section, spelled correctly. I suggest printing a draft of the program and passing it around during rehearsal so students can check the spelling of their name and make sure their name is on the program.
- Pieces you are performing with title, composer, and arranger
- Background info about music (program notes)—keep it brief
- Special thanks, upcoming concerts and other events

FESTIVALS

Festivals are a big part of the music program in many states. There are large group and solo & ensemble festivals, and select festivals like district, county, or all-state festivals. Each state has its own way of running these festivals. One thing all states have in common is deadlines for registering. Learn what the deadlines are, get them on your calendar, and work backward from the deadlines to ensure that you have enough time to communicate with your students and parents so they may prepare audition materials, and you can prepare the necessary paperwork and collect the necessary payment to send with the application materials.

Seek out mentoring from successful veteran teachers regarding timelines and preparations for festivals. Go to the festival websites, download the director files, and read the rules carefully!!! Learning the rules and requirements will help ensure a successful festival experience for you and your students. Work backward from the festival date to determine when your students will need to start learning the repertoire so that they are adequately prepared. Schedule a school performance the week before festival to share the music with the community and give students an additional performance opportunity. Invite a clinician to your school to help you and your students prepare for festival.

30.8 Concluding Thoughts

Teaching music will be a rich and rewarding journey for you if you make time for yourself, your family, and friends as you focus on developing your school orchestra program. Successful orchestra teachers pour a lot of time and energy into their students. Try to not let your program completely take over your life. Performances are important, but if your performance schedule is ruining your life, schedule fewer concerts. Learn to delegate tasks to students and parents you trust who want to help you succeed.

In conclusion, the secrets to building and maintaining your program are: 1) listen and learn from students, colleagues, administrators, parents and community members about the culture and traditions of the program when you take the position, 2) strive to be the most effective teacher you can be, and 3) remember that *effective* change occurs slowly over time. Stay focused on the students and helping all of them learn, and you will become the catalyst for a healthy and resilient orchestra program.

30.9 Discussion Questions

1. Write some questions to ask about recruitment and retention during your job interview.
2. What connections can be made between effective teaching and student retention?
3. Devise a recruitment procedure based on the seven questions posed in the chapter.

4. Based on the online resources for Chapter 30, describe how you can apply theories of motivation in your classroom to address your students' psychological and emotional needs.
5. In what ways will you build relationships with parents and community members?
6. Develop a rationale for a plan for seating strings that you can succinctly share during your job interview.
7. Identify relevant information about festivals in your state (assessment tools, deadlines, forms, links to music lists, etc.) and compile them into one folder.

OXFORD learning link

Visit the online resources for additional documentation and exercises to help expand learning and test your knowledge further: www.oup.com/he/powell_music1e.

CHAPTER 31

CULTURALLY RESPONSIVE TEACHING IN SCHOOL ORCHESTRAS

James Ray, Brian W. Kellum, and Karin S. Hendricks

Guided by Lind and McKoy's (2016) framework for culturally responsive music teaching, this chapter envisions an active role for string educators in cultivating inclusivity within school orchestra programs.

31.1 Scenario

Imagine a scenario where a student misbehaved during a rehearsal of Tchaikovsky's Serenade for Strings (Op. 48) during drill practice in the first movement at rehearsal letter D. The rehearsal came to a halt. The disruptive student had produced loud rhythmic beats, rapped percussively with the bow against the metal stand, and chanted nonsensical lyrics, rhyming in time to the music in hip-hop style. He felt pleased with himself, and other students chattered away about the disruption while smiling and laughing.

However, when he sought approval from the conductor/educator, the conductor/educator seemed irritated and incredulous and looked as if this student had betrayed the educator. All-district festival was a few short weeks away and the ensemble had been rehearsing the Serenade for a while, but the passage was neither in tune nor together. This was not this particular student's first such interruption. Moreover, other students were beginning to make beats and chant as well. Why then, during a critically important rehearsal? Did the students not understand the classroom expectations or have respect for rehearsal etiquette?

The Tchaikovsky needed refinement. The first violin and viola parts feature rapid staccato sixteenth notes that must align with one another through the delicate negotiation of the slurs alternating with lightly articulated off-the-string strokes, a quick sautillé. The unison cello and bass parts include a chromatic line of pizzicato eighth notes that must be played in tune and not rushed. The entire section is marked *p*, followed by a global *pp* as the second violins echo the opening sixteenth-note passage.

ASSUMPTIONS

With the student's disruption framed this way, and given the proximity of the all-district festival date, a typical response from teachers—now jarringly separated from our role as conductors—might be to reprimand. In this frame, discipline and attentiveness are the norm for a rehearsal setting. Teacher preparation programs and developmental texts (Newell, 2012) posit classroom management skills as a prerequisite for educators who expect productivity in the music classroom. We are taught to quickly address the issue by first assessing the severity of the disruption and then issuing an appropriate consequence, enabling the ensemble to return their attention to letter D. We believe that this action will avoid wasting valuable rehearsal time, return focus to the musical challenge, and, most important, win back the loss of control the conductor merits as the high priest or priestess of the podium.

There are several assumptions worth unpacking from this scenario. The educator assumes the stance that rehearsals are environments that should remain pristine, given the demands placed upon the final performance as adjudicated by the standards and expectations embedded within the Western classical tradition. Further, interruption of the rehearsal process could be viewed as an act of chaos, one that subtracts from the musical goals the conductor/educator has set for the ensemble. This chaos is assumed to be a net negative, implying the "hip-hop Serenade" as "less than" in the musical value it brings to the rehearsal space. Therefore, if the student has produced musicianship that disrupts, causes chaos, and fails to add value to the task at hand, then the student must be acting in defiance.

ALTERNATE REACTION

Now imagine this incident of musical misbehavior from another perspective. What if the spontaneous artistry behind the student's interruption were lauded as creative, even welcomed? Assuming the role of educator rather than conductor, teaching and learning are shared. A musical moment recognized, the rehearsal is paused to reflect upon and accept the expressiveness exhibited by the student. The teacher turns the interruption into an opportunity to channel the energy of the moment, praising the quality of the student's execution, cleverness, and contribution to Tchaikovsky's work. Tchaikovsky's Serenade has been introduced into the curriculum as a vehicle for such musical diversions rather than as a work to be recreated. The all-district festival's significance shifts: it becomes less an adjudication of students' ability to interpret and reproduce nineteenth-century style and more (or also) a showcase for students to demonstrate their own creative interpretation of the work.

In this view, the educator values the student's interpretation as enrichment rather than as a breach of tradition. The expectation for rehearsal is not about perfecting the Serenade, but rather about engaging it from the multiple perspectives of the teacher and the students. The value of an interpretive interruption is welcomed and encouraged, and therefore its social value is regarded as equal to or greater than that of the scheduled rehearsal itself, though the spontaneous outburst lies outside the rigid structural boundaries of traditional concert performance. The student, as a musician, gains confidence in the nurturing environment of creativity viewed as a multicultural expression rather than an act of resistance.

CHALLENGING OUR ASSUMPTIONS

Our conceptualization of culturally responsive teaching in school orchestra contexts is framed primarily by Vicki R. Lind and Constance L. McKoy's *Culturally Responsive Teaching in Music Education* (2016). Drawing upon foundational scholarship from general education (e.g., Gay, 2018), Lind and McKoy explore relevant implications across music education settings.

Gay (2018) describes culturally responsive teaching as that which both affirms and incorporates the cultural backgrounds that have already helped to shape the students entering our classrooms. Beyond merely acknowledging or "celebrating" those backgrounds, culturally responsive teachers adopt instructional practices that actively incorporate students' culturally informed perspectives and experiences. Gay explains that these incorporations enable high levels of achievement for students from diverse communities. Lind and McKoy (2016) identify a similar impact for music education, with students enabled to "access learning in ways that are respectful and congruent with different ways of knowing . . . broadening the curriculum to include diverse music genres and also looking at different ways of promoting musicality" (p. 30).

Growing demographic discrepancies between string teachers and school populations necessitate an explicit focus on culturally responsive string teaching. By the end of the last decade, the orchestra teaching profession remained more than 90 percent white (Smith et al., 2018). Meanwhile, the proportion of white students enrolled in public schools around the same time had fallen below 50 percent (de Brey et al., 2019). White students in orchestras remained a majority, but that majority was shrinking (Elpus & Abril, 2019; Smith et al., 2018). This disconnect undermines any notions about the extent to which teachers and students will enter the string classroom with similar assumptions, experiences, or expectations (see Lind & McKoy, 2016, p. 26). Accordingly, teachers face a growing imperative to both understand and make space for the backgrounds of students who are increasingly less likely to represent the dominant culture that has historically shaped our field.

31.2 Historical Context: An Elitist Orchestral Tradition

The orchestra tradition is rich in elitism, historically associated with primarily white people from middle- or upper-class backgrounds (Bull, 2019; Johnson, 2002). In many cases, in fact, classical music gatekeepers have maintained the social value of this art form by intentionally keeping it exclusive (Wang, 2016). Nonwhite, female, and/or lower-income individuals have gained limited access to educational and performance opportunities; those who have managed to overcome structural barriers have often been objectified and essentialized rather than being taken seriously for their artistry (Smith & Hendricks, 2021).

The elitist history of the orchestra has extended beyond representation in performance and consumption to include issues of philosophy and approach. The historical tradition of the orchestra, for centuries entangled with European history, has unfortunately mirrored many of Europe's imperialist and supremacist practices (Brown, 2007). Even as more female and nonwhite musicians have gained access to orchestral performance and education opportunities, many historical philosophies and approaches have remained—such as unquestioned dominance of Western Eurocentrism, the reverence of a "maestro" on the podium, and competitive practices ranking players against one another in divisive ways (Hendricks et al., 2014; Tsui et al., forthcoming).

More recently, however, many of these philosophies are being questioned and reimagined—and music educators are envisioning how this beloved orchestra experience might be more inclusive and welcoming of a more diverse array of people, musical styles, and educational approaches (e.g., Chapter 3; Chapter 26; Hendricks, 2018; Ray, 2020; Reed, 2019). This cultural expansiveness marks the latest evolution in a history of efforts toward diversity and multiculturalism in music education more broadly. In the early twentieth century, music teachers adopted an assimilationist approach, using European folk songs to homogenize the cultural identities of immigrants and others who were representative of socioeconomic and religious diversity (McCarthy, 2015). By the middle of the century, this "melting pot" approach had begun to give way to a recognition of individual students' musical goals and interests. The landmark Tanglewood Declaration (Choate, 1968, p. 139) reflected this shift, offering recommendations for an expanded repertoire encompassing more student-relevant styles and cultural influences. However, these recommendations remained based in a rationale that characterized students as "culturally deprived" (p. 139), reflecting the kind of deficit-based assumptions underlying a broader "salvationist" narrative that often characterizes Eurocentric interactions with non-majority cultural groups (see Kellum, 2021; Lind & McKoy, 2016; McKoy, 2017).

Culturally responsive teaching extends beyond Tanglewood in championing cultural pluralism: not only are the individual student's goals accounted for, but—as described in the opening scenario—their very ways of knowing and being are purposefully incorporated into instruction, including the repertoire studied (Lind & McKoy, 2016). Furthermore, in moving away from a stance of extreme individualism and a survival-of-the-fittest mentality, many educators are now considering how to facilitate experiences of self-efficacy (Hendricks, 2016) and collective efficacy (Ray & Hendricks, 2019) for all students, and focusing on creating musical experiences with care, compassion, and authentic connection (see Chapter 11). Culturally responsive teaching helps cultivate welcoming, vibrant, and engaging classrooms.

31.3 Enacting Cultural Responsiveness

Lind and McKoy (2016) describe a broad scope for culturally responsive music education that extends beyond the classroom to include forging connections across the school and broader communities. We limit our discussion, however, to the work and dispositions of orchestra teachers within their own classrooms and programs, framed around four themes outlined by Lind and McKoy: (a) the teacher's knowledge of *self*, (b) the teacher's knowledge of their *students*, (c) cultivating a supportive learning environment, and (d) designing a culturally responsive curriculum (see also McKoy, 2020, pp. 608–610).

TEACHER'S KNOWLEDGE OF SELF

Teacher self-knowledge and self-reflection are critical components of cultural responsiveness (Berg, forthcoming). Given the authoritarian role traditionally bestowed upon the conductor, it may not be second nature for orchestra teachers to step off the podium and engage in dialogue with students. However, continual self-monitoring can be key to helping teachers engage with students in culturally responsive ways. Self-checks might include continual questioning of assumptions (such as which musical styles or approaches are best) and avoiding any inclination toward a "pity" stance or "salvationist" narrative (Berg, forthcoming; Fairbanks, 2019; Chapter 11), instead embracing curiosity and a desire to learn together.

TEACHER'S KNOWLEDGE OF STUDENTS

While culturally responsive teachers necessarily draw upon the cultural backgrounds represented among their students, they should be equally cognizant of the variability in the degree to which anyone might express or identify with a given characteristic associated with their culture. This means avoiding presumptions about a student's individual interests based upon their perceived or self-associated cultural group. Ascertaining students' musical interests can be as simple as just asking them. Lind and McKoy (2016) encourage making direct inquiries, whether through formal surveys or informal conversation. Whatever a student's personal relationship to their heritage, it is worthwhile to educate ourselves about the variety of music they encounter in everyday life—such as what they listen to, or their music-making activities outside of school.

CULTIVATING A SUPPORTIVE LEARNING ENVIRONMENT

Orchestra students recognize and appreciate environments in which they are valued and cared for (Reed, 2019). We can promote such environments by fostering our programs' sense of community, including care for its individual members. This prioritization supersedes a laser focus on achieving any "artistic product" and thus may place culturally responsive dispositions at odds with imperialistic values discussed earlier—especially the traditional notion that a conductor's principal mission is to realize the composer's intent (e.g., Leinsdorf, 1981; Schuller, 1997). To be clear, the source of this apparent conflict is not whether music should be prepared and performed to a high level. Indeed, Lind and McKoy (2016) highlight the need to hold students accountable for meeting rigorous musical standards. Rather, culturally responsive music teaching regards high-quality artistry as a *by-product* of an environment that emphasizes care, empowerment, and personal relevance with respect to the musicians (students) involved.

Approaches to Competition

Musical competition is as old as American instrumental education and indeed was central to the proliferation of public school programs in the early twentieth century (Humphreys, 1989; Mark & Gary, 2007). Competition plays a prominent role in many schools, particularly at the secondary level, and thus raises important considerations in the context of creating culturally responsive learning environments. Students in whom cooperative values have been inculcated may feel threatened in environments that actively promote rivalries focused upon individual success (Lind & McKoy, 2016). While some responsively minded teachers might see reasons to minimize or eliminate musical competition, others still recognize value in competitive experiences. Teachers inclined toward either disposition can adopt culturally responsive practices, both within their own programs and externally between schools.

Internally, students often compete for ensemble placements and/or chair assignments. In a noncompetitive approach, teachers could determine ensemble membership by grade level rather than by audition, with chair assignments randomized or by rotation (see Yi, 2023). Teachers who prefer competency-based placements might seek to gauge the *potential* of an auditioning student in addition to the *proficiencies they demonstrate* at the time, especially when hearing students who may have had limited (if any) access to private study. Within ensembles, seating placement could occur by assessing all members of a section rather than one-on-one chair challenges. This more general method achieves dual objectives, informing the teacher's seating decisions while also gauging the progress of all students involved. These seating results could be ordered in a way that distributes students at various skill levels throughout the ensemble (see Chapter 3 and Chapter 30).

Teachers can substantially influence the degree to which students are impacted by contests *between* schools. While acknowledging that scores, rankings, certificates, and trophies will result from such performances, a teacher could choose to spend considerably more time encouraging students to prepare, perform, and reflect in ways that emphasize the best of their *own* abilities. Such deliberate choices can shape how students regard competitions, both individually and collectively. Above all, those choices should convey a sense of musical meaning that transcends any tangible reward, and that preserves for students a sense of belonging and social safety (see Hendricks, 2018).

CULTURALLY RESPONSIVE CURRICULUM

The orchestral curriculum itself must be both accessible and relevant to our students. In this section we address a pair of curricular considerations that are especially important in string programs: the value of rote teaching and the curriculum as represented by ensemble repertoire.

Rote Teaching

Imitative instruction is a fundamental element of string pedagogy, particularly at the beginning level (see MacLeod, 2019). Scholarship reviewed by Chappell (2020) indicates that teaching strategies based upon aural modeling increase a student's overall likelihood of string-playing success. Chappell's review also highlights the ubiquity of aural learning across a variety of musical styles, as well as the ways in which rote learning can provide more culturally sensitive entry points for students accustomed to musical traditions that do not rely upon written notation. Despite these benefits, Lind and McKoy (2016) observe that music teachers too frequently revert to written notation in introducing new music. In orchestras, such reversion becomes more tempting as repertoire increases in both length and complexity. Still, considering the effort required to learn and refine skills even beyond the initial years, aurally based musical activities retain instructional relevance. As we approach new rhythms, bowing styles, and expanded pitch ranges (via shifting, extensions, and new keys), much of the rationale we adopt in support of aural models at the beginning stages continues to apply (see Chapters 1, 3, 4, and 26–30).

Repertoire

Conversations about social justice in classical music often advocate for expanding the repertoire beyond works written by white men. Music educators' tendency to perpetuate a Eurocentric canon stems from factors including an emphasis on Western classical styles in teacher preparation (Chapter 26; Lind & McKoy, 2016; Ray, 2020), and practical challenges related to locating diverse repertoire appropriate for school groups (Marcho, 2020). Fortunately, identifying such repertoire has become more achievable with resources such as the Composer Diversity Database, which allows teachers and students to filter searches according to specific needs and interests. See https://www.composerdiversity.com/.

Composer diversity is but one of several ways we can be culturally responsive with respect to repertoire. Another approach is to regularly welcome students into the very process of repertoire selection, consistently inviting their choices or suggestions about selections that fit the scope of curricular goals. Having a say in programming provides students with tangible opportunities to exercise agency in the educational process, express their own musical interests, and bring varied interests to the fore through peer dialogue (Chapter 3; Rotjan, 2021). Teachers can also exhibit cultural sensitivity in how they discuss the musical selections ultimately programmed. Our language should reflect a sort of cultural egalitarianism, describing, for example, the artistic merits of a given piece as residing within the context of the style it represents, rather than in terms of some universal value. We can discuss the significance of Bach's Brandenburg Concertos as the apex of Baroque style without implying any hierarchical relationship with an arrangement of a popular tune in the same music folder.

31.4 Looking Forward: Toward a Community of Multiple Expressions

Viewed critically, traditionally accepted forms of orchestral music-making have been described as disconnected from everyday life (Snell, 2009), hegemonic and neo-colonial (Fairbanks, 2019), and at risk of perpetuating cultural and symbolic violence on marginalized and oppressed populations (Allsup, 2009; Jorgensen, 2003). Looking forward, however, we embrace a stance of mindful and purposeful anti-imperialism—one that challenges oppressive and/or marginalizing structures, and resists one-way approaches that are fast becoming antiquated. We seek to honor multiplicity and invite you, the reader, to do the same. As the Mayday Group (1997) states:

> *[M]usic and musical actions, when institutionalized, are transformed by a variety of ideological, ethical, economic, and pedagogical motivations and agendas. Any theory and practice of music education must successfully account for these phenomena, shed light on ways to critique them, and set in motion means of minimizing negative effects of institutions at the individual or social levels. ("4: The contributions made by schools" section, para. 1)*

31.5 Discussion Questions

1. What assumptions do I make about certain students? What assumptions do students make about themselves as musicians?
2. What do I say about certain students in the faculty room?
3. Do the student demographics in my program reflect those of the school more broadly? If not, what elements *within my program* could play a role?
4. What does cultural responsiveness look like during the initial stages of instruction (e.g., recruitment, instrument selection)?
5. What do I mean when I call some students "talented"?
6. What are some of the various musical abilities that my students display? How do they engage with music *beyond* the orchestra classroom?
7. What musical abilities have I previously taken for granted?
8. How do I analyze and address "disruptive" behavior in rehearsals?
9. What are some things that I struggle to teach my students, and whom might I ask for additional ideas about how to approach them?

OXFORD learning link

Visit the online resources for additional documentation and exercises to help expand learning and test your knowledge further: www.oup.com/he/powell_music1e.

PART IV.

Teaching Woodwinds

CHAPTER 32

PEDAGOGICAL CONSIDERATIONS FOR TEACHING WOODWIND STUDENTS

Cynthia L. Wagoner

This chapter will cover the process of teaching woodwind instruments, with a general understanding of teaching in heterogeneous settings. Teaching woodwind instruments requires a knowledge base of each of the instruments you will be teaching and the ability to use that knowledge to teach many instruments at once.

32.1 Organization for Beginning Woodwinds

WHICH INSTRUMENTS AND WHAT CLASSES?

There are many opinions about what specific woodwind instruments should be started with beginning band classes. My personal philosophy is that any instrument is a beginning instrument. Starting every instrument allows everyone to sound like a beginner at the same time.

Some directors do not start double reed instruments until after the first semester or first year, while others start with a variety of woodwind instruments, including tenor saxophones and double reeds. Some directors choose to begin with only flutes and/or clarinets and move students to other instruments after a short period of time. While starting with only two woodwind instruments makes it easier for the teacher and students to achieve success initially, allowing students to start on the instrument of their choice will often result in the students' having a greater motivation to achieve. These are decisions you will need to make carefully, considering where you are teaching and the traditions you might be inheriting in the school and community.

Another variable to consider when starting woodwind players is how your beginning woodwind classes will be arranged. Most of the beginning band classes I have observed were heterogeneous groups. Homogenous groupings (just flutes, for example) are rare in beginning band classes, but directors often hold a boot camp for beginners before school starts to give daily beginning lessons in homogenous groups. There are other considerations to think about when asking for specific classes for your band students. See 32.1, "Choosing and Organizing Beginning Band Classes," in the online resources, especially if you are given the opportunity to help create a class schedule for your students.

PLANNING FOR BEGINNING WOODWIND STUDENTS

The cost of participation with woodwind instruments is often high and can be prohibitive for many students, as reeds are continually needed to perform on all woodwinds except for the flute. When students sign up for band, have information available to parents on the cost of renting, leasing, or buying an instrument and how much reeds will cost for each instrument. Prepare for this by speaking with your local music store about what accessories you would like in each woodwind instrument case, from the specific type of reed, mouthpiece, and instrument swabs to reed cases, to be included in the rental price (see each individual instrument chapter for specific suggestions). It will be up to you to ensure that students and parents have the information available to them to order what they need online from a music store. You should also provide phone numbers or order forms for those without internet access. Speak with your administrators about the process of having accessories available at school to purchase and the approach you need to take if you are handling money.

Oboe and bassoon reeds are a special consideration. There may be double reed players in your area who can make reeds for your beginning students (called boutique reeds). The cost is a bit higher than that of manufactured reeds, but they help students produce a much better sound. Again, be sure you have communicated with parents or guardians so they are not shocked at the difference between single and double reed costs and include how many reeds a student could need for the first year. (For more information about oboe reeds, see Chapter 35; for bassoon reeds, see Chapter 36.)

Beginners will also need help with checking their instruments for maintenance issues. See 32.2, "Basic Woodwind Repair Kit," in the online resources for ideas to make sure you can keep your classes running as smoothly as possible. If you can spend some time learning simple woodwind repairs, it will be well worth the instructional time it will save both you and your students.

SETTING UP THE ENVIRONMENT FOR STUDENT SUCCESS

When setting up the room, I make sure that each beginner has a stand. Stands are not necessarily needed right away, but they will provide a place to stash the reed-soaking container (old clean pill bottles with a magnet glued to the side so they stay on the stand are perfect), a band notebook, and a hand mirror. I place students in a block where I can move easily between the students and still give them space to have their instrument case open beside or in front of them. This way, you can give quick assistance and walk freely among your students to give corrections, feedback, or praise. We want to set our students up for success on the instrument they are so excited to play.

One of the most important parts of our teaching is the ability to break down the technical executive skills that need to be learned and automated so that we can help students feel successful. This is just one approach to teaching woodwind instruments, and you will find that you will learn along the way what works the best for you and your students. Remember, your personal musicianship should always influence your teaching.

32.2 Skill Building: Technical Executive Skills for Woodwinds

Across woodwind instruments, single reeds, double reeds, and flutes, there will be different embouchures and voicings that can impact specifics such as the tonguing syllables you might choose to use and how you might explain the use of air. Each individual woodwind instrument chapter will help you understand the specific needs for each instrument.

However, when we teach in heterogeneous groups, we want to coordinate the similarities for our students when first introducing a concept and then give students in each instrumental section something more specific to work on as students gain control of the concepts and start to build muscle memory. *Technical executive skills* (see 32.3, "Technical Executive Skills," in the online resources) include posture, breathing, mouthpiece assembly, instrument assembly, embouchure and mouthpiece/head joint sounds, articulation technique, instrument carriage and hand position, and finally, learning first notes and establishing daily warm-ups. Each class period should review and reinforce the technical executive skills.

POSTURE AND BREATHING

The first two skills, posture and breathing, must be reinforced daily. Students need to be aware of what their bodies feel like while they are breathing and how to use their air. Learning how to take in air and how to expel it at different speeds and intensities is necessary, and each woodwind instrument is different in terms of controlling the airstream. The posture we take—sitting and standing—impacts the way in which we use our lungs and ultimately our control of the instrument. Therefore, we must check posture and practice breathing daily, building student understanding and ensuring that students are using proper air support and posture.

MOUTHPIECE ASSEMBLY

After we teach posture and breathing, we can ask the students to assemble the mouthpiece. Flutists can simply take the head joint out of the case, but reed players must learn how to care for the reed and assemble the reed, mouthpiece, and ligature. For clarinets, add the barrel to the mouthpiece before assembling anything else. This gives students something to hold onto. For saxophones, add the mouthpiece to the neck before assembling the reed. For oboe and bassoon, after soaking the reed for several minutes (new reeds need more time than those that have been broken in), use the "crow" of the reed or add the upper joint for the oboe and the crow of the reed, or add the bassoon's bocal, for mouthpiece assembly. The chart in Figure 32.1 lists mouthpiece assembly to prepare students for learning the embouchure.

FIGURE 32.1 Instrument set-up and concert pitch

Instrument Set-up	Concert Pitch
Flute head joint – stopped or open	A
Oboe reed only "crow"	C

Instrument Set-up	Concert Pitch
B♭ Clarinet mouthpiece and barrel	F♭
Alto Saxophone mouthpiece and neck	G♯
Tenor Saxophone	E
Bassoon reed only "crow"	G or A

EMBOUCHURE AND FIRST SOUNDS

Once the single reed mouthpieces have been checked for reed and ligature alignment, flutes can identify the head joint, and double reeds can place the reed on the upper joint or bocal correctly, you are ready to teach embouchure. I have found that combining modeling, broad and simple explanations, and giving individual feedback as you go works best. Students need the opportunity to experience and feel what the muscles of the mouth should be doing. Use hand mirrors to help students check what they feel, what they see, and what they hear.

I suggest having students practice long tones first as they are learning how to use the air with resistance from the instrument while holding an embouchure and voicing shape. I like to have all the instrument mouthpieces assembled so I can demonstrate. Work through the full group, small groups (rows or threes), and then individuals, with "my turn, your turn" so there is minimal talking on the teacher's part. The teacher can see and hear what is happening with each of their students and can give quick, in-the-moment feedback. Pass the tone around the room from individual to individual and listen to each instrument group, taking turns, then moving to rows and then individuals once more. Keep reinforcing proper breath and support for the air. As students become more confident with mouthpiece/head joint sounds, work toward making sure students are blowing the pitches for each instrument listed in Figure 32.1.

ARTICULATION

Preparation for articulation can happen during class by repeating rhythms and clapping, writing, and singing both melodies and rhythms. Build aural and notational skill sets by first singing rhythms on a pitch and having students sing back in imitation. I use "too" as a general syllable; use "too" for flutes and "tee" for clarinets to ensure better voicing for the best tone. Flute players must move the tongue against the hard palate right behind the front teeth. For single reeds, the tip of the tongue hits the tip of the reed from below (*not* between the reed and mouthpiece). Double reed players should place the tip of the tongue to the bottom of the reed, close to the tip, and articulate there. Do preliminary practice by saying "too" or "tee" aloud, feeling the tongue placement, then silently with air behind it, then practicing that with the instrument mouthpiece/head joint in playing position silently with air before trying to create a sound with the tongue starting each note. It is critical to have *air* behind the tongue. Continue to build on prior technical executive skills and remind students that air is released by the tongue to create the vibration on the reed or across the tone hole to create sound.

Once students figure out how to move the tongue to articulate, demonstrate articulated rhythms and have the students echo them back on their reeds/mouthpieces/head joints. Start with legato articulation, not a stopped staccato, accented, or hard tongue. Ask the students to slice the air/sound into pieces quickly and accurately, like a knife through butter. I have found having students start by using a faster tempo for articulation (quarter note = mm.120) helps them keep the air moving and then gradually have them slow it down (quarter note = 60). Use your eyes and your ears to find problems in articulation. There are some common mistakes for beginners. Flute players may use a lip articulation ("poo"), or the tongue may come between the teeth or lips ("thoo"). Listen carefully to the saxes and clarinets to make sure they are not anchoring the tip of their tongue against their bottom teeth, using the middle of the tongue to articulate (called "anchor tonguing"). If double reed players complain about feeling the tip of the reed blades, make sure they are coming *under* the bottom reed, not between the blades. Experiment with the syllable "toh" to help double reed students move the tongue down and out of the way of the reed. For more detail, see each individual instrument chapter.

Make sure you hear every student often while learning to articulate, as bad habits form quickly. Use "my turn, your turn" with articulation call and response in the full group, small groups, and finally individuals, listening carefully. Mix up your rhythms and meters, though you need to tell them you are changing meters—otherwise they will add a beat to simple triple examples. Don't just do simple duple combinations—students can imitate compound meters easily. Be inventive, as you are not reading the rhythms.

Just don't make them so complex or long that students lose sight of the act of moving the tongue correctly, especially at first.

Add one more layer right away to articulation to work on improvisation and aural acuity. I have each student improvise a rhythm in simple duple or simple triple time, and we all must play it back to the improvisor. The goal is to be accurate, not to confuse the group, so I may ask the student to try again if they do something too hard or unclear (it can happen occasionally). The goal for the group is successful repetition. If the group is large, I may choose a different set of students to improvise each day.

Once students are legato tonguing accurately, without stopping the air between notes, move to reading rhythmic notation. You might ask students to compose rhythms for the class to perform. Students may begin by imitating what they know currently, and that is acceptable. You could have the students place several measures together to create rhythmic phrases or create a rhythmic composition. Keep reinforcing the proper use of air, emphasizing the idea of the tongue slicing through the air. Plenty of creativity can happen while the students are working toward mastering articulation and tone production. Remember that with woodwind mouthpieces, we have a specific pitch in mind for each instrument, and those do not line up across different instruments. Therefore, the improvising and composing we do with our mouthpiece/head joint sounds will reflect rhythmic rather than melodic changes.

INSTRUMENT ASSEMBLY

Finally, teach instrument assembly. Videos provided with supplementary materials are good references for those who are not woodwind specialists and for your students when they are at home. I did not allow instruments to go home before students demonstrated they could assemble and disassemble the instrument correctly. I also made sure parents understood I would require instruments to stay at school until I knew their child could properly care for the instrument; that way you can avoid bent keys and stuck cleaning swabs. Give specific instructions for caring for the instrument after each use as well, including how to dry a reed and place it in a reed case. If you can't keep the instruments at school until students demonstrate mastery of assembly, change the order of the technical executive skills and teach assembly first, even if you will wait to use it.

CARRIAGE AND FINGER POSITIONS

Once the instruments are assembled, be specific about instrument carriage. Flutes, for example, are not held in a way that feels natural. Oboes are held at a slightly greater distance from the body than a clarinet. The alto saxophone doesn't need to be played to the side unless the person playing it is too small to hold it in front of them. Each instrument needs to be held appropriately for the tone production and air to work well and to assure the body is not under undue stress or tension.

It is important during carriage to help students place the fingers in the proper place on the instrument. I sometimes use the small paper adhesive dots in bright colors to indicate where the little fingers will rest. On closed-hole instruments, you can also use dots if students struggle to remember which keys to put their fingers on. Allow students to practice placing their fingers on the instrument and moving them up and down one at a time. I use R/L 1-2-3 and thumb, so I introduce that to students immediately. Practice adding the fingers of the right hand 1-2-3 and subtracting 3-2-1. This is especially important for flute players. Have them place the head joint on the left shoulder and the end of the flute on the right thigh and practice fingering first. This will help them find the appropriate keys before lifting the flute to the body.

If students have developed posture and breathing while both sitting and standing and are able to make good mouthpiece/head joint sounds, transferring those skills to the entire instrument will be relatively easy for them. If too many things are added too quickly, students develop bad habits that are hard to break.

FIRST THREE NOTES

What are the first three notes you are going to teach? This is open for debate, and I will offer my thoughts on starting all woodwinds together, but you will need to make this decision for yourself. You will have transposing instruments in a heterogenous class, so make sure you are aware of the transposition for each instrument. I like to use the concert pitches E♭, F, and G for the first three notes. For all students, moving more than one finger at a time in different directions takes a lot of practice. To coordinate the class with transposing instruments together, I put the chart shown in Figure 32.2 on the board.

FIGURE 32.2 **Transposition chart for beginning instruments**

Transposition: Instrument	Concert Pitch E♭	Concert Pitch F	Concert Pitch G
C: Flute, oboe, bassoon	E♭	F	G
B♭: Clarinet	F	G	A

Transposition: Instrument	Concert Pitch E♭	Concert Pitch F	Concert Pitch G
E♭: Alto Saxophone	C	D	E

For flutes, starting with written E♭5, F5, and G5 provides stability to both hands and encourages proper breathing and air control while using the fingers. For saxophones, the transposition to C, D, and E is not problematic if you use C5, D5, and E5. However, watch what they are doing with any fingers that are not pressing down a key and make sure the instrument is supported by the neck strap, not the right thumb, as they will need to toggle the left thumb for the D and E.

For clarinets, I like to have them play their C4, then work down the instrument, adding a finger at a time to play down to low G and F. I also mark the F key with a small sticker or dot (much like the ones string people use). *This takes time.* It is *not* the easiest way to start clarinetists. However, the extra time working through the chalumeau register pays off in dividends in the future, helping students move more easily over the break of the clarinet. It also does three things: (1) it requires students to blow through the entire instrument, (2) it gets proper finger position across the instrument quickly, and (3) it has the student balancing the instrument correctly with proper carriage immediately. You could start with throat tones (written G4 to B♭4 on the staff), but these notes are unstable in pitch and difficult to play with good tone, and the student must learn to balance the instrument on the thumb and chin, which won't help develop proper carriage or finger positions.

If double reed players can start in a separate class, oboes should use concert G major as the first tonal center, since concert G, A, B4, and C5 fit easily under the fingers. However, if they are starting with a full band class, flat keys it is, and oboists must work on the alternate F (forked F) immediately. I have always gone through and marked all beginning oboe music to designate the F fingering (diatonic/regular, left sliver, or forked) that I would like them to use, much like you might indicate what little-finger combination (left or right) you would like the clarinets to use. For bassoonists, the ideal key to start them in would be concert C major (C3, D3, E3, and F3), but again, this may not be feasible if you are starting them in the same class with flutes, oboes, clarinets, and/or saxes. Fingerings are idiosyncratic for each instrument, so keep a fingering chart handy to check yourself.

Teach one fingering at a time. Because you will need to teach a fingering to every woodwind instrument in the group, have a set routine for doing so. Ask students to put their fingers in the correct position and practice relaxing the fingers and re-placing them while you show the fingerings to the other instrument groups in the room. Once you have all the fingerings taught, have the students check each other's fingerings in pairs in the room. Once the fingers are in place with proper carriage and in playing position, start back with long tones, moving into simple articulated rhythms, then improvisation and/or notational rhythms, all while reinforcing air and posture. There is no need to introduce melodic notation at this point or to use a book. It is enough for a student to try to move their fingers and focus on the aural quality of sound. I have students start singing and often move between using my voice, a piano, and a woodwind instrument to demonstrate.

When the students can demonstrate one note (I usually start with concert F and move up or down from there), the second note may be introduced. Repeat the same process with the new fingering. Once a new fingering is added, I demonstrate and have students practice how to move between the two fingerings they now know. First, practice the finger movements. I have the flutes rest the head joint on their left shoulder and the foot joint on the right thigh so they can see their fingers until they are comfortable with the movement. Then move the instrument to the playing position and repeat the finger movements before adding air. All instruments should do this, with care taken with double reeds that the reed is placed in the mouth against the cheek or in the water container to provide a safe space. Single reeds should use their mouthpiece cover while practicing fingerings. Take your time to use both notes, moving between them, back and forth, singing before playing. Repeat the process with the third note, finally working up to teaching three-note "songs."

At this point, you should have established a warm-up routine that includes a posture check with breathing exercise, mouthpiece/head joint long tone and improvised articulations, full instrument warm-up with long tones, and articulated phrases with rhythms and familiar three-note melodies. I continue by introducing B♭, C, and D (the movement from C to D is difficult for flutes, as all the fingers must change) and repeat three-note songs in different tonal centers, both major and minor. Once the students learn more songs by rote, I will teach a simple harmonic accompaniment and allow them to learn a melody and an accompaniment and trade parts. They can perform in duets or quartets and perhaps make up their own harmony. The possibilities are endless, and we are still working on technical executive skills while focused on musical outcomes.

MOVING TO NOTATION

Once I have established strong aural skills with fingerings, we can move into notational reading. Along the way, I have already introduced rhythmic notation and moved to short melodic notation before I have students use a method book to work toward fluid notational literacy. This is important, because we have transposing instruments in the room together. The method book is a tool, and I chose the lines for both review and sight-reading opportunities to establish a routine for developing early sight-reading expertise, such as looking for tonal center, rhythms, and accidentals or other melodic signs, then audiating with fingerings, then singing with fingerings, and finally performing on the instrument. (See Chapter 7 for more detailed information.)

32.3 Summary

Setting up beginning band woodwind classes takes careful planning, from arranging meetings with the administration to decide which woodwind instruments you will start at the beginning of the year, to selecting which reeds, mouthpieces, and accessories are to be provided provided in rental instruments. More detailed planning should include careful scaffolding of the technical executive skills specific for woodwind instruments. Above all, remember that music is an embodied art form. We must feel it within our bodies and then create muscle memory to refine and build skill in technique and artistry. This takes time, practice, and patience.

Discussion Questions

1. What are some considerations in deciding whether to start double reeds and saxophones at the same time as flutes and clarinets?
2. What are some considerations to keep in mind when working with beginning woodwind students?
3. What are some of the technical executive skills that are important to teach beginning woodwind students?
4. What are the various rationales for which three notes to teach woodwind players first?
5. Why is it important to start developing aural skills with students before introducing music staff notation?

OXFORD learning link

Visit the online resources for additional documentation and exercises to help expand learning and test your knowledge further: www.oup.com/he/powell_music1e.

CHAPTER 33

PEDAGOGIES FOR TEACHING FLUTE

Cassandra Eisenreich

This chapter provides an overview of the fundamental aspects of flute playing, including recommendations and resources for beginning flute instruction.

33.1 Introduction

There are excellent flute resources for beginning band and instrumental methods that have been proven to be successful; however, many books introduce multiple topics simultaneously, which can be overwhelming for students. Teaching students how to create a sound on the headjoint can be difficult and modeling an ideal flute sound can be even more challenging. This chapter will provide approaches for teaching the flute to beginners with an emphasis on play, creativity, improvisation, and composition through a combination of kinesthetic, tactile, visual, and aural experiences.

33.2 Breathing and Air

The natural breath is quite different from how musicians need to breathe to play instruments. Breathing for flute playing is just as much about managing the air efficiently during the exhale as it is about the art of taking deep breaths. It is important to develop proper breathing techniques early on because the breath affects nearly every aspect of flute playing. When a student exhales to play a note, the air is cut on the wall of the flute, so that only about half of the air is sent into the instrument. Shoulders should be relaxed during the breathing process. Students should mark breaths in their music, since practicing the breath the same way every time helps them to stay consistent in their phrasing.

33.3 Toys, Games, and Exercises

There are many toys, games, and exercises that develop proper breathing techniques and airstream consistency in beginners. For younger students, fun breathing tools such as pinwheels and blowing ball/string toys are just as much a visual as a physical experience. For examples of breathing tools, please visit the online resources.

For slightly older students, the exercises in *The Breathing Gym*, by Sam Pilafian and Patrick Sheridan, available in book and DVD format and on YouTube, are an excellent resource for a serious breathing workout. When teaching proper breath support, it is best to provide these kinesthetic and tactile experiences without much explanation, since they naturally develop the physical sensation needed to support the sound. For more on support, see the section below on tone and intonation. To view a recommended breathing exercise for all ages and levels, visit the online resources.

33.4 Embouchure

There are several factors to consider when developing a flute embouchure, including what is happening on the outside (the appearance of the lips) and the inside (dental makeup and vowel shape, which includes the placement of the tongue). A great way to develop proper flute embouchure is to gently seal the wet part of the lips together and then freeze the shape of the lips immediately after saying the word "poo" or "pooh." Vocalize these first without the instrument by saying the word with an extended duration—almost as if singing—and then to do the same exercise with a consistent airstream and no vocalization. When the energy of the word "poo" or "pooh" is used, it creates an elliptical opening in the lips called the aperture. Students can experiment with the shape of the ellipse to find the best possible sound. Placing a hand in front of the airstream can help in assessing air consistency and intensity. Spitting rice is another approach that can be used to create the appropriate embouchure, aperture, and airstream. This technique requires students to place a grain of rice on the tip of their tongue slightly between their lips and allows them to feel the buildup of air used behind the tongue to spit the rice across the room. Regardless of the method, and among many other visual aspects of flute playing, using a mirror, taking photos, and making video recordings are all critical for establishing and refining the embouchure. To view a photo of the hand assessing the air angle and consistency, please visit the online resources.

All of these examples can be practiced alone, with the student's index (pointer) finger acting as the lip plate and/or angle of the air (a great physical sensation), with the Pneumo Pro Wind Director, created by Kathy Blocki, and/or the headjoint. Providing a correct visual model is important, but everyone has a different physical makeup, which will result in varying embouchure and aperture shapes. Some students will have an off-center embouchure. A prominent teardrop lip (also known as a cupid's bow) makes it difficult for an aperture to be formed in the middle of the lips, thus requiring a shift to one side. If the student lacks the ability to control the embouchure in the center because of how unnatural it feels, the most natural way of playing should be supported and developed, especially if the off-center embouchure is flexible enough to produce a quality sound in all registers. To view photos of the pointer finger supporting lip plate alignment and the angle of the air, please visit the online resources.

33.5 Articulation

"T" and "D" are the most common consonants used for single-tonguing articulation. Teachers can encourage students to experiment with different vowels that follow the point of articulation, as the vowels will change the shape of the inside of the mouth and have an impact on the overall sound and intonation. Students should speak the suggested consonant and vowel ("too" is a great transition from "poo") and then describe where they feel the point of contact with their tongue. Acceptable placements include feeling the tip of the tongue behind the teeth, where the teeth meet the gums, and slightly behind where the teeth meet the gums. It is easy to rely too heavily on the action of the tongue for articulation, so teachers should remind students that the sound is created by the air column. As when one places a finger under a faucet to interrupt a stream of running water, the tongue simply interrupts the stream of air at the point of articulation. The water coming out of the faucet does not stop, and neither does the air coming out of the aperture during exhalation. In classical flute playing, the tongue is only used to begin the note and should rarely be used to stop the sound (with the exception of some extended techniques and certain styles of playing).

Describing how to do something that students are not able to see can be difficult, so finding ways to model what is happening on the inside of the mouth can be helpful. Teachers can use one hand to show the shape of the inside of the mouth and the other, below it, to represent the placement and movement of the tongue. Showing the placement of the tongue at the point of articulation and its movement for the duration of the note helps students see what they are feeling inside their mouths and also helps to show that each note has three parts; the beginning, the sustained duration, and the release. Once the consonants and vowels are chosen, one can move through vocalizing first (singing the word with extended duration), then only using air (experimenting with various angles of air direction based on teacher guidance), and finally transferring those experiences to the Pneumo Pro and/or headjoint.

When teaching articulation for the first time, there are two schools of thought. Some books of instruction start with several shorter articulated notes in succession, while others choose to have students begin with long sustained notes. There are pros and cons to both approaches, but either can yield success if used methodically and with attention to detail.

33.6 Tone and Intonation

Listening to high-level performances is one of the best things students can do to develop their overall sound quality and musicality. Establishing a full and resonant tone in all registers with good intonation should always be a top priority, especially from the start of instruction. Students should learn their individual pitch tendencies as early as possible. If a note is consistently played too sharp or flat for an extended period of time, individuals are likely to begin hearing that sharp or flat pitch as correct. Visual tuners are helpful, but when one is supposed to be training the ear, *looking* at a device is not the best answer, since looking trains the eye more than the ear. Actively listening to professional flutists, accurate singing, and the proper use of drone exercises and a tuner can assist in establishing a good sense of pitch and beautiful tone. For a list of recommended flutists to listen to, please visit the online resources.

The combination of air, alignment, abdominal support, and vowels can have a dramatic impact on overall tone and intonation and should be the focus of instruction. These four areas are so impactful that they can collectively be referred to as the *battery* of flute tone and intonation (triple-A voltage—AAAv). The battery can be practiced without the instrument but should always be implemented when playing on the headjoint or full instrument.

1. A (air): The amount and direction of the air can be manipulated. Seeing and understanding how the upper and bottom lips work together to aim the air can have a profound effect on the quality of the sound. The bottom lip moves forward and backward (with the help of the jaw) to change the size of the aperture, which in turn changes the direction of the air. The top lip aims the air down and into the instrument. Students can place their hand out in front of them to feel the angle and intensity of the air.

2. A (alignment): The best alignment of the lip plate to the embouchure will vary. Students should experiment by shifting the flute up or down horizontally, rolling the flute in or out on the lip, very slightly increasing or decreasing the pressure of the lip plate toward the lip, sliding the flute left or right, and/or angling the flute in relation to the lips. Proper hand and body position also play an important role in this process.
3. A (abdominal support): Engaging the abdominal muscles while exhaling a steady stream of air is a common and often successful approach for many students. There are several familiar experiences that help to recreate this sensation:

   a. blowing up a balloon
   b. laughing
   c. coughing

4. V (vowels): When students experiment with vowels, it changes the shape of the inside of the mouth, which directly affects tone and intonation. Some refer to the shape of the inside of the mouth as a sensation such as having a large piece of fruit in the mouth or yawning, but there are many variations and adjustments beyond these examples. To view a chart exploring the different vowel sounds, visit the online resources. To view photos of the hand demonstrating vowels and the associated shape changes of the inside of the mouth, please visit the online resources.

33.7 First Sounds: Headjoint

The Pneumo Pro can help students develop proper embouchure, aperture, air direction, air consistency, and alignment. It can be used prior to or in combination with the headjoint to help establish a great tone and consistent intonation but is certainly not a requirement for students to be successful. Since working with the Pneumo Pro is a kinesthetic, visual, and aural experience, it provides a strong overall introduction to sound production that transfers directly to playing the flute.

Students must bring the Pneumo Pro to them for proper alignment, just as if they were playing on the headjoint. Generally, the edge of the embouchure hole on the lip plate should be placed where the bottom lip meets the skin; however, the placement of the lip on the lip plate varies according to the overall size of the lips. Some employ the "kiss and roll" method, where the embouchure hole on the lip plate is rolled in to meet the lips and then rolled out for proper placement. This process might work for some but cannot be adopted for all students, since the size of the lips and how the instrument is placed on them has a huge impact on overall control and flexibility. For larger lips the lip plate might be placed higher, and for smaller lips it might be placed lower. It is also helpful to place a small object on the top of the Pneumo Pro to ensure that students are holding it parallel with the floor. If the object falls, it is clear that the instrument is not being held properly. When young students hold the headjoint for the first time, they often try to change the placement of the instrument instead of adjusting their lips accordingly. Rolling the instrument in or out will direct the air to the various fans, but the resulting tone is often small, unfocused, and out of tune.

The goal of the Pneumo Pro is to help develop the correct angle, speed, and consistency of the air by directing the airstream to the attached fans. Even though a beginner's airstream is likely to set several fans in motion, the ability to isolate individual fans is the overall goal. The upper lip is what aims the air down to set the fans in motion. The angle of the airstream is adjusted up (by moving the bottom lip forward) and down (by moving the bottom lip back). The small and intricate movement of the jaw is what helps adjust the bottom lip forward to create a smaller aperture with a higher angle of air, and back to create a larger aperture with a lower angle of air. Once students have developed some flexibility and control on all fans, they should try to repeatedly isolate the lowest fan while focusing on the direction of the air, the speed at which the fan is spinning, and the length of time it spins. They should attempt to recreate this experience on the open headjoint by imagining they are isolating the lowest fan on the Pneumo Pro. The Pneumo Pro is not a necessity for developing a beautiful tone, but it will certainly support the process. If possible, students should have experiences with varied repetition and playful activities on the Pneumo Pro and headjoint before putting the instrument together. For photos of Pneumo Pro alignment, please visit the online resources.

33.8 Fun with First Sounds

The headjoint should be the focus of the first few lessons, and student progress on the headjoint should be monitored prior to their moving on to the fully assembled instrument. There are several effective techniques, games, and exercises that can be implemented using a little creativity and the headjoint alone. It is important for students to listen, watch, sing, and move through introductory concepts prior to labeling them or defining them in theory. The theory should come only after students have developed the ability to communicate and create with familiar skills and concepts. To view a list of ideas for initial headjoint work, please visit the online resources.

FIGURE 33.1 Open headjoint sound

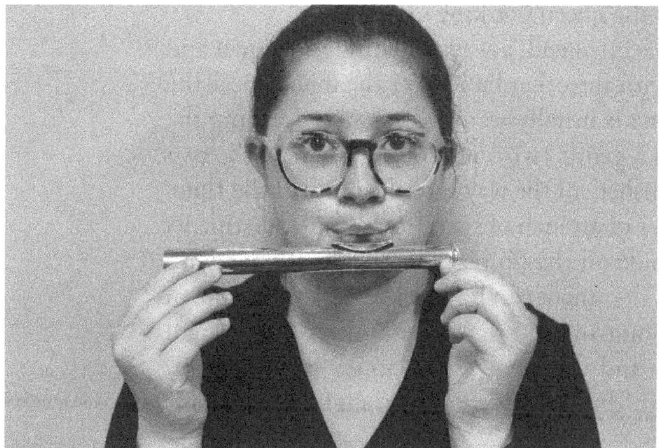

FIGURE 33.2 Closed headjoint sound

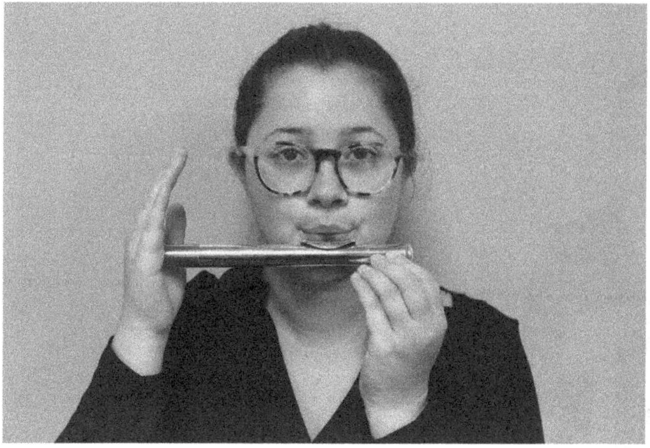

FIGURE 33.3 Sliding headjoint sound

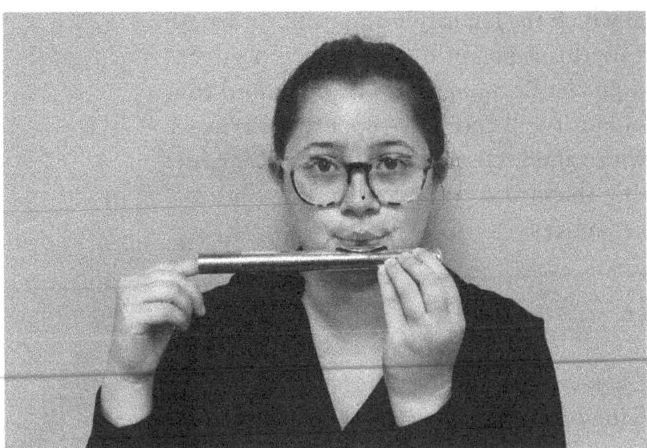

33.9 Assembly, Disassembly, and Maintenance

The flute is made up of three main parts: the headjoint, the body, and the footjoint. At the top of the headjoint sits the crown, which controls the placement of the cork and can drastically affect the tuning of the instrument. When teaching the instrument to a beginner, one can refer to the parts of the instrument in terms of royalty: every royal has a crown, a head, a body, and a foot, and nobody touches the queen's or king's crown.

Take the headjoint in one hand close to the open end, always avoiding the crown and lip plate. Now pick up the body of the flute with the other hand over the tenon (near the end that has fewer keys, where the brand name is usually stamped), always avoiding the keywork. Hold both sections firmly and with a gentle twisting motion assemble the two parts together. The headjoint should not be pushed all the way into the body of the flute. Leave approximately one-eighth to one-quarter of an inch of space to permit adjustments when tuning with others. The embouchure hole on the lip plate should be aligned with the long row of keys on the body of the flute. Alignment can be checked by looking down one end of the instrument. To put the headjoint in the same place every time, a small marking can be made on both the headjoint and the tenon for accuracy in alignment. Some brands already have arrows to assist with this process; however, slight adjustments may need to be made for each student.

FIGURE 33.4 Flute assembly, step 1

FIGURE 33.5 Flute assembly, step 2

FIGURE 33.6 Alignment of headjoint to body

Next, hold the footjoint in one hand, again avoiding the keywork, and take the rest of the flute by the tenon (where the headjoint and body overlap). Use a gentle twisting motion to attach the footjoint to the bottom end of the body. The rod of the footjoint should be aligned with the middle of the last key on the body (not with the rod). There is some flexibility with the placement of the footjoint based on the size of the right-hand pinky finger. Taking the flute apart should be done the same way: holding the instrument away from the keywork and using a twisting motion to separate the different parts. For information on flute care and maintenance, please visit the online resources.

FIGURE 33.7 Flute assembly, step 3

FIGURE 33.8 Flute assembly, step 4

33.10 Holding the Flute

Students should relax both of their arms and hands down to the side and notice the natural curve of the fingers and the placement of the thumb, specifically the right-hand thumb. This should be replicated when learning the proper hand position. The fingers should always be slightly curved, relaxed enough to hover over their respective keys, and able to move freely and quickly. The placement of the wrist and forearm should follow in alignment. When used for specific fingerings, the padded parts of the fingers will press down their designated keys. It is helpful to take a photo of this placement for students to reference at home. For an example of the natural curve of the hand, please visit the online resources.

LEFT-HAND POSITION

Let the palm of the left hand face in toward the body. The flute will rest on the bottom of the pointer finger between the first and second knuckle. The left-hand pointer finger will then wrap around to rest above the second key from the top of the body (from left to right). The thumb of the left hand will then gently press down the larger key on the side of the flute. The middle finger, ring finger, and pinky will fall into place after skipping an additional key at the top, and when used for specific fingerings, the padded parts of the fingers will press down their designated keys. For a photo of the left-hand position, please visit the online resources.

RIGHT-HAND POSITION

The right-hand position begins with the palm facing out, as if one were waving to someone across the room. The pointer finger, middle finger, and ring finger of the right hand are in charge of the last three keys on the body of the flute. The right-hand pinky controls all of the keys on the footjoint but spends most of its time pressing down the largest one, closest to the body of the flute. The natural C shape described is very important here, as it helps to develop proper technique. The thumb should be observed in its natural state in terms of its relationship to the fingers, and that shape should be replicated on the instrument. It is likely that the thumb will need to be adjusted slightly to the left or right of the pointer finger for maximum comfort, proper hand position, and ease of playing. The thumb can be placed on the side of the instrument or underneath but should not carry a majority of the weight of the flute or protrude out on the opposite side. For a photo of the right-hand position, please visit the online resources.

BALANCE POINTS

Once the correct hand position is established, balancing the instrument is the next step. There are three main balance points when playing the flute:

1. the lip/chin firmly against the lip plate
2. the left-hand pointer finger (carrying the majority of the weight of the instrument and pressing toward the body)
3. the right-hand thumb (on the side of the instrument pressing out or right beneath the instrument).

The right-hand pinky plays a role in balancing the flute, but since it is not used for every note, it should be considered a secondary balance point. Figure 33.9 demonstrates the proper hand and body position.

FIGURE 33.9 Hand and body position

HAND-POSITION HELPERS

It can be a challenge for students to know exactly where to place their fingers and to maintain proper hand position during study. If cleared with the family, students can use stickers, "BG Hand Position Cushions," or some other adhesive material on top of or beside the keys for a visual and kinesthetic representation of where to place their fingers. In addition to the designated keys, stickers or small pieces of adhesive material can be placed on the balance points discussed.

Thumbports and Bo-Peps are other great resources to help with finger placement. The Thumbport allows greater balance in holding the flute. It consists of a C-shaped shell and a thumblike extension. The Thumbport helps the player to place the right thumb at an efficient spot and provides additional support. There are three different types of Bo-Peps. The Bo-Pep Finger Rest (flat surface) and Bo-Pep Finger Saddle (curved surface) snap onto the flute to help eliminate cramping of the left index finger and extreme twisting of the left wrist. The Bo-Pep Thumb Guide snaps onto the flute to help with right-hand position and balance.

The Finger Position Corrector is a small piece of plexiglass that safely clips on to the flute to keep the fingers from moving too far away from the keys when playing. Sometimes the right-hand position can condense into the open C space between the thumb and the pointer finger. This placement angles the hand to the left toward the mechanism and can slow down technique. If the C shape becomes difficult for the student to maintain, a small beanbag or something of similar size can be placed inside the right hand to keep the space open.

FIGURE 33.10 Maintaining the natural curve of the right hand

Students who are initially struggling with the weight and awkwardness of the instrument might choose to hold the end of the footjoint with their right hand, or they may decide not to include the footjoint at all and hold the tenon at the end of the body of the flute with their right hand. This approach allows students to focus on the embouchure and left-hand position, including the recommended first three notes. For a more extensive list of helpful flute accessories and adaptations for hand position, please visit the online resources.

33.11 Bringing the Flute to You

Students should always maintain proper posture during flute playing. Beginners often move toward the instrument and lean to the left shoulder when they bring the flute up into playing position. It is important to always bring the instrument up to the face while keeping the head aligned with the spine and keeping shoulders relaxed. The chin should still face forward and away from the neck, and the elbows and the arms should be relaxed but not pressed against the body or angled up. As noted, the headjoint should be aligned with the majority of the keys on the body of the flute. If performing with a stand, it is recommended that it be about one flute's length away from the music, with the flute held parallel to the desk of the stand. For standing posture, the feet should be comfortably separated, with equal weight distributed. If looking at a stand, the left foot should face the stand and the right foot should angle out to the right side. For sitting posture, the chair can be angled to the right side of the stand and sat on normally, or the chair can face forward toward the stand and the body be angled to the right. It is important to sit on the edge of the chair. Both of these positions allow for proper alignment of the spine and natural space between the arms.

33.12 First Notes

There is a difference between method books for full group band instruction and small group or private lesson study. Band methods choose starting pitches that are a compromise based on all the other instruments that need to be taught in beginning band classes. The first three notes chosen for the flute are not always ideal in band method books (e.g., D, E♭, F), but they do make it possible for all the students to learn together in one setting. For small groups or private flute lessons, many flute-specific method books begin with B, A, and G. These are excellent first notes for several reasons:

1. The movement takes place all in one hand.
2. The movement includes adding a finger or taking one away (no cross fingerings or multiple finger movement initially).
3. All the notes are naturals.
4. The first three notes are the start of a G major scale.
5. They are in a great register for singing.
6. The fingerings for B, A, and G one octave higher are exactly the same.
7. Familiar three-note songs can be learned by ear.

To view a list of ideas for three-note games, please visit the online resources.

33.13 Conclusion

Playing the flute should be an enjoyable experience filled with creative opportunities that engage students on multiple levels and through diverse learning modalities. Working on fundamental skills through play-based instruction and varied repetition can help to keep students invested in, and enthusiastic about, the learning process. Method books provide a plethora of valuable information, but educators should feel encouraged to explore by going beyond the binding of the books to better serve their students.

33.14 Discussion Questions

1. Why is it important to demonstrate proper playing on the headjoint before adding the rest of the flute?
2. What are some ways to help students develop proper hand position?
3. Which play-based headjoint and three-note games might you implement in your beginning flute instruction and how might you build on them?

OXFORD learning link

Visit the online resources for additional documentation and exercises to help expand learning and test your knowledge further: www.oup.com/he/powell_music1e.

CHAPTER 34

PEDAGOGIES FOR TEACHING CLARINET

Cynthia L. Wagoner and Asia Muhaimin

This chapter includes specific language and provides an overview for successful skill building for teaching performance on the clarinet across public school participation in instrumental music.

34.1 Introduction

The clarinet is one of the workhorses of band literature, with a long history in classical, jazz, and klezmer music. In this chapter we will learn a bit about the clarinet and then address specifics on assembly and daily maintenance as teachers working with our students. We then attend to specifics on how to build skills for beginning clarinet students. Finally, we end with things to consider and remember as a teacher.

34.2 About the Clarinet

The B♭ clarinet is a transposing instrument. All the written pitches will sound a whole step (i.e., a major second, or M2) lower than written. The sounding pitch will be written a whole step (M2) higher than what we hear. Concert pitch is the sounding pitch. If you play a written pitch of C on the clarinet, it sounds a B♭ (M2 lower) on a piano (concert pitch). For more information, see 34.3, "Clarinet Family with Transpositions," on the book's online resources site.

The clarinet has a lovely wide range because it overblows an octave and a fifth; however, this means more fingerings to learn, because instead of an octave key, a register key is added, and new fingerings for the pitch and note name must be learned. There are four registers for the clarinet: chalumeau (E3–F♭4), throat tones (G4–B♭4), clarion (B4–C6), and altissimo (C♯6–C7). Each register brings its own challenges. For clarinet players' first year, the chalumeau, throat tones, and moving across the "break" from B♭4 to B-natural add up to a lot to learn, but if mastered well these skills will set students up for success in the future.

34.3 Assembling and Disassembling the Clarinet

ASSEMBLING THE CLARINET

Begin by showing and naming each part of the instrument: mouthpiece, ligature, reed, barrel, upper joint, lower joint, and bell. Demonstrate how to take the pieces out of the case and put them back one at a time until students recall the name, the location, and how each piece of the instrument should be placed into the case. Next, have students take the cork grease and place a light layer on each of the four tenon corks to make sure they are lubricated. When the corks are new, they are dry and need to be greased every day. Once the instrument is broken in, once a week will maintain the health of the corks.

It is best to build the instrument from the bell up, so that the most delicate part of the instrument is last, reducing the chances of breaking the reed. Point out the bridge key, which is the connecting metal lever between the upper and lower joints. It is easily bent, so take care to have students identify it and twist carefully left to right, not all the way around, to put these two sections together. It is much better to model each step of putting it together and taking it apart and then have the students then follow each step along with you. Remember to take the clarinet apart right away and place it back into the case, demonstrating proper assembly *and* disassembly for the clarinet.

ASSEMBLING THE BODY OF THE CLARINET

1. Take the bell in one hand and the lower joint in the opposite hand. Place your hand across the back of the lower joint to avoid placing your hands across the keys or the long rods along the side of the joint. With the cork pointed at the receiving end of the bell, twist with a back-and-forth motion until the two parts are flush with each other.
2. Take the upper joint in one hand. The portion of the upper joint with the bridge key will face toward the lower joint receiver. Find where the tone hole openings will line up. You will push the tone holes down with your fingers to raise the bridge key so that you can slowly twist back and forth until the bridge key is lined up across the joints and the instrument parts are flush with each other.
3. If you have not assembled the small instrument, place the barrel in one hand and twist it onto the upper joint of the clarinet, using a back-and-forth motion.

   a. Put the mouthpiece onto the barrel. The reed should not be on the instrument when you are assembling it in this way. Twist back and forth until the mouthpiece is flush with the barrel.
   b. Assemble the reed and ligature according to the instructions for the small instrument found on page 332.

4. If you have already assembled the mouthpiece with the barrel, put the mouthpiece cap on and slowly twist back and forth until the barrel is flush with the upper joint. The reed should be centered with the thumb rest on the back of the instrument.

CLARINET CARE AND DISASSEMBLY

Before sending any instrument home with a student, we suggest having a checklist for the assembly, disassembly, and care of the instrument. Every time the instrument is played, it needs to be swabbed out to remove the moisture. Take the reed off, wipe it off to remove any excess saliva, and place it in a reed holder. The metal anchor found on many swabs may damage the mouthpiece, so take the mouthpiece off before using the swab. Using a twisted tissue or paper towel, dry the mouthpiece out. Replace the ligature and mouthpiece cap and return to the case. Lukewarm soapy water may be used on the mouthpiece once a week as long as you avoid getting the cork wet but avoid disinfectant sprays, as they can damage the mouthpiece. A mouthpiece should be cleaned thoroughly at least once a week. Reminder: *never* get any cork wet!

Draw the swab through the rest of the instrument, still assembled, several times. Then take it apart, piece by piece, and wipe the moisture off the receiving and cork ends with the paper towel or tissue you used on the mouthpiece. Replace each piece. Throw out the tissue or paper towel. Have students check and make sure the swab is dry when they get home. We have occasionally found mold growing in cases in which a wet swab has been allowed to remain for long periods of time.

34.4 Making Noise: Learning to Play the Instrument

"Making noise" is a great way to start clarinet players off. Allowing the young musicians to familiarize themselves with the clarinet will ensure focus and long-term success. Developing the proper embouchure and producing sound on the clarinet is not always the easiest task for a beginner. They must find their own comfort in producing sound on the instrument first.

For the university woodwind class, Wagoner takes preservice teachers through the steps much as beginners, but with more information delivered and at a faster pace. You should consider how the technical executive skills (see Chapter 26) for the clarinet can be acquired *before* the addition of musical notation. The technical executive skills for clarinet players are posture, breathing, mouthpiece assembly, instrument assembly, embouchure and mouthpiece/head joint sounds, articulation technique, instrument carriage and hand position, and, finally, learning first pitches and establishing daily warm-ups.

POSTURE AND BREATHING

Posture and breathing should be taught before attempting to play, hold the instrument, or learn fingering positions. The proper posture while playing the clarinet is to sit on the edge of the chair with the feet flat on the floor and the back straight. If the student can stand easily from sitting without moving their feet or bending forward at the waist, posture is good. Breathing properly to produce a good clarinet sound requires practicing filling up the lungs and moving the air quickly to vibrate the reed. Instruct them to think of their air as a garden hose. When we place our thumb on the garden hose, we can stop the water, or we can let some of the water out with the thumb, whereupon it is released in a very fast and focused stream. The secret to good tone is the use of a fast, focused, laser-beam-like stream air. We recommend using the exercises in *The Breathing Gym*, by Sam Pilafian and Patrick Sheridan; it is available in book and DVD format and on YouTube.

MOUTHPIECE ASSEMBLY

Wagoner will ask students to watch as we name the five parts used for what we call the "small instrument," and then we practice finding each part by the name. The five parts of the small instrument are the mouthpiece, ligature, reed, cap, and the barrel. We now look at directions for assembly of the small instrument assembly.

STEPS FOR ASSEMBLING THE "SMALL INSTRUMENT"

1. Wet the reed by placing it in water for five minutes (I prefer not to have students hold the reed gently in the mouth, as it can split if they place it between the tongue and the roof of mouth and press too hard and saliva will break down the fibers of the reed.). Clean, empty pill bottles with or without their lids can work well to soak the reed in water. Wrap the bottle with washi or some other craft tape and glue on a magnet to make a soaking container for reeds that can stick to the music stand. Once the reed has been broken in, the soaking time does not need to be more than a minute or two.
2. Grease the cork on the mouthpiece. Place the mouthpiece (without the ligature) onto the barrel using a twisting motion.
3. Loosen (turning counterclockwise) the ligature screws about eight turns. Place the ligature on the mouthpiece (with the screws on the right) on the window side of the mouthpiece.
4. Have students demonstrate holding the reed with the flat side parallel to the floor and the tip aimed at the ceiling so they can see the writing on the flat side of the reed. Then have them show *you* the writing on the flat side of the reed (turning it around so the writing is facing away from them).
5. From the top of the mouthpiece down, slide the reed under the ligature. The emphasis is on inserting the fat end first, with the flat side against mouthpiece and the reed tip lined up with the tip of the mouthpiece. *Do not push down on the tip of the reed.*
6. Make the three checks:

    a. Tip: the hairline black line of mouthpiece should show above the reed. *Very* thin hair—too much is going to make the reed difficult to play.
    b. Rails: line up the rails (sides of the reed) with the sides of the mouthpiece.
    c. Ligature: the top of the ligature needs to be below the cut of the reed.

7. Gently tighten screws (turning clockwise) while periodically making the three checks outlined in steps 6a–6c above. Tighten the screw heads until there is resistance, then back the screw off a quarter of a turn. The ligature should sit just below the vamp (the wedge-shaped curve of the reed). Many mouthpieces will have ligature lines to assist with the placement.

INSIDER TIP: Remind students to use the mouthpiece cap whenever the reed is left on so that it is protected against chips or breaks. Check your students at each individual step of the process and use a checklist system for students to demonstrate they can do this without your help consistently.

CLARINET EMBOUCHURE

Have a set of small mirrors for students to visibly check their own work. Start with having students prepare their clarinet "band face" by saying the vowel "ah" and then "oo." The vowel "ah" opens the mouth and "oo" brings the corners in and the chin flat. Go through the steps listed in in the next section, having students check their progress in the mirror.

CLARINET EMBOUCHURE FORMATION

1. Open the mouth and make "Dracula" teeth.
2. Stretch the lower lip across the front of the bottom teeth, as if you are applying lip balm to the bottom lip.
3. Set the reed on the lower lip, right where the reed separates from the mouthpiece.
4. Check for "red" showing from the lower lip so the lip is not folded all the way into the mouth.
5. Set the upper teeth as an "anchor" so the mouthpiece doesn't move.
6. Seal the corners in toward the mouthpiece (think about tasting something sour) and recheck for the "red."
7. The chin should be flat and pointed toward the floor. The bottom lip is the table, the top teeth are the anchor, and the corners seal the deal!

Once you have worked on setting the muscles of the mouth, the "milkshake" exercise on the small instrument will prepare students to create a sound while producing the clarinet band face embouchure. Follow the steps outlined in the following section.

MILKSHAKE EXERCISE

1. Draw in air as if you were drinking a milkshake through a straw.
2. Freeze the muscle while inhaling through the corners of the mouth (bottom lip, = table; top teeth = anchor).
3. Blow air back through the mouthpiece and barrel.
4. Work to exhale for six slow counts and seal the deal with the corners.
5. Add corner and air pressure until concert F♭ sounds.
6. Reinforce upper-teeth anchor and check all points of embouchure formation.

SMALL-INSTRUMENT MOUTHPIECE SOUNDS

The proper pitch for the mouthpiece and barrel is a concert F♯. Little pressure from the lower lip is needed. The outer embouchure is the first step, but the second is the voicing or the "inner" embouchure. Once you have established a strong sense of the outer embouchure, follow the steps below to develop a student's voicing or inner embouchure.

INNER EMBOUCHURE (VOICING)

1. Imagine you are holding a little egg in your mouth. Think about the way that feels.
2. Feel the position of the egg on the tongue.
3. Imagine positioning the tongue to hold the egg. Think "hee" as a vowel so the back of the tongue is high.
4. You can also move the sides of tongue to the back teeth, using "hee" rather than "hoo," to direct the shape of the tongue in the mouth.
5. The position of the tongue will provide the openness the student should feel in the inner embouchure and allow air to move efficiently by directing it into the mouthpiece/reed.

ARTICULATION

Before assembling the clarinet, add articulation to the mouthpiece sounds using the small instrument. Moving the tongue can be more difficult. Have students practice verbalizing the word "tee" and practice several rhythms in call-and-echo with you. Then do that with "band face" and air, also in a call-and-echo. You might give students an opportunity to be the caller and move around the room to check for understanding.

Moving to the mouthpiece, have the students find the tip of the tongue to touch the reed tip, about a quarter of an inch from the top of the reed, right in the center. You can use a nontoxic marker to put a dot on the reed and have students create an embouchure and then create a sound, adding the tongue and then checking in the mirror to see where the tongue has touched the marker to check for accuracy. "The tip of the tongue to the tip of the reed" is a good instruction to repeat; just be sure students are not trying to tongue the very edge of the tip of the reed.

Watch the students carefully for movement of the chin or jaw; there should not be any "chewing" or changes in the embouchure. Legato tonguing should happen first, so keep the air moving and watch for pulses in the throat that could indicate the air is being controlled from there rather than being moved from behind the tongue. Long tones and control of the embouchure must be secure before articulation is introduced.

CARRIAGE AND FINGER POSITIONS

Make a C shape with your hands (think about the figurine hands found in Lego toys). Place your left hand in front of your chest and your right hand below, just above your waist. The left hand is on top and the right hand is on the bottom, *always*. Do this before moving on to finding the home keys for the fingers.

> **INSIDER TIP:** When you make a correction, repeat the mirror check so students will see the correction.

Teach Finger Home Keys

Before making sounds on the fully assembled instrument, have the students practice placing the fingers in the correct or "home" position on the instrument. Set the clarinet bell on the right knee and, with the mouthpiece cap on the instrument or without the barrel and mouthpiece, place the upper part on the left shoulder for support. The right thumb will later support the instrument by moving under the thumb rest on the lower joint right, about where the thumbnail meets the skin. This is above the knuckle of the thumb.

Have students begin with the right hand, remembering the "C" shape, and place the thumb at a 45-degree angle over the tone hole on the back of the clarinet. The thumb needs to be aimed at the two o'clock position so that the player can toggle the register key. Moving to the front of the instrument, place the first, second, and third fingers of the left hand consecutively from the top tone hole down. Have students rest the left-hand pinky finger on the E5/B4 key on the left-hand side of the instrument. Mark the pinky-finger key with a small sticker (a quarter-inch round color-coding label) to identify the proper key. Once students have placed their fingers down, have them press firmly and look at the pads of the fingers to see the ring of the open tone hole. It should leave a faint circle on the pad, or fattest part, of the finger.

Once you have established the fingers of the left hand on the instrument and the thumb of the right-hand position, add the barrel and mouthpiece and practice placing the instrument in playing position. The clarinet should be placed in the center line (left to right) of the body, with the bell held at about a 30- to 45-degree angle from the body. The elbows should be relaxed and away from the body. The student's head should be centered, and the instrument should be brought to the mouth, not the other way around, because we want the head and eyes looking straight ahead.

FIRST NOTES

Once the instrument is assembled, home keys have been identified for the right hand, and students can balance the instrument between their right hand and bottom lip/embouchure, we are ready to start with long tones, moving ever so slowly into legato tonguing. Tone quality and technique building is the most important aspect of clarinet playing, followed by finger dexterity and proper articulation. The introduction of long tones and legato tonguing can work to alleviate poor tone production and articulation struggles for young players.

The first five notes that can be introduced first *without notation* are written C4, D4, E4, F4, and G4. The first pitch of the written C4 (sounding B♭3) offers a young student a sense of comfort with holding the instrument, allowing them the security of supporting the instrument and not feeling that it might fall out of their hands. Introduce one note at a time, making sure to check posture, breathing, embouchure, carriage, finger position, and tone without articulation as you introduce a new note. Play long tones and have students sing the pitch while fingering it first, then play it. Start with applying proper breathing to long tones. Check students by playing "pass the long tone," where each student will hold the pitch right up to the count that the next person begins. This allows the teacher to hear each student individually. Once students feel secure with that one note, work on legato articulation, playing half-note and quarter-note rhythms at about quarter note = 60. As more pitches are learned, add more games, with you modeling and the students repeating what you play. Allow students to improvise half notes using one or two pitches, with the class echoing. Then add rhythms to the pitches. Work up to the first five notes, making sure you have students sing, finger, and play often. Build a repertoire of three- to five-note songs to enable students to learn aurally.

DAILY WARM-UP

A daily exercise once C4, D4, E4, F4, and G4 are learned should include a short review of executive skills at the level where the students can be most successful before moving on to simple slurred exercises. See 34.1, "Beginning Clarinet Exercises," on the book's online resources site.

Developing Each Register

Throat tones are stuffy and out of tune naturally on the instrument. There are resonant fingerings to help alleviate that, but it means manipulating more fingers, so add this to later lessons, avoiding it at the beginning. Gradually you can have students add all three right fingers and the F3/C5 key of the right hand to G4, G♯/A♭4, A4, A♯/B♭4. See 34.2, "Common Resonant Fingerings," on the book's online resources site. Working the pinky fingers also require understanding which fingering to use in a melodic setting. For more information, see 34.5, "Clarinet Pinky Keys," on the book's online resources site.

Preparation for the break happens by working in the chalumeau register; using proper finger positions (covering holes); using proper air support; using a reed with a hardness of at least 2½; and having the instrument in proper working order (e.g., no leaks in the pads). The proper finger position of the right hand should be reviewed, checking by pressing the pads of the fingers on the front keys for a count of 5 and then looking to see where the "circles" are.

INSIDER TIP: Say, "Here is a cool trick only clarinets can do," and have a student play B♭3 while you pop the register key for them. They get so surprised they sometimes stop blowing! At first, work with having them slur between B♭3 and F5, then A3 and E5, because with these notes it will be easier for them to find the clarion register. As the students develop confidence, start with F5 and E5 and move down to D5, C5, and B5, because the more fingers the students must manipulate, the more issues can arise. Teach fingerings for B4 (left) and C5 (right) by re-marking with dots to help them remember.

There are many wonderful resources for you to consider. See 34.6, "Teaching Clarinet Resources," on the book's online resources site.

34.5 Things to Consider and Remember as a Teacher

There are many things to consider when it comes to helping students choose a clarinet. It is not just about the clarinet itself: you should consider the type of mouthpiece, ligature, and reeds your students will have. In your first school community, encourage parents to avoid the "instrument-shaped objects" sold by the big-box stores. The keys are made of pot metal and will easily snap off, and nothing about the instruments' design will create a beautiful tone or an in-tune sound. For more detailed information, see 34.4, "Selecting an Instrument," on the book's online resources site.

All reed instruments depend on a good reed to create a good tone. Beginners' reeds should be a medium-soft to medium strength. As their embouchures strengthen, students should move to a harder reed (i.e., those with a higher number). Weak reeds also produce a flabby tone and flat pitches. When a reed is too hard, the student may play sharp, and the embouchure will fatigue easily, since the student will bite to produce and control the sound. A good reed at an appropriate strength will help students create a focused, consistent, characteristic tone comfortably. The student should always be able to play the reed comfortably, regardless of the strength.

INSIDER TIP: A reed that is too soft plays flat. A reed that is too hard plays sharp.

As a beginning band teacher, you should check reeds regularly and encourage students to throw away any that are frayed, chipped, cracked, discolored, or dirty beyond repair. Too often a clarinet player will only play on one reed every day and then decide to get a new reed the very day of the concert. Suddenly you are hearing that student squeak and squawk more often, all because they have been playing on a soft, unresponsive reed and now are working on something totally different and expecting the same outcome. Therefore, check student reeds regularly and encourage them to playing on different reeds on alternate days.

The goal of any music teacher should be to scaffold skills for our students so that they are able to make musical decisions and express themselves. To that end, help your future students by teaching the basic technical executive skills well at the beginning of their clarinet adventure. Then you can help your students soar musically while they use their clarinets to improvise and make meaningful music in multiple styles and genres.

34.6 Discussion Questions

1. What are some of the unique challenges of playing the clarinet?
2. How can you incorporate familiar melodies and popular tunes into beginning clarinet instruction?
3. What are different considerations for care and maintenance of the clarinet?

OXFORD learning link

Visit the online resources for additional documentation and exercises to help expand learning and test your knowledge further: www.oup.com/he/powell_music1e. A special thank you Douglas Moore-Monroe, Professor of Clarinet at East Carolina University, for his contributions to the online resources.

CHAPTER 35

PEDAGOGIES FOR TEACHING OBOE

Alison Robuck

This chapter provides instruction on teaching the oboe by including specific intonation exercises for students and teachers to play together, suggestions of modern solo repertoire for young students, and guidance on embouchure exercises and breathing exercises to play the oboe.

35.1 Introduction

I have often found that teaching oboe techniques class is fun because I enjoy being in the room with the energy and creativity of future teachers who will have the opportunity to teach future oboists. These students are quite advanced on their own instruments, and I love hearing them explore the oboe. My goal for music education students in the oboe techniques class is to create an opportunity for students to play and experience the oboe in a hands-on way that will give them time with the instrument and a good reed so that they can learn how to give future oboists their start on the instrument.

Oboists usually play a different instrument at first and then switch. Music education students come to oboe techniques class with a deep knowledge of their own instruments, and they can compare what they know about their own instrument to discover the similarities and differences with the oboe. Therefore, the exploration of the classroom provides them with knowledge about teaching their own future band students how to switch from their first (or second) instrument to the oboe. Each semester there are one or two students in the techniques class that play the oboe well, and that is a wonderful opportunity to teach the other students in the room how to encourage their students to become a beginning oboist by finding their voice with the oboe.

Oboists can begin to study the oboe without any prior knowledge of any other instrument. I have often taught sixth-grade oboists from the beginning of their musical training. The oboe can be taught right alongside all the other beginning instruments. I have had private oboe studios that had three students in each grade of middle school. The students build a sense of community together from the beginning of their studies, and it helps them not feel alone in their progress. Encourage students to play the oboe by starting them along with all of your other beginning instrumentalists.

It is important to learn how to play the instrument by listening to the oboe through musical literature. Orchestral literature is a wonderful addition to techniques class, not only to augment the listening list of music education students, but to also highlight the solo voice of the oboe within the symphonic tradition. Listen for the oboe solos from the symphonies of Mahler, Tchaikovsky, Beethoven, and Shostakovich. There are works that feature the oboe, such as the second movement of the Brahms Violin Concerto, the second movement of the Barber Violin Concerto, Stravinsky's *Pulcinella* Suite, and Beethoven's Third Symphony. Ravel's *Le tombeau de Couperin* and Rossini's *La scala di Seta* are standard pieces that an oboist will learn as they turn into advanced players. Richard Strauss's Oboe Concerto is considered to be one of the finest works featuring the oboe by a leading composer.

35.2 How to Play the Oboe

ASSEMBLY

There are four parts to an oboe: the reed, the upper joint, the bottom joint, and the bell. Assemble the oboe by beginning with the bell and the bottom joint. A small amount of cork grease is needed to gently slide the parts together. Put the bell in your right hand and place your right thumb on the open pad to close the pad on the bell so that the bridge key on the bell is opened wider before assembly. The two parts should connect and close together without too much effort. On the upper joint, put the ring finger of your left hand on the trill key to open the bridge key and then put the upper joint and the bottom joint together, being careful to watch the bridge keys throughout the assembly of these two parts. Finally, place the reed in the oboe. The plane of the oboe reed needs to be matched with the plane of the oboe so that it will be in a straight line. The cork of the oboe reed needs to be fully inserted in the reed well so that about one third of the cork remains outside of the oboe while most of the cork is fully inserted in the reed well. More of the cork is inside the reed well than outside. Hold the reed on the thread and the top portion of the cork as you place it in the oboe. A tiny amount of cork grease can be used to help slide the reed in the reed well if the cork is too big.

PLAYING POSITION

Hold the oboe with your elbows close to the sides of your body. The left hand holds the top joint, and the right hand holds the bottom joint. Hold the oboe at a forty-five degree angle and about six inches in front of the body. Curve each finger to hover over the keys. The pinky of the left hand rests over the A♭ key, and the pinky of the right hand rests over the low C key. The sides of the pointer fingers on both hands do not rest on the oboe or support the oboe in any way.

EMBOUCHURE

Say "or" to activate a round embouchure with upper and lower lip balanced in terms of controlling the reed. The oboe reed sits gently on the lower lip, and the oboist breathes with their mouth, raising their upper lip with the reed staying on the lower lip. Students can practice with the reed alone by holding the staple and putting the reed in their mouth in a playing position to create a C peep on the reed. They can take a little reed out of their mouth to create a B, B♭, or A as well. This simple reed exercise can help develop a student's embouchure without the oboe. The student can gain confidence in their embouchure by creating the C without holding onto the reed with their hand.

ARTICULATION

Articulation begins by withdrawing the tongue from the reed. The tongue is set between the opening of the double reed and withdraws to allow the sound. An awareness of where the reed is in the mouth is fundamental to developing correct intonation. The reed cannot be too far in or out of the mouth. The use of the tongue as a placement at the reed's opening helps to stabilize the location of the reed in the mouth.

BREATHING

Breathe deep breaths with your mouth. It helps to breathe as the conductor prepares the measure that you begin. Breathing over two or three beats sets up an excellent support system of air. Take every opportunity to breathe during the music's rests. Do not hold your breath. Keep your air moving in and out of your body.

1. How to:
   a. Inhale: silently say "how"
   b. Exhale: "to" creates articulation and air flow
2. "Sip sip sip sip" silent, pulsed inhales
   a. Four breaths inhaled in time to a tempo (quarter note =84); exhale for four counts
   b. Inhale four counts; exhale for six counts
   c. Inhale for four counts; exhale for eight counts

POSTURE

Proper posture is important whether you sit or stand. Keep your feet flat on the floor with energy in your toes and front of your legs. If you are seated, you have enough energy in your legs that you can stand up at any time. If you are standing, keep your feet pointed forward. Keep your shoulders back and down. The center of your chest should lead up and forward, while your neck stays in line with your spine and your chin points down to the floor.

35.3 Pedagogical Considerations

THE REED

The oboe reed needs to "crow" a C for ideal intonation.

1. Learn to crow the reed.
   a. The crow is found by placing the reed in the mouth so that your lips lightly surround the cane up to the thread. Blow into the reed and the crow will speak its true pitch. If it is a C, you will have a better opportunity for A440 accuracy. If you can achieve an octave C in the reed's crow, the reed will be a better reed.

HAND POSITION

Have an awareness of the half-hole from the beginning of learning to play the oboe.

First, take direct care to know the difference in the fingerings between C in the staff and C♯ in the staff. Then, roll the first finger on the left hand to vent the half-hole. The first finger on the left hand stays in contact with the metal of the key at all times. It rolls open and rolls closed to release the half-hole or to cover the tone hole completely.

ALTERNATE FINGERINGS

F♮ has three options: regular F, left F, and forked F.

1. Learn to use the three F fingerings in this order of preference:
   a. Regular F is the first choice.
   b. Left F is used when the D key needs to be used before or after F♮.
   c. Forked F is used to facilitate technique in fast passages where left F cannot be accessed as easily.

First Octave Key

1. Learn to use the first octave key with the left thumb placed just below the octave key on the wood of the oboe and resting on the octave key in a ready position to push the octave key to open the first octave vent. Use the first octave key for E♮, F♮, F♯, G♮, and G♯.

Second Octave Key

1. Learn to use the second octave key with the side of your left pointer finger for A♮, A♯, B♮, and C♮.

35.4 Starting to Play Without Teaching the Music Staff First

A beginner oboist needs time in the music to establish a healthy routine of good posture, air support, correct embouchure, correct intonation, and correct hand position and fingerings. I have written twelve exercises as examples of short opportunities to hear the teacher model and also lead the student in achieving these important aspects of beginning to play the oboe. The exercises are not melodies. Rather, they are opportunities for the teacher to demonstrate the tone and correct intonation of each of these notes, and for the student to echo each short brief statement. The teacher plays throughout the exercise on the top line, and the student plays the bottom line. These can be played completely by ear and not with the notation, so that the student does not have to read the music. The teacher can also freely create their own exercises to help their student. I have offered complete measures of rest in order to effectively teach comfort in finding time to breathe adequately.

My suggestion for instructors and students in collegiate technique classes is to incorporate playing small technique examples together in mirroring fashion so that students practice hand position and note learning without having to read the melodies found in the method book to learn how to begin to play the oboe. One or two exercises could be practiced each week. The intention of these exercises is not to play all of them in one practice session, but to isolate one idea to study with a particular exercise. The examples of exercises in notation can be led by the teacher without the students' reading the notes. Instead, the students can focus on the fingering chart, posture, breathing, and tone. The exercises are found in the online portion of this textbook, but I have included two of them here as examples of what you can find in the online textbook.

EXERCISES 35.1 AND 35.2

Start by playing the left-hand notes B♮, A♮, and G♮ in the staff, and also F♯, which adds the pointer finger of the right hand. I have added lots of measures for breathing so that students can catch their breath. They can also breathe between whole notes if necessary. I included two whole notes for students each time so that if the note doesn't respond the first time, they have time to prepare and try again for the second whole note. The measure of rest for the teacher is an opportunity to teach breathing out and in over measured counts with comfort and ease so that students will feel a sense of routine breathing before the next entry.

EXERCISES 35.3 AND 35.4

Add an ascending note with a C♮ or a descending note to F♯ in the staff, and then continue descending to low D. For these exercises, focus on hand position with control in the left-hand pointer finger and thumb as they hold the oboe. The left-hand pointer finger stays rounded and off the wood of the oboe. Only the first joint of the finger is on the first key. The right-hand fingers stay rounded and over the keys. The right hand can be as rounded as if you are holding a soda can. The fingers only touch the oboe when they are playing a specific note. The left pinky hovers over the A♭ key, and the right pinky hovers over the low C key.

FIGURE 35.1 Exercise 35.4

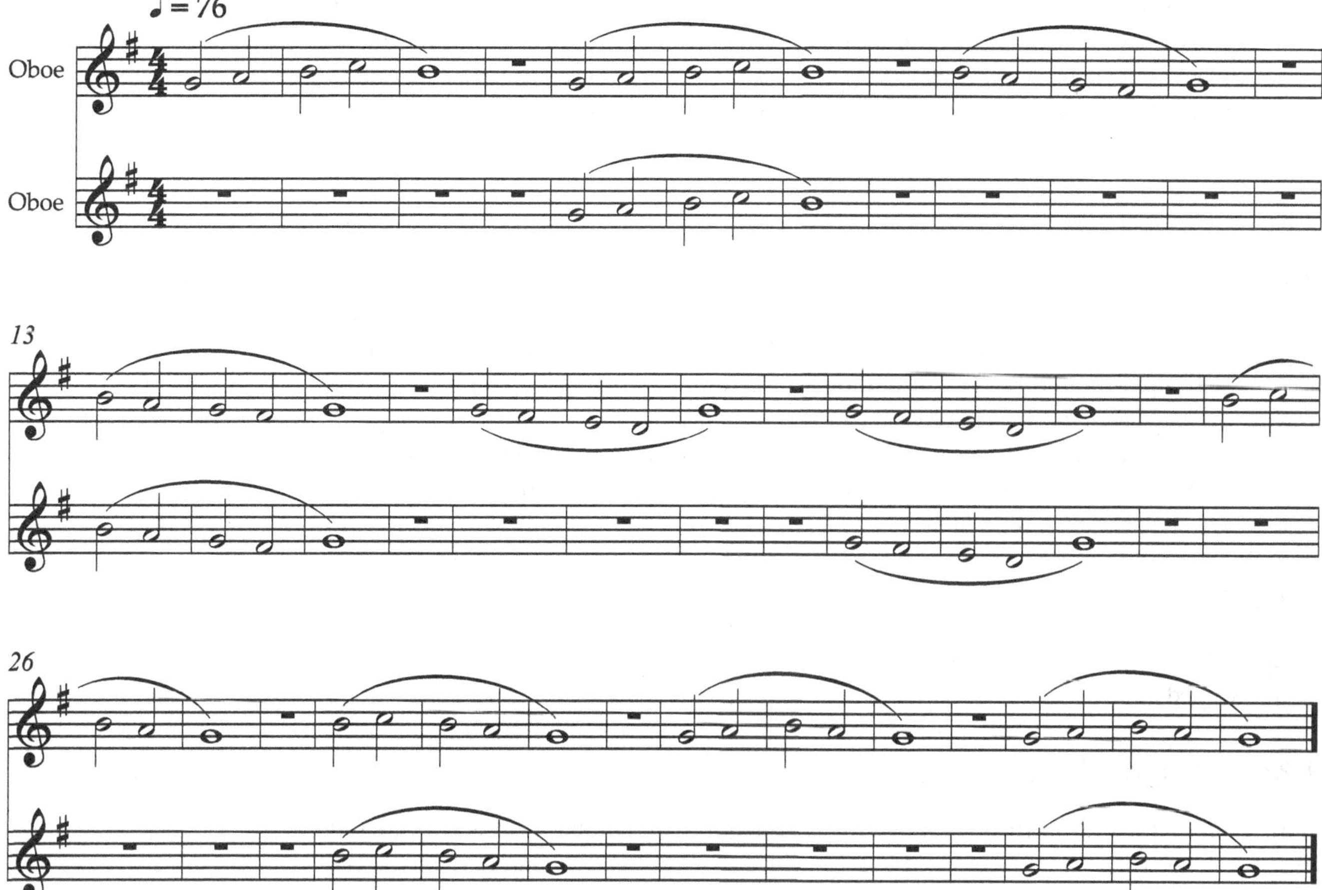

EXERCISE 35.5

Teach the half-hole on the oboe by using C♯ and D♮. The only movement between C♯ and D♮ is the right-hand pinky finger, so keep the right pinky over the C♯ key. The student has to coordinate many fingers when moving from C♯ to B. Having the knowledge of the simplicity of C♯ to D helps the student grasp the correct fingerings of these notes quickly.

EXERCISE 35.6 AND 35.7

Demonstrate the half-hole with the contrast between C♮ and D♮. Only D♮ needs the half-hole. The left-hand pointer finger stays in contact with the key as it rolls to open the half-hole for D and closes for the other notes. Exercise 7 uses C minor to teach the half-hole notes. This exercise is an opportunity to work on the change from half hole notes to a covered first finger on the left hand for C♮.

EXERCISE 35.8

E♮ and F♯ both need the first octave key. The left thumb rests just below the first octave key, and the student presses the key as needed.

EXERCISE 35.9

This exercise highlights F♮ and its use of the first octave key. This exercise also features half-hole E♭ and half-hole D to help students understand the rocking motion of their left hand to open the half-hole for E♭ and D and then close it again for F. The student must press the first octave key and cover the first tone hole to achieve the F. Their left-hand pointer finger stays in contact with the metal the entire time. They do not lift their finger off of the key but instead roll it open for the hole to vent. I am leaving whole measures open for breathing in order to practice relaxed and effective breathing and embouchure placement.

EXERCISE 35.10

This exercise is devised to allow the student to practice the difference between the two octave keys. The first four measures isolate correct intonation and placement of the higher register. Only use the second octave key for the first seven measures. The second octave key is used to play A♮ and B♮. The second octave key does not need the first octave key to be pressed to play A and B. The thumb can rest on the wood just under the first octave. In this exercise, the thumb is needed only for the first octave G♯ in measure 28. From measure 23 to the end, students are able to isolate and practice the change from the first octave key to the second octave key.

EXERCISE 35.11

A natural, B flat, and high C natural all use the second octave key. The first octave key is not needed at all.

EXERCISE 35.12

This exercise focuses on the second octave in A major, with emphasis on A natural and B natural and with some usage of G♯ and F♯ with the first octave. No use of the half-hole makes this a nice exercise of just the first and second octaves.

FIGURE 35.2 Exercise 35.12

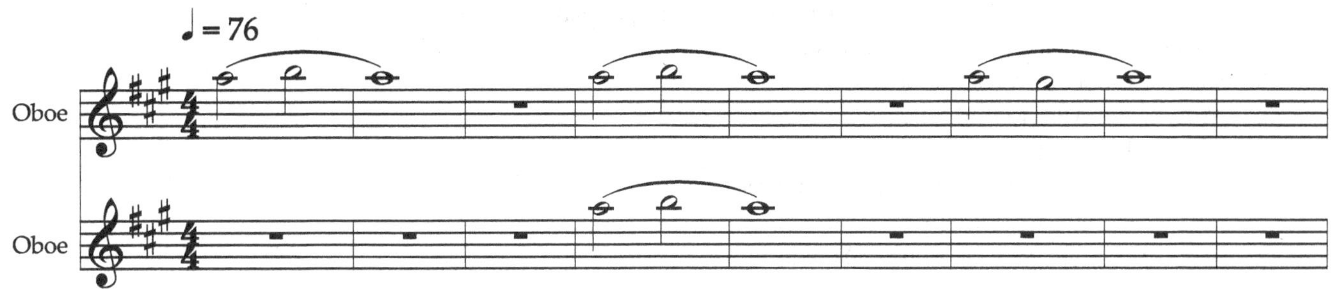

35.5 Exercises or Warm-Ups That Build Technique and Tone

1. Long tones
2. Ninths that resolve to the octave
3. Slurred major and minor scales in eighth notes throughout the range of the oboe. (I created an eighth-note pattern as a scale page, and it is available with this textbook's online materials. I created the scale page to offer plenty of clearly marked rests for breathing.) Playing slurred major and minor scales through the range of the student's ability in even eighth notes is a terrific way to create an even legato and sound concept throughout the notes on the oboe. I do not include a tempo marking or desired tempo goal, as I hope the students will find a freedom of expression and tone through this method of playing scales.

35.6 Lesson Ideas to Build Creative Musicianship

1. When students are learning notes, rhythms, or time signatures, I like to have them improvise around the new materials. Then I have them write their ideas into a brief melody of at least thirty-two measures.
2. Learning modes is a wonderful addition to the sound concepts that students encounter when they begin a new instrument. I teach students the Dorian, Phrygian, Lydian, Mixolydian, and Locrian modes with the first-space F♮ as the starting note, ascending to F at the top of the staff as the highest note and descending to F as the ending note of the mode.

3. There are many unaccompanied solo compositions for the oboe. The following list is just a brief selection of works demonstrating the variety of music found in this genre that can be accessible relatively early on in learning to play the oboe.
   a. *Circle of Memories*, by Rosalind Carlson
   b. Solo for Oboe, by Vivian Fine
   c. *Nuances*, by Alberto Guidobaldi
   d. *Absence*, by Mathieu Lussier
   e. *In Adoration of the Earth*, by Kathryn Potter
   f. *Arc en ciel*, by Kathryn Potter
   g. ". . . Is But a Dream," by Roupen Shakarian

35.7 Accommodation and Adaptations

1. An incredible resource for students who need adaptations for their instruments is an oboe repairperson. Repairmen and repairwomen have made adjustments to instruments throughout instrument making, and they know ways to accommodate an oboe (or English horn) for a student or professionals. They can also refer you to other repairpersons they know who can offer insight into a community of a wealth of knowledge capable of helping students find instruments that have been accommodated before for other people, and those repair ideas can serve them as well. Oboists buy and sell oboes fairly regularly, so it is possible to find an instrument that has been accommodated for someone else that can serve the needs of a new student oboist.
2. The availability of a wide variety of reed sellers offers an excellent opportunity in accommodation for young oboists. It is possible to purchase reed subscriptions, in which several reeds are mailed regularly to the student so that they are able always to have working reeds. My students who purchased three reeds every month have the greatest success as beginners in finding reeds that suit their personal embouchure. Students quickly learn what does and what doesn't work well for them. Once they find a reed maker who makes reeds that they like, they can purchase reeds regularly from small businesses online and have oboe reeds mailed right to their homes.
3. The weight of the oboe resting on the right thumb can present enormous challenges for students and professionals alike. There are a variety of products that can be purchased that can accommodate and aid the performer's hand position.
   a. Lorée adjustable thumb rest; connects to the oboe and lets the distance of the right thumb be adjusted to create a perfect fit for the individual's right hand.
   b. Lorée Dutch thumb rest.
   c. ERG-Oboe: Oboe and English horn support.
   d. Stick Support: attaches to the thumb rest; the stick descends from the oboe to rest on the chair where the musician is seated. It adjusts from ten inches to eighteen inches and weighs less than three and a half ounces.
   e. Floor peg: takes all of the weight of the instrument off the arms. It mounts securely to the oboe, hooks to the thumb rest, and is secured to the bell with an elastic strap.
   f. Protec Gel: thumb rest cushion.
   g. Neck straps made of elastic or nylon.
   h. Simple thumb rests such as the Thumbsaver can also add extra cushion to the oboe's thumb rest.

35.8 Discussion Questions

1. In techniques class, take the time to look at everyone's reeds on the first day before you start playing on them. What do the reed openings look like? Inspect your own reed. Is it easy to make a sound on the reed alone? This sound is called the "peep" of the reed. Can you make the reed peep easily?
2. Reexamine the reeds a few class sessions into the semester (maybe later the first week or at the start of the second week). How have the reeds changed? Are they easier or harder to play on? What can your instructor tell you about the changes that have taken place in the reed?
3. What orchestral works or wind ensemble compositions have you performed or listened to that offer sections featuring the oboe? Create a listening list as a class.

35.9 Suggested Activities

- Follow university oboe professors and their oboe studios around the country on Instagram and Facebook while participating in the oboe techniques class. You will see some of the greatest creative oboe minds of our day teaching and reaching out to oboe students.
- Attend an oboe recital at your university or at a nearby school.
- Watch a livestreamed performance of an oboe professor from a school of music at a leading university.

OXFORD learning link

Visit the online resources for additional documentation and exercises to help expand learning and test your knowledge further: www.oup.com/he/powell_music1e.

CHAPTER 36

PEDAGOGIES FOR TEACHING BASSOON

Robin Hochkeppel

This chapter presents a practical approach to starting a young student on the bassoon. The prospect of starting young students on the bassoon is undeniably a daunting one for novice and experienced music teachers alike. Owing to the complicated nature of the instrument, limited pedagogical training, and the fact that often only one player is started at a time, many teachers simply send beginning bassoon students to the practice room with a book and a fingering chart to learn on their own. It does not have to be this way. This chapter will unravel the mystifying reputation the bassoon has earned by presenting a practical pedagogical approach from someone who has been that middle school kid who started on the bassoon as well as a teacher starting her own students.

36.1 Introduction to the Bassoon

The knowledge required to start a beginner on the bassoon is not as complicated as one might imagine. This section focuses on ten instrument concerns as well as descriptions of accessories your students will need to get started.

INSTRUMENT BRANDS

As with any instrument, providing your students with a quality horn in working condition is a vital key to their success. Students commonly use school-owned instruments, which are often cheaper brands frequently neglected because of a lack of players, and almost certainly have fallen into disrepair. Because of its complicated mechanism, a bassoon that is out of adjustment can quickly become a nightmare that will frustrate your students into quitting before they have started. Providing your students with a well-built, quality instrument is ideal, but if you are stuck with what you have, I cannot stress enough having an experienced bassoon player test the horns you have. Even a talented high school student can judge an instrument's playability, needed repairs, and fickle tendencies. It is my experience that if you cannot upgrade, with a little bit of work almost any bassoon can transform into an acceptable working instrument for beginning students.

WOODEN VERSUS PLASTIC

Middle school kids are tough on their instruments, and the durability of plastic outweighs the minuscule tone differences between a plastic instrument and a wooden bassoon. For high school and beyond, wood is preferable, although I have had college students play on plastic bassoons with great success.

STRING-WRAPPED TENONS VERSUS CORK TENONS

A tenon is the smaller end of an instrument's joint, which fits onto the connecting socket. A solid fit of the tenon to the socket is vital to the playability of the instrument. There is much discussion among bassoonists on the pros and cons of string-wrapped tenons versus cork tenons, but the choice is personal and may depend on experience and/or climate. Refer to Table 36.1 for comparisons between string-wrapped and cork tenons.

TABLE 36.1 STRING-WRAPPED TENONS VERSUS CORK TENONS

String Pros	String Cons
Strengthens the tenons More flexible with weather changes String can be added or removed to adjust for swelling/shrinkage Generates a more resonant sound	String often comes undone and is easily pulled off if tampered with Adding/removing string can be difficult and require a repairman String-wrapped tenon joints are often tapered, so they must be pushed in all the way in order to stay put; no leeway for pitch adjustment Requires paraffin wax for lubrication, which is more cumbersome to apply than cork grease
Cork Pros	**Cork Cons**
• Less maintenance • Can seal better than string • Uses common cork grease for lubrication	• Structurally weaker than string • Can shrink or swell with weather changes; may require sanding or replacement • Generates a less resonant sound

ADAPTED BASSOONS

If you are starting younger students on the bassoon, I recommend purchasing an adapted bassoon, which is specifically designed for smaller hands. They include fewer keys, adjusted tone holes, extended plateau keys, and added roller keys that aid in smooth transitions between notes. Choose this option if you're sure these bassoons will never be used by older, more advanced students.

BODY LOCK

Some models are equipped with locking mechanisms that hold the wing and long joint together. This is optional and not standard.

WHISPER KEY LOCK

The whisper key lock, whose location depends on the model, is a highly useful mechanism which, as its name indicates, locks the whisper key down. The whisper key is the octave key on the bassoon (although it operates in the opposite way of the clarinet register key and the saxophone octave key-pushed down for low notes and lifted for high notes). The lock's function is to eliminate the continuous return to the whisper key when playing low-note passages;

this is fabulous for advanced players but complicated for beginners, because the mechanism can lock accidentally, making it difficult to produce high notes. If your bassoon has a whisper lock, educate your students on the possibility of accidental locking.

HAND REST OR CRUTCH

A hand rest or crutch is a small curved piece that attaches to the boot joint, providing stability to the right hand. This is an optional accessory, and its use is a personal choice that can depend on the player's hand size.

BOCAL

The bocal is the neckpiece of the bassoon which attaches to the wing joint and holds the reed. It is usually made of nickel silver and can make a huge difference in a bassoon's tone and intonation. A quality bocal can make a bad bassoon sound good, and a cheap or damaged bocal can make a good bassoon sound bad. Additionally, bocals come in varying lengths, which can drastically affect the intonation of a bassoon.

SEAT STRAP VERSUS NECK STRAP

I much prefer seat straps for securing the bassoon. A neck strap is hard on the neck, provides little stability, and makes the bassoon very difficult to hold up. A seat strap anchors the bassoon at the bottom, as opposed to the middle, and prevents the instrument from swinging back and forth erratically. Four variations of seat straps are discussed below.

Clip-On

This is my preferred method of attaching a seat strap. It requires that the boot protector cap have a small hole at the bottom in which a metal ring is attached. (I use ordinary binder rings.) The seat strap is then clipped onto the ring, as shown in Figure 36.1.

FIGURE 36.1 **Bassoon with clip-on strap**

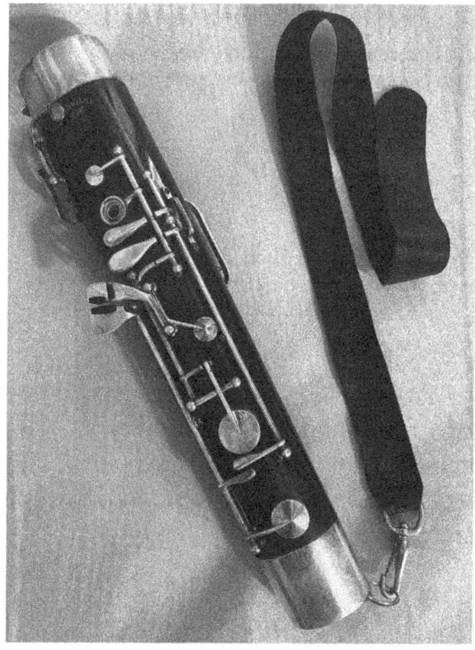

Boot Ring

This is used if the boot protector cap does not have a hole to clip a strap to. It is a large metal ring that slips over the boot and is tightened to stay put. The seat strap clips or hooks onto the metal ring. In my experience, the ring does not stay tightened and ends up moving up and down annoyingly.

Cup

This strap can also be used if the boot cup doesn't have a hole. A leather cup slips over the boot and is a sturdy option, although somewhat risky for young students, because the bassoon can slip out of the cup. Additionally, the cup can interfere with some of the lower keys.

Hook

A seat strap with a hook is the least desirable for young students. It is designed to hook into the hole in the boot cap. The problem is that it comes unhooked easily, leaving the bassoon at risk of crashing to the floor.

REEDS

In this section I will discuss four considerations: brands, composition, cases, and soaking containers.

Brands

Handmade reeds are preferable, but if it is not possible to acquire them, get a recommendation from a bassoon player in the area who can direct you where to get good-quality reeds.

Composition

Most players still play on cane reeds, which are made from natural materials, but synthetic reeds are definitely worth looking into. Synthetic reeds are made from composite materials and are intended to duplicate the sound of a cane reed. There have been many advances in synthetic reeds, and although the initial investment is greater, they will last much longer than a cane reed.

Storage Case

For added protection and to facilitate drying, reeds should be stored in a small case designed to hold at least four bassoon reeds (see Figure 36.2).

Soaking Container

In order to vibrate fully, reeds should be soaked in water for about as long as it takes to put the instrument together. Small containers are preferred, because the reed needs only about three-quarters of an inch of water—just enough to soak the blade almost up to the first wire. You can find specialized reed-soaking containers with music stand clips online for minimal cost (see Figure 36.2).

FIGURE 36.2 Reed storage case, soaking container with stand clip and basic reed tools

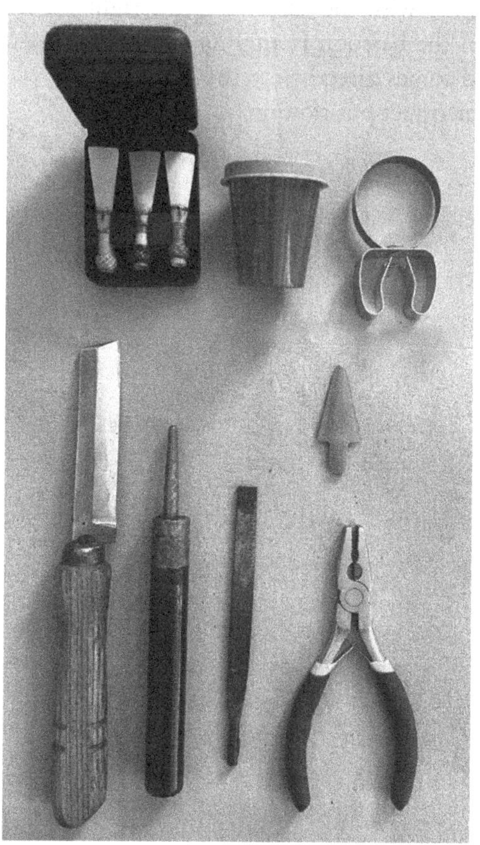

36.2 Teaching Beginning Bassoonists

You have an instrument, tested and repaired, complete with bocal, seat strap, a good-quality reed, and a soaking container. What's next? This section will demystify the process of starting that young bassoon student, addressing eleven different considerations.

ASSEMBLY

The bassoon breaks down into five main sections: the bocal, the boot, the long joint, the wing joint, and the bell. When assembling the bassoon, care should be taken not to bend the long rods. Cork grease (or paraffin wax for string) should be applied if there is resistance.

Set the boot joint firmly on the ground or on a chair. Attach the long joint first, then the wing joint (watch out for the long rods and whisper bridge key), then the bell (open the bridge key on the bell before inserting). The long joint and the wing joint can be attached at the same time only if there is a body lock. The bocal is attached last and should be aligned so the whisper key pad meets and seals the whisper hole. Great care should be taken when handling the bocal, which should be stressed to your young students from the beginning, as even minor dents can affect sound and intonation. Bends in the bocal are particularly menacing and difficult or impossible to repair. Students should be taught to always grab the bocal at the top of the bend to insert it in the instrument. When walking with their bassoon, the bocal should be stored in the bell.

BODY POSITION

Students should sit all the way back in the chair (never on the edge), chin up, eyes forward. The seat strap is placed in the middle of the chair with the bassoon to the right. Adjust the strap (pulling from the end) so that when the bassoon is angling across the body and resting on the side of the right thigh, the reed comes directly into the mouth (see Figure 36.3). Refer to Figure 36.4 for an example of incorrect positioning.

FIGURE 36.3 Correct body positioning

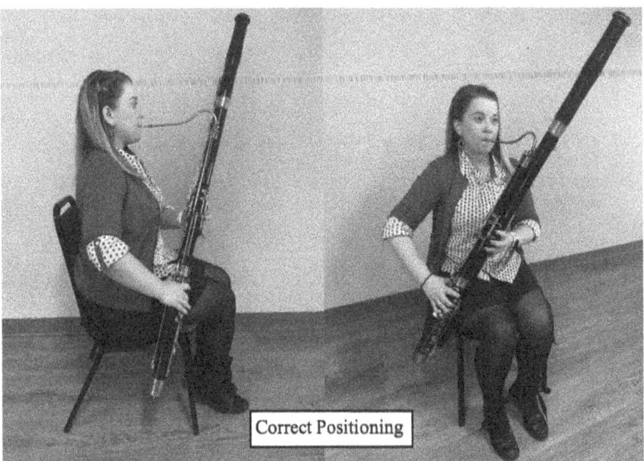

FIGURE 36.4 Incorrect body positioning

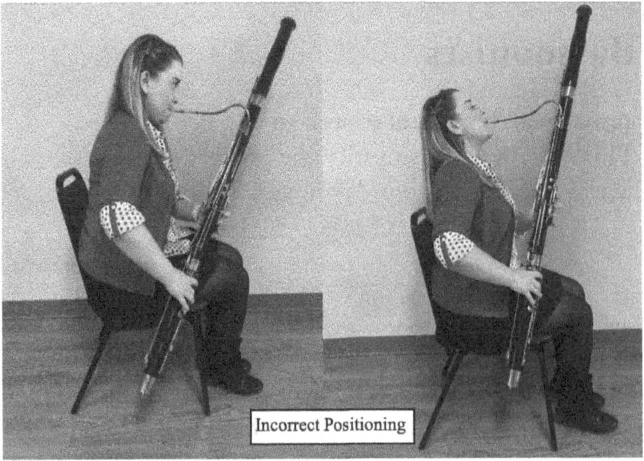

HAND POSITION

I use the following visuals to describe to my students how their hands should be formed around the instrument:

- Hamburger hands: pretend you're holding a triple-decker burger with both hands wrapped around it.
- Softball hands: shape your hand like you are holding a softball.
- Ballet hands: relaxed and curved.

EMBOUCHURE

When teaching the mystery of bassoon embouchure to young students, I try not to over explain. A short verbal description with a demonstration is all that's needed—it almost always happens naturally. It's just a matter of making a seal on the reed with the lips in an "o" so that air does not escape. The lips act as pillows, cushioning the teeth and providing firm, equal pressure all the way around the reed. Some approaches emphasize pulling the chin way back, creating an extreme overbite. In my opinion, the natural overbite is sufficient. Refer to Figure 36.5 for examples of correct and incorrect embouchure.

FIGURE 36.5 **Demonstration of correct and incorrect embouchure**

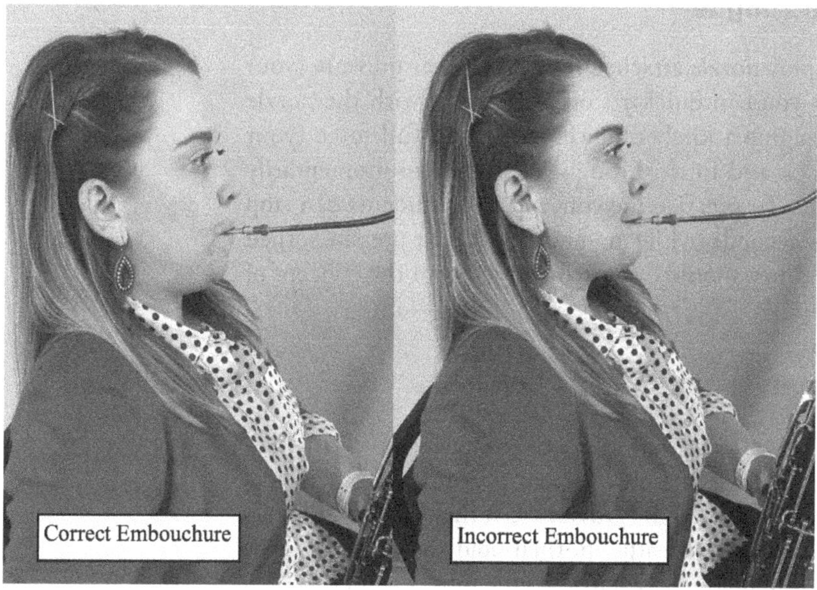

TEACHING EMBOUCHURE WITH THE WHISTLE/YAWN APPROACH

- Practice first without the reed. Place the index finger on the bottom lip, roll the lips over the teeth and form them around your finger in an "o" like you are whistling. Then yawn, keeping lips in the whistle form, cushioning the finger. This will pull the tongue down and open the mouth cavity, as if there's a golf ball in it.
- Use the same process with the reed, making sure to take at least three-quarters of the blade in the mouth. (The blade is the shaved part of the reed.)
- Breathe through the corners of the mouth and try to "crow" on the reed. (A "crow" is the multi-pitched sound that a reed makes when adjusted appropriately and/or the player is taking in the proper amount of reed.)
- Attach the reed to the bocal, hold the bocal at the bend, then repeat the process. Be sure the entry angle of the reed is straight into the mouth, not approaching from above or below.
- Attach the bocal to the bassoon and repeat.

BREATHING/AIR INTAKE

The bassoon takes a lot of air to create a big, full, resonant sound. I teach my students to breathe through the mouth so they can feel the cold air rushing into their lungs and to take in enough air to dive into a swimming pool and swim the length of the pool without coming up for a breath.

TONGUING

Tonguing should be taught to beginning band students in the first weeks of playing. If you don't introduce it early, it will not be a part of the natural process. The top of the tip of the tongue should touch the tip of the bottom blade of the reed. The tongue should not touch both blades in the center, nor should the back of the tongue be used. The tongue should be a minuscule interruption of the air pressure, just for the separation of notes. When learning to tongue, I first have my students practice without making a sound, just a "tuh tuh tuh" on the reed. After this is mastered, we add sound. When you teach tonguing, it's best to begin the note without using the tongue. The process of starting the tone with the tongue should follow soon after.

Separating the Notes with the Tongue

Tonguing is like using a hose with a spray nozzle attached to it. The water pressure (your airflow) is always on (sustained), but you can quickly stop and start it with the nozzle valve (your tongue). You can also imagine a kitchen faucet turned on full force (your airstream), then flick your fingers back and forth through the stream to momentarily interrupt the water flow (your tongue). To practice the concept, your students can stop the sound with their tongues for a few seconds (while maintaining the air pressure), then gradually decrease the stopping time. They should eventually understand the concept of separation but with notes still "touching."

Starting a Note with the Tongue

The concept that the tone on a wind instrument starts with the tongue is not really correct. Tone starts with the air, not the tongue. But a tone needs a starting point to avoid a vague and airy beginning, and that is what the tongue provides. On the bassoon, students should form the embouchure around the reed, breathe in, then hold the tongue on the reed. With sustained air pressure, the tongue is released to start the tone. Practice in slow motion, then speed up.

FINGERINGS AND FIRST NOTES

The fingering system on the bassoon is similar to the fingerings of the clarinet in the chalumeau register. If you are familiar with clarinet fingerings, it is just a matter of learning the few differences to get your student started. There are a lot of outdated and inaccurate finger charts out there, so I am once again recommending that you take yours to an experienced bassoon player for corrections and suggestions.

First Notes

The bassoon is the only band instrument that uses all ten fingers and thumbs to activate the keys. The thumbs alone are in charge of nine keys in the left hand and four in the right. This is a daunting notion for student and teacher alike! Never fear; the first notes are not much more difficult than on any other woodwind instrument. Additionally, the bassoon overblows at the octave, which provides some ease as students learn an expanded range.

Starting Students without a Method Book

Most beginning band method books start in the key of B♭, which has the bassoon learning B♭ and E♭ for their first notes. In a perfect world, my bassoon students would start in the key of C, where there are no accidentals to worry about. Students can start on F3 (just the whisper key) and simply add one finger at a time to walk all the way down to a low F2, easily concentrating on covering holes and producing good sounds. Simple songs can be learned by ear, giving students speedy success and confidence in the early stages.

Half-Hole

"*More half-hole!*" is a phrase I can often be heard exclaiming to my bassoon students of all ages. The half-hole is an octave key of sorts and enables a low note to pop an octave higher. When a player does not expose enough opening, an ugly, growly note somewhere between the two octaves occurs. The bassoon has three notes in the midrange that require the half-hole: F♯3, G3, and G♯3. Slide the left-hand first finger down until the note sounds clear and plays the correct octave (see Figure 36.6).

FIGURE 36.6 **"More half-hole!"**

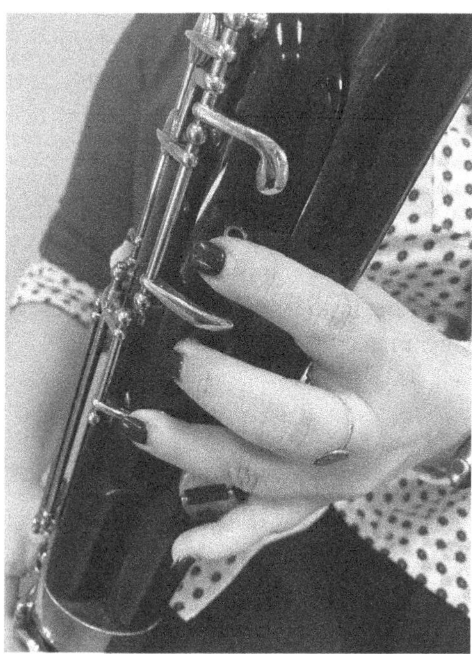

The rule is, whenever the half-hole is utilized, the whisper key is down. An exercise for practicing half-hole technique is illustrated in Figure 36.7.

FIGURE 36.7 **Half-hole technique exercise**

Note: If your students learned recorder in elementary school, they may already possess the half-hole technique that applies to bassoon!

INTONATION

In young students, poor intonation can be caused by many factors. Six common causes and solutions are discussed here.

Instrument

Bassoons are fickle instruments, and individual horns can have notes that are just out of tune. As mentioned previously, upgrading the quality as well as having a bassoon player try your instruments to determine pitch tendencies will save you a lot of grief.

Bocal

As mentioned in the bocal section, bocal length can affect overall intonation.

Reed

The reed can most definitely affect intonation. A reed that's too soft or too long will play flat, while reeds that are too hard or too short will play sharp. Tips for adjustment can be found in the reed adjustment section.

Embouchure

In general, the embouchure should adjust throughout the range of the instrument: looser, with a dropped jaw, for low notes ("ahh"); firmer for high notes ("ee"). Individual notes can be tweaked in either direction using this same concept. Beginning students often play flat because they have not mastered the firm "o" embouchure.

Air Support

As with any instrument, if the player is not using enough air support, intonation will suffer. Have your students take full breaths through the mouth and support the sound with consistent air.

Vent Keys

The bassoon has two vent keys on the wing joint that can be pressed to improve intonation and resonance dramatically. For resonance and pitch, add either key to E♭3. The top key added to G3 will improve intonation tenfold. These keys are also added to high notes as a student's range expands (see Figure 36.8).

FIGURE 36.8 **Vent keys**

FLICKING

Flicking, which is actually quickly tapping a key with the left thumb, is a concept that you may or may not want to teach in the first year, depending on your student. It is used for two purposes: (1) to "vent" certain notes to alleviate cracking, and (2) to enable slurring from a low note to certain high notes that don't require the whisper key. A2 is a note that I always flick to ensure that it won't crack. Additionally, I flick whenever I slur to a B♭2, B2, C2, or D2. The high A key (third left-hand thumb key) is flicked for A and B♭, and the high C key (fourth left-hand thumb key) is flicked for B, C, and D. To teach flicking, I use a systematic, slow-to-fast approach and use the word "tap" to calm down the motion. Refer to Figure 36.9 for some suggested exercises for practicing flicking.

FIGURE 36.9 **Suggested exercises for practicing flicking**

VIBRATO

Vibrato is an advanced concept, generally not required until a student is performing soloistic literature, and in my opinion, should not be taught until a student has mastered embouchure and tone. Bassoon vibrato is produced from the diaphragm and is a combination of relaxed intensity and lowered pitch.

BASSOON CARE AND CLEANING

General

- Never leave the instrument in extreme heat or cold.
- To prevent moisture from soaking the wood and penetrating the pads, try not to lay the bassoon flat during rests or after playing unless you swab it first.

- Always pick the bassoon up with one hand on the boot joint and one on the wing and long joint.
- Do not prop the instrument against a wall!

Cleaning and Swabbing the Instrument

It is very important that a bassoon be swabbed on a regular basis. Moisture is detrimental to the instrument as well as the pads. All joints should be swabbed, but the boot joint, which is a "u," will quickly fill with moisture and should always be cleaned after playing. To clean, pour the water out, drop a weighted silk swab into the bigger hole, rotate the boot so the swab snakes around the "u," then carefully pull the swab through. Avoid the fluffy stick swabs that you either push down into the joints or (gasp) actually leave in the joints in the case. Not only do the fibers come off and muck up the bassoon, but one can certainly understand the perils of storing a wet swab inside your instrument. Figure 36.10 shows an acceptable silk swab.

FIGURE 36.10 Bassoon swab and bocal cleaning items

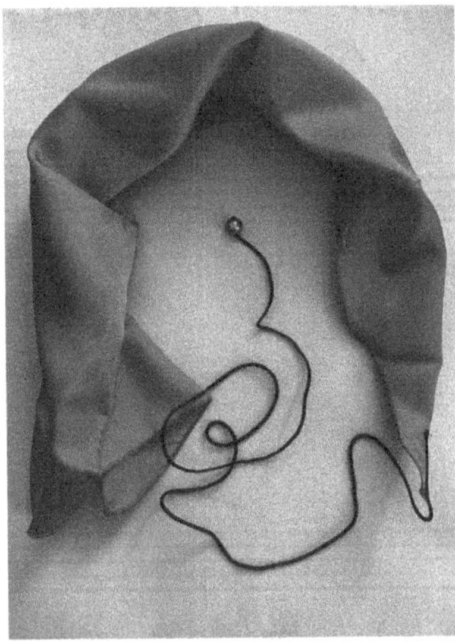

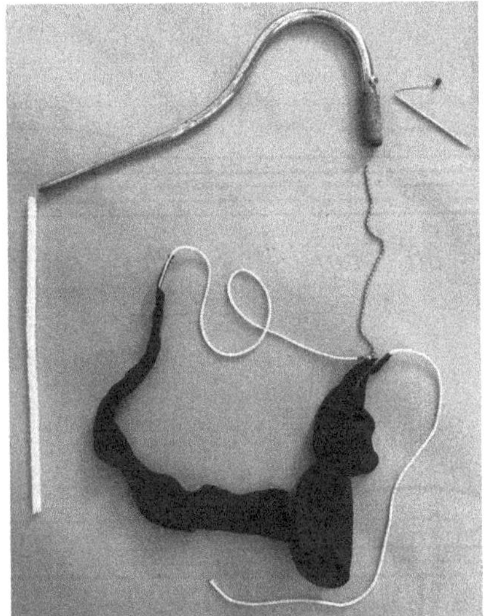

Cleaning and Swabbing the Bocal

To clean the bocal, use a bocal brush, pipe cleaner, or bocal swab and occasionally run warm water through it while being careful not to saturate the cork. The bocal pip (the metal bubble which juts out from the bocal and bridges the whisper key) can become clogged, which will affect a player's ability to produce the upper octave. A toothpick or straight pin carefully inserted into the hole will clear the opening (see Figure 36.10 for bocal cleaning items).

Cleaning and Swabbing the Reed

Reeds can and should be cleaned often, but for young students this is a risky activity, so I would suggest allowing only a warm-water rinse. For older students I suggest the following:

- Pour equal parts water and peroxide in a small bowl.
- Add about half an ounce of mouthwash.
- Soak the reeds in this mixture until the foaming subsides.
- Use a soft toothbrush to brush from the wire to the tip, removing debris from the grain.

REED ADJUSTMENT

The discussion of reed adjustment really would take up another whole book and requires a reed specialist to teach. However, there are small adjustments anyone can perform that can make a big difference in response.

Tip Opening

The number 1 adjustment I perform on my students' reeds involves the tip. If the tip is too closed (most common), the blades cannot vibrate, and no sound will come out. Too open, and the sound will be harsh and hard to play. To open the tip, gently push the sides of the reed at the first wire with fingers or small pliers, being careful not to split the reed with too much pressure. To close, do the opposite, pushing from the top and bottom of the first wire.

Shaving

With a little bit of knowledge, a good reed knife, and a plaque (a small, arrowhead-shaped piece that separates the blades for easy shaving), you can quickly make your students' hard reeds playable. The most basic thing you can do to adjust a hard reed is to evenly shave the entire reed, one small layer at a time. Test and repeat until it's just right. If the reed knife intimidates you, you can shave a reed with a small flat file or even fine sandpaper. Refer to Figure 36.2 for an example of simple bassoon tools.

36.3 Conclusion

My hope in writing this chapter is that the information provided will demystify starting young bassoonists and will encourage you to jump right in and start one or two. In my experience, you won't regret it. I cannot emphasize how much a strong, well-taught low-reed section, complete with bassoons, bass clarinets, contrabass clarinets, and low saxophones, will complement your low brass section and add beautiful resonance and fullness to your band's sound. Good luck!

36.4 Discussion Questions

1. Would you recommend plastic or wooden bassoons, and why?
2. Illustrate the pros and cons of string-wrapped versus corked bassoon tenons.
3. Is a neck strap or a seat strap the preferred method for holding a bassoon?
4. Describe the process of teaching bassoon embouchure to a beginner.
5. What are some easy reed adjustments that even a novice can perform on a bassoon reed for improved performance?
6. What is flicking for?
7. Should young students use vibrato? Why or why not?

OXFORD learning link

Visit the online resources for additional documentation and exercises to help expand learning and test your knowledge further: www.oup.com/he/powell_music1e.

CHAPTER 37

PEDAGOGIES FOR TEACHING SAXOPHONE

Nathan Holder

This chapter provides an overview of concepts and pedagogies for teaching the saxophone to beginning instrumentalists.

37.1 Introduction

The saxophone is one of the most iconic instruments in the world. Since it was invented in 1846 by the serial Belgian inventor Adolphe Sax, it has been used in a wide range of styles around the world. From the altissimo of Alex Han to the articulation of Tia Fuller, the saxophone has captured the imaginations of many. Believe it or not, there are over fifteen different types of saxophones, including the sopranos, altos, tenors, and baritones that many are familiar with. Lesser-known instruments such as saxellos, slide saxophones, conusaxes, and manzellos make up a family of instruments that musicians have made incredible music on for many years.

37.2 Setting Up the Saxophone

Help your students start their journey on the saxophone smoothly by helping them to understand how to set up and maintain their instrument. By advising them on reeds, ligatures, and mouthpieces and how they all work together, students can start quickly and efficiently. Perhaps most important, sharing this information can help students to take more control over their learning and develop their understanding of the instrument.

REEDS

Reeds come in different sizes depending on which saxophone you play. They are usually made from cane, a natural material, which means that no two reeds are the same. They will need to be replaced often (depending on usage), and since they are thin pieces of cane, they need to be treated with care. Many new students may need reminding that playing on a broken or chipped reed can lead to frustration: when the saxophone might squeak, or it might become difficult to produce a decent sound from the instrument. There are synthetic reeds available too, which last longer but feel very different from cane.

Reeds are generally graded by numbers according to how thick they are. The thinnest are graded 1, and they get thicker and stronger in 0.5 increments (1.5, 2, 2.5, 3, 3.5, etc). A common misconception is that the more advanced a player becomes, the thicker the reed needs to be. However, the relationship between a saxophonist and their reed is more about the quality of tone than how well someone can play. Every reed is different, and the more experienced players become, the quicker they will be able to understand the differences between strengths and even brands. Many players will say that in every box of ten reeds, they will find three or four really good ones to play in public, with some being used for practice, and some being thrown away.

To produce sound, a reed needs to vibrate. Moistening the reed before placing it on the mouthpiece helps it to vibrate more effectively. This can be done by placing the reed in water at room temperature, or by placing it in the mouth for up to twenty seconds.

The more advanced a player becomes, the better they will understand their own sound and the sound they want to produce. It should be a part of any teacher's pedagogy to help students understand how to craft the sound they want. This is done not only with the reed, mouthpiece, and ligature combination, but also with the musical environment a student is in or creates.

FIGURE 37.1 Saxophone reed

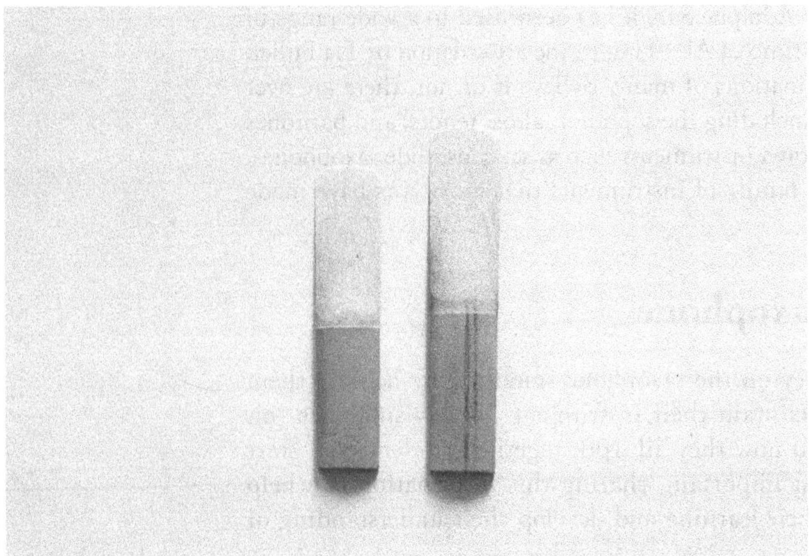

LIGATURES

Ligatures come in different shapes, sizes, and materials. While prices can range from $30 to $300+, with different manufacturers guaranteeing a "warm sound quality" or "control and flexibility," the main job of a ligature is to hold a reed securely onto the mouthpiece. Once a ligature is secured onto a mouthpiece, it should not be able to move.

FIGURE 37.2 Saxophone ligatures

MOUTHPIECES

There are typically two different types of mouthpieces. Those made of ebonite (a hard rubber) are typically a good choice for students attempting to play with darker and warmer tones. The other type of mouthpiece is made of metal, which often offers more projection and edge. Each mouthpiece's characteristic sound is affected by:

- the baffle: the part of the mouthpiece that is directly underneath the reed
- the chamber: the shape and size of the hollow part of the mouthpiece
- the tip opening: the distance between the tip of the mouthpiece and the reed
- the material from which it is made

FIGURE 37.3 Saxophone mouthpieces

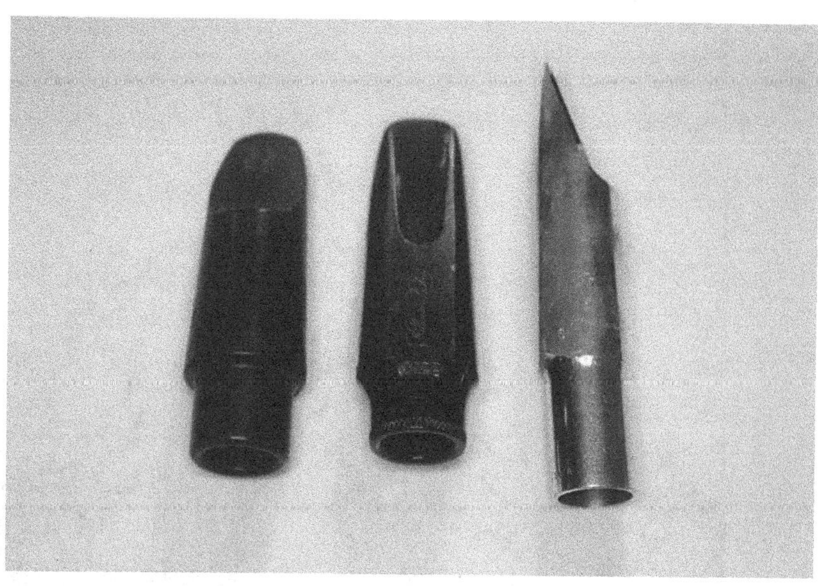

THE SET-UP

By set-up, I am referring to the combination of mouthpiece, reed, and ligature. Over time many saxophonists will change their set-up and in the process collect many mouthpieces and ligatures while searching for the perfect sound. It is important to remember that even the best players in the world are constantly trying to improve their sound, and it can take years for a player to begin to sound the way they want to.

The wider the tip opening, the more air is needed to make the reed vibrate against the mouthpiece and to produce a sound. The thicker the reed, the more air will be needed to make the reed vibrate. For many players, finding the perfect combination is a constant process of trial and error.

STRAP

The strap is there to hold the saxophone in place and relieve pressure on your right thumb. It should be placed around your neck before it is attached to the saxophone. Everyone feels comfortable with different strap lengths, so it is important to adjust the strap according to the individual. Aim to position the strap so that the mouthpiece rests in between the bottom lip and the chin (see Figure 37.4).

SETTING UP THE INSTRUMENT

First, place the ligature over the mouthpiece. Gently take a reed and slide it into place, holding it at its thickest point. When in place, the reed should sit on the mouthpiece, with the thinnest part in line with the edge of the mouthpiece. Turn the screw(s) on the ligature until the reed is securely in place (see Figure 37.5).

FIGURE 37.4 **Saxophone strap**

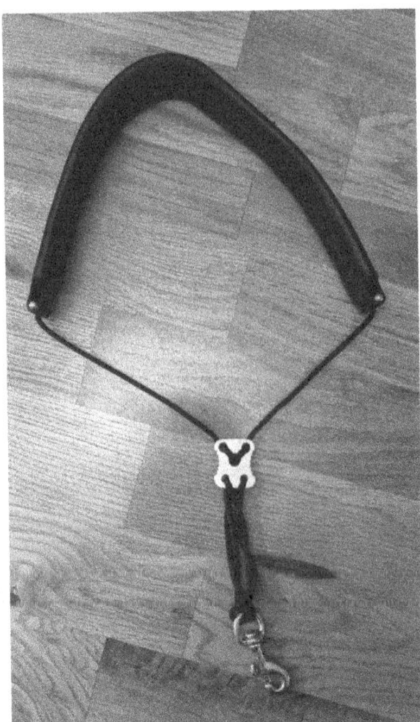

FIGURE 37.5 **Setting up the saxophone**

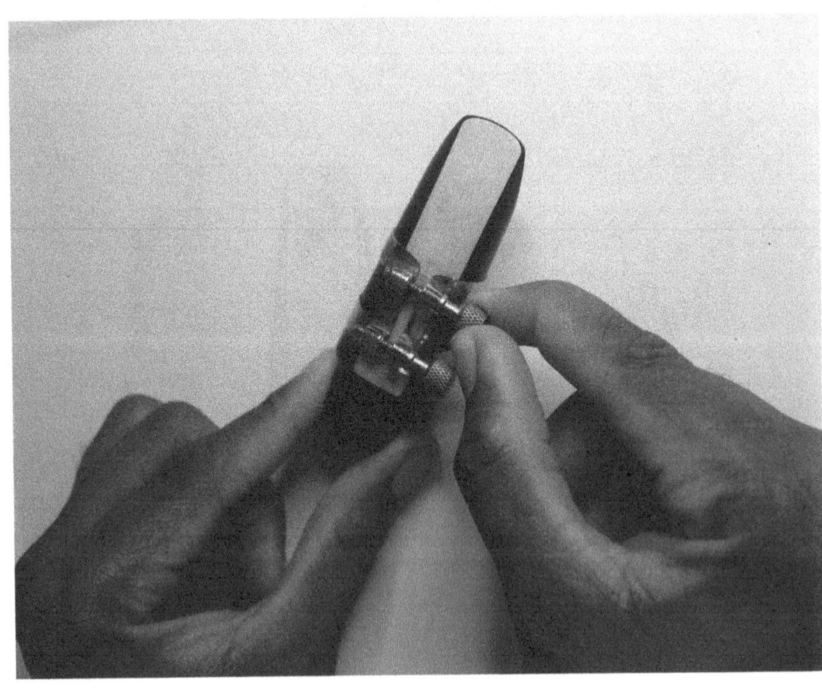

The mouthpiece attaches to the saxophone via the crook (also called the bocal), which is covered by a thin strip of cork. If it is difficult to attach it to the crook, there is special cork grease to help ease it into place. Alternatively, petroleum jelly or similar products will do the same job.

FIGURE 37.6 **Attach the mouthpiece via the crook**

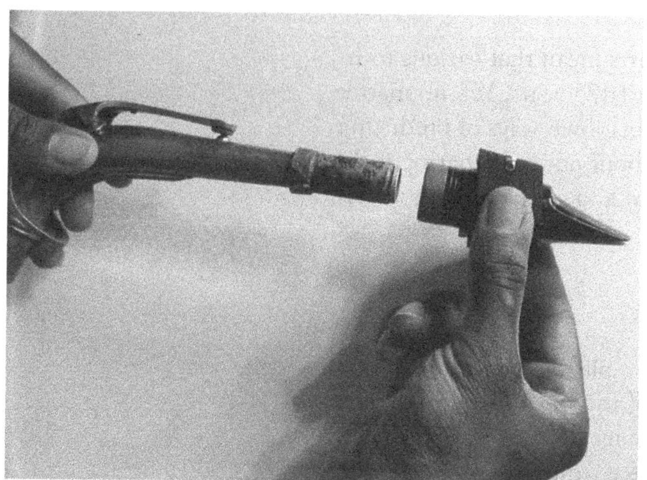

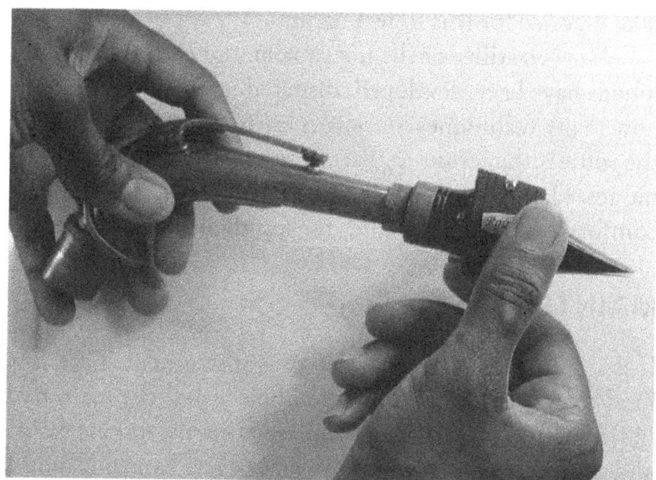

Once the mouthpiece is attached to the crook, put the brass end of the crook into the main body of the saxophone, making sure the pin key sits behind the crook key. By pressing on the octave key with the left thumb, the crook key should move toward the player.

FIGURE 37.7 **Put the brass end of the crook into the main body of the saxophone**

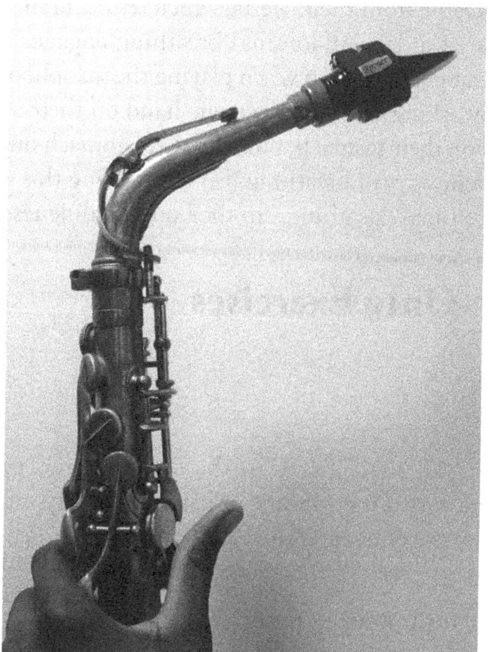

MAKING A SOUND

A good starting point is placing your two front teeth approximately halfway up the mouthpiece, with the bottom lip forming a barrier between the reed and the bottom teeth. There is no one correct embouchure; many players will change theirs slightly according to their mouthpiece, style of tune, or articulation.

To effectively and efficiently produce sound, make sure that no air is escaping from the corners of the mouth. Just as when you are whistling, the breath needs to be concentrated into a small area for enough air to travel through the mouthpiece and down into the rest of the instrument. If air is escaping, less air will be available to help the reed vibrate, which means there will be either a quiet, muffled sound or no sound at all. To correct this, tighten the corners of the mouth while blowing, which may feel almost like smiling. It can take practice for this to feel natural.

The versatility of the instrument and the customizable parts mean that various techniques have been developed, disputed, and adapted over the last 175 years. Yet, no matter how many techniques musicians learn, they will always find their own ways of producing the sounds they want to. Part of teaching this instrument is about not only sharing techniques, ideas, and repertoire that have worked for you, but also allowing a student to feel comfortable to discover and develop their own.

MAINTENANCE

It is important to take care of your instrument. Eating before playing can cause bits of food to get stuck inside the mouthpiece and the main body of the saxophone. The sugar in fizzy drinks and even fruit juices can leave residue inside the instrument, damage pads, and cause keys to stick. It is imperative to clean your mouthpiece regularly with antiseptic (or soap) and water and to clean the inside of the crook with a cleaning cloth. The better care is taken of the instrument, the less maintenance it will need. Try to use a microfiber cloth to help dry your pads every so often. Repairs can be expensive, and money is often cited as a reason students quit their music lessons. With good care and maintenance, a saxophone can last a lifetime.

BREATHING

In everyday life, most people breathe from their chests, which results in many short, shallow breaths throughout the course of a day. Abdominal breathing engages our diaphragms, which allows deeper and more supported breath when playing the saxophone. Help a student to understand the difference by asking them to place one hand on their chest and breathe. Then ask them to place a hand on their stomach, pushing their stomach out while breathing in. Talk about how these different ways of breathing feel when doing this with and without the instrument. See 31.1, "Abdominal Breathing," in the book's online resources.

37.3 Mouthpiece-Only Exercises

TONGUING

Holding just the mouthpiece, put some tissue in the chamber and practice tonguing rhythmically. This can be done with a metronome or listening to any music with a steady pulse. Try playing rhythms like the ones in Figure 37.8.

FIGURE 37.8 Exercise 1 for tonguing practice

These exercises can be expanded to include triplets and dotted rhythms; the metronome marking can also be increased. Adapt them to incorporate tunes and jingles that the student already knows, allowing them to connect familiar rhythms and melodies to the brand-new process of learning the saxophone.

BENDING NOTES

This is a great exercise to help strengthen embouchure. Encourage the student to blow into their mouthpiece, concentrating on maintaining a consistent sound. Experiment by compressing and loosening the jaw to change the pitch of that sound. Learning how to control this movement will help to give greater control when playing with the whole saxophone, and to develop an understanding of how to adjust the embouchure at different points on the saxophone.

LONG TONES

Playing long tones is a tried and trusted method of helping to build tone and strengthen embouchure. The saxophone can be very physically demanding, so working to strengthen the muscles involved in embouchure is incredibly important.

Starting to play long tones can be really useful. Saxophones are transposing instruments, which means that playing a C on a saxophone doesn't sound the same as playing a C on a nontransposing instrument like a piano or steel pan. C on a tenor or soprano saxophone will sound like a B♭ on a piano, and a C on an alto or baritone saxophone will sound like an E♭. A low F♯ is physically halfway up on an alto saxophone, but transposed it is also a concert A (or 440Hz). Using a tuner while playing all the notes on the instrument can help any student make sure that they are staying in tune. Try to start and end notes intentionally, aiming to start and stop the sound with the tongue to create a definite beginning and end. Try to focus on the word "too" and aim for a long, straight, round sound, as visualized in Figure 37.9.

FIGURE 37.9 **Visualize a long, straight sound**

The notes at the extremes of the saxophone are often some of the hardest to get to speak consistently. Practicing long tones on the lowest notes, such as B♭/A♯, B, C, C♯/D♭, and D, not only helps students practice abdominal breathing, but also helps develop their tone quality. Although this exercise sounds very basic, many top saxophonists still play long tones on these notes, expanding the exercise to include overtones, harmonics, and various rhythms. Playing long tones up and down the entire range of the instrument while using a tuner can also be beneficial. As previously noted, the intonation of the saxophone can vary, and this exercise can help to see where adjustments need to be made.

PLAYING IN OCTAVES

When you play higher-pitched notes on the saxophone, slight adjustments in the embouchure will need to be made to keep the saxophone in tune with an equal-temperament chromatic scale (the system which gives us twelve half steps in an octave). By playing simple exercises in octaves with a tuner, students can start to see how pressing the octave key isn't always enough. Small adjustments in the embouchure can help reduce the incidence of sharp and flat notes.

FIGURE 37.10 Playing in octaves

FROM C♯/D♭ TO D

For many, the notes which require the most fingers are the most difficult to play. This is because breath has to travel further for the air to escape and produce sound. When moving from middle C to middle D, extra support is required to not only produce the note, but to keep it in tune with the rest of the instrument. See the supplemental website for simple exercises to help strengthen the transition between octaves.

37.4 Playing by Ear

Not being able to read music staff notation is one of the biggest barriers to learning any instrument. While Western classical notation has become the default notation system used in many places around the world, many more musicians play by ear than read this specific type of notation. As a saxophone teacher, the default is often to immediately start to show a student a G (for example), instruct them to play it with a simple rhythm, and then slowly add an A, B, F and so on. This strategy has worked for many, but there are other ways to approach learning the saxophone.

We begin to develop our hearing in the womb, and the first sounds we produce are the attempted replication of the speech and sounds we hear around us. Many of us are born with the linguistic elasticity to learn languages we hear around us—we listen and speak before we read and write. What might it look like to avoid teaching through Western classical notation in the beginning and using a more aural approach instead?

CALL AND RESPONSE

Often the first few lessons will consist of trying to make a consistent sound with the instrument, getting used to holding it, and explaining the mechanics of breathing, tonguing, and posture. Once a student is comfortable with their instrument, using simple call-and-response phrases can be a fun way to practice all of the demonstrated techniques.

Playing a two- to four-note melodic phrase to a student and asking them to repeat it back can be a fun exercise that can be repeated and changed to incorporate different articulation, dynamics, timbres, scales, and keys. Not only can it work if a teacher plays a phrase to their student, but the roles can also be reversed, with the student playing phrases to the teacher. See Figures 37.11 and 37.12, which are the simple melodic phrases referenced. This approach can help students to:

- Keep a steady pulse
- Be aware of their articulation and intonation
- Improve understanding of different intervals
- Encourage creativity through improvising short phrases

FIGURES 37.11 and 37.12 Simple melodic phrases

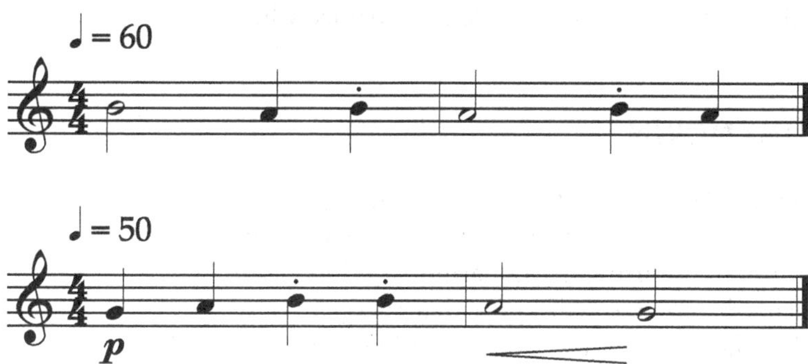

FAMILIAR MELODIES

Encourage a student to play a simple melody familiar to them. In this example we'll use "Mary Had A Little Lamb." By starting on A, we avoid any need to explain sharps or flats or involve notes such as A♭/G♯ or E♭/D♯. Show your student that the notes A, G, and F are the only ones they will need, and once they have played them a couple of times, leave them alone to figure out the melody. Encourage them to move up or down by using an object or a hand to show how the melody moves stepwise up or down.

The key is to let them figure it out, no matter how long it takes. The first few times you do this, it may take some time, but as you continue you can slowly introduce melodies with more notes, as well as scales, which will make the process easier. Scales then become about limiting note choices and providing context, rather than abstract concepts which rarely appear in their entirety in a lot of Western music.

This exercise can be set as homework, with no prescribed time allotted for practice. By doing this, you are implicitly telling your student that it is they who are in charge of their learning, instead of mandating, for example, that they practice for thirty minutes a day. There is a vast amount of learning that can take place outside of lessons if independent learning is established from the beginning as part of a teaching philosophy. If students feel as though learning can only occur in lessons, they can become overly dependent on the teacher. By posing challenges based upon their own interests, you can help students understand how to explore music without relying on notation—if there is even accurate notation available.

GUESS THE SONG

Ask a student to pick any song or melody they want and figure out the first verse or chorus by the next lesson. In the subsequent lesson, ask them to play the song and then you try to guess what it is. This gives students a measure of control over what they learn, and it will also help to expand your musical knowledge if they choose a song you do not know. Furthermore, it forces a student to think musically about a song. They will start to realize how precise we need to be as saxophonists when playing a melody, as each hesitation or poorly articulated note reduces the chances of someone recognizing the melody or song. This exercise need not be repeated until the song is "perfect." At an early stage of training the ear, it is more about being able to play in tune, hear nuance, and gain confidence rather than being able to play it perfectly. Depending on their knowledge of Western music theory, it may be useful for you to tell them what key the song is in or even to ask them to figure it out themselves.

Singing can be an essential part of learning any instrument, not just the saxophone. While we do not have to have the vocal range or dexterity of Lalah Hathaway or Kurt

Elling, being able to sing scales or melodies before playing them helps us to internalize the sounds before attempting to play them on the saxophone. The more familiar we are with a sound, scale, or song through singing it, the more we are able to recognize when we hear it again.

FROM THE FAMILIAR TO THE UNKNOWN

Starting from a place of comfort and familiarity for students can be an important launch pad to creativity. For example, if a student is very familiar only with the C major scale, asking them to be creative or even improvise using a a D harmonic minor scale can be difficult. Even though an experienced musician will know that there are only two notes' difference between these scales, those two notes can make a big difference to someone unfamiliar with the harmonic minor sound. Making a log and using scales that a student may be familiar with can take away a barrier to being creative from an early stage.

Similarly, using songs with which a student is already familiar can start the creative processes earlier. This is where communication with a student can be key. Having an idea of what style(s) or songs a student wants to learn, what they want to sound like, and what music they love can be an amazing starting point for the learning process, even if the song was not written for saxophone.

Fortunately, many people from around the world have covered popular songs such as "I Will Always Love You" (Whitney Houston) or "Thinking Out Loud" (Ed Sheeran), so there will often be various versions of these songs to listen to. By listening to different versions of familiar songs, a student can understand the ways different saxophonists have approached the same song. There will be some they gravitate to more than others, which can spark a conversation as to why one version resonated with them more than another. While it is useful to allow these conversations to flow naturally, it can be important to ask probing questions and, where appropriate, introduce musical language that may help a student express themselves differently.

- What did you like about the chorus?
- Why didn't you like it?
- What did you notice about the bass line?
- Why do you think the saxophonist played in a higher range in the second chorus and not in the first?
- How is Saxophonist X's version of this tune different from Saxophonist Y's?

These questions do not have to exclusively be about the saxophone either. Many teachers will be well aware that for many different reasons, only a small percentage of students will continue playing the saxophone (or any instrument, for that matter) after a couple of years. It is important to understand this and help students develop a general musicality and appreciation for music. The saxophone is simply the instrument, literally, that opens the door to a student's lifelong musical journey. There are many people who quit playing the saxophone because their teacher was fixated on having them play certain repertoire and never provided a space for exploration and questioning. When we start with the familiar and begin to unpack what a student already knows, we can move gradually to the unknown and help draw musical, historical, and/or anecdotal links between songs, styles, composers, performers, producers, record labels, and the like.

By using an ear-first approach, a student can focus on the elements of music that they find most intriguing, strange, or familiar. Although we can develop systems and pathways based on what we feel is right for a student, helping to expand on a student's natural interests is for me the core of what we do.

37.5 Listening

As mentioned previously, listening to other saxophonists can not only help students hear how various people play and approach the instrument, but can also help them decide what music or sound they want to pursue. Moving into the unknown, I will usually give a student an album or song to listen to that we will discuss over the course of a couple of lessons. Encouraging younger students to write short album or song reviews helps them not only to think more deeply about the music they listen to, but also to develop and practice handwriting, literacy, and general knowledge. Having this space to talk about music is something which is often missed, especially in ensemble lessons. Some people to listen to include:

- Candy Dulfer
- John Coltrane
- Grace Kelly
- Nubya Garcia
- Kirk Whalum
- Jess Gillam
- Kamasi Washington

LISTENING TO YOURSELF

The size of a room, the objects in a room, and other factors often mean that students do not have a clear idea of what they actually sound like. The sound that comes out of the saxophone bounces around a room or dissipates outdoors before the sound waves reach a student's ears. To get a clearer idea of your sound and tone, stand facing a corner in a room and play. Not only do you hear yourself louder, but students will be able to hear slight changes in embouchure in real time, as opposed to recording themselves and listening back. This allows them not only to hear themselves, but to critique their own sound outside the lesson.

That is not to say that recording isn't important. Encouraging students to record themselves playing all the previously covered exercises and their attempts at playing popular songs, riffs, or jingles can be a really important process. It can help students to develop critical hearing skills away from their teacher, with the added benefit of the teacher's being able to discuss these short recordings in a lesson together.

LISTENING TO OTHERS

It is rare that a saxophonist will express themselves with the soft tones of the jazz saxophonist Paul Desmond but listen only to the percussive tones of Fela Kuti. We often shape our sound according to the other saxophonists we listen to the most. Again, returning to the idea that learning an instrument could follow the same progression we naturally go through when acquiring language, understanding what we listen to when developing tone is important. Listening to saxophonists who have a tone similar to what a student wants to sound like can help not only develop tone quicker, but also give the student something to aim for (this also goes for styles of music). It is also interesting to find out what set-up (mouthpiece, reed, and ligature) another player uses. That is not to say that by having the same set-up as Camille Thurman or Kenny Garrett a student will sound like them, but there are often similarities in bits of equipment between saxophonists who play in similar styles.

Live Performances

Wherever possible, encourage your student to attend live performances whenever they can. The experience of hearing and seeing a professional saxophonist live can motivate a student in many different ways. There may even be the opportunity to speak to a performer, which can further inspire.

Opportunities for Performance

Encourage your student to perform whenever possible. It could mean playing a song at someone's birthday, playing in a church regularly, or even uploading to social media. The euphoria and disappointments that often come with performing are an important part of being a saxophonist, or indeed, any other kind of musician. Help students to understand that performances do not always have to be formal occasions. Playing in public is an essential part of being a well-rounded musician.

37.6 Discussion Questions

1. Why would it be important to discuss the expectations a student might have about learning the saxophone?
2. Is there one specific technique for the saxophone? How much leeway is a student "allowed" within a technique?
3. How important is it for your future students to feel your passion for the saxophone? How can you motivate them by sharing your learning journey?
4. Do you know somewhere to get saxophones repaired and maintained, that you can recommend to students?
5. Do you know how to diagnose or identify minor issues with the instrument (sticky pads, bent keys, leaks)?

OXFORD learning link

Visit the online resources for additional documentation and exercises to help expand learning and test your knowledge further: www.oup.com/he/powell_music1e.

PART V.

Teaching Brass

38. *Pedagogical Considerations for Teaching Brass Students* by Benjamin Yates
39. *Pedagogies for Teaching Horn* by Meryl Sole
40. *Pedagogies for Teaching Trumpet* by Steven Cunningham
41. *Pedagogies for Teaching Trombone* by Dunwoody Mirvil
42. *Pedagogies for Teaching Baritone and Tuba* by Jennifer Jester
43. *Culturally Relevant Pedagogy in Band* by Darrin Thornton

CHAPTER 38

PEDAGOGICAL CONSIDERATIONS FOR TEACHING BRASS STUDENTS

Benjamin Yates

This chapter provides an overview of brass instruments, preparing to teach brass instruments, ways to improve student learning, and ideas about helping beginning brass students.

38.1 Introduction

Teaching brass to music students requires a flexible, nimble mindset. Successful learners need to strike a balance between separating the various parts of sound creation, developing fundamental routines, and playing music on the instrument. They also need repetition of good playing habits and teachers who are attentive to music.

The following chapters will focus on each instrument in the brass family: trumpet, horn, trombone, and baritone/euphonium/tuba. Although each instrument has unique difficulties and solutions that arise in playing, the common areas for successful playing are extensive. All brass instruments amplify the fundamental sound made in the mouthpiece by buzzing the lips together to make a pitch. The buzz is wind passing through the body's oral cavity, past the teeth, and finally past a pucker in the lips. Musicians' body parts can be manipulated, changing the sound, tone, pitch, and dynamic. This introductory chapter focuses on general ways of manipulating these areas for success on the instruments, specifically for beginning brass players.

It will help all teachers of brass instruments to remember that brass instruments do not have octave keys or other ways of changing the octave. Therefore, beginning students can become frustrated trying to play in both high and low ranges. Teachers can focus on the ideal sound, range, and pitch using specific care and instruction, allowing students to execute the proper sound during performance.

38.2 How to Prepare as a Brass Teacher

Literature resources that support or introduce new teaching concepts are easily accessible. All brass instruments have professional associations that publish online articles and journal materials that can be useful to general music teachers and lesson teachers. These associations include:

- Trumpet: International Trumpet Guild, trumpetguild.org
- Horn: International Horn Society, hornsociety.org

- Trombone: International Trombone Association, trombone.net
- Tuba and euphonium: International Tuba and Euphonium Association, iteaonline.org

Music teachers can benefit by exploring each organization's website and watching the pedagogy videos. It is also helpful to read articles on the details of orchestral excerpts and on collegiate pedagogy. These ideas can be carefully applied to beginning lessons and will help the teacher become more knowledgeable and comfortable teaching brass instruments.

38.3 Finding Appropriate Literature and Methods for Brass Instruction

Many methods, solos, technique books, and etudes are written for brass instruments and beginning bands. These general method books will work well in most classrooms. By the time a general brass method book is adopted, teachers should be comfortable in the method's vocabulary and nomenclature.

However, finding specific method books for each instrument that also fit a student's individual needs is an important step. Some students may show more interest, either actively or through specific improvement, and can benefit from additional learning opportunities. Working with an increased level of interest is important; you should encourage all students and push them to improve at a rate that will sustain their interest and help them improve.

In addition to the general band method books, consider finding brass method books that work for specific programs. Here are some ideas to use in your search:

- Who wrote the book? (Books written by brass performers and pedagogues are usually the best options.)
- Does the method include sample audio and/or video?
- Does the method include popular music examples that students can connect with?
- Does the method include information contrary to the teacher's instruction?

Eventually student brass players will be ready for individual instrument methods. Specific recommendations will be made in the following chapters. However, teachers should consider the subjects covered by beginning methods, including the starting note of the method, the range introduced, and musical concepts such as time signature, key signature, measures, rests, and rhythms.

If a method book seems outdated or not up to your standards, find supplemental materials like popular music, music by underrepresented composers, or methods that offer composition and improvisation exercises. Several components of a beginning program should be researched when deciding on a new method book:

- What are the expectations of students progressing into secondary school, university, or professional settings?
- What are your goals for students?
  - Technical playing
  - Lyrical playing
  - Knowledge of the instrument
- What are the students' goals for playing the instrument?
  - Having a conversation with the student about individual goals for learning an instrument can help teachers decide which method book might be most appropriate for the class.

It is possible to find a balance between group and individual needs when choosing method books. Ideal programs typically find multiple methods that will work in the context of the ensembles and applied lessons and will also fit individual student needs.

In addition to learning the instrument in a beginning band class, students might also benefit from taking private lessons from a brass teacher—performers, teachers, college-age students, and graduate students can all provide valuable experience when teaching beginning and intermediate students. Before recommending a specific teacher for a student, ask to observe the teacher teaching a lesson to see if that person is a good fit for the student. Applied lessons can be intimidating for young students, so it is vital to find and recommend a teacher with the right mix of comfort and an ability to nurture and challenge a student.

38.4 Ideas for Teaching Beginning Brass Lessons

A plethora of resources exist to help music educators think about how they want to teach. However, many of the decisions about how to teach and approach an element of playing a brass instrument come at the time of instruction and can make a significant impact on students. Stay calm and allow students time to experiment with their new instrument. Students have different oral cavities, teeth and/or jaw structures, and bodies that can affect how they play brass instruments. The following information may help most students. Teachers will need to find a balance between encouraging all students and leaving room for mistakes.

Teachers and students will benefit from a list of goals for students to accomplish, including ways students want to use their music skills for the future. These goals can be determined with the student and teacher, or between the teacher and the entire brass section. Students respond well to knowing these goals. Teachers can identify ways for all students to find success and an interest in music. Some of these goals may include broadening students' understanding of music through the music around them and how it relates to the music they perform in the classroom.

It is important to broaden students' understanding of the music they are playing. This can be accomplished through allowing students to learn about the composer and the ways in which the music was originally used. Even method books contain music from different composers as well as music used in films and commercials. Allowing students to explore the musical connections outside of the written notes can help students better understand the music they are playing. It is also important to include music that is a reflection of the musical identities of your students. This can include music that the students already know, music that their families listen to, and music from your students' various cultures. Brass players at all levels (even beginning bands) can play culturally relevant melodies as they learn their instruments.

Great resources are available to help make these connections. Playing original recordings for students to hear can provide historical perspectives on music. Teachers can use films and online commercials that contain parts of the music students are learning. These are both ways to help students find success through enjoyment of music.

38.5 How Brass Instruments Work

As mentioned earlier, the fundamental sound of brass instruments comes from the buzz. The buzz is wind passing through the oral cavity, past the teeth, and past a pucker in the lips. However, many steps are needed before this happens to create a strong brass instrument sound.

THE BREATH

The air inhaled into the lungs will directly impact the output of wind to the buzz. All students need to learn to take big breaths. Students may become tense in the upper torso while taking a breath and keep that tension while playing the instrument; this leads to inefficient playing. Because the breath is the starting position for all playing, taking relaxed, full, efficient breaths and exhaling with only the tension needed to focus and energize the wind will lead to better tone, easier articulation, and increased range. The following sections and chapters will provide specific examples and ways of practicing this technique.

THE EMBOUCHURE

The embouchure is what puts the lips in position to buzz. This is a combination of the pressure of the wind being blown against the lips, the pressure of the front teeth against the lips (not necessarily hard, but giving form to the lips), the lip corners being set, the lip aperture being relaxed or tense as needed by pitch, and the mouthpiece rim.

In order to make an efficient buzz, the lips need to be puckered, as if one were blowing a pinwheel or blowing out a candle. This action sets the corners of the lips and provides the required tension in the facial muscles while allowing the aperture of the lips to buzz freely.

Caution: Players may try manipulating the pitch by moving the corners of the lips. Stretching the lips this way may provide quick improvement early on, but when more range is needed, there will be no room for the lips to stretch. This may also lead to using too much pressure on the embouchure with the mouthpiece, causing serious and potentially permanent damage. Discourage lip stretching by placing a small mirror on the music stand so students can watch their embouchure. Students will notice the lip movement and learn to use a wind-driven embouchure.

THE BUZZ

This is the sound created as the lips vibrate against the mouthpiece. It is a complex part of brass playing. Inhaled air is exhaled as wind, which passes through the trachea, the oral cavity, the front teeth, the lips, the mouthpiece, and the instrument.

To change the pitch of the buzz, the size of the oral cavity can be manipulated with the tongue. If the tongue rises, the wind will move faster past the lips and make the buzz higher, creating a higher-pitched note. If the tongue is lowered, the buzz will be lower, creating a lower note. It is difficult to imagine what is happening inside the oral cavity, so it is best to think about vowel sounds for changing pitches. Sounds for lower pitches include "oh," "ah," and "eh." Those for higher pitches include "oo," "ee," and "sss," the highest-pitched sound.

Brass players should practice vowel sounds by buzzing on the mouthpiece. Learning to focus on sound creation should be the first lesson. Using a visualizer or mouthpiece cutaway will increase efficiency of the air and buzz. More information on this topic is in the section "Concepts, Tools, and Techniques for Improving Brass Performance" at the end of this chapter.

THE TONE

The tone is the sound of the buzz amplified by the instrument. Most issues in tone are related to the buzz. Working on the buzz on the mouthpiece alone without the instrument will typically improve tone, as will working on improving breath and wind. However, mechanical instrument issues can sometimes affect tone and are unrelated to player error; including using the wrong valve or slide position, items stuck in the instrument, or a dirty horn.

THE HARMONIC SERIES AND BRASS INSTRUMENTS

The harmonic series on brass instruments includes all the partials, from the fundamental to the top of a student's range. Most beginning students will not start with the ability to play the fundamental pitch on their instrument. However, it is useful to use the harmonic series or overtone series to describe parts of the instrument. The harmonic series consists of open pitches played on the instrument, with no valve or slide changes. This can help the player find the best tone and sound on an instrument. Learning the intonation tendencies of the brass instrument early will improve ensemble pitch and accuracy.

VALVES OR SLIDE

As already stated, the pitch of the instrument is dictated by the buzz. However, brass instruments are played in tune by using valves or a slide. Each valve addition or extension of the slide will lower the pitch of the instrument. However, in order for the player to play in tune, the buzz must be at pitch. If a student is playing a note with the correct valve or slide position but buzzing the wrong pitch, they will be out of tune or play the wrong note.

THE MOUTHPIECE

The mouthpiece is the final part of the embouchure. Mouthpieces come in various sizes and styles, and from a plethora of makers. Beginning brass players should stick with basic mouthpieces, recommended in the ensuing chapters. Different mouthpieces will fit players' individual needs based on the physical characteristics of their embouchure (lips, teeth, and mouth shapes).

Measurements of mouthpieces include the rim width, cup diameter, cup depth, and size of the throat, backbore, and shank. All mouthpiece makers provide these mouthpiece measurements, and many companies selling mouthpieces provide comparison charts.

Teachers should consider having a variety of standard mouthpiece brands and sizes available for students to try. Beginning students should use a mouthpiece that is neither too small nor too large.

38.6 Brass Teaching: The First Lesson

WHAT DO YOU CALL THAT?

Prepare explanations of the different parts of the brass instrument and mouthpiece using a diagram from a method book of the student's instrument. Learning the vocabulary of a brass instrument will increase students' understanding of how to buzz on the mouthpiece, change pitch, and hold the instrument.

The following chapters on each instrument will use vocabulary that best describes the parts of the instrument and embouchure.

LESSON PLANS

Lesson plans are included in the following chapters and supplemental online materials.

Considerations for early lesson plans:

- Creating wind: inhalation and exhalation
- Holding the instrument efficiently
- Buzzing the mouthpiece
- Pitch-matching on mouthpiece
- Simple melodies on the mouthpiece

- Playing the first notes, matching pitch
- Playing higher and lower notes on the open instrument
- Pitch matching

SPARKING INTEREST IN BRASS PLAYING

It is beneficial for beginning players to hear and see examples of their instrument being played. Teachers can make sure all students have access to inspirational examples of brass instrument recordings. In addition, if parent or adult support is available at home, this could be part of practice time.

Finding different styles, ensembles, and types of music is also key to sparking interest in brass playing. Some of the example lesson plans can be starting places. Consider the types of music students may listen to on their own or at home as starting points.

38.7 Brass Teaching: Early Ensemble Considerations

Novice brass players will probably be part of a larger band ensemble. Ensemble practice and performance is an important part of learning an instrument and is key for most programs. However, several issues may arise when brass students play in a band, primarily because the instruments have similar roles in most beginning band works: the trumpet will typically have the melody, while the low brass will outline the basic chords of a tune. This leads to several deficiencies: tuba players miss out on how to play a full phrase with legato articulation; horn players may not learn the full, usable range of the instrument; and trumpet players may not learn to use the low range effectively or be able to count rests in a more complex work.

To solve some of these issues, strong instrumental programs and teachers often use mono-instrument ensembles (choirs of the same instruments) to work on these issues. In mono ensembles, instrumentalists can learn the full range of the instrument, work on specific tone-production issues, develop a higher understanding of note attacks and tonguing, learn complex and simple rhythms, and more, in a supportive environment. A brass ensemble can provide similar experiences for all brass players, away from percussion and woodwind instrumentalists.

These smaller ensembles also help keep students involved in music making rather than just fulfilling the basic needs of the band part. Smaller ensembles can also perform music students already listen to, including film, pop, and traditional music.

Additional ways of keeping beginning ensemble students involved in music making include learning works without sheet music. Again, this can allow brass players the time and focus needed to work on larger concepts of tone production, unified articulation, and intonation. It also provides a way for students to work on simple ear training, aiding the band greatly. Students can do this work in small groups or even in applied lessons. This is an opportunity for teachers to have students watch and listen to themselves while playing using a mirror and/or audio or video recorder. When students learn by ear, they can address the many physical or mental issues that come into play while performing.

38.8 Concepts, Tools, and Techniques for Improving Brass Performance

BREATHING

Wind is what creates the buzz and is directly related to tone. Diffused, slow, or lethargic wind will produce poor tone on the instrument. The ideal tone comes from a full breath that leads to energetic, spinning, and sufficient wind. Students may think taking a big breath means straining the body with tension. Instead, it's a way to keep the body relaxed and focused on the breath; taking a full breath encourages students to focus on the sound of a breath.

Two exercises will help students focus on the breath. First, start with one hand stretched away from the mouth and use it as a scoop to bring air into the mouth. The other hand rests on the lower abdomen to feel how the air is filling the lungs and body. In the second exercise, students place a hand vertically against the embouchure and inhale and exhale quickly against the resistance of the hand. This provides audible feedback for how much air a student is moving.

A centered, balanced, and relaxed posture is important for all brass players. It may help to have students start by standing when they practice the breathing exercises. Eventually, students can transfer the standing posture to an efficient seated posture.

For efficient breathing, the body needs room for the full chest cavity (front, sides, and back) to expand. The lungs hang from the upper back in the body. As they fill with air, other organs are pushed out of the way, mostly expanding the lower torso. When learning how to breathe for brass playing, students may raise their shoulders or become tense in the upper chest. Students will need help to find a more efficient way of breathing. One way to illustrate efficient breathing is to have students do some light aerobic exercise, like some jumping jacks, and ask them to observe the way the body inhales and exhales.

Exhaling and Buzzing Tools for Brass Players

Exhalation comes directly after the breath; there is no pause or holding of air. Ask students to practice this technique without instruments and while buzzing on the mouthpiece.

Buzzing

Buzzing depends on wind from the breath. Have students practice inhaling, forming an embouchure (keeping the corners set), and blowing at a piece of paper. The paper should move, helping to visualize the wind. This silly exercise is powerful. Try this with mouthpiece buzzing as well, showing that wind is passing the embouchure. Consider finding ways of encouraging students to match pitch, including buzzing a familiar tune, buzzing with a recording, and more.

Pinwheel

The pinwheel will visually show students how the wind passes the embouchure. If the pinwheel does not spin, the wind is not passing freely and could be stopped or distorted by the tongue, front teeth, or a tight aperture in the lips. Buzzing the mouthpiece into a pinwheel is another great way to check the wind.

Breathing Tube

Breathing tubes are useful for any breathing or buzzing exercise. The breathing tube also helps students find the needed space between the front teeth, allowing wind to pass through the oral cavity and past the lips, creating a buzz. Depending on the instrument and range, the distance between the top and bottom front teeth varies.

Incentive Spirometer

This medical tool exercises the lungs and measures the quantity of air inhaled or exhaled. Incentive spirometers can be found at medical supply stores, pharmacies, and many music stores specializing in brass instruments. The incentive spirometer can be turned upside down to measure the amount of air released from the lungs. A moving ball in the spirometer chamber helps students visualize the airstream coming from the lungs. Students can buzz into the incentive spirometer and measure how much air is leaving the buzz. The resistance of the device is adjustable, so a teacher can guide students into using an efficient air column.

Mouthpiece Rim Visualizer

A mouthpiece rim visualizer is a mouthpiece rim designed to be held against the lips for practice creating an embouchure and allowing teachers to observe the embouchure without the mouthpiece cup in the way. The visualizer can also be buzzed on for practice without the resistance of the mouthpiece cup and instrument.

Cutaway Mouthpiece

Similar to the rim visualizer, a cutaway mouthpiece can also help students improve their tone, range, and flexibility on all instruments. Several versions of this tool are available for all instruments, coming in general sizes similar to each instrument's mouthpiece. The cutaway mouthpiece allows students to observe how the embouchure is affected by extraneous movement, airstream efficiency, tongue position, teeth position, and more. The tool can significantly help students relax the embouchure, creating a wind-driven, flexible, and efficient buzz.

38.9 Conclusion

The purpose of this introductory chapter is to provide a brief introduction to brass instruments and prepare teachers who will teach brass instruments to beginning students. This context of the instruments, information about pedagogy, and ideas for teaching are for the first steps toward having successful lessons and ensembles for brass players.

The following chapters in this section will provide specific ideas for methods, teaching each brass instrument at all levels, and lesson plans for teachers.

OXFORD learning link

Visit the online resources for additional documentation and exercises to help expand learning and test your knowledge further: www.oup.com/he/powell_music1e.

CHAPTER 39

PEDAGOGIES FOR TEACHING HORN

Meryl Sole

This chapter provides an overview of teaching the French horn, covering the instrument's history, maintenance, playing basics and embouchure, and articulation exercises.

39.1 Introduction: French Horn Dreams Are Made of This

The classroom is dark and silent. I've turned off the lights and projector and lowered the video screen. I begin with the sound only. Sforzando! Silence. Sforzando! Silence. Then the fast, pulsating bass line. It's dark and haunting; the sound is dark and mellow. Twenty seconds later the melody enters in a low voice, and my students recognize the tune of "Sweet Dreams (Are Made of This)." Then I turn on the video to reveal four young women dressed all in black, running through a field, sleeping in bed in matching pajamas, rowing a boat, and running through the forest. The images flash between scenes, highlighting each player.

The group is called Genghis Barbie and is made up of four hornists who describe themselves as a "the leading post post-feminist feminist all-female horn experience." In addition to their impressive résumés and positions in leading orchestras, they are known for their arrangements of pop music from all eras, contemporary commissions, and classical works. Their live performances and videos feature classical, pop, rock, jazz, indie, alternative, punk, and electroacoustic music, as interpreted by a French horn quartet (see https://www.genghisbarbie.com/bio-page).

I don't begin my brass methods course with a recording of the legendary British hornist Dennis Brain playing Mozart or a video of Barry Tuckwell playing Richard Strauss and conducting a chamber ensemble with his horn tucked under his arm; I start my introduction to the horn by sharing *this* video because it is unexpected. The Genghis Barbie performance of the Eurythmics' 1983 new-wave, synth-pop hit is so full of possibility (search for 'Sweet Dreams (Are Made of This) by Genghis Barbie' on YouTube). It is modern. It shows what the horn can be and what players can do. The almost presto synth bass part is astounding on its own. My students usually remark that they can't imagine how the player has time to breathe. As each version of the vocal melody enters, my students say that they are impressed by the tone quality and the range. From low to high and bright to dark, the sound is varied and interesting. The harmonies are stunning and the highest vocal melody sings! The glissandos, the trills, the forceful yet controlled power are all mentioned as we discuss the video together.

I've been teaching brass methods for years and playing the horn for longer. I want my students to hear and see everything the horn can do—all of these possibilities. The horn can transcend musical genres and styles and gender stereotypes. This video performance isn't just fun, relatable and entertaining, it shows off what horn players can do; from their range, sound, role and boundless capabilities. Inspiration!

Activity 39.1: Students should search the web for diverse examples of horn playing across many styles of music. Discuss how the horn sounds in jazz music versus Western classical art music. Talk about some unexpected examples they encountered in their search.

This chapter focuses on the skills necessary for learning to both play *and* teach the horn. It is based on my years of experience in doing both of those things. Within each topic, I share suggestions of activities that can be done individually or as a group within the methods course. Additionally, there are a number of print and online resources that the reader may find useful and inspiring.

39.2 Background: A Horn That's Really Not So French

A little background to the instrument is useful as you begin your journey with the horn. Understanding the history and evolution of the instrument will inform your playing and support your knowledge base as you introduce the horn to your students later on in your teaching career. A landmark resource on the horn, *The Art of French Horn Playing*, was written by the legendary hornist Philip Farkas. See 33.1, "The Art of French Horn Playing," on the book's online resources site.

In the early 2000s there was a short-lived and unpopular political movement to rename French fries "freedom fries" for a number of reasons, including the fact the *frites* originated in Belgium and not France. Similarly, in 1971 the International Horn Society called for the French horn to be renamed "horn," as the "French" in French horn is used colloquially. It seems important to understand the ancestry of the horn. An early precursor to the modern horn is the shofar or ram's horn, where sound is amplified through the horn and can carry great distances. The shofar is still used in Jewish ritual. Another predecessor, the alphorn, which is a long wooden horn sometimes curved at the end, was used for early communication and at festivals and daily ceremonies. It may be recognized from 1990s commercials for Swiss cough drops.

The traditional hunting horn was used to bring order to an animal hunt, as different calls identified different animals as well as the start or end of a hunt. As the hunting horn developed, the tubing was modified to become circular and easy to carry and transport. The French were the first to lengthen the tube to create more notes. Unlike the trumpet, which features cylindrical tubing, the horn is conical in shape.

By the 1700s these horns were used in orchestras and operas to play fanfares and calls. The addition of crooks—tubes that could attach to the natural horn—allowed the player to play in different keys. The player would choose a crook that corresponded to the key of the music and then play pitches in the harmonic series. See 33.2, "The Natural Horn Resource," on the book's online resources site. Players could insert their right hands into the bell of the horn to raise or lower the pitch a half step, enabling them to play all the notes of the chromatic scale. This technique, called hand stopping, is still used today, especially for sonic effects, as it creates a distant and brassy sound.

In 1813 the horn evolved into the modern instrument we recognize today, complete with rotary valves that allow players the flexibility of playing all the chromatic pitches without hand stopping or carrying around a suitcase full of crooks. Each valve allows the player to alter the length of tubing that is blown through. Most beginning horn players start on a single F horn and move to the double horn (both the F and B♭ horn combined in one instrument) as they advance to a more intermediate level. As students advance to the double horn, they also learn different fingerings, which vary from the F horn fingerings.

One of the first discoveries a new horn player makes is that it is possible to play a pitch with numerous valve combinations. They also find out quickly that playing a pitch isn't as simple as depressing a valve. The combination of correct embouchure, air quantity and speed, ability to hear/sing the note, and the correct fingering all contribute to the ability to play a pitch correctly.

Activity 39.2: Students should conduct a web search to view images of the horn's ancestry, including alphorns, hunting horns, shofars, natural horns with crooks, and the modern horn (single, double, and triple).

39.3 The Basics of Playing: Breath and Buzz

You cannot get anywhere without wind. . . . If you think of a car, the wheels will not turn without an energy source—the engine. Brass players must have a source of energy, as there must be a vibrating column of air for the instrument to amplify and resonate. The musical engine is the vibration of the lips. However, the lips cannot vibrate without wind.

—*Arnold Jacobs,* Song and Wind

The legendary tuba player and teacher Arnold Jacobs' ideas about breathing and air apply not only to tuba playing but to horn playing as well. Air is indeed the source of energy that allows the player to create sound. I like to begin brass methods with breathing exercises because the air is so foundational to the ability to play. Proper inhalation along with a metered approach to the exhale is something that students should add to their practice session before they even pick up the mouthpiece or the instrument. Students can work on breathing through this simple exercise.

Activity 39.3: Using a metronome to keep a steady, slow beat students can inhale for four counts and exhale for eight, then progress to inhale for three counts and exhale for eight, and so on until they can inhale for an eighth note (half a count) and exhale for eight counts. Pay careful attention to the sound of the inhale. As they progress, they can lengthen the exhale to ten or twelve beats. After this exercise, it's useful to move on to the embouchure and buzz, where students can connect the air to vibration.

39.4 Embouchure and Aperture: Smile on the Inside Only

For horn players, the embouchure is the setting of the lip and face muscles that will aid them in vibrating at different speeds and intensities. Tighter muscles and faster vibration create higher pitches, while looser muscles and slower vibration create lower pitches. The front of the face should be flat, and the player should not smile or make a whistling shape with the lips. A simple pucker with firm corners is correct.

Activity 39.4: Students should first experiment with creating buzz on their lips without the mouthpiece. Give ample time to play around with low- and high-sounding buzzing. Be sure to talk about what elements contribute to a high-sounding versus a low-sounding buzz (aperture, air speed, etc.). Students can take turns buzzing for the group and sharing personal experiences of how to manipulate the register of the buzz. Ask the group, "How did you strengthen your buzzing? How did you change the register? How could you teach this skill to a beginner based on your experience?"

Once a solid buzz has been created, students can begin to experiment with the mouthpiece and its placement on the lips. The player should avoid using too much pressure or forcing the metal mouthpiece onto the delicate lips, as this will cause numbness and fatigue. A mouthpiece visualizer or one of the second-valve tuning slides can be helpful in demonstrating the proper embouchure, which consists of two-thirds upper lip and one-third lower lip. The lips should be slightly moist but not too wet. The following images show the correct mouthpiece placement as well as some common mistakes. Note that the second-valve slide makes an excellent mouthpiece visualizer.

FIGURE 39.1 **Correct horn embouchure (two-thirds upper lip, one-third lower lip)**

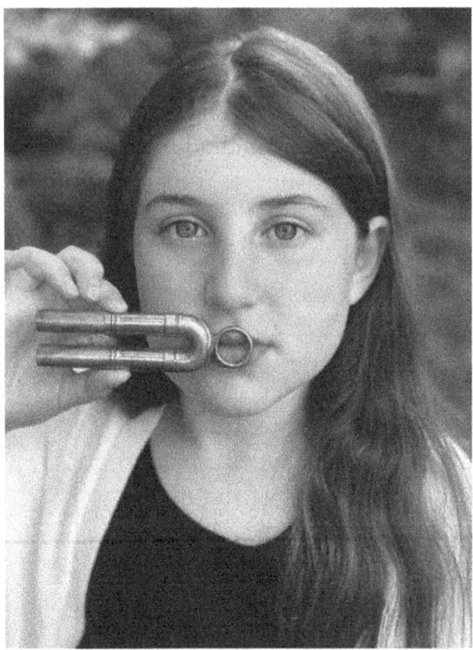

FIGURE 39.2 Incorrect horn embouchure

There are a number of excellent resources that demonstrate embouchure with many diverse lip shapes and sizes, and apertures (opening inside the mouthpiece). See 33.3, "Horn Matters on Mouthpiece Placement," on the book's online resources site.

Activity 39.5: Students can experiment with hearing, singing, and then buzzing pitches on their mouthpieces. Talk about connections between hearing/singing and buzzing a pitch. Some students will inevitably face challenges in matching pitches buzzed on the mouthpiece. Again, allow the group to share strategies and suggestions, keeping in mind that the experience of learning the skill will impact how they can teach the skill.

39.5 Starting the Sound: Articulations

Before the exciting moment of placing the mouthpiece into the horn's lead pipe, it may be useful to first introduce the concept of how we incorporate the tongue to articulate the beginning of each sound.

Activity 39.6: Students should try out different articulations sounds, such as "ta," "tu," "te," and "tsss," by closing their eyes and paying careful attention to the placement of the tongue inside the mouth and in relation to the top front teeth. Talk about which sound helps to create the most crisp, clean start to a pitch. Then add the articulations to the buzz on the mouthpiece. Students can compose simple rhythmic patterns to articulate and buzz, then perform as a "mouthpiece ensemble." They can also adapt popular songs to perform on buzz, such as hip-hop tunes with repetitive bass lines and rhythmic hooks.

39.6 How Do I Hold This Thing? Correct Posture and Playing Position

Before demonstrating the correct posture and playing position, I always allow my horn students the opportunity to freely explore the instrument and experience the excitement of amplifying the mouthpiece buzz through the horn. The mouthpiece should be gently inserted into the lead pipe with a small twist. Do not jam it in with force or you will quickly have to learn how a mouthpiece remover works.

> **Activity 39.7:** Give time and space for students to experience the joy of connecting the mouthpiece to the horn and creating sound. Allow them to play around with the valves and experience changes in pitch and volume.

IT'S TIME TO PUT JULIE ANDREWS IN YOUR BELL

After playing around with the horns, it's finally time to demonstrate the correct posture and position for playing. The student should be seated at the front of the chair, with both feet planted firmly on the ground. The left elbow should be hanging in a relaxed position, and the left index, middle, and ring fingertips should be placed on the valves, with the pinky underneath the pinky hook.

The placement of the right hand is always the trickiest skill to teach. The right hand should be slightly cupped; as a former student once remarked, it should "look like you are giving a royal wave, the kind of regal gesture that Julie Andrews might use to acknowledge a crowd." This image of the right hand led my students to rejoice in the silly idea that they have Julie Andrews inside their bell. With the right hand in this position, place the hand inside the bell with the back of the fingers touching the far side of the bell, still creating plenty of space and opening for the sound to pass. The bell can rest comfortably on the right thigh. Then sit up straight and bring the lead pipe to the mouth (do not move the head downward to meet the lead pipe).

FIGURE 39.3 **The Julie Andrews wave**

FIGURE 39.4 Proper posture with bell resting on the thigh

FIGURE 39.5 Incorrect posture

Activity 39.8: Students can create a short video of themselves assembling the horn and moving themselves into the correct playing position while narrating their steps. This activity will encourage students to think about how to describe the process and teach it to someone else.

39.7 It's Not Spit, It's Condensation

Horn players do not consciously spit into their instruments. Blowing moist air through twelve feet of metal tubing will result in pools of condensation or saliva that must be emptied regularly so that they do not create a gurgling sound while the horn is being played. Most instruments are equipped with spit valves that can be pressed as the player blows through the lead pipe to eliminate the condensation. Given the curved nature of many of the slides of the horn, it is common for the condensation to get trapped in the nooks and crannies of the slides. To empty the horn, it is best to remove the mouthpiece and tip the lead pipe to the right while removing the main tuning slide (you can find the main slide by tracing the lead pipe to the first removable slide) and emptying it.

Given the health precautions in place surrounding the COVID-19 pandemic, the issue and process of emptying horns must be handled in a safe manner. Some players are experimenting with tying plastic bags to their spit valves to catch and dispose of the condensation, while others are using paper towels or newspaper to catch the condensation so that they can dispose of it in a sealed plastic bag afterward. It's also important to have mouthpiece sanitizing spray on hand to disinfect mouthpieces quickly.

39.8 Common Maintenance Issues

In addition to removing condensation, horn players must do regular maintenance on their horns, which includes oiling the rotary valves, greasing slides, and completing basic cleaning of their instruments. For a video on basic horn maintenance and care, see 33.4, "My French Horn Gets a Bath," on the book's online resources site.

Some of the most common maintenance issues that horn players experience include stuck mouthpieces, broken valve strings, and dents. The videos at 33.5, "Tying French Horn Levers," and 33.6, "How to Remove a Very Stuck Mouthpiece," on the book's online resources site are excellent resources for addressing these issues, which can be easily remedied without a trip to the repair shop.

> **Activity 39.9:** Students can compete in a maintenance relay race. Set up the classroom with a number of horns with issues: remove slides, snip a valve string, bring in a few dented mouthpieces. Have students attempt to repair the issues!

39.9 Playing: Warming It Up

Warm-up and short practice sessions are important for beginners; it takes time to build strength and endurance on the horn. Since C, E, and G are played without valves on the horn, the open notes are a great place to start and warm up. It will allow the player to differentiate between the notes of the C major triad by experimenting with embouchure, ear, and air speed.

> **Activity 39.10:** Students can compose their own simple open horn exercises on the C major triad using different rhythms and patterns. Students can write these down and share with each other or create a call-and-response game where one player plays and the other imitates based on what they hear.

39.10 Long Tones

Long tones are a wonderful way to have students practice their exploration of pitch, intonation, dynamic abilities, and sound. Starting on a comfortable pitch, the player can consistently hold a pitch for a given count (eight to twelve beats), trying to maintain consistency of sound and intonation. Then the player can introduce a crescendo and decrescendo to work on increasing the sound and diminishing it in a controlled fashion. See "Horn Matters, The Art of Practice, Part II: Long Tones," on the book's online resources site.

39.11 Articulation Exercises

The following articulation exercise is a great way to practice clean, crisp tonguing using the syllable "tsss." The exercise may be repeated at different pitches in the upper and lower registers:

FIGURE 39.6 **Horn tonguing exercise**

39.12 Transposition

The most common horn that students will encounter, the F horn, is not at concert pitch but sounds a fifth lower than written. Therefore, the concept of transposition needs to be introduced to understand how the written parts (usually these are already transposed into F for the beginning player) compare to concert pitch. The basic concept is that the horn player produces a sounding concert B♭ when playing their written F. See 33.8, "French Horn Transposition Chart," on the book's online resources site.

Activity 39.11: Students can explore some books and online resources on transposition. A horn player can stand near a piano and play their middle C. Have another student find the pitch on the piano and then identify it. Compare the horn C and the pitch on the piano and discuss the difference. Repeat this with other pitches being played on the horn and identified on the piano. You can also find some simple melodies and have students re-write them in the key of F. Then try playing the transposed parts as a pianist plays the original. Do they sound the same now?

39.13 Review of the Methods

There are a large number of different method books that are available to the beginning horn player. Some of the most popular methods include *Accent on Achievement*, *Standard of Excellence*, and *Essential Elements*. Each is worth reviewing to see how the instruments are introduced and the various skills and concepts in this chapter are addressed for the young player. It's worthwhile to have methods that students will use and to explore a number of different methods as one important resource in the classroom. Students may also wish to examine well known resources on horn playing (Bachelder and Hunt, 2002; Caruso, 2002; Farkas, 1999).

Activity 39.12: Students can complete a review of a few popular methods to see how they differ in approach. Ask questions such as: What images are used throughout the books? What repertoire is selected, and does it represent a diverse range of styles? Does the method give students the chance to create, compose, and improvise? What elements are successful and what is missing from each method? If you were to design a method book for horn, what would it look like and what would it include?

39.14 Building Creative Musicianship

Upon review of existing method books, students may find that they themselves can be a wonderful resource for composing and arranging music for the beginning horn player. One activity that my students love is where they compose original melodies or arrange existing songs that are meaningful to them. Keeping in mind their playing abilities, students share melodies that are appropriate in range, register, and complexity. Each student takes turns teaching their melody to the group, adding additional parts and harmonies as the group progresses. This activity not only allows students to share music that is relevant and meaningful to them, but also engages their creativity, teaching, transposition, rehearsal, and performance skills. In a recent class meeting, my students worked on a student arrangement of ABBA's "Dancing Queen," learning the melody, adding in harmonies, and tapping into musicality through dynamics and phrasing. The class culminated with a performance and recording of the student project. One student remarked, "That was so much fun. We sounded great and it seems like we all really bought into the process."

Activity 39.13: Have students attempt the described melody project using compositions or arrangements that are fun and meaningful to them.

39.15 The Player as Teacher

The purpose of the undergraduate horn methods course is twofold. The students should learn the basic information and skills necessary to play the horn, but they must also take these new skills and explore how to teach them. My methods classes are filled with opportunities for the students to teach their new skills. For example, when one student has made progress on playing a scale slurred, staccato, and marcato, how can they teach this to another member of the group? Perhaps students can teach a friend or roommate who is not in the course and record the lesson.

In order to truly understand and describe the process of learning, I have found it helpful for students to reflect on the process of learning and teaching. Journals and video blogs are great resources for students to describe and detail their successes and challenges.

Activity 39.14: Students can write out lesson plans or maps for teaching a specific horn-related skill. Consider the approach and each step that is important for meeting the goal and how your own learning happened with regard to this. Then teach the lesson you planned. Consider how the actual teaching was different from the written lesson plan. Have the community of students share positive and constructive feedback for the mock lesson.

39.16 Final Thoughts

A horn methods course is typically filled with music education students from different backgrounds, each having a different life experience with a primary instrument. Tap into that diversity and use it to benefit the group. A vocalist will have great things to share about breath control, just as a clarinetist will be able to give great tips on articulation and tonguing. Each student needs the space and encouragement to explore the horn at their own pace. The horn is often considered to be one of the most challenging instruments to play. Students often experience frustration as they attempt to master the highlighted skills. But horn can be equally challenging to teach. So make sure you practice your playing *and* practice your teaching.

39.17 Discussion Questions

1. Compared to your primary instrument, what are the similarities and differences that you experienced in learning to play the horn?
2. Which horn skills did you find most challenging to master? Which horn skills were most challenging to teach? Why?
3. What do you enjoy most about the sound of the horn, playing the horn, and teaching the horn to others?
4. Consider keeping a journal to reflect on your experiences of learning to play and teach horn skills. Reflect on some of the suggested activities you may have tried from this chapter. What insights may be useful to your peers?

OXFORD learning link

Visit the online resources for additional documentation and exercises to help expand learning and test your knowledge further: www.oup.com/he/powell_music1e.

CHAPTER 40

PEDAGOGIES FOR TEACHING TRUMPET

Steven Cunningham

This chapter provides an overview of trumpet fundamentals and discusses essential practice techniques. The trumpet is a versatile, multigenre instrument, used in orchestras, wind ensembles, jazz bands, marching bands, popular music, mariachi, and more. In this chapter I begin with helpful tips on how to teach beginners to play the trumpet, starting with instrument assembly and care and progressing to teaching playing position, embouchure, and tone production. Technical exercises are also included.

40.1 Introduction to the Instrument

TRUMPET ASSEMBLY

When teaching beginners, I usually begin by introducing them to the parts of the trumpet: mouthpiece, shank, valves, lead pipe, bell, slides (main tuning slide and first, second, and third), and finger hook. To avoid damaging the instrument, I have the students place the trumpet case on a flat surface. Students should then take the trumpet out of the case by placing their left hand around the valve casing, because the left hand supports the weight of the instrument. Carefully twist the mouthpiece into the mouthpiece receiver.

Check the valve pistons to ensure that they are in the correct order. While holding the instrument, make sure that the valve pistons are in this order: the first valve is closest to you, the second valve is in the middle, and the third valve is farthest away from you. On each valve piston are plastic parts called valve guides, which lock the valve piston into its proper position. This is imperative; when the pistons are not in this order or the valve is facing the incorrect direction, the trumpet will be unplayable because there will be a blockage in airflow.

TRUMPET MAINTENANCE

Trumpet maintenance is just as important as practicing. Trumpet players should avoid eating food right before playing because the food will get in the instrument. If the food stays in the instrument for a long time, it will turn into mold. Playing a brass instrument with mold can affect the player's lungs and cause severe health problems. Other materials such as dirt, old lubricants, and bacteria are also hazardous to trumpet players' health. A dirty instrument will also be harder to play: dirt and debris will narrow the instrument's bore, and air blockage affects intonation. Following a simple cleaning routine can significantly decrease any chance of health problems and extend the life of your instrument.

Depending on how much the trumpet is played, I recommend cleaning the instrument once every two months. Disassemble the instrument and place all parts next to a bathtub or large sink. Fill the sink or tub with warm water and add liquid soap. Place all parts in the water, except for the valves, for approximately five minutes. Use a trumpet snake to clean all of the tubings. These devices are included in trumpet-cleaning kits. Drain the water, rinse all the parts out with warm water, and place them on a dry towel to dry. Put slide grease on all the slides and put them back on the trumpet. Then take a valve brush and clean the valve ports with warm water, being sure not to let any water touch the springs and pads. Place the valves on a dry towel and let them dry. Then apply valve oil to the valves and place them back in the trumpet (Hickman et al., 2006).

Trumpeters must oil their valves on a consistent basis to ensure that the valves do not stick while playing. Place the instrument on your lap with a towel or cloth to protect your clothes from oil stains. Loosen the top of the bottle of valve oil and set it aside so that it is easy to find. Unscrew a valve cap and gently raise the piston until you see the gray part of the valve body. Do not take the whole piston out—just enough to see the valve body. Put several drops of valve oil on the valve body and let it run down into the valve casing. Carefully reassemble the valve and place the valve oil top back on the bottle and tighten it.

PLAYING POSITION

Depending on the size of your hands, place either the left-hand ring or middle finger inside the ring on the third valve slide. With your right hand, hold the mouthpiece by the shank and twist it into the mouthpiece receiver. Form your right hand as if you were holding a tennis ball or the letter C. Place the right thumb between the first and second valve casings. Then place your right pinky finger on top of the hook.

EMBOUCHURE FORMATION AND PLACEMENT

The formation of the embouchure is critical for healthy brass playing and must be addressed at the beginning stages with utmost care. Have the student say the letter "m." Notice that the red part of the lips is slightly curled inward. Then, firm the corners while maintaining the lip position. Make sure that the teeth are not clenched, as there must be some space between the upper and lower teeth. The trumpet pedagogue David Hickman refers to this as the "pucker": "Correct trumpet pucker is not like whistling, as some methods describe. Although the facial muscles work in a similar manner to whistling, the trumpet embouchure requires that the lips be somewhat flat against the front teeth and slightly curled inward, whereas whistling normally causes the center of the lips to purse excessively outward from the teeth" (Hickman et al., 2006, pp. 13–14).

BREATHING TECHNIQUES

Proper posture is a prerequisite for any breathing technique. The shoulders should be down and relaxed. Avoid raising the shoulders or bringing them forward because that creates unnecessary tension.

Without the instrument, practice inhaling and exhaling. Inhale air with an "oh" syllable, then exhale. Repeat. On the exhale, articulate with a "tu" syllable. While holding the trumpet in playing position (set embouchure), inhale by opening the corners of the lips with an "oh" syllable. This is the basic breathing technique that trumpet players use while playing. Pay close attention to beginners, because they may be inhaling air with their noses while their embouchure is set.

40.2 Pedagogical Considerations

TONE PRODUCTION ON TRUMPET

What makes a good tone? Our goal is to create a resonant, vibrant sound. In order to achieve this, we must listen to professional trumpet players to develop a concept of the sound. If we know what we want to sound like, then it is easier to produce a good tone.

With one hand, take a piece of paper and hold the top part twelve inches from your face. While maintaining puckered lips, blow air out as if you were blowing out candles on a birthday cake. At this point, refrain from using the tongue and use a "hu" syllable. Keep blowing the air while maintaining the "u" syllable. If done correctly, the paper should flap back and stay in that position while the air is blowing.

Now repeat the same process and change the syllable to "tu." Notice that when we use the vowel "u" it brings the lips into the pucker formation. Form your embouchure, then take the mouthpiece and place it on the lips. Center the mouthpiece on the lips and make sure that both lips are inside the mouthpiece and stay there while playing. The mouthpiece placement may change due to dental structure. Blow air through the mouthpiece; this should produce a sound.

Most beginning trumpet methods instruct students to buzz their lips into the mouthpiece. This instruction can lead to a very pinched tone with a tremendous amount of tension. However, if done properly, buzzing can be a gateway to developing a beautiful and resonant tone. Buzzing the mouthpiece while playing the piano is an excellent way to work on tone production and ear training. These two items are essential to beautiful trumpet playing.

ARTICULATION

The most common syllable for clear articulation is "tu." The "t" syllable should be gentle, not forceful. Using the pedagogy of the former Chicago Symphony trumpeter Vincent Cichowicz is a natural way of introducing articulation. Cichowicz focused on using wind patterns to teach his students how to develop efficient tonguing. Without the trumpet, form the embouchure, breathe, and blow a musical phrase with only the wind and articulation. This process can also help trumpeters find their natural tongue placement. For smoother tonguing, trumpet players should use a soft "du" syllable to play legato phrases (Cichowicz et al., 2021, p. 35).

The tongue and air are at the forefront of brass playing. The tongue acts as a valve that releases the air through the lips and creates vibration; this vibration creates sound. There are three main types of articulation for trumpet players. Staccato, marcato and legato tonguing appear in all styles of music and should be practiced in every practice session.

Articulation Styles: Staccato, Marcato, Legato

Healthy terms for the staccato style would be "light" or "detached" as opposed to "short." Beginners tend to stop their airflow with their tongue to play in this style. Remember that the end of the note is short and still stopped by airflow, not the tongue. Marcato or "marked" tonguing should be loud and forceful. The tongue will release the air with more force. Remember that the tongue does not strike but releases the air. Legato means "tied together." The articulation should be smooth and connected without any separation in the sound. Trumpet players should use a "du" or "la" syllable in a light manner.

INTONATION

Intonation issues are directly related to the trumpet design and our ear training. Trumpet players should work with drones at A 440 by playing unison, and intervals such as major thirds, minor thirds, perfect fourths, and perfect fifths to realize that our ears can help us fix intonation issues, especially in ensemble playing. Having the ability to play and adjust pitch to match the ensemble is a very important skill that will improve over time. Advise students on the placement of their tuning slides and challenge them to tune to a drone so that they can hear if a pitch is in tune or not. This process is critical to developing their ear and awareness.

40.3 Starting to Play Without Teaching the Music Staff First

LEARNING BY EAR/CALL AND RESPONSE

To develop ear-to-hand skills, I suggest teaching students without musical notation in the beginning. This will encourage students to focus on fundamentals, tone quality, pitch, and associating the pitches with the fingerings. Learning how to read music and an instrument simultaneously can be overwhelming. Here I include a few suggestions for how to teach without notation.

- Teach one note at a time.
- Play ear-training games by playing notes and challenging students to match the pitches. Start with two notes, then expand as they progress on the instrument.
- Play rhythmic games as well. Tap a rhythm and ask them to copy it.
- Combine rhythm and pitch to make it more challenging.
- Once they are comfortable with mouthpiece buzzing, tell them to buzz along with their favorite songs.
- For advanced students, play an exercise and tell them to sing the notes while the demonstrator is playing, then apply to the mouthpiece, then possibly the instrument.

40.4 Exercises and Warm-Ups That Build Technique and Tone

LEAD PIPE BUZZING

Lead pipe buzzing can be a great introduction to playing the trumpet with a full, resonant sound with the least amount of effort. On a B♭ trumpet, remove the tuning slide and buzz a concert E♭ (F). Aim for a full, resonant tone without any tension. See Figure 40.1.

FIGURE 40.1 Lead pipe buzzing

MOUTHPIECE BUZZING

Mouthpiece buzzing can be a great tool to develop the embouchure and train the ear. If done incorrectly, mouthpiece buzzing has the potential to produce uncomfortable tension in the player's facial muscles if done too hard or too long. The goal is to buzz the mouthpiece with a full resonant sound and avoid "air" or "fuzz" in the sound. Figure 40.2 features buzzing exercises that utilize half steps and major triads.

FIGURE 40.2 Mouthpiece buzzing

LONG TONES

Long tones can be used to develop sound, control, intonation awareness, and embouchure strength. Playing long-tone exercises that feature dynamic changes with a metronome is extremely beneficial for developing these items. See Figure 40.3.

FIGURE 40.3 Long tones

LIP BENDS

Lip bends is the process of using our lips to force out a pitch that we are not fingering. This exercise strengthens the muscles of our face, range development, tone, and pitch centering which is critical to ensemble playing and playing in tune. This is similar to mouthpiece buzzing except on the instrument. See Figure 40.4.

FIGURE 40.4 Lip bends

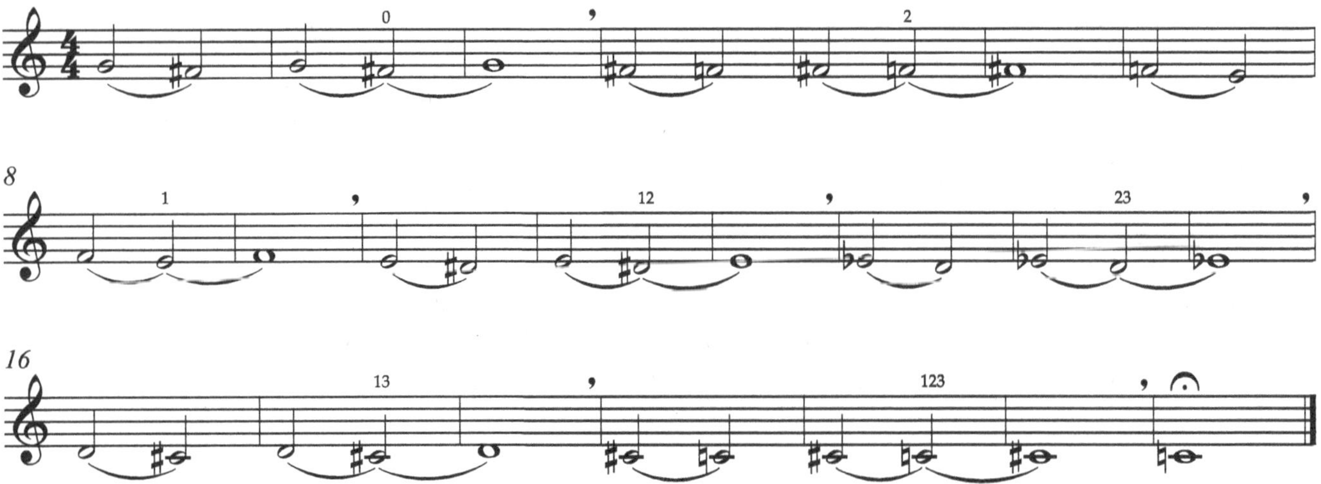

SLURS: VALVE AND LIP

We know that slurred notes are connected notes played without separation in sound. On the trumpet, the first note of the slur is the only note that is tongued. There are two types of slurs for trumpets: valve slurs and lip slurs. Valve slurs occur when trumpet players use different fingerings to change notes.

Lip slurs utilize the same fingering between two notes, allowing them to change partials without articulating or stopping the air on the same valve or slide position. Trumpet players have to change notes by varying embouchure tension, tongue position, and air compression. On the trumpet, there are seven different valve positions, each with a different harmonic series. By using all seven valve positions, the trumpet is able to play all chromatic tones. Trumpet players must execute a lip slur when there is a slur between two or more notes with the same valve position. Exercises that focus on lip slurs will help develop smooth playing and improve range and airflow (Hickman et al., pp. 29–30).

I prefer to think of lip slurs as tongue slurs, since we change notes with the shape of the tongue and air speed instead of relying on the lips to change the notes. The goal is to connect notes as smoothly as possible without using the lips. Trumpet playing is related to singing in that we need to change our syllables with the tongue. Imagine playing the following exercise with the syllables "ah–ee–ah–ee." See Figure 40.5.

FIGURE 40.5 Lip slurs

ARTICULATION

Articulation exercises are meant to develop an efficient tongue stroke that creates a clear attack. In order to do this on a consistent basis, trumpet players should practice different styles of articulation. Staccato, marcato, and legato articulations are the three main styles that must be practiced. Starting with legato articulations can help reinforce a gentle tongue stroke for marcato and staccato articulations. See Figure 40.6.

RANGE

Range will come in time. For beginners, it is more important to develop the embouchure with efficiency and patience. Playing simple slur exercises at a soft dynamic that goes to the top of the student's range can help with the concept of air compression for higher tones. See Figure 40.7.

FIGURE 40.6 Articulations

40.5 Lesson Ideas to Build Creative Musicianship

Listening to music is arguably the most important learning tool for aspiring musicians. Students who listen to professionals who play their instrument of choice on a consistent basis have a goal of what they want to sound like. The goal is to develop a sound concept and learn stylistic traits of multiple styles of music. Ensemble skills can be improved by learning how to listen. Section playing requires the ability to blend with other musicians. Listening also has a tremendous effect on intonation as well. I suggest using a drone reference for tuning instead of just looking at a tuner. By using a drone, students will learn how to actually play in tune by listening and making adjustments.

THE IMPORTANCE OF RECORDING

Recording our practice sessions can be a great tool. If we approach recording with positive and constructive thoughts, we can improve certain aspects of our playing instantly. Listening to recorded practice sessions develops our musical awareness and helps us make necessary adjustments to achieve the sound that we want.

40.6 A Guide to Trumpet Practice

Having a consistent practice routine is essential to developing strong fundamentals. Endurance, range, articulation, and sound suffer when trumpet players do not practice efficiently. Below is a sample practice routine that can be used every day.

SUGGESTED DAILY PRACTICE ROUTINE

Warm-Up (10 minutes)

1. Listen to a professional trumpet player
2. Breathing exercises

FIGURE 40.7 Range exercises

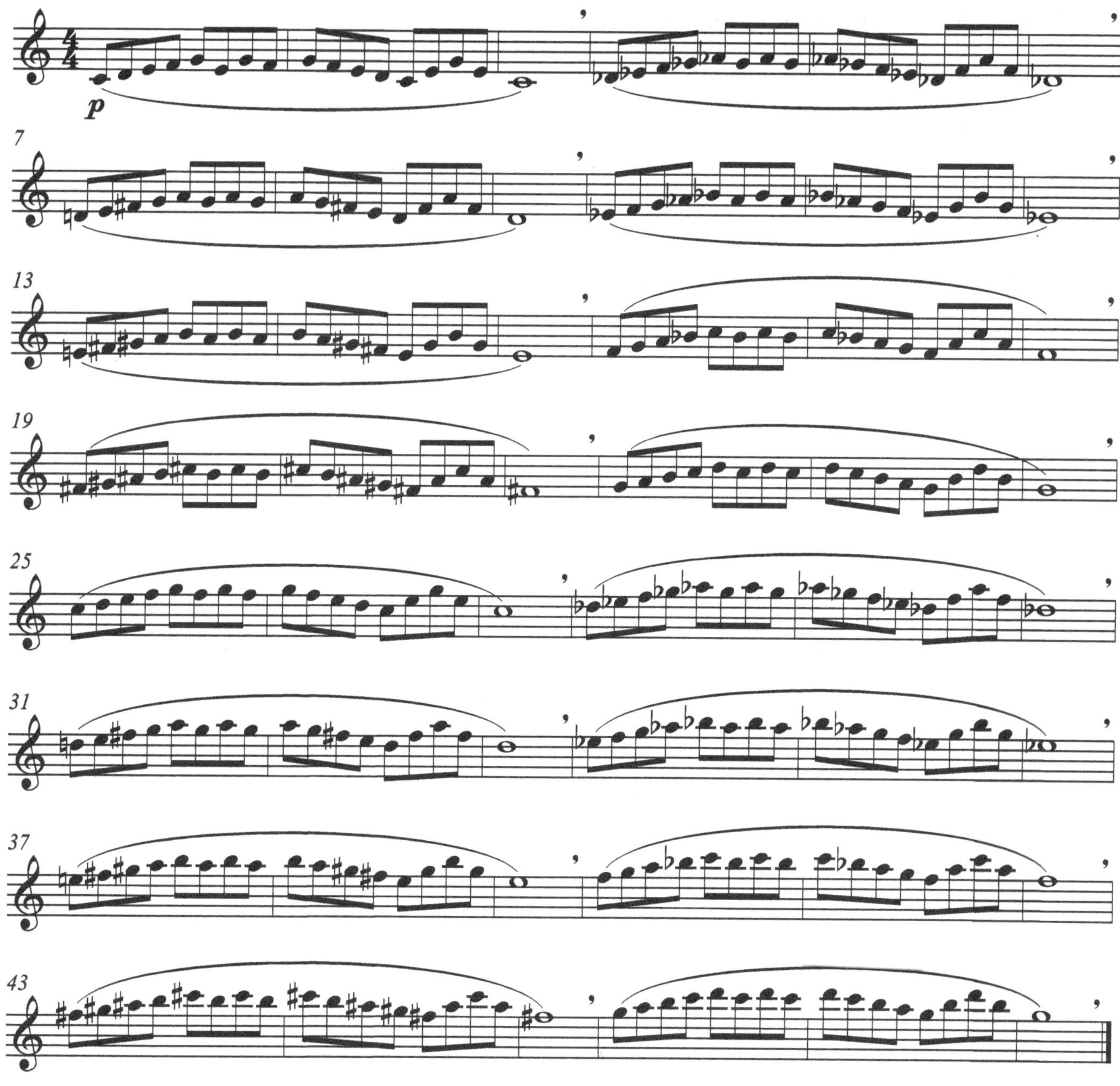

3. Lead pipe/mouthpiece buzzing
4. Long tones/lip bends
5. Lip flexibility
6. Articulation (scales, chords)

Rest (10 minute)
Musical practice (20 minutes)

1. Listen to recordings of repertoire
2. Practice trouble spots in pieces

40.7 Discussion Questions

1. What role does the trumpet play in a concert band?
2. What professional trumpet players do you listen to on a daily basis? Do you listen to different styles of music? What role does the trumpet function in those styles?
3. How often should you rest while practicing?
4. Have you tried to learn your favorite songs by ear?

OXFORD learning link

Visit the online resources for additional documentation and exercises to help expand learning and test your knowledge further: www.oup.com/he/powell_music1e.

CHAPTER 41

PEDAGOGIES FOR TEACHING TROMBONE

Dunwoody Mirvil

This chapter will outline sound pedagogical methods designed to assist middle and high school music directors in equipping their students with positive habits that focus on the finer details of trombone performance.

41.1 Introduction to the Instrument

TROMBONE ASSEMBLY

The trombone has three main parts: the slide, the bell, and the mouthpiece (Figure 41.1). It is advised that the slide and bell be assembled by resting the bottom of the slide on the floor using the rubber on the end of the slide. Then use the left hand to place the bell section into the slide's receiver before screwing the two sections together, as shown in Figure 41.2 (Colwell & Goolsby, 2002, p. 258). The angle between the bell and slide should be 90 degrees or less depending upon the player's hand size. When assembling the trombone, the student must be careful with the slide, for it is the most fragile part of the instrument. It can be dented by the slightest knock or bump, which can impair the intonation and performance of the slide movement.

FIGURE 41.1 The slide, bell, and mouthpiece

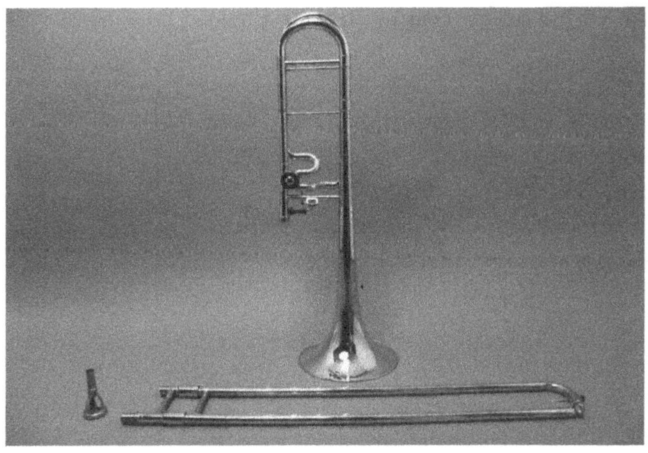

FIGURE 41.2 Left hand to grasp bell, right hand on slide

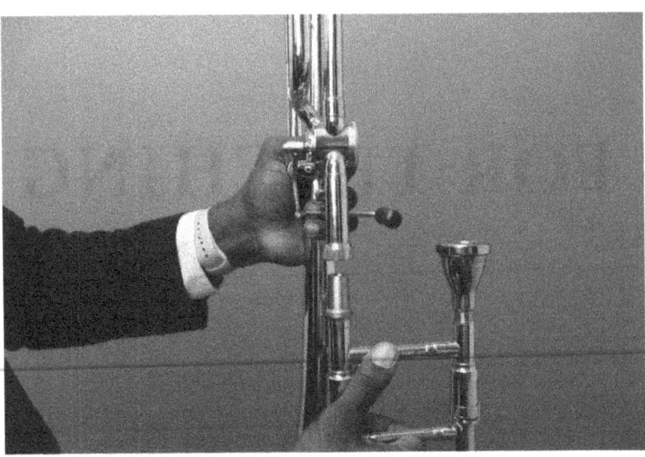

TROMBONE MAINTENANCE

There are several reasons that regular cleaning of the trombone is paramount. Dirt, debris from old lubricants, the accumulation of food particles in the instrument, and the rapid growth of bacteria and fungus can build up in the humid atmosphere of the trombone. If the instrument is not maintained properly, these materials can be hazardous to the trombonist's health, narrow the instrument's bore, pollute the moving parts, and corrode and degrade of the metal.

Here is a basic cleaning routine one can incorporate into their regimen (Note: This is advised for experienced students or teachers; please have the beginner consult their director, but be involved by watching the cleaning process):

1. Remove all slides. The slide is the most delicate part of the trombone and must always be handled with care.
2. Soak the instrument in a bathtub of warm (not hot) water. Add a mild soap (not detergent) to the water. Please keep in mind that detergent and hot water may cause the lacquer to peel. Let the trombone soak for a couple of minutes to loosen the debris.
3. Drain the soapy water and rinse the entire instrument several times with lukewarm water.
4. Wrap a cleaning rod with a kitchen towel or cleaning cloth to wrap around the rod. Ensure that the entire rod is fully covered to protect the inner and outer slide from scratches or damage from the rod.
5. After soaking, use a malleable snake brush with a rubber coating to clean the lead pipe and all tubing.
6. Dry all working parts with a soft, lint-free cloth.
7. After cleaning, lubricate with oil or slide cream. If slide cream is the lubricant of choice, place a dab of cream toward the slide stockings near the slide's end and the middle of the slide. The slide action is best when water is added to the mix.
8. Between cleanings, it is suggested that the inner slides be wiped regularly and sprayed with water as needed. Avoid moving the slides when they are dry.

LUBRICATING THE SLIDE

The slide can be lubricated with slide oil, cold cream, or a water-based cream. Most advanced trombonists prefer cold cream or a water-based cream over slide oil. The creams are inexpensive and work smoothly for a long time without care, whereas oil must be applied more often to keep the slide working efficiently. If the student chooses a water-based slide cream as the lubricant, apply the substance to the slide in the same manner as you would apply a cold cream. Ultimately, it is up to the trombonist to decide which lubricant is best for their instrument.

Steps for Applying Cold Cream or Water-Based Cream to the Slide

1. Spray the slide with water, then move the slide to spread the water.
2. Wipe all debris from the slide with a cloth and respray it with water.
3. Apply the cold cream or water-based cream on the "groove" of the inner slide (near the seventh position) and the middle of the slide (near the bell). The amount of cream should be no larger than a pea.
4. Move the slide back and forth to spread the cream.
5. Spray water on the slide again to prevent the cream from sticking in one area.

ROTOR MAINTENANCE

The rotor mechanism on the F attachment should be viewed as a high-powered engine for a luxury car. Most high-end sedans would take super unleaded or premium gas to maintain high performance. If the driver uses the lower-grade gas, the car will continue to run but will eventually face some engine issues. The case is similar when using slide, key, or valve oil on the rotor mechanism. The different viscosities of the oils mentioned can eventually affect the rotor. It is advised to use rotor oil on the rotor "engine." See Figures 41.3 and 41.4.

FIGURE 41.3 **Applying rotor oil through valve mechanism**

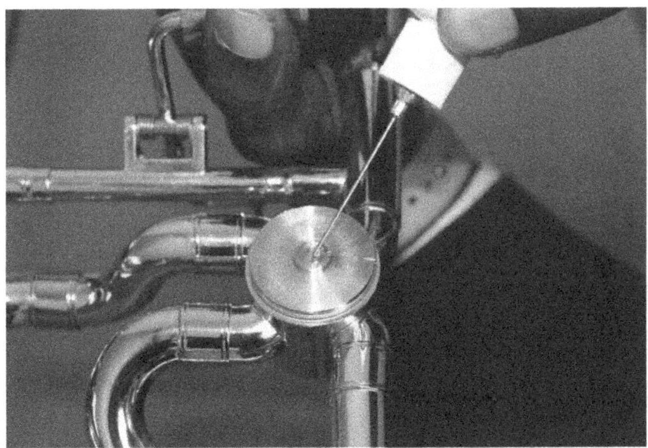

FIGURE 41.4 Applying rotor oil through tuning slide

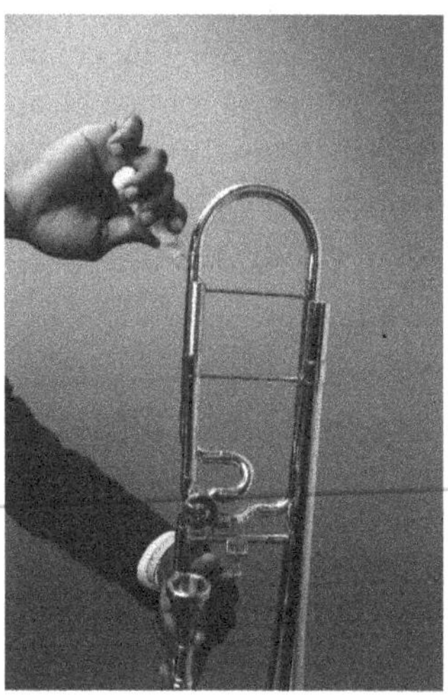

PLAYING POSITION: HOLDING THE TROMBONE

The way we hold the trombone can affect our performance efficiency; the more comfortable the player, the greater the potential for ease of play. The following steps provide a recommended approach on how to hold the trombone.

The Left Hand

- The left hand and arm are used to hold the trombone. The effort needs to be strong enough to support the instrument but not so much as to create unnecessary tension.
- Form your hand in the sign-language gesture for "I love you," as shown in Figures 41.5 and 41.6, and place the thumb around the bell brace or the F attachment lever, the

FIGURE 41.5 "I love you" in American Sign Language

FIGURE 41.6 Applying the sign while holding the trombone with the left hand

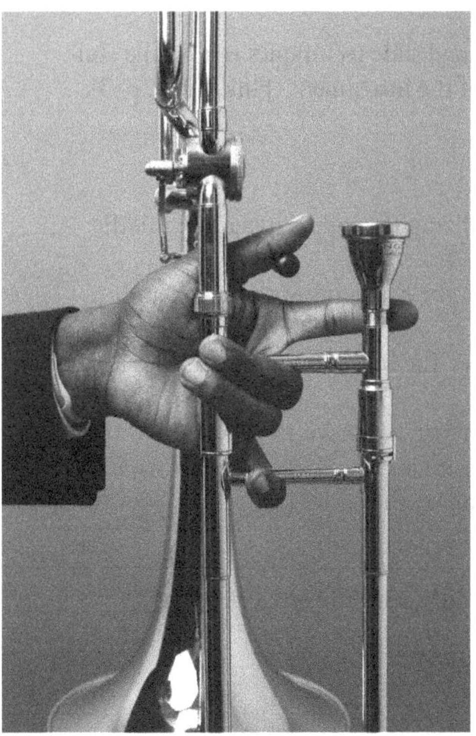

index finger against the side of the lead pipe near where the mouthpiece enters the instrument, and the pinky finger on the slide (either with or without the slide being locked). The middle and ring fingers grasp the instrument through the brace and curl into the palm.

- While the horn is in playing position, refrain from hunching the left shoulder, tilting the head, or twisting the neck to support the instrument's weight, as shown in Figure 41.7. Doing so can restrict breathing, tighten the throat, and contort the embouchure.

FIGURE 41.7 Holding the horn with the left hand while the slide is parallel to the ground

- Be careful not to use the right hand to help support the instrument. Doing so will affect the slide technique and cause the instrument to bounce when shifting positions.
- The development of the embouchure, breathing, and slide techniques rest on the ability of the left hand to support the entire weight of the instrument (Fink, 1970, p. 3).

The Right Hand

- The most effective way to hold the slide is by utilizing the index finger, the middle finger, and the thumb.
- While looking into the palm of your hand, place the first joint of the index and middle fingers at the bottom of the slide brace.
- Place the thumb on the bottom of the slide brace. The brace should touch the side of the thumb near the tip (Fink, 1970, p. 3).
- Doing this encourages more flexibility with the wrist, as shown in Figure 41.8. If the hand is placed around the slide by gripping with all five fingers (like a fist), it will affect the clarity of the tone and ability to move efficiently.

FIGURE 41.8 **Hold the slide with index, middle, and thumb**

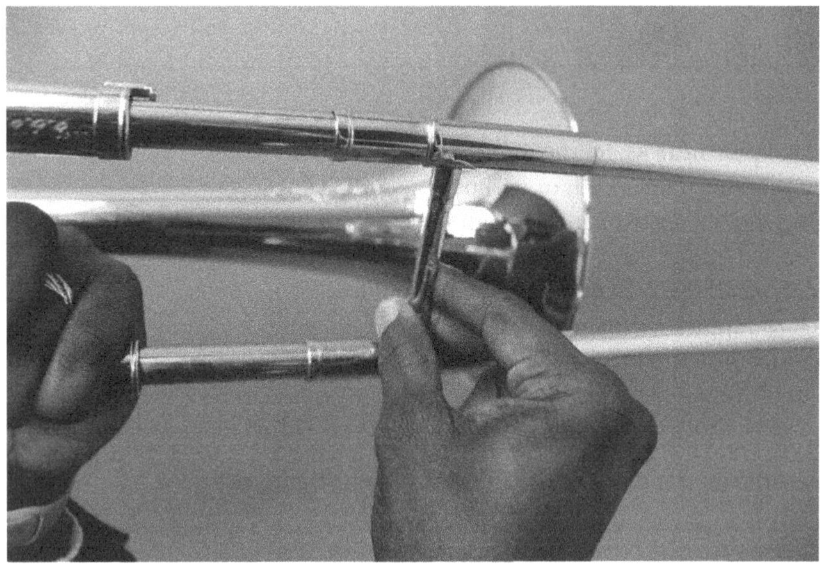

- To keep consistency and accuracy with the right-arm movement, the elbow needs to be kept at a 45-degree angle from the body in first position and should not be allowed to droop down next to the body (Bachelder & Hunt, 2002, p. 103).

EMBOUCHURE FORMATION AND PLACEMENT

The formation of the embouchure should be as natural as possible (Bachelder & Hunt, 2002, p. 21). If the essential physical prerequisites are met, it is unnecessary to contort the facial muscles to form an embouchure (Bachelder & Hunt, 2002, p. 21). The mouthpiece plays a crucial role in the structure of the trombonist's embouchure. The placement of the mouthpiece is contingent on the size and position of the player's teeth and lips, as well as an individual's register of concentration (Bachelder & Hunt, 2002, p. 23). The mouthpiece is usually placed with two-thirds of the upper lip and one-third of the lower lip, forming the embouchure (Colwell & Goolsby, 2002, 261). This basic set is similar to other lower brass instruments (baritone/euphonium and tuba), where the lips are relaxed across the front of the teeth.

The steps to forming an embouchure are as follows:

1. The embouchure is constructed as if pronouncing the letter "m" (Fink, 1970, p. 10).
2. While saying the letter, the jaw is in its natural, relaxed state, lowered, and the teeth are separated.
3. The lips should be slightly tensed and rolled in, more than they would when pronouncing the "m" in conversation (Fink, 1970, p. 10).
4. Then, while consistent air is being blown, the lips are pressed together until a lip vibration is made. The facial muscles are set in a combination of a pucker and a smile, which prevents the puffing of the cheeks and forms the corners of the embouchure (Fink, 1970, p. 10).
5. Be careful not to stretch the lips too much. Doing this will form an aperture that is too flat and wide, which will prevent the lip from serving as a cushion for the mouthpiece. This embouchure setting typically creates an edgy or thin tone for the performer (Colwell & Goolsby, 2002, p. 262).
6. The trombonist must also be aware not to jam too much of their lip into the mouthpiece or clench their teeth or jaw, for it will cause an uneven aperture that creates a stuffy, nasal tone (Colwell & Goolsby, 2002, p. 262).

THE APERTURE

The shape of the aperture of the embouchure plays a vital role in the student's overall sound. The aperture is the space near the center of the lips where the air transfers into the mouthpiece, and it should be as round as possible. To create a round aperture, the lips must have a slight pucker, and the jaw is lowered instead of clinching or biting. Having the lips stretched while forming an egg-shaped aperture will produce an airy and buzzy tone (Fink, 1970, p. 12). The tone is usually improved immediately when the trombonist thinks of rounding the embouchure, which affects the shape of the aperture (the buzzing portion of the lips).

41.2 Pedagogical Considerations

TONE PRODUCTION ON TROMBONE

The tongue's placement in the mouth plays a significant role in the trombonist's tone. If a student has a thin, pinched sound, it is possibly due to the tongue's being held too high in the mouth, as when pronouncing the syllable "ee" (Bachelder & Hunt, 2002, p. 26). This is typically the case when the student attempts to produce a middle- or low-register note using the syllable. One reason for this problem is that students are often told to start every attack using "t," which implies a mouth configuration of "ee" (Bachelder & Hunt, 2002, p. 26). The tongue position could be changed to either an "oo" or "aw" syllable to improve the sound (Bachelder & Hunt, 2002, p. 26). This is done by adjusting the space between the upper and lower jaws or moving the jaw slightly forward (Bachelder & Hunt, 2002, p. 26). The trombonist will know if the mouth cavity is too large for the pitch and volume intended when a fuzzy, airy sound is present.

ARTICULATION: THE USE OF THE TONGUE

Many trombonists tend to overarticulate, which causes the tongue to be their biggest adversary in many cases. It is important to note that the correct use of the tongue in brass articulation is similar to that for articulating in speech. Whether playing a single note or repeated notes, the trombonist should use the tip of the tongue (Bachelder & Hunt, 2002, p. 27). The middle and back of the tongue must remain relaxed in all passages, regardless of the difficulty (Bachelder & Hunt, 2002, p. 27). Any use of the back end of the tongue during articulation will cause a delayed response, which will ultimately slacken the tempo to some selection.

ARTICULATION AND VARIED TONGUING STYLES: LEGATO, MARCATO, LEGATO

There are three factors that contribute to producing a note: the embouchure, the air, and the tongue. When it comes to the style or type of articulation, it has everything to do with the tongue, not the air. However, the air plays a crucial role in the act of articulation, for without it one cannot articulate. When articulating, the air should be continuous and not pulsated, regardless of the type of articulation. It is important to note that the purpose of the tongue is to *shape* the articulation. The following information is a guide to the various syllables students should consider when articulating on the trombone:

The "T" Syllable: Staccato, Marcato, and Accent

- "tee": upper register
- "taa": mid-register
- "toe": low-register

The "D" Syllable: Tenuto (Long Accent)

- "dee": upper register
- "daa": middle register
- "doe": low register

The "N" Syllable: Legato

- "nee": upper register
- "naa": mid-register
- "noe": low register

SLIDE TECHNIQUE

One of the plagues facing trombonists is synchronizing the air, tongue, and slide movement to operate the instrument efficiently. Of these three factors, the accuracy of the slide tends to be the main issue with most novice trombonists. To have a good concept of proper slide technique, one must understand that it is about getting to the right place at the right time. Brass musicians, other than trombonists, can change from one note to the next with a rapid movement of the valves. Similarly, the trombonist must move the slide from one position to the next just as rapidly but typically moves too slowly. The slide's slow and lazy movement will produce micro-glissandos at the beginning and end of tones.

On the other hand, when asked to move the slide faster, most students tend instead to move *sooner*, which undercuts the full value of the note. To obtain the proper slide speed, one must wait until the last possible moment before moving to the new position, then move with pinpoint accuracy. Using a metronome and setting it to the sixteenth-note subdivision is an excellent tool in incorporating this approach. Utilizing this knowledge will eliminate the micro-glissandos between notes on the same partial.

THE F ATTACHMENT

The F attachment is a device consisting of extra tubing that is switched into the basic length of the trombone utilizing a thumb-operated valve or trigger (Colwell & Goolsby, 2002, p. 256). This device also adds a multitude of possible slide positions, offering alternative positions and trills for technically tricky passages (Colwell & Goolsby, 2002, p. 256).

The extra tubing added to the instrument lowers the pitch by a perfect fourth. However, the trouble with this invention is that the perfect fourth becomes progressively imperfect the farther the slide is extended (Aharoni, 1996, p. 7). Owing to the laws of acoustics and to compensate for good intonation, the distance between each position increases as the slide is extended (Aharoni, 1996, p. 7). It is known that the trombone on the B♭ side is designed to play seven different fundamental positions. Yet, with the F attachment activated, the slide is long enough for only six positions when the entire length, including the stockings of the slide, is used (Bachelder & Hunt, 2002, p. 97). Essentially, the instrument is too short to accommodate seven positions or seven different harmonic series on the F side of the instrument. The following information provides a detailed description of the placement of the slide positions with the F attachment activated (Bachelder & Hunt, 2002, p. 97):

- Low F, first position: slide closed; if the instrument has a spring on the slide, it may be necessary to push it in to get the low F in tune
- Low E, flat second position: approximately one inch beyond the regular second position
- Low E♭, flat third position: approximately two and a half inches beyond the regular third position (this position may be thought of as a short fourth position if this is an easier approach for the trombonist)
- Low D, sharp fifth position: about an inch short of regular fifth position (fourth position has been dropped)
- Low D♭, flat sixth position: approximately one inch beyond the regular sixth position
- Low C, flat seventh position: as far as possible to reach (the pitch will probably still be sharp)

41.3 Exercises and Warm-Ups That build Technique and Tone

Just as an athlete incorporates calisthenics to loosen up before an event and strengthen their muscles for future ventures, brass players need to include a warm-up routine in their practice regimen. The goal of the trombonist is to achieve the point where the lips are responding in a relaxed and comfortable manner throughout the entire register of the instrument.

An excellent daily warm-up routine should include but is not limited to mouthpiece buzzing, long tones, lip slurs, articulation exercises, and range studies. Concentrating on these exercises will enhance almost all the desirable elements of fine playing. It is important to note that practice requirements will differ depending on the trombonist's talent, the seriousness of their musical aspirations, and the strong and weak attributes of their playing. Regardless of their skill level, the student should establish a well-planned routine to loosen up the embouchure and coordinate all the playing factors.

MOUTHPIECE BUZZING

Mouthpiece buzzing is often recommended for trombonists (indeed, for all brass players) who want to develop better pitch placement, tone quality, and endurance. Incorporating this technique also prevents the cheeks from puffing out while keeping the corners of the mouth firm and chin flat (Colwell & Goolsby, 2002, p. 262). Subsequently, once students become comfortable with the buzzing technique, they should notice more secure pitch placement on the trombone and a fuller, more focused tone. While it has its benefits, this method is very demanding on the lips and should be done in moderation (five to ten minutes per day). It is also recommended that the student utilize a drone or piano while performing this technique to assist with centering the pitches. See Figure 41.9. For more notation examples to use with mouthpiece buzzing, see the book's online resources.

FIGURE 41.9 Mouthpiece buzzing

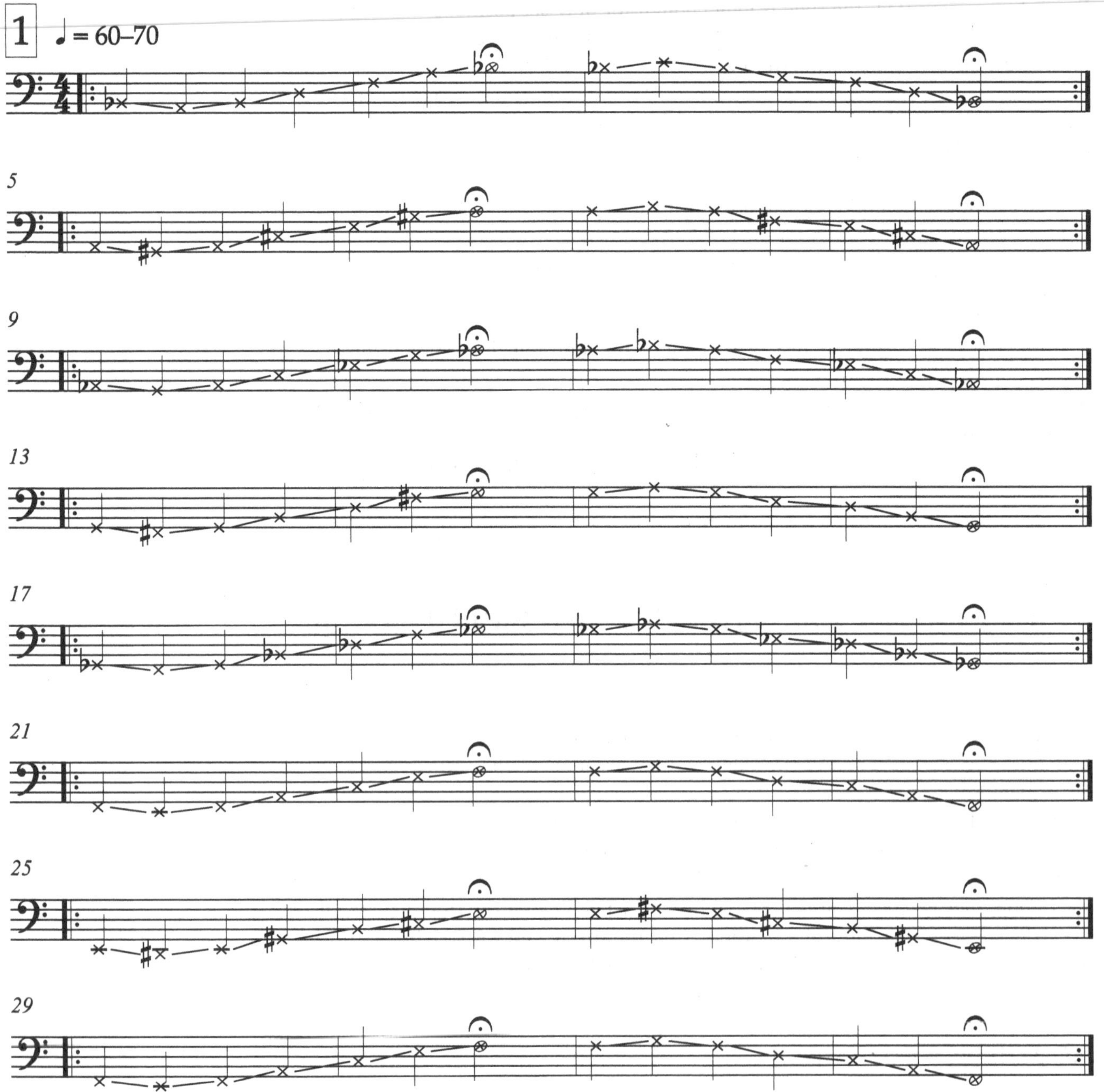

LONG TONES

Playing long tones is imperative. It is a great technique for coordinating the student's breathing, range, and dynamics throughout the entire register. The exercise can also test the player's endurance while improving their tone quality and intonation. While performing the following exercises, the student should relax their lips as they increase the volume to ensure that more of the lip surface will vibrate in proportion to the volume. If the student is not careful, tension can sneak into their playing, which in most cases goes unnoticed or is accepted out of habit. These exercises should be performed for a few seconds each and take less than five minutes to complete. See Figure 41.10. For more long-tone exercises, see the book's online resources.

FIGURE 41.10 Long tones

LIP SLURS

Lip slurs are the process of changing pitches within a harmonic series by adjusting the embouchure (which affects the air) only, without changing slide positions or valve combinations (Colwell & Goolsby, 2002, p. 208). It is recommended that trombonists practice lip slurs in all registers, starting in the middle register, then progressively extending the technique to the upper and lower registers. The following exercises should be performed at a moderate tempo in a controlled and relaxed manner to assist with precision. It is also suggested that the student use a metronome beating eighth notes on the following exercises to ensure evenness and smoothness of sound. Accomplishing this will also assist with maintaining the rhythmic integrity of the exercises. See Figure 41.11. For more lip slur exercises, see the book's online resources.

FIGURE 41.11 Lip slur

ARTICULATIONS

As defined in most dictionaries, articulation is how sound is connected—that is, the term refers not only to how a sound starts, but to how it ends (Colwell & Goolsby, 2002, p. 211). This is a critical concept to digest, because many brass players can start the pitch with their tongue while also using the tongue to end the note. Unfortunately, the latter approach produces an abrupt ending to the note, creating an unfavorable musical effect.

Let us apply this concept in algebraic terminology to provide a visual example. Regardless of the type of articulation, the air should be treated as the *constant*, and the tongue serves as the *variable*. We are aware that the constant (air) is fixed and does not change, whereas the variable (tongue) is a factor that is liable to change (creating staccato, legato, accent, etc.). The purpose of the tongue is to dictate the shape of the articulation.

It is also important to note that the tongue is best used in a forward, upward motion rather than back and forth. This will enable the tip of the tongue to be used when articulating while the middle and base of the tongue remain relaxed. Identifying this can assist

FIGURE 41.12 Articulation

the student in playing lighter and faster. See Figure 41.12. For more articulation exercises, see the book's online resources.

RANGE

When working on extending the range, much time and effort will be saved if the student approaches the technique by establishing a balance between speed of air, facial muscular strength, and the size of the aperture, which is affected by the embouchure. (Bousfield, 2015, p. 37). Physiologically, the lower jaw will rise incrementally so that the lip and teeth opening will become smaller, which assists with attaining a high range. This directs the angle of the airstream downward as the student goes higher in pitch. The aspiring trombonist must understand that to find success playing in the high register, one must spend time in the high register. Still, the technique must be done with diligence, intermittent rest, and alternate with low-register routines.

Developing an excellent low register on the instrument serves as a benefit to the student as much as an exceptional high register. A great approach in establishing a solid low register is to start in the middle register and work down without repositioning the lips on the mouthpiece. While playing in the lower register, the trombonist will need to push the jaw out slightly to align the lips and keep the tongue flat (Bachelder & Hunt, 2002, p. 27). The player should envision blowing hot air onto a cold window.

Incorporating this concept will assist in dropping the jaw and opening the throat, which will enable the player to increase the volume of warm air (the same effect as yawning). If the student plays with a clenched jaw, where the tongue is near the roof of the mouth, it tends to create a pinched and deficient sound. It is also important to note that the low register does not require the trombonist to force the air or overarticulate to respond. A relaxed embouchure paired with good breath control and capacity breathing will provide a good-quality tone in the low register. See Figure 41.13. For more range exercises, see the book's online resources.

WARM-DOWN

This aspect of the practice session is just as important as the warm-up but is often neglected by most novice trombonists. The warm-down process provides an opportunity to relax the lips and allow the blood to expel the acids from the embouchure muscles. Warm-down exercises could range from playing short exercises softly to playing long tones in the low register. Pedal tones are ideal for intermediate and advanced players to include in the warm-down process. Some of the warm-up exercises displayed earlier could be used in the warm-down routine; they can be taken down an octave or performed at a soft dynamic level.

FIGURE 41.13 Range

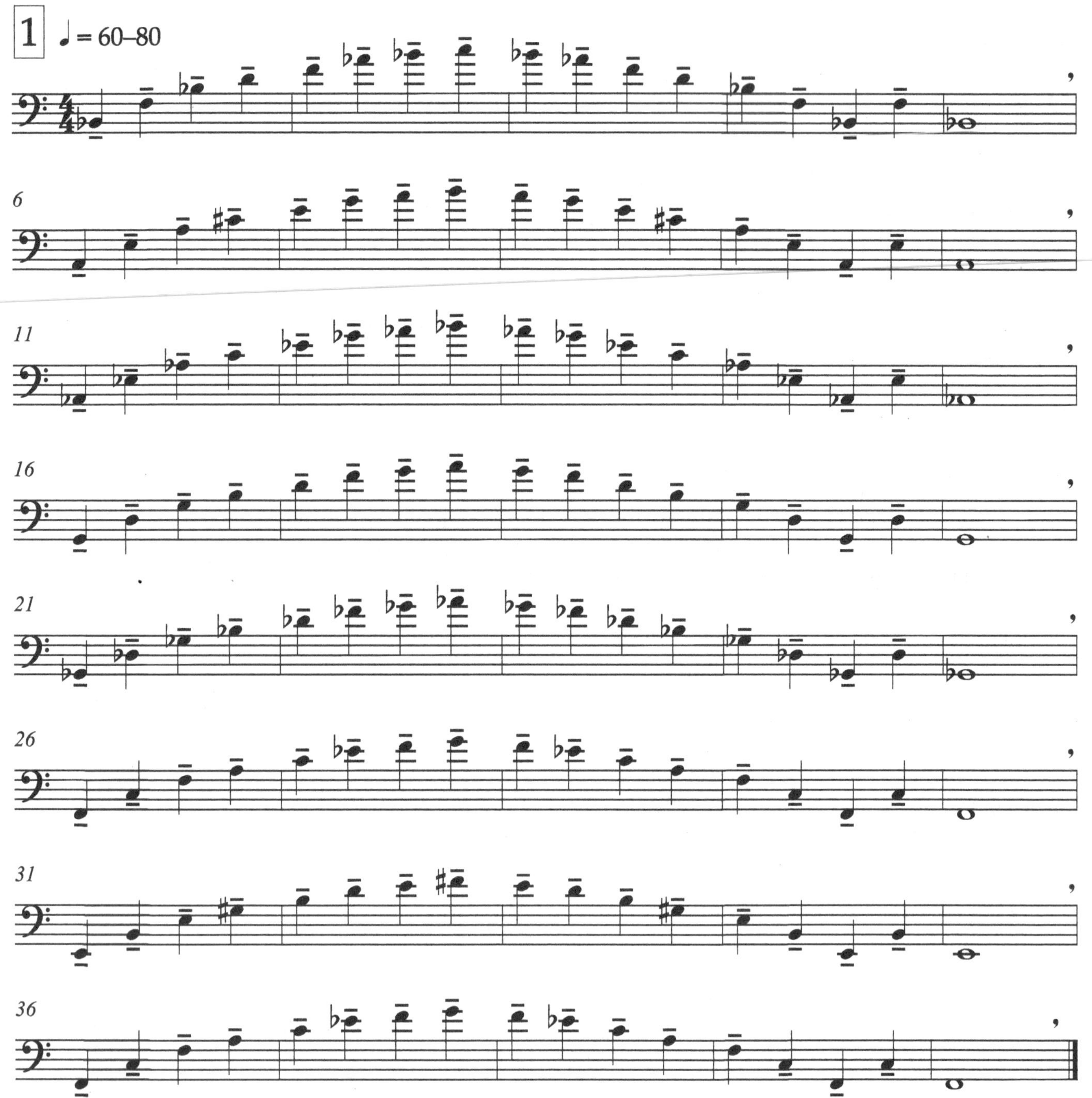

41.4 Lesson Ideas to Build Creative Musicianship

THE IMPORTANCE OF LISTENING

To develop a good tone, the student must have a concept of a quality sound. This is where listening is instrumental to the student's practice regimen: we tend to become the player we hear. Listening to high-quality recordings of professional trombonists plays a role in the maturation process of the young trombonist. It is suggested that the student listen to more than one style or player, since limiting themselves in that way often leads to a sound with a somewhat one-dimensional character. Instead, the student should listen to a number of different trombonists who play in a variety of styles, including classical, jazz, salsa, popular music, and others. This will encourage students to develop their sound based on the assortment of colors stored in their minds as an "ideal" trombone sound.

THE IMPORTANCE OF RECORDING

The benefit of recording is an approach that is often abandoned or avoided by many student trombonists. This is most likely attributable to their fear of hearing the deficiencies in their playing. Without the recording device, trombonists tend to think the sound being heard from behind the bell is the sound received by the audience.

To improve at any skill, whether it be music or other disciplines, the player, who is essentially the producer of their product, must not hide from their weaknesses; it is best to seek out the problem and correct it. Professional musicians often record themselves to accurately depict their performance sound and determine what can be improved. Using a recording device can assist the student in their pursuit of being a better musician, as it provides an honest representation of where they stand.

41.5 Discussion Questions

1. Which type of oil is considered best for the rotor mechanism on the F-Attachment trombone? Would other types of oil suffice?
2. How many fingers are needed to operate the slide? How is the overall performance affected by gripping the slide in the form of a fist?
3. What is the difference between the embouchure and the aperture? Does the embouchure affect the aperture or vice versa?
4. Accuracy of the slide movement is one of the top goals for every trombonist. What tool is mentioned in the chapter that assists with eliminating micro-glissandos, which can occur between notes on the same partial?
5. The trombone has seven identifiable slide positions on the B♭ side of the horn. However, the same instrument only possesses six slide positions when the F attachment is engaged. Why is this the case?

OXFORD learning link

Visit the online resources for additional documentation and exercises to help expand learning and test your knowledge further: www.oup.com/he/powell_music1e.

CHAPTER 42

PEDAGOGIES FOR TEACHING BARITONE AND TUBA

Jennifer Jester

This chapter provides an overview of the baritone and tuba playing positions, postures, embouchure, tone production, articulation, and intonation, and an introduction to playing without music and improvisation. It also includes technical exercises, practice tips, and personal anecdotes on switching instruments and supporting student choice regarding musical instruments.

42.1 Introduction to the Instrument

BARITONE AND TUBA ASSEMBLY

Baritones and tubas have two main parts: the body of the instrument, which includes the bell and valves, and the mouthpiece. The mouthpiece is inserted into the receiver. It is advisable to put the mouthpiece in while the instrument is on the lap so that the mouthpiece doesn't fall out. When taking the instrument out of the case, be careful of the bell, as it is the most fragile part of the instrument.

BARITONE AND TUBA MAINTENANCE

Cleaning

Baritone horns and tubas can go for months without being cleaned. The biggest culprit behind stuck valves is when a student eats prior to playing the instrument. This can lead to buildup inside the horn that causes the valves to stick. Encouraging students to wash their mouths out before playing will dramatically help keep the inside of the horn clean.

Taking the instrument to a music store for a chemical cleaning is the preferred method of cleaning and will yield a professional result. While it is possible for students to take the horn home and give it a bath, this requires disassembling the horn, cleaning it in the bathtub with mild liquid soap (such as Ivory), rinsing, and reassembling. This is much easier with baritones. When it comes to tubas, because of their size it can be impossible to get all the soap out of them without using a hose. The safest and most effective way is to have a professional cleaning if possible.

If you clean your horn at home, make sure that you put the valves in the correct valve casing. There are numbers on the outside of each valve, and the pistons also have numbers. If they aren't put back correctly, when the air won't flow through, and the horn will be unplayable until they are arranged correctly. Put slide grease back on the slides so that they glide in and out easily. Re-oil the valves, since the previous oil will have been washed off.

Maintenance

Baritones and tubas are similar to cars in that they need to have oil in order to run correctly. Use the starting point of the semester as a check in to see if all the valves are oiled. If there are rotary valves, they *must* have rotary valve oil. Rotary valve oil is lighter than regular valve oil and has a special applicator with a long needle for application.

For piston valves, unscrew the top casing and pull the valve up to oil it. Put oil all around the valve and return the valve, using the valve guide in the notch of the valve casing. Do not turn the horn upside down and drop oil into the valves, because the oil will run back out through the hole in the bottom of the valve. If the valve is still stuck, take the horn in for repair.

For rotary valves, oil them by oiling everything that is a moving part (there are three or four tiny joints per valve). Unscrew the back casing of the valve and put oil on top of the tiny area in the center that moves, then replace the casing. Drop light rotary oil into the valve by pulling out the tuning slide and dropping oil into the slide in the direction of the rotors. Press the valve so oil is worked into the rotor from the inside.

In *no* circumstance should you use pliers. Doing so without proper training can destroy the metal grooves of the horn. Please warn parents that *this can damage the horn forever.* When in doubt, use a repairperson.

PLAYING POSITION: HOLDING THE INSTRUMENT

Baritone or Euphonium

Notice how the euphonium is cradled—almost tucked under the left arm. The body is not twisted, the knees are parallel with the arms, and the head is in alignment (see Figure 42.1).

FIGURE 42.1 **Baritone held correctly**

In the online resources there are photos showing incorrect posture for holding the baritone. Can you identify what is wrong? What would you tell the student to do to fix it? See Figures 42.1, 42.2, and 42.3 in the online resources.

The baritone is an instrument that has to be held in a way that doesn't come naturally. It is critical to try to establish some of these habits early so the student has the best chance of success and also doesn't develop strange habits.

Euphoniums can have three valves at the top (top-action), four valves at the top (top-action), or three valves and one side action. Some older euphoniums and baritones can have front-action valves as well.

Tuba

Start by looking at the photos in Figures 42.2, 42.3, and 42.4. This set of photos is different because I wanted to show the natural way people sit in relation to where one sits with a tuba.

FIGURE 42.2 Tuba with mouthpiece too low

FIGURE 42.3 Tuba with mouthpiece too high

FIGURE 42.4 Tuba with mouthpiece too high

Notice where the bottom of the tuba is sitting. Is it on the chair? Below the chair? Is the student able to get to the tuba without contorting their body? Does the mouthpiece sit above or below the person's mouth when resting naturally?

Figures 42.5 and 42.6 are photos showing a tuba being held correctly by a seated player.

FIGURE 42.5 Tuba with mouthpiece just right

FIGURE 42.6 Tuba with mouthpiece just right (side view)

Figures 42.7 and 42.8 are photos of showing a player holding the tuba supported by a stand.

FIGURE 42.7 Player seated with tuba stand

FIGURE 42.8 Player seated with tuba stand (three-quarter view)

Figures 42.9 and 42.10 show a player standing with the tuba supported by a strap.

If the base of the tuba keeps slipping, consider using nonslip material such as drawer liner underneath the tuba.

FIGURE 42.9 Player standing, holding tuba supported by a strap

FIGURE 42.10 Player standing, holding tuba supported by a strap (side view)

POSTURE DO'S

- Sit toward the edge of the chair if using a tuba stand; if not using a stand, still sit toward the front of the chair.
- Consider using a chair pad to raise the player to the height of mouthpiece.
- Consider using a tuba stand to put the tuba into proper playing position.
- Consider a fully held tuba stand for smaller students who are unable to hold the instrument completely on their own.
- Keep the body relaxed and upright, not stretched or extended.
- The hand position should be relaxed and correct.

POSTURE DON'TS

- Don't lean back on the chair.
- Don't curve the torso back.

PLAYING POSITION ADAPTATIONS FOR BARITONE HORN PLAYERS

This isn't an adaptation for people specifically with physical limitations, but rather for anyone who might have a long torso, or just who needs assistance with the placement of their horn—which could be anyone. Become familiar with how a person should look when holding and playing a baritone.

Signs that someone might need help are when the student:

- Slouches down to meet the mouthpiece
- Sits with heels up to bring the horn to the playing position

- Is sitting with a completely twisted torso to get the horn to the playing position
- Always puts the horn on the right knee or leg to play

These all signals there might be a need for a euphonium pillow, a rolled-up towel, or wrist strap of some sort to help the student hold the instrument. The first three cause the player to be unable to take a big breath and can cause posture issues. It also just looks strange. Remember the basic posture concepts: sitting on the edge of the chair, torso upright, head facing forward, and bringing the horn to you, rather than you to it, which is what these three positions look like. There are euphonium pillows and wrist straps available online. I was a longtime user of euphonium pillows until I found the wrist strap. The strap allows me to stand and hold the horn in the same position as when I am sitting, which is not the case with pillows.

For examples of a student using a small pillow and a hand strap, see the online resources.

ADAPTATIONS FOR TUBA PLAYERS

Stands

The tuba is an unforgiving instrument if it does not fit your torso. A helpful solution is to use a tuba stand; it is a great way to lower the tuba to exactly where you need it. It holds the weight of the tuba below the chair, rather than on the chair or your lap. For photos of how stands can be placed to help hold the weight of the tuba, see the online resources.

Embouchure Formation and Placement

On mouthpiece positioning:

- Baritone: Form the embouchure by saying the word "hmmmm." The mouthpiece should meet the embouchure without any alteration of the head or jaw position.
- Tuba: Place the mouth at the halfway point on the mouthpiece. When the mouthpiece is positioned too low or high, it can dramatically affect the tone, leading to gurgling. Remind the student to use as light pressure as possible.

Don't puff your cheeks. This is called an "inflation" and is caused by the muscles not contracting. To remedy this, have the student say the "tu" syllable; the muscles will automatically contract.

BREATHING TECHNIQUES

One of my favorite breathing techniques to use is from the tuba player Michael Milnarik, who created a really useful set of low-brass exercises in a concise format called the "Milnarik Daily Routine," found at www.tubastudio.com under the section "Tuba Methods" or "Euphonium Methods." The daily routine exercises, in addition to the breathing exercises, are very simple to use and can be done with a metronome, and they really help a student feel the size of the horn and how much air they need to use very quickly.

Blow into the horn with all the valves pressed down (don't make a sound; it should be quiet, warm air) and then breathe in again. Now breathe out through the horn with all the valves open. From there, alternate blowing through the instrument with the valves pressed and then open. Use a metronome, and if the metronome is set in 4/4, breathe in on 4 and out on 1, 2, and 3. If the metronome is set on 3/4, breathe in on 3 and out on 1 and 2.

TONE PRODUCTION (BUZZING TECHNIQUES)

A small amount of buzzing (no more than three or four minutes) before playing is helpful to build embouchure muscles and start to understand the flow. For baritone and tuba buzzing, use only two fingers to hold the mouthpiece (i.e., don't wrap your hand around it) and then start with "sirens" or getting the student to make high and low sounds. Don't buzz too long, as this can be counterproductive. If the sound is weak, that means that too much air is escaping and the embouchure is inefficient. The next step after basic buzzing and sirens is to buzz simple nursery tunes, such as "Row, Row, Row Your Boat." It helps the student learn how to match pitch while buzzing, but also has a bit of articulation, since the pitches for "row, row, row" are repeated ones.

42.2 Pedagogical Considerations

TONE PRODUCTION ON BARITONE AND TUBA

Having an open oral cavity is key. Have the student visualize holding an apple in their mouth helps make a round, open sound.

ARTICULATION

Use of the Tongue

You can use "tu" or "pu" as the starting syllable to get the air moving and get the lips to begin vibrating. This is where repetitive articulation studies can be helpful.

For tuba, one exercise I use is "tu" (rest) "tu tu, tu."

The notes are the lightest, quietest articulations you can muster, and sometimes this exercise requires that your tongue be in between your lips just to get the note started. After that you can dial back the articulation to place the tongue behind the teeth.

Double Tonguing and Triple Tonguing

These are considered to be more advanced, and you wouldn't teach them to a beginning student. When teaching students double tonguing. use the syllables "tu ku, tu ku, tu" ("tk tk t"). When teaching triple tonguing, teach "tu tu ku, tu tu ku, tu" ("ttk ttk t").

Important: for triple tonguing, do not use the pattern "tu ku tu, tu ku tu, tu ("tkt, tkt t"). This can be disastrous for students who want to go on to play on a more advanced level.

VARIED TONGUING STYLES: LEGATO, MARCATO, LEGATO

Intonation

Practicing with a drone can be invaluable for low-brass students. Use a solid tone either from your metronome, or my favorite, tanpura drones, which can provide a practice buddy that can help with intonation problems. Go to YouTube and type in "tanpura drone" and the key you need. Here are some examples of how to practice with a drone:

1. Scales with drone: In the key of the drone, play scales over a drone. You can also change keys: play the scale over a drone in the wrong key (this is really great for listening—try a C scale with an F♯ drone).
2. Drone in the key of your piece: Play the piece with the drone.

LIP SLURS

Some of my favorite exercises include:

- Slow lip slurs: Take two partials and move between them slowly to work on the partial bend (great for beginners).
- Bugles: Start with an anchor note, such as high B♭ in the staff. That is the note you always return to and always slur, not tongue. Go up a partial, then back to your anchor note. Slur up two partials, then slur down to anchor note; keep doing this all the way up to the highest level that your student can go. This helps to build not only range but also flexibility. Once you've reached the highest point, then you can start over, using the descending chromatic sequence of valves (0, 2, 1, 12, 23, 13, 123).
- Lip flips: This takes the same idea as bugles, where you have an anchor note but are working at a faster tempo.

B♭, B♭ D B♭ ______________

B♭, B♭ D B♭ ______________

B♭, B♭ D, B♭ D, B♭ D, B♭ D, B♭ D, B♭ ______________

Memorize the pattern and then you can also use the descending chromatic sequence of valves to move through the chromatic partials.

42.3 Starting to Play Without Teaching the Music Staff First

Many band directors go through method books as a routine, but there is so much more to making music—especially the world of making music by ear. Without this element, students will not develop a way to internalize the music-making process. This requires a completely different set of synapses in the brain, and starting kids on basic improvisation early on can be absolutely invaluable to their musical education as well as helping them develop a real love for music.

STARTING POINTS

Start them with songs they know—not pop songs, but nursery tunes. As the decades come and go, so does whatever pop hit they might be into; the tried-and-true songs that aren't going away are the nursery tunes. It turns out they are also great to buzz your mouthpiece to, which helps the student develop more embouchure strength.

> Try small pieces of a chorus of a song. But if this is too difficult, you can rock, jazz, and funk up nursery tunes to make them cooler. Being familiar with the tune is key!

LESSON PLAN EXAMPLE

My favorite example to start with is "Row, Row, Row Your Boat." It is scalar, repetitive, and doesn't have many tricky jumps; we all know it; you can put it in all the keys to start teaching scales; and it's a great introduction to chord changes.

Procedure:

- Melody: Have them buzz and/or sing the song first.
- Dissection of melody: Use numbers or solfège. Dissect the melody using numbers. That high leap—what scale degree is that?
- Put harmony with the melody—have the student sing or buzz a harmony part. Have half the class sing the melody and the other half sing the harmony, then switch. Let them figure this out for themselves first. They may put harmony on the wrong thing but letting them mess up is part of the learning process.
- Dissection of harmony: Using a piano, let students help you play the right harmony. Play it all with just the tonic, then play it with all tonic and dominant all the way through. After that, hopefully you and the class can get it to the scaled-back version of mostly tonic through much of the song, dominant on the words "life is but a," and back to tonic on "dream."
- Dissection of chords: Identify the notes in the chord. When the chords are identified, have half the class play the arpeggiated chords and half play the melody. Then switch.
- Jazz up the harmony: Bring in new rhythm patterns, grooves, and so on. Have them repeat until comfortable.
- Improvisation: To start, give students parameters, such as "improvise on the first five notes of the scale"; in C these would be C, D, E, F, and G. Using "mass improvisation," where people are all playing at the same time, is great—it takes away the fear, and making a mess is fun. Remember, you still need half the class to play the harmony and rhythm parts.

These are ways you can expand on the improvisation:

- One-note wonder: Have them choose one note and improvise on just that note
- Expand this to two notes, three, and so on.
- Riff: Choose a tiny four-beat rhythm, and they play whatever notes they want to that rhythm.
- Partial scale prescribed notes.
- Partial scale prescribed notes with preset rhythm riff.
- Full scale.
- Full scale prescribed notes with preset rhythm riff.
- Expand to two or three preset rhythms that they can choose between.
- Try another key and start with these same ideas; they will have to rebuild their knowledge of the song/improvisation in that new key.
- Individual solos: When ready, students can try individual solos, because they have built a vocabulary of notes and rhythms.

- Avoid the "Happy Birthday" song. Inevitably it is one that will come up because we all know it, but it is full of pitfalls. It is in 3/4, which isn't a real groovy time signature; it has big leaps, which get tricky; and it starts on the dominant. Believe it or not, it is actually a pretty advanced song to take it apart and harmonize. That isn't to say your class couldn't get there, but just don't make it one of the first songs you do. Stick to zippier songs in 4/4.
- The blues: Use the song "C Jam Blues"; there are backing tracks available on YouTube and it is a very easy tune to learn.
- Take the first riff to Bruno Mars's "Uptown Funk."

42.4 Exercises and Warm-Ups That Build Technique and Tone

TONE, TECHNIQUE, AND ARTICULATION

Prescribed listening to solo recordings of a student's instrument can be invaluable. When making a sound on the euphonium or tuba, you want to help students get an idea of what the instrument should sound like. Speaking about a mellow, round, dark tone is very different than playing a recording of a professional playing the instrument, and nothing can replace the value of listening over a period of time to develop a mental image of what the instrument should sound like. The next step might be to have the student describe what they hear and notice from a recording and use their terminology.

IDEAS FOR LISTENING

- Euphonium: Steven Mead, David Childs, Demondrae Thurman, Hiram Diaz, Bastien Baumet
- Tuba: Roger Bobo, Gene Pokorny, Carol Jantsch, Velvet Brown

EXERCISES FOR TECHNIQUE

For beginning and intermediate slurring and tonguing exercises for both the baritone and tuba, see the online resources for this chapter.

42.5 Lesson Ideas to Build Creative Musicianship

THE IMPORTANCE OF LISTENING

Another idea for transcribing by ear with your band is to use "Soul Bossa Nova," by Quincy Jones. It can be easily dissected and is a great primer for basic form and bossa nova music; furthermore, it has parts for the whole band. It is basic enough that you could learn it in parts. Based on Brazilian-style parade-band music, this is a fun piece to learn by rote.

42.6 A Guide to Baritone and Tuba Practice

PRACTICING

Example of a practice strategy:
Begin with:

- Buzzing: two minutes. Use mouthpiece melodies from the teacher or known tunes; also use sirens and half-step slide up/down buzzing.
- Technical: Slow (way) down; play one note at a time; sing/hear the note and then play it; scale studies; scale in the key of the materials.
- Practice buddy tools:
  - Metronome work: With a metronome on, tap out rhythms, the music they are playing, and so on (could also be in the form of recordings to play along with).
  - Recordings to play along with: Smartmusic and other tools to utilize.
  - Using drones: Play scales, other pieces with drones (helps develop intonation skills).

42.7 Personal Stories and Anecdotes

ON SWITCHING INSTRUMENTS

My journey with the euphonium started in junior high after I had already spent four years learning to play the flute. While there were differences in the embouchure, it didn't prohibit me from playing both instruments at a high level in my state solo and ensemble festivals. Eventually my love for the euphonium won, and I started devoting my practice time to that instrument.

DON'T BE THE ROADBLOCK

There are many stories of students who are more or less forced into playing an instrument because "that's what the band director wanted" or "we had one at home." Or worse— "girls/boys don't play those instruments" or "those instruments are expensive to buy/maintain." Don't squelch someone's passion. If they resonate with a particular sound, then let them play it.

I was definitely in this situation as a beginning band student: we had a flute at home, so that is what I would play. However, when my mom asked what I wanted to play, I boldly said "DRUMS!" The response that followed was that "girls don't play drums." We live in a very different time now, and perhaps it would have been less of an issue, but those stereotypes are still out there. If the desire is there, somehow it will find a way into a person's life. Don't be the roadblock!

Discussion Questions

1. Discuss the progression of using improvisation to work with beginning students. Why would you not want to jump right to solo improvisation?
2. What are some accommodations or adaptations that could be used for the euphonium and tuba?
3. Was someone ever a roadblock to you in your instrument choice or anything else in your life? Do you know anyone to whom this happened? How did it make you or them feel? What did you or they do to adjust your or they situation or mindset? Do you have any musical roadblocks that you need to explore further now that you are an adult and can follow your passion?

OXFORD learning link

Visit the online resources for additional documentation and exercises to help expand learning and test your knowledge further: www.oup.com/he/powell_music1e.

CHAPTER 43

CULTURALLY RELEVANT PEDAGOGY IN BAND

Darrin Thornton

This chapter explores how the mindset of culturally responsive pedagogy can be applied to the band setting.

43.1 Introduction

The American band tradition stems from bands' historical relationship to the military (Allsup & Benedict, 2008), as mentioned in Chapter 11. Over time, military bands were developed in all branches served both public and military functions, providing opportunities for soldiers to be trained as musicians while serving their country. After World War I, as these men returned from their military tour to civilian society, many found work as band directors in school systems.

The mass production of marching and concert band instruments began around the same time. These companies made student versions of most instruments at a price point accessible to families and school districts, either individually or for their school program.

Publishing houses (Carl Fischer, Hal Leonard, etc.) met the need for what we call band music and methods materials. Band music was written with specific musical parameters relative to range, tessitura, and rhythmic complexity.

The band competition became a form of assessment for band programs. Bands adhered to a strict set of rules and regulations for each competition, including choosing performance selections from a prescribed repertoire list approved by the competition board or committees. These lists outlined the band's instrumentation.

These three elements—the military, instrument manufacturers, and publishing houses—combined to influence the history of school bands in America. Band rooms have similar elements today, from the rows of chairs, the music stands, and the choice of certain instruments to the cabinets filled with band music. Contests have been replaced with festivals, where the assessment is criterion-based (gold, silver, and bronze) instead of placement rankings (first, second, and third).

This history of band programs in the United States of America is important to remember as we consider how to approach a culturally responsive pedagogy for band. From this historical framing of how bands came to be in schools, we now focus on the historical purpose of bands in schools.

THE PURPOSE OF BAND

Participation in school band has evolved over time from a mostly white male endeavor to a more inclusive offering. However, the demographics of band programs have remained relatively consistent since the mid-1900s. Although there has been relative gender equity, the racial and ethnic representation has remained predominantly white, across the country, particularly with band curricula offered within the school day (Elpus & Abril, 2011).

"School band" is a catch-all phrase that refers to the entire band program in a school building and/or district. It is common for band programs to have more than one teacher assigned to them, depending on the size of the school district. Though the characteristics of band programs differ by local preferences and needs, most center a traditional concert band with the instrumentation needed to play school band literature. The role and purpose of the band program are important data when considering culturally responsive pedagogy, a point we will explore next.

The band program is often considered as a whole. However, what happens during the school day is accessible to everyone, whereas what happens outside of school hours is available only to those who can attend at those times.

Curricular school band offerings often entail traditional concert bands in the middle and upper grades. Depending on the size of the district and the number of band teaching staff available, jazz bands may be offered during the curricular day. At the younger grades, when students are beginners, the curricular band offerings may consist of small group lessons. What is offered during the official school day provides data points regarding the purpose of the curricular band program and what that district considers to be important.

Often the overall band program does not fit into a regular school day. In this case those offerings are either co-curricular, meaning they can be taken for credit, or extracurricular, meaning they are not credit bearing but there is still music instruction. This varies by school district and may provide insight into the purpose and relative importance of these offerings. Marching band is a good example of a school band offering that could be either co-curricular or extracurricular.

43.2 Culturally Responsive Mindset

Lind and McKoy (2016) use of term "mindset" with regard to the application of culturally responsive teaching in music education. Their approach encourages teachers to consider whom they teach, what they teach and why, how they teach, and which skills are most important for their students to learn. I urge music teachers to consider discussion questions 4–8, found at the end of the chapter, before designing a curricular response to teaching in any given setting. These questions require us as professionals to do the personal work of self-awareness, becoming aware of our teaching surroundings, and determining the best curricular approaches to meeting the needs of those we are teaching. This work represents the mindset Lind and McKoy describe in their approach. Elements of the mindset will be discussed in the following sections: personal work/disposition; awareness and cultural understanding of space; who are you teaching and what is important; pedagogical responses; and access, transfer, and lifelong skills.

PERSONAL WORK/DISPOSITION

One of the greatest challenges in teaching band is the reconciliation of what you value and consider to be critical to learn with what your students value and consider to be important. In education, we use the word "disposition" to describe a teacher's tendencies. Although most aspects of disposition are internal characteristics, people's dispositions are observed from their behaviors and actions in given situations. The way we position ourselves in relation to those around us demonstrates aspects of our disposition. Our preferences, biases, and philosophies influence our disposition, how it manifests in our teaching, and how we interact with learners, their families, and the community in which the learning is happening.

When considering the culturally responsive pedagogy mindset, we must first introspectively explore our personal disposition. We unpack the influences that have informed and framed who we are as teachers by interrogating our biases, identifying them in action, and articulating them clearly. As music teachers, we tend to enter the profession with a bias toward quality music as defined by our mentors and our classes in college and conservatory. Being consciously aware of this bias is helpful as we work to serve our students.

This personal work is the starting point for intentional culturally responsive pedagogy. It starts with you, the band director/teacher, not the students. Through your full, embodied self you will exist in the learning-teaching setting, and how you move through that space flows through your disposition. Thus, it is imperative that you understand your own self as fully as possible; realizing this will be an ongoing lifelong process. This personal work never ends.

AWARENESS AND CULTURAL UNDERSTANDING OF PLACE

The inward self-work is one aspect of the culturally responsive pedagogy journey. Another aspect deals with your disposition and how you situate yourself within your teaching context. Being aware of how your disposition manifests in that place is a critical element in determining how best to respond pedagogically.

Awareness is a reflexive skill requiring you to be cognizant of the environment and how your presence and actions affect those surroundings. Although you can't control how others respond to you, you can notice and make sense of those responses. Developing this reflective aspect of awareness gives you much-needed feedback both personally and regarding the assessment of your teaching effectiveness. Not all feedback is affirming, and making good use of the critical feedback is an important skill to develop. In teacher preparation programs, we are coached to take charge of the repertoire used to teach essential musical elements and concepts. As developing educators we often start with what we know, but what we know may not always be the best pedagogical response. Being able to read the context cues of a given setting (reflective awareness) is a valuable skill.

When accepting a teaching position, you are signing on to teach at the will of that school district. Your contract comes with the expectation that you will serve the students in your charge and the community in which the district is located. This is particularly true for band directors, who often display the processes and products of their music instruction in a very public fashion.

Each district has its own culture. School districts adjacent to one another may have very different cultures, so location is not the only determining factor relative to culture. Culture has a very broad meaning and context. Within the frame of this chapter, the term "culture" is used in reference to the music program, and the band program specifically.

Working up this type of profile on the culture of the band program and how it is situated within the school and community culture is critical. This allows you to then consider your disposition in relation to these findings as you begin planning your approach to stepping into the culture of this band program.

WHO ARE YOU TEACHING AND WHAT IS IMPORTANT?

After learning all you can about the culture of the band program and considering how you relate to it, it is time to take a deeper look at who you are responsible for teaching. Ascertaining who the learners are requires more exploration and assessment.

A wise mentor of mine often said, "You can't assume learners know anything you haven't taught them, and even then, you should double-check." As we think of delivering music instruction via band, it is important to know what your students may know and the musical skills they have had the opportunity to develop in the program to that point. This type of information can be gathered by exploring the curriculum plans, if they exist. You may be able to also speak with your band program colleagues who teach the students before they pass to you. If you are teaching at the beginning of the band program process, this could be a bit easier to ascertain; otherwise it may take some effort, depending on how the district program is organized. You should also speak with the elementary school general music teachers, choir teachers, and string teachers, as some students switch instruments. Then you can use similar rhythm counting systems and figure out if they sang, used solfège, Curwen hand signs, or other approaches, to make the transition easier for students.

Once you have gathered all the information you can without engaging with the learners, it is time to assess music skills and proficiency in the technical and musicianship realms. This step is laden with dispositional considerations, since we tend to develop assessments based on what we deem to be important. Consider broadening your assessment beyond traditional band skills and knowledge. Using the broadest sense of musicianship, you can explore learners' interests and what they consider to be important.

Although band may be the medium through which you teach music, it is not the only medium in learners' lives. School bands often have a not-so-positive reputation because many do not see the connections of band with music in life (Mantie & Tucker, 2008). For this and many other reasons, I strongly encourage you to take an interest in the ways those you teach engage with music in their lives. Furthermore, I encourage you to consider how they see the role of their band participation in their lives. This type of inquiry opens windows through which you can see how your work can enhance lives by connecting the musical elements you will develop with them through band to the music they encounter in their lives outside of school.

PEDAGOGICAL RESPONSES

Girded with the information gathered about your students, the culture of the band program, and your own awareness of your disposition, you are in a good position to consider how you will deliver band instruction in this space. Culturally responsive pedagogy is a mindset (Lind & McKoy, 2016). As such, you have the agency to be very intentional regarding your approach. Luckily, in most band programs you, as the teacher, have a great deal of latitude in what you teach and how you go about teaching it if you deliver what is expected within the band program culture. You may be told that there is not enough time to teach in a culturally responsive fashion and have a quality band program based on traditional assessment standards, but that is not true. Culturally responsive teaching and a quality band program are not mutually exclusive; it is possible to teach responsively and cultivate a quality music program that enables learners to carry their musical understandings far beyond their school years.

Acknowledging the musical knowledge and skills students bring to your classroom regardless of their level of expertise within the band context is important. Finding ways to celebrate their knowledge and tie it to the specific band knowledge or skill sets you are teaching is critical. With some intentional and creative maneuvering, you can bring the music of your students lives into the band context, engage them with exploring its musical elements, and make connections to what you are teaching them in school. Another advantage to teaching in a band setting is the variety of the musical offerings. Again, the traditional concert band is a great place to bring in musical examples from outside the traditional genre, apply them to the concert band instrumentation, see how the arrangements can come to life.

I often say that "style is everything." If you are playing a pop tune arranged for concert band, then it is the job of the players to make that pop tune sound like the original artist's version as much as possible. Clearly, it will not be possible to reproduce the tune exactly; however, it can still be styled in ways that indicate an understanding of the style and even the meaning of the song. This is one example of connecting school music with music happening outside the school.

In the final section of this chapter, we will explore further applications of culturally responsive pedagogy within the band setting. This mindset is informed by the personal work and the other investigations done before we ever set foot in the classroom with learners, and then the awareness we employ to learn all we can about who we are teaching, what is important to them, and how best to respond to what we learn.

43.3 Access, Transfer, and Lifelong Skills

CREATE AN ACCESSIBLE BAND PROGRAM

One element of culturally responsive pedagogy is providing access to the band program, regardless of when a student decides to join. There are many aspects of participating in band that we take for granted. Thinking through everything a student needs to participate in a band performance is a great exercise to illustrate this point.

The high school fall band concert information:

- The concert starts at 7:00 p.m.
- Students are required to wear a particular uniform.
- The warm-up call time at the school is 6:00 p.m., and transportation is not provided by the school district.

Based on this scenario, step back and do an access audit to help anticipate participation barriers for students. Why might a student not be able to attend this band program event?

The evening element presents many assumptions about family's abilities to get students back to school outside of school hours. Some parents work, others may not have personal transportation, others may not be physically able to drive their student back to school, and public transportation may not be available to the location or be safe for students traveling at that time of night. Even when the uniform requirement might seem reasonable and simple (e.g., white top, black pants or skirt, black shoes), that could be a hardship for some families. Even if this has been a tradition at a school for some time, it could be a barrier for some.

When we do this type of audit and challenge our assumptions, it is possible to uncover many access barriers. Taking a step further to provide a way for students and parents to voice barrier issues anonymously is helpful. The class happens during the day, but the assessment for the class happens in the evening. Even if you grant credit to a student who cannot attend a concert, you still deny them the opportunity to demonstrate their learning and be a part of the performance. Giving credit for being present at the performance alone is a questionable practice within a school context. Other academic subjects (math, English, etc.) do not give students a grade for showing up. Grades in music, like grades in other school courses, should be related to student growth and musical attainment.

Perhaps there are ways to move the assessment performance to the school day, then save the outside of school opportunities for optional extracurricular activities. For example, the concert could happen during normal band class time and be recorded for broadcast later, and/or you could work to set up carpools and fund rides for students and families who have transportation issues after school hours.

It is often hard for band programs to accommodate students who want to start learning to play a band instrument outside the prescribed entry point for that district. Many start beginners in mid-elementary grade years or at least by early middle school. This issue often creates a barrier to participation for a student who may have moved into the district later from a district with no band program, or for a student who simply decides late they wish to start a band instrument. Consider creative mentoring programs wherein new band students are coached by peers and catch up quickly (see the suggestions in Chapter 18 on peer mentoring). Other programs have resources to provide private lessons for the later starter and then find ways for them to jump right in and contribute as they can until their skills catch up with those of the other band students.

TEACH TRANSFERABLE MUSICAL SKILLS AND CONCEPTS

Developing the mechanics and technique to play music of any kind beautifully requires the mastery and execution of many skills and concepts. As mentioned, there are technique books and methods designed specifically for band instrumentalists. These methods prepare players to play traditional band literature. Following this historical trail to the music competitions and festivals that often serve as the assessment for the band and the program, we find the required literature on those competition lists often becomes the musical material focused on in band class.

This music may be of fine quality and merit, but it often does not represent literature and sounds that are relevant, or even familiar, to the students in the program. Historically, the literature on these lists is less often written by underrepresented composers or inclusive of a variety of genres. It is good to use as many different musical styles as possible to teach musical skills and concepts. Through commissioning projects, composers are being hired to write concert band music that draws from styles and melodies from a variety of backgrounds. Another way to access music from the lives of our students is to foster learning music by ear, as well as reinforcing the importance of music literacy.

Reading notation should not be favored over learning by ear; both should be encouraged. Learning music by ear gives students access and agency to explore any kind of music that interests them. This often gives students great incentive to develop technique and proficiency so they can play their favorite song long before they might develop the ability to read its notation. When students explore music, they get to choose, with the only stipulation that they play it on their "band instrument." They begin to make connections to the things you are doing in band. For more on this, see Chapter 6.

Discerning the difference between a concept and a skill is very important when considering culturally responsive pedagogy. The concepts are more transferable than are skills (Lonis & Haley, 2018). Take the *concept* of a crescendo versus the skills required to effectively *achieve* a crescendo. Understanding the concept of a crescendo as a compositional device and the many ways it is used in music is a necessary step in learning to play a crescendo. Having students find great crescendos in everyday life and bring them back for discussion in band is the type of exercise that requires demonstrated musicianship, but the product returned to class could be from any kind of music a student has access to.

This type of discovery opens the door to why a crescendo is present in a piece of music and how it may be characterized. With the understanding of why, we work on achieving the desired crescendo effect. This type of learning sticks and is carried into other musical contexts outside of band and school in a way that learning skills for a specific work does not (Allsup & Benedict, 2008; Lonis & Haley, 2018; Thompson, 1993; Westerlund, 2008).

CULTIVATE LIFELONG LEARNERS AND PARTICIPANTS IN MUSIC

The hope and dream of most band directors/teachers is for their students to continue participating in music long after leaving their school band program. Many times, especially in smaller school districts, the band directors have the same students from middle school through high school, if not longer. During that time we can spark and maintain musical interest and build musical skills and competencies that will last a lifetime.

Cultivating lifelong learners is the key to longevity in music participation. Band may be the medium through which we teach music, but it is important to teach *music*, not just band. Providing opportunities for students to use their musical skills outside of the traditional band context is important. Chamber group opportunities are a great way to cultivate the application of music skills and concepts students have learned, as they require everyone to deliver their own part without the security of having other players on the same part. The chamber group also provides an opportunity for the students in the group to make the musical decisions and choices without teacher direction.

Encouraging students to perform outside of school is also helpful in cultivating lifelong participation. Many band teachers will give their students extra credit for playing outside of school in their communities, such as in churches, at holiday functions, and the like. These experiences may plant the seeds for ways they can continue music making after they graduate from high school.

Some band teachers give opportunities for learning popular music instruments as well. This could be on Fridays or perhaps in units after the concerts in December and May. After four to six years of these opportunities, students will be able to flourish if they so choose.

Marching band is a great opportunity to participate during students' college careers as well and to be co-collaborators in the sports experience. The marching band also allows students to play many styles of music, including popular arrangements that they may have some say in picking out for the band to play. Although the band director usually selects the music for the marching band and writes the show, it is a good opportunity for students to be consulted, have input, and perhaps even have a hand in making the choices or producing the music or drill.

Jazz band also provides an opportunity to play different styles of music, and it is versatile and portable as well. Jazz bands and the smaller jazz combos can play just about anywhere and be student led. The skills of picking the music based on the occasion and negotiating how the performance will flow are ones students can draw upon later in life as they get together with others to play.

43.4 Conclusion

Culturally responsive pedagogy is a mindset. It is an intention from the start that is built into our practice. Teaching in this manner is not inherent to any genre, but band provides many opportunities to employ this culturally responsive mindset. It is not a prescriptive method and thus requires a great deal of the teacher: they have to do the personal work, the cultural exploration, and relationship building to develop a pedagogical response that is effective for their setting. The overall mantra: Do it with purpose from the start.

43.5 Discussion Questions

1. In the band programs of which you are aware, what offering is given the highest position or favor? How did you arrive at that determination?
2. Do the school band offerings mirror those of traditional concert bands from the mid-1900s?

3. Does participation in the band program you have in mind require resources beyond what the school can provide?
4. What are the historical activities and practices of the band program?
5. How involved is the community with the band program?
6. Is the band required to participate in school or community events, such as sporting events, homecoming, or holiday parades?
7. Who tends to participate in the curricular, co-curricular, and extracurricular band program offerings?
8. Which courses are offered for credit and during the regular school hours?

OXFORD learning link

Visit the online resources for additional documentation and exercises to help expand learning and test your knowledge further: www.oup.com/he/powell_music1e.

PART VI.

Teaching Percussion

CHAPTER 44

PEDAGOGICAL CONSIDERATIONS FOR TEACHING PERCUSSION STUDENTS

Virginia Davis and Daniel Smithiger

This chapter introduces two foundational percussion experiences for beginning students—snare drum and keyboard percussion—and discusses essential tips and techniques for teaching a beginner.

44.1 Introduction

The percussion family comprises instruments played by striking, scraping, and shaking. A percussionist is responsible for playing a large number of instruments, both small and large, that encompass a wide array of timbres and textures. Capable of both rhythm and melody, percussion instruments contribute excitement, energy, groove, color, and depth to an ensemble. One of the great things about percussion instruments is that they are found in almost every genre and style of music, making them some of the most versatile—and fun—instruments to play!

In this chapter we focus on initial experiences on the snare drum and keyboard percussion, as these are typically the foundational instruments for a beginning student. Skills on these instruments can then be transferred to other instruments in the percussion family with the necessary instrument-specific modifications indicated in the following chapters.

44.2 Preparing to Teach Beginners: Snare Drum

EQUIPMENT

Basic equipment for a beginning percussionist can come in various forms. The absolute minimum equipment necessary is a practice pad and a good pair of sticks.

Practice Pads

Practice pads come in different shapes, sizes, prices, and feels. The least expensive practice pads are black rubber with a raised center, intended to be placed on the head of a snare drum. Such a pad is adequate for the beginning student, but when the student begins playing bounces and rolls, it may need to be replaced with a pad that offers more resistance.

Other pads come ready to be placed on a stand, such as the RealFeel™ pad, with a bouncy rubber surface. Figure 44.1 shows a variety of practice pads.

FIGURE 44.1 **Different varieties of practice pads**

Sticks

Sticks for a beginning student should be carefully chosen. Avoid the common mistake of buying small sticks because the student is small. Sticks should be full-length concert snare drum sticks with a substantial width and weight—*not* the skinny, lightweight sticks commonly considered jazz sticks. Students should be able to feel the weight in their hands; this aids proper hand and stick position. Good sticks for a beginner include ProMark, Vic Firth, and Innovative Percussion brands. The stick sizing system is a confusing one even for percussionists, but ask at your local drum store for size 9A, 2B, SD1 Generals, IP-1, or a stick they believe is of a similar size.

Snare Drums

Good snare drums are manufactured by drum companies such as Pearl, Yamaha, Black Swamp, and Ludwig. A new drum should be purchased with a stand and a sturdy case. A used snare drum can be fine as well, as long as the shell of the drum is relatively free of dents, the snare system is intact, and the head is fairly new (without large dents and pockmarks). Heads can be replaced as needed; see 44.1, "Changing a Snare Drum Head," in the book's online resources. Good brands include Remo and Evans. Students should be encouraged to bring a new or used snare drum into their lesson in order to learn proper maintenance and tuning of their drum.

PLAYING POSITION

Acquiring the correct body, arm, hand, and stick position should be one of the most important goals of the first lessons. The teacher should verbally present these steps to a good playing position *every time the student sets up to play*, like a mental checklist: body, arms, hand, fingers, sticks. Soon students should be able to take themselves through the checklist independently. The teacher should correct improper playing positions gently but immediately, before bad habits become ingrained.

Body

The student's body should be relaxed and natural at all times. If a student feels or looks uncomfortable, something is wrong. Beginning students should stand while practicing and during lessons (rather than being seated in a chair or behind a drum kit) to ensure good posture and hand and arm position. The top rim of the instrument should be positioned approximately at the height of the student's hips; have the student place their hand on their belly button and raise the drum so that the rim lines up with the bottom of their hand. Figure 44.2 shows the correct height for a snare drum relative to the player's body.

FIGURE 44.2 Correct height for a snare drum

Arms

The forearms should be brought up (again, in a *relaxed* and *comfortable* way), with the elbows gently bent and the forearms in a triangular position going in toward the drum. The upper arms should hang naturally next to (but not touching) the body. Avoid sticking the elbows unnaturally out like wings. Shoulders should stay relaxed, not raised or scrunched. Figure 44.3 shows a student with arms and body ready to play.

FIGURE 44.3 Student with arms and body ready to play

Hands

Sticks should be held (try not to say *gripped*, for that implies unnecessary tension) with the bottom of the hand about an inch and a half from the end of the stick. Two types of snare drum holds are used, though we recommend matched grip for beginners. For matched grip, the student's hands should be positioned with the *tops* of the hands (knuckles) up, not the thumbs. The thumbs should rest on the side of the stick. Young students can be reminded of this by placing stickers on the tops of their hands and periodically asking them, "Can you see your stickers?" Figure 44.4 shows the correct hand position for matched grip.

FIGURE 44.4 Correct hand position for matched grip

In traditional grip, descended from an early style of military marching featuring a tilted snare drum, the left hand holds the stick in an underhanded fashion, coming up through the space between the thumb and first finger and extending between the middle and ring fingers. The wrist turns in a rotating motion, as if one were turning a doorknob. This grip is ideal for playing certain rudimental styles and is also seen in some jazz drum kit playing. Figure 44.5 shows the correct hand position for traditional grip.

FIGURE 44.5 Correct hand position for traditional grip

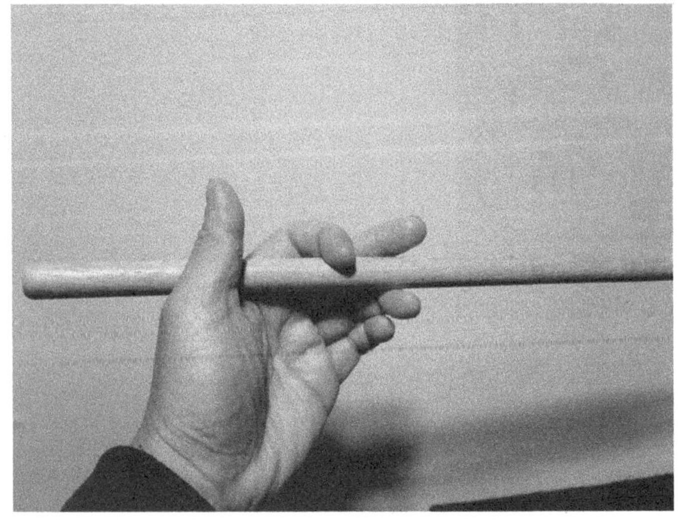

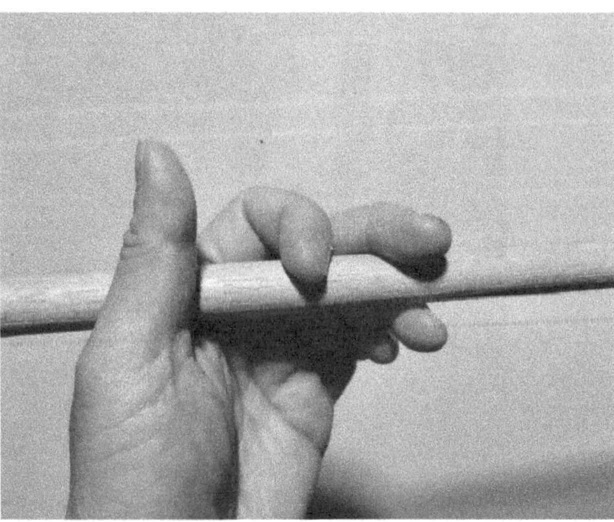

Fingers

In matched grip, it is very important that students place their fingers so that the thumb and forefinger are opposite each other on the sides of the stick and can contract against each other when needed. The main playing energy comes from the thumb and first fingers; the other fingers are used mainly for support and control. These fingers should curl loosely and naturally around the stick. In traditional grip, the thumb should contact the first finger to control the movement of the stick, while all the other fingers support the stick in its motion.

Sticks

Students should use the sticks as an extension of the arm, with the tips of the sticks being the point on a triangle. For a beginner, the tips of the sticks should aim for the center of the drum at all times. Figure 44.6 shows sticks held ready to play.

FIGURE 44.6 **Sticks held ready to play**

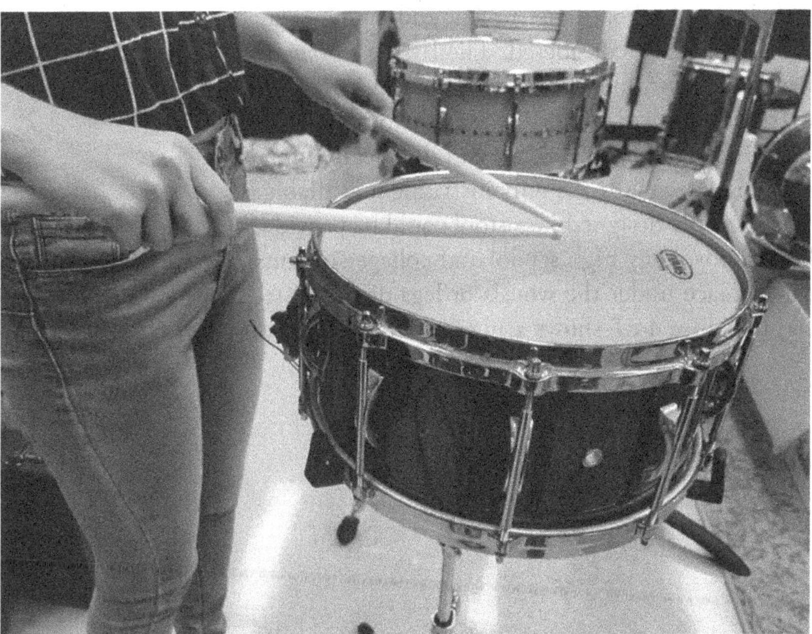

STROKE TECHNIQUE

Developing a good stroke takes time and practice. Modeling is an ideal way to demonstrate an accurate, relaxed stroke. Face the student (with your own drum) and take turns making single right-hand strokes, back and forth. Then switch to left-hand strokes. Call attention to body and hand position (discussed earlier) as well as stroke technique. A good basic stroke has these elements:

- Hands are relaxed and allow the stick to move a bit on its own.
- The stroke should start about six to eight inches above the drumhead.
- The stroke should be made mostly by the fingers and wrist, with some movement in the forearms. Very little upper-arm and shoulder movement should be used.
- The stick should come straight down and should naturally rebound from the drumhead, with a little help from the hand.
- The stick should return to playing position six to eight inches above the drumhead.

44.3 Preparing to Teach Beginners: Keyboard Percussion

The introduction of keyboard percussion instruments, also called *mallet percussion*, is essential for the beginning percussionist. The most common keyboard instruments available to percussion teachers and students are the glockenspiel (sometimes called bells), xylophone, vibraphone (or vibes), and marimba. Though each instrument does have special techniques unique to it, the considerations discussed in this chapter are appropriate for all these instruments.

SPECIAL CONSIDERATIONS FOR KEYBOARD INSTRUMENTS

Many aspects of keyboard technique are similar to the technique on the snare drum, including body position and how the mallets are held. Though keyboard mallets have different diameters, weights, and feels, they are held much like snare drumsticks (see the "Sticks" section earlier in this chapter). It is especially important to keep the tops of the hands facing upward and to hold the mallets in a relaxed triangular position. As with the snare drum, the keyboard player should avoid unnecessary shoulder and arm movement and allow their bodies, hands, and fingers to stay free of tension.

Before placing a beginning student behind a keyboard instrument and saying "Play," certain logistical features of the instrument must be considered. The first is *instrument height*. As with the snare drum, the keyboard instrument should be around hip height. Many xylophones, vibraphones, and marimbas are too tall for the average fourth-, fifth-, or sixth-grader. Using an instrument that is too tall (or too short) can drastically impair playing position and therefore the ability to play well. If the only instrument available is too tall and cannot be lowered, perhaps a specially designed step-stool could be provided. If the instrument is too short (as is the case for many high school and college students), percussionists commonly design blocks to place under the wheels or legs of the instrument to raise it to an appropriate height. Figure 44.7 shows a marimba at the correct playing height.

FIGURE 44.7 **Marimba at the correct playing height**

A second consideration is the *positioning of the instrument*. This is particularly important if the student is playing in an ensemble. The instrument must be placed so that the student's line of sight goes straight to the conductor. This may sound obvious, but many keyboard percussionists in beginning and intermediate groups are turned away from the conductor, making it difficult to see needed cues. Wherever students are placed, make sure they can see!

The last (and possibly most important) logistical consideration is the *placement of the music stand*. The music stand should be low: the music should sit just above the keys. Figure 44.8 shows the proper placement of a music stand with a marimba.

FIGURE 44.8 Proper placement of a music stand with a marimba

For most other percussion instruments, the music stand is placed higher so that the player's line of sight includes both the music and the conductor. Keyboard players, however, have a more important line of sight: that of their peripheral vision. Why? One of the most common difficulties for beginning keyboard players is not that they cannot read the pitches—it's that they can't look at the notes on the page and the keys on the keyboard at the same time. Looking only at one or the other leads to playing incorrect pitches, so many young keyboard players either give up playing keyboard instruments or begin to memorize all of their music instead of reading it. As a result, some keyboard students do not learn to sight-read well and are not prepared to play from written music.

To allow students to both read their part and see the keyboard, lower the music stand. Show the students that when they are looking at their music, they can see their mallets and the keyboard with their peripheral vision. Demonstrate peripheral vision for students by having them look at one point after another on the music stand while moving their mallets. How far up can they look and still see their hands? Usually students discover they need to look quite far above the music stand before their hands are out of their peripheral vision. Then bring the students' eyes back down to their music. After that exercise, it should seem very easy for a student to see their hands while reading the notes on the page.

44.4 Teaching Beginners: Developing Technique

STARTING TO PLAY WITHOUT TEACHING THE MUSIC STAFF FIRST: SNARE DRUM

Before introducing staff notation to the beginning percussionist, it is important to provide the student with fun, low-stress playing opportunities. Most students come in wanting to play music, so get started right away. Frequent playing helps build technique, and it is never too early to start playing for fun.

We enjoy starting with short echo exercises with beginning students. Play a short pattern (perhaps two beats long) and have the student echo it back. After a few of these, ask the student to play something for you to echo. We suggest doing this to a metronome or backbeat so that there is a natural rhythmic give-and-take between you, with minimal talking. Move to longer patterns, perhaps up to four or even eight bars over the course of the first several weeks. Use varied tempi for the backbeats and model elements such as dynamics and accents, as well as relaxation and proper technique. Echo playing can be followed by call and response. Encourage the student to play a different but complementary pattern in response to yours. Later, when the student begins reading notation, help the student learn how to write these patterns out to create their own compositions.

Another good exercise is to warm up by playing steady strokes at various tempi. Starting with quarter notes, have the student play a steady beat while concentrating on good technique. We then like to move the student into steady eighth notes and even sixteenth notes as they become ready. This helps the student become accustomed to playing regular, even, controlled strokes at a steady pace while developing needed automaticity. To make this more enjoyable (and musical), we suggest playing along with popular music tracks in place of a metronome. Perhaps the student could direct you to music they enjoy, and you can provide additional tracks with different tempi and feels. As with the echo exercises, you can ask the student to play with different sticking patterns or stick heights and use musical elements as they play.

STARTING TO PLAY WITHOUT TEACHING THE MUSIC STAFF FIRST: KEYBOARD PERCUSSION

Most students are naturally interested in new instruments, especially the large ones like the xylophone, vibes, or marimba. If possible, perform something (even scales or arpeggios) to demonstrate the sound of the instrument. Investigate its sound production properties, discuss the origins of the instruments and the differences among different keyboard instruments if you have several available, and let the student experiment. Many scales, dyads, and arpeggio patterns can be learned without staff notation and are great for developing dexterity and fluidity at the keyboard.

As with snare drum, students should be encouraged to play creatively, for fun. Echo patterns using only a few known notes can be a good way to become comfortable with the keyboard and with new notes, in addition to being great for ear training. Keep the range of notes small at first and encourage all attempts at copying what they hear. As an alternative to echo exercises, try playing a simple pattern in a loop and letting the student take time to work it out until they match you.

Improvisation at the keyboard can be facilitated by using backing tracks (many are available on YouTube or Spotify) in various keys. Help the student determine what notes work within a given tonality and model improvisation, perhaps by starting with call-and-response patterns, and work up to "trading fours" (taking turns playing four-measure solos), as in the jazz tradition. Again, once students are working with notation, encourage students to write down their improvisations to create their own music.

PEDAGOGICAL CONSIDERATIONS: SNARE DRUM

Common Mistakes Made by Beginning Students

Problem: Gripping the stick tightly with all the fingers, keeping the stick from making a natural rebound.

Solution: Encourage students to relax their middle, ring, and pinky fingers, using the thumb and first finger to hold on. This is not to say, however, that the ring and pinky finger be allowed to fly off the stick or stick out! They should curl around the stick, but loosely.

Problem: "Flailing," or starting the stroke from too high off the drum.

Solution: Flailing produces a great lack of control and an unacceptable volume. Stick height can be brought down by encouraging less arm and shoulder movement or placing your stick about a foot above the drumhead and instructing students to start and end their stroke below it. A stick-height line can also be drawn on a mirror. Sticks should start in a triangle position, parallel to the floor—*not* perpendicular. Go through the playing position checklist often and practice playing at different stick heights.

Problem: "Sticking to the drum," or pressing the stick to the drumhead instead of rebounding.

Solution: Try telling the student to imagine the drumhead is hot and the stick must be lifted off to avoid burning. Use modeling to show a proper rebound. Other tips include relaxing the grip somewhat, bouncing the stick off the head to demonstrate rebound, and having a student practice with a hand drum before returning to sticks (for some reason, sticking to the drum is less common when using only the hands).

PEDAGOGICAL CONSIDERATIONS: KEYBOARD PERCUSSION

The method for introducing staff notation for keyboard percussion is similar to those used for other keyboard instruments, such as the piano. While we will not prescribe a particular method here, we encourage teachers to focus on the needs of the student, as music reading is never a one-size-fits-all endeavor. Whatever notes you start with, it is important to introduce them one at a time. Allow enough time for the students to practice each note and memorize both its position on the staff and its location on the keyboard. Introducing too many new notes at once can be overwhelming, and students may resort to compensating for their confusion by writing in note names.

The student should *say the note name out loud* as they play. This helps keep their eyes on the page. You may wish to tell them, "I don't care if you play a wrong note, as long as you're moving in the right direction and *say* the right one." This helps alleviate the fear of playing wrong notes that causes staring at the keyboard. If the student gets very off track, have him/her look down and quickly reorient during rests.

PREPARING FOR SNARE DRUM ROLLS

The snare drum roll is one of the most common special techniques used in percussion. It is executed by bouncing the sticks in a rapid but controlled manner that creates a sustained sound.

Two basic types of snare drum rolls exist: the open roll and the closed roll. Open rolls are commonly used in rudimental and marching percussion and feature a discernible double bounce: it should be possible to count the number of strokes in an open roll. Closed rolls are used in symphonic and concert snare drum playing and create a sustained buzz: percussionists work to make these as smooth as possible by using an even, multiple-bounce stroke. Both types of rolls are important for a percussionist to learn and be able to execute.

For the beginner, it is usually easier to begin the fundamentals of rolling by learning the multiple-bounce closed roll, and learning the open roll after a basic closed roll can be comfortably executed. The roll-preparation exercises in the online resources can be used for both closed and open rolls, so the teacher may use them first to teach the closed roll and then use them again to teach the open roll. See 44.2, "Open and Closed Rolls," in the book's online resources.

To teach the closed roll, ask the student to bounce each stick on the drumhead by loosening the fingers and allowing the stick to bounce. The thumb and first finger should help control the bounce. The other fingers should release their hold on the stick but remain curled to guide the stick into position. The student should use the fingers and wrist to give the stroke some downward momentum instead of merely dropping the stick and letting it bounce. The resulting multiple bounce stroke is called a "buzz."

To practice the multiple-bounce stroke along with a student, start with one hand and trade buzzes back and forth with the student. This provides the student with a model of the correct sound and look of a buzz stroke. Try to sustain a long buzz by starting from eight inches above the drum and allowing the stick to bounce until it stops. The longer the stick bounces, the more multiple bounces will be created. Beginning students should attempt for as long a buzz as possible. This will help rolls to sound more sustained.

Open rolls should be approached in the same way closed rolls are learned; the only difference is that instead of playing a multiple-bounce buzz, the stick plays a quick double bounce.

44.5 Discussion Questions

1. Should beginning percussionists start on both snare drum and keyboard percussion simultaneously? Why or why not? What might be some benefits or challenges of starting on only one instrument? What are the benefits or challenges of starting on both together?
2. If a student shows greater interest in either snare drum or keyboards, should they be allowed to specialize? Why or why not? If not, what are some ways you might help students reach a higher comfort level on the other instrument?
3. Why is it important to spend so much time on proper playing position, hand and finger position, and stroke technique in the beginning?

OXFORD learning link

Visit the online resources for additional documentation and exercises to help expand learning and test your knowledge further: www.oup.com/he/powell_music1e.

CHAPTER 45

PEDAGOGIES FOR TEACHING PITCHED AND NON-PITCHED ORCHESTRAL/BAND PERCUSSION

Virginia Davis and Daniel Smithiger

This chapter provides an overview of the most common concert percussion instruments and their characteristic sounds, playing techniques, and mallet options.

45.1 Introduction

The percussion section is a vital part of a band or orchestra. Percussion players, usually standing and frequently in motion, command an exciting array of musical instruments with a variety of timbres. An effective percussion section is a cohesive group; only when working together cooperatively can a section meet its musical challenges.

As your percussionists learn, always expect sensitive and musical playing from the section. Percussionists should learn phrasing, sound color, tone, and even "breathing" with wind and string players. To augment the sometimes technically unchallenging parts found in many band and orchestra works, consider forming a percussion ensemble with your students to teach chamber music skills, as well as involving students in drum kit playing (see Chapter 23), to allow students to stretch their technical abilities.

45.2 Accessibility Options for Percussion Instruments

Percussionists are known for their creative problem-solving when it comes to their instruments. Many percussion instruments are accessible to students with disabilities if some modifications are made. For example, for students challenged in their hands or arms, silicone bands can be used to assist in holding sticks, or gloves can be fitted to the student in which sticks and mallets can be held using Velcro or other materials. Percussion instruments can all be played from a seated position when needed, and stools and chairs of various heights are widely available. Many percussion parts tend to be ostinato-based and could be taught by ear and memorized by students with sight challenges, while hearing-challenged students can be successful on instruments that produce low vibrations, such as the bass drum, as well as on other drums and keyboard percussion instruments. Evelyn Glennie, a highly respected percussionist, is profoundly deaf and still has a successful career in music.

45.3 Battery

SNARE DRUM

The snare drum is one of the most visible and ubiquitous percussion instruments in the band and orchestra. A snare drum consists of a shell of wood or metal and features a top ("batter") head, typically made of synthetic material, and a bottom ("resonant" or "snare") head made of thin synthetic film, both secured to the drum with counter-hoops, tension rods, and tension casings. The snare system consists of wires lying flush against the bottom head, which causes the characteristic rattle of the snare drum. A snare strainer mechanism is used to tighten and loosen the snares against the head and can be released to separate the snares from the head altogether.

Snare drummers build technique by practicing "rudiments"—essential proficiencies and sticking patterns that prepare players for the techniques that they will encounter in band and orchestra music. Most teachers begin with the standard twenty-six American drum rudiments, but rudiments number into the forties, with new rudiments being created by drummers in the marching arts in particular. After a basic rudiment is mastered, drummers typically practice the pattern "open to closed," meaning starting slowly and gradually increasing the tempo to as fast as the player can execute the rudiment, then gradually decreasing the tempo back to the start. Common rudiments for beginners include flams, ruffs and drags, diddles, and rolls.

BASS DRUM

The bass drum is a large, double-sided drum with a low, deep tone. Concert bass drums typically range from twenty-eight to forty inches in diameter and are placed on a stand. Heads for a bass drum are usually made of a synthetic calfskin, such as the Remo FiberSkyn™ or Renaissance heads. Percussionists play the bass drum with a large mallet, usually wrapped in felt, lambswool, or leather. The hardness of the mallet and the material used depends on the amount of articulation needed for the part being played. One mallet is typically used for general playing, though players frequently use two mallets to execute rolls. Rolls on the bass drum are always single stroked, never bounced; the sustained sound is produced by using the natural resonance of the head. The bass drum is an important instrument to practice, as it can be vital to the sound of an ensemble. A bass drummer needs to be able to watch the conductor closely while following the written part and have an impeccable sense of time.

Bass drum mallets are held with the thumb facing up and the other fingers curled lightly around the shaft, pointing toward the floor. Hold the mallet firmly but without unnecessary tension. Figure 45.1 shows a correct bass drum mallet hold.

A bass drum stroke should come primarily from the wrist, with some wind-up and follow-through from the arm as needed for the dynamic marking. Like other percussion instruments, most bass drums have a "sweet spot," ideal for general playing. It can usually be found just off-center, in the middle third of the drum's circumference. Rolls are played closer to the rim, while strong, loud shots can be played directly in the center. Figure 45.2 shows bass drum mallets ready to execute a roll.

FIGURE 45.1 Correct bass drum mallet hold

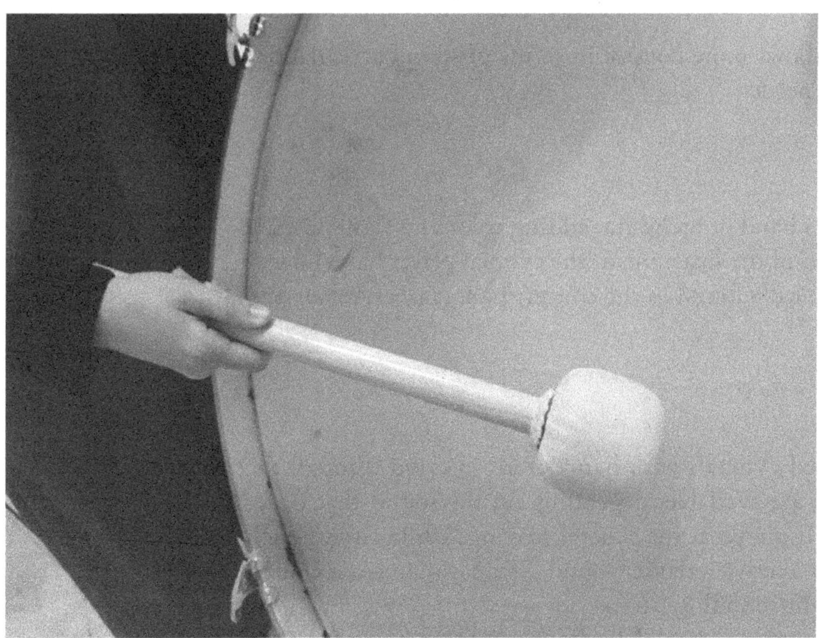

FIGURE 45.2 Bass drum mallets ready to execute a roll

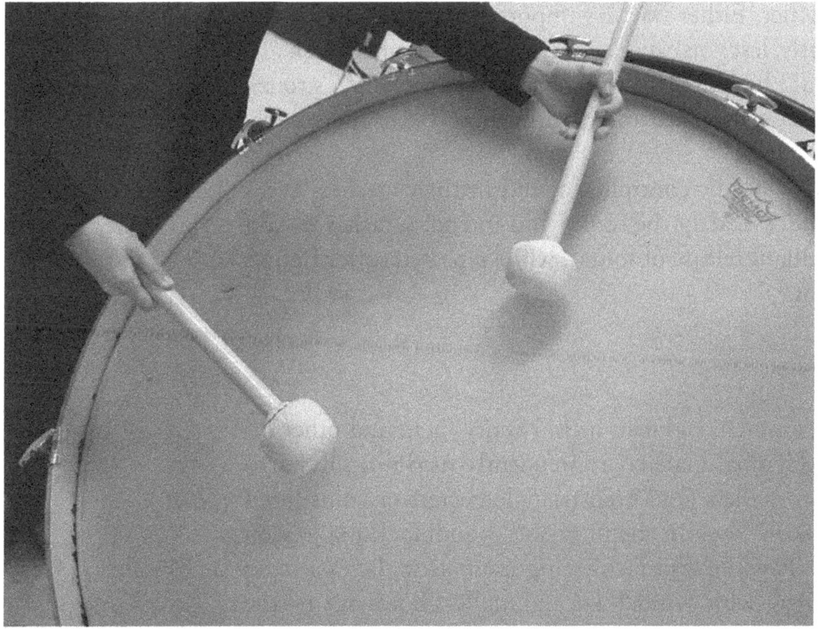

Muffling the bass drum is important for shaping the duration of the notes and controlling the amount of articulation for a given passage. Some players like to clip a small towel to the rim that gently rests on the head and controls the resonance, but we also like to muffle manually. We suggest using the non-playing hand to dampen the drumhead. Players can reach around a smaller bass drum to touch the back (resonant) head to muffle it; others place their hand directly on the top area of the batter head near the rim as needed. Some players like to muffle with a soft cloth, mitt, or chamois in their hand. Still others choose to muffle the head by applying their knee to the bottom area of the head while playing—some bass drums come with a little plate attached to the stand for the purpose of stabilizing one's foot while knee-muffling.

We find that manual muffling allows more control in terms of sound articulation, note length, and executing accents as needed.

CYMBALS

The cymbals play an essential role in a band or orchestra, adding color and flash. Owing to the timbre and dynamic possibilities of the instrument, the cymbal player has a powerful role. Two types of cymbals are typically found in the concert hall: crash cymbals and suspended cymbals.

Crash Cymbals

Crash cymbals consist of two matched cymbals with hand straps inserted through the center holds. Varied sizes of cymbals are available, depending on the sound that is desired: eighteen-inch Viennese cymbals are great for general playing, while twenty-inch Germanic cymbals are appropriate for a heavier, darker sound. Smaller-diameter cymbals are perfect for marches and other bright-sounding parts.

Cymbal players rest the instruments in a special cradle stand or on a padded table when not playing. To play, the cymbal player holds the cymbals by the straps (without inserting the hands into the loops) about one to five inches apart, depending on the dynamic marking, at approximately a 45-degree angle to the body. Many players hold the lower cymbal still and propel the higher cymbal toward it, just off-center. Other players move the two cymbals toward each other. Either way, it's important not to connect the cymbals exactly together, simultaneously, lest you experience the dreaded cymbal lock. To muffle after a crash, the cymbals should be quickly dampened against the player's torso. For this reason, we suggest that concert attire have any hard buttons and zippers safely out of range.

Cymbal players practice attaining a steady, controlled sound in their crashes, as it's important in orchestral music to produce exactly the sound you intend. Crashes should have a single, strong impact with a brilliant release of sound, while repeated softer figures should sound controlled and consistent.

Suspended Cymbals

Suspended cymbals are found in sixteen-inch, eighteen-inch, twenty-inch, and other diameters, secured on a cymbal stand. Cymbal mallets are frequently medium-soft yarn-wrapped mallets, with harder or softer mallets (and even triangle beaters or coins) used for specialized sounds. We love the Ron Vaughn medium-soft woodblock mallets on a cymbal, as they produce smooth rolls while also facilitating more articulate passages when needed. A player should experiment with cymbal size and mallet choice to find the desired color.

For rolls, strike the cymbal near the edges. Slower strokes are used for quiet rolls, while louder rolls and crescendos require strokes of increasing speed and momentum. Cymbal rolls are always executed as single-stroke rolls. For single "splash" notes, try striking the edges of the cymbals with hands opposite each other, at precisely the same time, and then experiment with one hand at the edge and one hand closer to the bell. Many different tone colors and sound blends are possible on these instruments. See 45.2, "Suspended Cymbal Rolls," in the book's online resources.

45.4 Keyboard Percussion

MARIMBA

The marimba is a keyboard percussion instrument that can have a range of four octaves, four octaves and a third, four octaves and a fifth, or five octaves. The bars are made from Honduras rosewood or a synthetic material such as the Musser brand's Kelon™. The bars are generally played using yarn mallets, the softness of which is determined in part by the octave in which one is playing and the amount of articulation desired. The holding position of two marimba mallets is very similar to that of matched grip on a snare drum: thumbs should remain on the side of the shaft, palms down, and fingers loosely wrapped around each stick. The bars of the marimba, as well as other keyboard instruments, are normally played in the centers, over the resonators. Players should experiment, though, to find the sweet spot on the bars. Always be sure to keep hands and body relaxed and maintain an open fulcrum, meaning keeping a small space open between the thumb and index finger. This is essential for a fluid stroke. Remember that you should lift your mallets off of the marimba bars quickly to allow the bars to vibrate without interference, as keyboard instruments generally do not facilitate a natural rebound as when striking a drum head.

XYLOPHONE

The xylophone can range from two octaves and a fifth up to four octaves. Bars are typically made of dense, hard rosewood or a synthetic blend such as Musser's Kelon™. The instrument is transposing, which means it sounds one octave higher than the written notes. Articulation on the xylophone should be delicate; a polyball mallet is preferred. As with the marimba, mallets should be lifted off of the bars quickly.

GLOCKENSPIEL

The glockenspiel (concert bells) is a mallet instrument with bars made of steel or other metal. The range covered is two octaves and a fifth to three octaves and a fifth. The bells are a transposing instrument, as the sound of the bells is two octaves higher than the written pitch. Generally, glockenspiels should be played with hard plastic mallets. Avoid brass or metal mallets, as these are made for special circumstances and not for everyday playing.

VIBRAPHONE

A keyboard percussion instrument including bars made of metal, the vibraphone has a range of two octaves and fifth to four octaves. It is a nontransposing instrument, and its primary distinction from other mallet instruments includes a motor that operates a butterfly wheel to create vibrato. A pedal is used to dampen notes, similar to the piano.

CHIMES

Chimes (also known as tubular bells) are long, tuned metal tubes. Their sound is similar to the sound of church bells. The range of the instrument is typically one octave and a fourth (C4–F5). The tubes are struck with a rawhide or hard plastic mallet at the very top edge of each bar.

45.5 Timpani

The timpani (plural; the singular is "timpano") consist of two to as many as five or six drums, usually arranged low to high. Sometimes called "kettle drums" because of their large copper bowls, these instruments have been a vital part of orchestral music since the seventeenth century, though they are much older than that. Timpani feature calfskin or synthetic heads stretched across the bowls and secured under the rim with tension rods and tension casings. Timpani are pitched instruments; the interior drawbars, which are attached to a pedal mechanism, allow the drumheads to be tightened and loosened within a given pitch range. Most timpani have tuning gauges to help the player determine the approximate note, though some do not, and most players learn to fine-tune the pitches by ear using a pitchpipe, tuning fork, or battery-operated tuner.

Timpani mallets are usually made with wood or bamboo shafts with heads of varying sizes, weights, and coverings. Mallet heads are typically made of wood or cork and are covered with felt of different thicknesses to allow the player to adjust the tone and articulation of the sound. Harder mallets for special uses can be tightly wrapped flannel or just wood tips. Mallets can be held with the French grip (the most common), with thumbs on top and fingers perpendicular to the floor. Figure 45.3 shows the French grip for timpani mallets.

FIGURE 45.3 **French grip for timpani mallets**

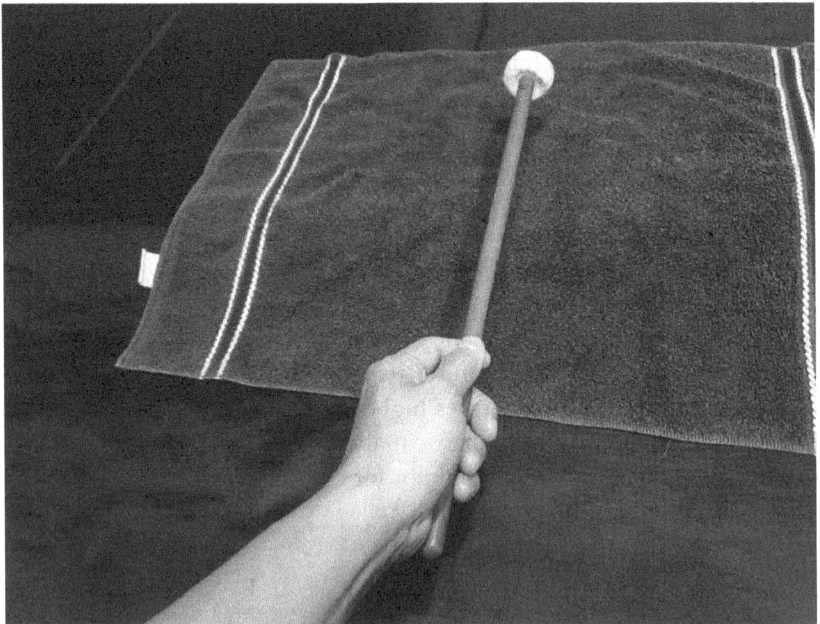

The German grip is similar to a matched snare drum grip. Figures 45.4 and 45.5 show the German grip.

Timpanists can be seen with a range of mallet choices available on a small table near their instrument, covered with a soft cloth to prevent extraneous noise. Figure 45.6 shows an array of timpani mallets.

When playing the timpani, a player should find the sweet spot on the head, usually a third of the way between the rim and the center. Timpani strokes should allow as much resonance as possible from the drum, so the player's job is to make sure the mallet strikes the head without hand or arm tension and then naturally rebounds off the head with a little helper "flick" from the wrist. Rolls are always single stroke. Timpanists devote much practice to executing a smooth single-stroke roll, made more difficult on the higher-pitched drums by tighter heads. Timpani rolls frequently feature a crescendo and complete their

FIGURE 45.4 German grip 1

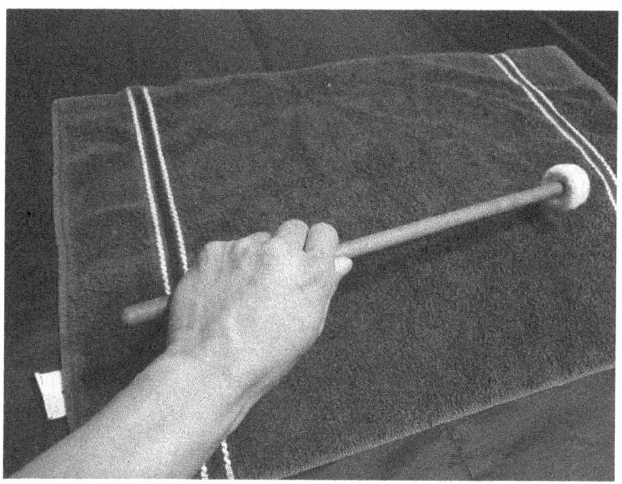

FIGURE 45.5 German grip 2

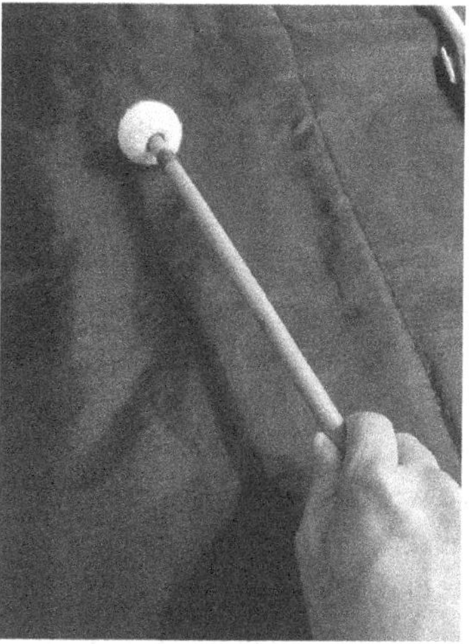

FIGURE 45.6 Array of timpani mallets

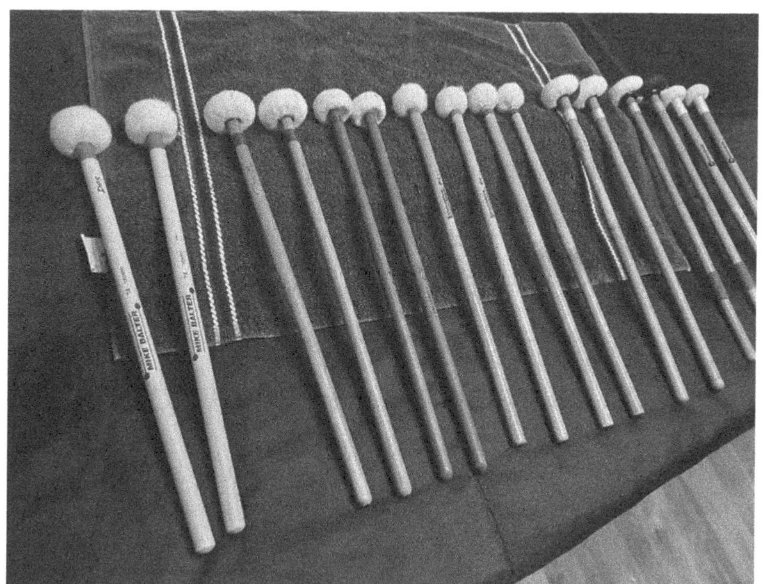

climax by striking a higher drum, so this is a technique students should practice. Other timpani exercises help the student move smoothly between drums, learning when to alternate hands, use the same hand, or cross the hands over each other. It is important that the timpanist listen to and match their strokes to the ensemble, especially the low strings and brass, as timpani parts frequently double or accentuate other instruments' parts. Players muffle the timpani with their fingers to adjust the note's duration; it takes practice to do this quickly yet gently enough that the muffling itself does not produce noise.

Timpani can be played standing, but most players prefer to perch on a special stool, turning freely so the player can orient properly to the drums and work the pedals. Stools can be adjusted to the player's height so that he or she can achieve a comfortable orientation to the instrument.

45.6 Auxiliary

TRIANGLE

The triangle is an instrument consisting of a single bent piece of metal (usually steel or metal alloy) in the expected shape. Good triangle brands include Abel, Grover, and Black Swamp. Triangles are mounted onto a clamp or clip, hanging from thin wires. Wires can be gut, nylon (such as fishing line), string, or other material. Like other percussion instruments, the triangle sounds best when allowed to resonate freely, so any hanging system should be designed so as to impact the vibration of the instrument as little as possible. That being said, we recommend a double-wire system (perhaps with only one contacting the instrument and the other a located bit below it as a safety measure), as wires have a tendency to break at the most inopportune times; a falling triangle is a mortifying, cacophonous sound featured in many percussionists' worst nightmares.

Generally, a good triangle sound is one with as much sparkling overtone as possible. This can be achieved on a good-quality instrument with careful attention to mallet choice and playing spot. Triangle beaters come in various materials, weights, and thicknesses, all of which affect the sound. A percussionist should have a selection of beaters in order to find the right one for the desired tone. Triangles should be played either on the bottom center of the instrument or on the unbroken side. Practice is needed to achieve a consistent sound. For rolls, place your mallet in an unbroken corner and move the beater rapidly back and forth. See 45.3, "Triangle Technique," in the book's online resources.

Some players clamp the triangle to a music stand, but unless "music stand" is a sound called for in the score, we suggest holding the triangle with your hand whenever possible. Conductors and audience members like to see the instrument being played, and the sound carries better when the instrument is elevated. Therefore, hold the triangle high; many players try to sight the conductor through the center of the instrument or just past their hands. Fingers can be used to dampen the sound when needed for sharp cutoffs and to control the duration of the notes but otherwise should stay clear of the vibrating instrument.

TAMBOURINE

The tambourine is made with a frame of wood, metal, or plastic interspersed with jingles made from brass, copper, silver, or other light metal. Most orchestral tambourines come with a single head stretched across the frame, though tambourines used in popular music are frequently made without heads. Heads come in calfskin or synthetic materials. Good-quality tambourines include the Grover and Black Swamp brands. For general playing, strike the tambourine with an open hand against the head in the middle third of the area. Strong, "popped" notes can be produced by striking the center with your fist, while quiet notes can be played near the frame with your fingers. Tambourines can be tuned by adjusting the tension on the head, usually by applying heat such as from a heating pad. Most tambourines like a little humidity; heads can crack in arid conditions.

A rolling sound is frequently called for in tambourine parts. Some tambourine rolls can be played by shaking the instrument: hold the instrument by clamping your hand around the frame and turn your wrist rapidly in the manner of opening a doorknob. Sometimes the rolling sound can be punctuated by striking it with the other hand at the beginning or end of (or sometimes intermittently during) the roll. Rolls can also be produced by dragging your thumb across the head in a bumping or skipping motion, causing the head and jingles to vibrate. Achieving this special effect takes practice and usually no small amount of beeswax on the head. See 45.4, "Tambourine Technique," in the book's online resources.

45.7 Other Accessories

WOODBLOCK, TEMPLE BLOCKS, AND SLEIGH BELLS

One of the best parts of playing in a percussion section is the number of small accessory instruments and sound effects that percussionists get to play. Too numerous to detail here, accessory percussion can add fun and exciting timbres to the concert stage. One such instrument is the woodblock. This single piece of resonant wood is a type of slit drum typically carved out of teak, maple, other hardwood, or even plastic. It is played with a wood, rubber, or fabric mallet depending on the desired sound. The temple blocks are a collection of woodblocks, mounted on a stand. They usually number four or five in ascending pitches and can be heard in classic pieces such as Leroy Anderson's "Sleigh Ride." Another instrument heard in that piece and on many a holiday pops concert is the sleigh bells. Sleigh bells are a collection of small bells fastened to a stick with a handle. They are typically shaken to achieve their wintery sound. Shake sleigh bells by holding them horizontally on each side and shaking up and down; or hold the bells pointed toward the floor with the handle in one hand while striking the top of the holding hand with your fist. This tends to produce a more controlled sound with an articulate attack. Other accessory instruments include claves, maracas, cowbells, castanets, ratchet, vibraslap, and whistles of all kinds.

45.8 Discussion Questions

1. Percussion parts can be minimal in some band and orchestra literature. How can you keep your percussion students engaged and learning during rehearsals?
2. What are some ways to encourage sensitive, musical playing from the percussion section?
3. Percussion students are responsible for keeping track of numerous instruments, large and small. How might you help students organize their instruments to be ready for rehearsal on time and to facilitate a quick and easy tear-down after class?
4. Do you believe it is better to have percussion students specialize on a particular instrument or to have them rotate instruments during class? Why?

OXFORD learning link

Visit the online resources for additional documentation and exercises to help expand learning and test your knowledge further: www.oup.com/he/powell_music1e.

CHAPTER 46

PEDAGOGIES FOR TEACHING LATIN PERCUSSION

Aixa Burgos

This chapter provides an overview of Latin percussion instrumentation, playing techniques, and common rhythm patterns played in Latin music.

46.1 Introduction

For several years our education system has seen an increasing number of students whose families have immigrated to the United States from Latin American countries. This, along with the rise of native-born Latin Americans, has slowly been transforming the US education system. Part of that transformation has been research and implementation of several English as a Second Language and English to Speakers of Other Languages (ESL/ESOL) programs and, in most recent years, the incorporation of Latin American culture in the education process through approaches such as culturally responsive teaching and culturally sustaining pedagogy. Music education must also adapt to the diverse cultures of Latin America. Although it is important that students receive traditional music education, a curriculum dominated by Western music traditions can isolate minority students and be very limiting for nonminority students. Incorporating the rich history, stylistic variety, and unique rhythms of Latin music into music education curricula will benefit not only Latin American students, by linking identities and strengthening interactions, but other demographics as well. Benefits for non–Latin American students include broadened music preferences, increased receptivity to new music, and satiation of their appetite for music that aligns with what's current.

As a percussionist, I have encountered many situations where the ability to play Latin percussion instruments and rhythms has been critical in providing me opportunities for work in the professional arena. The variety of Latin percussion instruments and rhythms can provide distinct nuances and vibrant musical colors that classical percussion instruments and rhythms cannot. An example of this is seen in the many composers around the world who have incorporated Latin percussion instruments into their classical compositions (think of, e.g., Bernstein's *West Side Story* Suite and Carlos Chavez's *Sinfonía India*). Thus, fluency in and command of Latin percussion instruments and rhythms are extremely valuable in the performance workforce and in many different styles of music worldwide.

I have also encountered the misconception in music education that Latin percussion instruments and playing techniques are simple and easy to learn. This idea that anyone can grab a bongo and become a Latin percussionist overnight is false. It is important to understand that Latin percussion instruments require the same amount of effort and study as a traditional band or orchestra instrument; one is no less sophisticated or complex than the other. This chapter is dedicated to providing accurate and important information on common Latin percussion instruments, along with basic patterns, playing techniques, and pedagogical approaches that can be utilized in the music education classroom for a diverse and rich musical experience. I really hope you enjoy.

¡Un abrazo!

46.2 Ideas for Learning and Exercises on Latin Percussion Instruments

Imitation is a wonderful way for students to learn Latin American rhythms since these rhythms are repeated throughout the music. As you teach each rhythm, vocalize it first and have your students vocalize it back. This will allow students to memorize the rhythms which will be helpful once they are ready to apply the rhythm to the instrument. Some rhythms may seem intimating; however, they are easy to memorize, and imitation will help facilitate that.

Call and response is an excellent strategy for beginning improvisation on Latin Percussion instruments. In order for call and response to not feel intimidating to the student or teacher, it is important to start using very simple rhythmic patterns and add more complex ones little by little over time. Once students are comfortable participating in call and response as a whole group with you, allow them to lead call-and-response sessions in their own groups.

46.3 Congas

FIGURE 46.1 Name and size of each conga drum

Drum Name	Standard Size
Tumba (*or Tumbadora*)	12½ inches, largest sized drum
Conga (*the term "conga" is also used to refer to all conga drums*)	11¾ inches, medium sized drum
Quinto	11 inches, smaller sized drum
Requinto	10 inches, smallest sized drum

TUNING THE DRUMS

Conga drums (see Figure 46.1) are tunable, pitched instruments, and can therefore be tuned to the key signature of the piece of music being played. Understanding the pitch register of each conga drum will allow you to determine which note to tune each drum. Figure 46.2 shows the pitch registers for each drum which are ranges of where each drum sings best.

FIGURE 46.2 **Pitch registers for each conga drum**

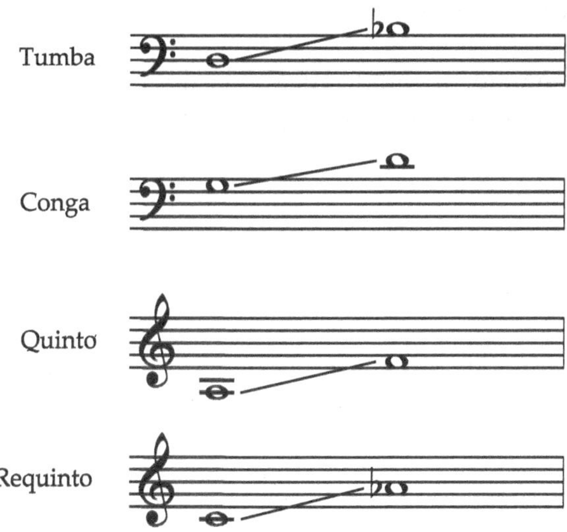

HOLDING THE CONGA DRUMS

See "Holding the Conga Drums," in the book's online resources.

TONES OF THE CONGA DRUM

There are five essential tones one can begin to master when learning conga drumming: open tone, muted tone, open slap, muted slap, and bass tone. Below I will describe how to produce each tone. See "Tones of the Conga Drum," in the book's online resources.

1. Open tone: warm, open, long sound
   - Open your hand and let it assume its natural curve.
   - Keep all your fingers together, including your thumb.
   - Place your hand on the edge of the drum, using the curve of your thumb as a guide to show how much of your hand will be on the drumhead.
   - Try to gently grab the drumhead (this will give your hand some firmness).
   - Keeping your hand in this position, lift and strike the drum on the spot where your hand was.
   - After striking, lift your hand again and let the sound ring.
2. Muted tone: shortened open tone
   - Open your hand and let it assume its natural curve.
   - Keep all your fingers together, including your thumb.
   - Place your hand on the edge of the drum, using the curve of your thumb as a guide to show how much of your hand will be on the drumhead.
   - Try to gently grab the drumhead (this will give your hand some firmness).
   - Lift the palm a little so that only the hand is making contact with the drumhead.
   - Strike the drum as you would for an open tone.
   - Once you strike the drum, keep your hand on the drumhead and press down. This will produce a clear pitch while stopping the drum from ringing.
   - Since the muted tone is essentially a muted open tone, it is recommended to focus on creating a good open tone before muting it.

3. Open slap: high-pitched; combines the tone of the drum with its harmonics
   - Allow your hand to take the shape of an igloo.
   - Your hand must remain firm; your fingertips must remain loose.
   - Keep the thumb against the index finger.
   - Strike the drum, turning the hand slightly inward, toward the edge of the drum.
   - The tips of the fingers will bring out the harmonics, while the shape of your hand (the igloo) will amplify the sound.
   - After striking, lift your hand and let the sound ring.
4. Muted slap: shortened open slap
   - Allow your hand to take the shape of an igloo.
   - Your hand must remain firm; your fingertips must remain loose.
   - Keep the thumb against the index finger.
   - Strike the drum, turning the hand slightly inward, toward the edge of the drum
   - The tips of the fingers will bring out the harmonics, while the shape of your hand (the igloo) will amplify the sound.
   - After striking the drum, gently grab the drumhead to stop the sound from ringing.
5. Bass tone: dark, low tone
   - Flatten your hand, bringing your thumb close so that its shape has a natural contour.
   - Strike the drum with your palm at the very center of the drumhead, letting the sound ring.
   - Make sure the drum is elevated off of the floor (fully or at an angle) to allow a deeper, more sustained bass tone.

THE CLAVE

The clave (pronounced "CLA-veh") is the most essential component in Latin music, since all Latin music is written based on and around it. Common rhythmic patterns are played in two-bar phrases that are determined by the clave. The two types of claves are clave 2-3 (Figure 46.3) or clave 3-2 (Figure 46.4). All rhythmic patterns introduced in the upcoming sections will include the corresponding clave for each. See "The Clave," in the book's online resources.

FIGURE 46.3 Clave 2-3

FIGURE 46.4 Clave 3-2

SOUND VOCABULARY AS A PEDAGOGICAL APPROACH

In most cultures throughout history, with very few exceptions, rhythms have been taught orally and by rote, not written down but passed down through vocalizations that would imitate the sound of the instrument. The sound vocabulary introduced in this section closely resembles the sound the conga drum makes thus facilitating the ability to convey accurate characteristics of the tone qualities for the drum and the rhythms to be played. Students should first vocalize the rhythm, then transfer onto the conga drum. *If you can say it, you can play it.* This process will also facilitate memorization of rhythms with proper tone. The sound vocabulary that will be used for teaching conga rhythms (abbreviating left hand as LH and right hand as RH here and elsewhere in the chapter) is:

1. *Chu*: muted bass tone, palm on conga or quinto (LH)
2. *Ca*: muted flat slap on conga or quinto (LH)
3. *La*: muffled muted slap on conga or quinto (RH)
4. *Been*: open tone on conga or quinto (RH)
5. *Beep*: muted tone on conga or quinto (RH)
6. *Lah*: open slap on conga or quinto (RH)
7. *Chun*: open bass tone, palm on conga or quinto (RH)
8. *Boom*: open tone on tumba (or lowest) drum (RH)
9. *Boop*: muted tone on tumba (or lowest) drum (RH)

BASIC PATTERNS FOR SELECT MUSICAL STYLES

In most repertoire, the conga part consists of a desired rhythmic style (or simply "Latin music") written above the staff, and each measure has slashes where the rhythm is to be played. It is assumed that percussionists are aware of and able to play the rhythmic patterns or musical style written in the music. Musical breaks, however, are always written out in traditional notation. Figure 46.5 shows an example of this.

FIGURE 46.5 Example of musical breaks written in traditional notation

Tumbao

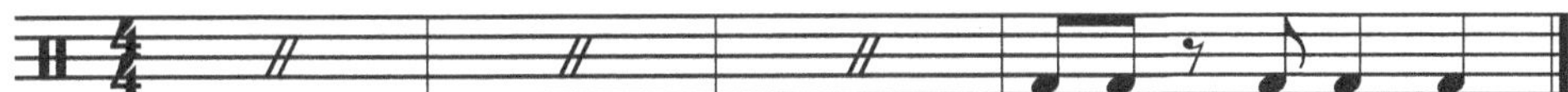

The next few sections will introduce common rhythmic patterns played on the conga drum. See "Basic Conga Patterns," in the book's online resources for written notation. For pedagogical purposes and proper playing technique, I will include the sticking above the rhythm and sound vocabulary for each rhythm example.

Tumbao/Marcha

This is the most important pattern to learn on the conga drums and the foundation of many other styles. Arguably the most popular rhythm on conga, it can be played in mambo, guaracha, cha-cha-cha, Latin rock, and even pop music. See "Basic Conga Patterns: Tumbao/Marcha," in the book's online resources.

Bolero

This is used for ballads; it is played at a slower tempo with two drums. The bolero pattern can be played utilizing clave 2-3 or clave 3-2. See "Basic Conga Patterns: Bolero," in the book's online resources.

Bomba

This is an Afro–Puerto Rican rhythm used in traditional music and dances of Puerto Rico. The bomba pattern can be played utilizing clave 2-3 or clave 3-2. See "Basic Conga Patterns: Bomba," in the book's online resources.

A Caballo

Literally translated as "by horse," this is a driving pattern used in merengue as well as many other styles throughout Latin America. See "Basic Conga Patterns: A Caballo," in the book's online resources.

Apambichao

Also referred to as *pambiche* or *merenge apambichao*, this is a pattern that originated in the Dominican Republic; it is used in merengue music. This pattern utilizes a stick for all right-hand strikes. The stick will strike the drumhead as well as the rim of the drum. See "Basic Conga Patterns: Apambichao," in the book's online resources.

Guaguancó

Originating in Cuba, this pattern can be played in a variety of ways with different clave patterns. Common clave patterns used are *son* clave 3-2 and rumba clave 3-2. See "Basic Conga Patterns: Guaguancó," in the book's online resources.

Songo

This is s a combination of the mambo pattern and the guaguancó. See "Basic Conga Patterns: Songo," in the book's online resources.

Bossa Nova

Originating in Brazil, bossa nova was inspired by a combination of traditional Brazilian rhythms and jazz. See "Basic Conga Patterns: Bossa Nova," in the book's online resources.

46.4 Timbales

FIGURE 46.6 **Name and size of each timbale drum**

Drum Name	Standard Size
Timbales (*most common*)	14 inches-15 inches and 13 inches-14 inches
Timbalón	15 inches-16 inches
Timbalitos	10 inches-12 inches

TUNING THE DRUMS

Timbales are pitched instruments, and their tuning is based on the key signature of the music being played (see Figure 46.6 for the name and size of each of the timbales). It is important to tune them in relation to the music being played so that their sound becomes part of the music. Tune the higher-pitched drum first to make sure you have a clear, crisp tone. Then tune the lower-pitched drum to the interval that works best in relation to the music you are playing. Figure 46.7 demonstrates recommended intervals and pitches for timbale tuning.

FIGURE 46.7 Recommended intervals and pitches for timbale tuning

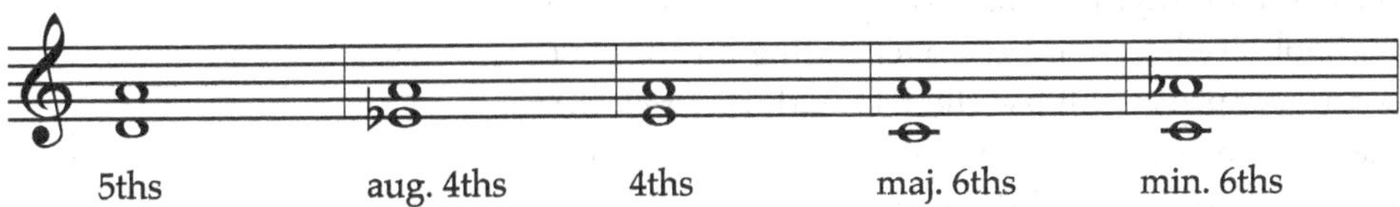

CASCARA PATTERN

The rhythm that is played utilizing the metal sides (shell) of the timbales is called the cascara pattern. See "Cascara Pattern," in the book's online resources. When playing cascara, there are a few things to keep in mind:

- Strike the shell surface in the space between the tuning lugs.
- Strike the shell using the part of the stick that is about an inch and a half from the tip so that the tone is sharp and crisp.
- Using different parts of the stick will change the tone of the cascara.

BEATING SPOTS FOR THE TIMBALES

Playing on different areas of the drum surface will produce different tones. There are five playing areas to choose from:

1. About one inch from the rim
2. Off-center
3. Center
4. Above-center
5. About one inch from the rim (farthest away)

These beating spots can also be applied to rim shots. See "Beating Spots for the Timbales," in the book's online resources. Here are three examples of beating spots and stick angles that will produce distinct tones:

1. Strike the drum at a sharp angle with the tip of the stick to produce a high-pitched rim-shot.
2. Strike the drum at a slight angle, hitting the rim about an inch and a half down from the tip of the stick to produce a sharp, powerful rim shot.
3. Strike the rim of the drum flat using half the length of the stick to produce a dark sound.

BEATING SPOTS FOR THE COWBELL

Playing on different areas of the cowbell will also produce different tones. It is important to find the "sweet spot" on the bell. See "Beating Spots for the Cowbell," in the book's online resources. There are four playing areas to choose from:

1. Striking the bell with the tip of the stick one inch from the top will produce a light, ringing tone.
2. Striking the bell two inches from the top will produce a darker, lower tone.
3. Playing over the mouth of the bell with about one inch of the stick sticking out of the bell will provide a full sound.
4. Playing the bell on the top of the mouth will produce a light and resonant sound.

BASIC PATTERNS FOR SELECT MUSICAL STYLES

The next few sections will introduce common rhythmic patterns played on the timbales. See "Basic Timbal Patterns," in the book's online resources. Depending on the rhythm being played, there will be times where the player will use the RH with the stick for the cascara pattern and their LH on the drum or with a stick to keep time. For pedagogical purposes and proper playing technique, I have included the RH sticking on the top and the LH sticking on the bottom.

COMMON RHYTHMIC PATTERNS FOR TIMBALES

- Mambo (clave 2-3)
- Mambo (clave 3-2)
- Cha-cha-cha (clave 2-3 and 3-2)
- Bolero (clave 2-3 and 3-2)
- Bomba sicá (clave 2-3 or 3-2)
- A caballo (clave 2-3 or 3-2)
- Guaguancó (son clave 3-2 or rumba clave 3-2)
- Songo (son clave 3-2 or rumba clave 3-2)
- Bossa nova

46.5 Bongos

FIGURE 46.8 Name and size of each bongo drum

Drum Name	Standard Size
Hembra (*female*)	8 inches–9 inches (lower pitched drum)
Macho (*male*)	6 ¾ inches–8 inches (higher pitched drum)

TUNING THE DRUMS

Bongos, like timbales, are also pitched instruments that can be tuned; however, there are a few things to keep in mind when tuning the bongos:

- The register of the bongo is determined by the size of the drum.
- Make sure that the sound of the bongo is high and "crispy."
- For the macho (higher-pitched drum), the best notes are F5 up chromatically to an A5 (see Figure 46.8 for the names and sizes of each of the bongos).
- For the hembra (lower-pitched drum), the best notes are B♭4 up chromatically to a E♭5.

RECOMMENDED INTERVALS AND PITCHES FOR TUNING

These are listed in Figure 46.9 order of preference from left to right.

FIGURE 46.9 Recommended intervals and pitches for tuning

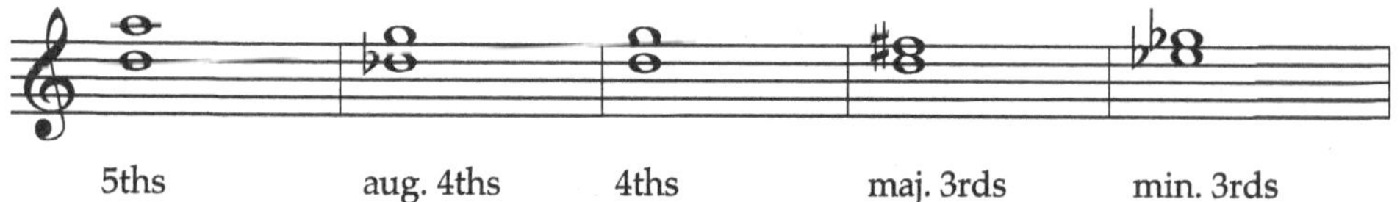

TONES OF THE BONGOS

There are five essential tones one can begin to master when learning how to play the bongos. See "Tones of the Bongos," in the book's online resources.

HOLDING THE BONGOS

See "Holding the Bongos," in the book's online resources.

SOUND VOCABULARY AS A PEDAGOGICAL APPROACH

The sound vocabulary for the bongos is as follows:

1. *Li*: muffled and/or muted high pitch, one to three fingers, on the high drum (LH)
2. *Ca*: muted high pitch with the hand on the center of the highest drum (LH)
3. *Co*: muted low tone with the palm close to the center of the high drum (LH)
4. *Boo*: muted tone on the low drum using one of the middle three fingers (RH)
5. *La*: high open tone on small drum played close to edge for a crisp "rim-shot-like" sound (RH or LH)

These sound can be achieved in either of two different ways:

1. Use the LH in a palm-to-hand rocking motion while the RH plays using just the fingers.
2. Use only the hands to imitate all the sounds.

BASIC PATTERNS FOR SELECT MUSICAL STYLES

Figure 46.10 shows the basic patterns for marcha/tumbao/martillo (LH in rocking motion with palm and hand).

FIGURE 46.10 **Basic patterns for marcha/tumbao/martillo**

This bongo pattern can be used for the following musical styles:

- Mambo (clave 2-3 or 3-2)
- Cha-cha-cha (clave 2-3 or 3-2)
- Guajira (clave 2-3 or 3-2)
- Bolero (clave 2-3 or 3-2)
- Bomba (clave 2-3 or 3-2)
- A caballo (clave 2-3 or 3-2)
- Guaguancó
- Songo

46.6 Cowbell

The cowbell or *campana* is an important component in Latin American music. In salsa music, you will typically see the bongo player switch to the cowbell when the music switches to the chorus/refrain of the piece, mambo section, horn solos, or other heightened sections of the piece.

HOLDING THE COWBELL

There are two different styles of holding the cowbell. Either can be used, depending on the player's preference and comfort. See "Holding the Cowbell," in the book's online resources.

SOUNDS OF THE COWBELL

- High: strike with the cowbell stick on the bottom, closed end of the cowbell for a high sound
- Low: strike with the cowbell stick on the top, open end of the cowbell (also referred to as the mouth) for a low sound

BASIC PATTERNS FOR SELECT MUSICAL STYLES

The next few sections will introduce common rhythmic patterns played on the cowbell. See "Basic Cowbell Patterns," in the book's online resources. For pedagogical purposes and proper playing technique, I have included the RH sticking on the top and the LH sticking on the bottom.

COMMON RHYTHMIC PATTERNS FOR TIMBALES

- Mambo (clave 2-3)
- Mambo (clave 3-2)
- Cha-cha-cha (clave 2-3 or 3-2)
- Guajira (clave 2-3)
- Guajira (clave 3-2)
- Bomba (clave 2-3 or 3-2)
- Songo
- A caballo (clave 2-3 or 3-2)
- Guaguancó

46.7 Maracas

The maraca is a very underestimated instrument, often seen as a toy. In Latin America maracas are truly virtuosic instruments that can also be used as accompaniment. Usually the best maraca players are the singers in the band. When learning how to play the maraca, it is important to always focus on the sound that you are producing.

HOLDING THE MARACAS

Hold one maraca in each hand by the handle. The head of the maraca should be facing up. See "Holding the Maracas," in the book's online resources.

PLAYING TECHNIQUES

- Staccato/short eighth-note patterns: Flick your wrist in a short, quick downstroke, as if tapping something. Alternate downstrokes with each hand. See "Maraca Playing Techniques," in the book's online resources.
- Swish/roll: Turn the maracas upside down, keeping the head pointing to the ground, and swirl the maracas in a small circular motion. See "Maraca Playing Techniques," in the book's online resources.

BASIC PATTERNS FOR THE MARACAS

See "Basic Patterns for the Maracas," in the book's online resources.

46.8 Güiro and Guira

The güiro is an instrument used in many Latin American countries and musical styles. The güiro is traditionally made out of a gourd; however, they are currently available in plastic and fiberglass for durability. Some musical styles require güiro. For example, the cha-cha-cha cannot exist without güiro, just as rock cannot exist without electric guitar. The güira is different from the güiro: it is from the Dominican Republic and is made out of metal.

HOLDING THE GÜIRO AND STICK

On the back side of the güiro are two openings. Hold the güiro with your non-dominant hand. Place your thumb into the top opening and your middle finger into the bottom opening. The güiro should be resting in your palm. The opening of the güiro should be slanted, pointing upward. The scraping stick is held with your dominant hand. Wrap your index finger around the stick as you would a drumstick. See "Holding the Güiro and Stick," in the book's online resources.

HOLDING THE GÜIRA AND GANCHO

The güira usually has a handle on the back. Hold the güira with your non-dominant hand. The gancho is held with your dominant hand. Wrap your fingers around the wooden part of the gancho and leave the metal wires of the gancho uncovered. See "Holding the Güira and Gancho," in the book's online resources.

SOUND VOCABULARY

The sound vocabulary for the güiro and güira is as follows:

1. *Cha*: quarter-note value, downward stroke with stick; quarter notes played either full value or staccato
2. *Cha-ya*: eighth-note value, short down-up stroke on the guiro/a with stick/gancho

BASIC PATTERNS FOR MUSICAL STYLES ON GÜIRO

The next few sections will introduce common rhythmic patterns played on the güiro. See "Basic Güiro Patterns," in the book's online resources.

- Basic and most frequently used pattern: used for styles such as salsa, *son*, cha-cha-cha, and bolero

- Cinquillo Rhythm: used for a musical style called danzón
- Rumba

BASIC PATTERNS FOR MUSICAL STYLES ON GÜIRA

- Merengue
- Bachata
  - Derecho (also known as caminando)
  - Majao
- Mambo

46.9 Claves

The name of this instrument is synonymous with the rhythm pattern introduced at the beginning of the chapter. What is important about the claves is the concept of the clave and its role in Latin American music. Claves produce a very sharp, penetrating, clear sound that can stand out in large ensembles. Although the playing technique and rhythms are simple, the claves should be played by a strong musician, as they are central to keeping the entire ensemble together.

HOLDING THE CLAVES

There are many variations of rhythm and sound possible with the claves. Holding the clave properly is essential in sound production. The player must hold one clave on each hand, using the fingertips in order to enhance the instrument's resonance. The non-dominant hand should be under the dominant hand. The clave on the non-dominant hand is stationary and does not move. While holding the clave in the non-dominant hand, it is important to make a hollow with the hand, holding the clave with the fingertips only and allowing the curve of the palm to act as a resonator. The dominant hand will hold the clave and will be used to strike the clave on the non-dominant hand. See "Holding the Claves," in the book's online resources.

BASIC PATTERNS FOR MUSICAL STYLES

The next few sections will introduce common rhythmic patterns played on the claves. See "Basic Clave Patterns," on the book's online resources.

BASIC PATTERNS FOR THE CLAVES

- *Son* Clave 2-3
- *Son* clave 3-2
- Rumba clave 2-3
- Rumba clave 3-2

46.10 Discussion Questions

1. What do you know, or think you know, about Latin music?
2. In what ways do Latin American music and Latin percussion instruments relate to the music you listen to?
3. What do Latin American music and Latin percussion instruments reveal about Latin American people and culture?

OXFORD learning link

Visit the online resources for additional documentation and exercises to help expand learning and test your knowledge further: www.oup.com/he/powell_music1e.

CHAPTER 47

PEDAGOGIES FOR TEACHING STEEL PAN AND STEEL BANDS

David Knapp

This chapter provides context for including steel band within a music education program and highlights important topics from the author's coauthored (with Adam Grisé) steel band curriculum *Introduction to Steel Band* (2009), available through Engine Room Publishing.

47.1 The Steel Band Movement

The steel band movement is a fascinating story of colonialism, race, class, and material culture, animated by a narrative history that celebrates the vibrant contributions that Trinidad's African population has made to its culture. Though steel pan was once looked down upon by upstanding society and even outlawed for a time, it is now Trinidad and Tobago's national instrument and for many a source of national pride. Essential to this trajectory is a master narrative pertaining to struggle and overcoming adversity (Stuempfle, 1995). Steel bands now extend across the globe and across genres, creating a rich tapestry of diverse musical practices.

The steel band movement began in a specific place and time in Port of Spain, Trinidad, during the 1930s and 1940s. There, young afro-Trinidadians—the descendants of slaves—performed their lower-class *jammete* Carnival through syncretic musical practices that blended West African musical traditions with the French Catholic pre-Lenten Carnival masquerade. These early steel bandsmen—as they were all men at this time—took to the streets with their pitched *tamboo bamboo* to mark out polyphonic rhythms on *booms*, *foulés*, and *cutters*. As often happened, these bamboo would wear out on the cobbled streets in the neighborhoods of St. James, Woodbrook, and Laventille. So the young revelers would take whatever scrap metal was available to them, as it was more durable on the road.

Though the precise provenance of the first steel pan is open for debate, it is certain that it came from the observation that repeated beating on metal tins, and most likely a cookie tin, created a stretched surface on the metal, producing an altered pitch. In each successive year, young inventors from masquerade bands with such colorful names as Alexander's Ragtime Band and the Invaders would debut their musical innovations during Carnival. Early steel pans had names like "ping-pong" and "dud-up," onomatopoeias of their simple sounds. They soon evolved into diatonic instruments and then fully chromatic instruments with names such as "tenor," "double seconds," "guitar," and "bass"; these make up today's multiphonic steel orchestras.

47.2 Steel Band Methods and Materials

Regarding pedagogy, steel bands occupy a space similar perhaps to that taken up by other genres in music education, such as jazz band. Members of a steel band learn their parts using a chart, with a concert or gig in mind. Like a jazz band, the director of the band is decentered and is usually there only to count in the band and provide cues. And like jazz band, steel band presents opportunities for more student-centered approaches than are typical of large ensembles such as concert band. Improvisation has been a mainstay of steel bands since the beginning of the art form and continues today; many steel band charts contain solo sections for students. Beyond explicit sections for improvisation, there is room for student creativity thanks to the involvement of steel band members in a tune's arrangement. Though many charts are available for bands to perform, there are fewer expectations that the players will strictly adhere to the page, and members of a band are often free to make informed choices about strumming patterns, dynamics, and form. Even the existence of a score is not assumed. Notation in steel band is relatively new. To this day in Trinidad and Tobago, most performers in steel bands learn highly complex charts by rote. Though these practices may be less common and challenging for some students, learning by rote may lead to important learning outcomes for students who are overly reliant on the page. In practice, most steel band directors employ a combination of these two methods in their classrooms. For more insight into steel band methods, Chris Tanner's *Steel Band Game Plan* (2005) explores ideas for starting and building a program, including effective classroom strategies. Additionally, my aforementioned *Introduction to Steel Band* provides a solid foundation for student success, including a student textbook, teacher's manual, and individual method books for each instrument.

Though there are many instrument layouts across the different registers of steel pans, school steel bands are typically made up of tenor, double tenor, double seconds, triple guitar, and six bass. Procuring these instruments is less of a challenge than it used to be, and there are more pan builders now than ever before. Still, a band of ten pans will cost between $10,000 and $20,000, and it can take more than a year for the instruments to be built by hand. Figure 47.1 shows the most common layouts for these instruments, as well as their ranges and musical functions.

In a typical musical arrangement, the tenor pan performs the melody of the tune, with double tenor playing in unison, doubling an octave below, or harmonizing the melody. The next two instruments, the double seconds and triple guitars, most commonly perform strumming patterns. In a steel band, strumming functions much like a rhythm guitar, performing both a harmonic and rhythmic purpose. However, the rhythms strummed in a steel band are often more syncopated and interlocking.

The first four patterns in Figure 47.2 are in cut time, which is typical for older calypsos and some soca. All of these patterns are readily apparent in Trinidadian popular music. The cuatro strum, for example, is prominent in music from the golden age of calypso (the late 1930s through the 1950s) and can be heard on the accompanying cuatro, a four-stringed instrument from Venezuela. These patterns are also sometimes played in common time by simply doubling them. The last strumming pattern is in common time and emerged during the 1970s as Trinidadian popular music began to increase in tempo and rhythmic complexity. Even though tempos increased, the older rhythmic patterns persisted. The artful combination of these patterns across different instruments and different sections of a tune can lead to a sweet-sounding band.

FIGURE 47.1 Common steel pan layouts with ranges and musical functions

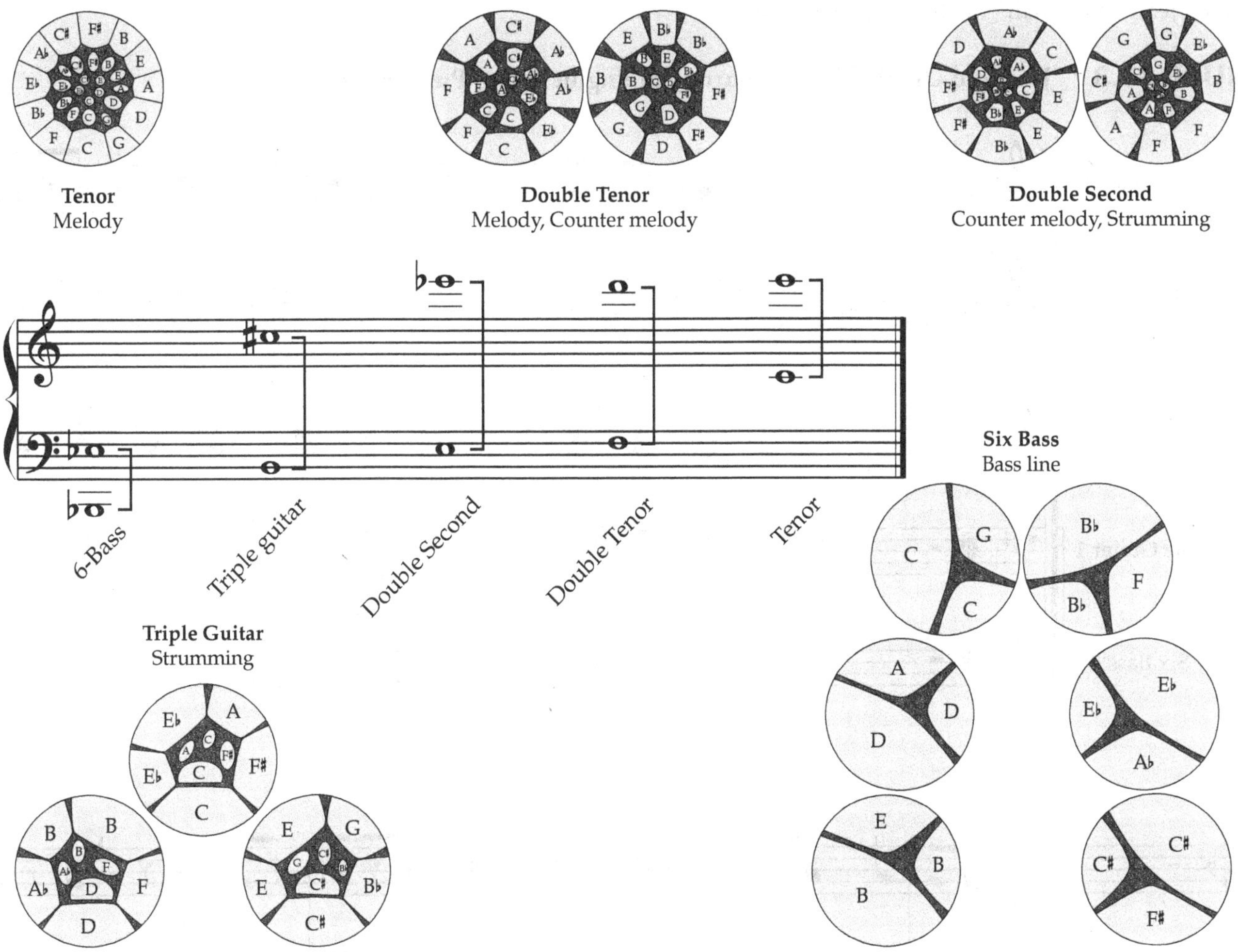
Tenor
Melody
Double Tenor
Melody, Counter melody
Double Second
Counter melody, Strumming
6-Bass
Triple guitar
Double Second
Double Tenor
Tenor
Six Bass
Bass line
Triple Guitar
Strumming

FIGURE 47.2 Common steel band strumming patterns

Three Strum
Soca Strum
Cuatro Strum
Off-Beat Strum
Back-Beat Strum

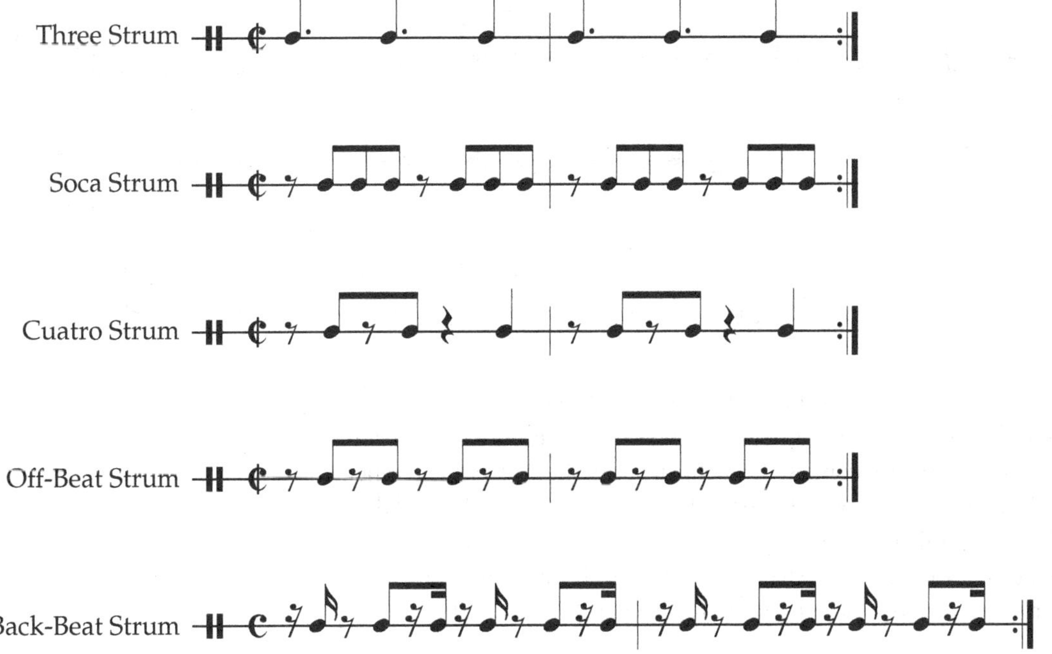

Finally, among the common instruments, the bass pans perform a role typical of a string or electric bass. Figure 47.3 is an example of a simple arrangement of the famous calypso "Jean and Dinah" by the Mighty Sparrow.

FIGURE 47.3 **"Jean and Dinah," verse. Courtesy of Engine Room Publishing**

In addition to the rhythmic patterns performed by the "backline" in Figure 47.3, the driving force of a steel band's groove is the engine room. The engine room consists primarily of a drum set, iron (i.e., brake drum), congas, cowbell, and scratcher. These instruments, combined with the backline, function to push the band forward, set the groove, and dictate the band's dynamics. The rhythmic patterns played by the engine room vary according to genre and tune. For a lengthier discussion of steel band styles and the engine room, take a look at the teacher's manual to *Introduction to Steel Band* (Knapp & Grisé, 2009).

47.3 Diversity through World and Popular Music

Proponents of steel band in music education advocate for the ensemble by relying on a world-music rationale, citing its exogeneity and its ability to instruct students about a foreign musical culture (Williams, 2008). Yet, it's not clear to what extent steel band teachers in the United States include this history in their teaching. Without a steel band pedagogy that makes full descriptions of Trinidadians' musical practices possible, multicultural music education is stripped of its value, leaving a tropicalized representation of a complex musical culture. Lessons that center this culture might confer something about calypso, Afro-Trinidadian musical traditions, the steel band movement, and colonialism. This multicultural approach to steel band goes beyond treating the music as the object of study and instead seeks to instruct students in the musical practices of another place.

Yet, circumscribing steel band within the confines of world music limits our understanding of it as a popular music genre. From the beginning of the movement in the 1940s and 1950s, steel bands performed popular music. On the road during Carnival, steel bands pounded out the most popular melodies for revelers on the street. This included the popular calypsos of the day as well as Latin pop and music from the Broadway stage and Hollywood movies. Popular music continues to play a central role in steel band music. The annual Panorama competition, which occurs the Saturday before Lent, showcases dozens of the best steel bands in Trinidad and Tobago performing complex arrangements of that year's most popular soca anthems.

A multicultural approach to teaching steel band, then, includes a focus on popular music. This connection provides an opportunity for directors to extend steel band musical practices to their students' own popular music. While engaging responsibly in learning about the music of another culture, school steel bands can also be a site for culturally responsive teaching by inviting students into musical processes, such as selecting and arranging repertoire. A concert program that blends world and popular music approaches might include historical calypsos such as "Jean and Dinah," contemporary socas such as Farmer Nappy's "Hookin Meh," and contemporary popular music, from Adele to Bruno Mars to The Weeknd to whatever it is that your students are listening to.

47.4 Discussion

Our field continues to wrestle with issues of diversity. Two important philosophical movements that have been calling for diversifying the curriculum are multiculturalism and popular music pedagogy. While these philosophical orientations have not been adopted evenly across our field, they remain important and evolving orientations as music pedagogy contends with its relationship to a diverse and diversifying society.

In some corners of our curriculum—including steel band—the combination of these two orientations may prove to be generative in connecting students' own musical experiences to those from other cultural backgrounds. This philosophy of steel band pedagogy combines students' own music making with the vibrant history of the steel band movement. Instead of recreating steel band as a musical practice separate from their own experiences, students are able to incorporate musical processes central to steel band.

Finally, owing to the proliferation of steel bands in academic settings, there are plenty of resources to support music educators who want to expand their curriculum. In addition to the aforementioned resources, there are music publishing houses that cater to school steel bands; see Engine Room Publishing (engineroompublishing.com) and Pan Ramajay (ramajay.com) for collections of excellent variety of curated charts.

47.5 Discussion Questions

1. How might rote- and note-based music learning be combined in teaching a steel band ensemble? What other ensembles also use a blended approach?
2. What are the different instruments in a steel band? What are the musical functions of the pitched steel pans, and how are they used to arrange a tune? What are some of the various non-pitched percussion instruments, and what are they collectively called?
3. How might the philosophical rationales of multiculturalism and popular music be combined in a steel band ensemble? What learning opportunities would this afford students? Are these opportunities similar or different from those available from other ensembles and curricular offerings?
4. What roles do race, class, nationality, and identity play in the history of steel band? How could this history be used to support student learning outcomes?

OXFORD learning link

Visit the online resources for additional documentation and exercises to help expand learning and test your knowledge further: www.oup.com/he/powell_music1e.

PART VII.

Ensemble Rehearsal Techniques

CHAPTER 48

MODERN BAND REHEARSAL TECHNIQUES

Scott Burstein

This chapter provides an overview of pedagogical considerations for teaching modern band.

48.1 Introduction

Teaching a large modern band can be challenging beyond the typical unfamiliarity with the repertoire or lack of traditional curricular resources. The way in which popular music instruments (guitar, bass, drums, keyboards, vocals, and technology) are used in school is unlike more traditional instruments and ensembles. For example, the violin in the orchestra or the saxophone in jazz bands are part of larger sections, and this in turn is part of a much larger ensemble, whereas popular music groups outside of the classroom (e.g., rock bands) rarely have more than four or five members. In most public school classrooms, it is often necessary to include a large number of students for a variety of reasons, including enrollment minimums.

I taught popular music ensembles at the high school level for twelve years before my current role as director of teaching and learning for a large popular music nonprofit organization; I also directed the first-ever All National Honors Ensemble for modern band (Powell, 2021). In addition to teaching ensembles that varied by size, instrumentation, and age of the members, I have also observed hundreds of other modern band ensembles around the country. All these groups of students taught me a lot about the ins and outs of modern band. Based on these experiences, I will spend the rest of this chapter discussing the three most common options for teaching a large popular music ensemble: single instrument–focused, balanced large ensembles, and smaller individual bands in one class. I will discuss some of the pros and cons of each and give suggestions for repertoire selection, facilitation, and balance of teacher- and student-led direction.

48.2 Single Instrument–Focused Modern Band

The most common classes that use popular instruments in K–12 music classrooms in the United States are guitar ensembles and keyboard classes. In most cases, neither class actually focuses on popular music, instead opting to concentrate on classical repertoire.

However, there are many ways which even a single instrument–focused class can work well for learning specific instrumental skills, with just some minor additions and repertoire choices. I recommend that any single instrument–focused class add in a bass and drum set. This immediately can add some depth to the sound of the group. Let's look at guitar classes and keyboard classes separately.

For a guitar class, adding an electric bass is a no-brainer, since many of the chords and concepts from guitar transition smoothly to the bass, and it is often easier at first just focusing on one note per chord and learning basic grooves. For adding in a drum set, start by having the whole class work on body percussion to get the basic backbeat, or have each student use a pair of drumsticks and play basic rhythms on chairs or the floor. Once students have mastered the basics of these two instruments, I recommend alternating bassists and drummers throughout each class, giving everyone a chance to expand their musical knowledge.

In keyboard class, sometimes a drum set will be tough to fit into a keyboard lab, but usually each keyboard has drum patches, so some students can play the drum part on the keys themselves. Bassists can help fill out the sound early on while beginning students focus on playing chords.

In both guitar and keyboard modern bands, instruction should be varied, with a focus on composition, improvisation, and basics of repertoire. However, since these classes are largely composed of students playing one instrument, much more attention to instrument-specific skills can be utilized, and lesson planning for these skills through popular repertoire can make or break a class. One of the most important skills a teacher of popular music can have is the ability to find new student-centered repertoire and identify specifics from the song to teach the necessary skills. For example, a keyboard class that is beginning to work on arpeggiation might look to something like Adele's "Someone Like You," or a guitar class working on simple pentatonic riffs could work on the post-chorus guitar melody in American Author's "Best Day of My Life." Both of these songs might not be student centered, but they are examples of songs that during their prime were pervasive in my classroom, and the same types of examples can be found with current hits. As recommended throughout this book, make sure you talk to your students about the music that they are listening to and when possible use music chosen by students to demonstrate musical concepts.

Approximation (modifying the music to meet the student's needs) and scaffolding (allowing students of mixed ability to play together, supporting each other) should be key ingredients to making these classes work for students at various skill levels (Burstein & Powell, 2019). These concepts can best be understood through examples. Let us look at the 2016 hit "Heathens," by Twenty One Pilots (which can be found in section 2 in *Modern Band Method*, Burstein et al., 2020), taught through the lens of a keyboard course. As mentioned earlier, one or several students could either play percussion or emulate it on a keyboard patch. Meanwhile, there are a few other important parts students could play, working on different skills for each. Some students could read the vocal melody, either through simple iconic notation using just letter names or with traditional five-line-staff notation. The bass line is fairly simple, mostly half and whole notes that for the most part repeat throughout, which could be played with just one hand or in octaves. Then the harmony itself is a progression from C to Am to E, arpeggiated with broken chords. Students can either play them as root-position chords or can work on voice leading and inversions.

Once students have a basic understanding of the parts of the song, they can mix and match these different parts, which is where the fun comes in. Students can self-select the parts they want to play and will likely try to work on more and more challenging arrangements as they go on, but all students can play and sing the song together as a large ensemble. For assessment, teachers can develop a rubric that assigns grades based on how many different parts students can play, and more advanced students can work on singing while playing the chords, or playing the chords and the bass, or even playing the melody with the right hand and the bass part or chords with the left hand. As long as students are combining their approximated parts together in a scaffolded setting, the result will be a full, musical arrangement that allows students to develop a variety of important keyboard skills. Students can even go a step further and change up the form or add improvisatory breaks, or even a modulation.

While popular music is a vast and diverse repertoire of genres, many primary student–centered songs focus on repetitive phrases of two to four chords; these phrases are often the same for both the verse and the chorus. This is a gross simplification of the depth of even the most radio-friendly pop songs, which often endure owing to their amazing production or ear-worm melodies, but it does mean that beginning students can play a lot of songs from the outset with very little knowledge, particularly since so many of these songs are diatonic and can easily be transposed to friendly keys (G, D, or A major on guitar, C on keyboard). For this reason, the very approach to learning songs should be different than that of a typical performance ensemble, which focuses on four or five pieces a semester for adjudication and concert. Effective modern band classes will look at songs at the micro and macro level. For every song learned to completion and for performance, there should be between ten and twenty others that are brought up specifically for pedagogical purposes, such as to introduce a new chord or skill. Instead of learning and mastering these songs, single phrases or even single bar riffs can be the focus. After all, what modern band teacher has not had a student excitedly showing off their musical knowledge to their peers with a variety of two-bar melodies rather than an entire three-minute performance?

Using snippets as well as full songs can help create a good structure for the organization of class time. For example, in my classes I would typically start each class with a warm-up while they walked in, often a simple melody written on the board from a familiar song, which they had to identify and learn to play. I could extend this lesson by using different iconic notations for them to decipher, and then they would notate it in another (e.g.. I could write it in guitar tablature and they could notate it on a staff). This set up expectations from the moment they walked into my class; they would go grab their instrument while I took attendance, we would play together after they rehearsed it for two to five minutes, and then we would move on.

Next, we could review the previous day's songs before adding in new techniques or chords through new repertoire. This could lead to vamping a chord progression for extended periods of time, giving me an opportunity to walk around the room and assist students who might have been potentially struggling, and meanwhile a couple of students at a time could improvise either on electric guitar (I would have a couple ready to play at the front of the class) or by turning their volume up on the keyboard. We could then focus on composition, either as a group or individually, using a variety of different composition games (such as rolling a die and playing a power chord starting on that fret, or writing a chord progression based on three successive rolls where the number rolled was the harmony they would play). Once again, composition could be a simple five-minute activity or could build to a much larger composition they would work on successively, building week by week. Finally, we could end the class by working on the repertoire songs for the concert, some of the songs they determined they wanted to put their time into really working on for performance in front of parents and peers.

48.3 Balanced Large Modern Band

The second type of modern band class I recommend is the large balanced class, where there is a fairly even distribution of instruments throughout. For instance, in a class of between twenty-five and thirty-five students, you might have three or four drummers or percussionists, three or four bassists, six to eight guitarists, six to eight keyboards, four or five vocalists, and a handful of other instruments such as ukulele, horns, or strings. There are a lot of challenges with building an ensemble this way, but a lot of advantages as well.

The largest disadvantage is figuring out how to start the basics of this class if it is primarily beginning students. I recommend having stations where students can work together within their instrument group; the teacher can float between these stations to assist the students and keep them on task. I would also recommend having students change instruments throughout, pushing for students at the outset to become versatile multi-instrumentalists. The guitar group can switch to keyboard while keyboard jumps to bass and drums, and so on. As the class progresses, typically by about the fifth week, students can start to gravitate toward "home" instruments as the larger ensemble really starts to form.

Classes can be set up similarly to the organizational scheme in the previous section, starting with sight-reading repertoire, but now potentially including short modern band charts for two- to four-bar sections, often highlighting one instrument. For example, the song "Low Rider" might be on the board with the groovy bass line, guitarists can work on a new strumming pattern with the single-chord song, keyboards can play the horn melody, and the drummers can work on Latin grooves or incorporate the auxiliary percussion.

Unlike the single-instrument focus, in this approach there is a lot more opportunity to have long sessions of playing without stopping while students jump from instrument to instrument. For instance, if you have multiple drum sets, one student can switch out with another while the rest of the drummers keep the groove; the same goes for all the other instruments. With practice students can make a full rotation and get through all the instruments, learning all the parts to a song. As students become more skilled, they can start expanding on some of their favorite songs and work on arranging them, adding in sections where some instruments are tacit, including an instrumental break, or even creating mash-ups.

The balanced approach to modern band really shines as students become more advanced, since then they can take all their musical skills and knowledge not only to craft great arrangements, but also to choose their own repertoire, find and/or create their own charts, and figure out how to put on the best show. This was the approach I took with the inaugural All National Honors Ensemble (ANHE) for modern band. The ensemble featured four vocalists, four guitarists, four keyboards, three drummers, and three bassists. Many of the students doubled on other instruments, such as flute, sax, or trumpet, which they took into account in the arrangements. Before we all finally met up for three days of in-person rehearsals and a concert, the students made repertoire suggestions via a simple online form and then voted on songs, which I then, as the facilitator, used to create a balanced set list that showed their diverse skills. We also had some of the students submit their own songs, and the group voted for which ones to include.

Once the rehearsals began, my assistant director and I largely let the students run rehearsals, mainly directing their time and giving suggestions after run-throughs. The first day was dedicated mostly to trying to play through the songs they had already worked on independently. By the end of the day, they had talked as a group through suggestions for changing the form and instrumentation, who would take solos and when, and which songs they would try to recreate note-for-note versus ones they would remake for themselves. They also spent a lot of time working with the original composition, taking the original and, with the songwriter's blessing, finding ways to help expand the writer's vision.

The second day started off as review and implementation of the previous day's ideas and eventually turned to one of the most neglected parts of music education ensembles: showmanship. We rehearsed choreography, discussed outfits, and practiced letting loose, often a big challenge when there is no audience. However, in my experience, if students do not work on this in rehearsal, they will not be able to just turn the stage presence on when they are in front of an audience. By the third day we were able to fine-tune the performance and put on an amazing show.

The students in this ensemble were clearly very advanced and motivated, but the general outline should be applicable to all classes. Students can collectively pick the songs. Motivated individuals can help craft the arrangement, vie for solos, or write songs for the group. The musicians should be allowed to use their ears and their critical thinking skills to discuss and make changes during rehearsals (I highly recommend filming rehearsals and reviewing them together). And, most important, make sure they work on stage presence. Stage presence rehearsals are some of my fondest memories as an instructor, and they should also be a fun and democratic process. Some ways to make this inspired and fun are keeping a prop closet so students can get extra silly, or having them all lip-sync to performances of the songs, unplugged, to give it their all. Have half the class perform while the other watches, and then they can give constructive feedback to the group.

The timeline for the ANHE ensemble was very short, but rehearsing songs in the music classroom can take place over the course of weeks or an entire semester. It helps to set goals early on, but do not be afraid to change it up—for instance, if a song they picked in September does not seem that fresh or interesting come December. Flexibility is key.

48.4 Smaller Individual Bands

This final class approach is one I ran during some of my last years of teaching, which I subsequently wrote about in my dissertation (Burstein, 2016). After teaching "guitar" class for years, I had a lot of very advanced students who wanted an opportunity to really work on being in a band. Our school had run a successful Battle of the Bands for multiple years, and it was a natural extension to give these garage bands a place to play in an educational setting year round. While most of the students in the class were intermediate or advanced players, there were a few beginners mixed in who found great ways to work with the others. I also had a few students that took the class to learn to be managers—working on the business end of groups, setting up gigs, and promoting the bands.

The class was set up into five-week sections, and each section had the same basic layout. The forty students would break into eight bands, and each band would perform at lunch on the student quad at the end of the section. The final section had a concert at the Hollywood rock club Whisky a Go Go. At the conclusion of each five-week section, students had to change bands, and they could not pair up with the same group. I also structured each section so it had a genre theme, and while I set them up (classic rock, alternative, "new" music, and finally a genre of their choice), I would recommend letting the students choose the themes for the sections.

Once the sections were set, the pace of each section was similar. The first week they would work on just choosing their songs as a band, which included finding the music and rehearsing it. This time was largely spent with their bands; I only worked to help point them in the direction of some recommendations for music or how to learn their parts, with some individual instruction. The second and third weeks were typically spent in rehearsals, with groups getting specific time slots for working with me directly as a producer; the rest of the time they would work in practice rooms. During the fourth week they would perform for each other, with each group giving critique and recommendations. The final week leading up to the show was largely about stage presence and pacing for getting on and off the stage quickly, so that the show had smooth transitions.

Lots of nonplaying aspects were covered in this class, and it greatly benefited their outside-of-class skills. From the first day of class (after introductions and syllabi), I told the students that they would need to set up and tear down all the gear each day, since this was also my concert band classroom. That first day it took them the rest of the period to set up, and the second day it took them almost half of the period to set up, at which point I told them they would have to try again and make it much faster. They got the hint, and no longer did the guitarist plug in and make noise, but learned to help the drummer. Vocalists learned about placement of not just the mic, but also the bass and keyboards. Everyone worked in tandem, so they all learned how to set up and take down every instrument, how to sound-check it, and how to work well together. They also learned a lot of valuable skills in terms of how to rehearse as a band: listening to each other, not playing while someone was talking, and how to work on small sections of a piece that needed it rather than just playing through songs over and over again. Forcing students to change bands every five weeks also ensured that they learned about band (and social) dynamics. They had to compromise with each other and identify songs that may not have been their top choice but that fit the skill set of the musicians. They learned how to bring out the personality of each performer to put on the best show.

I found that the students grew by leaps and bounds throughout this course, learning not only how to be amazing independent musicians, but also to support each other and create a community, and to use that to find success where they did not think they could. Some of the more traditional students from concert or jazz band were initially flummoxed when presented with this do-it-yourself attitude of choosing songs and finding music, whereas some of the students whose only musical experience was at home jamming really shone. Many of the students reported that for the first time they were seen as leaders.

There are some challenges with this approach to instruction, to be sure. First, the teacher needs to be comfortable mostly being hands-off, largely acting as facilitator. A lot of the time the class will look chaotic, and it is important to direct the flow while letting this creative process grow. Instruments and space can be a major impediment, I was lucky enough to have a few practice rooms, but often students would literally practice acoustically with drumsticks on the floor right outside the classroom door. Probably the most important considerations are to make sure that respect is present at all times for everyone: everyone must be included, and all feedback should be positive and constructive. There is no room for dissing other bands, and the class needs to always think of itself as a collective.

48.5 Final Considerations

No matter which approach to modern band you take, the core concept for success should be present throughout: student-centered. That means there should be a focus on song choices that they know and love, with classes largely facilitated rather than taught, where musical and rehearsal choices are dictated by their needs, and songs are approximated for their level and scaffolded so they can choose how they interact with the musical whole. It also means a supportive environment where students' own musical tastes are encouraged, and that starts with the instructor. It is not enough to let students just share what they love about songs, but language such as "good" and "bad" songs must be eliminated, since music is a personal choice. There is no right and wrong when it comes to music preference, and any arguments about one music's being better than another are elitist and will just lead to the students shutting down. Similarly, if the students feel like the instructor does not value their musical choices, it opens the door to other students' also making fun of their choices and will ruin the ever-important safe environment necessary for a modern band.

Learning how to balance student needs in this way and to trust the students to lead the process will take time and will constantly evolve, but it is essential so that the modern band does not become just another teacher-led educational model that is far removed from how popular music actually exists in the real world. Good luck on your journey!

48.6 Discussion Questions

1. In what ways are the approaches to facilitating single-instrument, small-group, and large-group modern bands similar? How are they different?
2. How are the described music classes similar to and different from your experiences as a student in a musical ensemble?
3. What are some of the most important pedagogical approaches to remember when facilitating a modern band?

OXFORD learning link

Visit the online resources for additional documentation and exercises to help expand learning and test your knowledge further: www.oup.com/he/powell_music1e.

CONCERT BAND REHEARSAL TECHNIQUES

Quincy C. Hilliard

This chapter focuses on the key elements for developing a strong concert ensemble: tone, intonation, balance, and technique.

49.1 Introduction

Rehearsal techniques for the middle and high school bands should center on the teaching of fundamentals: tone quality, intonation, balance, and technique. The elements must also be taught in this order. At the beginning of the school year, these elements should be the primary focus. See Table 49.1.

TABLE 49.1 SUGGESTIONS FOR TIME SPENT ON TEACHING FUNDAMENTALS VERSUS MUSIC

	Aug.	Sept.	Oct.	Nov.	Dec.	Jan.	Feb.	Mar.	Apr.	May
Fundamentals	90%	80%	80%	50%	30%	40%	30%	20%	20%	20%
Music*	10%	20%	20%	50%	70%	60%	70%	80%	80%	80%

*I suggest that the music chosen for August, September, and October center on pieces that allow students to work on tone, intonation, balance, and blend.

In looking at the chart, you will notice that in November–December and February–May there is more of a focus on the teaching of music; this is to allow you to concentrate on concert performances or assessments. Although this is a month-by-month chart, the percentages should also serve as the day-to-day rehearsal focus. Note: I suggest keeping technical demands to a minimum when teaching tone. If an ensemble starts to struggle with technique, tone and intonation will suffer. Therefore, focusing on fundamentals at the beginning of the year will help set students up for success; then, starting in late October and early November, the director can start focusing on music for the winter concert.

Directors must understand that they are dealing with young musicians and that these musicians must continually develop their fundamentals and techniques. Until all the students are able to practice these fundamentals on their own, these fundamentals should be worked on in class every day.

Just as athletes get in shape by focusing on drills that include weightlifting, muscle-building exercises, and calisthenics, musicians perform calisthenics and drills that get them in shape, focusing on producing good tone, intonation, and technique. Sometimes it is difficult to get the students to accept these drills. The director must reinforce the concept that if they do not play with good fundamentals as a group, the performance of the music will be poor. If an athlete is out of shape, their performance during competition will also be poor. Establishing a good daily routine of drills will ensure that the ensemble develops the proper techniques to be successful. This daily routine must center on development of tone quality, intonation, balance and blend, and technique drills.

49.2 Tone Quality

Tone quality is defined as getting the most beautiful characteristic tone from your instruments. Tone quality is the *first* and the *most important element* in becoming a successful musician and/or ensemble. Tone quality consists of three elements: correct posture, good breathing habits, and embouchure development. Since these three elements should have been covered in the first year of playing, we are now going to reinforce them in an ensemble environment. Correct posture (PPP—proper playing position) should be the first element that the director teaches (Hilliard, 2003). PPP refers to sitting tall (no wrinkled stomach) on the edge of the chair, both feet flat on the floor, and holding still. This is of the utmost importance in developing a good tone. It should be noted that the students only need to be in this position when they are actually playing. When the director is talking or making announcements, they can be a bit more relaxed in their seated position.

BREATHING EXERCISES

Next, the director should focus on exercises and drills to develop a good tone. The following drills are examples that can be used in an ensemble setting.

Breathing Exercises Without the Instrument

This is an excellent way to begin a rehearsal. Have the ensemble come to the proper playing position, then slowly inhale deeply (using the diaphragm and expanding the abdomen, not the lungs) for four counts, hold still for four counts, and then exhale for four counts. If done correctly, the exhaled air will be warm, not cold. Have the ensemble repeat this exercise several times. The following chart shows variations of this exercise.

	Inhale	*Hold*	*Exhale*
Young players	2 counts	4 counts	8 counts
Young/advanced players	1 count	4 counts	12 counts
Advanced players	1 count	4 counts	16 counts

Breathing Exercises with the Mouthpiece

Repeat the previous drill with the ensemble using the mouthpiece only. The following drills can be done without the hold and on the mouthpiece only. During this drill, the director can check for correct mouthpiece placement and for the correct embouchure.

	Inhale	*Play*
Young players	4 counts	4 counts
Young players	2 counts	8 counts
Advanced players	1 count	12 counts
Advanced players	1 count	16 counts

Long-Tone and Scale Exercises

Long tones can be practiced through the use of scales and scale patterns. Once the students have learned their scales, it is important that the following drills be completely done from memory, only looking at the pattern as it is written. This will help the students conceptualize the scales from memory and eventually lead them to play their scales from muscle memory. The methods in Figures 49.1, 49.2, and 49.3 will also reinforce good breathing habits. Note that the number patterns refer to scale degrees.

FIGURE 49.1 Very young ensemble

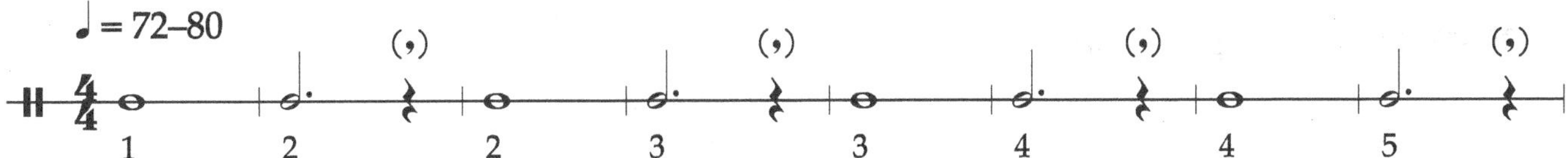

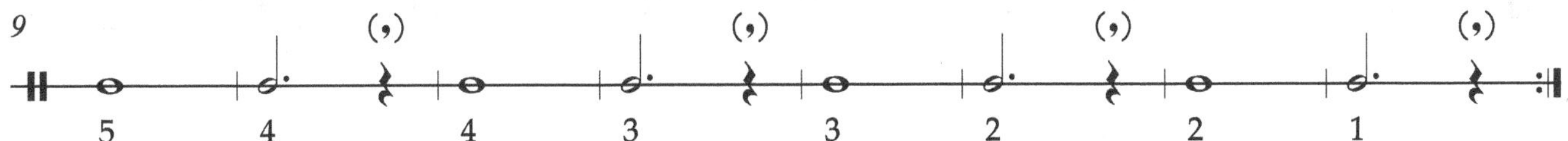

FIGURE 49.2 Young ensemble

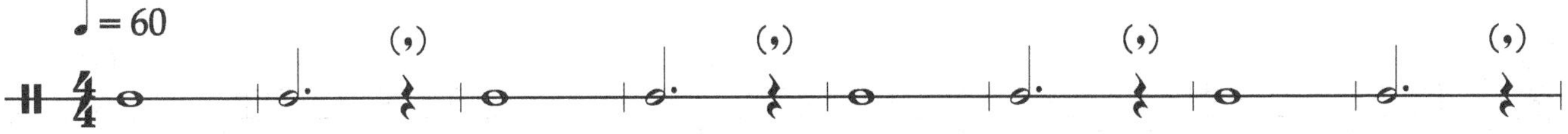

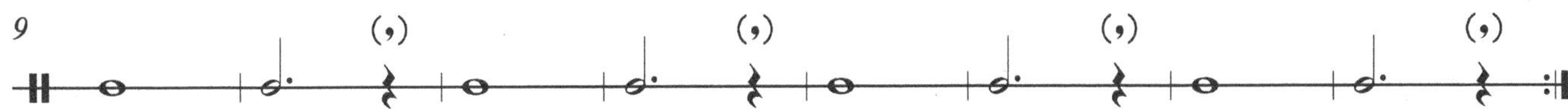

FIGURE 49.3 Advanced ensemble

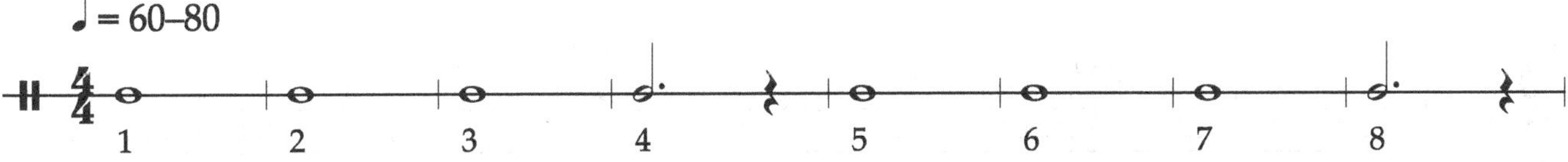

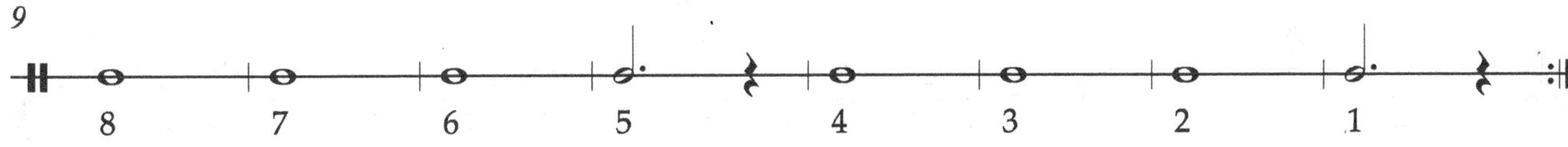

THE F WARM-UP AND THE B♭ WARM-UP

The F warm-up and the B♭ warm-up are often used as long-tone exercises. These exercises are usually done in unison. The director can write out or find these exercises in method books or workshop handouts. The exercises in Figures 49.4, 49.5, and 49.6 are written at concert pitch. It should be noted that the same drills can be done using any scale.

FIGURE 49.4 Very young ensemble

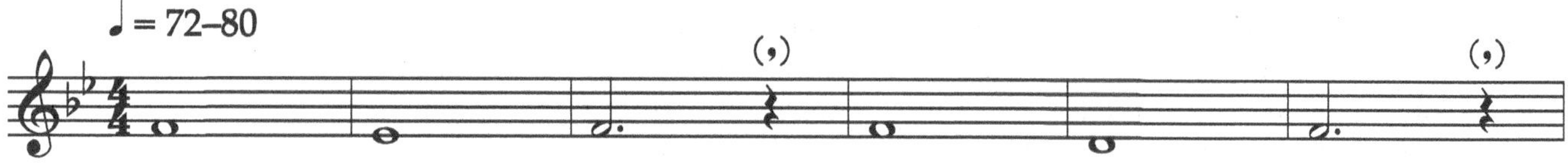

FIGURE 49.5 Young ensemble

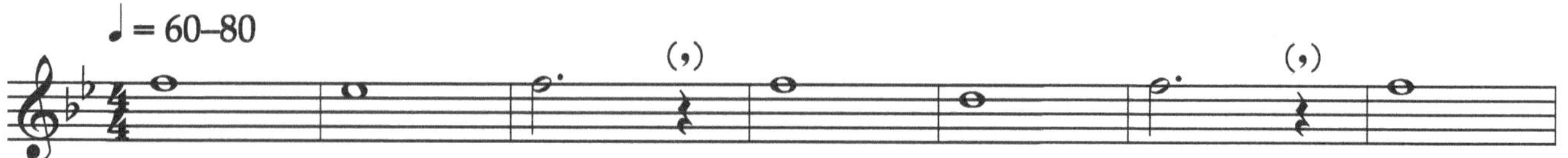

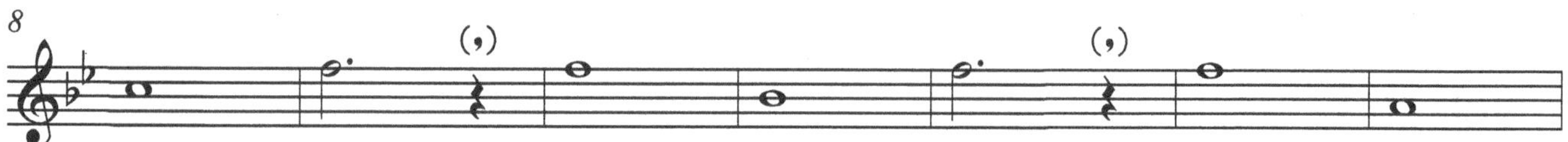

FIGURE 49.6 Advanced ensemble

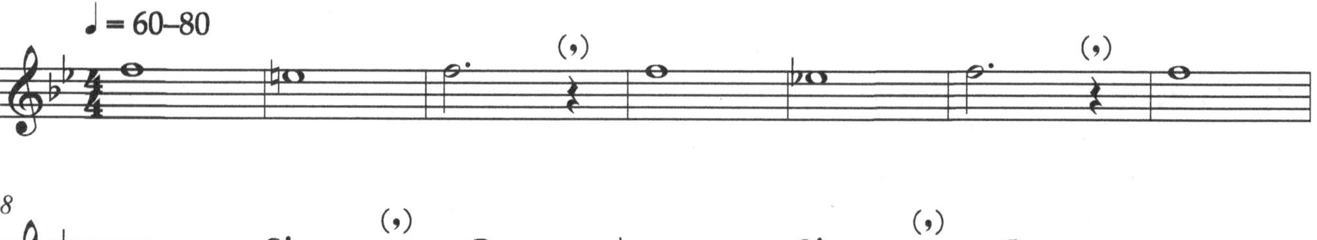

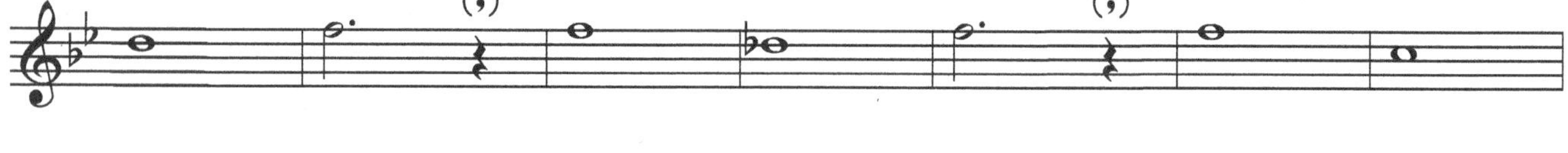

LIP FLEXIBILITY EXERCISES

Lip flexibility exercises are imperative for developing a good tone on brass instruments. Lip slurs, as they are commonly called, must be done every day. These exercises build strong brass embouchures, which will in turn lead to a beautiful brass tone. Another technique is to do these exercises on the mouthpiece by itself, to gauge center of pitch and placement. There are several published exercises and method books with lip flexibility drills. I have published two such resources: one for young players, *Fundamental for Ensemble Drills*, and another for advanced players, *Superior Bands in Sixteen Weeks.*

49.3 Intonation

You cannot tune a bad tone! Until the students are getting a characteristic tone on their instruments, it would be a waste of time to work on tuning the ensemble. I am convinced that 80 percent of the intonation problems that occur in an ensemble are related to tone quality—posture problems, breathing problems, bad embouchure, and/or lack of embouchure development. The remaining 20 percent can be attributed to the instrument makeup and problem notes with intonation on every instrument. In some cases, to help intonation, it would be a good idea to have all the clarinet and saxophone players play on the same brand of mouthpiece and use the same ligature. A bad mouthpiece can make an expensive instrument sound bad, but a good mouthpiece can make a mediocre instrument sound good.

Once the students have a good tone, intonation problems will be minimal. Intonation is an individual problem. Each student should strive to solve all the major pitch problems on their instrument. One way to achieve this is to have each student take an intonation test on their instrument. The only book that has an intonation test is *Superior Bands in Sixteen Weeks* (Hilliard, 2003). The book outlines how to complete the test and gives suggestions for solving pitch problems on each instrument. Some notes on an instrument have inherent intonation problems, as seen in *Superior Bands in Sixteen Weeks* (Hilliard, 2003). Today most students have a cell phone. There is no excuse for them not having a tuner app on the phone that can be used to correct individual pitch problems. In addition, some of the pitch problems can be correct through alternate fingering(s).

A good way to start building ensemble intonation awareness is to have the students listen and match pitches and make sure there is no oscillation (dissonance) between the pitches. The director should first model in tune and then out of tune for the students showing them if a pitch is flat or sharp. This can start with the first note of the B♭ scale. First, listen and match pitches within the section (like instruments). After the students are doing well with this exercise, the director can expand the drill to cross sections (unlike instruments). This exercise should continue until all of the notes of the concert B♭ scale have been covered and corrected on all of the instruments in the ensemble.

It would be a good idea to spend about a week on each pitch of the B♭ scale matching, listening, and making adjustments.

49.4 Balance and Blend (Phrasing through Breathing)

Balance is the ensemble ability to play without students or sections overpowering each other. Blend is the ability of the various members of the ensemble to work in harmony with each other. If tone and intonation are problems, then there will be problems with balance and blend. The balance pyramid (Figure 49.7) can aid both director and students in understanding their role in establishing a good ensemble balance.

FIGURE 49.7 The balance pyramid. Taken from W. Francis McBeth, *Effective Performance of Band Music*, published by Southern Music

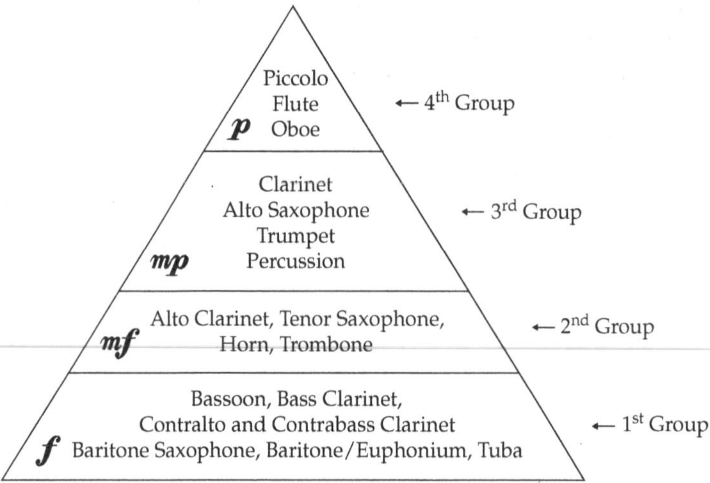

Here are three rules of balance that students should know and memorize:

1. *Listen to yourself.* Your sound should not overpower the ensemble. If it does, make adjustments to play softer.
2. *Listen to your section.* The section should not overpower the ensemble. If it does, the section should make adjustments to play softer.
3. If blend and balance are still a problem, the section or individual might be playing with poor tone quality and/or have intonation concerns. The section or individual should make adjustments with air flow, posture, embouchure, reed, tuning slide, barrel, or mouthpiece (Hilliard, 2003).

Using the balance pyramid, the director should follow these four points:

1. Start by using a tuning note (concert B♭ or concert F).
2. Later on, other notes can be used with the pyramid.
3. Always start by using the first group of the pyramid, followed by the second group, then the third, and finally the fourth. The director should teach the students to listen and play to blend rather than play louder within your group or louder than the previous group.
4. Use compare and contrast techniques to reinforce the sound of good balance. Allow the group to experiment with incorrect balance and instruct the ensemble to listen. Now play with the correct pyramid balance to hear the difference (Hilliard, 2003).

A good way to teach good balance and blend is through the use of chorales and/or ballads. In doing so, the director is able to teach not only balance and blend, but also phrasing, through good breathing habits. In teaching a chorale or ballad, the student should follow these steps with regard to correct breathing:

1. Never breathe at a bar line.
2. Never breathe at the end of a slur unless it is followed by rest.

The concept I am trying to teach the students, and the ensemble, is to take a breath after four measures. Young groups can start with two measures. This idea helps the student to develop the habit of long breathing, thus producing a good tone and better intonation. I often tell students if they must breathe, take a quick breath while sustaining a note to avoid breathing at a bar line or at the end of a slur. Chorales and ballads are also excellent exercises for teaching long tones and developing good tone quality and balance.

Here are few suggestions for chorales for different age groups:

Elementary ensemble:
    Quincy C. Hilliard, *Eight Chorales for Elementary Band* (FJH Music Publishers), 2004

Young ensemble (these chorales grow with your ensemble):
    Quincy C. Hilliard, *Ten Chorales for Beginning and Intermediate Band* (Kjos Music Publishers), 1993

Advanced ensemble:
    Quincy C. Hilliard, *Twelve Chorales for Developing Band* (FJH Music Publishers), 2001
    Quincy C. Hilliard, *Chorales and Rhythm Etudes for Superior Band* (FJH Music Publishers), 2004

There are also many chorale books and exercises on the market to aid in the teaching of balance. Directors should explore as many as possible until they find one that they enjoy using.

49.5 Technique

Technique is listed fourth because having good technical skills without good tone is worthless. Technique is a forever-growing process for the individual musician as well as the ensemble. The more technique each individual musician possesses, the more difficult literature the ensemble will be able to play. The only difference between a middle school ensemble and an advanced high school ensemble (both with good tone and intonation) is the technical expertise of the advanced ensemble as opposed to the limited technical expertise of the middle school ensemble.

49.6 Rhythm

Teaching students to count has always been a challenge for the director. I suggest that directors choose a counting system that they are comfortable with and stay with that system so as not to confuse the students. Also, the system should have a clear and concise method for teaching the subdivision of the beat. It has been my experience that students can count note values, but what they have a problem with is counting patterns that have rests and notes. Students should be taught that rests are *counts of silence*. In other words, you must continually count all the time, even during rests, when performing. When working with younger ensembles, it is a good idea to start teaching rhythm on a small scale. Having the students learn a rhythm a day is a good start. The director writes a rhythmic pattern on the board. This can also be reinforced by having the students copy the rhythms down and keep them in a journal or notebook. For instance, let's examine how to teach the rhythm pattern in Figure 49.8.

1. The director writes the pattern on the board.
2. The students copy the pattern in their notebook or journal.
3. The director discusses the counting of the rhythm, with student input.

FIGURE 49.8 **Rhythm teaching example**

4. Have the students write in the counting pattern on the board.
5. Have the students clap the rhythm.
6. Have the students sing the rhythm.
7. The director can select students to clap or sing the pattern individually.
8. Call on sections to clap, sing, or play the pattern.
9. Have the ensemble clap and sing the pattern.
10. Finally, have the ensemble play the pattern.

These rhythm patterns can start with two, four, six, and finally eight measures for young students. As this exercise progresses, the director can have the students create their own patterns. These patterns can be written on the board and taken through the same process. This concept can also be used to teach rhythm in selections that you are going to perform before you give the music to the students. This idea works well not only with young ensembles but with advanced groups as well. Once the ensemble has a chance to outgrow the rhythm-a-day drill, it would be a good idea to explore some rhythm books for the group.

These books are excellent books for teaching rhythm:

Young ensemble:
 Timothy Loest, *Rhythms and Beyond* (FJH Music Publishers, 2004)

Young and advanced ensemble:
 Quincy C. Hilliard, *Counts of Silence*, (Wingert-Jones Publications, 2023)

Advanced ensemble:
 Quincy C. Hilliard, *Chorales and Rhythm Etudes for Superior Bands* (FJH Music Publishers, 2004)

At the time of writing of this book, there is an online sight-reading program called the Sight-Reading Factory. The rhythms range from easy to advanced. I am sure that there will be other online sight-reading programs in the future. The director can seek out other websites and books to use with their ensemble.

Scales are an excellent way to teach students technique and range. Eventually, advanced students should learn all twelve major and minor scales and the chromatic scale. These scales must be learned to audition for honor groups and college admission to music schools.

In playing a single scale, it is important to establish a breathing pattern. For example, one breath up and one breath down the scale for young ensembles, depending on the pattern. As the ensemble becomes more advanced, each scale should be played up and down in one breath. Advanced players should strive to play each scale up and down two to four times in one breath, depending upon the rhythmic pattern and tempo. This idea will reinforce good breathing habits.

One of the most effective ways to use scales to teach technique is to play scales in thirds. This will advance the students' and ensemble's technical skills tremendously. Also, playing scales in thirds will aid in the precision of the ensemble. In addition, playing arpeggios will increase range and technique. This concept is more of an advanced technique for an advanced ensemble.

Here are some technique books for these exercises:

Quincy C. Hilliard, *Superior Bands in Sixteen Weeks* (FJH Music Publishers, 2003) (scales in thirds and arpeggios)
Quincy C. Hilliard, *Scales and Tuning Exercises for Superior Bands* (FJH Music Publishers, 2009)

Since scales must be learned by wind instruments, the percussion students should be introduced to rudiments. Rudiments are the equivalent of scales for percussion. The director can select a different rudiment to play with each scale until all the primary rudiments are learned. Technique is an ongoing pursuit for the individual player as well as for the ensemble. It should be noted that the more advanced techniques that the individual player can command, the more advanced music the ensemble will be able to perform.

49.7 Other Rehearsal Concepts

Stylistic concepts should also be taught. This will aid the student and ensemble to effectively perform music in the correct style. The young ensemble should begin with two styles of playing—legato and marcato. Legato is a smooth and connected style that will require the student to emphasize a long tonguing attack, such as "tOO" or "dOO." This will provide more of a connected approach to the playing, with very little separation between the notes and can first be taught during the warm-ups using scales and long tones. Next, the use of chorales and ballads can be used to reinforce this concept. The marcato style is more a lift, bounce, and separate style found in the playing of a march. Ernest Cantu, a director from Brownsville, Texas, describes this style as a "march" style. In a lecture to my class, he stated:

> *"The march style is a lift-and-bounce style. The idea of lift deals with a tone longer than an eighth note. A quarter note would release on the 'up' part of the beat. A half note would release on the 'up' part of the second beat. The idea of bounce deals with the length of the eighth note. The length of the eighth note in a march style is comparable to what you hear when bouncing a ball. You can also compare eighth notes to short bursts of air from a spray can. This will also help with support of march-style eighth notes."*

The march style can be introduced using the scales as the subject matter. After using the scale, the director can choose a march composition for students to reinforce this concept.

For the advanced ensemble, the concept of style will vary according to the piece chosen for performance. The ensemble should be introduced to many styles, for example—Baroque, Classical, Romantic, twentieth and twenty-first century, English-style marches, chamber music, transcriptions, and so on. Many of these styles can be taught with the aid of recordings where available.

Directors can listen to many interpretations of the same compositions and choose one they like or take a combination of all and come up with their own interpretations.

49.8 Discussion Questions

1. List other breathing exercises that can be done without the mouthpiece. List other long-tone exercises. Discuss how lip flexibility drills can be done on the mouthpiece only.
2. List other methods that can be used to encourage students to listen for intonation problems. Discuss the importance of intonation in a performance. List some ideas that students can use to correct their own intonation problems.
3. Discuss why the pyramid concepts are so important in developing a good ensemble sound, including the importance of the pyramid concept as it relates to sectional balance and examples of bad balance within an ensemble.
4. Discuss other technique books that can aid in developing good technique. Should minor scales be taught to the advanced ensemble? Discuss different approaches to teach the chromatic scales.

OXFORD learning link

Visit the online resources for additional documentation and exercises to help expand learning and test your knowledge further: www.oup.com/he/powell_music1e.

CHAPTER 50

JAZZ BAND REHEARSAL TECHNIQUES

Lonnie Easter II

This chapter examines effective teaching strategies for jazz ensembles.

50.1 Introduction

The primary objective of this chapter is to provide preservice music educators (particularly those with limited jazz experience) with practical instructional strategies that will assist them in directing a jazz ensemble while promoting cognitive, psychomotor, and affective domain development in their future jazz students. These techniques are grounded in twenty-first-century practices and are intended to provide clear and concise references to strategies for increasing rehearsal effectiveness and overall student learning, especially in jazz improvisation. These ideas have been added to my band-director toolkit over many years of trial and error teaching jazz as well as listening to and studying great jazz instructors. Additionally, while the concepts presented are transferable to any level, the emphasis will be on beginning and intermediate ensembles.

> As you read this chapter, please consider that we live in an unprecedented information era and have access to an infinite number of resources for inspiration, reference, and teaching jazz at our fingertips (Weist, 2019). There is a wealth of materials available (e.g., recordings, videos, innumerable jazz books, and a plethora of online websites that offer both synchronous and asynchronous jazz pedagogical material) that music educators may utilize to enhance their pedagogical content knowledge in jazz. In addition to utilizing this chapter, I strongly encourage you to take advantage of these resources.

50.2 Establishing, Maintaining, and Achieving Educational Objectives during the Jazz Rehearsal

Our primary objectives as music educators should be to motivate students to reflect critically on their classroom performance, to relate classroom activities to prior, current, and future experiences, and to facilitate success. These notions include and are equally applicable to jazz instruction. As with any other ensemble rehearsal, it is our responsibility as jazz educators to provide direction that results musically in the most cohesive and consistent ensemble sound, guides transitions, specifies our expectations as conductors, and accurately interprets the composer's or arranger's intentions (Stevenson, 2019). Given that improvisation is the foundation of jazz and presents significant cognitive, perceptual, and motor sequencing challenges, we should also devote adequate time to training our students in this art.

Jazz educators should prioritize opportunities for students to develop the following skills when teaching jazz: (a) cognitive—related to knowledge (e.g., reading chord changes, jazz nomenclature and figures, rhythms, articulations, etc.); (b) psychomotor—related to motor skills (i.e., the physical execution of the cognitive information on an individual instrument); and (c) affective—related to feelings, emotions, and attitudes (i.e., processing motivation, anxiety, and other factors while learning to interact with other musicians spontaneously creating music) (Mantz, 2011). Students will need these abilities to negotiate the higher-order cognitive processes inherent in jazz music. When students grasp guiding principles and concepts, they may develop the ability to think by themselves and resolve problems without your aid. This streamlines the learning process and prepares the student to work independently as a musician (Schmidt, 2019b).

IMPROVING THE EFFICIENCY OF JAZZ ENSEMBLE REHEARSALS

It is widely accepted that success is difficult to achieve without both long- and short-term planning, especially in music education. I am sure you have encountered the 7 Ps at some time throughout your musical career, particularly when dealing with ensemble directors. If not, I am happy to be the first to introduce you to them: "Proper Planning and Preparation Prevents Painfully [I learned it as 'Piss'] Poor Performance" (Cousins, 2018). Preparation is critical for increasing the effectiveness of your rehearsals. Determine in advance your objectives for each selection you choose to perform, keeping in mind both musical and, more significantly, educational objectives, always aiming at the improvement of higher-level cognitive functioning. Again, be sure that your developmental objectives result from both short- and long-term educational planning.

There are minimal differences between how jazz ensemble directors should prepare for rehearsals and how traditional symphonic band directors should do so. The more time we allow to study the score, listen to recordings, and analyze what is happening, the more efficient the rehearsal will be. Create a rehearsal schedule, determining which components of the tunes to focus on and how much time to dedicate to each. Always ask yourself, "What skills or concepts do the students need to know in order to execute the piece effectively?" These skills and concepts (meter/rhythm, articulations, stylistic considerations, dynamics, phrasings, solo section chord changes, and historical context, among others) should be incorporated into your preparation.

You should consider what content will be new, reviewed, and transferable between the selections you are working on. Subsequently, develop adequate assessments to ensure that your students comprehend the material. Far too frequently while studying jazz, students struggle to connect what they read on the page, what they hear, and what they play. We can assign a student a solo transcription to study. They may be able to nail it technically with their playing technique; however, if the student does not comprehend what is being played and why, we have missed a significant portion of the educational objective.

The most critical part of organizing your rehearsal time is to adapt to the needs of the students. The amount of time to devote to warm-ups, developmental activities (e.g., tone production or improvisation skill development), rehearsing charts, and promoting other essential abilities is entirely dependent on the general performance level of your students, the frequency of ensemble rehearsals, and the group's performance schedule (Schmidt, 2019b). Warm-up exercises that are clear and concise and that help students to focus on the conceptual and stylistic challenges inherent in jazz are recommended. When leading students through warm-up exercises or chart rehearsals, instructors should emphasize all six aspects of the jazz language: rhythm, articulation, dynamics, balance, phrasing, and improvisation.

50.3 Suggestions for Tightening the Ensemble Sound and Technique

Understanding the links between time, style, phrasing, and balance will contribute significantly to your student's growth and development. To begin, correct the notes. I have discovered that if I implement a sixty-second noodle approach, I can save a significant amount of rehearsal time; it gives the band one or two minutes to noodle the difficult passage in their part and resolve whatever note difficulties they are having with the figure being played. I also frequently employ the holding-notes technique—having those who play the questionable notes sustain them one at a time. Issues will become visible quickly and may be rectified.

Ensure that you have taken the time to unify accents (particularly essential in soli sections), dynamic nuances, cut-offs, and other articulations in the distinct sections of the chart. Ascertain that the section has denoted these items in their proper locations in pencil. Analyze horn section parts for similarities in rhythm or harmony. When aligning figures that must be coordinated within and across sections, it might be beneficial to inform the impacted players of how things fit. If necessary, I suggest utilizing the one-on-one approach to connect each section member to the lead—lead player with the second, lead player with the third, lead player with the fourth, and so on. Additionally, ensure that breathing locations are unified: mark in breathing places to ensure consistency in phrasing.

50.4 Suggestions for Drums, Bass, and Piano

DRUMS

The drummer shoulders a great deal of responsibility. When that responsibility is simplified to its most fundamental purposes, two primary functions emerge: maintaining time (i.e., playing the groove and ensuring that the ensemble swings) and delineating the form (e.g., cymbal crashes and fills that signal the beginning of phrases or choruses). I spend considerable time helping drummers and the ensemble comprehend that the set player defines the group's dynamic, degree of intensity, and style. When speaking with most experienced jazz drummers, particularly when discussing jazz set pedagogy, you will discover that most will tell you the quickest way for a student to improve is to listen. Listening to recordings of professional jazz ensembles in various styles will assist your drummer (and your band) in progressing. As the director, you must direct your students' listening. Listening only once or twice will have little effect on their performance. Provide stylistic examples and instruct the students on what they should be listening for. These considerations should be made in both your long- and short-term planning.

If you have minimal familiarity with jazz percussion pedagogy, my recommendation is to refrain from directing your students to stress the high hat on 2 and 4 or the ride cymbal in this manner unless the song has a strong 2 feel with heavy downbeats on 1 and 3. Exaggerating the offbeats will shift the balance in the opposite direction and impede the swing. Again, I recommend that your students utilize the wide range of resources available (books, lessons, online asynchronous materials, YouTube, etc.). John Riley is the author of two jazz drumming books well endorsed by professional drummers, *The Art of Bop Drumming* (Riley, 1994) and *Beyond Bop Drumming* (Riley, 1997). Additionally, from a pedagogical standpoint, a book I recommend to assist music educators with limited drum set expertise (and the rhythm section in general) is Fumi Tomita's (2019) *The Jazz Rhythm Section*.

BASS

The bass is essentially the timekeeper, as the bass part is typically composed of steady quarter notes, eighth notes, or other repeated patterns (Crotts, 2019). That steady pattern (in the form of a walking bass line) generally provides a precise reference point for listening for pace. The bassist and drummer of your ensemble should be in sync with each other, giving the band its groove or swing. The majority of the middle and high school jazz ensembles (beginning to advanced) charts have been written with an educational focus in mind. The bass line has been fully realized, whether it be a walking bass line or some other style. Specific older charts may only contain chord changes; it is up to you as the director to either write out the bass line or teach your bassist to interpret changes and walk a bass line. While there are multiple ways to interpret walking bass lines, I added a basic formula to my toolkit years ago, and it generally works very well when training inexperienced bassists:

1. Beat 1: Determine the tonality of the chord (major, minor, dominant, half-diminished, diminished) and play the root.
2. Beat 2: Play any other chord tone. While playing the third or the seventh chord tone is recommended, as these are the most important ones aside from the root, you may undoubtedly add randomization by playing the fifth. Keep in mind the chord's tonality and make appropriate adjustments to these notes (e.g., in a dominant chord, the seventh is lowered a by half step).
3. Beat 3: Repeat step 2 with a different chord tone than is played on beat 2.
4. Beat 4: Play a leading tone to the next chord. In most cases, this works, playing a half step above or below the root of the next chord. They can also be diatonic steps or the fifth (dominant) of the next chord.

While this formula works in most circumstances and is meant to provide a legitimate starting point for directors with limited bass experience, it will quickly become repetitive. As indicated previously in the drum section, I advise you to encourage your students to utilize the numerous resources available for learning walking bass lines, and that you avail yourself of them as well.

PIANO

Jazz ensemble piano parts can be notated in various ways, ranging from completely notated music to parts with chord symbols and slashes. The latter format is typically the most difficult for a beginning jazz pianist and instructors with minimal experience to understand. While you are likely proficient at navigating the piano and identifying the notes in the given chord (via your theory courses), jazz voicings were most likely not emphasized throughout your piano instruction. Remember that your ability to model what you teach is your most valuable asset. It is worthwhile to establish oneself as a suitable example (Schmidt, 2019a).

As a beginning point, I recommend the two-hand, four-note, drop-2 voicings for developing jazz pianists. Drop-2 voicings are created by constructing a seventh chord voicing in a closed position and dropping the second note from the top an octave. For example, if you have an F major seventh chord (typically notated FMaj7, FM7, or FΔ), which consists of the first, third, fifth, and seventh notes of the F major scale (F, A, C, and E), in a drop-2 voicing the chord would be respelled C, F, A, E, with C and F being played in the left hand and the A and E in the right.

Once your pianist has comprehended this concept, change the voicing to first inversion and substitute the ninth for the root (in this case, G for F). After mastering accurate spelling and voicing of chords, the next critical skill your pianist (as well as your guitarist) needs to master is comping. This moves the piano away from the root and out of the way of your bass player, which is a skill they will need as they advance.

50.5 Teaching Improvisation Skills during the Ensemble Rehearsal

Often developing jazz ensemble instructors within the confines of a rehearsal can overlook or completely disregard the most critical element of our jobs: to ensure that our students are learning the art of jazz. This is not to suggest that concepts are not learned when preparing music for a concert or performance; nevertheless, the very essence of jazz is again improvisational. This spontaneous creation of music is at the top of Bloom's Taxonomy, Webb's Depth of Knowledge (DOK), and any other theoretical or conceptual framework your educational department requires you to study. Jazz educators should be intentional in their planning processes to design student learning objectives, activities, and assessments that align with these principles and enhance students' capacity to improvise.

As a jazz director, you will always have a small handful of students who excel at improvisation and are eager for additional knowledge. Regardless of how much you encourage or incentivize, other students are apprehensive about improvising in front of either their peers or people in general. Your responsibility is to provide a positive environment and well-designed instructional exercises that enable students to grasp the fundamentals of improvisation and feel comfortable taking turns attempting it. To incorporate all possible techniques and strategies for teaching jazz improvisation would take not a single chapter in a single book but multiple volumes. There is no one-size-fits-all strategy, but my most basic advice for designing exercises to teach improvisation is to construct exercises with the purpose of developing (a) technique, (b) linking harmonic context, and (c) practical phrase creation.

The following instructional exercise is a highly efficient and effective method for teaching jazz improvisation and creating an environment where all students feel comfortable while adhering to rehearsal time restrictions. After a warm-up, I suggest employing this exercise sequence, using ten to fifteen minutes of rehearsal time.

> This technique does not, in and of itself, reinvent the wheel. It synthesizes several jazz educators' techniques (those of Jamey Aebersold, David Baker, Jerry Bergonzi, Chad Lefkowitz-Brown, and Lorenzo Ferrero, among others). This approach is also presented in its most basic form and assumes that students already know how to construct the basic five seventh chords and/or have a sheet containing all the major scales and formulas to build the chords.

The sequence is as follows:

Using a jazz standard or the chord changes to a tune the students are rehearsing, instruct students to build a "JIGsaw" (jazz inversion grid) sheet. A JIGsaw grid (inspired by a jigsaw puzzle, which consists of several parts that must be put together) is formed by stacking the chord changes (four measures at a time using basic seventh chords) in each inversion and, if applicable, the accompanying scale. This procedure can and should be altered as your students progress. The ability to improvise corresponds to Webb's Depth of Knowledge (DOK) levels 3 and 4 and Bloom's Taxonomy's application, analysis, evaluation, and creative components. At the same time, improvising students demonstrate more complex and abstract thinking in their musical performance and attain a level requiring complex reasoning that includes planning, investigating, and analyzing results (STANCOE, 2021). Figure 50.1 shows an example of a JIGsaw grid comprising the first four measures of a B♭ rhythm-changes progression for E♭ alto saxophone.

FIGURE 50.1 **JIGsaw grid example: first four measures of B♭ rhythm-changes progression, alto saxophone solo**

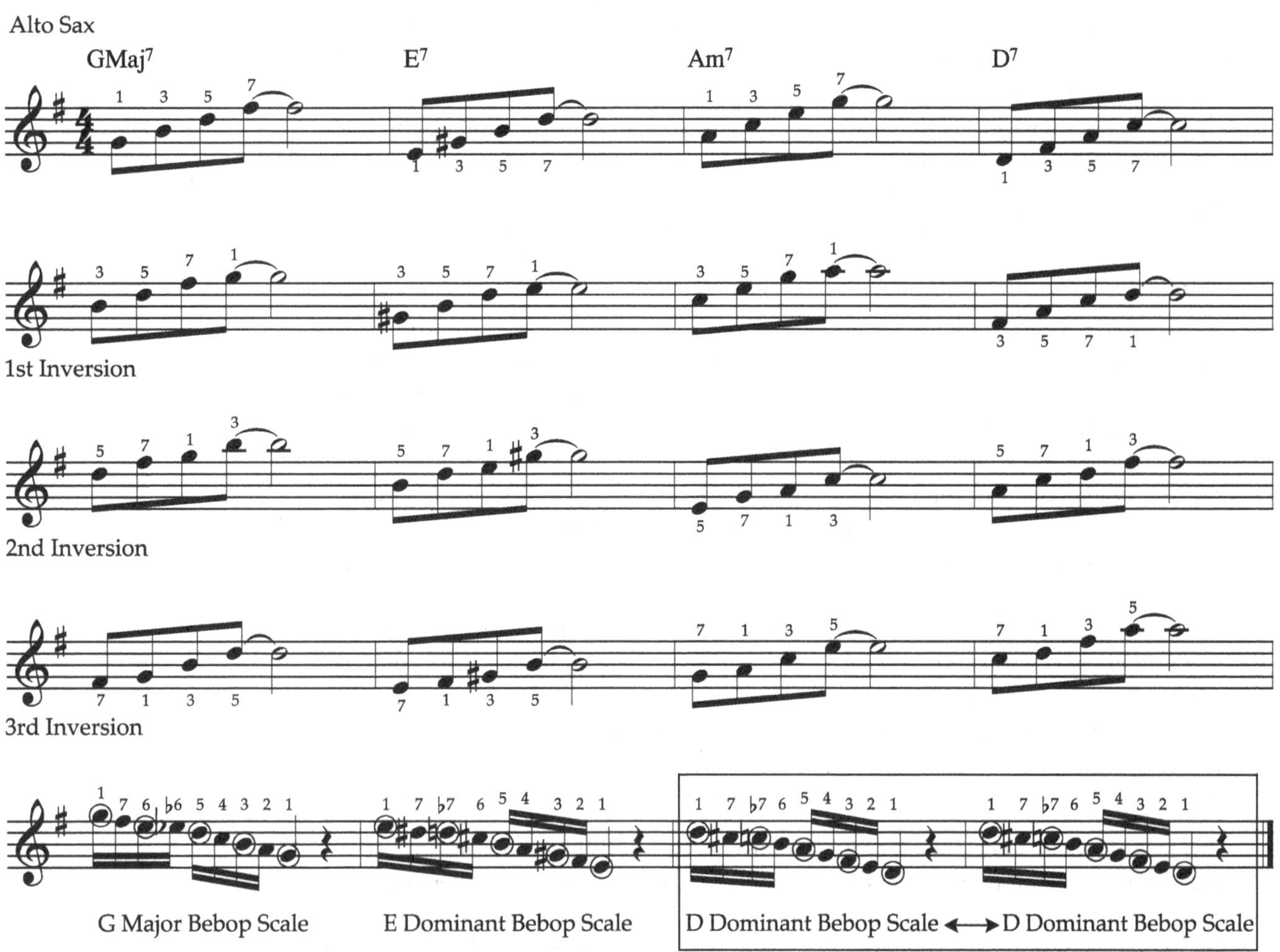

A JIGsaw grid should be assigned and assessed as both a written and a played exercise. As a written take-home assignment or an in-class assessment, students are given the chord changes to undertake and instructed to write down the correct chord spellings for those four measures, labeling the first, third, fifth, and seventh notes of each chord in each inversion, ensuring that each student has access to every chord in root position and first, second, and third inversion. As students advance, they should also write the corresponding scales for every chord. This enables the instructor to verify that the students comprehend the changes both intellectually and aurally.

While a minor bebop scale exists and may be played over the third measure, for the sake of keeping things simple and succinct, the D dominant bebop scale was utilized over the A minor chord—a common jazz shortcut.

As a playing assignment or assessment, the exercise can be performed by playing the four measures in one of its many variations:

1. Playing a solo only on the roots
2. Playing a solo only on the thirds and sevenths
3. Playing each chord progression ascending and descending (instruct students to read every measure backward for descending)
4. Combining the inversions creatively by reading one measure in one system and the next measure in another
5. Playing the scale ascending and descending (instruct students to read every measure backward for the descending scale) from each chord tone

This practice promotes the development of the cognitive, psychomotor, and affective domains in your students. It serves as a guideline for improvisation but still allows students the autonomy to be creative in their choices, training them to be able start every chord on any chord tone in the bebop scale (the fundamental basis of the jazz language). More important, from the educational perspective, it creates a rehearsal environment wherein all students should feel more comfortable playing in front of each other as the exercise builds. If a student struggles or is still apprehensive, I provide more guidance by introducing rhythmic concepts. I generally engage them in call-and-response activities or construct spontaneous rhythmic exercises in which a two-measure rhythm is written down. The students then play that rhythm and reverse it in the subsequent two measures. This immediately establishes a rhythmic relationship between students' phrasing, and their style of play becomes considerably more melodic. Additionally, I recommend applying the practice in multiple tiers to fit your students' varied developmental stages. A three-tiered system (e.g., beginner, developing, and advanced) is one such example, with the beginning tier consisting of just one of the exercises with suggested base and accelerated (pushed to the extent of their ability) tempos. The developing tier may include additional exercises or more than four measures in addition to the specified base and accelerated tempos (faster than the beginner level), whilst the advanced tier would follow suit, increasing the activity.

As your students' progress, you can increase the complexity of the activity by introducing more advanced concepts such as:

1. Replacing the roots with ninths
2. Varying the order in which notes are played inside the chord (e.g., in root position play [1,5,3,7], instead of [1,3,5,7])
3. Displacing an octave (e.g., in first inversion, instead of playing [3,5,7,1], play [3,7,1,5], with the 5 being placed an octave higher)
4. Adding enclosures or approach tones

This activity also supports the acquisition of practical voice-leading skills in developing students. Students may readily identify the best voice-leading options based on the variation they choose (e.g., if we begin with the GMaj7 chord in first inversion, students can easily see and hear an example of effective voice leading when choosing the E7 in second inversion; see Figure 50.2). Another example is shown where the Am7 in first inversion produces good voice leading to the D7 in third inversion (see again Figure 50.2).

FIGURE 50.2 JIGsaw grid with voice-leading examples

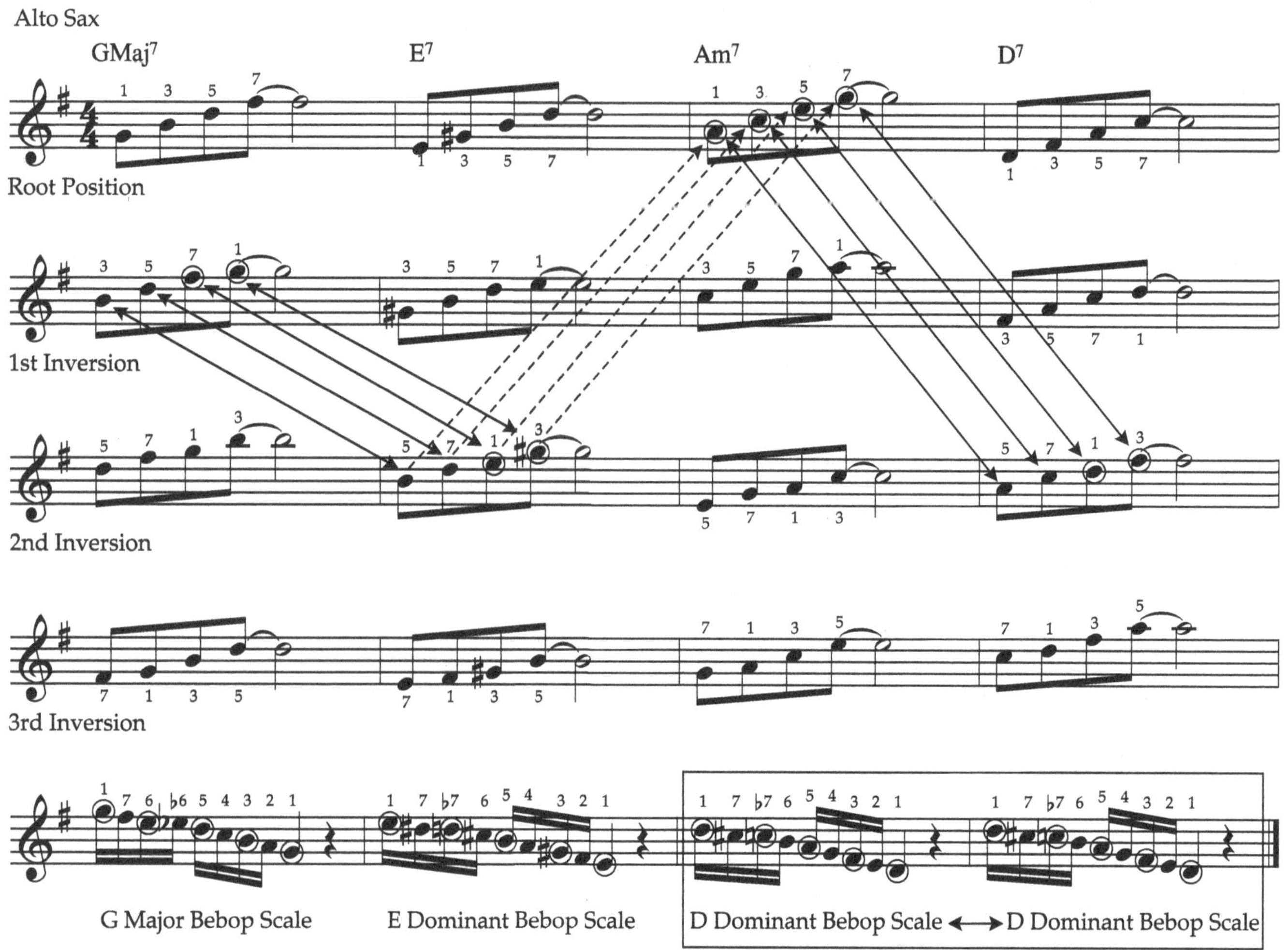

Additionally, introducing elements of color into the use of the grid has proven effective. When color is included, students comprehend voice-leading concepts and play scales from different chord tones more effectively.

When utilizing this exercise, I recommend devoting a week to every four measures, depending on the frequency of your rehearsal schedule. The following week, go to the composition's next four chords or measures. Repeat this process until you have gone through all the chord changes in the tune. If a measure has two chords, integrate them into a single measure and have the students execute it in double time. Typically, I utilize an app (e.g., iReal Pro or iPracticePro) to sustain individual chords or repeat a chord progression as a practice guide when performing these playing exercises. Drummers are not let off the hook: they perform the exercise on vibraphone or piano. Additionally, I provide each student a link to a track produced using iReal Pro or iPracticePro to practice at home (if they do not have access to the apps). This technique has aided tremendously in developing the performing and instructional aspects of improvisation in jazz ensembles I have directed.

50.6 Conclusion

You, the certified music educator, are fully responsible for the ensemble's success from the start. No amount of practice technique, discipline, or privilege in terms of demographics can compensate for an educator's musical deficiencies. As a result, educators need to maintain a continuous program of personal development. Additionally, the instructor needs to be prepared with the appropriate music for each rehearsal. There is always someone with more expertise than you around the corner, so tap into their knowledge. Develop a strong network of individuals with a diverse range of experience. This is one of the most valuable items an aspiring music and/or jazz educator can have. If you want to grow and develop, approach those with experience in areas you lack, remain modest, ask questions, and learn. We are educators, and thus we are all lifelong learners; ask questions, and you will obtain answers.

Never stop discovering new bands, composers, jazz musicians, and arrangers. Listen to college bands and other good bands in your area. Documenting tunes you enjoy is a fantastic approach to becoming acquainted with them. Attending seminars, workshops, and concerts at conferences will also help you acquire knowledge and inspiration. This enables you to generate new ideas while supporting your colleagues and developing partnerships that can assist you in moving forward.

50.7 Discussion Questions

1. Discuss your learning experiences within jazz ensembles during your middle/high school experiences. Was there a method implemented to teach improvisation?
2. Discuss creating a rehearsal plan based on a jazz ensemble score (instructor provide score). Emphasize essential rhythms, articulations, dynamics, balance, phrasing, etc.
3. Discuss creating a basic JIGsaw grid based on the solo changes to the chosen tune.

OXFORD learning link

Visit the online resources for additional documentation and exercises to help expand learning and test your knowledge further: www.oup.com/he/powell_music1e.

CHAPTER 51

MARCHING BAND REHEARSAL TECHNIQUES

Kelvin D. Jones

This chapter provides strategies for rehearsing a marching band.

51.1 Introduction

Marching band is the most visible music program in most school districts. Whether it is the pageantry of flags, the energy of the drums, the spirit from the wind players, or just the excitement from music at a sporting event, the marching band serves as a source of pride for schools and communities alike. Due to the number and variety of people that are present at sporting events, people will judge the validity of your entire music program, fairly or otherwise, on the quality of the marching band, so you need to treat this group with the same high standards one would an indoor concert, orchestra, or jazz ensemble.

As the former director of the University of Wisconsin's marching band and director of bands at Drake University, Don Marcouiller (1958), mentioned in the book *Marching for Marching Bands*: "More people will see their work here [on the marching field] than on the concert stage. More people will judge the music program of the school on the basis of the marching band than on the concert organizations. The marching band is, in a sense then, the showcase of the music program" (p. 3). This highly visible entity not only acts as a supporter of sporting events, most commonly football, but can also serve as the preliminary point for fundraising, community outreach, engagement, recruitment, cultural experiences, and much more.

51.2 Goal Setting

"Success is not an accident, success is a process."

Before you start ordering music, securing drills, arranging, or choreographing the flags for halftime, you should have a solid grasp of what the goals and expectations for the program should be. What is your philosophy for the program? Before you can plan anything, you must first solidify how you envision your program will function and what it will look like. From there you can decide on the areas of most importance to attack with your ensemble, whether visually or musically.

For example, will your program focus on competitive events like marching competitions and festivals? If so, then fundraising goals will need to be at the forefront as travel, drill, props, equipment, choreographers, and uniforms can be costly when the band is competing at a high level. Or maybe you value competitive marching events less and instead want to focus on other endeavors. Regardless, the students will embrace the values of their teachers. Whatever the teacher emphasizes, the students will follow along, so being clear about those expectations is vital from the very beginning.

Once clear on your philosophy and vision of the program, you should define clear goals, expectations, and objectives regarding what you'd like to see in a rehearsal on a daily basis. An example is creating SMART Goals for rehearsals (Yemm, 2013)—things that are Specific, Measurable, Attainable, Relevant or Realistic, and Timely. See Chapter 8 for more details on SMART goals.

51.3 Organization

"If you fail *to plan, you are* planning *to fail!"*

—Benjamin Franklin

This is a vital step, and one that many educators gloss over. Having a plan tells you which steps you need to take in order to get to your goals (refer to Chapter 2 of this book for planning goals). Being organized helps put your plans into motion in a clear and hopefully concise way. When starting off the school year after organizing your music library and inventory lists, you should begin developing your band handbook. This will serve as a guide to all the necessary information for important stakeholders, that is, students and parents. If constructed and used properly, this handbook can save the director countless hours of answering questions or disturbing notices and visits. As Greg Martin (2016), director of athletic bands at West Chester University, remarks, "A well thought out and executed band handbook should contain the answer to just about any question a student or parent might have over the course of the year." Your handbook should include, but certainly not be limited to, the following:

- Welcome letter
- Mission statement
- Ensemble and rehearsal information, expectations, auditions, and requirements
- Detailed attendance policy and grading procedure
- Leadership
- Uniforms
- Band boosters
- Staff bio(s)
- Forms such as absence request procedure, medical release, challenge procedure if applicable
- Full-year calendar for all band-related events: marching, concert, jazz, solo and ensemble, percussion ensemble, honor band, festivals, and so on

BAND CAMP

This is where you set the standard of instruction for the entire season. The former director of the Marching Illini at the University of Illinois Gary Smith states (2016), "Successful marching ensembles result from a mastery of the fundamentals of musicianship and marching." Band camp is usually the only time you can have approximately two weeks of full, uninterpreted days of instruction with the students to ingrain concepts. Once school officially starts, there will be numerous other factors attracting the student's attention; at camp, you can spend your time teaching marching fundamentals, instilling music fundamentals, and, most important, implementing your philosophy and vision for the program. You should have a detailed and meticulous plan for how you'd like to implement each concept. This should be included in your handbook as well so that everyone has clear instructions on how to execute maneuvers, whether it is a formal command like calling the band to attention or how to properly execute the desired horn carriage.

Also of importance is how you plan to sequence your instruction. Have a specific procedure on how instruments and equipment should be cared for when performing and also when not performing. For example, when students are given the command "Stand by," this means students will cease talking and await instruction given by the director or staff member. When students are given the command "Set," this means they snap to attention to get ready to perform. Just using these two operating terms," "Stand by" and "Set," helps unify instruction and create a system of procedures to help with rehearsal efficiency. Smith (2016) outlines examples of activities to accomplish at band camp:

- Issuing instruments, music, uniforms, equipment and supplies
- Training leaders and defining their responsibilities
- Distributing season schedules, handbooks, and fundraising materials
- Discussing roles, regulations, goals, philosophies, and purpose
- Defining rehearsal procedures, warm-ups, tuning processes, and work ethic
- Refining music fundamentals
- Teaching and refining marching fundamentals
- Reviewing traditions, cheers, cadences, school songs, and membership requirements
- Reading and memorizing drill charts
- Memorization of music (if applicable)
- Hosting special guest clinicians or specialized instructors
- Meeting band parents, coaches, and school administrators
- Taking pictures and/or videos for press release and promotional purposes

51.4 Classroom Instruction

There should be a consistent set of expectations, procedures, and standards to follow on a daily basis. Specific ideas should be tweaked to hit your specific goals, but the basic procedure and outline should be the same. A good rule of thumb is to reexamine specific goals weekly to see if any adjustments need to be made. Here are some aspects to focus on during your daily rehearsal.

WARM-UPS

Regardless of the performance medium, the basic music fundamentals of tone, intonation, balance, blend, articulation, and the like should be continually refined and developed. Incorporating these activities into the daily music regimen will go a long way toward developing desired musicianship qualities throughout the ensemble. One idea is to use breathing exercises for wind players to understand how airflow works by supporting the sound with adequate air. Another idea is to incorporate long tones and lip slurs for brass players and technical dexterity exercises for woodwinds.

Good bands play in tune regardless of whether they are indoors or on the fifty-yard line. This can be achieved by a daily dose of chorales and understanding pitch centers and tendencies so it is important to develop aural skills among all musicians. Listening for pitch also impacts listening for balance and blend as well. Be sure to have technique exercises for the percussion to perform as well, whether they involve finding creative ways to incorporate rudiments into the warm-ups or creating grooves that reinforce concepts performed in music from the show. I call this "giving students their vitamins in the guise of candy." Scales, lip slurs, and other warm-ups and fundamentals can get boring, so finding creative ways to reinforce these concepts will be vital. Another technique is to take something that is a tricky spot in the school or performance music and break that down into a warm-up exercise. Maybe the rhythm in a particular passage is giving the group trouble. Take that rhythm and make a composite rhythmic exercise out of it, then transfer that back to the original for the students. Another technique is to mark time during warm-ups so that students can get used to marching and feeling the pulse while playing.

REHEARSAL TECHNIQUES

Another exercise that can help refine clarity of articulation for the ensemble is distinguishing syllables for articulations. For example:

- "Doo" = legato
- "Dee" = accent
- "Dah" = marcato
- "Dit" = staccato

When you speak each syllable example, the tongue goes to a specific spot within your oral cavity, which helps clarify the articulation at hand. This is important when performing on the field over a hundred feet away from the audience. You want to be sure the written staccato is still clear and distinguishable.

As indicated earlier, having a procedure for the sequenced instruction of feedback is important. If you have a staff or even just student leaders, having a clear procedure for when they can give feedback is crucial in order not to have people talking over one another. A tool for this can be incorporating a time for field comments. For example:

- You (the director) cut off the group.
- You give a couple of big comments and then say, "Field comments," which signals the time for leaders on the field to give specific commands they saw as well, whether these leaders are hired staff or students.
- After thirty to forty-five seconds you can call them back by saying, "Stand by."
- You then reinforce the comments you made before and proceed to the next rehearsal segment.

This not only allows students to pay attention to you but also emboldens your staff to give constructive criticism and feedback to the group. Often they see things you can't and can provide insight into aspects you may have missed. The alternative is having staff members talk over you, and this is never a good idea. The big goal for any music rehearsal, not just marching, is to keep them fast-paced but lighthearted, so that students stay engaged, keeping their focus on playing fundamentals—tone, intonation, articulation, balance, blend, and technique—that can be transferred to any setting. Below is an example of a lesson plan for a fifty-minute class:

- Three minutes: breathing exercises
- Five minutes: long-tone exercises, playing and then singing
- Five minutes: lip slurs for brass and dexterity exercises for woodwinds

- Five minutes: scales and chorales
- Five minutes: tonguing exercises
- Five minutes: rhythm exercises
- Twenty minutes: music
- Two minutes: quick announcements and dismissal

Helpful hint: When possible, have your students march in place while playing during your warmup to get used to marching while playing. For many students this is a foreign concept and needs to be developed over time.

51.5 Auxiliary Units

Many programs have additional units with the marching that add much flair and glamor to the organization, such as color guard, flags, dancers, and/or front-line ensemble along with the drumline. However, many directors may not have experience working with these auxiliary units. If you have the resources or funding, you can outsource this to someone else, who can add value to these sections if you are not comfortable leading them on your own. Even if you do have experience with such groups, it is still advantageous to hire someone to work with them to take one more thing off your plate. Nonetheless, you still need to have a baseline of knowledge for each subgroup under our direction, whether you have experience with them or not.

Establishing a solid color guard program may seem daunting to someone who has not had any experience twirling a flag or teaching choreography. If you have no experience with color guard and flags, you can start by visiting a high-level color guard instructor in your area and ask questions. If there is none in your area, reach out to a trusted colleague, ask for their recommendations on whom to speak with, and set up a time to meet in person or virtually. This can also be your resource for potential color guard instructors for your school moving forward by asking if they know of anyone they'd recommend to serve as your instructor.

Smith (2016) highlights that with any of your auxiliary units, you will want to develop procedures for auditions, equipment and supplies, staff, show design, and rehearsal techniques. Auditions will likely take place in the spring semester of the school year. You will need to decide on a few factors. Will you allow musicians to be part of the guard, or are they to be strictly non–band instrumentalists? Will you have clinics leading up to the actual audition? If so, then incorporating a four-day clinic, Monday through Thursday, to teach concepts and having the actual audition on that Friday will be helpful. Also, what will be the ideal size for your guard? A typical marching band of 120 musicians will have a color guard of around twenty members. Ideally, more students will audition than will be taken on the team.

Upon the recommendations of your instructor (or conversations with other experts), figure out what you'll need in the way of equipment and supplies. This can include PVC pipe, tape, practice flags, performance flags, bags, uniforms, make-up, decorations, markers, rifles, sabers, swing flags, and more. Other rehearsal strategies are to have camps dedicated specifically to the subgroups throughout the summer so you or your instructor can work exclusively with them. There should also be movement, equipment, and marching exercises for each group. Movement exercises should include stretching to help increase flexibility and prevent injury, especially lower-body exercises. Equipment exercises involve taking the equipment and warming up by using the equipment to move with in a coordinated fashion. Marching exercises function similarly fashion to the equipment exercises—to get the body accustomed to moving in time. Ideally, concepts including glide step, backward march, jazz step, jazz running, frappés, tendus, pliés, and so on can be taught to the entire band program.

During rehearsals, you can incorporate the auxiliary units into the whole-band warm-up routine by doing technique exercises in conjunction with each basic warm-up activity. If the band is performing a Remington (long-tone) exercise, the guard can do a drop spin technique exercise while the drumline performs rudiment exercises. The same can apply to dancers if you have them under your supervision as well. For the drumline and/or front ensemble, you should have some basic knowledge of their performing fundamentals, whether it is a butterfly on the quad drums, a double paradiddle on the snare drum, or a soft mallet roll on the marimba. It is vital to create an environment where all the auxiliary units feel that they are part of the program. Too much distance or a lack of attention to what they are doing can subconsciously create a void and rift between groups. It is important to avoid this and have every entity feel welcome and part of the big picture, so be diligent in incorporating each unit within your normal rehearsal routines.

51.6 Discussion Questions

1. What are the things you value in a marching band program? Heavy competitions, no competitions, corps-style band, traditional, one halftime show all year, multiple halftime shows, performing multiple stand tunes, indoor drumline, winter guard, something else?
2. What are the pros and cons of having band students in the color guard?
3. What music fundamentals do you work on as an individual musician that can be effective for a large marching ensemble?

OXFORD learning link

Visit the online resources for additional documentation and exercises to help expand learning and test your knowledge further: www.oup.com/he/powell_music1e.

STRING AND ORCHESTRA REHEARSAL TECHNIQUES

Joel Schut and Rebecca B. MacLeod

This chapter provides an overview of common string ensembles and recommended string rehearsal strategies.

52.1 Introduction

This chapter will focus on the most common types of orchestra ensembles found in public schools as well as successful string teaching strategies that can be used in a variety of musical environments. While fundamental pedagogy will help any string teacher improve their students technically, an understanding of string specific rehearsal skills and strategies can help teachers be successful across the string teaching landscape. The world of string playing and teaching includes many formats, traditions, and collaborative opportunities and may include chamber music groups, string quartets, chamber orchestras, fiddle circles, jazz combos, and large symphonic ensembles that include wind, brass, and percussion. A healthy string program is one that provides many different opportunities for students to participate in music making.

52.2 Common String Ensembles

STRING ORCHESTRA

The string orchestra is the most common type of ensemble found in public schools. The orchestral bowed-string family consists of violin, viola, cello, and double bass. Commonalities among these four instruments provide opportunities for a well-blended sound, parallel skill development, and a strongly homogenized rehearsal process. Harp may be included at times. A common string orchestra rehearsal ordering includes tuning, a warm-up, and repertoire study. Tuning is best preceded by an individual student warm-up and followed by a group warm-up. The group warm-up is generally used to extend technique and musicianship. String orchestra warm-ups ideally allow separate focus on the development of right- and left-hand skills in addition to aural training and ensemble skills. A wealth of classical string orchestra and chamber ensemble literature exists dating back hundreds of years, in addition to current works for string orchestras.

FULL SYMPHONY ORCHESTRA

The string orchestra can be expanded to include wind, brass, and percussion players. Much literature exists for symphony orchestra. This ensemble provides great listening challenges learning to blend textures and colors across instrument families. Wind, brass, and percussion players must learn to play soloistically because they frequently play one on a part. Similarly, string players need to learn to listen in new directions and balance to single-voiced parts. Rehearsal ordering follows a format similar to that used for string orchestra, though tuning is traditionally led by the oboe using either a single A or a B♭ as well as the A.

MULTIPLE STYLES

Including diverse musical styles is one way to provide a comprehensive musical experience representative of all students. String instruments can be found in a variety of musical styles and across many cultures, such as old-time, Irish, Northern Indian classical, jazz combos, mariachi, electric rock, tango, and many more. Engaging in music making from different cultures may necessitate that students become collaborators in the process, teaching one another, sitting in a less formal arrangement, or working in smaller groups. "Culturally relevant teachers utilize students' culture as a vehicle for learning" (Ladson-Billings, p. 161) Efforts should be made to bring tradition bearers—musicians from the culture being studied—to collaborate with the students.

Music and culture are inextricably linked, so the music director must have a thorough understanding of the music being learned, including the context in which it was created, as well as a deep understanding of their students and their cultural backgrounds, strengths, interests, and experiences. Including regular conversations with students about music that is relevant to them is an important element of culturally responsive teaching and enables teachers to design instruction that is more meaningful. Furthermore, as Abril (2006) posits, allowing students to experience "the means by which music is taught, learned, and performed" within a culture honors the musical tradition of the people represented by the music and should be included as part of the learning process. For example, many musical styles are transmitted through aural traditions, so teaching music by rote may be an important element of that musical process. If families have musical expertise, formal or informal, consider having them present to the class, thereby building bridges between home and school. For more on culturally responsive teaching in school orchestras, see Chapter 43.

52.3 Fundamental String Rehearsal Strategies

A popular axiom is that "good teaching is good teaching." Many elements of effective rehearsals such as delivery, pace, sequence, assessment, and feedback easily transfer between settings. However, when diagnosing string instrument sound, musical problems can frequently be narrowed further to right- or left-hand technical issues (Allen 2001). Consider the following common strategies.

DIAGNOSING STRING SOUND

String ensemble sounds can be both wonderful and disorienting! The triage triangle (see Figure 52.1) provides a hierarchical system for assessing and addressing issues in the string rehearsal. Each concept in the pyramid builds upon the previous one. For example, it can be nearly impossible to improve intonation if the fundamental tone quality is inadequate. Likewise, students may have trouble producing a beautiful tone if there are issues with their body format or instrument set-up.

FIGURE 52.1 Triage triangle sound diagnostics

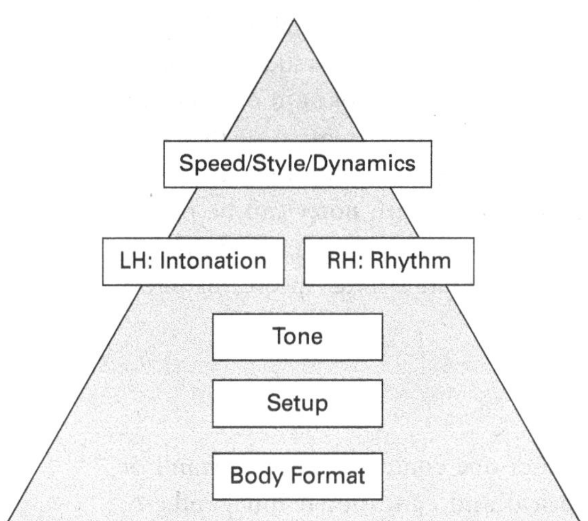

Teachers who listen foundationally to string sound can help diagnose problems, prescribe meaningful solutions, and separate symptoms from cause. By utilizing the triage triangle for sound diagnosis, combined with an understanding of sequential string pedagogy, the director will be better able to determine what to rehearse.

REHEARSAL STRATEGIES FOR THE LEFT HAND

Issues related to pitch, intonation, and vibrato can be addressed through left-hand isolation strategies. For example, rehearse pizzicato or use separate bows note by note in a slower rhythm. Occasionally shifts may need to be isolated or fingerings reconsidered. Left-hand issues related to pitch accuracy, facility, and consistency may frequently be solved by providing a more strategic fingering. Recommend fingerings that shift on the smallest musical interval, facilitate easier string crossing patterns, or create similar sound colors (MacLeod 2019). Proficient string players are intimately aware of the location of half steps; this is particularly true of violin and viola players, as this interval frequently requires neighbor fingers to almost touch. Finger patterns provide the framework for the left hand, and a thorough understanding of what finger pattern is needed will increase students' pitch accuracy. For information on left-hand set-up and strategies, see Chapter 28; for more about shifting and vibrato, see Chapter 29.

REHEARSAL STRATEGIES FOR THE RIGHT HAND

Issues related to tone, rhythm, and articulation can be addressed through right-hand isolation. For example, practice playing the rhythm of a musical passage on a single open string (or multiple open strings if the passage has string crossings). Air bow while singing or saying the note name, bow direction, or bow distribution. Rehearse complicated slurred bowings separately for accuracy. Divide by stand and have one player play as written and the other the simplified rehearsal version, then have them switch. For continued refinement, ensure students' bow direction, placement, and contact point are unified.

The terms "save" and "spend" are frequently used to describe the amount and speed of bow needed to produce a good tone. Long tones or long slurred passages require students to save their bow. A unique rehearsal challenge to strings may be that the left hand is playing sixteenth notes, while the right hand is playing a long slur. The teacher should consider the rhythmic responsibilities of both hands in order to correctly diagnose the music problem. For information on right-hand set-up and strategies, see Chapter 27.

String players are able to produce more than thirty articulations (Rabin & Smith 1990). The majority of bow strokes begin from the string, with exceptions such as ricochet and col legno. Students often overlook the need for off-the-string strokes to originate *on* the string in an ensemble context. Refine specialty strokes such as tremolo so that they have multiple placements, lengths, and speeds. Similarly, teach the ability to slide among style spectrums on common strokes. For example, spiccato eighth notes can be played many different ways, including weighted rock bounces, light classical springs, and rhythmic fiddle chops. Explore longer/shorter, faster/slower, and louder/softer spectrums across common strokes.

TEACH AND REHEARSE FOR TRANSFER

Transfer is the ability to take an idea or concept from one context and understand or recognize that same idea in another context. Musical and educational independence is predicated on the ability to make transfers for technical and musical purposes. The homogenous nature of string ensembles increases opportunities to teach explicitly for transfer because sound production techniques are similar for all four bowed-string instruments. Integrating transfer as a core element of the rehearsal process helps speed progress, builds skills across all instruments, and helps students become independent musicians able to refine their playing in ways specific to their instrument.

To increase student opportunities to transfer learning, rehearsals should be conceptual, focusing on the central musical elements or technical skills that we hope students will internalize, such as tone, rhythm, style, intonation, balance, and ensemble skills. The principles of tone production (point of contact, angle of bow, weight, and speed), as outlined in the ASTA curriculum (Benham et al. 2011) can be introduced to all students simultaneously and applied to almost any piece of music. Teaching students to save their bow to produce a long tone or move their contact point toward the bridge for a bigger sound are examples of techniques that can be taught conceptually to the entire class simultaneously.

Students learn to transfer best when given the opportunity to make connections and find examples. For instance, a young fifth-grade student was once teaching his classmates to play "Lightly Row" for the first time. After he sang the note names "A F♯ F♯, G E E" to them, he explained that "the next part is basically the D major scale, [*singing*] D E F♯ G A A A." This is a perfect example of transfer: this student was able to identify the D major scale within a song without being told by the teacher.

Providing multiple examples of a musical idea in succession across different pieces of music is an excellent way to encourage students to transfer. Once students have been presented with a concept, they need opportunities to immediately apply the information in a musical context. For instance, if the rehearsal is focused on producing a sustained, legato sound, then students may be taught how to play with a slow bow during warm-up, then be immediately asked to apply that technique to a musical passage that requires a long, slow bow. The rehearsal must be sequenced logically so that students can explicitly make these connections.

> Student retention often requires modeling transfer. Consider rehearsing all similar themes back-to-back, emphasizing changes in instrumentation, register, and orchestration. Rehearse similar bowing applications throughout the work. Rehearse similar pitch challenges and key centers back-to-back.

REHEARSAL PACING AND SEQUENCING

Preparing for an effective rehearsal includes planning, sequencing, and pacing learning experiences that support technical and musical growth. Students stay engaged when they are actively participating and the instruction is sequenced for maximum student success. Bob Culver's energy profile (1989) provides an ideal framework for planning and managing time across a rehearsal (Culver 1989) (see Chapter 4, Figure 4.2). The energy profile stipulates that rehearsals begin with a medium energy level, transition to a lower energy where students are focused and can engage with more complex and difficult material, then conclude the lesson with high energy and high success.

To establish an ideal energy profile, first notice the energy with which students enter the rehearsal space. Match their energy level as they enter the room, then engage the students with review or an activity that will allow them to be successful. The sense of success will prepare students emotionally to tackle something new or more challenging. The middle portion of the rehearsal is the best time to address more difficult passages. Establish a desirable difficulty pace where students are challenged by new skills and experiences but avoid traps of overt frustration. Before the end of rehearsal, work to drive the pacing and energy to a higher level with a sense of student accomplishment. This could mean putting sections back into tutti context, performing a rehearsed section with no stops, or pivoting to a motivating, further-along, or easier piece. Avoid placing new information at the end of rehearsal. Students often return to subsequent rehearsals reflecting the energy with which they left the prior rehearsal.

Classroom management can be linked to issues with rehearsal pacing, energy profile, and logical sequencing. For example, an entire rehearsal with extensively challenging material may lead students to feel unable to succeed and act out due to frustration. Similarly, a rehearsal without challenge may lead students to act out due to boredom. See Chapters 1 and 4 for more information on rehearsal energy profiling.

> The exact length of time spent in each rehearsal period (review, extension, or motivation) is dependent on the developmental age and ability of students. For beginners, these may look like equal parts. For middle school and high school players, the middle extension may be longer. Regardless of age, all feature the core moments of review, extension, and motivation. While this flow may appear spontaneous to students, it is achieved through careful teacher planning.

COMMUNICATION AND PRECISE LANGUAGE

Rates of verbal instruction and student performance impact pacing. From the research literature we know that experienced music teachers use less verbal instruction than novice teachers (Goolsby 1999) that students are more off task during periods of teacher talk (Nápoles 2007), and that students prefer rehearsals with less teacher talk and more opportunities to perform (Witt 1986). Effective music teachers spend 32-45 percent of rehearsal time using verbal instruction and allow students to actively perform for the majority of rehearsal.

There are numerous strategies that teachers may use during rehearsal to limit descriptive explanations. Demonstrate with an instrument or vocally, or have a student model by proxy. Use effective conducting gestures that are congruent visually with what is expected of the students' bow arm. When providing verbal instruction, speak precisely and concisely, using as few words as possible. Use a "who/where/what" ordering, which helps deliver content in the manner in which the brain most easily identifies, locates, and applies information. Provide focused action items delivered in less than thirty seconds between student performance trials. Use direct, vivid, and imaginative language that sticks in the memory and allows for future code work development (e.g., "elephantine accents," "effervescent arm weight tone"). Avoid redundancy by allowing a single breath to communicate each main instruction.

The use of code words or "bowcabulary" is an effective tool to minimize excessive verbiage during rehearsal. Knowledge of string-specific vocabulary is helpful. Generate code words and phrases in the warm-up process for use during repertoire rehearsal. Common orchestra rehearsal code words include "from the string," "bow lane 5," "subdivide sixteenths," "no break," "shape of the line," and the like.

DEVELOPING STRING ENSEMBLE UNITY

There are five key rehearsal skills that string students should develop that will contribute to positive and effective rehearsals in which ensemble unity is at the center: breathing/moving, subdividing/counting, listening/adjusting, watching/matching, and musicianship/motivation. These five skills are not listed in order of priority; they are all equally important characteristics of high-level ensembles. How these skills are developed vary slightly between string and wind players because of the visual nature of string playing, where so many musical elements can be seen in the motion of the bow, such as articulation, rhythm, and tone. We have assembled some of our favorite strategies for teaching and reinforcing these skills. See 52.2, "Rehearsal Strategies for Strings Supplemental Materials," in the book's online resources for more.

BREATHING/MOVING

Wind players naturally require good breath support in order to create a characteristic tone. String players should also breathe to initiate sound and communicate across the ensemble. In addition to an intake of air, string players should have a corresponding motion that mimics the preparatory beat provided by the conductor. Shoulder instruments can lift their scroll, and low string instruments, their head. Giving a clear visual measurement, such as, "give me a 6-inch scroll lift" will encourage students to practice a gesture that is more effective. Have students imagine that their scroll or head is attached by a string to the conductor's baton and practice moving in tandem.

The breathing/moving exercises listed in 52.2, "Rehearsal Strategies for Strings Supplemental Materials," in the book's online resources can be tailored to students' needs. To create a sense of ensemble pulse or bow speed matching, consider "Pass the Beat." Explore "Follow the Leader" to develop ensemble awareness and leadership observation. Consider "Start Without the Conductor" to initiate student-led movement and cueing. With all breathing/moving exercises, make sure to transfer the role among players to encourage all students to breathe and lead from the front to the back of each string section.

> When conducting strings, it can be highly effective to increase the use of horizontal space. This demonstrates bow usage in a similar plane to which string bows naturally make sound. Similarly, work to execute preparatory gestures only as much as musicians need to move. Model and match breath and upper strings' scroll movement.

LISTENING/ADJUSTING

No skill is more important to a musician than listening. But to what should students listen? How should they listen? Students need opportunities to identify different elements of music when they are not playing as well as when they are. Encourage students to assess what role they are playing: melody, countermelody, accompaniment, rhythmic motor? Ask score questions about the music to teach students how to listen. Have them play a section of music, then ask, "Who had the melody?" "When did you hear two sections in rhythmic unison?" "Where did you notice the melody in octaves?"

Tailor the listening/adjusting exercises listed in 52.2, "Rehearsal Strategies for Strings Supplemental Materials" in the book's online resources to students' needs. Use "Intonation Detective" and "Imposters Among Us" as motivational games for listening awareness. Explore "Backup Singer" as a game for melodic and harmonic balance. Similarly, "The Rule of Octaves" provides students with a practical goal framework to transfer into new scenarios.

> There is a difference between hearing and listening. Work to guide students' listening skills, teaching them what to listen for and how to use the information they are hearing. Additionally, teach them to listen in multiple dimensions (vertical alignment, horizontal harmony, and sagittal balance). Have them practice listening for parts that are not played by their primary instrument or in their native tessitura. If you are an upper-register player, listen for the bass; if you are a lower-register player, listen for the interplay of the middle voices; and so on.

SUBDIVIDING/COUNTING

Teachers regularly ask students to subdivide, but do students know what that means? To constantly subdivide takes an incredible amount of mental energy and requires discipline. Students need audible examples of what it means to subdivide, and they need to demonstrate the ability to subdivide audibly for the teacher.

The subdividing/counting exercises listed in 52.2, "Rehearsal Strategies for Strings Supplemental Materials," in the book's online resources can be tailored to students' needs. For developing internal pulse, consider "Metronome Game Outside/Inside" and the "Counting X" game. For creating rhythmic listening and rhythmic accuracy within parts, use "Human Metronome." To control rushing and expand musical shaping, explore "Insert Rests."

> Strive to teach subdivision in a musical way. All rhythms can have shape, emphasis, and resonance. Additionally, rhythm can be paired with dynamic and ensemble watching and listening. Model these skills and provide specific examples of where and how to achieve subdividing and counting success.

WATCHING/MATCHING

Visual cues are incredibly helpful to string players because not only can we see the conductor's gesture, we also can see the bow stroke of our fellow players. String players must learn to watch for bow placement, articulation, and bow speed. String players should be encouraged to watch their principal players and one another at least as much as they watch the conductor.

Tailor the watching/moving exercises listed in 52.2, "Rehearsal Strategies for Strings Supplemental Materials," in the book's online resources to student needs. For creating awareness of preparatory beats in time and space, use "Toss a Ball." For matching another player, use "Mirror Game" or "Bow Twins." To refine matching while playing, explore "One Inch Rule" and "Freeze." Develop section leadership and matching using "Bow Change Drones." For accuracy and unity, have fun with "Share a Bow."

> Students often listen most carefully to where directors are focusing their visual attention. Help students know where to put their eyes and their ears will follow. Give specific things to look for and praise positive noticing. Be specific about location and goals and make watching and matching explicit. When students know where to watch and how to match they become increasingly confident and proud of their ensemble community.

MUSICALITY/MOTIVATION

Why did we pair musicality with motivation? Because playing musically *is* motivating, and students have to be motivated in order to reach their peak musical potential. Rehearsals must go beyond notes, rhythms, and bowings, but for that to happen, students must be engaged and keenly aware of the music and the other musicians in the room.

The musicality/motivation exercises listed in 52.2, "Rehearsal Strategies for Strings Supplemental Materials," in the book's online resources can be tailored to students' needs. For developing audiation and inner musicianship, use "Play Only the Down Beats." For students struggling to keep up or hesitating, use "Play the Essence Notes." "Tonal Pillars" are helpful for establishing musical moments learned as ensemble goals. Use "Relay Rehearsal" to foster independence and teamwork. Finally, many "Ensemble Seating" and "Setup" opportunities exist and can be tailored to student or musical needs. For section unity, consider section circles. For part independence, consider chamber pods. For listening across a full orchestra, consider moving wind players to the podium, surrounded by strings. For waning student motivation, provide three minutes to rearrange as a flattering cartoon of the director.

> It is all too easy to get lost in the mechanics of a piece. Help students to not lose track of the musical why by finding ways to teach, rehearse, and connect with music in a way that makes both music and musicians feel alive and vital. Commit to musical decisions and develop a plan with students to share the meanings of the music with listeners.

52.4 Conclusion

Incredible music-making opportunities exist across the string rehearsal landscape. The multitude of styles and repertoire inclusive to string players allows directors to keep expanding their skills and interests across a career. An understanding of string technique and a complimentary rehearsal process will help directors regardless of musical background. Moreover, further cultivation and exploration of string teaching possibilities helps further develop string teaching into an ever-expanding space for creativity and inclusion.

52.5 Discussion Questions

1. What types of string ensembles might you find in school music programs?
2. How can a wide variety of musical styles be incorporated in the string classroom?
3. Describe three rehearsal strategies to help students develop their rhythm skills.
4. Describe three rehearsal strategies to improve students' intonation skills.
5. How might the triage triangle help diagnose issues in rehearsal?

OXFORD learning link

Visit the online resources for additional documentation and exercises to help expand learning and test your knowledge further: www.oup.com/he/powell_music1e.

MARIACHI ENSEMBLE REHEARSAL TECHNIQUES

Sergio Alonso

In this chapter, the author emphasizes the sociocultural aspects of mariachi music's multidimensional performance contexts in providing an overview of hybridized teaching strategies that develop mariachi students' technical and practical skills.

53.1 Introduction

No other form of Mexican music stirs excitement, emotion, and *alegría* like mariachi. Music educators seeking to enhance their programs with nontraditional ensembles may consider mariachi an ideal source for fun and exciting music making. Teachers, students, and community members may reap the rewards of a culturally relevant music alternative by implementing a high-quality mariachi program, but teaching popular and/or folk music in schools comes with unique challenges. Before delving into the world of mariachi music, teachers may do well to consider the social and cultural aspects of mariachi transmission and performance.

As with conventional school music programs, proper technique, Western notation, and competition will likely persist at the center of formal mariachi education's curricular and pedagogical priorities. This practice is in stark contrast to the genre's apprenticeship learning model, where musical knowledge is transmitted informally, aurally, and independently from educational activities in schools (Campbell & Soto Flores, 2016). In school settings, skills that help define the mariachi musician, such as accompaniment, transposition, and improvisation, often give way to skills deemed "legitimate" by the educational system (Rodriguez, 2006).

A complete mariachi education, in contrast, allows for the acquisition of musical knowledge and technical skills typically developed within formal settings without losing sight of the importance of orality in the mariachi tradition (Soto Flores, 2015). Teaching toward *todo conocimiento* ("complete knowledge") involves a teaching-learning hybrid that incorporates formal and informal practices, implements both note and rote methods, and acknowledges the beliefs and values within the mariachi music culture. In this chapter I posit a holistic and comprehensive approach to mariachi music that recognizes the genre's traditional forms of transmission, the sociocultural aspects of mariachi's multidimensional performance contexts, and the contextual knowledge and practical skills those spaces demand.

53.2 Instrumentation

Teachers should exercise care in developing students' instrumental skills as they relate to mariachi practice. Although an in-depth exploration of authentic mariachi instrumental performance is beyond the scope of this chapter, the following sections address salient technical, stylistic, and notational considerations of each mariachi instrument.

TRUMPET

Marked jaw vibrato and staccato articulations are the most distinguishing aspects of mariachi trumpet playing. Trumpeters can cultivate a steady and fluid vibrato at varying speeds by performing long tones while dropping and raising the jaw at progressively faster rhythms. Students should avoid producing a vibrato that is too fast and jittery and an amplitude that is too wide and pronounced. The mariachi trumpet *picado* articulation is accented and short. However, unlike the "tu" articulation of other genres, mariachi trumpeters employ a "tut" to stop the sound with the tongue. See 53.1, "Trumpet Performance," in the book's online resources.

VIOLIN

Although mariachi draws on Western classical techniques, students should consider some devices to achieve proper interpretation and style. Requiring more arm weight than classical technique, the mariachi violin *jalón*, or downbow, is generally heavy and aggressive. Such is the case when playing the most representative mariachi genre, the *son*, where hard and raspy attacks work in tandem with *caballito*, or a swinging "horse gallop" eighth note, phrasing. For other genres, such as the *bolero*, lyrical phrasing, soft to moderate accents, smooth and seamless bow changes, graceful vibratos, and diversity of dynamics are well suited. See 53.2, "Violin Performance," in the book's online resources.

GUITARRÓN

Although this bass guitar–type instrument can feel cumbersome and taxing to some students, correct posture and technique allow comfortable and efficient playing. Teachers may guide students to stand tall with feet shoulder width apart and knees slightly bent. Hips should also push slightly forward with shoulders back and relaxed. The strap is secured over the right or the left shoulder and across the back. The instrument rests toward the right side of the abdomen, with the soundboard at a roughly 45 degree angle. The right forearm rests on the soundboard edge, with the hand over the tone hole and the thumb fully extended.

Modern guitarrón playing utilizes a double-stop plucking technique where musicians execute most pitches in octaves. A proper right-hand *jalón*, or pluck, consists of the index finger and thumb pulling two strings simultaneously, save A, B♭, and B, where the middle finger and thumb pluck the first and sixth strings, and G and G♯, where the thumb plucks the fourth string only. When reading guitarrón notation, students should assume this practice regardless of the indicated pitch. For example, a guitarrón player executes an A in octaves, whether it is notated on the first space or the fifth line of the bass staff. See 53.3, "Guitarrón Performance," in the book's online resources.

VIHUELA, GUITAR, AND GUITARRA DE GOLPE

The five-string vihuela and nylon-string guitar comprise the modern *armonía*, or harmony section. Although the guitarra de golpe, a five-string guitar, also forms part of the section, its use in contemporary practice is nearly obsolete. Mariachi notation combines rhythmic guitar instruments under the collective staff name, "armonía," or simply "guitars." In line with the section's harmonic function, armonía sheet music employs chord symbols over rhythmic notation.

Vigorous chordal strumming is foundational to mariachi rhythmic guitar performance, where the right-arm and -hand movement centers on wrist rotation. Whether using the standard pick typically used by guitar performers or the index finger pick often employed by vihuela players, the wrist remains slightly bent, so the hand is at approximately a 45 degree angle in relation to the string plane. Whereas guitarists strike the strings with a pick, vihuela players strike with a slightly bent index finger when down-strumming and with an extended thumb when up-strumming. Guitarists form chords in open-string positions for the left hand, except for when chords call for barre positions.

Specialized strumming techniques are vital to the mariachi essence. The *redoble*, a sixteenth-note rhythmic pattern, is common in various styles, especially the *son*. The rapid down-up-down strumming pattern requires a relaxed hand free of residual tension. The *apagón* muting technique involves the dampening of the strings with the rounded, fleshy part at the base of the thumb. Although the technique is used sparingly in different styles, it is essential to *huapango* rhythmic structure. The *rasgueado* fanning technique resonates in various styles, particularly the *son jarocho*. Vihuela players should strum with an open hand and "scratch" across the strings with the nails of the ring, middle, and index fingers and follow through with the thumb. Guitarists may fan with the ring and middle fingers, then follow through with the pick. See 53.4, "Guitar Performance," in the book's online resources.

HARP

Commonly tuned in C or G major, the diatonic thirty-six-string *arpa jaliscience*, or Jalisco harp, ranges from G1 to G6. With the adaptation of sharping levers, B♭ or E♭ tuning allows a broader range of key possibilities. The fundamental technique is consistent with the harp's traditional function as a bass and harmonic accompaniment instrument. The left hand performs bass lines, usually with the ring finger and thumb plucking in octaves, while the right hand outlines the harmony with four-voice chords.

Harp melody often advances by way of *brinco*, where the right hand jumps up and down the string plane as the fingers engage synchronously. Finger-independent melodic figures are also common in some styles. A diverse array of techniques and effects, such as arpeggios, tremolos, glissandos, and others, also characterize modern mariachi harp practice. Basic harp notation employs the grand staff, finger designations (e.g., "one" indicates thumb, "two" is the index finger, "three" is the middle finger, and "four" is the ring finger), and chord names. Notation may alternate between traditional harp notation when executing melodic lines, and guitarrón and armonía notation when performing bass and harmonic accompaniment. See 53.5, "Harp Performance," in the book's online resources.

53.3 Music Planning and Preparation

Mariachi music offers performance opportunities for students of all levels. Many standard songs are within the technical reach of beginning and intermediate students, while other pieces challenge even the most advanced instrumentalists. By planning for songs of varying degrees of difficulty and preparing music that addresses students' diverse skill levels, teachers meet the needs of all students, develop their ensembles' repertoire, and prepare students for future community music making.

SELECTING APPROPRIATE REPERTOIRE

Song difficulty levels often align with mariachi musical genres. Rhythmic structure, melodic complexity, harmonic vocabulary, and other musical devices contribute to students' technical challenges. Mariachi educators and students may benefit greatly from selecting music that matches the instrumentalists' and vocalists' skill levels (Fogelquist, 2008). Students may assist in the music selection process by suggesting songs, genres, and artists they enjoy.

Beginning Students

In its slow tempo in common time, simple rhythm, and limited harmony, *canción ranchera*, a popular mariachi genre, is ideal for beginning students. "Volver, volver," "Por un amor," and "La diferencia" are among the most beloved.

Beginning and Intermediate Students

Like the 4/4 ranchera, the waltz-like ranchera in 3/4 meter, or *ranchera valseada*, is suitable for beginning students. Excelling students may also benefit from the seemingly endless list of classics that fall under this accelerated ranchera variant, including "El rey," "Ella," and "Paloma negra."

Intermediate Students

The *ranchera polqueada*, or polka-like ranchera, provides a festive element to any intermediate ensemble with its upbeat tempo. "Caminos de Michoacan," "El herradero," and "Si tu también te vas" are time-tested favorites. The *corrido*, a narrative genre, tells of personal experiences and historical events. "El caballo blanco," "Gabino barrera," and "Corrido de los Perez" are some of the many possibilities. Colombian *cumbia* music also aligns with intermediate students' skill levels and gives audience members danceable options during celebratory events. "Mariachi loco" is far and away the most popular among mariachi aficionados.

Intermediate to Advanced Students

The bolero is synonymous with romantic music and optimal for developing intermediate-to-advanced students' understanding of complex vocal and instrumental harmonies. Through its use of chromaticism, tonicization, and modulation, the bolero adds a level of musical sophistication to the mariachi repertoire with songs such as "Besame mucho," "Sabor a mi," "Solamente una vez," and countless others. *Vals*, or waltz music, also presents major and minor key modulatory complexities over a relatively simple rhythmic foundation. "Sentimiento," "Dios nunca muere," and "Viva mi desgracia" are among the most popular.

Polkas are also instrumental options that serve to develop melodic instrumentalists' dexterity. Whereas "Jesusita en Chihuahua" and "Las perlitas" are workable favorites, other, more demanding pieces such as "La chuparosa" and "Honor y patria" require that the trumpet and violin players pay meticulous attention to their musical complexities. Commonly known as *son jalisciense*, or *son* from Jalisco, the *son* is mariachi music's quintessential genre. Rooted in *sesquiáltera*, a hemiola rhythmic structure, and driving eighth-note phrases, the *son* challenges students with technical and stylistic intricacies derived from mariachi music's traditional folk idiom. "El son de La Negra," mariachi music's emblematic song, is a must.

Advanced Students

In many respects the huapango is the most demanding of all standard mariachi genres. Syncopated counterrhythms, stylized rhythmic-guitar muting techniques, elaborate violin passages, and falsetto singing allow teachers to showcase their most skilled vocalists with songs like "El pastor" and "Cielo rojo" and to demonstrate violinists' instrumental prowess with the fast-tempo variants heard in songs like, "Serenata huasteca," and "La noche y tu." A close relative of the huapango, the *son jarocho* is also an ambitious option for highlighting advanced students. "El cascabel" and the internationally famous "La bamba" are staples within the *son jarocho* style.

Besides the cumbia, mariachi incorporates other international styles into its canon. The rhythmically and harmoniously complex *joropo* from Venezuela and Colombia has long influenced mariachi music. Rhythm guitar players may significantly benefit from the likes of "La bikina," "La fuente," and "Mi ciudad." The *pasodoble*, of Spanish origin, offers trumpet players a space to display their musical pageantry with pieces such as "El dos negro," "El zopilote mojado," and "España cañi." The Cuban *danzón* has also influenced mariachi in challenging instrumentals like "Nereidas" and "Juarez."

MARIACHI MUSIC TRANSCRIPTIONS

Although there is increasing demand for written mariachi music among educators, a mariachi sheet-music publishing industry remains virtually nonexistent. The newly established Mariachi Education Press is the only publishing company dedicated to mariachi education materials and resources. Lacking published mariachi music, educators can benefit from attending mariachi conferences, such as the Tucson International Mariachi Conference, the Mariachi Spectacular de Albuquerque, and the Las Cruces International Mariachi Conference, where mariachi professionals provide high-quality transcriptions as part of the events' educational workshops. Veteran mariachi educators also archive sheet music from past conferences and many other sources (Fogelquist, 2008). Social network sites allow prospective mariachi teachers to access educational resources from experienced mariachi educators. Facebook mariachi network groups include:

- Mariachi Resources, www.facebook.com/groups/mariachiresources
- Mariachi Directors Group, www.facebook.com/groups/394713693980346

MUSICAL ACCOMMODATIONS

No matter how judicious and painstaking teachers are in researching and selecting appropriate music, some standard arrangements may not be suitable for all instrumentalists. Depending on the compositional nature of a particular song and the individual proficiencies of group members, musical elements may need adjusting to accommodate individual players, singers, or entire sections. Mariachi educators may tailor the music to fit students' varying skill levels by modifying and adapting individual parts. The following suggestions are ways teachers can make changes without diminishing the music's integrity and essence:

- Trumpet section: Limiting trumpets to one voice, lowering sections or entire parts by an octave, or inverting two voices can aid trumpet players with limited range and endurance. Alternating sections with the violins also allows trumpet players to rest in between passages.
- Violin section: Selecting music or transposing to the violin-friendly major keys of D, A, and G while limiting the parts to first position serves beginning violinists. Emphasizing detaché bowing, reducing to one or two voices, and lowering parts by octaves may also support students' rhythm and intonation.
- Harmony section: Transposing songs to the major keys of G, D, A, and E and minor keys of A and E will allow guitarists to play primary chords in open positions. Additionality, armonía players can simplify unfamiliar extended chords (e.g., min7, Maj7) by focusing on triads. For guitarrón players, playing in the major keys of F, C, G, and A will avoid scales and primary triads that require the most challenging pitch positions, C♯/D♭ and D♯/E♭. Guitarrón and harp players can also focus on outlining chords with roots and fifths in place of walking bass lines.
- Vocalists: Establishing appropriate keys sometimes centers on vocalists' needs. Teachers can expect to transpose songs up between a fourth and a sixth to accommodate young, soprano, and alto voices. In some instances, such as when developing boys begin to experience voice changes, teachers may have to lower keys.

53.4 Rehearsal Techniques

Western European thought and practice have historically informed mariachi music education. As such, mariachi educators may draw on many of the concepts presented in this book. Part I provides educators a wealth of information relevant to teaching and learning mariachi music, including transferable pedagogical practices in Chapter 1, student learning concepts in Chapter 3, and caring and compassionate teaching in Chapter 11. Parts III and IV are particularly useful for developing mariachi trumpeters' and violinists' musicianship and technical skills.

The following exercises focus on the guitarrón, armonía, and harp and the ways in which the rhythm section may be integrated into typical warm-up and scale exercises to develop technique and genre-specific style.

WARM-UPS

Contextualized scales allow students to develop their technical and stylistic understandings of mariachi genres by focusing on the musical characteristics of a particular song of study. Song style and key should be guiding factors when designing an appropriate warm-up. For instance, Figure 53.1 depicts a bolero warm-up in G major, a preparatory exercise for "Si nos dejan" in a soprano or alto vocalist's key. The following exercise is only a structural guide. There are countless ways teachers can adjust trumpet and violin rhythms, articulations, phrasing, and dynamics in varying keys while protecting the integrity of the rhythmic and harmonic framework. See 53.2 ("Ranchera"), 53.3 ("Ranchera valseada"), 53.4 ("Ranchera polqueada"), 53.5 ("*Son*"), and 53.6 ("Huapango") in the book's online resources for additional sample exercises.

FIGURE 53.1 Bolero warm-up in G major

PREPARING FOR A PERFORMANCE

Mariachi groups play in significantly different scenarios, and the context may influence song selection and how teachers and students prepare for a performance. Most familiar to school music groups is a presentational or stage performance (e.g., school assembly, civic event, community festival, concert, or competition), which provides an opportunity to showcase student artistry through a predesigned and performer-driven show. A participatory performance (e.g., festive gathering, serenade, funeral, or mass) allows audience members to actively engage by requesting songs and even performing with the mariachi.

Presentational Performance

Rehearsing for a concert or competition allows teachers and students the freedom to carefully craft a well-selected, cohesive, and tightly executed collection of songs. The teacher is responsible for addressing the fundamental aspects of instrumental performance (e.g., tone quality, intonation, articulation, rhythmic precision and tempo, note accuracy, and technique) and tending to the finer points of ensemble musicality (e.g., interpretation, style, balance, blending, phrasing, expression, and dynamics). In preparing for a stage performance, teachers and students would do well to:

- Balance the repertoire: Design a set list that presents a variety of musical styles. Create a pleasant flow by combining upbeat genres with slower, lyrical songs.
- Emphasize stage presence: A confident, charismatic, energetic, and uniform ensemble captivates audiences. Students should avoid negative gestures such as grimacing and slouching.
- Practice stage movement: Students will enhance their professionalism by practicing how to move throughout a sound-equipped stage and properly use instrumental and vocal microphones.
- Provide a stage plot: Diagrams help stage managers and sound engineers best prepare for a show. As illustrated in Figure 53.2, the typical configuration is an arc with the violins on the left, trumpets center, and rhythm guitars on the right. For proper microphone positioning, stands with boom arms may be used for all string instruments (Alonso, 2008, pp. 30–31).

FIGURE 53.2 Mariachi stage plot

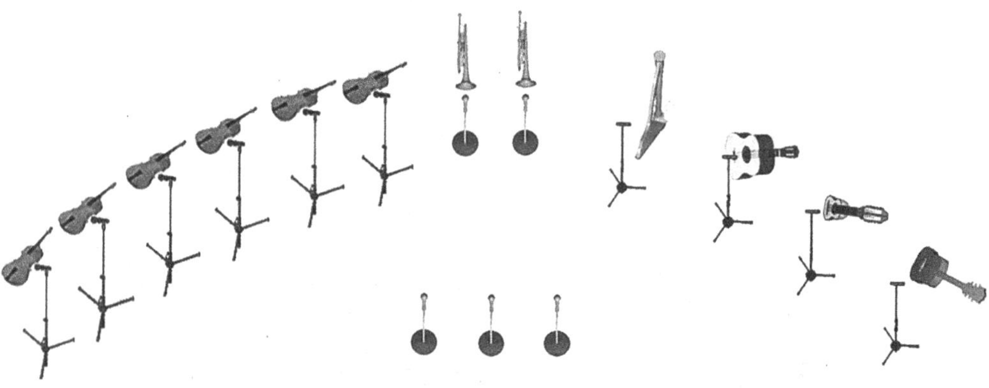

Participatory Performance

Student mariachi ensembles may perform in private engagements involving audience participation. The event host and other listeners will likely request songs and sometimes may even ask to sing. This dynamic poses a unique challenge to student mariachi musicians, who often do not have the skills or references to navigate within client-driven settings (Rodriguez, 2006). However, teachers may strategically prepare students by rehearsing music that clients may request based on the nature of the event (Alonso, 2008). For instance, a "Día de Las Madres" serenade will call for songs that fit the Mother's Day theme, while a "Día de La Virgen de Guadalupe," for a mass for the feast of the Virgin of Guadalupe, requires adherence to sacred music. Teachers and students should prioritize repertoire development over ensemble cohesiveness and invest less time polishing a few challenging songs and more time learning numerous standards.

- Celebratory events: Birthday parties and formal social occasions are only some of the many festive events where mariachis resonate. "Las mañanitas" and "En tu día" are birthday standards, while "Alejandra" is a waltz favorite for a *quinceañera*, a girl's formal fifteenth-birthday celebration.
- Serenatas: Romantic boleros and love-themed rancheras are most appropriate for courtship serenades. "Gema," "Hermoso cariño," and "Tres regalos" are among the many options.
- Masses: The *misa Panamericana* or mariachi mass is typical of Catholic weddings, baptisms, and quinceañeras. The ensemble accompanies religious service with liturgical songs such as "Señor Ten Piedad," "Cordero de Dios, and "Ave María."
- Funerals: Mariachis help people mourn the loss and celebrate the life of the dear departed. Context-appropriate music includes "Un día a la vez," "Te vas angel mio," and "Nadie es eterno" (Alonso, 2008, pp. 32–33).

53.5 Fostering Contextual Knowledge and Practical Skills

Mariacheros de todo conocimiento, which translates as "mariachi musicians with complete knowledge," understand the different spaces and the nuanced manners of transmission, practice, and performance (Rodriguez, 2006). Although nothing compares to the educational potential of experiential learning among a community of practitioners, teachers may cultivate students' *colmillo* ("chops") by drawing on hybrid approaches to develop contextual knowledge and practical skills inherent in mariachi music's multidimensional performance contexts.

NOMENCLATURE AND COLLOQUIALISMS

Mariachi musicians utilize a fixed-*do* solfège system to identify pitches, chords, and keys. The tonic, dominant seventh, and subdominant are identified as *primera*, *segunda*, and *tercera*, respectively. Musicians also use key and chord identifying terms such as *segunda de sol* for the dominant seventh of G major. *Circulo* references the I–vi–ii–V^7 chord progression, while a term such as *circulo de la* places the progression in a specific key, such as A minor. *De arriba* indicates the beginning of a piece, *al bajón* tells musicians to begin together by following a guiding gesture, *sale* signifies the end of a piece, and *de cajón* references the typical way of performing a passage or song in the oral tradition of mariachi.

MEMORIZATION AND ROTE LEARNING

Playing music by memory is integral to mariachi practice. Students should therefore strive to memorize songs and perform without sheet music. Teachers may cultivate students' memorization skills by integrating rote learning that draws on fixed-*do* solfège and mariachi terminology. By learning simple rancheras by ear, for example, students draw on mariachi practitioners' informal ways of knowing to enhance their musical intelligence.

Rote learning also involves selecting, listening to, copying, and performing mariachi music from audio and video platforms. YouTube is an invaluable source of music and educational resources. VihuelaTv and Taylor Fuentes are among the most popular channels offering mariachi instrumental tutorials.

ACCOMPANIMENT, IMPROVISATION, AND TRANSPOSITION

Mariachi performance spaces often require musicians to perform unfamiliar songs and accompany event participants, which sometimes entails improvisation and on-the-spot transposition to vocal range–appropriate keys. Proficiency in improvisation and transposition requires years of practice. However, students may begin to develop their abilities by referencing scale degrees and harmonic functions. *Salidas de cajón*, or standard endings, may serve as a springboard for students to develop their accompaniment, improvisation, and transposition skills (see Figure 53.3).

FIGURE 53.3 **Salida de cajón: Ranchera**

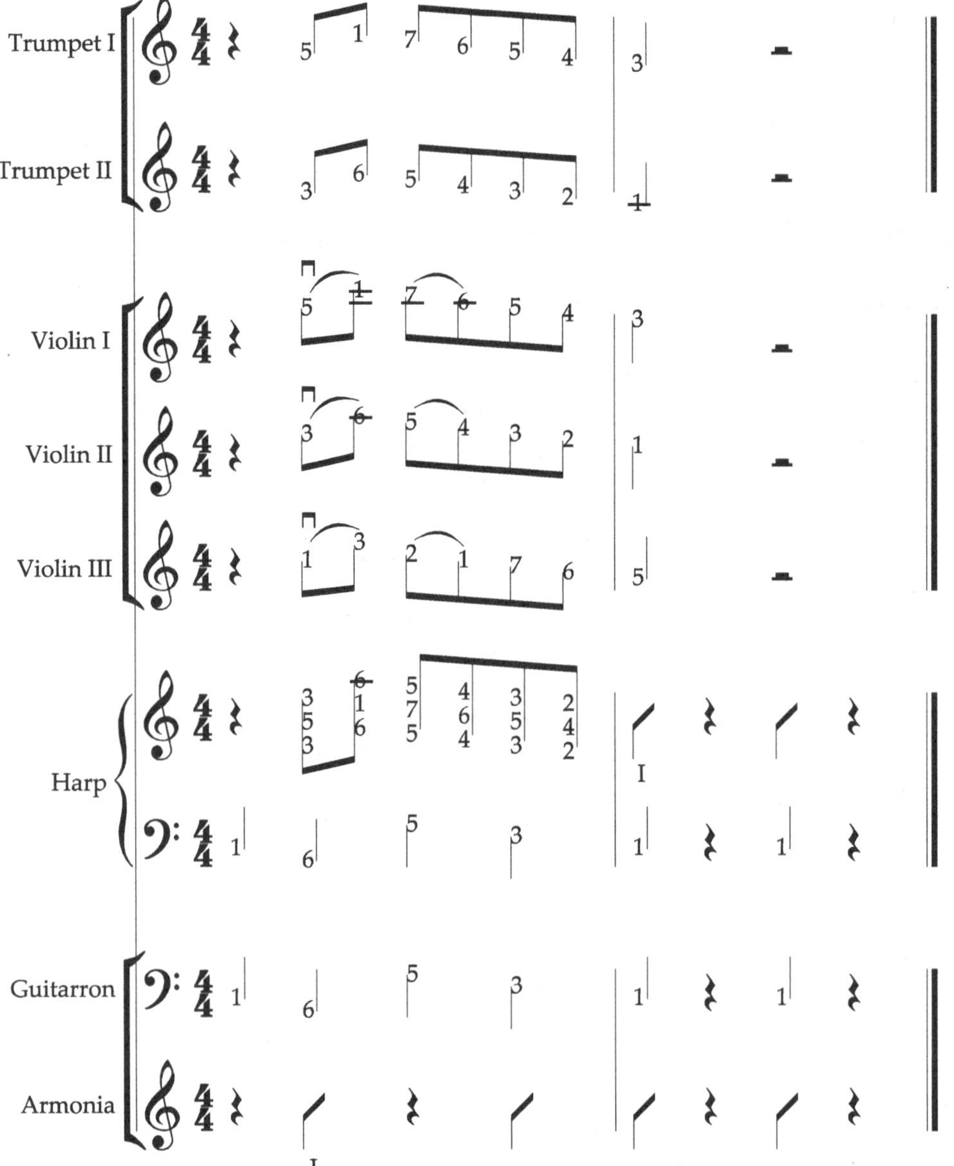

Ranchera music is the most popular among singing aficionados and ideal for practicing transposition. The transposition exercise presented in 53.8 of the online resources eliminates key and pitch references, replaces note heads with scale degrees, and substitutes Roman numerals for chord names. By unbinding the passage from specific keys, pitches, and chords, students rely on their prior knowledge of scales and chords, and begin to develop a deeper understanding of pitch and chordal relationships. Teachers may verbalize the scale degrees and practice this exercise in mariachi music's most employed major keys: C, G, D, A, E, F, and B♭. See 53.9, "Salida de cajón for an example of music notation that replaces note heads with scale degrees. See Ranchera valseada"; 53.10, "Salida de cajón: Ranchera polqueada"; 53.11, "Salida de cajón: Bolero"; 53.12, "Salida de cajón: *Son*"; and 53.13, "Salida de cajón: *Son*" in the online resources for additional exercises.

53.6 Conclusion

Mariachi rehearsal techniques strategically align with the kinds of performances students engage. Said another way, *what* and *how* students prepare largely depends on *where* they will play. Although assemblies, shows, and concerts at school or in the community will likely comprise the greater part of performance activities, students' music-making experiences may also include client-driven social gatherings. Teachers and students may work together to prepare for a lifetime of music making in diverse performance contexts by implementing formal and informal rehearsal techniques that foster technical and practical skills.

53.7 Discussion Questions

1. Reflect upon the types of mariachi genres that most speak to you, your family, and your community. What kind of mariachi music is your favorite and why?
2. Describe how mariachi music is similar to and different from other music you listen to in terms of instrumentation and performance contexts.
3. Comment on learning by note versus learning by rote. What are some advantages and limitations of learning songs through Western notation? What are some advantages and limitations of learning songs by ear?
4. Discuss how musical knowledge and performance context are interrelated. What kinds of knowledge and skills are necessary for presentational contexts? What kinds of knowledge and skills are necessary for participatory contexts?

OXFORD learning link

Visit the online resources for additional documentation and exercises to help expand learning and test your knowledge further: www.oup.com/he/powell_music1e.

CHAPTER 54

MUSICAL THEATRE PIT ORCHESTRA PREPARATION AND PERFORMANCE

Herbert Marshall

This chapter primarily focuses on instrumental music teachers' responsibilities for preparing and conducting a musical theatre pit orchestra.

54.1 Introduction

One of the culminating experiences for high school music and arts departments is the high school musical. Few activities integrate so many different performing, visual, and technical artists into one unified event. A key component to making live musical theatre a unique experience is live accompaniment by a pit orchestra. This is also an opportunity to collaborate with colleagues as well as to perform for thousands of community members. While there are unique challenges to producing musical theatre in high school, the potential for growth in your instrumentalists and refinement of your own rehearsal and conducting skills make this genre worth your time and energy.

54.2 Context

Typically, school productions are led by four colleagues: the producer, the director, the music director, and the choreographer. Because musical theatre productions are complicated and costly, it is best to involve a group of colleagues to share responsibilities. Often the music responsibilities are shared among three persons: the vocal coach, the pit orchestra coach, and the accompanist. Any of these individuals may end up conducting the performances. For the sake of this chapter, let us assume you have an excellent accompanist who can play for staging, choreography, and vocal rehearsals. Further, you have an excellent colleague who will coach all the vocal solos and ensemble singing, then turn the singers over to you when they begin to do entire scenes or acts on stage. Thus, this chapter will focus on your role as pit coach and conductor. Your responsibilities include:

1. Analyzing scores (and scripts) for consultation in selecting an appropriate work
2. Analyzing the chosen score to determine what the instrumentation should be, where the pit should be placed, and what amplification and mixing will be used

3. Deciding if any of the books are beyond what is developmentally appropriate for your students, meaning you need to hire a professional
4. Auditioning the pit players and setting up a rehearsal schedule
5. Minor arranging or orchestrating to account for slight changes in instrumentation
6. Rehearsing the pit orchestra
7. Gradually integrating the other elements (vocalists, actors, and dancers)
8. Setting up the pit's performance space and transitioning to this location
9. Incorporating elements of the orchestration into rehearsals, eventually providing full accompaniment to rehearse scenes and acts
10. Taking on more control of the show during tech week as all the other visual and technical elements are added
11. Conducting performances
12. Collecting rental materials to be returned and dismantling the pit

As we examine the skills and understandings that help make you an effective music director, let me be transparent about a few philosophical positions. You might not share them, but they guide how I approach musical theatre, and they will help explain why I am guiding you in this direction. First, I am a student-centered educator; the students' safety and success are most important to me. Second, in musical theatre all performers, artists, and technicians are in the service of telling a great story and communicating this to the audience—a unified, harmonious pursuit. Third, I prioritize live music making, including live rehearsal accompaniment, without the use of back tracks, enhancements, or recorded accompaniment in performance. I want live performing artists to be the backbone of what makes live theatre an exhilarating and engaging event for performers and audience.

54.3 Skills and Understandings

SCORE AND SCRIPT ANALYSIS

Offer to be part of the team that reads perusal copies of scripts and scores to choose the musical, a process that begins months before you announce a musical or set an audition date. Your producer may order perusal copies from the copyright holders (see the list later in the chapter for their websites). Make notes about the script in terms of the number of roles, the story, and the appropriateness of this material for your community. Note that it is not permissible to change language and situations from the copyrighted script. If there is not already a simplified high school version available, then the authors expect you to perform the play as they wrote it. There are hundreds to choose from, so pick one that is appropriate and educational for your community. Share your expertise with the show selection committee.

The score is almost always condensed, so you will have to intuit the orchestration based on the published list of orchestra books, the instrument indications in the score, what you hear on a good live stage recording, and your own musical instincts. Note that film adaptations of musicals often feature enhanced orchestration, so base your analysis on the Broadway cast album or as close as you can come to it. Analyze the score the same way you would a major work for your ensemble: instrumentation, range, tessitura, key signatures, rhythmic complexity, solos, and so forth. For pit orchestras, you need also consider doubling—particularly in the woodwind books, keyboard parts and what sounds they need to generate, and the complexity of the percussion book(s) and how many instruments they require. For most of the play, the pit accompaniment is supporting the singers. When you have extended pit music without singers or actors, however, it is the orchestra that will need to sustain all the musical and emotional energy, such as in large dance segments, full ballets, long scene changes, the overture, the entr'acte, and interludes. Your orchestra needs to be proficient enough to play these segments as a chamber ensemble.

Because you have read the script, you will note where specific instruments or sounds are mentioned as part of the story and if the pit is producing this sound. Sound effects like car horns and thunder are often recorded and produced by the sound technician. However, you cannot produce *Anything Goes* without an excellent trumpet soloist, *1776* without an excellent violinist, or *The Phantom of the Opera* without an impressive organ setting on your keyboard. And think of all the instruments Harold Hill names as he advocates for instrumental education in *The Music Man*. Ideally, they should all be in your orchestra.

TRY YOUR HAND AT MUSIC DIRECTION

Using the resources at your school or community library or from your theatre colleagues, assemble a script, score, and cast recording (audio or video) of a musical that might be produced in school or community theatre. Using your analytic and educator skills, determine:

1. Are there words or situations that would be problematic in your high school?
2. Copy the orchestration from the score or the theatrical licensing agency website. Using your knowledge of orchestration and your musicianship, determine an actual orchestration based on musical integrity and practical limitations of players, space, and time. Justify your choices.
3. Using your own state standards for what is developmentally appropriate for a high school instrumentalist—perhaps the criteria from a solo and ensemble list, aligning with what might be a level 5 or 6 on the New York State School Music Association list—determine which books would need to be played by yourself or another professional. In some cases, determine which books would need to be transposed for different instruments (an oboe book played by a clarinetist) or split (woodwind 1 split among a flutist, clarinetist, and alto saxophonist, and so forth).

AUDITIONS AND SCHEDULING

Building a pit orchestra should be a combination of invitation and audition. Most students will not know this repertoire or its level of difficulty, so the director should invite those who will benefit from this experience. Teaching students to audition, however, is valuable, and they will thoroughly learn some important passages before rehearsals begin. Your producer has the option to order the orchestra books as early as necessary (with a small fee added) so that you can prepare actual parts. Make a short audition packet that includes any solos, technical passages, and a variety of keys and styles from the score. This makes participation in the pit similar to the audition process actors go through and gives them a head start on difficult passages.

As part of the audition process, survey their availability for rehearsals. A typical schedule is two or three rehearsals a week, with at least one rehearsal being the full pit. Other rehearsals may be sectionals. You will need to coordinate with your colleagues regarding space and time constraints. The production team determines major rehearsals before tech week when they are running major scenes or acts and when it is time to integrate the pit into the rehearsal. Make sure all your pit musicians are available for these essential rehearsals, tech week, and all performances. If you create a culture of community within the pit and the overall production company, students will be eager to spend time on this endeavor and connect with their peers. A common theme in research involving musical theatre participation is the sense of community it engenders and the strong familial ties that develop among participants (Ryan, 2014; Ogden, 2008; Van Houten, 1999).

TRY YOUR HAND AT MUSIC DIRECTION

Take an existing audition rating scale you have used and adapt it for pit orchestra.

Using the score and recording you analyzed before or a new one from a contrasting style or time period, create audition packets for one player from each of three to five instrument groups: woodwind, brass, percussion, strings/guitar/harp, and keyboard. In each packet, include two short, contrasting excerpts and relevant technique exercises. You probably do not have access to actual orchestral books, so you will need to transpose from the condensed piano/vocal score. If, however, your school or community theatre owns some orchestra books from an operetta, opera, or oratorio, you could use them for this project.

ARRANGING AND ORCHESTRATION

Chapter 15 has more detail on this subject, but my remarks here are specific to musical theatre. Musical theatre has many examples of short chorales, hymns, and ballads that lend themselves well to trying your hand at arranging for instruments with voices. Examples include "Public Enemy Number One" from *Anything Goes*, "My Funny Valentine" from *Babes in Arms*, "Once in the Highlands" and "Brigadoon" from *Brigadoon*, "Hymn for a Sunday Evening" from *Bye Bye Birdie*, "Chess Hymn" from *Chess*, "Only Us" from *Dear Evan Hansen*, "Anatevka" from *Fiddler on the Roof*, "More I Cannot Wish You" from *Guys and Dolls*, "Ribbons Down My Back" from *Hello, Dolly!*, "Atención" from *In the Heights*, "Dear One" from *Kiss of the Spider Woman*, "One by One" from Disney's *The Lion King*, "Feed the Birds" from *Mary Poppins*, "Hills of Tomorrow" from *Merrily We Roll Along*, "Tender Shepherd" from *Peter Pan*, "Hail Poetry" from *The Pirates of Penzance*, "Mis'ry's Comin' Around/When I Die Let Me Rest" from *Show Boat*, "Edelweiss" from *The Sound of Music*, and "She Used to be Mine" from *Waitress*.

TRY YOUR HAND AT MUSIC DIRECTION

1. Musical theatre has benefited from the talents of some great orchestrators, such as Robert Russell Bennett. Listen to his concert works such as *Suite of Old American Dances*, *Carol Cantatas I–IV*, *Symphonic Songs for Band*, and *String Quartet* (1956). Compare these to some of his famous Broadway orchestrations: *Oklahoma!*, *Girl Crazy*, and *The Sound of Music*. Many see him as the person who established the sound and style of classic-era Broadway musicals, winning two Tony awards, an Oscar, and an Emmy along the way.

2. Arrange a section of one of the pieces listed above or something of your own choosing for voice(s) and instruments. Consider the importance of the voice in telling the story, literally, and the role of the instrumental accompaniment to provide support, tone, and mood to help convey meaning. You might arrange for a classic rhythm section of piano, bass, and percussion, a string quartet, a woodwind quintet, or the complete Broadway chamber orchestra, which is over twenty players for the larger theatres (Pogrebin, 2003).

COORDINATION WITH THE VOCAL COACH, CHOREOGRAPHER, AND DIRECTOR

As with any complex project, communication is essential. As rehearsals progress, minor changes and adjustments are made. The worst waste of time for directors and cast is to work out these changes during tech week, when everyone is focused on the first performance. To avoid this, be in constant communication with your colleagues for updates—at least once a week. The vocal coach may need tempo adjustments, phrasing changes, or a starting pitch for a tricky entrance. The choreographer may need to know more about the percussion book to incorporate movements that mirror accents or may need you to repeat a vamp or be aware of a visual cue to start a section. The director may need more or less scene-change music, want to cut a verse in a reprise, or need to find specific spots in the overture or entr'acte for curtain cues. In your script and your score you will make many marks (or use sticky notes) to keep track of these adjustments.

REHEARSING THE PIT ORCHESTRA

The rehearsal process is not that different from your preparation for rehearsing other small ensembles, but there are a few unique elements.

- Most musicals are about three hours of performance featuring about one hour of music. Think about your timeline for preparing a one-hour concert program and you will know the time and effort required.
- There are a handful of pieces in which you are mostly autonomous, such as the overture, entr'acte, bows, exit music, and some short interludes and scene-change music. For everything else, you are in support of the vocalists, dancers, or actors. However, the music director is usually the only member of the production team who is performing the show *live* with the cast and crew. Thus, it is helpful for you to have a fundamental knowledge of the whole show to support the company.
- In your score analysis, note when material is revisited. This can come in the form of a literal reprise with new verses or a main melody used for scene-change music or to prepare the audience for something that is about to happen. Sometimes the scene-change music is an entirely different tune but is used several times. Typically, the material for the overture, entr'acte, bows, and exit music includes the essential tunes from the show, reorchestrated so that the instrumentalists have the melody *and* accompaniment.
- Given this practice of recapitulation, you do not need to rehearse the book from beginning to end. You can start with the hardest pieces or the pieces that return the most. Once a theme is learned, rehearsing its reprise is easy. Pieces with difficult techniques, rhythms, and keys require more time for players to build confidence.

Balance your rehearsals with difficult and accessible pieces, new numbers to tackle, and familiar numbers to refine. Do remember to rehearse the show in order eventually so that doublers, percussionists, and keyboard players can practice all the physical and technical adjustments they will make from piece to piece.

- Keyboard and vocal skills are helpful in rehearsing the pit. An acoustic piano is not a timbre used in most orchestrations, but it is one we are accustomed to for rehearsals. If you can play from the condensed score while you are rehearsing, that will help drive the musicians and fill in parts they will hear in the finished product. Please sing, especially the introductions, recitatives, and ballads, so the instrumentalists will learn to phrase with the vocalists and listen for specific word cues. Some orchestrators double the vocal line with an instrument. If the vocalist is confident, it is fine to have the players tacit for some or all of the vocal solos (or even play something else).
- Most Broadway musical recordings (and some live productions) are available online. It is helpful for the instrumentalists to listen to these to get a sense of context for the end result. Either curate a listening list yourself or remind them that some numbers may be transposed, and the film versions of musicals are often different from the stage version of musicals.

TRY YOUR HAND AT MUSIC DIRECTION

Musical theatre is an opportunity for instrumentalists to try expressive and extended techniques. Thus, it is a broadening experience for them and a teachable moment for you. Brass players will use different types of mutes, as well as double tonguing, growls, raspberries, and other effects. String players will use mutes and different bowings, articulations, and bow placements to achieve different effects. You may also need to mic them, which is often a new experience in high school. Percussionists will often have a huge array of instruments, some of which will be new to them. Consider investing in electronic percussion to let your percussionists explore this technology—it is an advantage in a pit because it is versatile and takes up less space. Guitarists may be asked to bring numerous instruments and special effects technology and to learn different styles. A complicated show like *Shrek the Musical* will challenge any young guitarist. Woodwind players will have technically demanding parts, but the greater challenge for young players is doubling. The classic Broadway era's jazz-oriented composers were used to big-band woodwind players. Within the five woodwind books, players were expected to play piccolo, flute, alto flute, recorder, oboe, clarinet, bass clarinet, English horn, bassoon, and soprano, alto, tenor, and baritone saxophones. If you have a jazz ensemble that uses doubling, this will be a wonderful extension for them. For those who want to learn to double, start early—perhaps the summer before. Others may prefer to transpose, which will not be the right timbre but will still allow an oboe part to be played by clarinet, or a bassoon part to be played by baritone saxophone. As a last resort, order three copies of the woodwind 1 book and give them to a flutist, a clarinetist, and a saxophonist to split.

As a music educator, every opportunity to expose your students to new genres and advanced techniques makes them more versatile players and may lead to a career playing in theatre. Consider the aforementioned techniques and equipment. For your own instrument family, put together a guide for what an intermediate or advanced player needs to know or acquire to perform effectively using a variety of extended techniques. Share this guide with your peers.

INTEGRATING THE ELEMENTS OF INSTRUMENTAL MUSIC, VOCAL MUSIC, DRAMA, AND MOVEMENT

There is efficiency and safety in rehearsing the elements separately. The longer you stay separate, however, the harder it is to coalesce to tell a story in a unified, purposeful way. As the pit musicians become confident on pieces, start to invite vocalists or dancers into your space to try things together. Take your score and sit behind the accompanists in the voice, movement, or acting rehearsals and start to mark interpretation and style choices, note how many times vamps are played, and notice how dialogue transitions in and out of musical numbers. All of this helps you be prepared to collaborate.

Depending on the score, it is not necessary to integrate the entire pit into the cast rehearsals all at once. For many shows, just adding the percussion and bassist to your regular rehearsal accompanist is a great way to gradually introduce more timbres and texture to what the actors are hearing. In addition, percussionists often have sound effects that need to be timed with specific words or actions, so they will need extra rehearsal time. Next, add important solo strings or winds that must coordinate with vocalists for balance, phrasing, and timing. In this manner you can gradually build the orchestra without overwhelming the cast and wasting some of the players' time. It is also valuable for the pit musicians to watch a rehearsal on stage. They should come with a music stand and their book and see how their parts fit with the overall story and action, which will greatly inform their playing and help them understand the overall context of the production.

A sitzprobe is a term (borrowed from opera) for a rehearsal that integrates the instrumental and vocal elements, normally without staging or movement. It can be done with the orchestra in the pit and the cast, seated, on the stage. But it is usually the last rehearsal I do before moving the orchestra into the pit, and it means an entire day off the stage for the crew to finish set installation. I use the largest rehearsal room I can find and place the orchestra and cast in such a way that the cast can see who and what are making the sounds and who they need to listen to in order to hear pitches or improve rhythmic accuracy. Typically everyone is seated, but I have the vocalists stand while singing.

I highly recommend this kind of rehearsal to you as a chance to refine all the musical interpretations, a rehearsal for the vocalists to concentrate on beautiful singing without the added dimensions of blocking and choreography, and for community building among musical performers. You might structure the rehearsal to go straight through the show, leaving out some long instrumental numbers, or you might structure the rehearsal to go from the largest numbers to the smallest, so that ensemble vocalists and supporting leads can leave once their responsibilities are done. Either way, this should be an opportunity for high-level music making and a celebration of all the progress that has been made.

TRY YOUR HAND AT MUSIC DIRECTION

Using the score and recording you analyzed before or a new one from a contrasting style or time period, create a sitzprobe master seating plan for orchestra and vocalists in a large, flat room. Analyze two or three large ensemble numbers to note which instruments double which voice parts. Guide the vocalists and instrumentalists to know where to listen to be in sync with their colleagues, including helping them with any octave transpositions. You can even have people move to be physically near each other while they perform. When the actors are on stage, the pit is typically out of sight or invisible because of the blinding lighting. The actors need to be able to *see* the conductor and *hear* the instruments clearly in order to perform their best. This rehearsal is probably your only opportunity to teach this important strategy.

FROM TECH WEEK TO MAILING BACK THE BOOKS

During tech week, all the technical elements come together to bring the production to life. These include lighting and sound, costumes, scenery, props, special effects, makeup, and so forth. Much of the show's pace and sequence depends on you, the conductor. You can also mouth words to singers or prompt a nervous actor with a line from the script. Rarely is there supposed to be silence in a live musical. Thus, either you should be playing, or you might prepare something extra or improvised to play during an unexpected brief delay. If there is a disaster, like a fire alarm, injury, or mechanical failure, you or the stage manager will be the person to stop the show, bring down the curtain, and solve the problem. I always conduct the show from a score with *many* instructions in it, as well as having a stand beside me with the complete script, which has even *more* instructions.

If you have not yet explained some basic signals to your orchestra, particularly for vamping, now is the time. They need to know a signal to keep "repeating" (usually your index finger tracing a circle in the air) and the signal for "last time" (usually a closed fist). These you will do with your non-conducting hand (Marshall, 2016). Players need to memorize vamps so that they can watch and pick up on last-minute instructions to repeat or go on. You may need other signals, such as numbers for different pieces or sections of a piece, and so forth.

There may be cuts or additions to the orchestra books. It is very disruptive for players to manage everything they are playing as well as read scribbles and arrows. Thus, you should make these cuts as minimal and simple as possible. Keep a spreadsheet of all the changes and give it to the players so that they can make the markings. Date the handouts so that they are using the latest version. At least one licensing agency is currently sending out inexpensive copies of orchestra books that you do not have to erase, as they are all recycled when you return them. For most shows, the books must be treated with care until returned, and you pay a hefty fine if a book is damaged or lost. Therefore, impress upon the players to write lightly in pencil and use sticky notes, all evidence of which they must remove before they return the book back to you.

Setting up the pit is building- and play-specific, so it will suffice to say that it is crucial that you be able to see and communicate with all instrumentalists and the entire stage, and that they all be able to see you—at least from the bottom of your conducting plane to your forehead. Given space constraints, seat the instruments with some attention to how directional instruments will project. If your hall is very live, you may want the brass to project perpendicular to the stage rather than out at the audience. If the floor is hard, consider putting carpet remnants or moving blankets under the brass and percussion. Finally, consider the sight lines of the audience so that you are not blocking anyone's view of the stage and neither are other standing musicians (bassists) or tall instruments (bass, tuba, harp, and chimes). To avoid being a distraction, the pit orchestra dresses in black and turns off their phones.

TRY YOUR HAND AT MUSIC DIRECTION

As a collegiate musician, you are very valuable to reinforce high school and community musicians in pit orchestras, accompany a rehearsal, be an assistant vocal coach, help with choreography, or assist with the many technical aspects of a production. The best way to learn about being a music director and about musical theatre in general is to volunteer your time to work on a production. You will learn new repertoire, hone your skills, and make a significant contribution to a worthwhile endeavor. They are not likely to come seek you out, so reach out to a theatre company near you and contribute your time and talents!

Your most important assets for tech week and performances are your musicianship and your understanding of the score and script. There are, however, other tools that may be useful. For making adjustments to the books, have soft pencils, soft erasers, sticky notes, paper clips, and staff paper. Try to keep food out of the pit area, allowing only water to hydrate. Bring some extra valve oil, reeds, strings, and tools. Assuming you are using stand lights, you will need extra bulbs and a complex network of extension cords and power strips. A flashlight might come in handy if the lighting blows all the circuit breakers and the building is plunged into darkness.

Despite those allusions to disaster, the moments I spent conducting high school musicals were some of my most cherished memories. By the middle of tech week, the student-centered conductor will accept what the production has achieved and help students recognize and celebrate how far they have come—all of the students. These include the ninth-grader pulling the curtain, the quiet senior mending costumes, the novice tapper, the newly changed baritone, the harried stage manager, the leads, and your hard-working orchestra! You are their most discerning audience, as you have seen the show from the first read-through; you know what is *supposed* to happen; and you have seen every tech rehearsal and performance. By helping them be aware of their growth, you help them be confident to share this story with an audience and be proud of their achievements. This cast, this orchestra, this show, are ethereal and will vanish when the final curtain comes down, but the way they feel about their time together in the production will propel them to new and exciting experiences in the arts.

54.4 Discussion Questions

1. What is it about musical theatre that is compelling or annoying to you?
2. Do you recall the vocalists and instrumentalists being aligned or being in competition?
3. Does it change your approach and interpretation when you are essentially an accompaniment ensemble and your music is programmatic?
4. What are the mentoring opportunities for your students if you hire a few essential specialists to play alongside them in the pit?
5. What are some of the unique recruiting and community connections possible through musical theatre?

54.5 Resources

As of 2023 there are three major theatrical licensing agencies. Other than very early musicals and operetta—that are in the public domain and can be performed without paying royalties—most plays produced in grade 6–12 school and community settings are licensed through these agencies. They have extensive websites and resources and are constantly adding to their catalogs.

Concord Theatricals: https://www.concordtheatricals.com/
Music Theatre International: https://www.mtishows.com/

Theatrical Rights Worldwide: https://www.theatricalrights.com/

For updates on licensing rights, additional companies, and other musical information, refer to the website https://www.musicals101.com/ curated by historian John Kenrick.

For a more thorough examination of music direction, including vocal preparation, timelines, templates, warm-ups, vignettes, and marking examples, see Marshall (2016).

OXFORD learning link

Visit the online resources for additional documentation and exercises to help expand learning and test your knowledge further: www.oup.com/he/powell_music1e.

BIBLIOGRAPHY

Introduction

Bruner, J. S. (1960). *The process of education.* Harvard University Press.

Colwell, R. (1969). *The teaching of instrumental music.* Appleton Century Crofts.

Dewey, J. (2013). *The school and society and The child and the curriculum.* University of Chicago Press.

Grunow, R., Gordon, E., & Azzara, C. D. (2001). *Jump right in: The instrumental series teacher's guide.* GIA Publications.

Vygotsky, L. S. (1966). Genesis of the higher mental functions. Abridged translation. In P. H. Light, S. Sheldon, & M. Woodhead (Eds.) (1991), *Learning to think,* 32–41. Routledge and Open University Press.

Vygotsky, L. S. (1978). *Mind in society: The development of higher psychological processes.* Harvard University Press.

Chapter 1

Bakker, A. B. (2005). Flow among music teachers and their students: The crossover of peak experiences. *Journal of Vocational Behavior, 66,* 26–44.

Bruner, J. S. (1960). *The process of education.* Harvard University Press.

Conway, C. M. (2019). *Teaching private lessons: A manual for teachers.* Conway Publications.

Csikszentmihalyi, M. (2008). *Flow: The psychology of optimal experience.* New York: Harper Perennial Modern Classics.

Custodero, L. A. (2002). Seeking challenge, finding skill: Flow experience and music education. *Arts Education Policy Review, 103*(3), 3–9.

Dewey, J. (2013). *The school and society and The child and the curriculum.* University of Chicago Press.

Evelein, F. G., & Korthagen, F. A. (2015). *Practicing core reflection: Activities and lessons for teaching and learning from within.* New York: Routledge.

Gillespie, R. (2003). Repertoire-based warm-ups. In D. Littrell (Ed.), *Teaching music through performance in orchestra,* vol. 2 (47–67). GIA Publications.

Gordon, E. E. (1971). *The psychology of music teaching.* Englewood Cliffs, NJ: Prentice-Hall.

Gordon, E. E. (1999). All about audiation and music aptitudes: Edwin E. Gordon discusses using audiation and music aptitudes as teaching tools to allow students to reach their full music potential. *Music Educators Journal, 86*(2), 41–44.

Johnston, H. (2012). The Spiral Curriculum. Research into Practice. *Education Partnerships, Inc.* https://files.eric.ed.gov/fulltext/ED538282.pdf.

Millican, J. S., & Forrester, S. H. (2018). Core practices in music teaching: A Delphi expert panel survey. *Journal of Music Teacher Education, 27*(3), 51–64.

Millican, J. S., & Forrester, S. H. (2019). Music teacher rankings of selected core teaching practices. *Journal of Music Teacher Education, 29*(1), 86–99. https://doi.org/10.1177/1057083719867682

Pestalozzi, J. H. (2012). *How Gertrude teaches her children.* Hardpress Publishing.

Raiber, M., & Teachout, D. (2014). *The journey from music student to teacher: A professional approach.* Routledge.

Ritter, F. L. (1884). *Music in England and music in America,* vol. 2. Reeves' Music Publications.

Suzuki, S. I. (1983). *Nurtured by love: The classic approach to talent education* (W. Suzuki, Trans.). Warner Bros. Publications. (Original work published 1969.)

West, C. (2015). Developing internal musicianship in beginning band by teaching the "Big 5." *Music Educators Journal, 101*(3), 101–106.

West, C. (2016). Sound foundations: Organic approaches to learning notation in beginning band. *Music Educators Journal, 102*(4), 56–61.

Chapter 2

Abu-Khader, S. (2019). *Musical bridges—Crossing the divide of where fear meets music: How autoethnography contributes to an evolving cultural identity through multiple musical worlds.* Ph.D. diss., University of Toronto (Canada). ProQuest Dissertations and Theses Global, Publication No. 2316054434.

Bandura, A. (1977). *Social learning theory.* General Learning Press.

Castañeda Lechuga, C., & Schmidt, M. E. (2017). Cultural straddling: The double life of a Mariachi music education major. In B. C. Talbot (Ed.), *Marginalized voices in music education* (pp. 80–98). Routledge.

Darling-Hammond, L., & Bransford, J. (eds.) (2007). *Preparing teachers for a changing world: What teachers should learn and be able to do.* John Wiley & Sons, Inc.

Day, C., & Gu, Q. (2010). *The new lives of teachers.* Routledge.

Day, C., Kington, A., Stobart, G., & Sammons, P. (2006). The personal and professional selves of teachers: Stable and unstable identities. *British Educational Research Journal, 32*(4), 601–616.

Evelein, F. G., & Korthagen, F. A. (2014). *Practicing core reflection: Activities and lessons for teaching and learning from within.* Routledge.

Ferguson, K. (2003). Becoming a string teacher. *Bulletin of the Council for Research in Music Education, 157,* 38–48.

Garrett, M. L., & Palkki, G. (2021). *Honoring trans and gender-expansive students in music education.* Oxford University Press.

Haston, W., & Russell, J. A. (2012). Turning into teachers: Influences of authentic context learning experiences on occupational identity development of preservice music teachers. *Journal of Research in Music Education, 59*(4), 369–392. doi.org/10.1177/0022429411414716

Hibbard, S. L. (2017). *Music teacher presence: Toward a relational understanding.* Ph.D. diss., University of Michigan. ProQuest Dissertations and Theses Global, Publication No. 10760119.

Korthagen, F. A. J. (2004). In search of the essence of a good teacher: Towards a more holistic approach in teacher education. *Teaching and Teacher Education, 20*(1), 77–97.

Korthagen, F. A. J., & Nuijten, E. (2022). *The power of reflection in teacher education and professional development: Strategies for in-depth teacher learning.* Routledge.

Lakoff, G., & Johnson, M. (1980). *Metaphors we live by.* University of Chicago Press.

Meijer, P. C., Korthagen, F. A. J., & Vasalos, A. (2009). Supporting presence in teacher education: The connection between the personal and professional aspects of teaching. *Teaching and Teacher Education, 25,* 297–308.

Millican, S., & Pellegrino, K. (2015). Curriculum and assessment in preservice music teacher education. In C. M. Conway (Ed.), *Musicianship-focused curriculum and assessment* (pp. 457–485). GIA Publications.

Millican, J. S., & Pellegrino, K. (2017). Band and orchestra teachers' instrument playing inside and outside the classroom. *Bulletin of the Council for Research in Music Education, 214,* 19–40. https://doi.org/10.5406/bulcouresmusedu.214.0019

Olsen, B. (2008). How reasons for entry into the profession illuminate teacher identity development. *Teacher Education Quarterly, 35*(3), 23–40.

Palkki, J. (2015a). "Negotiating the closet door": The lived experiences of two gay music teachers. *Visions of Research in Music Education, 26.* http://www-usr.rider.edu/~vrme/v26n1/visions/Palkki_Negotiating_Closet_Door.pdf

Palkki, J. (2015b). "If it fits into their culture, then they will have a connection": Experiences of two Latina students in a select high school choir. *Research & Issues in Music Education, 12*(1), article 5. http://ir.stthomas.edu/rime/vol12/iss1/5

Palmer, P. J. (2017). *The courage to teach: Exploring the inner landscape of a teacher's life.* John Wiley & Sons.

Parkes, K. A. (2015, February). Teacher-efficacy: The importance of developing teacher identity in pre-service music teachers. Paper presented at the Texas Music Educators Association's 2015 Annual Convention, San Antonio, TX.

Paul, S. J., Teachout, D. J., Sullivan, J. M., Kelly, S. N., Bauer, W. I., & Raiber, M. A. (2001). Authentic-context learning activities in instrumental music teacher education. *Journal of Research in Music Education, 49,* 136–145.

Pellegrino, K. (2011). Exploring the benefits of music-making as professional development for music teachers. *Arts Education Policy Review, 112*(2), 79–88. https://doi.org/10.1080/10632913.2011.546694

Pellegrino, K. (2014). Examining the intersections of music making and teaching for four string teachers. *Journal of Research in Music Education, 62*(2), 128–147. https://doi.org/10.1177/0022429414530433

Pellegrino, K. (2015). Becoming music-making music teachers: Connecting music making, identity, well-being, and teaching for four student teachers. *Research Studies in Music Education, 37*(2), 175–194. https://doi.org/10.1177/1321103X15589336

Pellegrino, K. (2019a). Becoming music teachers in a supportive String Project community. *Journal of Music Teacher Education, 28*(3), 11–27. https://doi.org/10.1177/1057083718803638

Pellegrino, K. (2019b). Music teacher identity development. In C. M. Conway, K. Pellegrino, A. M. Stanley, & C. West (Eds.), *The Oxford handbook of preservice music teacher education in the USA* (pp. 269–293). Oxford University Press.

Pellegrino, K., Johnson, E., Wagoner, C. L., & Powell, S. R. (2021). Music teacher resilience: Identity transitions during the early years of teaching. In P. M. Jenlink (Ed.), *Understanding teacher identity: The complexities of professional identity as teacher* (pp. 163–186). Rowman & Littlefield.

Pellegrino, K., & Russell, J. A. (2015). String teachers' practices and attitudes regarding their primary string instrument in settings inside and outside the classroom. *Bulletin of the Council for Research in Music Education, 204,* 9–26. https://doi.org/10.5406/bulcouresmusedu.204.0009

Raiber, M., & Teachout, D. (2014). *The journey from music student to teacher: A professional approach.* Routledge.

Rodgers, C. R., & Raider-Roth, M. B. (2006). Presence in teaching. *Teachers and Teaching, 12*(3), 265–287.

Sammons, P., Day, C. W, Kington, A., Gu, Q., Stobart, G., & Smees, R. (2007). Exploring variations in teachers' work, lives, and their effects on pupils: Key findings and implications from a longitudinal mixed methods study. *British Educational Research Journal, 33*(5), 681–701.

Schmidt, M. (2005). String teachers' lesson-planning processes: An exploratory study. *Journal of Research in Music Education, 53,* 6–25. doi:10.1177/002242940505300102

Schmidt, M. (2010). Learning from teaching experience: Dewey's theory and preservice teachers' learning. *Journal of Research in Music Education, 58*, 131–146.

Taylor, D. M., Talbot, B. C., Holmes, E. J., & Petrie, T. (2020). Experiences of LGBTQ+ students in music education programs across Texas. *Journal of Music Teacher Education, 30*(1), 11–23. https://doi.org/10.1177/1057083720935610

Talbot, B. (Ed.). (2017). *Marginalized voices in music education*. New York, NY: Routledge.

Wagoner, C. L. (2021). Preservice music teacher identity construction through metaphor. *Journal of Music Teacher Education, 30*(2), 24–36. doi.org/10.1177/1057083720982278

Wenger, E. (1998). Communities of practice: Learning, meaning, and identity. Cambridge University Press. https://doi.org/10.1017/CBO9780511803932

Chapter 3

Austin, J. R., & Berg, M. H. (2006). Exploring music practice among sixth-grade band and orchestra students. *Psychology of Music, 34*, 535–558.

Bandura, A. (1977). *Social learning theory*. General Learning Press, New York.

Bruner, J. S. (1960). *The process of education*. Harvard University Press.

Burnette, J. L., Russell, M. V., Hoyt, C. L., Orvidas, K., & Widman, L. (2018). An online growth mindset intervention in a sample of rural adolescent girls. *British Journal of Educational Psychology, 88*, 428–445. doi: 10.1111/bjep.12192

Conway, C. (2003). Good rhythm and intonation from day one in beginning instrumental music. *Music Educators Journal, 89*(5), 26–31.

Culver, R. (1989). *The master teacher profile: Elements of delivery at work in the classroom*. Madison: University of Wisconsin-Madison Division of University Outreach.

Darling-Hammond, L., & Bransford, J. (2007). Preparing teachers for a changing world: What teachers should learn and be able to do. Hoboken, NJ: John Wiley.

Dewey, J. (2013). *The school and society and the child and the curriculum*. University of Chicago Press.

Dweck, C. S. (2008). *Mindset: The new psychology of success*. Ballantine Books.

Edgar, S. N. (2013). Introducing social emotional learning to music education professional development. *Update: Applications of Research in Music Education, 31*(2), 28–36.

Edgar, S. N. (2017). *Music education and social emotional learning: The heart of teaching music*. GIA Publications.

Goldstein, T. R., Lerner, M. D., & Winner, E. (2017). The arts as a venue for developmental science: Realizing a latent opportunity. *Child Development, 88*, 1505–1512. doi: 10.1111/cdev.12884

Hallam, S., Rinta, T., Varvarigou, M., Creech, A., Papageorgi, I., Gomes, T., & Lanipekun, J. (2012). The development of practising strategies in young people. *Psychology of Music, 40*(5), 652–680.

Hargreaves, D. J., MacDonald, R., Miell, D., McPherson, G. E., & Welch, G. F. (2018). Musical identities mediate musical development. *Music and music education in people's lives: An Oxford handbook of music education* (vol. 1), pp. 124–142. Oxford University Press.

Holochwost, S. J., Bose, J. H., Stuk, E., Brown, E. D., Anderson, K. E., & Wolf, D. P. (2021). Planting the seeds: Orchestral music education as a context for fostering growth mindsets. *Frontiers in Psychology, 11*. https://doi.org/10.3389/fpsyg.2020.586749

Lakoff, G., & Johnson, M. (1980). *Metaphors we live by*. Chicago: University of Chicago Press.

McLeod, S. A. (2019, July 11). *Bruner—Learning theory in education*. Simply Psychology. https://www.simplypsychology.org/bruner.html

Miksza, P. (2007). Effective practice an investigation of observed practice behaviors, self-reported practice habits, and the performance achievement of high school wind players. *Journal of Research in Music Education, 55*(4), 359–375.

Millican, J. S., & Forrester, S. H. (2018). Core practices in music teaching: A Delphi expert panel survey. *Journal of Music Teacher Education, 27*(3), 51–64.

Millican, S., & Pellegrino, K. (2015). Curriculum and assessment in preservice music teacher education. In C. M. Conway (Ed.), *Musicianship-focused curriculum and assessment* (pp. 457–485). GIA Publications.

Oare, S. (2012). Decisions made in the practice room: a qualitative study of middle school students' thought processes while practicing. *Update: Applications of Research in Music Education, 30*(2), 63–70.

Rohwer, D., & Polk, J. (2006). Practice behaviors of eighth-grade instrumental musicians. *Journal of Research in Music Education, 54*(4), 350–362.

Stapleton, L., & Stefaniak, J. (2019). Cognitive constructivism: Revisiting Jerome Bruner's influence on instructional design practices. *TechTrends, 63*, 4–5. https://doi.org/10.1007/s11528-018-0356-8

Smith, F. (1998). *The book of learning and forgetting*. Teachers College Press.

Tan, J., Yap, K., & Bhattacharya, J. (2021). What does it take to flow? Investigating links between grit, growth mindset, and flow in musicians. *Music & Science, 4*. https://doi.org/10.1177/2059204321989529

Tharp, R. G., & Gallimore, R. (1991). *Rousing minds to life: Teaching, learning, and schooling in social context*. Cambridge University Press.

Thompson, I. (2013). The mediation of learning in the Zone of Proximal Development through a co-constructed writing activity. *Research in the Teaching of English*, https://www.researchgate.net/publication/264337590

Vygotsky, L. S. (1978). *Mind in society: The development of higher psychological processes*. Harvard University Press.

Vygotsky, L. S. (1986). *Thought and language* (rev. ed.). MIT Press.

Vygotsky, L. S. (1991). Genesis of the higher mental functions (abridged trans.). In P. H. Light, S. Sheldon, & M. Woodhead (Eds.), *Learning to think*, pp. 32–41. Routledge and Open University Press. (Essay originally published in 1966.)

West, C. (2015). Developing internal musicianship in beginning band by teaching the "Big 5." *Music Educators Journal, 101*(3), 101–106.

West, C. (2016). Sound foundations: Organic approaches to learning notation in beginning band. *Music Educators Journal, 102*(4), 56–61.

Reese, J. (2007). The four Cs of successful classroom management. *Music Educators Journal, 94*(1), 24–29.

Regier, B. J. (2021). Preservice music teachers' self-efficacy and concerns before and during student teaching. *International Journal of Music Education, 39*(3), 340–352. https://doi.org/10.1177/0255761421990787

Chapter 4

Berg, M. H., & Miksza, P. (2010). An investigation of preservice music teacher development and concerns. *Journal of Music Teacher Education, 20*(1), 39–55.

Csikszentmihalyi, M. (2008). *Flow: The psychological of optimal experience.* Harper Perennial Modern Classics

Culver, R. (1989). The master teacher profile: Elements of delivery at work in the classroom. University of Wisconsin–Madison Division of University Outreach.

Ginott, H. G. (1965). *Between parent and child: New solutions to old problems.* Macmillan.

Hilliard, Q. (2005). *Superior bands in sixteen weeks.* FJH Music.

Pellegrino, K. (2010). *The meanings and values of music-making in the lives of string teachers: Exploring the intersections of music-making and teaching.* Ph.D. diss., University of Michigan. ProQuest Dissertations and Theses Global, Publication No. AAT3429263.

Pellegrino, K. (2011). Exploring the benefits of music-making as professional development for music teachers. *Arts Education Policy Review, 112*(2), 79–88. https://doi.org/10.1080/10632913.2011.546694

Pellegrino, K. (2014). Examining the intersections of music making and teaching for four string teachers. *Journal of Research in Music Education, 62*, 128–147. https://doi.org/10.1177/0022429414530433

Pellegrino, K. (2015a). Becoming music-making music teachers: Connecting music making, identity, well-being, and teaching for four student teachers. *Research Studies in Music Education, 37*(2), 175–194. https://doi.org/10.1177/1321103X15589336

Pellegrino, K. (2015b). Becoming a music teacher: Preservice music teachers describe the meanings of music-making, teaching, and a tour experience. In M. R. Campbell & L. K. Thompson (Eds.), *Analyzing influences: Research on decision making and the music education curriculum* (pp. 69–96). Information Age Publishing.

Pellegrino, K. (2015c). Student, cooperating, and supervising teacher perceptions of educational and musical interactions during student teaching. *Journal of Music Teacher Education, 24*(2), 54–73. https://doi.org/10.1177/1057083713508653

Pellegrino, K. (2019). Becoming music teachers in a supportive String Project community. *Journal of Music Teacher Education, 28*(3), 11–27. https://doi.org/10.1177/1057083718803638

Raiber, M., & Teachout, D. (2014). *The journey from music student to teacher: A professional approach.* Routledge.

Chapter 5

Benham, S. J., Wagner, M. L., Aten, J. L., Evans, J. P., Odegaard, D., & Lieberman, J. L. (2021). *ASTA string curriculum: Standards, goals and learning sequences for essential skills and knowledge in K–12 string programs.* American String Teachers Association.

Chapter 6

Clauhs, M. (2018). Beginning band without a stand: Fostering creative musicianship in early instrumental programs. *Music Educators Journal, 104*(4), 39–47.

Clauhs, M., Powell, B., & Clements, A. C. (2020). *Popular music pedagogies: A practical guide for music teachers.* Routledge.

Cremata, R., & Powell, B. (2016). Digitally mediated keyboard learning: Speed of mastery, level of retention and student perspectives. *Journal of Music, Technology & Education, 9*(2), 145–159.

Gordon, E. E. (1999). All about audiation and music aptitudes: Edwin E. Gordon discusses using audiation and music aptitudes as teaching tools to allow students to reach their full music potential. *Music Educators Journal, 86*(2), 41–44.

Jacobi, B. S. (2012). Kodály, literacy, and the brain: Preparing young music students to read pitch on the staff. *General Music Today, 25*(2), 11–18.

Kivijärvi, S. (2019). Applicability of an applied music notation system: A case study of Figurenotes. *International Journal of Music Education, 37*(4), 654–666.

National Association for Music Education. (2014). Core Music Standards Glossary. Accessed May 28, 2021, https://www.nationalartsstandards.org/sites/default/files/NCCAS%20 GLOSSARY%20for%20Music%20.Standards%201%20column.pdf

NCCAS. (2014). National Core Arts Standards: A conceptual framework for arts learning. National Coalition for Core Arts Standards. Accessed May 2, 2021. https://www.nationalartsstandards.org/sites/default/files/NCCAS%20%20Conceptual%20Framework_0.pdf

New York State Education Department. (2021). Arts Standards Implementation Resources. Accessed March 26, 2020. https://www.nysed.gov/curriculum-instruction/arts-standards-implementation-resources.

West, C. (2016). Sound foundations: Organic approaches to learning notation in beginning band. *Music Educators Journal, 102*(4), 56–61.

Chapter 7

Duke, R. A. (2009). *Intelligent music teaching: Essays on the core principles of effective instruction.* Learning and Behavior Resources.

Garofalo, R. J. (1983). *Blueprint for band: A guide to teaching comprehensive musicianship through school band performance.* Meredith Music.

Millican, J. S. (2012). *Starting out right: Beginning-band pedagogy.* Scarecrow Press.

Millican, J. S. (2013). Describing wind instrument teachers' thinking: Implications for understanding pedagogical content knowledge. *Update: Applications of Research in Music Education, 31*(2), 45–53.

National Coalition for Core Arts Standards. (2014). *National Core Arts Standards: Harmonizing instruments.* https://www.nationalartsstandards.org/sites/default/files/Music%20Harmonizing%20Instruments%20at%20a%20Glance%203-4-15.pdf

National Coalition for Core Arts Standards. (2015). *National Core Arts Standards.* National Core Arts Standards.

Pagliaro, M. J. (2014). *The instrumental music director's guide to comprehensive program development.* Rowman & Littlefield.

Raiber, M., & Teachout, D. (2014). *The journey from music student to teacher: A professional approach.* Routledge.

Wisconsin Music Educators Association. (2021). *Comprehensive Musicianship through Performance (CMP).* https://wmeamusic.org/cmp/

Chapter 8

Covey, S. (2020). *Seven habits of highly effective people* (4th ed.). Simon & Schuster.

Yemm, G. (2013). *Essential guide to leading your team: How to set goals, measure performance and reward talent* (pp. 37–45). Pearson Education.

Chapter 9

Clark, R. (2004). *The excellent 11.* Hyperion.

Fain, J. (2018). Motivation & leadership: An interview with Jessica Fain. *Instrumentalist*, November, *73*(4), 7.

Wilcox, L. (2018). "Top Five Strategies for Motivating Students." *National Board for Professional Teaching Standards*, July, 4.

Chapter 10

Silveira, J. M., & Gavin, R. (2016). The effect of audio recording and playback on self-assessment among middle school instrumental music students. *Psychology of Music, 44*(4), 880–892.

Williams, D. A. (2014). Another perspective: The iPad is a REAL musical instrument. *Music Educators Journal, 101*(1), 93–98.

Chapter 11

Allsup, R. E., & Benedict, C. (2008). The problems of band: An inquiry into the future of instrumental music education. *Philosophy of Music Education Review*, 156–173. https://www.jstor.org/stable/40327299

Berg, M. (2009). Strings attached: The reality show. In J. Kerchner & C. Abril (Eds.), *Musical experiences in our lives: Things we learn and meanings we make* (pp. 165–181). Rowman & Littlefield.

Bryk, A., & Schneider, B. (2002). *Trust in schools: A core resource for improvement.* Russell Sage Foundation.

Burstein, B., Agostino, H., & Greenfield, B. (2019). Suicidal attempts and ideation among children and adolescents in US emergency departments, 2007–2015. *JAMA Pediatrics, 173*(6), 598–600. https://doi.org/10.1001/jamapediatrics.2019.0464

Centers for Disease Control (2021). Preventing childhood abuse and neglect. https://www.cdc.gov/violenceprevention/childabuseandneglect/fastfact.html

Costello, E., Erkanli, A., & Angold, A. (2006). Is there an epidemic of child or adolescent depression? *Journal of Child Psychology and Psychiatry, 47*(12), 1263–1271. https://doi.org/10.1111/j.1469-7610.2006.01682.x

Davis, T. E. (2020). *Self-assessment in jazz improvisation: An instrumental case study of professional jazz musicians in a jazz combo setting.* Ph.D. diss., Boston University. ProQuest Dissertations and Theses Global, Publication No. 28149451.

Deci, E. L., & Ryan, R. M. (1985). *Intrinsic motivation and self-determination in human behavior.* Plenum Press.

Dirks, R. L. (2020). *A phenomenological study of adolescent anxiety and depression through the lived experiences of novice and experienced high school music educators.* Ph.D. diss., University of Kansas. ProQuest Dissertations and Theses Global, Publication No. 27960293.

Goswami, U. (2008). Neuroscience and education. In Jossey-Bass Publishers (Eds.), *The Jossey-Bass reader on the brain and learning* (pp. 33–50). Jossey-Bass.

Hendricks, K. S. (2018). *Compassionate music teaching: Motivation and engagement in the 21st century.* Rowman & Littlefield.

Hendricks, K. S. (2021). Authentic connection in music education: A chiastic essay. In K. S. Hendricks & J. Boyce-Tillman (Eds.), *Authentic connection: Music, spirituality, and well-being* (pp. 237–253). Peter Lang.

Hendricks, K. S. (2023). A call for care and compassion in music education. In K. S. Hendricks (Ed.), The Oxford handbook of care in music education (pp. 5–21). Oxford University Press.

Hendricks, K. S., & McPherson, G. E. (2023). Reconsidering ability development through the lens of diversity and bias. In K. S. Hendricks (Ed.), The Oxford handbook of care in music education (pp. 410–422). Oxford University Press.

Hendricks, K. S., Smith, T. D., & Stanuch, J. (2014). Creating safe spaces for music learning. *Music Educators Journal, 101*(1), 35–40. https://doi.org/10.1177/0027432114540337

Jennings, P. A. (2019). *The trauma-sensitive classroom: Building resilience with compassionate teaching.* W. W. Norton.

Leahy, S. E. (2021). *Neurodidactics in elementary music classrooms: A mixed-methods study*. Ph.D. diss., Boston University.

Lewis, M., Weight, E., & Hendricks, K. (2022). Teaching methods that foster self-efficacy belief: Perceptions of collegiate musicians from the United States. *Psychology of Music, 50*(3), 878–894. https://doi.org/10.1177/03057356211026744

McGrath, C., Hendricks, K. S., & Smith, T. D. (2016). *Performance anxiety strategies*. Rowman & Littlefield.

Mental Health America (2021). *Quick facts and statistics about mental health*. https://www.mhanational.org/mentalhealthfacts

Noddings, N. (2013). *Caring: A relational approach to ethics and moral education* (2nd ed.). University of California Press.

Payne, D. P., Lewis, W., & McCaskill, F. (2020). Looking within: An investigation of music education majors and mental health. *Journal of Music Teacher Education, 29*(3), 50–61. https://doi.org/10.1177/1057083720927748

Ray, J., Kellum, B. W., & Hendricks, K. S. (2023). Culturally responsive teaching in school orchestras. This volume, pp. 299–305.

Rosenberg, M. B. (2003a). *Life-enriching education: Nonviolent communication helps schools improve performance, reduce conflict, and enhance relationships*. PuddleDancer Press.

Rosenberg, M. B. (2003b). *Nonviolent communication: A language of life* (2nd ed.). PuddleDancer Press.

Ryan, R. M., & Deci, E. L. (2000). Self-determination theory and the facilitation of intrinsic motivation, social development, and well-being. *American Psychologist, 55*(1), 68–78. https://doi.org/10.1037/0003-066X.55.1.68

Smith, T. D. (2021). Teaching through trauma: Compassion fatigue, burnout, or secondary traumatic stress? In D. Bradley & J. Hess (Eds.), *Trauma and music education: Haunted melodies* (pp. 49–63). Routledge.

Twenge, J., Joiner, T., Duffy, M., Cooper, A., & Binau, S. (2019). Age, period, and cohort trends in mood disorder indicators and suicide-related outcomes in a nationally representative dataset, 2005–2017. *Journal of Abnormal Psychology, 128*(3), 185–199. https://doi.org/10.1037/abn0000410

van der Kolk, B. A. (2014). *The body keeps the score: Brain, mind, and body in the healing of trauma*. Viking.

Chapter 12

Allsup, R. E. (2012). Music education and human flourishing: A meditation on democratic origins. *British Journal of Music Education, 29*(2), 171–179. https://doi.org/10.1017/S0265051712000034

CASEL (2003). *Safe and sound: An educational leader's guide to evidence-based social and emotional learning programs*. Collaborative for Academic, Social, and Emotional Learning.

Dewey, J. (1916). *Democracy and education: An introduction to philosophy of education*. Macmillan.

Green, L. (2008). Group cooperation, inclusion and disaffected pupils: Some responses to informal learning in the music classroom. *Music Education Research, 10*(2), 177–192. https://doi.org/10.1080/14613800802079049

Jellison, J. A., Draper, E. A., & Brown, L. S. (2017). Learning together: The instinct to do good and peer-assisted strategies that work. *Music Educators Journal, 104*(2), 15–20.

Payne, R. K. (1998). *A framework for understanding poverty*. RFT.

Piaget, J. (1952). *The origins of intelligence in children* (M. Cook, Trans.). International Universities Press. (Original work published in 1936.)

Topping, K. J., & Ehly, S. W. (2001). Peer assisted learning: A framework for consultation. *Journal of Educational and Psychological Consultation, 12*(2), 113–132. https://doi.org/10.1207/S1532768XJEPC1202_03

Vygotsky, L. S. (1978). *Mind in society: The development of higher psychological processes*. Harvard University Press.

Chapter 13

Bear, G. G., Mantz, L. S., Glutting, J. J., Yang, C., & Boyer, D. E. (2015). Differences in bullying victimization between students with and without disabilities. *School Psychology Review, 44*, 98–116.

Downing, J. (2008). *Including students with severe and multiple disabilities in typical classrooms* (3rd ed.). Paul H. Brookes.

Eisenberg, M. E., Gower, A. L., McMorris, B. J., & Bucchianeri, M. M. (2015). Vulnerable bullies: Perception of peer harassment among youths across sexual orientation, weight, and disability status. *American Journal of Public Health, 105*(9), 1784–1791.

Fox, N., & Ysseldyke, J. (1997). Implementing inclusion at the middle school level: Lessons from a negative example. *Exceptional Children, 64*(1), 81–98.

Janssen, I., Craig, W. M., Boyce, W. F., & Pickett, W. (2004). Associations between overweight and obesity with bullying behaviors in school-aged children. *Pediatrics, 113*, 1187–1194.

Kaikkonen, M. (2016). Music for all: Everyone has the potential to learn. In D. V. Blair & K. A. McCord (Eds.), *Exceptional music pedagogy for children with exceptionalities, international perspectives* (pp. 10–11). Oxford University Press.

Kennedy, C., & Horn, E. (Eds.). (2004). *Including students with severe disabilities*. Allyn & Bacon.

Malecki, C. K., Demaray, M. K., Smith, T. J., & Emmons, J. (2020). Disability, poverty, and other risk factors associated with involvement in bullying behaviors. *Journal of School Psychology, 78*, 115–132.

McCord, K. A. (1997). Adapting music technology for students with learning disabilities. *Proceedings of the Fourth International Technological Directions in Music Education Conference*. IMR Press.

Peterson, J., & Hittie, M. (2010). Inclusive teaching: The journey toward effective schools for all learners (2nd ed). Pearson Education.

Robinson, J. P., & Espelage, D. L. (2012). Bullying explains only part of the LGBTQ-heterosexual risk disparities: Implications for policy and practice. *Educational Researcher, 41*, 309–319.

Chapter 14

Buchanan, L., Bui, Q., & Patel, J. (2020, July 3). Black Lives Matter may be the largest movement in U.S. history. *New York Times*. Accessed December 2, 2021, https://www.nytimes.com/interactive/2020/07/03/us/george-floyd-protests-crowd-size.html

Coronavirus report. (2021, December 2). SmartNews. Accessed December 2, 2021, https://coronavirus.smart-news.com/us/

Dale, E. (2021). *Covid-19 & social distancing music making resources*. NAMM.org. Accessed December 2, 2021, https://www.namm.org/playback/advancing-music-making/covid-19-social-distancing-music-making-resources

Elpus, K., & Abril, C. R. (2011). High school music ensemble students in the United States: A demographic profile. *Journal of Research in Music Education, 59*(2), 128–145.

Freire, P. (1972). *Pedagogy of the oppressed*. Herder & Herder.

Garoutte, L., & McCarthy-Gilmore, K. (2014). Preparing students for community-based learning using an asset-based approach. *Journal of Scholarship of Teaching and Learning*.

Hannan, M. (2012). Expanding the skill set. In *Life in the real world: How to make music graduates employable*. Common Ground.

Lind, V. R., & McKoy, C. L. (2016). *Culturally responsive teaching in music education: From understanding to application*. Routledge.

Mackun, P., Comenetz, J., & Spell, L. (2021, August 12). *More than half of U.S. counties were smaller in 2020 than in 2010*. The United States Census Bureau. https://www.census.gov/library/stories/2021/08/more-than-half-of-united-states-counties-were-smaller-in-2020-than-in-2010.html

McNeil, B. (2021). *Aural skills pedagogy in the wind band: A survey of secondary and collegiate wind band conductors' perceptions and strategies*. Ph.D. diss., Auburn University.

Mills, J., & McPherson, G. E. (2006). Musical literacy. In G. E. McPherson (Ed.), *The child as musician: A handbook of musical development*. Oxford University Press.

The NCES fast facts tool provides quick answers to many education QUESTIONS (National Center for EDUCATION STATISTICS). National Center for Education Statistics (NCES) Home Page, a part of the U.S. Department of Education. (n.d.). ttps://nces.ed.gov/fastfacts/display.asp?id=372#College_enrollment

Pike, P. (2015). The ninth semester: Preparing undergraduates to function as professional musicians in the 21st century. *College Music Symposium*. Accessed August 21, 2021, https://www.jstor.org/stable/26574399

US Census Bureau (2021, August 17). *Local population changes and nation's racial and ethnic diversity*. The United States Census Bureau. https://www.census.gov/newsroom/press-releases/2021/population-changes-nations-diversity.html

Whitehead, B. (2021). Black music matters. *College Music Symposium, 61*(1), 86–88. https://www.jstor.org/stable/27041504

Chapter 15

Azzara, C. (1999). An aural approach to improvisation. *Music Educators Journal, 86*(3), 21–25.

Cribari, P., & Layton, R. (2019). *The elemental style: A handbook for composers and arrangers* (Part 1). Sweet Pipes.

Ellington, D. (1973). *Music is my mistress*. Doubleday.

Goodkin, D. (2002). *Play, sing, & dance*. Schott.

Gordon, E. E. (2012). *Learning sequences in music: A contemporary music learning theory*. GIA.

Hannah, W. (2007). The new Bloom's taxonomy: Implications for music education. *Arts Education Policy Review, 108*(4), 7–16. https://doi.org/10.3200/AEPR.108.4.7-16

Kennan, K., & Grantham, D. (2002). *The technique of orchestration* (6th ed.). Prentice Hall.

McConville, B. (2015). The kindergarten approach to arranging music. *College Music Society, 55*.

Miller, R. (2015). *Contemporary orchestration: A practical guide to instruments, ensembles, and musicians*. Routledge.

Robinson, N., Bell, C., & Pogonowski, L. (2011). The creative music strategy: A seven-step instructional model. *Music Educators Journal, 27*(3), 50–55.

Suzuki, S. (2018). *Nurtured by love: The classic approach to talent education* (W. Suzuki, Trans.; 2nd ed.). Suzuki Method International.

Wiggins, G., & McTighe, J. (2005). *Understanding by design* (expanded 2nd ed.). Association for Supervision and Curriculum Development.

Chapter 17

Benham, J. L. (2016). *Music advocacy: Moving from survival to vision*. GIA Publications.

Elliott, D. J., & Silverman, M. (2019). *Music matters: A philosophy of music education*. Oxford University Press.

Helding, L. (2020). *The musician's mind: Teaching, learning, and performance in the age of brain science*. Rowman & Littlefield.

Chapter 18

Clauhs, M., & Cremata, R. (2020). Student voice and choice in modern band curriculum development. *Journal of Popular Music Education, 4*(1), 101–116.

Cremata, R. (2017). Facilitation in popular music education. *Journal of Popular Music Education, 1*(1), 63–82.

Dammers, R. J. (2010). A case study of the creation of a technology-based music course. *Bulletin of the Council for Research in Music Education, 186*, 55–65.

Elpus, K., & Abril, C. R. (2019). Who enrolls in high school music? A national profile of US students, 2009–2013. *Journal of Research in Music Education, 67*(3), 323–338.

Gramm, W. (2021). *Peer mentoring in modern band.* Ph.D. diss., Boston University.

Mantie, R., & Tucker, L. (2008). Closing the gap: Does music-making have to stop upon graduation? *International Journal of Community Music, 1*(2), 217–227.

NAMM (2020). Global Report. Accessed February 12, 2022. https://ww1.namm.org/sites/www.namm.org/files_public/resources/2022%20NAMM%20Global%20Report%20Executive%20Summary.pdf

Powell, B. (2019). Breaking down barriers to participation: Perspectives of female musicians in popular music ensembles. In Z. Moir, B. Powell, & G. D. Smith (Eds.), *Bloomsbury handbook of popular music education* (pp. 337–350). Bloomsbury Academic.

Powell, B. (2022). A history of Little Kids Rock and modern band. *Journal of Historical Research in Music Education.*

Powell, B., & Burstein, S. (2017). Popular music and modern band principles. In G. D. Smith, Z. Moir, M. Brennan, S. Ramabrran, & P. Kirkman (Eds.), *The Routledge Research Companion to Popular Music Education* (pp. 243–254). Routledge.

Springer, D. G. (2016). Teaching popular music: Investigating music educators' perceptions and preparation. *International Journal of Music Education, 34*(4), 403–415.

Chapter 19

Bernard, C. F., & Cayari, C. (2020). Encouraging participatory music making through differentiation on the ukulele. *General Music Today, 64*(1), 21–28. doi:10.1177/1048371320926608

Chapter 20

Gramm, W. (2021). *Peer mentoring in modern band.* Ph.D. diss., Boston University. https://open.bu.edu/handle/2144/42042

Mok, A. (2010). *Enculturation and learning in music: The attitudes, values and beliefs of four Hong Kong socio-musical groups.* Ph.D. thesis, University of London.

Chapter 21

Groening, M., Brooks, J., & Simon, S. (Aus.), & Anderson, M., & Moore, S. (Dirs.). (2014, November 23). *The Simpsons* (season 26, episode 8), *Covercraft.* Gracie Films, 20th Century Fox Television.

Chapter 22

Bastien, J. (1997). *Bastien piano basics: Piano level 1.* KJOS.

Burstein, S., Hale, S., Claxton, M., & Wish, D. (2020). *Modern band method: Keyboard; A beginner's guide for group or private instruction.* Hal Leonard.

Clauhs, M., Powell, B., & Clements, A. C. (2020). *Popular music pedagogies: A practical guide for music teachers.* Routledge.

Evans, L. (2013). *Crash course in chords.* Hal Leonard.

Faber, N., & Faber, R. (2001). *Adult piano adventures: A comprehensive piano course; Level 1.* FJH.

Music Will. (2023). *Downloadable Teacher Resources.* Accessed April 10, 2023, *https://musicwill.org/already-a-music-will-educator/downloadable-teacher-resources/*

Palmer, W., Manus, M., & Lethco, A. V. (1987). *Alfred's basic piano chord approach: A piano method for the later beginner.* Alfred.

Pianote. (2008). Accessed April 10, 2023, https://www.youtube.com/c/PianoteOfficial/videos

Tomlins, T. (2004). *Basic piano chord chart.* Santorella.

Chapter 24

Allsup, R. E. (2008). Creating an educational framework for popular music in public schools: Anticipating the second-wave. *Visions of Research in Music Education, 12*(1), 2.

American Academy of Teachers of Singing. (2009). *In support of contemporary commercial music (nonclassical) voice pedagogy.* http://www.americanacademyofteachersofsinging.org/academy-publications.php.

Baldwin, J. (2021). Accessing and building mix in choirs and singing groups. In S. Holley, K. Reinhert, & Z. Moir (Eds.), *Action based approaches in popular music education* (pp.131–136). F-Flat Books.

Benson, E. A. (2020). *Training contemporary commercial singers.* Compton.

Dimon, T. Jr. (2018). Anatomy of the voice: An illustrated guide for singers, vocal coaches, and speech therapists (illustrated ed.). North Atlantic Books.

Edwards, M. (2014). *So you want to sing rock 'n' roll: A guide for professionals.* Rowman & Littlefield.

Errico, M. (2022). *Music, lyrics, and life: A field guide for the advancing songwriter.* Backbeat Books.

Hess, J. (2019). Popular music education: A way forward or a new hegemony? In Z. Moir, B. Powell, & G. D. Smith (Eds.), *The Bloomsbury handbook of popular music education: Perspectives and practices* (pp. 29–44). Bloomsbury Academic.

Hoch, M. (Ed.). (2018). *So you want to sing ccm.* Rowman & Littlefield.

Holley, S. (2019). *Coaching a popular music ensemble.* McLemore Ave Music.

Hughes, D. (2010). Developing vocal artistry in popular culture musics. In S. Harrison (Ed.), *Perspectives on teaching singing* (pp. 244–258). Queensland: Australian Academic Press.

Hughes, D. (2017). Art to artistry: A contemporary approach to vocal pedagogy. In G. D. Smith, Z. Moir, M. Brennan, S. Rambarran, & P. Kirkman (Eds.), *The Routledge research companion to popular music education* (pp. 177–189). Routledge.

LeBorgne, W. D., & Rosenberg, M. (2014). *The vocal athlete* (1st ed.). Plural Publishing.

LeBorgne, W. D., & Rosenberg, M. (2019). *The vocal athlete* (2nd ed.). Plural Publishing.

Lewis, S. (2014). *The rise*. Simon & Schuster.

Malde, M., Allen, M., & Zeller, K.-A. (2016). *What every singer needs to know about the body* (3rd ed.). Plural Publishing.

Murnak, R. (2021). Let me see you move! Adding movement and blocking to a popular music performance. In S. Holley, K. Reinhert, & Z. Moir (Eds.), *Action based approaches in popular music education* (pp. 59–64). F-Flat Books.

Reinhert, K. (2019). Singers in higher education: Teaching popular music vocalists. in Z. Moir, B. Powell, & G. D Smith (Eds.). *The Bloomsbury handbook of popular music education: Perspectives and practices* (pp.127–140). Bloomsbury Academic.

Reinhert, K., & Gulish, S. (2021). Songwriting for music educators. F-Flat Books.

Russo, F. A., Ilari, B., & Cohen, A. J. (2020). *The Routledge companion to interdisciplinary studies in singing*, vol. 1, *Development*. Routledge.

Smith, G., & Shafighian, A. (2014). Creative space and the "silent power of traditions" in popular music performance education. In P. Burnard (Ed.), *Developing creativities in higher music education: International perspectives and practices* (pp. 256–267). Routledge.

Woodward, S. C. (2017). Social justice and popular music education: Building a generation of artists impacting social change. In G. D. Smith, Z. Moir, M. Brennan, S. Rambarran, & P. Kirkman (Eds.), *The Routledge research companion to popular music education* (pp. 139–150). Routledge.

Chapter 25

Claxton, M., & Hale, S. (2021). *Modern band measures of success*. Little Kids Rock.

Crumly, C. (2014). Student-centered versus teacher-centered learning, in C. Crumly, P. Dietz, & S. D'Angelo, *Pedagogies for student-centered learning: Online and on-ground*, 3–20. https://doi.org/10.2307/j.ctt9m0skc.5 Augsburg Fortress Publishers.

Culturally relevant pedagogy. Culturally Relevant Pedagogy—Educator Excellence (CA Dept of Education). (n.d.). Accessed October 29, 2021, https://www.cde.ca.gov/pd/ee/culturalrelevantpedagogy.asp

Seaman, P., Copeland, S., & Gao, L. (2021). Teaching with intent: Applying culturally responsive teaching to library instruction. *Portal: Libraries and the Academy, 21*(2), 231–251.

Chapter 26

Benham, S. J., et al. (2011). *ASTA string curriculum guide*. ASTA.

Dweck, C. S. (2008). *Mindset: The new psychology of success*. Ballantine Books.

Gillespie, R. (2003). Repertoire-based warm-ups. In D. Littrell's (ed.) *Teaching Music through Performance in Orchestra*, vol. 2, (pp. 47–67). GIA Publications.

Hopkins, M., & Pellegrino, K. (2019). Teacher preparation for beginning strings. In C. M. Conway, K. Pellegrino, A. M. Stanley, & C. West (Eds.), *The Oxford handbook of preservice music teacher education in the United States* (pp. 765–783). Oxford University Press.

Chapter 27

Rabin, M., & Smith, P. (1990). *Guide to orchestral bowings through musical styles*. Really Good Music.

Chapter 28

Hamann, D. L., & Gillespie, R. (2018). *Strategies for teaching strings: Building a successful string and orchestra program* (4th ed.). Oxford University Press.

Hopkins, M. (2019). *The art of string teaching*. GIA Publications.

Lyle, D. (2018). *The Bornoff approach: A comprehensive curriculum for string orchestra*. FASE.

Rolland, P., Mutschler, M., Colwell, R., Johnson, A., & Miller, D. L. (1971). *Development and trial of a two year program of string instruction*. University of Illinois. Office of Education, U.S. Department of Health, Education, and Welfare. https://files.eric.ed.gov/fulltext/ED063323.pdf

Segado, M., Hollinger, A., Thibodeau, J., Penhune, V., & Zatorre, R. J. (2018). Partially overlapping brain networks for singing and cello playing. *Frontiers in Neuroscience, 12*, 351–366.

Zweig, M. (n.d.). Mimi Zweig String Pedagogy. www.stringpedagogy.com

Chapter 29

Fischbach, G. F. (2002). *The art of vibrato*. Neil A. Kjos.

Fischbach, G. F., & Frost, R. S. (1997). *Viva vibrato!* Neil A. Kjos.

Whistler, H. S. (1989). *Introducing the positions for violin*, vol. 1, *Third and fifth Position*. Rubank.

Chapter 30

Abeles, H., Hoffer, C., & Klotman, R. (1995). *Foundations of music education* (2nd ed.). Schirmer Books.

Adey, C. (1998). *Orchestral performance: A guide for conductors and players*. Faber & Faber.

Cook, B. V. (2013). *An examination of factors contributing to orchestra students' attrition in transition from elementary to middle school.* (Unpublished master's Thesis.) University of Michigan, Ann Arbor.

Cooper, L. G. (2004). *Teaching band & orchestra: Methods and materials.* Chicago: GIA Publications.

Eccles, J. S., & Wigfield, A. (2002). Motivational beliefs, values, and goals. *Annual review of psychology, 53*(1), 109–132. https://doi.org/10.1146/annurev.psych.53.100901.135153

Hamann, D. L., & Gillespie, R. (2012). Strategies for teaching strings: Building a successful string and orchestra program (3rd ed.). Oxford University Press.

Hamann, D. L., Gillespie, R., & Bergonzi, L. (2002). Status of orchestra programs in public schools. *Journal of String Research, 2*, 9–35.

Holz, E. A., & Jacobi, R. E. (1966). *Teaching band instruments to beginners.* Prentice-Hall.

Hopkins, M. (2019). *The art of string teaching.* GIA Publications.

Kjelland, J. (2001). But what about the sound? Toward greater musical integrity in the orchestra program. In D. Littrell, L. R. Racin, & M. Allen (Eds.), *Teaching music through performance in orchestra.* GIA Publications.

McPherson, G. E., & Davidson, J. W. (2006). Playing an instrument. In G. E. McPherson (Ed.), *The child as musician: A handbook of musical development* (pp. 331–351). Oxford University Press.

Selby, C., Rush, S., & Moon, R. (2016). *Habits of a successful orchestra director.* GIA Publications.

Chapter 31

Allsup, R. (2009). Rough play: Music and symbolic violence in an age of perpetual war. *Action, Criticism, and Theory for Music Education, 8*(1), 35–53. http://act.maydaygroup.org/articles/Allsup8_1.pdf

Berg, M. H. (forthcoming). Fostering care through core reflection. In K. S. Hendricks (Ed.), *The Oxford handbook of care in music education.* Oxford University Press.

Brown, J. (Ed.). (2007). *Western music and race.* Cambridge University Press.

Bull, A. (2019). *Class, control, and classical music.* Oxford University Press.

Choate, R. A. (Ed.). (1968). *Documentary report of the Tanglewood Symposium.* Music Educators National Conference.

Chappell, E. (2020). Research-to-resource: The importance of aural learning in the strings classroom. *Update: Applications of Research in Music Education, 38*(3), 5–8. https://doi.org/10.1177/8755123320908687

de Brey, C., Musu, L., McFarland, J., Wilkinson-Flicker, S., Diliberti, M., Zhang, A., Branstetter, C., & Wang, X. (2019). *Status and trends in the education of racial and ethnic groups 2018.* National Center for Educational Statistics. https://nces.ed.gov/pubs2019/2019038.pdf

Elpus, K., & Abril, C. R. (2019). Who enrolls in high school music? A national profile of U.S. students, 2009–2013. *Journal of Research in Music Education, 67*(3), 323–338. https://doi.org/10.1177/0022429419862837

Fairbanks, S. (2019). *Schooling habitus: An auto/ethnographic study of music education's entanglements with cultural hegemony.* [Doctoral thesis, Cambridge University]. Apollo. https://doi.org/10.17863/CAM.42088

Gay, G. (2018). *Culturally responsive teaching: Theory, research, and practice* (3rd ed.). Teachers College Press.

Hendricks, K. S. (2016). The sources of self-efficacy: Educational research and implications for music. *Update: Applications of Research in Music Education, 35*(1), 32–38. https://doi.org/10.1177/8755123315576535

Hendricks, K. S. (2018). *Compassionate music teaching: Motivation and engagement in the 21st century.* Rowman & Littlefield.

Hendricks, K. S., Smith, T. D., & Stanuch, J. (2014). Creating safe spaces for music learning. *Music Educators Journal, 101*(1), 35–40. https://doi.org/10.1177/0027432114540337

Humphreys, J. T. (1989). An overview of American public school bands and orchestras before World War II. *Bulletin of the Council for Research in Music Education, 101*, 50–60.

Johnson, J. (2002). *Who needs classical music? Culture choice and musical value.* Oxford University Press.

Jorgensen, E. (2003). *Transforming music education.* Indiana University Press.

Kellum, B. (2021). *A phenomenological investigation of access and participation: Music education in El Sistema, Venezuela's system of youth orchestras* [Doctoral dissertation, University of Illinois Urbana-Champaign]. Illinois Digital Environment for Access to Learning and Scholarship. https://hdl.handle.net/2142/115313

Leinsdorf, E. (1981). *The composer's advocate: A radical orthodoxy for musicians.* Yale University Press.

Lind, V. R., & McKoy, C. (2016). *Culturally responsive teaching in music education: From understanding to application.* Routledge.

MacLeod, R. B. (2019). *Teaching strings in today's classroom: A guide for group instruction.* Routledge.

Marcho, T. (2020). *Socially responsible music repertoire: Composer gender diversity in instrumental ensembles* (Publication No. 28287761) [Doctoral dissertation, The Ohio State University]. ProQuest Dissertations and Theses Global.

Mark, M. L., & Gary, C. L. (2007). *A history of American music education* (3rd ed.). Rowman & Littlefield Education.

MayDay Group (1997). *Action for change in music education.* http://maydaygroup.org/wp-content/uploads/2014/08/ActionForChange1997.pdf

McCarthy, M. (2015). Understanding social justice from the perspective of music education history. In C. Benedict, P. Schmidt, G. Spruce, & P. Woodford (Eds.), *The Oxford handbook of social justice in music education* (pp. 29–46). Oxford University Press.

McKoy, C. L. (2017). On the 50th anniversary of the Tanglewood Symposium. *Journal of Music Teacher Education, 27*(1), 3–6. https://doi.org/10.1177/1057083717719073

McKoy, C. L. (2020). Race, ethnicity, and culturally relevant pedagogy. In C. Conway, K. Pellegrino, A. M. Stanley, & C. West (Eds.), *The Oxford handbook of preservice music teacher education in the United States* (pp. 603–623). Oxford University Press. https://doi.org/10.1093/oxfordhb/9780190671402.013.28

Newell, D. (2012). *Classroom management in the music room.* Neil A. Kjos.

Ray, J. (2020). Advancing antiracism in the secondary school orchestra program. *American String Teacher, 70*(4), 13–17. https://doi.org/10.1177/0003131320963078

Ray, J., & Hendricks, K. S. (2019). Collective efficacy belief, within-group agreement, and performance quality among instrumental chamber ensembles. *Journal of Research in Music Education, 66*(4), 449–464. https://doi.org/10.1177/0022429418805090

Reed, E. A. (2019). Culturally responsive teaching within rural, suburban, and urban orchestra programs. *American String Teacher, 69*(1), 35–40. https://doi.org/10.1177/0003131318816087

Rotjan, M. (2021). Deciding for or deciding with: Student involvement in repertoire selection. *Music Educators Journal, 107*(4), 28–34. https://doi.org/10.1177/00274321211013879

Schuller, G. (1997). *The compleat conductor.* Oxford University Press.

Smith, B. P., Mick, J. P., & Alexander, M. L. (2018). The status of strings and orchestra programs in U.S. schools. *String Research Journal, 8*(1), 15–31. https://doi.org/10.1177/1948499218769607

Smith, T. D., & Hendricks, K. S. (2021). Diversity, inclusion, and access. In G. E. McPherson (Ed.), *The Oxford handbook of musical performance* (pp. 528–549). Oxford University Press.

Snell, K. (2009). Democracy and popular music in music education. In E. Gould, J. Countryman, C. Morton, & L. S. Rose (Eds.), *Exploring social justice: How music education might matter* (pp. 166–183). Canadian Music Educators' Association.

Tsui, A., Hess, J., & Hendricks, K. S. (forthcoming). "I just wanna live my life like it's gold": Anti-racist music education. In K. S. Hendricks (Ed.), *The Oxford handbook of care in music education.* Oxford University Press.

Wang, J. (2016). Classical music: A norm of "common" culture embedded in cultural consumption and cultural diversity. *International Review of the Aesthetics and Sociology of Music, 47*(2) 195–205.

Yi, T. S. (2023). Alternative seating practices: Pedagogy of the back of the orchestra. *Music Education Research.* Advance online publication. https://doi.org/10.1080/14613808.2023.2187042

Chapter 39

Bachelder, D. F., & Hunt, N. J. (2002). *Guide to teaching brass.* Alfred Music Publishing.

Caruso, C. (2002). *Musical Calisthenics for Brass.* Hal Leonard Corporation.

Farkas, P. (1999). *The art of French horn playing.* Alfred Music.

Frederiksen, B. (1996). *Arnold Jacobs: Song and wind.* Windsong Press.

Chapter 40

Hickman, D. R., Nielsen, H., & Pepping, A. (2006). *Trumpet pedagogy: A compendium of modern teaching techniques.* Hickman Music Ed.

Cichowicz, M., Dulin, M., Rolfs, T., & Knopp, L. (2021). *Vincent Cichowicz: Fundamental studies for the developing trumpet player.* Hal Leonard.

Chapter 41

Aharoni, E. (1996). *New method for the modern bass trombone single valve in F (with E section); Double valve in E, E♭ or D; Independent double valve (in line); New: Single valve with sliding E extension.* Noga Music.

Bachelder, D. F., & Hunt, N. (2002). *Guide to teaching brass.* McGraw-Hill.

Bousfield, I. (2015). *Unlocking the trombone code.* Warwick Music.

Colwell, R. J., & Goolsby, T. W. (2002). *The teaching of instrumental music.* Prentice Hall.

Fink, R. (1970). *The trombonist's handbook.* Accura Music.

Chapter 43

Allsup, R. E., & Benedict, C. (2008). The problems of band: An inquiry into the future of instrumental music education. *Philosophy of Music Education Review,* 156–173. https://www.jstor.org/stable/40327299

Elpus, K., & Abril, C. R. (2011). High school music ensemble students in the United States: A demographic profile. *Journal of Research in Music Education, 59*(2), 128–145. https://doi.org/10.1177/0022429411405207

Lind, V. R., & McKoy, C. (2016). *Culturally responsive teaching in music education: From understanding to application* (1st ed.). Routledge. https://doi.org/10.4324/9781315747279

Lonis, D., & Haley, A. (2018). *Due but not done: Selected resources for instrumental music teachers* (8th ed.). Music Mentors International.

Mantie, R., & Tucker, L. (2008). Closing the gap: Does music-making have to stop upon graduation? *International Journal of Community Music, 1,* 217–227.

Thompson, K. P. (1993). Media, music and adolescents. In R. M. Lerner (Ed.), *Early adolescence: Perspectives on research policy and intervention* (pp. 407–418). Lawrence Erlbaum Associates.

Westerlund, H. (2008). Justifying music education: A view from here-and-now value experience. *Philosophy of Music Education Review, 16*(1), 79–95.

Chapter 47

Knapp, D., & Grisé, A. (2009). *Introduction to steel band.* Engine Room.

Stuempfle, S. (1995). The steelband movement: The forging of a national art in Trinidad and Tobago. University of Pennsylvania Press.

Williams, K. (2008). Steel bands in American schools: What they are, what they do, and why they're growing! Steel drum ensembles promote multicultural music education and attract a wide range of students. *Music Educators Journal, 94*(4), 52–57.

Chapter 48

Burstein, S. D. (2016). *Transformation of habitus and social trajectories: A retrospective study of a popular music program.* Ph.D. diss., University of Southern California. USC Digital Library. http://digitallibrary.usc.edu/cdm/ref/collection/p15799coll40/id/320915

Burstein, S., & Powell, B. (2019). Approximation and scaffolding in modern band. *Music Educators Journal, 106*(1), 39–47.

Burstein, S., Hale, S., Claxton, M., & Wish, D. (2020). *Modern band method.* Hal Leonard.

Powell, B. (2021). Modern band: A review of literature. *Update: Applications of Research in Music Education, 39*(3), 39–46.

Chapter 49

Hilliard, Q. C. (1993). *Ten Chorales for Beginning and Intermediate Band.* Kjos Music Publishers.

Hilliard, Q. C. (2001). *Twelve Chorales for Developing Band.* FJH Music Company.

Hilliard, Q. C. (2003). *Superior bands in sixteen weeks.* FJH Music Company.

Hilliard, Q. C. (2004). *Eight Chorales for Elementary Band.* FJH Music Company.

Hilliard, Q. C. (2004). *Chorales and Rhythm Etudes for Superior Band.* FJH Music Company.

Hilliard, Q. C. (2009). *Scales and Tuning Exercises for Superior Bands.* FJH Music Company.

Hilliard, Q. C. (2015). *Fundamental for Ensemble Drills.* Print Music Sources.

Hilliard, Q. C. (2023). *Counts of Silence.* Wingert-Jones Publications.

Loest, T. (2004). *Rhythms and Beyond.* FJH Music Company.

Chapter 50

Cousins, J. (2018). *Strategic plan template: Elements to include; Proper planning and preparation prevents painfully poor performance.* https://medium.com/swlh/proper-planning-and-preparation-prevents-piss-poor-performance-95049e1c40c2

Crotts, C. (2019). *Jazz ensemble rehearsal tip: What to listen to?* https://nottelmannmusic.com/jazz-ensemble-rehearsal-tip-what-to-listen-to/

Mantz, B. D. (2011). *The jazz taxonomy.* Ph.D. diss., California State University, Long Beach. ProQuest Dissertations and Theses Global, Publication No. 890203251.

Riley, J. (1994). *The art of bop drumming.* Alfred.

Riley, J. (1997). *Beyond bop drumming.* Alfred.

Schmidt, R. A. (2019a). Jazz piano. In C. West & M. Titlebaum, *Teaching school jazz: Perspectives, principles, and strategies* (pp. 199–208). Oxford University Press.

Schmidt, R. A. (2019b). Pedagogical language of jazz. In C. West & M. Titlebaum, *Teaching school jazz: Perspectives, principles, and strategies* (pp. 39–48). Oxford University Press.

Stanislaus County Office of Education (STANCOE) (2021). Depth-of-knowledge in the fine arts. https://www.stancoe.org/sites/default/files/instructional-support-services/resources/california-state-standards/CSS_dok_arts.pdf

Stevenson, R., (2019). Roxanne Stevenson: Chicago State University. In M. J. Papich & R. Adamsons, *Rehearsing the jazz band* (pp. 98–112). Meredith Music Publications.

Tomita, F. (2019). *The jazz rhythm section: a manual for band directors.* Rowman & Littlefield.

Weist, S. (2019). Steve Weist: University of Denver. In M. J. Papich & R. Adamsons, *Rehearsing the jazz band* (pp. 113–137). Meredith Music Publications.

Chapter 51

Marcouiller, D. (1958). *Marching for marching bands.* Wm. C. Brown.

Martin, M. G., & Smolinsky, R. L. (2016). *Marching band techniques: A guide to the successful operation of a high school band program.* Schiffer Publishing.

Smith, G. (2016). *The system: Marching band methods.* GIA Publications.

Yemm, G. (2013). *Essential guide to leading your team: How to set goals, measure performance and reward talent* (pp. 37–45). Pearson Education.

Chapter 52

Abril, C. R. (2006). Music that represents culture: Selecting music with integrity. *Music Educators Journal, 93*(1), 38–45.

Allen, M. L. (2001). A pedagogical model for beginning string class instruction: Revisited. In D. Littrell & L. R. Racin (Eds.), *Teaching music through performance in orchestra*, vol. 1 (pp. 3–13). GIA Publications.

Benham, S. J., Wagner, M. L., Aten, J. L., Evans, J. P., Odegaard, D., & Lieberman, J. L. (2011). *ASTA string curriculum: Standards, goals and learning sequences for essential skills and knowledge in K–12 string programs*. American String Teachers Association.

Culver, B. (1989). *The master teacher profile: Elements of delivery at work in the classroom*. University of Wisconsin-Madison, Division of University Outreach, Department of Continuing Education in the Arts.

Gay, G. (2010). *Culturally responsive teaching: Theory, research, & practice* (2nd ed.). Teachers College Press.

Goolsby, T. W. (1999). A comparison of expert and novice music teachers' preparing identical band compositions: An operational replication. *Journal of Research in Music Education*, *47*, 174–187. doi: 10.2307/3345722

Ladson-Billings, G. (1995). But that's just good teaching! The case for culturally relevant pedagogy. *Theory into Practice*, *34*, 159–165. doi:10.1080/00405849509543675

MacLeod, R. B. (2018). The perceived effectiveness of non-verbal, co-verbal, and verbal string ensemble instruction: Student, teacher and observer views. *Journal of Music Teacher Education*, *27*(3), 169–183. 1–15. https://doi.org/10.1177/1057083717739790

MacLeod, R. B. (2019). *Teaching strings in today's classroom: A guide to group instruction*. Routledge.

Nápoles, J. (2007). The effect of duration of teacher talk on the attitude, attentiveness, and performance achievement of high school choral students. *Research Perspectives in Music Education*, *11*, 22–29.

Rabin, M., & Smith, P. (1990). *Guide to orchestral bowings through musical styles*. Really Good Music.

Spradling, R. L. (1985). The effect of timeout from performance on attentiveness and attitude of university band students. *Journal of Research in Music Education*, *33*, 123–137. doi: 10.2307/3344732

Witt, A. C. (1986). Use of class time and student attentiveness in secondary instrumental music rehearsals. *Journal of Research in Music Education*, *34*, 34–42. http://www.jstor.org/stable/3344796

Chapter 53

Alonso, S. (2008). Preparing for a performance. In W. Gradante (Ed.), *Foundations of mariachi education: Materials, methods, and resources* (pp. 25–34). Rowman & Littlefield Education in partnership with MENC.

Campbell, P., & Soto Flores, L. (2016). Mariachi music: Pathways to expressing Mexican musical identity. In H. Schippers & C. Grant (Eds.), *Sustainable futures for music cultures* (pp. 271–301). Oxford University Press. http://doi.org/10.1093/acprof:oso/9780190259075.001.0001

Fogelquist, M. (2008). Choosing appropriate repertoire. In W. Gradante (Ed.), *Foundations of mariachi education: Materials, methods, and resources* (pp. 15–23). Rowman & Littlefield Education in partnership with MENC.

Rodriguez, R. (2006). *Cultural production, legitimation, and the politics of aesthetics: Mariachi transmission, practice, and performance in the United States*. Ph.D. diss., University of California, Santa Cruz. ProQuest Dissertations and Theses Global, Publication No. 3219648.

Soto Flores, L. (2015). *How musical is woman? Performing gender in mariachi music*. Ph.D. diss., University of California, Los Angeles. ProQuest Dissertations and Theses Global, Publication No. 3728332.

Chapter 54

John, R. (2014). Part of it all: The high school musical as a community of practice. *Visions of Research in Music Education*, *24*, 1–29. http://www.rider.edu/~vrme/v24n1/visions/John_High_School_Community_of_Practice.pdf

Marshall, H. (2016). *Strategies for success in musical theatre: A guide for music directors in school, college, and community theatre*. Oxford University Press.

Ogden, H. (2008). Vivid moments long remembered: The lifetime impact of elementary school musical theatre. Master's thesis, Queen's University, Ontario.

Pogrebin, R. (2003, February 5). Showdown over orchestra size looms on Broadway. *New York Times*. https://www.nytimes.com/2003/02/05/theater/showdown-over-orchestra-size-looms-on-broadway.html

Van Houten, K. (1999). *High school musical theatre and the meaning students give to their involvement*. Ph.D. diss., New York University. UMI 9935665.

INDEX

Figures and tables are indicated by "f" and "t" following the page numbers.

B

D

E

J

K

N

O

P

Q

R

S

U